Herodotus and Imperial Greek Literature

Herodotus and Imperial Greek Literature

Criticism, Imitation, Reception

N. BRYANT KIRKLAND

OXFORD
UNIVERSITY PRESS

Oxford University Press is a department of the University of Oxford. It furthers
the University's objective of excellence in research, scholarship, and education
by publishing worldwide. Oxford is a registered trade mark of Oxford University
Press in the UK and certain other countries.

Published in the United States of America by Oxford University Press
198 Madison Avenue, New York, NY 10016, United States of America.

© Oxford University Press 2022

All rights reserved. No part of this publication may be reproduced, stored in
a retrieval system, or transmitted, in any form or by any means, without the
prior permission in writing of Oxford University Press, or as expressly permitted
by law, by license, or under terms agreed with the appropriate reproduction
rights organization. Inquiries concerning reproduction outside the scope of the
above should be sent to the Rights Department, Oxford University Press, at the
address above.

You must not circulate this work in any other form
and you must impose this same condition on any acquirer.

Library of Congress Cataloging-in-Publication Data
Names: Kirkland, N. Bryant, author.
Title: Herodotus and imperial Greek literature : criticism, imitation,
reception / N. Bryant Kirkland.
Description: New York : Oxford University Press, 2022. |
Includes bibliographical references and index.
Identifiers: LCCN 2022000226 (print) | LCCN 2022000227 (ebook) |
ISBN 9780197583524 | ISBN 9780197583548 |
ISBN 9780197583517 (hardback) | ISBN 9780197583531 (epub)
Subjects: LCSH: Herodotus—Influence. |
Greek literature—History and criticism.
Classification: LCC PA4004 .K53 2022 (print) | LCC PA4004 (ebook) |
DDC 880—dc23/eng/20220316
LC record available at https://lccn.loc.gov/2022000226
LC ebook record available at https://lccn.loc.gov/2022000227

DOI: 10.1093/oso/9780197583517.001.0001

For my parents, Lisa and Nelon,
And in memory of my grandparents,
Jiles Ellsworth Kirkland and Roberta Singer Gibson

Contents

Acknowledgments	ix
Introduction: After Herodotus	1
1. The Ethics of Authorship: Herodotus in the Rhetorical Works of Dionysius of Halicarnassus	35
2. Dionysius's Global Herodotus	73
3. Parallel Authors: Plutarch's "Life" of Herodotus	105
4. Hellenism in the Distance: Herodotean Fringes in Dio Chrysostom's *Borystheniticus*	152
5. Removable Eyes: Lucian and the Truths of Herodotus	186
6. Anacharsis at Border Control	236
7. Acts of God: Pausanias Divines Herodotus	261
8. Pausanias in Wonderland	296
Epilogue: Herodotus without End	331
Bibliography	337
Index of Passages	363
Subject Index	373

Acknowledgments

This book would be unthinkable apart from the many people who have contributed to its realization over several years. It is a true joy to record my thanks to these persons—teachers, fellow scholars, students, friends, and my family.

The roots of my interest in Herodotus go back to a 2008 seminar taught in London by Simon Hornblower and Chris Carey. Those sessions prompted a fascination with Herodotus as a narrator and thinker that, competing interests notwithstanding, has not waned.

The question of how certain ancient writers thought about and with Herodotus, and why their reckonings might be worth studying, became a formal focus during graduate school. This book has its basis in a Yale doctoral dissertation supervised by Emily Greenwood, to whom I owe a permanent debt of gratitude. Emily's bravura intellectual range, generous trenchancy as a reader, and deeply ethical sense of scholarly purpose have been an enduring inspiration. This project would not have seen the first spark of life without her extraordinary mentorship. From my time at Yale, I am also thankful to Victor Bers, Egbert Bakker, Pauline LeVen, and Irene Peirano Garrison. Egbert and Pauline offered critique on the final dissertation that later helped me chart its path toward being a book, and Irene has been and remains an encouraging influence. Finally, Chris Kraus deserves singular mention. At a pivotal stage, she graciously applied her keen eye to several chapters of the manuscript. Over and above her generosity as a reader, her wise (and often witty) counsel during the past decade has meant very much to me.

My colleagues and students at UCLA have emboldened me to write a different book from what I might otherwise have undertaken, and I thank them all collectively. I wish to thank the graduate students in seminars I led on Herodotus and Lucian, with particular thanks to Jasmine Akiyama-Kim, Andrew Lifland, and Collin Moat for help with proofreading and indexing at different points in this project. Among my colleagues, I am very grateful to David Blank, an uncommonly precise reader and scholar, whose patient advice and sharp good sense have saved me from many wayward moves. I am also thankful to Giulia Sissa, a generous and wide-ranging interlocutor, for many wonderful conversations. Amy Richlin, in her glint-eyed wisdom, helped steer me straight in my early days at UCLA, and I remain grateful. Sarah Morris, John Papadopoulos, Francesca Martelli, Chris Johanson, Brent Vine, and Sander Goldberg have all at different times offered advice or a friendly ear. I also wish to thank Lydia Spielberg, Sarah Beckmann, Adriana Vazquez, and Ella Haselswerdt, as well as Sam Beckelhymer and Simos Zenios, for their support and companionship. To Kathryn Morgan I owe a considerable debt of thanks—for countless conversations, for encouragement and advice at many turns, and for generously reading and incisively commenting on portions of the manuscript despite her other pressing obligations. Finally, I am especially grateful to Alex Purves for her inspiring and vibrant sense of what makes literature interesting—and for her generous collegiality and friendship.

In coordination with UCLA's Faculty Development Office, my home department sponsored a Junior Faculty Manuscript Workshop in the spring of 2021. The two manuscript readers from that workshop deserve special mention. Ewen Bowie brought his encyclopedic (and infectiously genial) erudition to bear on page after page. His observations, corrections, questions, and suggestions have improved the book in countless ways. Likewise, I owe tremendous thanks to Janet Downie, who has a gift for seeing synoptically and for asking the kinds of questions that don't go away. Her lucid scholarly acumen has sharpened this book on numerous fronts.

Many thanks are due to Stefan Vranka at Oxford University Press for his initial receptivity and abiding patience as well as his remarkable efficiency and clarity throughout the process. I am deeply grateful to the Press's two expert readers, Tim Rood and Jason König, for their thoughtful, sharp-eyed, and thorough reports, which did much to improve this book. I also thank Jubilee James, Brent Matheny, and all others involved in production, especially Wendy Keebler for her meticulous copy-editing.

I wish to thank the staff of the Charles E. Young Research Library in Los Angeles, without whose help, particularly during pandemic closures, completing the manuscript would have been impossible. My thanks also go to the marvelous staff of the Fondation Hardt in Vandoeuvres, Switzerland, where a stay in March 2019 afforded me the quiet and relief from ordinary daily duties to rewrite portions of chapter 3.

Over the years, several people have generously offered comments on portions of this project at different stages or have discussed ideas or bibliography that ultimately informed this book. I am grateful for their comments

ACKNOWLEDGMENTS xi

and for various conversations and exchanges—some brief, some extended and recurrent. In particular, I thank Emily Baragwanath, Chris Baron, Josh Billings, Artemis Brod, Cynthia Damon, Anthony Ellis, Markus Hafner, Kyle Khellaf, Larry Kim, John Marincola, Michael McOsker, Karen ní Mheallaigh, Chris Pelling, Chris van den Berg, Kenneth Yu, and Laura Viidebaum. Audiences in New Orleans, Edinburgh, Carlisle, Gambier, Boulder, South Bend, and Los Angeles have heard portions of this project and posed many questions, none of which I claim to have answered fully.

At a personal level, several people in the field deserve mention for uplifting, challenging, and sustaining me over the years: Margarita Alexandrou, Tom Biggs, Jessica Blum-Sorensen, Keyne Cheshire, Martin Devecka, Maya Gupta, Carolin Hahnemann, Ben Jerue, Peter Krentz, Jeanne Neumann, John Oksanish, Adam Serfass, Michael Toumazou, and Erika Weiberg.

Outside the academy, a few exceptional persons have kept me going, more than they might know. I owe so much to these steadfast friends: Andrea Applebee, Jenny Francoeur, Marc Serpa Francoeur, Steve Kaliski, Michelle Levin, and Jonathan Rodkin.

My family has supported me in every way imaginable, including in the pursuit of my interests, however odd they have sometimes seemed. During the latter stages of writing, two inspiring grandparents—both tremendous influences on me—died after great long lives. Roberta Singer Gibson and (the Reverend) Jiles Ellsworth Kirkland were autodidacts who passed on a fervor for learning. Many books in my library were once theirs, and in writing this monograph about, in part, the meanings of tradition and the inextricable entanglements with one's influences, I have sensed the presence of them both, beyond their earthly lives. I also wish to thank my deep-hearted sister Amanda for her insight, affection, and steady belief in me. Above all, I thank my parents, Lisa Endriss and W. Nelon Kirkland, who have each in their own very different ways shown what it means to live with curiosity, humor, imagination, and integrity. For their unswerving love I am profoundly grateful, more than I could ever say.

I owe special thanks to Matthew Dryer for permission to use Moira Dryer's *Fingerprint* for the cover image. I am grateful to the staff of Van Doren Waxter in New York for helping me source the image. My thanks to Brill for permission to reproduce, in modified form, portions of chapters 1 and 2 that previously appeared in *Mnemosyne* and to Johns Hopkins University Press

xii ACKNOWLEDGMENTS

for permission to reproduce in chapter 3 material that previously appeared in the *American Journal of Philology*. Translations of Ancient Greek and Latin are my own, unless otherwise indicated. For passages from the original German, French, or Italian I quote published translations if they exist (as cited in the Bibliography), but in cases for which no published English translation exists, translations are my own. The text of Herodotus is the Oxford Classical Text of N. G. Wilson. Texts of Imperial authors are indicated in the relevant chapters.

Introduction

After Herodotus

Lydia Davis's 2002 short story "Certain Knowledge from Herodotus" consists of a single line capped by a colon: "These are the facts about the fish in the Nile:"[1] The remainder of the page is blank. Like the fish in question, the facts seem to have swum away, if they were ever there in the first place. Readers unfamiliar with Herodotus may experience relief in the story's extreme brevity. But before flipping the page, they may wonder: Is this funny? What's the gag? What am I assumed to know about Herodotus to get it? Even for readers more comfortable with Herodotus, questions multiply. Is the joke that Herodotus says nothing true about the fish? Why shrink the sprawling text of Herodotus down to a single, improbable topic? And what's this about "certain knowledge"? Does it include the seeming certitude of Davis's own assertion that "These are the facts"? Or is this "certain" as in "just one piece of"—a certain bit from—the ancient writer? Readers are left to puzzle over the terms on which Davis wagers the jape of her "story" and whether they need to have read much Herodotus at all. Maybe it is enough merely to know the broad brushstrokes of his reputation—and then turn the page.

Davis's miniature offers just one among the myriad responses that Herodotus of Halicarnassus has garnered over the roughly 2,500 years since he set forth the results of his inquiry in the expansive work known as the *Histories*. Already closer to his time, we find another reader troubled by truth—and, it turns out, by Herodotus's fish. In *Generation of Animals*, Aristotle makes passing mention of Herodotus and of an absurd story that some boatmen cling to: "The fishermen join the chorus and repeat the same old senseless story (εὐήθη . . . λόγον) that we find told by Herodotus the fabulist (ὁ μυθολόγος), to the effect that fish conceive by swallowing milt" (*Gen.*

---

[1] Davis 2009: 325.

Herodotus and Imperial Greek Literature. N. Bryant Kirkland, Oxford University Press. © Oxford University Press 2022. DOI: 10.1093/oso/9780197583517.003.0001

2 HERODOTUS AND IMPERIAL GREEK LITERATURE

An. 3.5.755b6).[2] The idea of Herodotus as μυθολόγος, now almost inertly familiar, is part of a genealogy of critique that goes back even before Aristotle. If Davis's story echoes Aristotle's comment on Herodotus's silly story, Aristotle's formulation, as many readers will recognize, replays one of the earliest reactions to Herodotus, the probable allusion by Thucydides in claiming to distinguish himself from "prose writers who have composed more for attractive hearing than for truth" (1.21.1).[3] Conceding that his own account may sound "less pleasurable for listening," Thucydides announces that his *History* will at least be marked by an absence of "the fabulous" (τό . . . μυθῶδες, 1.22.4), or what the standard Greek–English lexicon describes as "the domain of fable."[4] The μῦθος that you will not find in Thucydides is there in Herodotus, he implies, and Aristotle's own passing description a generation or two later has a way of backing him up.

Such responses have come, after a fashion, to form their own tradition and to control aspects of our reading: from the "domain of fable" to the "fableteller" about fish to mysteriously "certain" facts, Herodotus has himself become fabled—and more often than not for his own supposed fabulism. Thucydides-to-Aristotle-to-Davis offers a seemingly linear model, but even in such schemata, strange receptive echoes arise. Consider Aristotle's theorizations of history-writing in the *Poetics*, which link the genre with particulars, to be distinguished from poetry's timeless universals (1451b6–7). A universal, Aristotle says, "is defined by the kind of thing that a certain sort of person happens to do or say, according to either probability or necessity. . . . A particular is what Alcibiades did or what he experienced" (ἔστιν δὲ καθόλου μέν, τῷ ποίῳ τὰ ποῖα ἄττα συμβαίνει λέγειν ἢ πράττειν κατὰ τὸ εἰκὸς ἢ τὸ ἀναγκαῖον. . . . τὸ δὲ καθ' ἕκαστον, τί Ἀλκιβιάδης ἔπραξεν ἢ τί ἔπαθεν, 1451b7–11). Even if Thucydides's text is among those evoked by the mention of Alcibiades, and thus slotted into Aristotle's category of history, Aristotle's

---

[2] μυθολόγος adjoins two words that in Homer often seem interchangeable, only later parting ways in the verse of Pindar, according to one lexicographical interpretation: LSJ s.v. μῦθος II.2; cf. LSJ s.v. μυθολόγος.

[3] See Gabba 1981: 50; Marincola 1997: 21 n. 100, 226; and Hornblower 1991: 56–58 for the reference to Herodotus. The Herodotean jingles of Thucydides's methodological statements bring into sharper focus his implicit target: Herodotus's proemic τὰ γενόμενα ἐξ ἀνθρώπου τῷ χρόνῳ ἐξίτηλα γένηται is echoed in Thucydides's τῶν τε γενομένων τὸ σαφὲς σκοπεῖν καὶ τῶν μελλόντων ποτὲ αὖθις κατὰ τὸ ἀνθρώπινον, and Thucydides's "events of some future time" (τῶν μελλόντων ποτέ, 1.22.4) recalls Herodotus's "what may happen in time" (τῷ χρόνῳ . . . γένηται). On Herodotus in this passage, see Hunter 1982: 227–28.

[4] As Priestley 2014: 200 notes, the scholiast on this passage glosses Thucydides's ἀγώνισμα as "the sweet tale" (τὸν γλυκὺν λόγον) and interprets it as a reference to Herodotus; see Dickey 2007: 55. For the wider influence of Thucydides's views, see Momigliano 1966 [1958]: 130–31.

INTRODUCTION 3

discussion of poetry's universal probability and necessity at times edges remarkably close to Thucydides's own formulations. For if by Aristotle's lights poetry concerns what someone may well say with respect to probability and necessity, Thucydides may be seen, retrospectively, to have conceived of his own speech-writing as similarly dependent on a probable universalism: "In the way I thought each would have said what was especially required in the given situation" (ὡς δ' ἂν ἐδόκουν ἐμοὶ ἕκαστοι περὶ τῶν αἰεὶ παρόντων τὰ δέοντα μάλιστ' εἰπεῖν, 1.22.1).[5] Likewise, the emphasis Thucydides places on likely recurrence (1.22.4) and futurity (κτῆμα ἐς αἰεί, 1.22.4) have him sounding, in Aristotelian terms, rather more like a philosophical poet than Aristotle's historian.[6] On one reading, then, Aristotle subtends Thucydides's own implicit charge against Herodotus: that it is a work that played to a particular moment, contra Thucydides's own strong emphasis on generations to come.[7] As a result, the apparent reverberations of Thucydides in Aristotle seem to ratify the Herodotus/Thucydides distinction that Thucydides himself was keen to establish, affirming Thucydides's own sense of disruption—albeit in an unexpected way, casting him as poetic and philosophical against the paratactic particulars of Herodotus.[8]

Reading forward, we thus find ourselves reading backward as well. Even the vaguest inclination toward accepting Thucydides's self-differentiation from his prose predecessor will affect a reader's broader encounter with other ancient critical pronouncements about *historia*. Many readers meet Aristotle *with* Thucydides, and they re-encounter Thucydides *with* Aristotle—in turn digesting Thucydides's own "reading," as it were, of the *Poetics*. Such entanglements and circularities of intertext are familiar to readers of classical literature.[9] It is indeed these very entanglements, felt presences, and implicit

---

[5] The phrase from 1451b9 repeats Aristotle's words at 1451a38, where he defines what "may happen" as the things that are "possible in accordance with probability or necessity" (τὰ δυνατὰ κατὰ τὸ εἰκὸς ἢ τὸ ἀναγκαῖον).

[6] Similar to poetry that relies on τὸ εἰκός (*Poetics* 1451a38, b9), the usefulness of Thucydides's *History* depends on the probability that events to come at some point will recur "in similar or approximate fashion" (τοιούτων καὶ παραπλησίων ἔσεσθαι, 1.22.4) and on the probability that even unknown particulars, in the speeches, at least, can be surmounted through knowledge of "the necessary things" (τὰ δέοντα).

[7] See also *Poetics* 1451b6–7. Herodotus was certainly interested in universals (concerning human behavior, customs, and many other topics); see esp. Węcowski 2004. For Aristotle's interpretation of Herodotus and his association of philosophy with poetry, see Bartky 2002.

[8] Compare Aristotle's comments in the *Rhetoric* on Herodotus's "strung-along" (εἰρομένη) style, which seem to reinforce a sense of history's side-by-side particulars (3.9.1, 1409a24–b1). On some of the reductiveness of the Herodotus–Thucydides binary, see Rood 2009: 172–74; Rood 2020: 21–26.

[9] See, for comparison, the comments of Charles Martindale concerning Homer and Virgil: "If we take the case of Homer and Virgil, the weak thesis would be that Virgil gives us powerful insights

4 HERODOTUS AND IMPERIAL GREEK LITERATURE

echoes between and among texts that shape interpretation, controlling, coloring, and at times confounding one's sense of how to read. This book aims to explore some of that blended encounter—the multidirectional transit of receptive reading—as it concerns that great and nearly mythological figure known as Herodotus.

Predetermining Herodotus

Herodotus provoked immediately and enduringly. Despite (or because of) its associations with poetry, its whiff of the "fabulous," and the ways in which it is distinctly not Thucydidean, Herodotus's *Histories* has become its own possession for all time. The foregoing prologue notwithstanding, this book will not be fixated on Herodotus as the foil to Thucydides. Many of the reception acts by the authors studied herein often creatively divagate from that familiar paradigm, or at the very least show a flexibility for thinking about and through Herodotus in ways that extend beyond the binary that Thucydides insinuates in his chapters on methodology.[10] Granted, the belief that Herodotus failed to live up to the standards of his successor Thucydides shapes a major part of his *Nachleben* and cannot be ignored, and indeed many have traced the reception history of Herodotus through the works of later historiographers.[11] Yet this book does not proceed neatly down that path, in part from the conviction that tracing Herodotus through traditional historiographic channels leads to a certain circularity: a reception study focused on historiographic influence unduly confines Herodotus to the very genre in which, per Thucydidean and many modern standards, he is often doomed to fall short.[12]

into Homer; the strong thesis, that, since Virgil, no reading of Homer, at least in the West, has been, *or could be*, wholly free of a vestigial Virgilian presence—not even one given by an interpreter not directly familiar with Virgil's poems—because the Homer-Virgil opposition is so deeply inscribed, both in the exegetical tradition and in the wider culture, because the two texts are always and already culturally implicated" (Martindale 1993: 8).

[10] The opposition anyway elides the complexity of relation between the two writers and aspects of their intellectual afterlives. See Rood 2020: 25, "The very conception of opposing Herodotean and Thucydidean traditions in antiquity should be rejected"; see further pp. 26–27 for consideration of how marking passages as "Herodotean" in Thucydides "serves to reinforce rather than to deconstruct the preconceived idea of a separation of two branches of historiography." Dionysius of Halicarnassus, however, will often rely on the binary; see chapters 1 and 2.

[11] For such analyses, see, e.g., Drews 1973: 97–140; Hornblower 2006: 312–15.

[12] See Gabba 1981: 50, commenting on Thucydides and Polybius as analogues for later readers, "precisely because their historical method is close to our own."

INTRODUCTION 5

In this schema, as was well described by Arnaldo Momigliano, Thucydides repeatedly wins out for intellectual substance, while Herodotus shines for his charming style: "The father of history was never, or almost never, recognized as a model historian, because he was not considered trustworthy, even by his admirers."[13] Assumptions about the meaning of stylistic imitation, however, can generate their own limitations. Already prior to Momigliano's alignment of Herodotus with style, Felix Jacoby had in a discussion of Herodotus's transmission history linked the Imperial era with Herodotus's reception along rhetorical and stylistic lines.[14] Now, for all the comprehensiveness of Jacoby's synthesis, including a catalogue of Herodotus's principal postclassical manifestations (col. 513, lines 15–62), Jacoby's concern lay with the constitution of Herodotus's text, not with Herodotus's role as a literary figure or intertextual presence during the Imperial era. Yet such positivist focus results in an assessment of Herodotus's post-Hellenistic reception as "without great significance," marked by Herodotus's "lopsided importance as a stylistic model."[15] To be sure, Jacoby's characterization of Imperial imitations as rhetorically or stylistically focused is apparently intended as a neutral description, since his concern lay with the value of postclassical receptions for constituting the text. But viewed from a wider angle, Jacoby's characterization of Herodotus's stylistic influence among Imperial authors might be felt to chime with later views of Imperial literature as so much empty rhetorical activity worth little interpretive attention.[16] Moreover, Jacoby's developmental arguments about Herodotus—according to which his ethnographic inquiry eventually matures into history-writing—may set up an implicit hierarchy by which other elements of Herodotus's *Histories* (and their reception) are conceived as inferior to that of the work's ultimate subject, the history of the Persian Wars.[17] The positions delineated by Jacoby and Momigliano are thus

[13] Momigliano 1966 [1961–62]: 213. Compare Ehrhardt 1988: 851–52. See further Momigliano 1958 (= Momigliano 1966: 127–42); Momigliano 1978; Rood 2020: 22–27, 29, and esp. 23, with helpful attention (nn. 14, 16–17) to Momigliano's own evolving thought on and modification of the Herodotus–Thucydides opposition.

[14] Jacoby 1913: cols. 504–20; see esp. col. 513.

[15] Jacoby 1913: col. 513, lines 63–66, "Für H. selbst ist diese ganze nachhellenistische Benutzung und Imitation ohne große Bedeutung, da sie kaum je etwas für den Text ausgibt"; col. 513 lines 66–68 to col. 514 lines 1–2, "Wohl aber hat die einseitige Geltung als Stilmuster und in der Rhetorenschule alles, was die Philologie an H. getan hat, noch gründlicher vernichtet, als dies selbst bei Thukydides geschehen ist." Moving beyond positivist concerns with the text, Murray 1972 indicated fruitful avenues for exploring Herodotus's role in Hellenistic literature, paving the way for Clarke 1999a: 56–72; West 2009; Priestley 2014; Hornblower 2015: 19–20; and now Morrison 2020.

[16] See, e.g., Reardon 1971: 3–4, citing representative views.

[17] On Jacoby's Herodotus, see Fornara 1971: 4; Hornblower 2006: 309–11; Rood 2020: 27–29. For consideration of Jacoby's critical frameworks (particularly as they relate to *Fragmente der griechischen*

6 HERODOTUS AND IMPERIAL GREEK LITERATURE

indicative of a tendency that risks pigeonholing Herodotus either as a lesser Thucydides or as a stylistic model for postclassical (read: less compelling) writers.[18] This framework would seem to exclude a variety of questions, including that of how Imperial stylizations of Herodotus encompass particular modes of thought—how evocations of Herodotus, that is, function as ways of *thinking like* Herodotus, in addition to or rather than merely sounding like him.

In an effort to avert the circularity of sidelining Herodotus in the terms used by Thucydides, and to fill out a segment of his reception history that explores the situated meanings of imitation among epigoni not directly or exclusively concerned with writing history or with the afterlife of the Persian Wars, this book traces some of the ways in which Herodotus was more than just nice to read and was, in fact, intellectually important for later writers. This will mean looking to his reception outside traditional historiography proper. I have chosen to pursue various close engagements with Herodotus that illuminate aspects of his broad reach. Yet any study of Herodotus's afterlife must bow to selectivity. My own method of study favors focused close readings of particular works over survey chapters that give only passing attention to a multitude of sources. Some texts familiar from Herodotean reception studies, including Plutarch's *On the Malice of Herodotus* and Pausanias's *Periegesis*, will receive focused attention, but others, including Lucian's *On the Syrian Goddess* and Aelius Aristides's *Egyptian Oration*, will not.[19] I hope all the same to offer, through encounters with various Imperial Greek authors writing beyond the bounds of historiography, a capacious idea of Herodotus's influence in sundry manifestations across genre.

Historiker), see Marincola 1999: 285–86 (on ethnography), 290–301. See Priestley 2014: 4–5 and Marincola 2012b: 2–3 on challenges to Jacoby's developmental model.

[18] Both Bowersock 1989 and Hornblower 2006 push back against what Bowersock calls Momigliano's "indefensible" belief that "Herodotus's reputation in antiquity was generally bad" (408). Still, Bowersock and Hornblower (albeit to a lesser extent) mainly trace Herodotus's imitators among historians, especially Arrian.

[19] One could doubtless also pursue various Herodotean aspects of Philostratus, Antonius Diogenes, Arrian, and others. Certain authors included in this study, including Plutarch and Lucian, have outputs so large as to necessitate further selectivity (as discussed in the particular chapters devoted to these writers). For a catalogue of Herodotus's Imperial presences, see Ehrhardt 1988: 853–55.

INTRODUCTION 7

Critical Continuities?

Any notion of reception (of Herodotus or any author) depends on critical judgments of that author that are themselves subject to revision. In recent decades, scholars have come to appreciate Herodotus as a writer more meaningfully multivalent and altogether more slippery than simplistic claims about truth or falsehood would imply.[20] To a certain degree, Herodotean polysemy was something already appreciated by ancient critics and imitators, too, but not always by the imitators that later generations would deem worth attending to. Across various chapters, we shall see that a kind of Herodotean complexity was constructed by a cluster of authors—including Dionysius of Halicarnassus, Plutarch, Dio Chrysostom, Lucian, and Pausanias—writing in Greek while living amid Roman rule between roughly 30 BCE and 200 CE. These five writers, divergent in style, genre, aim, and interest, exhibit a set of nuanced relationships with Herodotus that in their different ways prefigure the complexity that later audiences would also recognize in him.

Yet in tracing critical continuity between modern and ancient judgments, one tendency has tilted toward a sense of shared critique. Ancient readers, including Plutarch or Lucian, are implicitly and explicitly affirmed for having problems with Herodotus, while his more sanguine acolytes, including Dionysius and Pausanias, have at times had to count among their various shortcomings the very fact of their positive engagement with the author of the *Histories*. Take Dionysius. As a consequence of his positive assessment of Herodotus, he has himself been subject to rather harsh assessment. In his 1985 Loeb Classical Library edition of Dionysius's critical works, editor Stephen Usher remarks on Dionysius's view that Herodotus was superior to Thucydides in his choice of subject, writing that there

> could be no clearer indication of the intellectual weakness of the rhetorical mentality than this extraordinary statement, which has long been the object of deserved scorn and adds nothing to Dionysius's own stature as a critic, or indeed as a historian.[21]

---

[20] A number of studies evidence the tidal shift in the perception of Herodotus as a serious intellectual force, among them (but not limited to) Immerwahr 1966; Fornara 1971; the essays in the 1987 *Arethusa* volume on Herodotus; Gould 1989; Harrison 2000; Thomas 2000; Irwin and Greenwood 2005; Baragwanath 2008; Harrison and Irwin 2018; Pelling 2019; Kingsley forthcoming.

[21] Usher 1985: 350.

8 HERODOTUS AND IMPERIAL GREEK LITERATURE

Usher lifts various perturbed sentences from Thomas Hobbes, who in the preface to his translation of Thucydides had written, "I think there was never written so much absurdity in so few lines [as those written by Dionysius in favor of Herodotus]."[22] The implication is that the authoritative past, including the judgment of no less than Hobbes, weighs in the editor's favor in belittling Dionysius. Similarly, its harsh tone notwithstanding, Plutarch's jeremiad *On the Malice of Herodotus* might easily supply modern-day fodder for critique of Herodotus's accuracy on certain points.[23] As Donald Russell once noted in passing, Plutarch's essay "contains in its opening sections one of the most revealing accounts of the principles of ancient historiography that we possess."[24] Although these "principles" have been carefully parsed (and their utility in large part deconstructed) in the scholarship, especially that of John Marincola, they may nonetheless provide the reader with an image of Plutarch's proto-academic credentials, the sense that he is somehow in agreement with "our" skepticism. If Dionysius can be read as a gullible simpleton, Plutarch might be read as the shrewd anticipator of Detlev Fehling.[25]

Equally, it is tempting on the more positive, recuperative side of reading to draw analogies between past and present, but in this book, I will try to take the Imperial writers first on their own terms without being entirely tone-deaf to a sense of critical continuity. In ideal circumstances, the study of Herodotus's reception is not about whether various ancient authors were "right" in their judgments but rather about how the categories of perceived rightness have been configured and sustained. Consequently, the study of the ancient reception of Herodotus is also bound up with the reception of the ancient authors who received Herodotus and with how we have been conditioned to read *them*—whether (as in the aforementioned case of Dionysius) because of their perceived failures to interpret according to later standards or because they have been deemed lesser for other reasons. One hoped-for result is that by studying different Imperial receptions of Herodotus, we might challenge some of the conventional wisdom about the talents of Imperial critics and writers and possibly challenge, in certain instances, the conventional wisdom regarding their (and our) ways of interpreting Herodotus.

---

[22] From *The English Works of Thomas Hobbes* (1843), Vol. 8, xxvi. See Matijašić 2018: 100–102.

[23] For inquiry into some of Plutarch's handling of Persian Wars material, see Pelling 2007; Marincola 2010; Marincola 2016.

[24] Russell 1966: 182.

[25] Fehling 1989 [1971].

INTRODUCTION   9

In the remainder of this introduction, I explore some of the general ideas behind this book's approach to (1) reception, (2) imitation, and (3) the nature of Herodotus's authorship. The scope of intended provocation may at times exceed the bounds of what I am able to cover in the book, but I have erred on the side of generality in the hope that some of the following might prove applicable to reception studies beyond mine. I conclude with an outline of the Herodotean sensibility that this book draws out from the ancient sources.

Reception

Reception studies has become an institutionalized feature of classical studies. Hans-Georg Gadamer's notion of hermeneutic self-awareness, familiar to many classicists, remains a foundational summons, namely that "the abstract antithesis between tradition and historical research, between history and the knowledge of it, must be discarded. . . . [W]e have to recognize *the element of tradition* in historical research and inquire into its hermeneutic productivity."[26] As Gadamer famously propounded, the conditions for thinking about literary history are defined already within that literary history: "Real historical thinking must take account of its own historicity," for "understanding is, essentially, a historically effected event."[27] As I have already begun to suggest, the "element of tradition" and the question of critical continuity have particular application in the case of Herodotus, whose reception history has often conformed to a recurrent pattern of assumptions about the kinship between ancient and modern judgments. The patterns of a particular reception history (such as "the Persian Wars as exemplary, ergo Herodotus as exemplary," or "Herodotus as lesser, ergo his positive critics as lesser," etc.) can form their own instance of what Gadamer, albeit in a different valence, describes as the classical, "something raised above the vicissitudes of changing times . . . a consciousness of something enduring":[28]

[26] Gadamer 1975 [1960]: 294 (emphasis added). See Martindale 1993: 7, with remarks on how his own study builds on that of Gadamer's student Hans Robert Jauss, but in Martindale's case with greater attention to Jacques Derrida and to the deferral of closed meaning.

[27] Gadamer 1975 [1960]: 310. Understanding involves the recognition of what Gadamer calls "effective history" (*Wirkungsgeschichte*), the consciousness that one's own hermeneutics is situated historically in a "historicality" (*Geschichtlichkeit*), one that has itself been "effected" by past readings and interpretations.

[28] On Gadamer's use of the term *classical*, see Holub 1984: 41–45. For a summary of Jauss's rejection of such essentialism—the "classical creed of the canonical work as the aesthetic incarnation of a universal essence"—and his querying of the "canonical conception itself," see de Man 1986: 57 (source of quotations).

10 HERODOTUS AND IMPERIAL GREEK LITERATURE

So the most important thing about the concept of the classical (and this is wholly true of both the ancient and the modern use of the word) is the normative sense. But insofar as this norm is related retrospectively to a past greatness that fulfilled and embodied it, it always contains a temporal quality that articulates it historically.[29]

Although Gadamer nods to the "temporal quality that articulates" classicality "historically," a largely conservative, normative concept of the classical prevails here, as Barbara Herrnstein Smith observed in a well-known essay, applying Gadamer's own concept of historical self-consciousness back to Gadamer:

> It is hardly, however, as Gadamer implies here, because such texts are uniquely self-mediated or unmediated and hence not needful of interpretation but, rather, because they have already been so thoroughly mediated— evaluated as well as interpreted—for us by the very culture and cultural institutions through which they have been preserved and by which we ourselves have been formed.[30]

While Smith's analysis of a "thoroughly mediated" classicality may now sound axiomatic in literary studies, one could argue that a somewhat static notion of classicality has long shaped the reception history of Herodotus in particular, owing to both his subject matter and his perceived genre. In antiquity and beyond, many readers, especially those taken with the supposed moralizing legibility of the Persian Wars as a victory of valor over hubris, virtue over indiscipline, have used Herodotus to project a normative sense of "significance" onto that which "cannot be lost and . . . is independent of all circumstances of time."[31] This significance can cut in different directions. It can inhere in Herodotus's reifying the Greek victory in the Persian Wars and, in this sense, offering up a "timeless" image of Greek greatness, unity, and triumph. Already, Dionysius and Plutarch partake of this interpretative mode, albeit in different ways and with different purposes. Nor has the triumphalist hermeneutic disappeared; it remains a live phenomenon among, for instance, certain American conservatives who appeal to the past as a repository of "unchanging" values.[32]

---

[29] Gadamer 1975 [1960]: 299.
[30] Smith 1983: 29. See generally 29–30.
[31] Gadamer 1975 [1960]: 299.
[32] Witness Strauss's 2005 *The Battle of Salamis: The Naval Encounter That Saved Greece—and Western Civilization.* Compare Lacey's 2011 *The First Clash: The Miraculous Greek Victory at*

INTRODUCTION 11

At the other end, however, Herodotus's classicality can be construed for what he *fails* to achieve. On this reading, the *Histories* helps to clarify the importance of accuracy and truth in historiographic methodology—owing to its apparent inconsistency or absence in Herodotus. This angle of Herodotean fixation is evident especially in the positivist debates around Herodotus's accuracy, in the scholarship of Fehling and Stephanie West, and in the rebuttals of W. K. Pritchett and Robert Fowler.[33] Herodotus's canonicity can thus be read as exemplary and counter-exemplary all at once. In either case, though, a classicizing gist for Herodotus is reiterated, either in laudatory terms for his magnifying achievement or in rueful terms for his deficiencies in light of what he might have accomplished. Especially as it applies to the negative reception of Herodotus—as a writer who fell short of his genre's calling, even as he both births and precedes the terms of that calling—Gadamer's urgings only reinforce the need for continued (self-) consciousness of our "historically effected" understanding of Herodotus's afterlife. His framing reminds us that a "classical" Herodotus exists and, simultaneously, that such existence relies on the contingencies and needs of particular hermeneutic moments.[34]

Taking into account the provocations of Gadamer's successor Hans Robert Jauss, who extended Gadamer's emphasis on the necessary (self-)historicizing of critical processes, we might view Jauss's call for a "critical revision if not destruction of the received literary canon" to include not only the canon of literary works but also the *canons of criticism* that have accrued around them.[35] After all, even Jauss's proposal to situate a work amid the "horizon of expectations" from (or against) which it was first elaborated does not delimit a clearly articulated set of aesthetic standards that greeted a work.[36] Any

---

Marathon and Its Impact on Western Civilization, endorsed in jacket copy by Donald Kagan and Victor Davis Hanson and similar in tone to Hanson 2002.

[33] Fehling 1989 [1971]; West 1985; Pritchett 1993; Fowler 1996: 80–86.

[34] See, for instance, Matijašić 2018: 177–79 for consideration of second- and third-century rhetorical treatises that omit Herodotus as a model: those of Rufus of Perinthus and Valerius Apsines of Gadara mention only Thucydides and Xenophon, while the Anonymous Seguerianus includes only Thucydides. As Matijašić goes on to conclude, weighing the fate of Theopompus, Ephorus, and others, "Being excluded from the school curriculum meant, at this stage [second century CE] of the history of classical texts, falling out of the canons of historiography" (Matijašić 2018: 183).

[35] Jauss 1982 [1970]: 20. See also Porter 2006c, a vigorous call for the continued nuancing of ancient classicizing movements.

[36] See de Man 1986: 58–59, who reads the process of historical description as characterized by Jauss as an interplay of knowing and not knowing, a condition he calls "duplicitous epistemology," asserting that the "historical consciousness of a given period can never exist as a set of openly stated or recorded propositions" (58). Cf. Martindale 1993: 9, who comments that Jauss

12 HERODOTUS AND IMPERIAL GREEK LITERATURE

original horizon of expectation must in turn be coordinated onto a set of prior expectations that were themselves unconsciously shaped.[37] Herodotus may be credited with catalyzing a new set of expectations, with his irruptive text reframing earlier collective "answers" to questions of memory, history, and knowledge, but such "answers" are themselves only pointed up *as contingent* by the very fact of Herodotus's intervention.[38] Imperial Greek writers, for their part, in their simultaneous attentiveness to and frequent dissatisfaction with the conventions of tradition, help to broker a "critical revision" of Herodotus's canonicity, including the standards of critique that had gathered around his name. Even if we are always blind to our own horizons, we can nonetheless attempt to become more conscious of our expectations of Herodotus—what he means, how he was read for different purposes, how we wish to read him—through the mediating readings of past readers, including Imperial Greeks.

Reputation and Reception

Herodotus "surely never sank from view" in antiquity, in the words of Simon Hornblower.[39] He had a reputation; a story is there to tell, something that cannot be said for every ancient writer. Various studies have traced this reputation as it is represented by explicit remarks in later sources.[40] But the very fact of Herodotus's reputation somewhat complicates the question of reception, to the extent that there is a temptation to mistake the former for the latter.[41] Naturally, features of Herodotus's reputation—that is, the explicit

"exaggerates the knowledge which we can have of earlier readers, thereby reverting to a positivism which it supposedly rejects."

[37] De Man 1986: 59: the "preconscious or subconscious expectations are always collective and therefore, to a degree, 'received.'"

[38] The metaphor of "answers" is that of de Man (1986: 59).

[39] Hornblower 2006: 306.

[40] I intend the term *reputation* not pejoratively but descriptively, to refer to those studies that have emphasized explicit pronouncements by ancient (or modern) authors about Herodotus as key to understanding something of his esteem or infamy: see esp. Momigliano 1958 and Riemann 1967 (the most complete record of ancient references to the author).

[41] Martindale has noted how certain reflexive assumptions about the term *reception* have cohered into an undertheorized set of practices, writing that "disappointingly, fewer students of reception than I had hoped have taken up RTT's [*Redeeming the Text*, 1993] challenge to theorize, and much that is written within reception studies conforms, relatively inertly, to traditional positivistic inquiry" (2013: 170–71). He has continued to insist, across a series of reviews and articles (2007, 2010, 2013), on the need to rethink the term periodically, to ensure a clear relationship between practice and purpose.

INTRODUCTION 13

judgments pronounced on him—play an integral role throughout this book. I will want, however, to distinguish between reputation, which tends toward the taxonomic, and reception, which often calls out for interpretation and may exist in implicit tension with the explicit particulars of reputation.

Let us first recall some of the fundamental aspects of Herodotus's ancient reputation, inasmuch as its contours interact with reception. While Herodotus's controversial repute is well captured in Josephus's remark that although various writers attack each other, "everyone accuses Herodotus of lying," there has been some debate about how generally liked or disliked Herodotus was among ancient audiences.[42] If we glance outside traditional literary texts, we might indeed come away with a positive impression. We know, for example, of a bust of Herodotus that stood in the Pergamene Library, constructed in the first half of the second century BCE, a place second in prestige only to the Library at Alexandria, and we know of Roman-era coins from Halicarnassus featuring Herodotus on the reverse.[43] We also know of specifically Halicarnassian pride that springs forth in a Hellenistic inscription from Rhodes, the so-called Literaten-Epigramm, possibly by Antipater of Sidon (*IG* XII 1, 145; *SEG* 36, 975):[44]

Assyria (has) the stone-mound of Semiramis.
But the city of Ninos did not bring forth an Andron, neither did
Such offspring of the Muses shoot from the ground among the Indians.
Primeval Babylon did not nourish a mouth like that of Herodotos, which is
    even sweeter, nor
Panyassis with his sweet words, but the rugged earth of

---

[42] Josephus, *Against Apion* 1.16: ἐν τοῖς πλείστοις ψευδόμενον ἐπιδείκνυσιν . . . Ἡρόδοτον δὲ πάντες. Further references to slander against Herodotus can be found in Murray 1972: 205 n. 6. See also the judgment of Aphthonius at *Prog.* 8.8 (quoted in Matijašić 2018: 175): "Who then would compare Herodotus to him [Thucydides]? The former narrates for pleasure, the latter speaks all things for the purpose of truth" (εἶτά τις αὐτῷ παραβάλοι τὸν Ἡρόδοτον; ἀλλ' ἐκεῖνος μὲν διηγεῖται πρὸς ἡδονήν, ὃ δὲ πρὸς ἀλήθειαν ἄπαντα φθέγγεται).

[43] See Murray 1972: 204; Priestley 2014: 25; on the coins, see Richter 1965: Vol. 1, 147, figs. 821–24.

[44] See Ebert 1986; Isager 1998: 16.
    [lacuna: unknown number of lines missing]
        λάινο[ν Ἀ]σσυρίη [χῶμ]α Σεμι[ρά]μιος·
    ἀλλ' Ἄνδρωνα οὐκ ἔσχε Νίνου πόλις, οὐδὲ παρ' Ἰνδοῖς
        ῥιζοφυὴς Μουσέων πτόρθος ἐνετρέφετο·
    [κοὺ] μὴν Ἡροδότου γλύκιον στόμα καὶ Πανύασσιν
        ἡ[δυ]επῆ Βαβυλὼν ἔτρεφεν ὠγυγίη,
    ἀλλ' Ἁλικαρνασσοῦ κραναὸν πέδον· ὧν διὰ μολπὰς
        κλειτὸν ἐν Ἑλλήνων ἄστεσι κῦδος ἔχει
    [lacuna]

14   HERODOTUS AND IMPERIAL GREEK LITERATURE

Halikarnassus did. Through their songs
does she enjoy a renown among the cities of the Hellenes. (trans. Isager)

In a similar text, the so-called Salmakis Inscription (*SEG* 48. 1330; *SGO* 01/12/
02), dated to the second century BCE, Halicarnassus again applauds Herodotus
among other figures of local renown, honoring him with the nickname the
"prose Homer of history" (Ἡρόδοτον τὸν πεζὸν ἐν ἱστορίαισιν Ὅμηρον, col.
2, line 43) in the context of the "other good men of good descent" to whom
Halicarnassus gave birth (ἄλλους τ' ἐξ ἐσθλῶν ἐσθλοὺς τέκε, line 55).[45] The
view of Herodotus's epic and poetic qualities registers in essentially the same
terms as those of Longinus's *On the Sublime*, in which Herodotus is likewise
compared to Homer (*Subl.* 13.3).[46]

Further in this line of upbeat examples, one might look to a later inscription from Aphrodisias, dated to 127 CE, honoring one C. Iulius Longianus,
whom the Halicarnassians wished to make an honorary citizen (*IAph* 2007
12.27, 27 March AD 127 = *MAMA* viii 418):[47] "[I]t has been resolved that
Gaius Julius Longianus be honored with the other grants of citizenship and
honors, the greatest that the laws permit, and with bronze statues which
are to be put up both in the most notable places of the city and in the precinct of the Muses and in the gymnasium of the ephebes next to the ancient
Herodotus" (ἐν τῷ τῶν Μουσῶν τεμένει καὶ ἐν τῷ γυμνασίῳ τῶν ἐφήβων
παρὰ τὸν παλαιὸν Ἡρόδοτον, trans. Bowie). The honors accorded Longianus
are clearly meant to parallel, and indeed reach their pinnacle with, the esteem
accorded Herodotus. The inscription's call for a presentation of his books in
the library and the references to educating the city's youth elevate Longianus
to a position comparable to Herodotus, whose statue among the ephebes was
meant to encourage local pride and whose works were no doubt studied from
a young age.[48]

Indeed, along with many other classical authors, Herodotus features recurrently in *progymnasmata* and clearly occupied a foundational role

---

[45] On the inscription, see Isager 1998; Lloyd-Jones 1999; Gagné 2006; Priestley 2014: 186–88.

[46] Note, however, that Longinus questions whether Herodotus is the only writer who can be considered Homeric (μόνος Ἡρόδοτος Ὁμηρικώτατος ἐγένετο;), perhaps suggesting that he is refining
the *communis opinio* in offering up Stesichorus, Archilochus, and Plato.

[47] I am thankful to Ewen Bowie for alerting me to this inscription (on which see Roueché
1993: no. 88, 225–27). See also Bowie 1989: 202; Bowie 2008a: 18–19.

[48] On the gymnasium at Aphrodisias, see Chaniotis 2015, esp. 115–19. On the fundamental role of
Herodotus in *progymnasmata*, see Jacoby 1913: col. 513, lines 38–40 ("H. ist in der Rhetorenschule
traktiert und hat Stoffe für die rednerischen Jugendübungen geliefert"); Gibson 2004: passim with
117 and n. 59; Matijašić 2018: 168–79.

in rhetorical education.[49] In the exercises of Aelius Theon (first to second centuries CE), for instance, Herodotus provides moralizing anecdotes in addition to modeling ekphrasis, arguments in refutation, and the representation of character (*prosopopoieia*).[50] He enjoys a high stature for Theon, who describes him (along with Thucydides and others) as encompassing all divisions of history-writing.[51] Still, one may question whether in such educational contexts it was primarily for historical purposes that students read Herodotus. While almost fifty Herodotus papyri have been published, the nearly double number of Thucydides papyri may suggest that Herodotus was less well read than his arguably more difficult successor.[52] In light of the papyrological evidence, West has argued that "those who read Herodotus tended to do so in an unhistorical way," rather with an emphasis on rhetorical and entertainment value.[53] In any case, the evidence of both the *progymnasmata* and the papyri undoubtedly indicates the importance of Herodotus in educational contexts while also demonstrating the prevalence of his early, potentially more entertaining and "fantastical" books.

These various pieces of evidence help to construct a largely positive profile of Herodotus's ancient renown, in which he is seen as by turns learned and venerable. Yet they might on their own fail to indicate Herodotus's decidedly mixed reputation, notable often for derision as much as celebration. Moreover, even the clear-throated endorsements carry nuances that call up recurrent and not always decidedly positive motifs of Herodotus's wider repute. His classification as the "prose Homer of history" in the Salmakis Inscription, for example, while intended as positive, provided a sobriquet whose value could cut different ways, as Jessica Priestley has shown.[54] Likewise, the range of Herodotean endorsement, from Pergamum to

---

[49] Webb (2001: 290) has described how the *progymnasmata* provided "a set of common narratives, personae and values to appeal to," allowing for identification with and internalization of past authors. See further Bompaire 1958: 161–221; Reardon 1971: 165–70; Pernot 1995; Morgan 1998: 191–92; Cribiore 2001: 220–25; Kennedy 2003: ix–xvi.

[50] See Riemann 1967: 111–14, 117–24; Kennedy 2003 at Aelius Theon §§ 66, 67, 91–92, 115, 116, 118.

[51] See Kennedy 2003: 68, § 104P; Matijašić 2018: 171–72 on genealogy, political history, myth, *memorabilia*, and "comprehensive" (περιεκτικός) narrative. Cf. Matijašić 2018: 175 on Aphthonius's exercises, in which only Thucydides is called a συγγραφεύς (*Prog.* 12.1).

[52] See Wilson 2015: xii–xiii, indicating further unpublished papyri held at Oxford.

[53] West 2011: 77. See Matijašić 2018: 205–7. Among the scraps, Herodotus's first book predominates, perhaps surprising given Imperial nostalgia for the Persian Wars narrative that largely fills Books 5–9: thus Wilson 2015: xiii. Pace Wilson, see Matijašić 2018: 209 with n. 95, stressing that the educational context in which most papyri were produced had a rhetorical focus, for which prologues would have been useful.

[54] See Priestley 2014: 188 on the "variety of different ways," including "admiring" and "less flattering" lights, in which Herodotus's association with Homer could be understood.

16 HERODOTUS AND IMPERIAL GREEK LITERATURE

Halicarnassus to Aphrodisias, points on the one hand to the binding force of his canonicity but also, on the other, to the fact that it was among distinct locales that Herodotus's value was affirmed and possibly disputed: like his predecessor Homer, a man "much contested" and "of many fatherlands" (περιμάχητος . . . καὶ πολύπατρις, Eust., Il. 1.6.6–7 = 4.20), Herodotus was claimed and fought over in different places.[55] Given that one of Plutarch's chief criticisms of Herodotus has to do with his alleged misrepresentation of Plutarch's own Boeotia in the Persian Wars narrative, it is conceivable, in the context of these local inscriptions, that if we had a "Boeotia Inscription" on Herodotus, it might well have cast him in a different light.[56]

The chronological and geographic spread of these *testimonia* furthermore brings home the fact that canons of value require renewal. Herodotus's reputation moves through time, never a static donnée but always a changeable quality whose worth is subject to reassertion. The bronze statue of Longianus sat in explicit proximal relation to Herodotus, affirming Longianus's high status while also *reaffirming* Herodotus's value and, by implication, the value that redounds to the young men who use the gymnasium in the presence, as it were, of the famed writer. Each inscription or reference promotes a new statement of worth that stands in its own relation, influenced by the position of the reader, to other evaluative poses. The most hackneyed assertion of reputation carries an agenda. Supposedly innocuous laudations interact with the authority of the past—affirming it, defying it, reformulating it, and sometimes generating various puzzles. After all, what does it mean to compare Herodotus to a figure so varied, vast, and contestable as Homer? Which qualities, exactly, of Homer make Herodotus "most Homeric"? What were ephebes in the gymnasium meant to take away from "ancient Herodotus"— truth, pleasure, or something else?

Herodotus's afterlife has thus tended to persist rather more as a paradox of ambivalent celebration than as an unalloyed commemoration.[57] Famously, Cicero's *pater historiae* was also, in the same breath, the author of a work filled with *innumerabiles fabulae*, "countless tall tales" (*De legibus* 1.1.5).[58] Herodotus could function simultaneously as progenitor of and disgrace to historiography. Even for the author of *On the Sublime*, Herodotus

---

[55] Priestley 2014: 19–50.

[56] See Plutarch, *On the Malice of Herodotus* 854F, with Wardman 1974: 192; Marincola 1994: 202; Ingenkamp 2016.

[57] See Bichler and Rollinger 2000: 114–15 for this tension in Herodotus's ancient reputation.

[58] *quamquam et apud Herodotum patrem historiae et apud Theopompum sunt innumerabiles fabulae.* See further Diodorus Siculus 1.66.10, 1.69.7; Strabo 1.2.35, 11.6.3; Hermogenes 2.12.

INTRODUCTION 17

continuously slips between categories, at some junctures an exemplum of sublimity for, say, his use of hyperbaton (*Subl.* 22.1), the second person (26.2), or hyperbole (38.4), while at other times he is guilty of various lapses in dignity, including smallness of soul (4.7) and insufficiently elevated phrasing (43.1).[59] Photius, in his ninth-century CE *Bibliotheca*, captures well the ambivalence that had accrued over time:

> I read the nine books of the *History* of Herodotus, in name and number identical with the nine Muses. He may be considered the best representative of the Ionic, as Thucydides of the Attic dialect. He is fond of old wives' tales and digressions (κέχρηται δὲ μυθολογίαις καὶ παρεκβάσεσι πολλαῖς), pervaded by charming sentiments (ἡ κατὰ διάνοιαν γλυκύτης διαρρεῖ), which, however, sometimes obscure the due appreciation of history and its correct and proper character (εἰ καὶ πρὸς τὴν τῆς ἱστορίας κατάληψιν καὶ τὸν οἰκεῖον αὐτῆς καὶ κατάλληλον τύπον ἐνίοτε ταῦτα ἐπισκοτεῖ). Truth does not allow her accuracy to be impaired by fables (μύθοις) or excessive digressions from the subject. (*Bibl.* codex 60, 19b 16–25, trans. Pearse, adapted)

Photius lights upon the fundamental tension of Herodotus's reputation, its combination of "charming sentiments" and flawed truthfulness. Herodotus lingers as irresistible and likable, even as we are told that he stands far from reliability. The taxonomy of paradox swirls around his reputation; the questions provoked by that paradox are the domain of reception.

Kinetic Reception and Hypotextual Activation

Implicit and indirect imitations contribute to understanding Herodotus's reception as much as—and often in interesting friction with—explicit judgments about him. The broad reception framework adopted by Richard Hunter in his study of Hesiod offers a useful parallel for this study. Referring to "the Hesiodic," Hunter writes that the "result of my sense of this ancient sense [of the Hesiodic] is that the 'voices' I will be discussing in this book differ very greatly in their distance from the Hesiodic text, whether that

---

[59] The complications of Herodotus for Longinus stand in contrast to his straightforward presentation of Thucydides as a consistent model of sublimity in the realm of historical writing (14.1), in particular for his use of hyperbaton (22.3), the present tense (25.1), and hyperbole (38.3).

18   HERODOTUS AND IMPERIAL GREEK LITERATURE

be measured in shared vocabulary or authorial consciousness of the presence of a Hesiodic trace."[60] Likewise, for what I designate at the end of this introduction as "the Herodotean," the possibilities of activation are many. They are not limited to shared phraseology or to authorial consciousness of the Herodotean presence. Rather, given the frequently controversial status Herodotus occupied (the charming liar, the malicious raconteur), indirect and submerged aspects of his reception deserve particular attention, inasmuch as they may have constituted a strategic means of accessing an author of whom direct imitation will at times have been undesirable.[61] The inflections and resonances of Herodotus for which I argue are not, to be sure, an exclusive focus by Imperial authors, but they are a repeated and insistent force.

Two guiding formulations of reception frame this study. The first I call kinetic reception. This refers to the relation between inherited reputation, explicit criticism, and a receiving author's own imitative acts. Kinetic reception is the interactive "movement" or tension between critical expectation or overt expression and actual appropriation. Imitation itself may be readily apparent, but often it is implicit, detectable in the submerged, unannounced deployment of the target text's ideas, formulations, narrative structures, and overall feel. The reader may detect harmony, friction, or something else altogether between reputational expectation and receptive act, between, on the one hand, how a text seems to affirm or deny Herodotus's reputation and, on the other hand, how that text in fact relates or *acts* in regard to that expectation. As a brief example, take Thucydides's apparent "correction" of the story of Harmodius and Aristogeiton (*History* 6.54–59), recalling Herodotus's own version (*Histories* 5.55). As Hornblower has observed, the story as told by Thucydides exhibits Herodotean qualities in its narrative shape, detailing, and tone—indeed, of a fashion rather different from most of Thucydides's narrative.[62] Thucydides's engagement with his predecessor affords an instance of kinetic reception in which he points to (and contributes to) the reputation of Herodotus—by correcting and one-upping him, in line with

---

[60] Hunter 2014: 34. Hunter goes on to note, again in terms relevant to conceptualizations here, how "the varied riches of the *Works and Days* provoked a matchingly rich ancient response, both at the level of explicit interpretation and of creative imitation" (39).

[61] For the risks of direct Herodotean imitation, see the comments of Hutton 2005b: 204 and Elsner 2001a: 128.

[62] See esp. Hornblower 2010: 433–40 (and ad loc. 6.54–59, with further bibliography) with his specific comment at 435: "From the literary point of view, the Herodotean features of the excursus are notable . . . and are surely the clue to part of his programme in these chs." Rood 2009 offers an excellent analysis of Thucydides's intertextual relationship with Herodotus.

INTRODUCTION   19

his apparent criticism at 1.22.4—while adding complexity to his own self-differentiation by writing his correction *in the very style* of the corrected. This blurred sense of past author as both rejected force and incorporated presence is a mark of kinetic reception.[63]

Second, and related to this style of blurred imitation, is what we might call hypotextual activation, borrowing terminology from Gérard Genette.[64] Genette talks of how the hypertext, the imitating work, can evoke its imitated hypotext "more or less perceptibly without necessarily speaking of it or citing it."[65] Such unmarked allusion is common enough in the works of Imperial authors. Rather more of interest to me here, however, is the *activation* that such hypotexts produce. By hypotextual activation I mean the various moods, nuances, and unresolved opacities—the "allusive reverberations," in Stephen Hinds's phrase—evoked already in the original work or more specifically the part of the text to which a later author makes allusion.[66] The receptions for which I argue, in the later chapters especially (concerning Dio, Lucian, and Pausanias), often exemplify this reception dynamic. Dio's activation of Herodotus's account of Scythia and its geographic environs does more than merely establish a learned backdrop for his *Borystheniticus*; rather, the intellectual puzzles of that very backdrop are integral to the structure and thought of Dio's oration. Likewise, Lucian's *True Histories*, for all its sweeping evocation of the *Histories*, depends especially on specific allusions made early in the text to Herodotus's account of Egypt, thereby summoning as key to its own meaning Herodotus's uncanny narratorial role in Book 2, suspended between traveling inquirer and embodied participant.

The concepts of kinetic reception and hypotextual activation in this book place a strong emphasis on Herodotean imitation outside traditional historiographic channels. Reception occurs in the space between what an author may feel he is *supposed* to think about Herodotus from heritable expectations and how that author, through imitation of Herodotus, in fact registers fidelity to or rupture from that tradition. "Correction" of

---

[63] Compare the remarks of Goldhill 1993: 151 on the ways in which classical texts "enter later culture all too often as a series of authoritative and authorising quotations: the tag, the motto." Although the context of Goldhill's argument differs from mine, there is a parallel sense with kinetic reception that receiving authors can advert to the "tag" or "motto" of a particular author's role in the canon, even as their own appropriations may also undermine, query, invalidate, or reformulate the "motto" by which we recognize said author.

[64] Genette 1997 [1982].

[65] Genette 1997 [1982]: 5.

[66] Hinds 1998: 50. See generally Hinds 1998: 21–51, including 46–51 on the "non-inert reading" of *topoi* (46).

20 HERODOTUS AND IMPERIAL GREEK LITERATURE

Herodotus can sometimes exist in interesting tension with other markers of imitation and presence.[67] The active appropriation of Herodotus in unexpected places and modes creates a new horizon of expectations and a new iteration of the Herodotean aura, in turn allowing readers to locate the dispersal of Herodotus in new places.[68] But rather than viewing Herodotean imitation in dour Benjaminian terms, the copy destroying the original, the reproductions of Imperial writers have, rather, the effect of increasing what Sharon Marcus has in a different context called the "halo of the multiple": "By virtue of being multiplied, celebrities come to seem unique; their apparent singularity is *intensified* by copying. The more versions of them we see, the more distinctive they come to seem. Copies do not dim the celebrity's halo; they brighten it."[69] Far from diminishing Herodotus, multiplication limns his singularity.

Imitation

What can Imperial Greek authors contribute to our understanding of a historically effected, kinetically received Herodotus? Since Ewen Bowie's groundbreaking 1970 article on the meaning of the past to Imperial authors,[70] our understanding of the ways in which these authors manipulate their literary heritage, as a means of navigating the anxieties of what Walter Benjamin might have labeled their *Jetztzeit*, has advanced considerably.[71] In the decades following Bowie's article, one observes a declining tendency to indict Imperial literature as repetitive or derivative, overly determined by an attempted classicizing conformity with the past.[72] Instead, Imperial Greek literature is now seen as a dynamic site of cross-generic fertilization, creativity, and intellectual brio.[73] As part of this sophisticated replay of past texts and genres, an elevated self-consciousness of literary canonicity animates writing of the Imperial era. As Bryan Reardon once noted of Imperial writers,

---

[67] Compare Hinds 1998: 2, 17–21, with reference to polemical correction.

[68] On reception and the "two-way process of understanding," see Martindale 2013: 171.

[69] Marcus 2019: 127 (emphasis in original).

[70] With Bowie 1970, compare Veyne 1999, esp. at 532–41.

[71] "[H]istory is the subject of a structure whose site is not homogeneous, empty time, but time filled by the presence of the now [*Jetztzeit*]" (Benjamin 1950: 261). The *Jetztzeit* is itself shaped by historical consciousness, and in turn "knowledge" of history is filled, in a recursive loop, by the present.

[72] On the negative reactions to Imperial literature, see Reardon 1971: 3–4.

[73] The bibliography is vast and varies with specific authors: two broadly conceived influential studies are Goldhill 2001 and Whitmarsh 2001b; see already Reardon 1971.

"The Greeks had always been conscious of their tradition; it is the intensity of this awareness that is new."[74] The five authors studied in this book offer a self-conscious take on the uses of literature and the literary past. Theirs marks an extended cultural moment of self-reflexivity that parallels the one proposed by reception studies, a self-consciousness by which questions of authority and rupture, continuity and creativity, come to the fore. In examining Herodotus's reception among these Imperial authors, we are witness to a series of critical moments in which Herodotus's status and meaning are (re)formulated by writers convinced of a "classicality" into which they might inscribe themselves while also aware that such classicality—by virtue of its inclusion of apparently problematic writers such as Herodotus—could raise flags about the value of their own self-inclusion. In each instance, these authors have a sense of the cumulative horizons of expectation regarding the acceptability of Herodotus, even as they are necessarily operating within invisible horizons of their own.

But what unifies these five writers? Even if we were to frame the period of Imperial literary production according to the rhetorical appellation, it is open to debate how the authors of this study would fit Jacoby's *Rhetorenschule*.[75] Dionysius, for instance, although anticipating some of the intellectual concerns of the so-called Second Sophistic (in particular the focus on a kind of Atticism), is not normally counted among its authors.[76] Of the others examined, Dio Chrysostom is sometimes identified as a sophist and is the only one of the authors studied here who appears in the direct spotlight of Philostratus's *Lives of the Sophists*.[77] To the extent that they participated in sophistic performance culture, the other authors examined in this book did so more as writers than as rhetors, and it is for this reason (as well as with attention to wider shifts in our classifications) that I prefer the

[74] Reardon 1971: 18, "Les Grecs avaient toujours été conscients de leur tradition; c'est l'intensité de cette conscience qui est nouvelle."

[75] Granted, an education in rhetoric does likely unify this study's authors—see, e.g., Reardon 1971: 29 on rhetoric's "total hold on education" ("une emprise totale sur l'éducation")—but it does not delimit their idiosyncrasies.

[76] See, however, Reardon 1971: 78–80 for Dionysius's framing of certain enduring concerns. See also Connolly 2007b: 159–61 (with comments on Dionysius at 155): "That the quest to define and lay claim to 'pure Greekness' partly drives the Atticism and archaism of Greek rhetorical culture in the Roman empire seems obvious. At the same time, as we have seen, Atticism is a movement with roots in first century Rome" (160–61).

[77] Failure to appear in the *Lives of the Sophists* does not, of course, mean that one was not a sophist; the absence of Lucian, some of whose works fit the sophist model (see Anderson 1993: 10), likely indicates nothing more than the arbitrary classifications of Philostratus, on which see Anderson 1993: 13–21; Eshleman 2012: 125–48. On Plutarch as unlikely to have been a sophist, see Russell 1972: 6–7.

22 HERODOTUS AND IMPERIAL GREEK LITERATURE

term *Imperial* over *Second Sophistic*.[78] As Tim Whitmarsh has noted, in an essay on Pausanias, "We should remind ourselves periodically that there was in reality no single 'Second Sophistic,' no unified movement of which Greek intellectuals were card-carrying members."[79] It is hoped that although the scope of this book is limited to a few select authors, they manage to convey something of this non-unity, that the varied receptions possible for the multifaceted Herodotus affirm Whitmarsh's observation that there is no unified movement. Rather, in the diversity of their concerns, the recurrent recourse to Herodotus conjures the ways in which his own multifarious text spoke to the variety of interests among these writers.

Still, one might ask whether the engagement with Herodotus only reprises questions of Imperial conformity, revanchism, and hibernating obsession with the past. The studies of Reardon (1971) and Whitmarsh (2001b) have done much to reimagine the contours of literary ingenuity among Imperial Greeks and to complicate the contention that Imperial imitation reveals principally its own non-dynamism.[80] In this regard, I wish to flag two further models of imitative creativity from comparative literary studies that help to frame the receptive acts studied in this book.

The first is that discussed in Edward Said's essay "On Originality," published in *The World, the Text, and the Critic* (1983). Said urges a "transformation of the imaginative terms by which we can now understand originality."[81] In elaborating his capacious view of creativity, one that turns away from a Platonic model of imitation-and-copy, Said adduces modernist literature and its tendency to manipulate the literary past for creative transmutation. Although his choice of example comes from an era distant in time and detail from those studied in this book, the broad outlines of his observations have a kinship with Greek literature of the Roman Empire:

---

[78] *Imperial*, however, introduces the problem of seeing these writers as always writing to, against, under, etc., Roman power, a topic that deserves its own nuancing: see, e.g., Veyne 1999, esp. 556–63, for discussion of coexistent negative representations of Roman hegemony and more sanguine depictions of the emperor. In some instances, including Dionysius, Rome comes directly to the fore, but in others (Lucian, Pausanias), the interpretability of the works studied vis-à-vis Roman political power conjures more speculation than specificity. Reardon's remark (1971: 17) holds in many instances: "Sauf certaines exceptions, la littérature grecque de cette période ignore Rome. Non pas totalement, mais presque; le fait est significatif."

[79] Whitmarsh 2015: 49. See further Porter 2001: 90–92; Whitmarsh 2005: 6–10; Whitmarsh 2013: 2–5.

[80] See, e.g., Reardon 1971: 4, discussing the bias of later readers toward an interest in Roman imperial power, to the neglect of a serious interest in Imperial Greek literature. On Imperial belatedness and creativity, see Whitmarsh 2001b: 41–89.

[81] Said 1983: 135–36.

INTRODUCTION   23

the best way to consider originality is to look not for first instances of a phenomenon, but rather to see duplication, parallelism, symmetry, parody, repetition, echoes of it—the way, for example, literature has made itself into a topos of writing. What the modern or contemporary imagination thinks of is less the confining of something to a book, and more the release of something from a book in writing. This release is accomplished in many different forms: Joyce releases the *Odyssey* into Dublin, Eliot frees fragments from Virgil and Petronius into a set of jagged phrases. The writer thinks less of writing originally, and more of rewriting. The image for writing changes from *original inscription* to parallel script, from tumbled-out confidence to deliberate fathering-forth . . . from melody to fugue.[82]

Said's vivid description corresponds in several ways to the characteristic markers by which scholars have come to describe Imperial Greek literature, with its capacity for harnessing an idea of originality into a rewriting of the past. In this book, we will variously find instances of duplication (in, say, Dionysius's evocations of Herodotus's ethical persona), parallelism and repetition (in Plutarch's evocation of the Persian Wars), parody (in Lucian's ludic exposure of historiography's narrative fissures), and an endless variety of echoes (such as the many that course through Dio and Pausanias). Through many means, we witness a "release of something . . . in writing," a proliferation of the past that offers a "parallel script" to the Herodotus of the fifth century, the melody of his *Histories* transformed into the fugue of his variegated reception across literary criticism, manifesto, satire, comic dialogue, and travelogue. Said will go on to speak in terms that conjure a notion of boundlessness:

> Since our self-perception as writers has changed from being *lonely begans* . . . to being workers in the *already-begun* (the always already), the writer can be read as an individual whose impulse historically has been always to write through one or another given work, in order finally to achieve the independence, like Mallarmé, of writing that knows no bounds.[83]

The famed self-consciousness of Imperial Greek literary production is surely evidence of an "already-begun" sense of authorship, but one in

---

[82] Said 1983: 135.
[83] Said 1983: 136.

24 HERODOTUS AND IMPERIAL GREEK LITERATURE

which, as Said implies, a path of creative freedom lies in writing through one's precedents.[84]

Likewise expanding on this notion of "writ[ing] through one or another given work," Colin Burrow has explored the complexities of creativity rooted in imitating authors from the past. As with Said, Burrow's interest lies not in mimesis as traditionally defined but rather in the question of how certain writers imitate and take on the presence of other writers. Burrow similarly focuses on how *imitatio* may be seen not in the Platonic, negative terms of the *simulacrum* but rather more in the fecund terms of creativity, locating imitation at the "diffuse fringes" of inventive reworking.[85] As he observes, and as is essential to this study, "Imitating authors are also readers."[86] Imitating (and we might say receiving) authors do not merely (re)create; they also imagine and interpret, and in their "adaptive imitation," they make of past authors what Burrow calls a "subjunctive principle."[87] At multiple points in this study, we may hear the authors in question essentially asking, "What would Herodotus do?" For Burrow, and for this book, the dynamics of imitation need not be confined to straightforward verbal repetitions and borrowings. They may refer, rather, to formal concerns, rhetorical and argumentative structures, patterns of thought, and the effort to generate the perceived *effect* of a text without necessarily copying its details.[88]

This latter mode—generating the effect of a prior work—involves what Burrow, with reference to experimental psychology, distinguishes as *emulation*, " 'observing and attempting to reproduce results of another's actions without paying attention to the details of the other's behavior' ":[89]

> "Emulation" in this sense is now generally distinguished from what experimental psychologists term "imitation," in which the mannerisms or gestures of the person imitated are replicated. . . . It can entail grasping

[84] Compare Reardon 1971: 5: "It is precisely this [i.e., a respect for tradition] for which the Greeks of the period [of the second century] are reproached, *assuming there is no other mark of greatness than originality*" ("Et c'est précisément cela qu'on reproche aux Grecs de l'époque, *en supposant qu'il n'y a pas d'autre marque de la grandeur que l'originalité*") (emphasis added). See also Webb 2001: 314 on how ancient school exercises "encouraged an attitude toward the texts of the classical canon as an open source of tradition, part of the student's cultural property, with which he was expected to engage, and not as a static, untouchable monument."

[85] See Burrow 2019: 1–34 and esp. 1–4 on the complexity of imitation, including its capacity to be constituted by "parody, forgery, and mimicry" (3); "diffuse fringes" at 3. See also Hinds 1998: 48, cautioning against "intertextualist fundamentalism—which privileges readerly reception so singlemindedly as to wish the alluding author out of existence altogether."

[86] Burrow 2019: 2.

[87] See Burrow 2019: 2–4; "adaptive imitation" and "subjunctive principle" at 9.

[88] See also Morrison 2020: 18 on "the wide range of types of relationship texts can have with one another."

[89] Burrow 2019: 12, quoting Arbib 2012: 185.

the principles which underpin a particular text and extrapolating from them a set of practices for generating a new text. Those principles might be a large scale-set of relations between the different elements of an earlier text, or a rhythmic pattern, or a rhetorical structure, or any of the innumerable features of a text that constitute a "style." They *might* include verbal correspondences, but need not do so.[90]

Taking into account the creative expansiveness accorded imitation by Said and Burrow, I will view Herodotus's Imperial reception—already outside the bounds of traditional historiographic channels—as part of the inspired flowering of Herodotean discourse. The creative responses of later authors bespeak a kind of freedom within the allusive "system" of Imperial literature, to borrow once again from Said: "Thus the ultimate, perhaps infinite goal of writing is a Book conceived of as a bibliosystem, a kind of activated library whose effect is to stimulate the production of forms of disciplined, gradually actualized freedom."[91] Amid the bibliosystem and "activated library" of Imperial authors, the multifariousness of Herodotean reception indicates to some extent the range of issues provoked by the *Histories*, encompassing, among other matters, the ethical responsibilities of authorship, the murky relation between seductive narrative and the truth, the nature of foreignness, and the consequences of registering wonder in narrative. What Said ultimately calls the "formidably complex originality of writing as . . . it counters nature" is summoned in the diversity of responses to Herodotus that, in their turn, defy, reinscribe, or rewrite past interpretations.[92]

Herodoteanism

The Transdiscursive, Global Herodotus

The diversity of responses to Herodotus emerges from the various purposes of authors who interact with him. In a certain sense, that variety is a key element of Herodotus's own interpretability. But variety produced about and

---

[90] Burrow 2019: 12–13. Compare Webb 2001: 309–10 on ancient school exercises as encouraging " 'acting like' rather than 'producing a copy of,' " putting the "student in continuity with the authors he read" (309).

[91] Said 1983: 139. Compare Reardon 1971: 7 (citing Bompaire 1958: 63) on mimesis as "reference . . . to literary heritage" ("référence . . . au patrimoine littéraire"). See further Reardon 1971: 9 and Bompaire 1958: 93 on "enlarging the notion of mimesis" ("d'élargir la notion de Mimésis").

[92] Said 1983: 139.

26 HERODOTUS AND IMPERIAL GREEK LITERATURE

in relation to Herodotus is also variety enabled in some sense *by* Herodotus. We might therefore frame the diversity of Herodotean intellectual progeny in terms of what Michel Foucault once called a transdiscursive author:[93]

> [O]ne can be the author of a theory, tradition, or discipline in which other books and authors will in turn find their place. These authors are in a position that I will call "transdiscursive." . . . They are unique in that they are not just the authors of their own works. They have produced something else: the possibilities and the rules for the formation of other texts.[94]

Herodotus, as many have argued, put a distinctive stamp on the emerging practices of writing up inquiry, "fathering" a tradition that would obviously evolve but many of whose essential features would endure.[95] His unleashing of the "possibilities and the rules for the formation of other texts" positions him as a "discourse-founding" author. Some aspects of this discursive distinctiveness were illuminated in a 1996 article by Fowler, whose conclusions about the *Histories* well fit Foucault's identification of writers who generate a new set of discursive questions and realize a new genre for posing them: "[A]wareness of the disagreement or absence of sources as a general problem requiring theoretical attention and the development of critical tools is not found in either poets or early mythographers. It *is* found in Herodotus."[96] While Fowler's concern was primarily with the Herodotean "voiceprint," evident in his adverting to the set of possibilities and critical voices from which Herodotus would distinguish himself, we can extend the

---

[93] Foucault 1977. To my knowledge, the only contemporary critic of Herodotus to have brought up Foucault's ideas on transdiscursivity is David Chamberlain (Chamberlain 2001). See the passing comment at Chamberlain 2001: 6 n. 3, on Herodotus as a "founder of discursivity" and further 30–32, quoting Foucault. See also 6 n. 7. Compare Hawes 2016: 324–25, discussing a genealogical paradigm of genre and arguing that Herodotus is himself a product of his time (rather than a creator ex nihilo) and that responses to him are "diffuse" and "networked": "Imitation is both layered and nuanced. . . . We might think of these allusions [to Herodotus] offering not a response to Herodotus *tout court*, but to a particular *idea* of something distinctly Herodotean" (emphasis in original; all quotations from 324).

[94] Foucault 1977: 113–14, "[O]n peut être l'auteur de bien plus que d'un livre—d'une théorie, d'une tradition, d'une discipline à l'intérieur desquelles d'autres livres et d'autres auteurs vont pouvoir à leur tour prendre place. Je dirais, d'un mot, que ces auteurs se trouvent dans une position 'transdiscursive.' . . . Ces auteurs ont ceci de particulier qu'ils ne sont pas seulement les auteurs de leurs oeuvres, de leurs livres. Ils ont produit quelque chose de plus: la possibilité et la règle de formation d'autres textes."

[95] See the suggestive remarks of Morrison 2020: 17–22, 26–34, on Herodotus as a *modello-codice* (borrowing from G. B. Conte), "a text which functions as the representative of a genre or type, and therefore as a fundamental set of rules or expectations (a code) against which a later text defines itself" (19).

[96] Fowler 1996: 79 (emphasis in original). See 72, 76–80, for the Herodotean "voiceprint."

range of transdiscursivity that Herodotus would help inaugurate in prose. This might include works that engage with definitions of Greekness, problematize the narrator's epistemology or the relationship between myth and history, or raise questions about the relationship between observation and judgment, subject and object. In tracing the Herodotean conceptualization of these and other ideas across different genres, we gain a richer sense of his transdiscursive reach.

These varied provocations from Said, Burrow, and Foucault also prompt reflection on the ultimate indeterminacy of authorship. Foucault famously asked, "What is an author?" and we might in many cases in this book ask, "Who is an author?" or even "Who is *the* author?" In certain instances, we will encounter moments of allusion or imitation so richly realized, the feel of Herodotus so spectrally present, as to blur the line between Herodotus and Dionysius, or Herodotus and Lucian, or Herodotus and Pausanias. Reading among the latter, we might, despite differences in dialect and subject, feel that we are reading the former, or that he is somehow cooperating with his emulator. To approach such moments with rigorous expectations of novelty or innovation is to downplay the expectations of ancient audiences, among whom such imitation was often desired.[97] So embedded are the Imperial imitations that at times Herodotus seems to *write with* later writers as much as they write back to him. The felt quality of a shared text, of an uncanny co-authorship, may leave one with the sense that for the five writers examined in this book, an idea of authorship inheres in, or sets among its seminal aspirations, the effort to sound (sometimes obviously and sometimes more quietly) like someone else, to write through and with precedents, while at the same time moving in new directions, unraveling the fabric of the hypotext. At various junctures—Dionysius's attempt to appeal to the layperson, Dio's evocations of the opacities of Scythia, Pausanias's evocations of the divine, and elsewhere—Herodotus and his reader-imitators shade into each other. Yet the result is far from a flat or simplistic redundancy; rather, these Imperial writers often create in their interactions with Herodotus a richly hued penumbra. Source and emulation generate a new and layered composite.

To bring in, lastly, one further theoretical framing that will prove relevant at different points, it will be useful, in conceiving of a broad Herodotus who inspires response from a range of authors across various works, to

---

[97] See Webb 2006 for the kinds of learned expectations of imitation that ancient Imperial audiences would have maintained.

28 HERODOTUS AND IMPERIAL GREEK LITERATURE

think (however seemingly anachronistically) in terms of world literature, of a "global Herodotus" whose appeal to different writers was indissoluble from the political changes wrought by the rule of the Roman Empire. In his 2004 essay "To World, to Globalize: Comparative Literature's Crossroads," Djelal Kadir locates the origins of a notion of world literature in Herodotus's *Histories*:

> The world, and certainly the notional world of narrative, were already subject to critical revisioning and territorial displacement as early as the fifth century B.C. when Herodotus' perception of a shifting *oikoumene*, or world as home, led him to compose the inquiring narratives that would form the founding acts of historiography and the narrative genre of history.[98]

Kadir identifies in Herodotus a concept of plurality, one marked by the "vicissitudes" of "feeling at home in the world" amid a larger "transcultural metamorphosis" among Greeks.[99] For Kadir, this Herodotean plurality

> could well serve as an index to the multiplication of what, for his culture, had been a unitary and singular world. Herodotus experienced that shift first hand as alert observer in a public sphere whose subtle accommodation of Greek and Carian syncretisms suddenly became culturally and ethnically refracted as his native city of Halicarnassus passed into imperial Persian governance.[100]

Although one may quibble with aspects of this characterization, such as the concept of "unitary" world as against one of syncretism "suddenly" under Persian rule, the tendency of Kadir's observation squares with what many—including the authors studied here—have arguably recognized in Herodotus: a broadness of viewpoint, a cosmopolitan intellectual girth that upsets any easy attempt to see his work as advocating any one consistent perspective. This "global" Herodotus offers Imperial Greek authors opportunities to view the transformations of their *oikoumene* in the mirror of

---

[98] Kadir 2004: 3.

[99] On globalism and hybridity in Herodotus, see also McWilliams 2013.

[100] Kadir 2004: 3. Cf. Rood 2020: 21–23: while not entirely rejecting the notion of a "wide-ranging" (21) Herodotus, Rood observes how putative contrasts between Herodotus and the "narrow" Thucydides are "most commonly evoked in treatments" of their approaches to ethnography (21), a point of supposed difference that Rood's essay problematizes.

INTRODUCTION   29

Herodotus. Whereas François Hartog's mirror permitted Herodotus and his Greek readers to refract otherness through the lens of an *interpretatio Graeca*, I suggest that Imperial Greek writers could variously hold up as mirror to their own world the plurality and many-sidedness of Herodotus's text. That is, rather than turning to the *Histories* for a simple and coherent notion of "Greekness," later Greeks (in particular, Dionysius, Dio, and Lucian) could filter an expansive sense of Hellenism (and difference) through Herodotus's own polyvocality. The "mirror of Herodotus" thus becomes a mechanism for witnessing the "transcultural metamorphosis" that is surely evident in the literary productions of Imperial Greeks.

Toward the Herodotean Sensibility

The polychrome quality of Herodotus's *Histories* has arguably produced intellectual progeny so diverse as to court ubiquity. The reception of Herodotus is, in some sense, a reception of uncontainability. As Jane Lightfoot has observed, "imitating Herodotus does not determine a set of straightforward stylistic choices . . . [and] could extend from merely echoing the occasional catch-phrase to more thoroughgoing imitation of matters of dialect, diction, style, or content; or it might have respect to areas other than language altogether."[101] Lightfoot's liberal range of possibilities is worthy of the author in question. Yet even so capacious a conception as Genette's expansive remark that "*it is impossible to imitate a text*, or—which comes to the same—*that one can imitate only a style: that is to say, a genre*" bumps up against Herodotus's variegated, self-imploding inhabitation of genre.[102]

As a general rule, this study aims at tracing a wide-ranging philological, thematic, and trans-generic reception, one that countenances intertextual echo, thematic reverberation, intellectual and formal resonances, and Burrow's aforementioned "effect" of a text. The book falls roughly into two halves. The first three chapters (on Dionysius and Plutarch) largely involve explicit Herodotean criticism, although I attend as well to both authors' Herodotean imitations. The second half treats three authors (Dio, Lucian, and Pausanias) who exhibit more implicit receptions. The book thus moves from enunciated Herodotean reception toward more embedded

---

[101] Lightfoot 2003: 95.
[102] Genette 1997: 83, cited at Burrow 2019: 12 (emphasis in original).

30 HERODOTUS AND IMPERIAL GREEK LITERATURE

reception acts, although the receptions of the latter three writers can and should be read against the more explicit critical framework of Dionysius and Plutarch.

In each chapter, I am eager to keep in view not just *how* Herodotus is received, the poetics of his reception, but also *why* he is so received, the hermeneutics of his intellectual afterlife, and what kind of work that reception act is doing.[103] I am keen to place these Herodotean tesserae in the mosaic of kinetic and hypotextual reception, to elucidate how acts of receiving Herodotus (even moments of rejection) are nonetheless often conducted in a manner evocative of Herodotus, sometimes making of reception a double act, one both explicit (talking about Herodotus) and implicit (talking like Herodotus). Yet some limitations are essential. Although I track an array of Herodotean echoes, this is not a book about language or the Ionic dialect. And while I study the different ways later authors take up particular intellectual pursuits evident already in Herodotus, this is not a book of Herodotean positivism—did Herodotus get *x* topic "right"? Rather, I am concerned with the kinds of issues Herodotus's work stimulated in later authors and with their attempts to entertain those issues, especially in moments of kinetic reception that, lit by the Herodotean back-glow, recall the very spirit of the author under scrutiny or whose ideas are on the table.

What are the discourses that Herodotus's transdiscursive text helps to inaugurate? What kinds of writerly sensibility are continued and transformed through the vivification of Herodotean style? A succinct, if unsatisfactory, answer would be that "the Herodotean" encompasses the cornucopia of concerns that later authors and critics care to extrude from his text. But this is only to beg the question, what are those concerns? Although my chapters are author-based, it will emerge that each pursues a theme and that certain thematic threads tie this book together. In lieu of traditional chapter synopses, then, and at the risk of the very reductiveness that I would suggest the invocation of Herodotus can dispel, I outline as a guide to reading some of what emerges as the Herodotean in this study. The following are some areas around which Imperial interpretations often revolve. They are variously engaged by different writers and should not be seen as either exhaustive or mutually exclusive.[104]

---

[103] For these distinctions and their application to *Rezeptionsästhetik*, see de Man 1986: 55–58.

[104] Bibliography in this section is purposefully scant; see instead the individual chapters.

INTRODUCTION   31

1. *The Herodotean sensibility has to do with a strong idea of authorship and authority, and with the ethics of writing.* All writing has to do with authority. But among the earliest prose authors from ancient Greece, Herodotus has had certain qualities attributed to him. The Herodotean voice marks a distinctive turn in ancient Greek literature and is a robust and strongly felt presence in his work.[105] An active, judging presence, exuding attitudes and tones that range from chatty to solemn, combative to humble—such is the irrepressible voice of the *Histories*. In my chapters on Dionysius and Plutarch especially, I contend that this voice helps to reify the sense of Herodotus as a moral agent in his work. The overtness of his projected authority becomes a stimulus to Dionysius and Plutarch, whose responses to Herodotus's moral force differ in their judgments but rely on a similar premise of ethical authorship.[106] Likewise, for Dio, Lucian, and Pausanias, the heft of Herodotean presence affords each writer the chance to define his own authority through a co-opted version of its precedent. For Dio, this will mean adopting the moral authority of the Herodotean traveling and ethnographic mode. Lucian, for his part, attempts self-definition through apparent contrast (one kinetically combined with his adroit Herodotean mimicry), while for Pausanias, the appropriation of Herodotus's voice, in its very earnestness, shows just how different the reactions to the perceived power of that voice could be.

2. *The Herodotean sensibility has to do with charm and accessibility but also with a certain elusiveness, irony, and ambiguity.* Benjamin hints at something of Herodotus's elusiveness in his essay on the storyteller: "Herodotus offers no explanations. His report is the driest. That is why this story from ancient Egypt [regarding Cambyses and Psammenitus] is still capable after thousands of years of arousing astonishment and thoughtfulness."[107] Benjamin's description is suggestive of what one might call Herodotean *entranceability*, the ability for his narrative to entrance and, through its surface simplicity of style, to be entered into. Indeed, in the explicit judgments of ancient readers, Herodotean style is often "sweet," "charming," "graceful," and, especially in contrast to a

---

[105] See the classic studies of Dewald 1987; Marincola 1987; Fowler 1996. Further, Dewald 2002; Goldhill 2002: 11–44.

[106] In a way, their responses anticipate the recent turn in critical studies toward an affirmation of authorship: see Burke 1992; Burke 1995. See also Biriotti and Miller 1993: 5–7; McCann 1993; Goldhill 1993.

[107] Benjamin 1936: 90.

32 HERODOTUS AND IMPERIAL GREEK LITERATURE

writer such as Thucydides, easygoing and accessible.[108] The felt qualities of Herodotean style, by the assumptions of ancient criticism's ethical tendency, afford a notion of a good-spirited, gentle-minded author. For Dionysius, this is essential: the writerly life that he locates in Herodotus is one of admirable achievement, one that properly disposes the past by making it accessible to the "layperson" (ἰδιώτης). Plutarch, too, recognizes Herodotus's charm and gracefulness, but for him, this proves to be precisely the problem. The likable surface of Herodotus's text obscures the author's ill spirit. Dio, in his lone explicit reference to Herodotus (*Or.* 18.10), flags a quality of obliqueness that applies to aspects of his own corpus, one that itself combines smooth prose with sometimes barbed moral seriousness. For Lucian, charm is also a strategy of elusiveness and irony: having his day with Herodotus means romping through the ways in which charm allows him to divert, deflect, and leave readers uncertain. And if, finally, Pausanias is for some a quintessentially charmless writer, his consistent Herodoteanism contributes nonetheless to his difficulty: invoking the divine, for instance, or inscribing a set of alternatives to explain a particular phenomenon, Pausanias reiterates Herodotean qualities while also deferring ultimate adjudication. Herodotus in the hands of his receiving agents is both an open, freeing source and one whose own proliferations produce open-ended results.

3. *The Herodotean has to do with the ambivalence of "otherness" and with the slippery determination of the self and the truth.* Herodotus likes the oddball: strange animals, arch utterances, unexpected habits, reversals. At the same time, his capacity to flag otherness is met by a like capacity to collapse differences, to make the Greeks seem strange, and to reveal foreign peoples as sometimes familiar.[109] He exhibits chameleonlike qualities on such questions as the morality of empire, the consistency of identity (in his various accounts, for instance, of Athenian Pelasgianism), and the nature of the "differences" between Greeks and non-Greeks. Herodotus's engagement with such issues prefigures questions of Hellenic identity and self-definition under Roman rule.[110]

---

[108] See Pernot 1995: 127–28; Priestley 2014: 198 n. 47; Tribulato 2016: 178.

[109] See Pelling 2019: 142–45.

[110] Discussion of identity has been a staple of the scholarship on Imperial Greece. See Dench 2017 with further citations, but also fundamentally Woolf 1994; Jones 2004. One senses in Whitmarsh 2001b and Whitmarsh 2013 an impatience with the topic of identity, or at least a desire to theorize it more radically, for which see Whitmarsh 2001a (esp. 300–304) and Connolly 2007a: 28–32.

Accordingly, there is good reason to ask how Herodotus, whose text implicitly probes questions of Greek self-definition,[111] proved serviceable to Imperial writers acutely interested in questions of Hellenism. Dionysius, for instance, embraces Herodotus's cosmopolitan text as part of his own blended sense of Greco-Roman identity. Greeks are a form of both self and other for Dionysius, who transmutes Greek virtues into those of the Romans, while leaving open the possibility that the new Greeks—the Romans—can surpass those of old. In Plutarch's case, one aspect among Herodotus's many qualities of weirdness (ἀτοπία) is his enthusiasm for difference. For Plutarch, this trait scans as one of his chief flaws—that of being φιλοβάρβαρος (an insult that ironically anticipates other more redemptive readings of Herodotus's broadmindedness, including Dio's). If Plutarch is perturbed by Herodotus's love for difference, Lucian embraces it. In his *True Histories*, *Scythian*, and *Anacharsis*, he offers a sustained improvisation on the slippages of Herodotean sensibility, one that moves nimbly between interest in and perspectival inhabitation of "otherness." Meanwhile, while the qualities of strangeness would seem to many readers rather muted in Pausanias's *Periegesis*, it is nonetheless the case that his intense interest in religious matters shuttles his readers to a realm of the ineffable, as he trains his autoptic eye not on the oddities of the periphery but on the enduring mysteries of the center.

4. *The Herodotean has to do with magnitude, wonder, the beyond, the global—in short, that which approaches the sublime.* Herodotus approaches the unsayable. His text gestures at limits; it reaches boundaries physical and cognitive. Yet to mark wonder may also be to denote a form of temporary comprehension: the *understanding* that something is marvelous or strange. While Herodotus is well known for his preoccupation with the wondrous—the various things that fall into the category of θώματα—it is also the case that the entirety of his text charts its way through a wonder, the improbable repulse of the Persian invasion by allied Greek city-states. The invitation to marvel—the socialized, outward gesture of Herodotus's denominating wonder—is reflected in the critical engagement that each of his later receiving authors commits in relation to him. Dionysius's attraction to Herodotus, for instance, depends in part on his sense that his predecessor had a proper sense of scope and

---

[111] See Thomas 2001a.

magnitude in writing up both Greece and Persia, in turn informing his own interest in writing up the monolith of Rome. Plutarch, in turn, sees in Herodotus's choice of subject an appropriate grandeur but a failed execution, while Dio's sense of a cosmic Hellenism (in his *Oration* 36) replays some of the grand scale of Herodotus's Greek-and-barbarian world. Lucian's vivification of Anacharsis—whose first prominent appearance in Greek literature arises in the pages of Herodotus—summons a variety of questions about borders, identities, and the marvels that lie beyond one's own cognitive strictures. And rounding matters off, a strong sense of wonder pervades Pausanias, for whom it is none other than Greece itself, not distant lands or unseen realms, that is charged as a site of awe. Several centuries after Herodotus expressed his own capacity for astonishment, Pausanias's text revitalizes, amid the twilight of Greeks' power, the panoply of marvels still present in their own midst.

1

The Ethics of Authorship

Herodotus in the Rhetorical Works of Dionysius of Halicarnassus

Anomalous among ancient critics, the first-century BCE Roman émigré Dionysius of Halicarnassus offers a consistently sanguine appraisal of Herodotus, a fact that has not always inspired later readers to look favorably on Dionysius himself.[1] Although he does not devote a discrete treatise to Herodotus, Dionysius carves out, through various acts of attention across several works, an integral role for Herodotus in the construction of his own authorial persona and classicizing program, articulated amid a period of profound cultural change in Dionysius's adoptive Rome.[2] The question is why. What does Herodotus *do* for Dionysius, and why does it matter for understanding both authors? Although for some time Dionysius was not regarded as a sufficiently serious critic to merit the kind of attention such questions might entail, he has in recent years attracted nuanced consideration in the effort to understand his critical and historiographic agendas.[3] Along with the renewed regard for Dionysius's ambitions comes the opportunity to reconsider the kind of Herodotus he constructs, its relevance for Dionysius's literary program, and its meaning for the afterlife of the author of the *Histories*.

---

[1] See the introduction, quoting Usher 1985: 350. Dionysius's judgments occur in the wider context of a literary culture that often placed a high value on Thucydides: Weaire 2005: 256–63, with Cic. *Brut.* 287–88, *Orat.* 30–32. Dionysius was surely aware of Herodotus's problematic afterlife, and his various acts of reception amount to an almost contrarian response (noted in passing by Hadas 1954: 213); see, e.g., Momigliano 1990: 40 on those who "threw mud" on Herodotus. For Dionysius's rhetorical works, I follow the text and numeration of Aujac's Budé editions (Aujac 1978–1992).

[2] On Dionysius's alertness to the fusion of identities and cultural complexity, see Bowersock 1965: 131–32. On Dionysius as a writer in his Augustan context, see Hunter and de Jonge 2019a. Dionysius's longest extant discussion of Herodotus is at *Pomp.* 3, discussed later. Dionysius may have intended further treatment of Herodotus in *On the Ancient Orators*; see *Orat. Vett.* 4.4, "I shall discuss each author separately, starting first with the orators and then, if space allows (ἐὰν δὲ ἐγχωρῇ), the historians."

[3] For the (now largely outmoded) negative view of Dionysius as a critic, see Pritchett 1975: xxiii–v. Among recent studies devoted to Dionysius's literary-critical and historiographic programs, see Fox 1993; Fox 2011; Wiater 2011a; Wiater 2011b.

Herodotus and Imperial Greek Literature. N. Bryant Kirkland, Oxford University Press. © Oxford University Press 2022.
DOI: 10.1093/oso/9780197583517.003.0002

36 HERODOTUS AND IMPERIAL GREEK LITERATURE

In this chapter and the next, I situate Dionysius's esteem for Herodotus within the wider compass of his own thought. I argue that Dionysius's reception acts evince a habitual preoccupation with authorial ethics, the purposes of imitation, and—ultimately—the relationship between writing and power, text and empire. Herodotus sits at the convergence of Dionysius's interrelated ideals of moral and aesthetic value. Across his works, Dionysius both articulates and appropriates a Herodotean sensibility, that of a genial and what I will call ethical narrator who exercises a broad-minded approach to his subject. Dionysius's criticism also figures the *Histories* as a text that could speak to imperializing aspects of Roman power.[4] Dionysius's reception thus derives from something more than hometown pride or a predetermining "rhetoricality" that left him no choice but to uphold his forebear.[5] Rather than (or rather more than) exalting Herodotus merely as a good stylist, and rather than taking Herodotus's classicality as a given, Dionysius himself contributes to shaping something of a notion of Herodotus as "classical," in the process revealing ways in which that classicality comported with certain ideological pressures of Dionysius's own moment.[6] Dionysius depicts Herodotus as though Herodotus were himself a critic who chooses the right topic and the proper manner of disposing it. This interpretive tendency redounds to Dionysius's self-portrait as critic and affords analogy between the two: Dionysius chooses the "right" authors, much as Herodotus selected the "right" events and style in representing history. Both choose to depict a proper vision of the past.

Dionysius's Herodotus

Across a range of categories, Dionysius holds Herodotus in high regard. In this first section, I focus on how Dionysius's construction of the Herodotean persona adumbrates what we might call a "writerly life," a set of interrelated ethical and aesthetic authorial choices that manifest in literature. Dionysius's critical works open a space for thinking about *ethos* as something a writer determines or shapes, instead of merely possessing. As Dionysius constructs

---

[4] The *Histories'* role in imperial(izing) thinking has a long afterlife (see, e.g., Skinner 2020).

[5] Usher (1985: 71 n. 5) passingly intimates that a common hometown accounts for Dionysius's fealty to Herodotus; see also Hadas 1954: 213–14 for "local patriotism" (213).

[6] See Wiater 2019: 77 on Dionysian canon formation: "'The classical' is imposed on the material, not found in it." See Wiater 2019: 65 on the "complex of aesthetics and political and moral values" and the "structure of feelings" (borrowing from Raymond Williams) that they enable.

THE ETHICS OF AUTHORSHIP 37

it, the relationship between one's life and the written word is not so much a matter of directly transferring one's immutable character into style; rather, one's style depends on *deliberate choice* (προαίρεσις), a willed disposition toward one's subject and readers that shapes a writer's ethics of representation.[7] A hint of this interrelation of life and literary choice makes an appearance in the preface to Dionysius's *On the Ancient Orators*:

> I shall make an attempt to say these things, taking as the subject for my treatise one of universal interest, adopted with others in mind, and of potentially great benefit. It is the question of who the most noteworthy of the ancient orators and historians are, and what their deliberate choices both in life and literature were, and what we ought to choose and avoid from each.... (*Orat. Vett.* 4.1–2)

> ταῦτα πειράσομαι λέγειν, ὑπόθεσιν τοῦ λόγου κοινὴν καὶ φιλάνθρωπον καὶ πλεῖστα δυναμένην ὠφελῆσαι λαβών. ἔστι δὲ ἥδε, τίνες εἰσὶν ἀξιολογώτατοι τῶν ἀρχαίων ῥητόρων τε καὶ συγγραφέων καὶ τίνες αὐτῶν ἐγένοντο προαιρέσεις τοῦ τε βίου καὶ τῶν λόγων καὶ τί παρ᾽ ἑκάστου δεῖ λαμβάνειν ἢ φυλάττεσθαι....[8]

Dionysius foregrounds deliberate life choices (προαιρέσεις τοῦ τε βίου) in his effort to determine the literary men "most worthy of narration."[9] The preface conveys that it is not exclusively literary features that Dionysius will examine or literary choices as a one-to-one lens onto life choices. Invoking both categories, not strictly separable from but rather bound up with each other, broadens the usefulness of his criticism and squares it with his emphasis on "universal interest" (κοινήν) and human good (φιλάνθρωπον),

---

[7] See Fox 1993: 41; Hunter 2019: 38, 40, 49; Wiater 2019: 64. To be sure, the connections of life and literature, character and discourse, form a recurrent nexus in ancient criticism, as articulated in the formulation of Seneca the Younger: *talis hominibus fuit oratio qualis vita* (*Ep.* 114.1). Compare Dionysius's own statement that "everyone reasonably believes that one's words are the images of one's mind" (ἐπιεικῶς γὰρ ἅπαντες νομίζουσιν εἰκόνας εἶναι τῆς ἑκάστου ψυχῆς τοὺς λόγους, *Ant. Rom.* 1.1.3.10). See generally Russell 1981: 159–68, and compare Porter 2016: 223 on the "writerly soul." Dionysius's emphasis on προαίρεσις perhaps offers, however, a slight twist on the idea represented by the Senecan apothegm: his criticism of especially Herodotus and Thucydides, as we shall see, suggests that an author's literary output is not so much a reflection of a fixed quality but arises rather from a flexible willed disposition, which itself becomes imitable. Compare Burrow 2019: 66 on "re-instantiat[ing] the moral virtues of the *paradeigma*."

[8] I favor Reiske's emendation τῶν λόγων over the τοῦ λόγου printed by Aujac. See Hidber 1996: 125–26.

[9] Dionysius's ἀξιολογώτατοι has a Herodotean flavor, recalling an author frequently interested in things "noteworthy" (λόγου ἄξιος and ἀξιόλογος): see Hdt. 1.133.2, 2.138.2, 4.28.2, 8.35.2, 8.91.

38 HERODOTUS AND IMPERIAL GREEK LITERATURE

in a treatise that aspires to greatly benefiting people (πλεῖστα δυναμένην ὠφελῆσαι).[10] The collocation (τοῦ τε βίου καὶ τῶν λόγων), both terms dependent on the philosophically rich προαίρεσις, merges for Dionysius's reader the biographic and the literary—and, as we shall see, the moral and the aesthetic—into a common sphere of choice, as both text and *ethos* become models. Mere identification of the right authors does not suffice; one must know which qualities, ethical and aesthetic, are worth adopting from each.[11] At the outset of his treatise, then, Dionysius is raising multiple possibilities and implying that the authors, styles, and lives worthy of imitation are not a given. Authorial choice as it passes into literature becomes the point at which the critic judges another's style as the manifestation not of an unchanging soul but of an exercised freedom.[12] A "writer's capacity to express himself" bespeaks his προαίρεσις, the choices that shape the χαρακτήρ.[13] Indeed, just as Dionysius "takes on" (λαβών) a subject (ὑπόθεσιν τοῦ λόγου), and just as authors make their choices, so must the reader learn to take on (δεῖ λαμβάνειν) virtues from life and letters.

While scholars have long recognized Dionysius's approbation of Herodotus, the details of how and why Dionysius constructs Herodotus's writerly life and deliberate disposition, combining at once a choice for loftiness and accessibility, deserve attention. Some of the most illustrative examples of Dionysius's representation of Herodotus's ethical and aesthetic soundness appear in the latter half of the *Letter to Gnaeus Pompey*, where

---

[10] The fusion of style and content, aesthetics and ethics, is part of the political and public life envisioned by Dionysius, wherein philosophically inclined men are active in the public square, and the styles of their speeches reflect the content of their thought (*Orat. Vett.* 1.1). See Wiater 2019: 74–75. One might compare aspects of Dionysius's rhetorical-political program with that of Cicero; see Leo 1901: 221–23. Yet even if Dionysius's program is aimed at developing men for public life, his treatises emphasize figures from the past and their writerly lives far more than the practical effects of their styles in public settings (Wiater 2019: 73).

[11] Compare Dionysius's formulation at *Pomp.* 1.2: "I shall tell you what I feel about all who direct the power of their thoughts to the common good in their effort **to straighten out our lives and words**" (ἐπανορθοῦντες ἡμῶν βίους τε καὶ λόγους).

[12] Compare Dewald 1987: 150 on the way Herodotus's authorial interruptions remind readers that "Herodotus' narrative is not an unmediated transcription of *res gestae* but a set of authorial choices."

[13] Quoting Porter 2016: 223. I part ways somewhat with Porter's n. 118 on the same page, where in the course of distinguishing χαρακτήρ from *le style est l'homme même*, he writes that the "ancient virtue of style among rhetorical critics has very little to do with ethics in a moral sense. . . . Dionysius shows very little interest in the state of his writers' souls *per se*." This underserves Dionysius's programmatic προαιρέσεις τοῦ τε βίου καὶ τῶν λόγων (*Orat. Vett.* 4.2) and his larger interest in virtues that can apply to both literature and everyday interaction, such as clarity of speech (see *Thuc.* 49.3) or emphasizing topics that provide moral uplift to others (*Pomp.* 3.2). Dionysius's interest in narratorial behavior betrays a cognizance of writers as people whose lives one can imitate; narratorial ethics are not cleanly separable from those of social life.

THE ETHICS OF AUTHORSHIP 39

Dionysius offers his fullest surviving assessment of historians, including Herodotus, Thucydides, Xenophon, and Theopompus.[14] Dionysius claims that these chapters (*Pomp.* 3–6) reproduce his earlier discussion from *On Imitation*, concerning "which men—philosophers or poets, historiographers or rhetoricians—ought to be imitated" (*Pomp.* 3.1).[15] In his extended discussion of Herodotus's and Thucydides's choice of subject, for instance, Dionysius imparts his moral judgment of the two authors by evaluating the very premise of each writer's work. Dionysius hints at the idea that writers behave according to an inner ethic, a choice to follow one line of thought or the other, leaving a trail of consequences for readers:

For anyone writing history, the first and so to speak most necessary task of all is the selection of a subject that is noble and pleasing to readers. In my view Herodotus did this better than Thucydides. For the former has brought forth a common history of the doings of Greeks and barbarians, "in order that neither human events become faded, nor their deeds," just as he said: for the proem itself is both the start and end of his history. Thucydides writes a single war, one that is neither noble nor fortunate: indeed, a war which ought not to have occurred, and, short of that, one that ought to have been committed to silence and oblivion and ignored by successive generations. That he has chosen a bad topic is something he himself makes clear in his introduction, for he says there that many Greek cities were devastated because of the war, some by foreigners, others by their own peoples, and that there was more expulsion and slaughter than ever before, in addition to more earthquakes, droughts, plagues, and other kinds of calamity. Consequently, readers of his introduction feel alienated by his subject, since it is concerning Greece, after all, that they are about to read. To the extent that the written account showing forth the marvelous deeds of the Greeks and barbarians is superior to that announcing the lamentable, awful sufferings of the Greeks, to that very extent is Herodotus superior in discernment to Thucydides in his choice of subject. (*Pomp.* 3.2–6)

---

[14] For an outline of the topics discussed at *Pomp.* 3–6, see Walker 2012: 265–66; Matijašić 2018: 73–78.

[15] Inasmuch as Dionysius claims to have lifted the *Pompey* passage from what is likely his earliest work, he provides a kind of self-affirmation of the centrality of his comments on Herodotus to his criticism (see Matijašić 2018: 75, "Herodotus is preferred . . . throughout the whole treatise"). On the self-quotation, see Sacks 1983: 66–70, 76–80. On the relationship between the *Letter to Gnaeus Pompey* and the *On Imitation*, see Heath 1989a; Weaire 2002; Matijašić 2018: 70–72.

40　HERODOTUS AND IMPERIAL GREEK LITERATURE

πρῶτόν τε καὶ σχεδὸν ἀναγκαιότατον ἔργον ἁπάντων ἐστὶ τοῖς γράφουσιν πάσας ἱστορίας ὑπόθεσιν ἐκλέξασθαι καλὴν καὶ κεχαρισμένην τοῖς ἀναγνωσομένοις. τοῦτο Ἡρόδοτος κρεῖττόν μοι δοκεῖ πεποιηκέναι Θουκυδίδου. ἐκεῖνος μὲν γὰρ κοινὴν Ἑλληνικῶν τε καὶ βαρβαρικῶν πράξεων ἐξενήνοχεν ἱστορίαν, ὡς μήτε τὰ γενόμενα ἐξ ἀνθρώπων <ἐξίτηλα γένηται> μήτε ἔργα, καθάπερ αὐτὸς εἴρηκε· τὸ γὰρ αὐτὸ προοίμιον καὶ ἀρχὴ καὶ τέλος ἐστὶ τῆς ἱστορίας. ὁ δὲ Θουκυδίδης πόλεμον ἕνα γράφει, καὶ τοῦτον οὔτε καλὸν οὔτε εὐτυχῆ, ὃς μάλιστα μὲν ὤφειλε μὴ γενέσθαι, εἰ δὲ μή, σιωπῇ καὶ λήθῃ παραδοθεὶς ὑπὸ τῶν ἐπιγιγνομένων ἠγνοῆσθαι. ὅτι δὲ πονηρὰν εἴληφεν ὑπόθεσιν, καὶ αὐτός γε τοῦτο ποιεῖ φανερὸν ἐν τῷ προοιμίῳ· πόλεις τε γὰρ δι᾽ αὐτὸν ἐξερημωθῆναί φησι πολλὰς Ἑλληνίδας, τὰς μὲν ὑπὸ βαρβάρων, τὰς δ᾽ ὑπὸ σφῶν αὐτῶν, καὶ φύγαδας καὶ φθόρους ἀνθρώπων ὅσους οὔπω πρότερον γενέσθαι, σεισμούς τε καὶ αὐχμοὺς καὶ νόσους καὶ ἄλλας πολλὰς συμφοράς. ὥστε τοὺς ἀναγνόντας τὸ προοίμιον ἠλλοτριῶσθαι πρὸς τὴν ὑπόθεσιν, Ἑλληνικῶν μέλλοντας ἀκούειν. ὅσῳ δὲ κρείττων ἡ τὰ θαυμαστὰ ἔργα δηλοῦσα Ἑλλήνων τε καὶ βαρβάρων γραφὴ τῆς τὰ οἰκτρὰ καὶ δεινὰ πάθη τῶν Ἑλλήνων διαγγελλούσης, τοσούτῳ φρονιμώτερος Ἡρόδοτος Θουκυδίδου κατὰ τὴν ἐκλογὴν τῆς ὑποθέσεως.

In this opening passage of Dionysius's discussion of Herodotus in the *Letter to Gnaeus Pompey*, Dionysius enunciates a sense of transdiscursive unity that links up historical deeds and the choice to record them. The passage implies connection between ἔργα as "accomplishments" recorded—including their moral quality—and the ἔργον of the historian's "work" or "task," with its own attendant moral weight: historians recount ἔργα, but their own most important ἔργον involves choice of topic.[16] Narrative emerges as the result of a *decision* that conveys the author's judgment of what is good. The passage thereby indicates a key quality of Dionysius's own critical disposition, oriented toward identifying τὸ καλόν in both its moral and aesthetic spheres and toward identifying what is good for the benefit of his readers. In this case, Dionysius underscores that Herodotus chose a nobler, morally more beautiful subject.[17] The καλόν neatly enfolds Herodotus's moral and aesthetic superiority, and the qualities of the ὑπόθεσις redound to the historian himself.

---

[16] Compare Bakker 2002: 26–27 on the "reciprocity between on the one hand the intentions of the Greeks and barbarians engaged in the making of history and on the other hand the intentions of Herodotus himself in making his *historiē*" (26).

[17] At various points, I translate the word καλός as "beautiful" when it seems to call for that sense, but the slippage in Dionysius between nobility and beauty is persistent.

THE ETHICS OF AUTHORSHIP   41

Dionysius therefore assigns the historian his own critical "task" in choosing a topic in conformity with τὸ καλόν. In a certain sense, the historian operates on a contiguous moral plane as the actors of his work, and historians subsequently, like the characters of their texts, become subject to moral evaluation.

By contrast, the claim that Thucydides alienates (ἠλλοτριῶσθαι) readers allows Dionysius to analogize implicitly between the regrettable Greek-against-Greek hostility of Thucydides's narrative and the parallel hostility Thucydides shows his audience, in his failure to choose a "pleasing" (κεχαρισμένην) subject.[18] In his rejection of Thucydides's chosen topic, Dionysius does not exculpate Thucydides's skills qua historian while separately condemning the war. Instead, Dionysius describes how *both* subject and writer are blameworthy, binding the two together, Thucydides's moral failure and the disaster of the Peloponnesian War itself.[19] That war, Dionysius asserts, ought never to have occurred *and* ought to have been consigned to silence by those living in its wake (σιωπῇ καὶ λήθῃ παραδοθεὶς ὑπὸ τῶν ἐπιγιγνομένων ἠγνοῆσθαι). Thucydides's literary ἔργον is seen in direct relation to the war's ἔργα and thus worsens an already abysmal (πονηράν) event. Dionysius emphasizes, then, in this contrast between Herodotus and Thucydides, that each had a choice: the mere occurrence of events does not (for Dionysius) necessitate transcription.[20]

The end of the passage furthers the association of topic and author, content and *ethos*, by hypotactically coordinating into one sphere of superiority the marvelous Greek achievement and Herodotus's choice of subject matter. Event and text are brought into parallel: "To the extent that the written account showing forth the marvelous deeds of the Greeks and barbarians is superior to that announcing the lamentable, awful sufferings of the Greeks, to that same extent is Herodotus superior in discernment to Thucydides in his choice of subject." Snaking through this sentence is a near-quotation of Herodotus's proem: Dionysius embeds the historiographic phrasing from

---

[18] For some, Dionysius offers nothing more than a "rhetorical" understanding of history; see, e.g., Kennedy 1994: 161 and more generally Woodman 1988; Fox and Livingstone 2007. Cf. chapter 2 on Dionysius's "rhetoricality" and his own historiographic project.

[19] On Dionysius's reception of Thucydides at *Pomp.* 3, see de Jonge 2017: 646–49; Matijašić 2018: 88–97.

[20] To be sure, once the topical choice is made, events may demand an account that places the writer under necessity; see, e.g., Polybius 1.4.1 on the obligation (δεῖ) to offer a single historical vision (μίαν σύνοψιν) in response to a seemingly all-encompassing Rome; compare Lucian, *Hist. conscr.* 50 on the need to have a mind like a mirror that accurately reflects reality. Dionysius's highlighting of the writer's deliberate action here will inflect his own self-portrait as a well-intentioned author who does not alienate his readers (see the section on "Dionysius as Herodotus" later in this chapter).

42 HERODOTUS AND IMPERIAL GREEK LITERATURE

Herodotus into his own judgment: τὰ θαυμαστὰ ἔργα . . . Ἑλλήνων τε καὶ βαρβάρων (*Pomp.* 3.6) ≈ ἔργα μεγάλα τε καὶ θωμαστά, τὰ μὲν Ἕλλησι, τὰ δὲ βαρβάροισι (Hdt. proem). Phraseological reverberation reinforces Dionysius's moral point. By echoing Herodotus, Dionysius aligns his critical judgment with that of the very historian he praises: the critic's assessment is mapped onto historical judgment from the past.[21] The set of parallels solidifies the implication that Dionysius, casting his critical eye over literary history, chooses correctly, much as Herodotus did.[22] Thus, Dionysius limns a blended set of categories: the ἔργα of history and the ἔργον of history-writing; criticism of historiography and historiography as criticism.[23] Dionysius's vision applies both to the sweeping subject matter of the *Histories* and to the composite of authorial choice and textual articulation that he would (have his reader) imitate.

As the *Letter* proceeds, Dionysius continues to elevate Herodotus's writerly life by implying that he, again like a critic, exercised a superior understanding of the tradition predating him and therefore the imitative possibilities before him:

> In no way is it possible to say this: that Thucydides came to this writing through necessity. For although he knew other matters to be nobler, he nevertheless did not want to write on the same topics as the others. Quite the contrary: in his prologue he belittles ancient deeds, and declares that those brought to completion in his own time were the greatest and most awe-inspiring. And it is clear that he does so willingly and by choice. However, Herodotus for his part did not make this choice, despite the fact that Hellanicus and Charon, authors preceding him, had published on the same

[21] Compare Porter 2016: 236 on Dionysius's habit of quotation: "Quotations are for both writers [Dionysius and Longinus] the framework within which the past is staged and allowed to come to life repeatedly and performatively." Dionysius's tendency, as at *Pomp.* 3.6, to embed submerged reverberations contributes to this sense of activating the literary past.

[22] Hunter 2019 (esp. 41, 43, 46) advances a similar argument about the parallelism Dionysius establishes between his own critical judgment and that of Thucydides. Weaire 2005 likewise argues with respect to Dionysius's *On Thucydides* that the treatise offers a "display of *mimēsis* of Thucydides, a *mimēsis* characteristic of Dionysius in being a discriminating process of adopting the best in the model and discarding the rest" (263). I share both Hunter's and Weaire's belief in the historiographic imitative traces that permeate Dionysius, but I find the emphasis on Thucydides as Dionysius's model hard to reconcile not only with Dionysius's more consistent acclamation of Herodotus but also with the *Thucydides* essay's various ways of finding him problematic; see esp. *Thuc.* 49–51. On the inconsistency of Thucydides's status in Dionysius's rhetorical treatises, see Sacks 1983: 80–83.

[23] This blend is well captured by Fox (1993: 42): "Modern distinctions between writing, life, written history, actual historical events, subject matter, and historical account furnish a vocabulary inappropriate for comprehending the absence of distinctions and holism which the mimetic theory of composition assumes."

topic. But he was not deterred: rather, he decided to trust himself to carry out something greater, and that is exactly what he has done. (*Pomp.* 3.6–7)

οὐδὲ γὰρ οὐδὲ τοῦτο ἔνεστιν εἰπεῖν ὅτι δι' ἀνάγκην ἦλθεν ἐπὶ ταύτην τὴν γραφήν, ἐπιστάμενος <μὲν ὡς> ἐκεῖνα καλλίω, βουλόμενος δὲ μὴ ταὐτὰ ἑτέροις γράφειν· πᾶν γὰρ τοὐναντίον ἐν τῷ προοιμίῳ διασύρων τὰ παλαιὰ ἔργα μέγιστα καὶ θαυμασιώτατα τὰ καθ' αὑτὸν ἐπιτελεσθέντα φησὶν εἶναι, καὶ φανερός ἐστι ταῦτα ἑκὼν ἑλόμενος. οὐ μὴν Ἡρόδοτός γε τοῦτο ἐποίησεν, ἀλλὰ τῶν πρὸ αὐτοῦ συγγραφέων γενομένων Ἑλλανίκου τε καὶ Χάρωνος τὴν αὐτὴν ὑπόθεσιν προεκδεδωκότων οὐκ ἀπετράπετο, ἀλλ' ἐπίστευσεν αὑτῷ κρεῖσσόν τι ἐξοίσειν· ὅπερ καὶ πεποίηκεν.

Dionysius again asserts the importance of choice (ἑκὼν ἑλόμενος) by flatly rejecting the notion that Thucydides's subject came upon him by necessity (δι' ἀνάγκην ἦλθεν). Thucydides's willful rupture from tradition remains a decision to avoid the topics that others had chosen. Dionysius charges him with "tearing to pieces" (διασύρων) the "ancient accomplishments" (τὰ παλαιὰ ἔργα) recorded by the likes of Herodotus, effectively saddling Thucydides both with a failure to pick the right topic and with the failure to honor what came before him. For Dionysius, imitation of the past need not mean a compromise on originality.[24] Herodotus indeed emerges for Dionysius as the better imitator, the superior classicist, we might say.[25] Herodotus was not deterred from choosing the same subject as that chosen by writers before him but chose, rather, to believe he could represent it better. In Dionysius's intimate indication of Herodotus's writerly life, the latter "decided to trust himself" (ἐπίστευσεν αὑτῷ, *Pomp.* 3.7). Herodotus, then, not only understands the necessity of choosing a good topic, but he also understands how to replicate the past as a literary *tradition* by choosing topics previously treated. He finds a middle ground between outright imitation and Thucydides's arguably more abrupt break from the literary past.[26]

[24] On Dionysius's sensitivity to poor imitations, see comments on Xenophon and Theopompus with regard to their predecessors (*Pomp.* 4–5).
[25] For similar observations, albeit with different emphases, see Wiater 2011a: 132–49, esp. 147–48; Hunter 2019: 41. On Dionysius's construction of fifth-century writers as themselves already classicizing, see Kim 2014.
[26] Dionysius underscores the depravity of Thucydides's deliberate choices in his claim that "Thucydides operates so grudgingly as to assign the apparent causes of the war to his own city, even though he could have assigned the causes to many other starting points" (οὕτω γε φθονερῶς, ὥστε καὶ τῇ πόλει τῇ ἑαυτοῦ τὰς φανερὰς αἰτίας τοῦ πολέμου περιάπτειν, ἑτέραις ἔχοντα πολλαῖς ἀφορμαῖς περιάψαι τὰς αἰτίας, *Pomp.* 3.9).

44 HERODOTUS AND IMPERIAL GREEK LITERATURE

In fact, Dionysius accords so much positive credit to Herodotus that even when his text ventures into unsavory territory, style can save him. Consider a passage in Dionysius's essay *On Literary Composition* in which the critic, discussing the power of the arrangement of words, adduces Herodotus's story of Gyges and Candaules:

> Not only was the matter lacking in dignity and inappropriate for literary treatment, but it was also vulgar, morally hazardous, closer to turpitude than to beauty. Yet it is told so skillfully, and it has become something better to hear described than to see happen. (*Comp.* 3.14)

> τὸ πρᾶγμα οὐχ ὅ τι σεμνὸν ἢ καλλιλογεῖσθαι ἐπιτήδειον, ἀλλὰ καὶ ταπεινὸν καὶ ἐπικίνδυνον καὶ τοῦ αἰσχροῦ μᾶλλον ἢ τοῦ καλοῦ ἐγγυτέρω· ἀλλ' εἴρηται σφόδρα δεξιῶς, καὶ κρεῖττον γέγονεν ἀκουσθῆναι λεγόμενον ἢ ὀφθῆναι γινόμενον.

Herodotus, through a kind of literary alchemy, can overcome even an undignified topic (οὐχ . . . σεμνόν) that morally endangers his readers, as he transforms the low and visually rebarbative into an aesthetically accomplished aural experience (κρεῖττον . . . ἀκουσθῆναι). Dionysius's choice of example steers the historian's emphasis on autopsy (albeit, in this case, a hazardous kind of prurient looking) into a morally safe reading experience.[27] In Dionysius's formulation that the story becomes better to hear described than to see happen, he also appears to offer an echo of a passing comment by Candaules in Herodotus's account, namely that "humans happen to find their ears less persuasive than their eyes" (ὦτα γὰρ τυγχάνει ἀνθρώποισι ἐόντα ἀπιστότερα ὀφθαλμῶν, 1.8.2). The recall of this Herodotean detail reinforces Dionysius's point that because of Herodotus's dexterous rendering (εἴρηται σφόδρα δεξιῶς), readers *can* now trust their ears. This validation of aural sensation in Herodotus is all the more important insofar as elements of the (unseen) classical past, for someone of Dionysius's day, repeatedly depend on acoustic evocation, on the past's audibility through texts.[28] Thus, for all the foregrounded emphasis on choice of topic at *Pomp.* 3.2–6, Dionysius's assertions here about Herodotean style imply that topic alone is not coextensive with the moral integrity of his work. Dionysius leaves open a door

---

[27] The Gyges and Candaules story was an educational staple, as can be judged from its appearances in *progymnasmata*: see Theon 91–92; Gibson 2008: 22–23 at no. 16 for Libanius.

[28] I owe this point to an exchange with Christopher van den Berg.

THE ETHICS OF AUTHORSHIP   45

through which others, including himself, can elevate content by means of sound style.

Refining Sensibility: Herodotus's Flexible Disposition

Returning to the *Letter to Gnaeus Pompey*, let us consider a final instance of how Dionysius establishes the literary persona of Herodotus as both ethically and aesthetically cogent as well as one that can exercise moral flexibility. In his comparison of Herodotus and Thucydides, Dionysius closes his treatment of subject matter with a brief discussion of "the attitude (διάθεσις) of the writer himself, which he adopts toward the things about which he writes" (τὴν αὐτοῦ τοῦ συγγραφέως διάθεσιν ἣ κέχρηται πρὸς τὰ πράγματα περὶ ὧν γράφει, *Pomp.* 3.15). He goes on:

> Herodotus's disposition toward his material is everywhere fair: it takes pleasure in good things and feels pain for bad things. That of Thucydides, by contrast, is something willful and harsh, nursing a grudge against his native city for his exile.... (*Pomp.* 3.15)

> ἡ μὲν Ἡροδότου διάθεσις ἐν ἅπασιν ἐπιεικὴς καὶ τοῖς μὲν ἀγαθοῖς συνηδομένη, τοῖς δὲ κακοῖς συναλγοῦσα. ἡ δὲ Θουκυδίδου διάθεσις αὐθέκαστός τις καὶ πικρὰ καὶ τῇ πατρίδι τῆς φυγῆς μνησικακοῦσα....

Dionysius expands the notion of a writerly life by connecting the author's emotional and sympathetic capacities to the work at hand. Herodotus has the virtue of intimating his emotional and sympathetic capacities qua narrator: he *pre*-reads, as it were, for readers, guiding them in how to react by taking pleasure in the good and feeling anguish toward bad events. Dionysius reminds us that Herodotus's mimetic burden involves duties not only to his material but also to his own self *in relation to* that material. The writing up of his inquiry is one of Herodotus's obligations; but through an enfolding of his disposition into written text, the critic also emphasizes the historian's attitude as an aspect of imitation by which the historian must prove himself a responsible author.[29] Although a critical focus on the historian's

---

[29] On the attitude of the historian as a recurrent feature of ancient literary criticism, see Woodman 1988: 40–45; Luce 1989: 21–23; Marincola 1997: 18–19. On the historian's character in relation to his work's mimesis, see Gray 1987: 473, with Arist., *Rh.* 1378a 6–13. A proper disposition constitutes

46 HERODOTUS AND IMPERIAL GREEK LITERATURE

attitude appears to have been an enshrined aspect of ancient assessments of historians, Dionysius's recognition implicitly instantiates the historian's attitudinal presence as part of Herodotus's achievement. Insofar as Dionysius attributes to Herodotus various choices, he attributes to him a legibility of attitude that attaches to his authorial persona.

Moreover, Dionysius's use of διάθεσις, in line with his recurrent use of προαίρεσις, reinforces the pliancy of the writerly life. An attitude is not an inevitability. Indeed, διάθεσις can be illuminated by a distinction from the Peripatetic tradition. In the *Categories* (8b25–9a13), Aristotle differentiates inveterate, long-standing ἕξις from the relatively changeable διάθεσις:

> Let it be said then that trained habit and disposition constitute a unitary idea of quality. Trained habit differs from disposition insofar as it is more stable and enduring. . . . Dispositions, on the other hand, are said to be those things which are easily shifted and quickly undergo change . . . . (*Cat.* 8b26–28, 35–36)

> ἓν μὲν οὖν εἶδος ποιότητος ἕξις καὶ διάθεσις λεγέσθωσαν. διαφέρει δὲ ἕξις διαθέσεως τῷ μονιμώτερον καὶ πολυχρονιώτερον εἶναι. . . . διαθέσεις δὲ λέγονται ἅ ἐστιν εὐκίνητα καὶ ταχὺ μεταβάλλοντα . . . .

Aristotle will go on to say that while habits can be reckoned as dispositions, dispositions cannot be reckoned as habits (9a10–13). Dionysius's use of διάθεσις should not, accordingly, imply inflexibility on the author's part, nor figure him as incapable of doing anything except expressing an unchangeable nature.[30] Rather, by his choice, the historian *disposes himself* in his work toward a particular ethic. That Dionysius mentions the διάθεσις of the historian only reinforces his broader emphasis on the deliberations of style. Herodotus does not simply possess a genial character that makes him ineluctably benevolent toward the good and pained by the bad; he *assumes* those attitudes.

part of what Wiater 2011b: 63–64 has called Dionysius's attempt to establish a "bond" among his readers, citing the work of Benedict Anderson's "imagined communities": for Dionysius and "the Greek reader he envisages," the expectation is that "historiography enable[s] them to establish an intimate connection with tradition by establishing an emotional bond with the (classical) past through the process of reading." To Wiater's notion of a bond between Dionysius and his reader, I would add the importance of a bond between Dionysius's readers and the authors he parlays: readers are invited to have sympathetic reactions to certain ancient models, based on the critic's curating of their dispositions.

[30] Compare Burrow 2019: 68.

THE ETHICS OF AUTHORSHIP   47

Hence, for Dionysius, texts are choices that emanate from their authors, who are themselves depicted as ethical entities. This judgment of authorial dispositions and writerly choices reflects back on Dionysius qua critic. For when Dionysius goes on to state that Herodotus represents character better than Thucydides (Ἡρόδοτος δὲ τά γε ἤθη παραστῆσαι δεινότερος, *Pomp.* 3.18), one senses an implied parallel with Dionysius, insofar as *he* has been portraying the historians' attitudes, choices, and characters for us.

Beyond System: The Layperson's Herodotus

We have seen some of the ways in which Dionysius characterizes Herodotus. By this I have meant how Dionysius describes the deliberate choices of Herodotus and how he imputes to him a character—a stamp of attitude and style—that issues from conscious moves to be a particular kind of author. Accordingly, we have examined this characterization in a double sense, in terms of both Dionysius's description of Herodotus's style itself, and his discussion of style as an indication of the writerly life and chosen disposition that inform the *Histories*.[31] I wish now to consider how Dionysius's consistent preference for Herodotus allows him to present his fellow Halicarnassian as accessible to the so-called layperson. I restrict my analysis here to portions of two works, *On Literary Composition*, where a focus on Herodotus's accessibility is explicit, and *On Thucydides*, where the connection between the layperson and Herodotus is detectable but less overt.

The question of accessibility raises that of perception: what degree of sophistication is required of Dionysius's readers to appreciate the characteristics he identifies in ancient authors? Important in this regard (if difficult to parse) is Dionysius's occasional recourse to the concept of ἄλογος αἴσθησις, which we might render as "intuitive perception," something that Dionysius apparently believes is available to ordinary listeners and readers.[32] Regardless

---

[31] On χαρακτήρ in relation to ἦθος and λέξις, see Worman 2002: 29–35. On the concept of χαρακτήρ in Theophrastus and the way it feeds into the later rhetorical tradition, see Burrow 2019: 65–66.

[32] On ἄλογος αἴσθησις, see de Jonge 2008: 195, 382–84; Wiater 2011a: 345–46. On reconciling ἄλογος αἴσθησις with Dionysius's apparently ordered critical system, see esp. Schenkeveld 1975 and Damon 1991. Schenkeveld argues that Dionysius's criticism lacks a coherent system, while Damon contends, with specific attention to ἄλογος αἴσθησις, that a system exists, only incompletely. On the eclectic nature of Dionysius's critical system, see Walker 2012: 217–18. See also Walker 2012: 255–56 for the valuable distinction that, at least for *On Literary Composition* (§§ 9, 19, 24, 32), Dionysius tends to invoke αἴσθησις "as a final appeal" (255) and as the "bedrock standard of judgment" (256)

48 HERODOTUS AND IMPERIAL GREEK LITERATURE

of how one interprets the term ἄλογος αἴσθησις, its invocation reinforces the sense that Dionysius's critical process depends on interlocutors and is, fundamentally, part of an open-ended system, subject to revision, amplification, and the pressures of dialogue.[33] Dionysius anticipates challenges from readers as part of his flexible critical procedure. Indeed, across his literary-critical corpus, the formal presentation of his pronouncements feels more dialogic than magisterial.[34] He presents his interpretive activity as processual, its changes and apparent inconsistencies reflecting interaction with and consciousness of his readers. Indeed, the epistolary format of several treatises (*On Thucydides*, *On Literary Composition*, the *Letter to Gnaeus Pompey*, the *First* and *Second Letter to Ammaeus*), along with the frequent direct addresses to readers, frames Dionysius's criticism as a process of critical "textuality" concerning ancient works.[35]

As part of his strategy of emphasizing the possibilities of give-and-take between himself and his readers, and in service to this flexible mode, Dionysius puts forth a Herodotus notable for his accessibility and clarity, a layperson's Herodotus. In articulating his preference for a writer who in Dionysius's own judgment made his work highly readable, Dionysius in turn intimates *his* own cognizance of readers. Together with his stress on his high ethical and aesthetic virtues, Dionysius intimates, for instance, the fact that Herodotus's commendable qualities enjoyed broad appeal and were known to a wide audience. Recall that Dionysius applauds Herodotus's skill in the Gyges and Candaules story (*Comp.* 3.14) for transforming unsavory material into

---

that "technical analysis and theory cannot overrule . . . but can only try to elucidate" (256). In his *On Thucydides*, by contrast, αἴσθησις is both "test and starting point" (262) and may be supplemented or enhanced by technical study.

[33] See generally Wiater 2011a: 279–351.

[34] See, e.g., Weaire 2005 for a consideration, in part, of the ways in which Dionysius's *On Thucydides* can be read in its socio-historical context as a response to a request from his prominent Roman friend Q. Aelius Tubero. Compare also de Jonge 2017: 651. On Dionysius's social and intellectual milieu more broadly, see Goold 1961; Bowersock 1965: 122–39; Wisse 1995: 78–80 (contra Goold 1961); Hidber 1996: 5–7; de Jonge 2008: 25–34; Wiater 2011a: 22–29.

[35] For the language of fluid "textuality" and fixed "texts," see Gurd 2012: 6–7. On open-endedness and the reader's engagement in Dionysius, see further Wiater 2011a: 279–303. The *Letter to Gnaeus Pompey* and the *Second Letter to Ammaeus* are responses to readers' requests for revision and clarification (see *Pomp.* 1; *Amm.* II. 1, 17.2). That Dionysius makes such a showy response of his open, dialogic propensities in a treatise (*Amm. II*) covering Thucydides contrastively highlights his own authorial virtue vis-à-vis the obscurities of the author in question, who preferred, for instance, "metaphorical, unclear, archaic, and strange" diction (τροπικὴν καὶ γλωττηματικὴν καὶ ἀπηρχαιωμένην καὶ ξένην λέξιν, *Amm. II* 2.2 = *Thuc.* 24.1). See Fox 2019: 182: "In line with his views of historiography in his essays, his approach privileges an Herodotean interest in plurality and reader engagement, over a more authoritarian Thucydidean method."

THE ETHICS OF AUTHORSHIP   49

something less prurient. Dionysius's replay of the story recapitulates a tale that Dionysius himself thought base (ταπεινόν) but which he assumes his readers were likely to have known well (and perhaps to have enjoyed). The Gyges example is useful for Dionysius in making a moralizing point about Herodotus *and* because its sauciness, however lowbrow, guarantees broad appeal.

Even passing comments contribute to Dionysius's strategy of depicting Herodotus as a popular author. When Dionysius adduces sentences concerning Croesus the Lydian from the *Histories* (Hdt. 1.6, at *Comp.* 4.7–11) to exemplify an aspect of word arrangement, he notes in passing that he chooses the example from Herodotus on the grounds that it is "known to many" (γνώριμός ἐστι τοῖς πολλοῖς, *Comp.* 4.8). Though hardly an arresting comment, in the context of various references to Herodotus's accessibility in the essay, it gains in significance by contributing to an overall effect. Several chapters further on, Dionysius makes another passing remark on Herodotus's style that again may at first scan as banal: "The compositional style of Herodotus has both these qualities: it is both pleasing and beautiful" (ἡ δὲ Ἡροδότου σύνθεσις ἀμφότερα ταῦτα ἔχει, καὶ γὰρ ἡδεῖά ἐστι καὶ καλή, *Comp.* 10.5). The significance here has to do with the specific combination of pleasure (ἡδεῖα) and beauty (καλή). References to pleasure and charm surround Herodotus's ancient reputation, but they do not always ring positive.[36] Charm can deceive, and pleasure can lure a reader into unedifying material. Such were precisely Dionysius's concerns with the Gyges and Candaules story. Accordingly, Dionysius's passing collocation of the two elements here redeems the moral risks of pleasurable reading: Herodotus is both pleasurable *and* morally beautiful. His pleasure is moreover accessible, while Thucydides puts his readers off (*Pomp.* 3.2; *Thuc.* 27.1).

To reinforce his point that a feeling for the pleasurable is widely accessible, Dionysius in the next chapter brings in examples from what he claims are his own experiences in "very popular theaters, filled with a diverse and uncultured crowd" (ἐν τοῖς πολυανθρωποτάτοις θεάτροις, ἃ συμπληροῖ παντοδαπὸς καὶ ἄμουσος ὄχλος, *Comp.* 11.8). In these spaces, Dionysius claims, he has come away with the impression that in all humans there is a natural connection to and sense for (φυσική . . . οἰκειότης) good melody and rhythm. He uses the example of a harpist and a reed player booed by

---

[36] Compare Plutarch's grudging admission of Herodotus's charm before reminding his readers of the bad character it conceals: *de malig. Herod.* 874C. See also Demetrius, *On Style* 181.

50 HERODOTUS AND IMPERIAL GREEK LITERATURE

an audience for hitting one false note (*Comp.* 11.8). Throughout the passage, Dionysius underlines the ability of ordinary people to perceive these solecisms (ἐπὶ δὲ τούτοις ἅπασι τῷ πρέποντι, *Comp.* 11.6; ἅμα πάντας ἀγανακτοῦντας καὶ δυσαρεστουμένους, *Comp.* 11.10), even if the same people lack the requisite technical skills to go onstage and play correctly themselves:

> Why is this? It is because the latter is a matter of specialized knowledge, in which we do not all have a share, while the former [i.e., perceiving wrong notes] is a matter of feeling, which nature has given to all. (*Comp.* 11.9)

> τί δή ποτε; ὅτι τοῦτο μὲν ἐπιστήμης ἐστίν, ἧς οὐ πάντες μετειλήφαμεν, ἐκεῖνο δὲ πάθους, ὃ πᾶσιν ἀπέδωκεν ἡ φύσις.

Although not specifically mentioned here, the idea of ordinary perception is akin to the ἄλογος type. Situating this passage in the flow of what has preceded, we recognize that insofar as Herodotus is imbued with the kinds of qualities discernible to a wide audience, he is the sort of writer whom even a member of that diverse and uncultured crowd (παντοδαπὸς καὶ ἄμουσος ὄχλος) might have appreciated. Dionysius later declares, "I am convinced that everyone knows that variation is the most pleasing and beautiful feature in writing. I take as an example all of Herodotus's writing, the entirety of Plato's, and all that of Demosthenes" (ὅτι γὰρ ἥδιστόν τε καὶ κάλλιστον ἐν λόγοις μεταβολή, πάντας εἰδέναι πείθομαι. παράδειγμα δὲ αὐτῆς ποιοῦμαι πᾶσαν μὲν τὴν Ἡροδότου λέξιν, πᾶσαν δὲ τὴν Πλάτωνος, πᾶσαν δὲ τὴν Δημοσθένους, *Comp.* 19.11–12). Herodotus exemplifies the trait that "everybody knows" to be the most pleasing and in relation to μεταβολή succeeds where Thucydides fails.[37] Even if his "everybody knows" is another exaggerated cliché, Dionysius nonetheless conveys the sense that Herodotus pleases his readers and plays to their sense of the good.

---

[37] See *Pomp.* 3.12, with discussion in the next chapter: "Thucydides, stretching on through a single war, proceeds without taking a breath, stringing together battle after battle, preparation scene after preparation scene, speech after speech, with the result that he wearies his readers' minds" (Θουκυδίδης δέ, πόλεμον ἕνα κατατείνας, ἀπνευστὶ διεξέρχεται μάχας ἐπὶ μάχαις καὶ παρασκευὰς ἐπὶ παρασκευαῖς καὶ λόγους ἐπὶ λόγοις συντιθείς, ὥστε μοχθεῖν [μὲν] τὴν διάνοιαν τῶν ἀκροωμένων). See also *Thuc.* 50 on the uselessness of Thucydides's style (χαρακτήρ), "suited neither to political debates nor to private exchanges" (οὔτ᾽ εἰς τοὺς πολιτικοὺς ἀγῶνας ἐπιτήδειος … οὔτ᾽ εἰς τὰς ὁμιλίας τὰς ἰδιωτικάς).

THE ETHICS OF AUTHORSHIP 51

Finally, in the same treatise, Dionysius acclaims Herodotean style as one in which the choice of words corresponds to how things are in nature, thereby suggesting an almost non-mimetic kind of reading experience unencumbered by difficulties of stylization (οἷα ἡ φύσις τέθεικεν σύμβολα τοῖς πράγμασιν, *Comp.* 3.16). Herodotus's art lacks artifice. Likewise, Herodotean substance and style collapse together when Dionysius writes that his "thoughts are in no way grander than the things in and of themselves" (τὰ νοήματα μηδὲν σεμνότερα εἶναι ἢ οἷά ἐστιν, *Comp.* 3.17). This correspondence between subject and style, outward reality and its transfer into prose, creates continuity between the world as observed by Herodotus (and subsequent readers) and that world's articulation on the page. Dionysius, in emphasizing Herodotean artlessness, underscores the accessibility of his lauded model as well as the sense that reality as it is perceived by everyday people finds its way into his work. Herodotus is both well known (γνώριμος) and well *knowable*, a special author who remains open to the non-specialist.

The Layperson in *On Thucydides*

The focus on the layperson (ἰδιώτης), the ordinary reader, recurs in an important series of distinctions laid out in *On Thucydides*. Early in the treatise, Dionysius defends his own power, despite falling short of the abilities of the authors under examination (τῇ δυνάμει λειπόμεθα, *Thuc.* 4.1), to criticize ancient models. He writes that he need not state the obvious, that "the layperson is no less able a critic of many works than the artist himself, at least as for such works as are grasped by intuitive perception and emotion" (ὅτι πολλῶν ἔργων οὐχ ἥττων τοῦ τεχνίτου κριτὴς ὁ ἰδιώτης, τῶν γε δι᾽ αἰσθήσεως ἀλόγου καὶ τοῖς πάθεσι καταλαμβανομένων, *Thuc.* 4.3).[38] Now, the specification would seem limited—reinforced by Reiske's emendation of the particle γε for the manuscripts' δέ—referring only to the subset of literary works that are accessible to the ordinary person. But the seeming limitation is actually rather a broad category in Dionysius's works, as the foregoing discussion of *On Literary Composition* makes clear. Such works as appeal to

---

[38] Compare Porter 2010: 207–8 on *Lys.* 11 and ἄλογος αἴσθησις: "Dionysius has in mind a developed perceptual faculty for language, with language understood as an enriched phenomenon that is capable of registering multiply enhanced aesthetic effects (musical, visual, and other)" (208). See other instances of the term or related terms: *Thuc.* 27; *Lys.* 11; *Comp.* 22; *Dem.* 24. Compare Cicero's description of the layperson and the skilled critic of oratory at *Brut.* 183–200.

52 HERODOTUS AND IMPERIAL GREEK LITERATURE

intuitive perception are, initially at least, all works; whether they succeed in reaching their audience is a matter of whether their style aids or hinders ἄλογος αἴσθησις.

Two passages from *On Thucydides* drive home Dionysius's ideas about the layperson. The first concerns the judgment of Thucydidean style. While Dionysius commends Thucydides, he does so in terms that unmistakably conjure his praise elsewhere of Herodotus, revealing him to be the implied touchstone by which Thucydides's various successes are measured:

> These and similar passages appeared to be worth emulating and imitating, and I am convinced that the man's elevation, eloquence, impressive force, and other virtues are at their peak in such passages. My proof derives from the fact that every mind is moved by this type of style. Neither the intuitive critical faculty, by which we are naturally equipped to apprehend that which is pleasing or grating, is alienated from it, nor is the reasoning faculty, by which the beautiful thing in each art is perceived. Those altogether inexperienced in public discourse would not be able to mention any word or expression that displeases them, nor could the most extravagantly learned (who look condescendingly upon the ignorance of the masses) blame the elaboration of this style, but mass and elite will agree on the same notion. Even your ubiquitous layperson will not take displeasure in the usual coarseness, tortuousness, and unfollowability of his style, while the rare specialist, who has had an unusual training, will not fault it as base, vulgar, and artless. Instead there will be complete agreement with respect to the judging and intuitive faculties, by both of which we deem it right that everything in art must be judged. (*Thuc.* 27.1–4)

> ἐμοὶ μὲν δὴ ταῦτα καὶ τὰ παραπλήσια τούτοις ἄξια ζήλου τε καὶ μιμήσεως ἐφάνη, τήν τε μεγαληγορίαν τοῦ ἀνδρὸς καὶ τὴν καλλιλογίαν καὶ τὴν δεινότητα καὶ τὰς ἄλλας ἀρετὰς ἐν τούτοις τοῖς ἔργοις ἐπείσθην τελειοτάτας εἶναι, τεκμαιρόμενος ὅτι πᾶσα ψυχὴ τούτῳ τῷ γένει τῆς λέξεως ἄγεται, καὶ οὔτε τὸ ἄλογον τῆς διανοίας κριτήριον, ᾧ πεφύκαμεν ἀντιλαμβάνεσθαι τῶν ἡδέων ἢ ἀνιαρῶν, ἀλλοτριοῦται πρὸς αὐτό, οὔτε τὸ λογικόν, ἐφ' οὗ διαγιγνώσκεται τὸ ἐν ἑκάστῃ τέχνῃ καλόν. οὐδ' ἂν ἔχοιεν οὔθ' οἱ μὴ πάνυ λόγων ἔμπειροι πολιτικῶν εἰπεῖν ἐφ' ὅτῳ δυσχεραίνουσιν ὀνόματι ἢ σχήματι, οὔθ' οἱ πάνυ περιττοὶ καὶ τῆς τῶν πολλῶν ὑπερορῶντες ἀμαθίας μέμψασθαι τὴν κατασκευὴν ταύτης τῆς λέξεως, ἀλλὰ καὶ τὸ τῶν πολλῶν καὶ <τὸ> τῶν ὀλίγων τὴν αὐτὴν ὑπόληψιν ἕξει. ὁ μέν γε πολὺς

THE ETHICS OF AUTHORSHIP 53

ἐκεῖνος ἰδιώτης οὐ δυσχερανεῖ τὸ φορτικὸν τῆς λέξεως καὶ σκολιὸν καὶ δυσπαρακολούθητον· ὁ δὲ σπάνιος καὶ οὐδ' ἐκ τῆς ἐπιτυχούσης ἀγωγῆς γιγνόμενος τεχνίτης οὐ μέμψεται τὸ ἀγεννὲς καὶ χαμαιτυπὲς καὶ ἀκατάσκευον. ἀλλὰ συνῳδὸν ἔσται τό τε λογικὸν καὶ τὸ ἄλογον κριτήριον, ὑφ' ὧν ἀμφοτέρων ἀξιοῦμεν ἅπαντα κρίνεσθαι κατὰ τὰς τέχνας.

Dionysius's positive assessment here of Thucydidean style differs from his generally dour view elsewhere. Yet even in this instance of apparent praise, aspects of Dionysius's judgment of Thucydides the man (τοῦ ἀνδρός) are figured negatively.[39] Dionysius's praise for Thucydides does double duty as implicit praise for Herodotus by singling out the later historian for certain qualities in which he mirrors his predecessor. The reader who is conditioned to expect the "coarseness, tortuousness, and unfollowability of his style" (τὸ φορτικὸν τῆς λέξεως καὶ σκολιὸν καὶ δυσπαρακολούθητον) here notes the exceptional and, in certain instances, *Herodotean* qualities for which Thucydides is lauded. Dionysius uses certain Herodotean critical buzzwords, some of them established in his own critical oeuvre, in effect allowing various motifs associated with Herodotus's penumbra to "talk back" to Thucydides. For instance, he links the intuitive with the pleasant (ἄλογον . . . ἡδέων) and the rational capacity with beauty (τὸ λογικόν . . . καλόν), coupling the two critical faculties with the very things—pleasantness and beauty—for which he elsewhere endorses Herodotus (see earlier, καὶ γὰρ ἡδεῖά ἐστι καὶ καλή, *Comp.* 10.5). Recall that being both pleasurable *and* beautiful proves significant, given the dangers associated with pleasurable reading. The passage also imparts a sense of loftiness in its opening roll call of virtues (τήν τε μεγαληγορίαν . . . τὴν καλλιλογίαν καὶ τὴν δεινότητα). This means that when Thucydides is at his best, he is only ever achieving what Dionysius elsewhere proclaims about Herodotus: "Herodotus has sublimity, beauty, magnificence, and what is specially called 'the historical mold'" (ὕψος δὲ καὶ κάλλος καὶ μεγαλοπρέπειαν καὶ τὸ λεγόμενον ἰδίως πλάσμα ἱστορικὸν Ἡρόδοτος ἔχει, *Pomp.* 4.3).[40] Dionysius furthermore asserts that the passage

[39] Cf. *Thuc.* 29 and 33, which assert that Thucydides's convoluted phrasing becomes a source of annoyance for the reader. See also Marcellinus, *Vit. Thuc.* 35 on Thucydides's deliberate (ἐπίτηδες) intention to be obscure (ἀσαφῶς). Dionysius's criticisms here of Thucydides's style bear some resemblance to his criticism of what he takes to be Plato's late, mannered style, ornamented and failing to benefit the common good (see *Pomp.* 1–2).

[40] On Dionysian sublimity, see de Jonge 2012; Porter 2016: 213–39, esp. 224. On Dionysius's sensational reaction to reading Demosthenes, whose speeches can make him feel like an ecstatic Corybant (*Dem.* 22.2–5), see Wiater 2011a: 231–33; Wiater 2019: 68–72.

54 HERODOTUS AND IMPERIAL GREEK LITERATURE

of Thucydides he has just quoted appeals to both the educated and the layperson alike, and neither is able to find fault with various qualities. The opinions of the περιττοί, who usually "look condescendingly upon the ignorance of the masses," will for once harmonize with those of the many, and vice versa. This again means that Thucydides is chiefly to be praised only when he matches the broad accessibility of Herodotus. Accordingly, Dionysius's view that anyone may, by means of both intuitive and technical criteria, discern the qualities of pleasantness and beauty in certain passages of Thucydides only reinforces his points elsewhere about Herodotus's accessibility.[41]

An even more clarion evocation of Herodotean accessibility comes toward the end of the work. As part of a broader discussion of Thucydides's style in relation to public life (*Thuc.* 49–51), Dionysius offers a memorable series of images of what life would be like if ordinary people in their private affairs tried to imitate Thucydides. Dionysius's argument has the effect of recapitulating and reinforcing some of his critical judgments about Herodotus. After asserting that Thucydidean style is not only useless for matters of public discourse (οὔτε γὰρ ἐν ταῖς ἐκκλησίαις χρήσιμόν ἐστι τοῦτο τὸ γένος τῆς φράσεως, *Thuc.* 49.2; see generally 49.1–2), he reveals a further dimension between life and literature, style and *ethos*:

> Nor is [Thucydides's style useful] in private exchanges, in which we discuss everyday life with fellow citizens, friends, or relatives, when we describe something or other about the things that have happened to us, consult about some urgent matter, advise, encourage, or take pleasure in what is good and feel pain for misfortunes. I leave off mentioning how even the mothers and fathers of persons speaking this way would not repress their disgust, but would beg for interpreters, as though listening to a foreign language. (*Thuc.* 49.3)

> οὔτ' ἐν ταῖς ἰδιωτικαῖς ὁμιλίαις, ἐν αἷς περὶ τῶν βιωτικῶν διαλεγόμεθα πολίταις ἢ φίλοις ἢ συγγενέσιν διηγούμενοί τι τῶν συμβεβηκότων ἑαυτοῖς ἢ συμβουλευόμενοι περί τινος τῶν ἀναγκαίων, ἢ νουθετοῦντες ἢ παρακαλοῦντες ἢ συνηδόμενοι τοῖς ἀγαθοῖς ἢ συναλγοῦντες τοῖς κακοῖς·

---

[41] Compare Wiater 2011b: 66, with similar observations about Dionysius's technique in *Pomp.* of "correct[ing] Thucydides' version of the events by rewriting the structure of Thucydides' account along the lines of the basic structure of Herodotus's work." See further Wiater 2011b: 66 n. 14 for an example of how Dionysius's Herodotean plaudits seep into the critical language he aims at Thucydides. See also Irwin 2015: 6, who discusses—but does not stress the Herodotean resonance of—Dionysius's contention that it is "worth marveling over" (θαυμάζειν ἄξιον, *Thuc.* 9.5) Thucydides's failure to recognize that season-by-season narrative division would create obscurity.

THE ETHICS OF AUTHORSHIP   55

ἐῶ γὰρ λέγειν, ὅτι τῶν οὕτως διαλεγομένων οὐδὲ αἱ μητέρες ἂν καὶ οἱ πατέρες ἀνάσχοιντο διὰ τὴν ἀηδίαν, ἀλλ᾽ ὥσπερ ἀλλοεθνοῦς γλώσσης ἀκούοντες τῶν ἑρμηνευσόντων ἂν δεηθεῖεν.

Throughout the treatise, even as Dionysius has proclaimed Thucydides as one above all interested in truth (*Thuc.* 8.1), the critic nonetheless creates for his readers the impression of Thucydides's poor choices that by contrast only shore up the positive choices of Herodotus.[42] The image of parents calling for interpreters to explain their children's abhorrent utterances offers no exception. The style of Thucydides shows itself incompatible with and hostile to ordinary communication and life. Insofar as it would fail to consider someone else's needs in certain exigencies (e.g., consulting on an urgent matter, advising, encouraging, etc.), the imitation of Thucydidean style would amount to an interpersonal, even ethical, failure. The idea that Herodoteanism, by contrast, is in better accord with normal life is not simply implicit. In fact, Dionysius's description of private life offers direct echo of his description of Herodotean sensibility from the *Letter to Gnaeus Pompey*:

συνηδόμενοι τοῖς ἀγαθοῖς ἢ συναλγοῦντες τοῖς κακοῖς (*Thuc.* 49.3)

≈

ἡ μὲν Ἡροδότου διάθεσις ἐν ἅπασιν ἐπιεικὴς καὶ <u>τοῖς μὲν ἀγαθοῖς συνηδομένη, τοῖς δὲ κακοῖς συναλγοῦσα</u> (*Pomp.* 3.15)

To the extent that Dionysius claims to have lifted the *Pompey* passage on historians from his *On Imitation* and to the extent, in turn, that the *On Thucydides* is likely a mature work, Dionysius's use of this phrase three times across his corpus implies a consistently held belief about the harmony between the emotional tendencies of ordinary citizens and the Herodotean disposition. The climactic echo in this passage thus reinscribes Herodoteanism upon the life of the layperson. The admirable sensibilities of their lives—"taking pleasure in what is good and feeling pain for others' misfortunes"—cohere with the disposition of the man behind the *Histories*.

---

[42] Dionysius's judgments in *Thuc.* 49–51 are similar to those of Cicero at *Orator* 30–32. As is the case with Dionysius, Cicero remarks on the uselessness of Thucydides for public speaking (*nihil ab eo transferri potest ad forensem usum et publicum*, 30) and the obscurity of his syntax (*ipsae illae contiones ita multas habent obscuras abditasque sententias vix ut intellegantur*, 30), and he manages to convey the extent to which his opinion stands in defiance of trendy (and ignorant) belief: *ecce autem aliqui se Thucydidios esse profitentur, novum quoddam imperitorum et inauditum genus ... at laudatus est ab omnibus* (30–31).

56　HERODOTUS AND IMPERIAL GREEK LITERATURE

Dionysius's critique, then, of the elitism of Thucydides's style suggests that his own critical disposition inclines toward the broadly engaging rather than the exclusively specialized. This is brought out at a final stage in the treatise when Dionysius ties Thucydideanism to tyranny and oligarchy rather than democracy (*Thuc.* 51.1). Thus, even if, as Gavin Weaire has argued, Dionysius's audience was a class of well-to-do *philologoi*, there remains nonetheless a pronounced emphasis in Dionysius's treatise on clarity, accessibility, and the literary usefulness for the ἰδιώτης.[43] If Thucydides's writing is only for the "well educated" (εὐπαιδεύτων, 51.1), the common life is deprived of reading something potentially useful (χρήσιμον . . . ἀναιροῦσιν ἐκ τοῦ κοινοῦ βίου), and his work becomes the preserve of the few, "just like cities under oligarchies or tyrannies" (ὥσπερ ἐν ταῖς ὀλιγαρχουμέναις ἢ τυραννουμέναις πόλεσιν, *Thuc.* 51.1). And it is on these counts that Thucydides, however much an exemplary truth-teller, comes up short. Dionysius promotes instead a literary ideal of broad accessibility. In light of his strong critique of Thucydides precisely for his stylistic impenetrability, Dionysius's self-portrait as a socially responsive, open-minded critic who can judge even as a layperson (*Thuc.* 1–4) comes across as evocative of the very man he describes when characterizing Herodotus.

I have explored how Dionysius's overt reception of Herodotus centers on considerations of deliberate choice, dispositional flexibility, and the importance of accessibility—all aspects of his interest in the writerly life and in narratorial ethics. The attention Dionysius gives to Herodotus makes of him something far more than the whipping boy of mendacity or an easy-going precursor to a supposedly more mature Thucydides. Rather, Dionysius foregrounds authorial disposition and the choices that, passing into words, become the means by which a reader judges style as an exercised freedom. Dionysius should thus be credited with helping to shape an image of Herodotus on ethical and not simply stylistic grounds. That he did this in apparent defiance of various critical orthodoxies casts him not only as a bolder critic than often imagined but also as one alert to some of the critical perceptions that would later accrue to Herodotus.[44] I have also observed in

[43] Weaire 2005: 263.

[44] One such critical view against which Dionysius may have positioned himself is that voiced in the treatise of Demetrius called *On Style* (Περὶ ἑρμηνείας), variously dated to the late Hellenistic or early Imperial period but which, per Innes (at Russell and Winterbottom 1972: 172), "almost certainly precedes Dionysius of Halicarnassus." (See further Dührsen 2005; Dihle 2007.) In *On Style*, Herodotus is described (in a fashion similar to that of Dionysius at *Pomp.* 3.11, 3.21) as an imitator of Homer but rather more negatively as one who has copied Homer in a plagiarizing fashion (Demetr., *Eloc.* 112–13).

THE ETHICS OF AUTHORSHIP 57

passing that Dionysius's recognizing of choice is self-reflexive. The fact that Thucydides comes across as an ambivalent figure evidences Dionysius's own freedom as a critic: Dionysius can make his *own* choice to buck the conventional wisdom of his time, which largely saw Thucydides as superior.[45] In turn, his laudation of Herodotus's excellence betrays not an unthinking fealty of one Halicarnassian for another but rather the active critical judgment that Dionysius, applauding Herodotus, encourages in his own readers.

Dionysius as Herodotus

Dionysius's rhetorical treatises often channel features of the authors they examine.[46] We have already seen how Dionysius's valuations are occasionally laced with the language or mannerisms of various writers, as if the author under scrutiny were joining Dionysius in reinforcement of his judgments.[47] Despite the preferred position that Dionysius bestows on Herodotus, however, Herodotus's prominent interactive role, as it were, in shaping Dionysius's narratorial identity remains underexamined. In this second part of the chapter, I consider how Dionysius's channeling of a Herodotean disposition contributes to his self-presentation in his literary treatises, such that his own voice comes to sound like the past. In tracing Dionysius's conjuring of Herodotus, it will help to think in terms of kinetic reception: the relationship between what Dionysius may have felt he was expected to say about Herodotus, what he actually says about Herodotus, and his appropriation and imitation of the author. As with his self-modeling on others, Dionysius's various Herodotean traits harmonize his oeuvre with the tradition on which he renders judgment.[48] He enlivens

---

[45] See Weaire 2005: 257: "*Aemulatio* of Thucydides was a salient feature of the Latin literary scene that greeted Dionysius upon his arrival in 30 BC. The most prominent historian of the previous decade had been Thucydides' obsessive imitator Sallust. . . . This popularity means that Sallust is a valuable indicator of the particular Roman sensitivities to which Dionysius offered a challenge." See also de Jonge 2011: 456–59 on "Thucydidism" in first-century BCE Rome.

[46] On Platonic imitations, see Worman 2015a: 301–3; Worman 2015b: 282–93. See Weaire 2005 and de Jonge 2017 on Thucydidean presences. Ek 1942: 1–4 argues for Dionysius's own practice of imitation as one of "Verwandlung und Mischung" (4), albeit with a focus on the *Roman Antiquities*. Compare also Luraghi 2003 (esp. 181–85) for Dionysius's imitation of Herodotus in the *Roman Antiquities*.

[47] Compare Irwin 2015: 6, positing Dionysius's wish to "conduct a Thucydidean demonstration, indirect and through innuendo, for the astute reader . . . of how to read, and read through, Thucydides' masterful rhetoric." See also Wiater 2019 (esp. 63–68) on Dionysius's "abstracting" of a classical ideal for his own present.

[48] Compare Burrow 2019: 69–70 on adopting "the dispositions (moral and political as well as stylistic) of an earlier author rather than simply echoing his or her words."

58 HERODOTUS AND IMPERIAL GREEK LITERATURE

and gives argumentative ballast to his advice on imitation by means of his own imitations that animate antiquity.

At a fundamental level, Dionysius's recurrent conversationality and dialogism run parallel to what scholars have recognized as Herodotus's own open-ended, heteroglossic *Histories*.[49] Indeed, near to Dionysius's own time, the author of *On the Sublime*, commenting on Herodotus 2.29, cites Herodotus's ability to connect intimately with his reader:

> Do you see, reader, how when he carries your spirit with him he leads you across places and makes hearing into sight? Every passage of this sort, directly addressed to the reader, situates the listener in the very midst of the action. (*Subl.* 26.2)[50]

> ὁρᾷς, ὦ ἑταῖρε, ὡς παραλαβών σου τὴν ψυχὴν διὰ τῶν τόπων ἄγει τὴν ἀκοὴν ὄψιν ποιῶν; πάντα δὲ τὰ τοιαῦτα πρὸς αὐτὰ ἀπερειδόμενα τὰ πρόσωπα ἐπ᾽ αὐτῶν ἵστησι τὸν ἀκροατὴν τῶν ἐνεργουμένων.

In his own addresses to his readers and in his consistent attempts to involve his audience, Dionysius also displays a capacity to "situate the listener" in the midst of the critical action, as it were, and this is one of the key ways in which Dionysius, already extolling Herodotus explicitly, enacts a Herodotean persona across his critical corpus. Moreover, in addition to his direct engagement with the reader, Dionysius's tendency toward variation and digression, alongside narratorial comments on (the limits of) his own authority, repeatedly bring to mind classic Herodotean narratorial features. Dionysius's rhetorical works thus exhibit various watermarks—unmarked imitative acts—that support his own interest in a polyphonic reading, an experience by which readers sense the voices of the past speaking in and through the work before their eyes. Dionysius's reverberations of the Herodotean voiceprint implicitly expand the already roomy exemplarity that Dionysius explicitly grants him, as Herodotus's authorial tone is blended with the narrative mannerisms of the one who praises him.

But what did imitation mean to Dionysius, and how do its meanings help us to understand his imitation of Herodotus? For Dionysius, imitation need

---

[49] See Lateiner 1989: 30–35, 55–108; Baragwanath 2008: 1–26.

[50] Compare Longinus's formulation with later discussions of ἐνάργεια in *progymnasmata*; see Kennedy 2003: 14 (Aelius Theon § 71), 86 (Hermogenes § 22), 166 (Nicolaus § 68), and 187 (John of Sardis § 24).

THE ETHICS OF AUTHORSHIP   59

not constitute an inferior mode of literary activity.[51] Rather than registering disjunction, imitation done rightly marks proximity and similarity between imitator and source.[52] Yet Dionysius's self-presentation as an author devoted to enabling imitation will have run certain risks. For in the mimetic act lurks potential inauthenticity, as brought to the fore in his *On Dinarchus*:[53]

> In general terms, one can distinguish between two different types of imitation with respect to ancient models: one is natural and results from thorough communication and familiarity; the other is closely connected to it, but is based on the rules of the art. Concerning the first, what can one possibly say? And about the second, one could say the following: that a certain innate charm and freshness extend over all original models, but in replications, even when they reach the height of imitation, there is nevertheless present from the start something contrived and unnatural. (*Din.* 7.5–6)

> ὡς δὲ καθόλου εἰπεῖν, δύο τρόπους τῆς διαφορᾶς τῆς πρὸς τὰ ἀρχαῖα μιμήσεως εὕροι τις ἄν· ὧν ὃ μὲν φυσικός τέ ἐστι καὶ ἐκ πολλῆς κατηχήσεως καὶ συντροφίας λαμβανόμενος, ὃ δὲ τούτῳ προσεχὴς ἐκ τῶν τῆς τέχνης παραγγελμάτων. περὶ μὲν οὖν τοῦ προτέρου, τί ἄν τις καὶ λέγοι; περὶ δὲ τοῦ δευτέρου, τουτὶ ἂν ἔχοι τις εἰπεῖν ὅτι πᾶσι μὲν τοῖς ἀρχετύποις αὐτοφυής τις ἐπιτρέχει χάρις καὶ ὥρα, τοῖς δ' ἀπὸ τούτων κατεσκευασμένοις, κἂν ἐπ' ἄκρον μιμήσεως ἔλθωσι, πρόσεστίν τι ὅμως τὸ ἐπιτετηδευμένον καὶ οὐκ ἐκ φύσεως ὑπάρχον.[54]

Imitation admits of two types, natural (φυσικός) and technical (ἐκ τῶν τῆς τέχνης παραγγελμάτων).[55] The former results from "thorough

---

[51] See Doran 2015: 64.

[52] See Halliwell 2002: 292–96, concluding that for Dionysius, mimesis could be "true" and "natural," like the things it purportedly imitates, and could thus "be as good a model as reality itself" (295). Halliwell does not discuss the passage at *Din.* 7.5–7. See further on Dionysius's concept of imitation Hidber 1996: 56–75; Whitmarsh 2001b: 71–75; Delcourt 2005: 43–47; and esp. Wiater 2011a: 65–92.

[53] See, e.g., Plato, *Resp.* 598b–e, 603a10–b1, 605a8–c3, with Halliwell 2002: 37–71.

[54] Aujac emends ἐπιτρέχει for ἐπιπρέπει (1992: 169 ad loc. 131.2): "Le verbe ἐπιτρέχειν semble tellement lié chez Denys à χάρις et à ὥρα (cf. V [= *Dem.*] 5.3, 13.7, 41.3, et encore VII [= *Thuc.*] 5.4) qu'il a semblé pertinent ici de le substituer à ἐπιπρέπειν que porte F." Usher's translation as "emanates" (Usher 1985: 271), despite his printed text, nonetheless carries the sense that Aujac's emendation imparts.

[55] On the *Dinarchus* passage, see Wiater 2019: 66–68, whose reading emphasizes the possibility of Dionysius and his community's fulfilling a transferable notion of the classical in their present

60 HERODOTUS AND IMPERIAL GREEK LITERATURE

communication and familiarity" with its model, as if by constantly rereading and studying an author, a later writer might unintentionally produce a near-degree imitation.[56] Dionysius's treatises surely exhibit something of this deep familiarity and long-term acquaintance with various ancient writers.[57] But while imitation derived from precepts cannot recover the inborn grace of the original models, one may wonder whether "natural" imitation shares in the "innate" (αὐτοφυής) charm of its models.[58]

The comments from *On Dinarchus* deserve comparison with a remark from *On Imitation*, taken by many to be (among) the earliest of Dionysius's writings, in which Dionysius praises Herodotus for his "natural spontaneity" (τῷ αὐτοφυεῖ): "For pleasurableness, persuasiveness, charm, and natural spontaneity, Herodotus is in my view the winner by far" (ἡδονῇ δὲ καὶ πειθοῖ καὶ χάριτι καὶ τῷ αὐτοφυεῖ μακρῷ διενεγκόντα τὸν Ἡρόδοτον εὑρίσκομεν, *Imit.* fr. 3.3).[59] Reading backward from the *Dinarchus* passage, in which original models are said to possess an innate charm, we see that the celebration of Herodotean charm in *On Imitation* takes on a special meaning; one of Dionysius's original models is effectively endowed not only with charm but also with the very innate quality of spontaneity that is itself *descriptive of* charm in the *On Dinarchus* passage. Herodotus, qua "charming" writer, emerges in Dionysius's schema as an especially "natural," almost ur-natural, model. Such acclamation resonates with expressions of Dionysius's belief, cited earlier, that Herodotus's choice of words corresponds to how things are in nature (οἷα ἡ φύσις τέθηκεν σύμβολα τοῖς πράγμασιν, *Comp.* 3.16) and that his "thoughts are in no way grander than the things in and of themselves" (τὰ νοήματα μηδὲν σεμνότερα εἶναι, ἢ οἷά ἐστιν, *Comp.* 3.17). Setting

time. Even as Dionysius correlates the two imitative modes here (ὃ δὲ τούτῳ προσεχής), it is clear elsewhere that an author's originality is an essential criterion in judging whether to adopt him as a model. See, e.g., Dionysius's *First Letter to Ammaeus,* which tries passim to counter the suggestion that Demosthenes owes his skills to imitation of Aristotelian rhetorical theory.

[56] Compare the suggestive fragment from *On Imitation* in which imitation is defined as "an activity that molds [or "reproduces": ἐκματτομένη] the exemplar through theoretical concepts" (μίμησίς ἐστιν ἐνέργεια διὰ τῶν θεωρημάτων ἐκματτομένη τὸ παράδειγμα, fr. 2, Aujac 1992: 27). See Russell 1980: 10.

[57] See Gabba 1982: 47 on the breadth of Dionysius's theory of imitation, "valid within a wide range of classical writers, including non-Attic authors."

[58] On the importance of original models to Dionysius, see Usher 1974: xx–xxii. On the concept of χάρις in Dionysius, see Viidebaum 2019.

[59] On the date and publication of the *On Imitation,* see Bonner 1939: 25–38; Aujac 1978: 22–28; Weaire 2005: 247 n. 3; de Jonge 2008: 20–23; Matijašić 2018: 69–70; Hunter and de Jonge 2019b: 1. The probability that the *On Imitation* is an early, if not the earliest, work foregrounds Herodotus's programmatic importance in Dionysius's thinking; see, however, Matijašić 2018: 69–70 for Dionysius's publishing the *Letter to Gnaeus Pompey* before publishing, but after writing, *On Imitation* Books 1–2.

THE ETHICS OF AUTHORSHIP   61

these descriptions alongside the collocations of Herodotus with charm that Dionysius mentions elsewhere (see *Dem.* 41.3; *Comp.* 3.13–14, 12.8–12; *Pomp.* 3.14; *Thuc.* 23.7), it is clear that Herodotus occupies special status as a natural model for Dionysius. In identifying Dionysius's own imitations of this particular author, then, we see a writer who centers his own potentially natural and "spontaneous" imitations on an already impeccable paragon.

Submerged Imitation

In Dionysius's self-modeling on the past, the often unmarked or non-explicit presence of classical models populates his texts in terms similar to Gadamer's idea of imitative self-effacement: the copy, Gadamer writes, "has its real function not in the reflective activity of comparison and distinction, but in pointing, through the similarity, to what is copied."[60] Dionysius parries the potential shortcomings of technical imitation, and edges closer to a "natural" form, by means of what I call submerged imitation, a form of subtle mimesis that avoids explicit summoning of the model.[61] In this case, rather than imitating an author outright in dialect or topic, Dionysius echoes classical writers so as to ground his authority and foster a sense of proximity to the past.[62] In his imitation of historians, philosophers, and rhetors in his literary-critical treatises, Dionysius avoids overt genre-based imitation but nevertheless shows his "thorough communication and familiarity" with past masters. Indeed, we have seen already instances of submerged imitation in Dionysius's use of embedded Herodotean language and theme as part of his critical adjudications, as if allowing Herodotean phrasing to structure his own judgments. Recall his assessment of the Persian Wars' superiority to the Peloponnesian War that lifted a line from Herodotus (*Pomp.* 3.6 ~ Hdt. proem) and how his reference to the acoustics of the Gyges and Candaules story conjures the thematic contrast between seeing and hearing already present in Herodotus's version (*Comp.* 3.14 ~ Hdt. 1.8.2). Dionysius's submerged

---

[60] Gadamer 1975 [1960]: 139.

[61] With the concept of submerged imitation, compare Hidber's idea of Dionysius's "eclectic mimesis" (1996: 85–87) in discussing Dionysius's historiographically inflected preface to *On the Ancient Orators*, though not ostensibly a historiographic text: "Und schliesslich dient die in der kunstvollen, verschiedene Stilhöhen demonstrierenden Form des historiographischen Prooemiums gestaltete Praefatio mit ihren zahlreichen literarischen Anklängen auch als Beispiel und Muster für das Gestaltungsprinzip der eklektischen Mimesis" (87).

[62] Compare Tamiolaki 2015 (esp. 932–33) on Lucian's adoption in his treatise *How to Write History* of Thucydides's persona.

62 HERODOTUS AND IMPERIAL GREEK LITERATURE

imitation thus departs from more conventional strategies of Herodotean imitation, such as writing in Ionic or about the Persian Wars. Instead, it allows Dionysius to act both as a critic, set at a presumed distance from the authors under critique, and as a mimetic artist, who fashions his own literary persona by subsuming qualities and stylistic facets of the very writers he appraises.

A sustained example appears in a substantial epitomized passage from the opening of Dionysius's *On Imitation*.[63] Here the submerged presence of Herodotus goes unnamed but saliently anticipates his prominent role in various Dionysian rhetorical treatises:

[1] It is necessary for us to read the ancient authors in order to furnish for ourselves not only the content for our writing but also to enable emulation of particular expressions. [2] For the reader's soul, through continuous observation, draws off the likeness of an author's distinctive style, the sort of thing that the old story says happened to the rustic's wife. The story is that an unattractive farmer feared that he would father children like himself, and this fear taught him the art of having attractive children. For he crafted good-looking images and got his wife into the habit of looking at them. After she spent time doing this, he would go to bed with her, and the beauty of the images produced attractive children. [3] So is similarity born from imitation, whenever someone emulates what seems of good quality in each of the ancient writers, and channeling, so to speak, a single flow from many springs, he conducts this into his soul. [4] It behooves me to back up this story with a real-life example. Zeuxis was a painter and admired by the people of Croton. When he was painting a nude of Helen, the Crotonites sent their young women to him so he could see them naked, not necessarily because all of them were beautiful, though it is also unlikely that they were all unattractive. Whatever quality of each young woman was worthy of depiction, these he collected into a single bodily image, and from the selection of many parts he in his skill brought together a complete form. [5] So it is also possible for you, as if at the theater, to seek out forms of beautiful bodies and pluck out the superior part of their souls, and by collecting together the feast of your broad learning to mold not an image that will become faded with time, but the immortal beauty of art. (*Imit.* Epitome fr. 1.1–5)

---

[63] For the fragments and epitome of the *On Imitation*, see Aujac 1992: 25–40. On this passage, see Whitmarsh 2001b: 75; Hunter 2009: 109–14. See also Porter 2006b: 338–43.

THE ETHICS OF AUTHORSHIP 63

[1] ὅτι δεῖ τοῖς τῶν ἀρχαίων ἐντυγχάνειν συγγράμμασιν, ἵν᾽ ἐντεῦθεν μὴ μόνον τῆς ὑποθέσεως τὴν ὕλην ἀλλὰ καὶ τὸν τῶν ἰδιωμάτων ζῆλον χορηγηθῶμεν. [2] ἡ γὰρ ψυχὴ τοῦ ἀναγινώσκοντος ὑπὸ τῆς συνεχοῦς παρατηρήσεως τὴν ὁμοιότητα τοῦ χαρακτῆρος ἐφέλκεται, ὁποῖόν τι καὶ γυναῖκα ἀγροίκου παθεῖν ὁ μῦθος λέγει. ἀνδρί, φασί, γεωργῷ τὴν ὄψιν αἰσχρῷ παρέστη δέος, μὴ τέκνων ὁμοίων γένηται πατήρ. ὁ φόβος δὲ αὐτὸν οὗτος εὐπαιδίας ἐδίδαξε τέχνην. καὶ εἰκόνας πλάσας εὐπρεπεῖς, εἰς αὐτὰς βλέπειν εἴθισε τὴν γυναῖκα· καὶ μετὰ ταῦτα συγγενόμενος αὐτῇ τὸ κάλλος εὐτύχησε τῶν εἰκόνων. [3] οὕτω καὶ λόγων μιμήσει ὁμοιότης τίκτεται, ἐπὰν ζηλώσῃ τις τὸ παρ᾽ ἑκάστῳ τῶν παλαιῶν βέλτιον εἶναι δοκοῦν, καὶ καθάπερ ἐκ πολλῶν ναμάτων ἕν τι συγκομίσας ῥεῦμα τοῦτ᾽ εἰς τὴν ψυχὴν μετοχετεύσῃ. [4] καί μοι παρίσταται πιστώσασθαι τὸν λόγον τοῦτον ἔργῳ· Ζεῦξις ἦν ζωγράφος, καὶ παρὰ Κροτωνιατῶν ἐθαυμάζετο· καὶ αὐτῷ τὴν Ἑλένην γράφοντι γυμνὴν γυμνὰς ἰδεῖν τὰς παρ᾽ αὐτοῖς ἔπεμψαν παρθένους· οὐκ ἐπειδήπερ ἦσαν ἄπασαι καλαί, ἀλλ᾽ οὐκ εἰκὸς ἦν ὡς παντάπασιν ἦσαν αἰσχραί· ὃ δ᾽ ἦν ἄξιον παρ᾽ ἑκάστῃ γραφῆς, ἐς μίαν ἠθροίσθη σώματος εἰκόνα, κἀκ πολλῶν μερῶν συλλογῆς ἕν τι συνέθηκεν ἡ τέχνη τέλειον [καλὸν] εἶδος. [5] τοιγαροῦν πάρεστι καὶ σοὶ καθάπερ ἐν θεάτρῳ καλῶν σωμάτων ἰδέας ἐξιστορεῖν καὶ τῆς ἐκείνων ψυχῆς ἀπανθίζεσθαι τὸ κρεῖττον, καὶ τὸν τῆς πολυμαθείας ἔρανον συλλέγοντι οὐκ ἐξίτηλον χρόνῳ γενησομένην εἰκόνα τυποῦν ἀλλ᾽ ἀθάνατον τέχνης κάλλος.

The passage's thematic content, critical idiom, argumentative structure, and final Herodotean phrasal turn together constitute an act of submerged imitation, reinforcing the very practice of imitation explicitly under examination. First, the passage contains, much like the opening of Herodotus's *Histories*, stories others tell (φασί, 2) about women, including a version of the Helen story. Both authors draw connections between the viewing of women and issues of wider thematic importance to their texts: just as Herodotus's seesaw of retributive actions proves programmatic for the *Histories'* emphasis on reprisal, so does Dionysius employ similarly folksy imagery to enumerate principles of programmatic importance to his criticism, including, it would seem, the applicability of his precepts to ordinary laypersons (here represented by the rustic image-maker).[64] As Leslie Kurke has argued of Herodotus

---

[64] In Herodotus's case, of course, these images are rejected (*Histories* 1.5) as insufficient or inappropriate (see Węcowski 2004: 151, 155), but the gambit of their introduction perhaps has an alluring and captivating effect on readers and undoubtedly flags the theme of τίσις that remains operative throughout his text.

64 HERODOTUS AND IMPERIAL GREEK LITERATURE

(in relation to Aesop), a focus on demotic, "low" content is a marker of the *Histories*, especially in its early books.[65] Such low imagery was a feature of Herodotean content on which Herodotean imitations could draw.[66] While Dionysius's ideas of imitation here are surely indebted to Plato, as Hunter has shown, the imitation itself, in theme and phraseology, has roots in a Herodotean mode centered on preserving that which is best.[67] Here both the fundamental element of careful literary study (represented by the woman's habituation with the beautiful εἰκόνες) and the necessity of proper technical application (represented by Zeuxis's collage of different "worthy" parts into a whole), anticipating the passage from *On Dinarchus*, are mediated through demotic analogies. The story of the farmer and the nude images is a story of triangulated beauty and the consequences of coerced viewing, further recalling Herodotus's use of the story of Gyges and Candaules as another thematic introduction to his work.[68] Dionysius emphasizes successful imitation as a process whereby someone brings together disparate parts into one harmonious whole, whether the reader (καθάπερ ἐκ πολλῶν ναμάτων ἕν τι συγκομίσας ῥεῦμα, 5) or Zeuxis (κἀκ πολλῶν μερῶν συλλογῆς ἕν τι συνέθηκεν, 4), a mode of creation remarkably parallel to the very quality for which Dionysius lauds Herodotus in crafting the *Histories* as "one body" (ἓν σῶμα, *Pomp.* 3.14 ~ ἐς μίαν . . . σώματος εἰκόνα, fr. 1.4) from many parts.[69]

The shift from μῦθος and λόγος (2, 4) to ἔργον (4), a contrastive pair that betokens historiographic "proof-telling" (πιστώσασθαι), enhances the passage's echo of Herodotus's own prologue and its intention to record against perishability:

τοιγαροῦν πάρεστι καὶ σοὶ καθάπερ ἐν θεάτρῳ καλῶν σωμάτων ἰδέας **ἐξιστορεῖν** καὶ τῆς ἐκείνων ψυχῆς ἀπανθίζεσθαι τὸ κρεῖττον, καὶ τὸν τῆς πολυμαθείας ἔρανον συλλέγοντι οὐκ **ἐξίτηλον χρόνῳ γενησομένην** εἰκόνα τυποῦν ἀλλ᾽ ἀθάνατον τέχνης κάλλος. (*Imit.* fr. 1.5)

≈

Ἡροδότου Ἁλικαρνησσέος **ἱστορίης** ἀπόδεξις ἥδε, ὡς μήτε τὰ γενόμενα ἐξ ἀνθρώπων **τῷ χρόνῳ ἐξίτηλα γένηται** (Hdt. proem)

---

[65] Kurke 2011: 382–97.

[66] For a focus on humble characters in imitation of Herodotus, see Griffin 2014: 6–9 and Kirkland 2018: 306–7, both on the Pseudo-Herodotean *Life of Homer*.

[67] On Platonic elements in this passage, see Hunter 2009: 107–27, esp. 110–14.

[68] The emphasis on the effects of viewing also replays a theme strongly represented throughout Herodotus's work; on viewing and visuality in Herodotus, see Immerwahr 1960; Anhalt 2008; Kirk 2014.

[69] I discuss the imagery of the unified body (*Thuc.* 5.5; *Pomp.* 3.14) in detail in chapter 2.

THE ETHICS OF AUTHORSHIP   65

The practitioner of mimesis must "seek out" or "inquire into" (ἐξιστορεῖν) the forms of bodies and "pluck out" the superior portions of soul.[70] From these various sources, the reader (or writer) molds something that will not fade with time (οὐκ ἐξίτηλον χρόνῳ γενησομένην). Dionysius's phrasing neatly imitates Herodotus's already synesthetic formulation (the adjective connotes physical decay, as of pigment; see LSJ s.v. A), appropriate to a multi-sensory passage: images in mind "birthing" the images of actual people; reading as a process of channeling streams into a great flow; "seeking out" beautiful bodies in a theater to form an everlasting image of beauty. Hence, as Dionysius opens out his technique to the reader and would-be imitator, his submerged Herodotean resonances establish his own mimetic bona fides and hint at something of the (Herodotean) persona he elsewhere develops. The felt evocations of Herodotus confirm the concord between Dionysius and the ancient canon, between the writer's present and the authored past, and invite through Herodotean phrasing (οὐκ ἐξίτηλον χρόνῳ) the possibility that imitations themselves can take on a lasting, monumental quality. Through submerged imitation, Dionysius demonstrates his own "longstanding soulful acquaintance" (ψυχὴ ... συνεχοῦς παρατηρήσεως) by which he has "drawn off" the likeness of the Herodotus's style (τὴν ὁμοιότητα τοῦ χαρακτῆρος ἐφέλκεται), as theoretical principle and actual practice work to ratify the effectiveness of his endorsements.

Sounding Dionysian, Sounding Herodotean

As features of submerged imitation, aspects of Herodotus's narratorial behavior inform Dionysius's rhetorical treatises: the consistent use of variation and digression; comments on reliability or authority; and direct, often open-ended engagement with the reader. I highlight in this section some areas of correspondence between the two authors. Despite differences in context and genre, readers familiar with Herodotus's narrative style are likely to feel aspects of it percolating through the works of Dionysius. The effect of such correspondences is to reinforce Dionysius's acclamation for Herodotus by crafting treatises that in their digressive open-endedness and genial regard for the reader evoke sensations of one of Dionysius's lauded literary exemplars.

---

[70] Hunter 2009: 121 also notices the echo and discusses the use of the word ἐξιστορεῖν.

66 HERODOTUS AND IMPERIAL GREEK LITERATURE

Recall that when Dionysius highlights the use of digressions, he praises Herodotus (among others), in a passage seen earlier (*Comp.* 19.11–12): "I am convinced that everyone knows that variation is the most pleasing and beautiful feature in writing." Dionysius's references to "fluid variations" (ποικιλίαις εὐρωωτέραις, *Comp* 19.12) in Herodotus, Plato, and Demosthenes affirm that digressions are narrative virtues not limited to any one genre.[71] It comes as little surprise, then, that Dionysius wanders in his treatises, reinforcing his own strong emphasis on variation (μεταβολή and ποικιλία; see, e.g., *Comp.* 19.1, 10, 12, 13), a concept that encompasses a relatively wide definitional range in his works.[72] To be sure, in Dionysius's critical writings, μεταβολή often refers to minor stylistic and linguistic details, but the word can embrace matters of content, too. Varieties of expression (σχήμασι πολυειδεστέροις) may constitute breaks from an established syntactical or phrasal norm, but more broadly, Dionysius connects the idea of variation with how an author facilitates a reader's movement through a text. This concern again applies to the historian's sense of his reader's needs and the choices made to serve them:

> The third matter that the man who writes history must see to is the question of what he ought to include in his composition and what he ought to leave out. I think Thucydides fell short in this matter, too. For Herodotus understood that any narrative of great length **provides its listeners' spirits with pleasure if it takes certain pauses**, but that if it is limited to the same set of events, even if it is particularly successful, reading is beset with a feeling of satiety. Herodotus wanted to make his writing dappled, being a follower of Homer. Certainly, if we pick up his book, we are led through to the very last syllable, and we always are eager for more. (*Pomp.* 3.11)

---

[71] With regard to Herodotus, choosing at random a section of the *Histories*—say, the narrative covering the Ionian Revolt (5.28–6.32)—one can easily isolate any number of episodic or digressive "pauses" that interrupt the more straightforward tale of the Revolt proper: the story of Doreius as background to the story of Cleomenes (5.42–48), the expulsion of tyrants as background to understanding Athens (5.55), and the narration of Athenian activity before Aristagoras's arrival (5.65). Even by the loosest definition, instances of narrative μεταβολή can be found throughout Herodotus. On digression in Herodotus, see Cobet 1971; de Jong 2002: 255–58; Khellaf 2018: 169–70 (and 194–96 for Dionysius's comments on digression in Theopompus).

[72] For conceptualizations of μεταβολή in the Dionysian corpus, see *Comp.* 19, *Dem.* 46–47, and *Pomp.* 3, with reference to historians. See also Ros 1938: 29–40. Although Ros acknowledges (37) that the word has connections to history-writing, and specifically to the content as well as the style, he lays strong emphasis on stylistic (λεκτικός) components ("Stilkomponenten"). Given, however, the preeminent importance Dionysius attaches to subject matter in his comparison of Herodotus and Thucydides at *Pomp.* 3.2–6, it would be inappropriate to ignore Dionysius's views on the applicability of variation to matters of content.

τρίτον ἐστὶν ἀνδρὸς ἱστορικοῦ <ἔργον σκοπεῖν>, τίνα τε δεῖ παραλαβεῖν ἐπὶ τὴν γραφὴν πράγματα καὶ τίνα παραλιπεῖν. δοκεῖ δή μοι κἂν τούτῳ λείπεσθαι Θουκυδίδης. συνειδὼς γὰρ Ἡρόδοτος, **ὅτι πᾶσα μῆκος ἔχουσα πολὺ διήγησις ἂν μὲν ἀναπαύσεις τινὰς λαμβάνῃ, τὰς ψυχὰς τῶν ἀκροωμένων ἡδέως διατίθησιν,** ἐὰν δὲ ἐπὶ τῶν αὐτῶν μένῃ πραγμάτων, κἂν τὰ μάλιστα ἐπιτυγχάνηται, λυπεῖ τὴν ἀκοὴν τῷ κόρῳ, ποικίλην ἐβουλήθη ποιῆσαι τὴν γραφήν, Ὁμήρου ζηλωτὴς γενόμενος· καὶ γὰρ τὸ βιβλίον ἢν αὐτοῦ λάβωμεν, μέχρι τῆς ἐσχάτης συλλαβῆς ἀγάμεθα καὶ ἀεὶ τὸ πλέον ἐπιζητοῦμεν.

As if anticipating something of the views of Hayden White on narrative structure and historiographic meaning, Dionysius recognizes how narrative shaping affects readerly perception.[73] The description boils down to a discussion of variety in historical writing, focused on decisions of subject matter and topic (see *Pomp.* 3.12). Herodotus's laudable "pauses," as with his word choice, reorient the perception of content and can even improve the putatively uplifting narrative. Through his ἀναπαύσεις, Herodotus shows what Dionysius perceives as an admirable awareness of his readers' potential to feel pleasure (τὰς ψυχὰς τῶν ἀκροωμένων ἡδέως διατίθησιν). He also displays in Dionysius's eyes a commendable understanding of the importance of the literary tradition, for his own "dappled" writing is cited as an outgrowth of his being an emulator (ζηλωτής) of Homer. Once again, genre need not restrict Dionysius's prescriptions. Herodotus can follow Homer, and Dionysius can follow Herodotus. In this regard, Dionysius continues to situate his critique in the light of choice, through which the critic casts Herodotus as actively "wanting" (ἐβουλήθη) to infuse his work with variety and thereby benefit his reader. Dionysius finds in Herodotus's frequent (and sometimes derided) proclivity to digress further evidence of the sound writerly life described earlier.[74]

For their part, Dionysius's own critical writings exhibit ample variation alongside two other aforementioned criteria of Herodotean narrative behavior, namely, comments by the narrator on his own authority and direct engagement with the reader. Dionysius's many references to disruption and incompleteness, alleged challenges from his readers, and anticipations of readerly activity cumulatively construct his reader-conscious persona.

---

[73] Fox 1993 also suggests ways in which White's work (esp. White 1973) is relevant to Dionysius's historiographic concerns.

[74] For ancient judgments of Herodotus's digressive tendency, see Plutarch, *de Herod. malig.* 855C–D; Marcellinus, *Vit. Thuc.* 48–49. See also the comment of Quintilian on Herodotus's style as diffuse (*fusus*, 10.1.73).

68 HERODOTUS AND IMPERIAL GREEK LITERATURE

Dionysius sees a change in topic, for instance, as a necessary deference to his reader; he need not delay with countless examples, as when discussing Homer's diction: "There are many such passages in the poet, as I am confident everyone knows. It is sufficient for me to cite these passages alone as a reminder" (τοιαῦτα δ' ἐστὶ παρὰ τῷ ποιητῇ μυρία, ὡς εὖ οἶδ' ὅτι πάντες ἴσασιν· ἐμοὶ δ' ὑπομνήσεως ἕνεκα λέγοντι ἀρκεῖ ταῦτα μόνα εἰρῆσθαι, *Comp.* 3.12). He avoids lingering on another topic a few paragraphs later, following his discussion of Herodotus: "That's enough concerning these matters" (καὶ περὶ μὲν τούτων ἱκανὰ ταῦτα, *Comp.* 3.18).[75] Even when he finishes a topic, Dionysius can indicate the possibility of the reader's active role in perpetuating it: "I think I can let go this topic for the time being. However, it is possible for anyone who so wishes to investigate how prose style can undergo the same change as poetry when the words are preserved but their arrangement altered" (ταῦτα μὲν οὖν ἐάσειν μοι δοκῶ κατὰ τὸ παρόν. ὅτι δὲ καὶ ἡ πεζὴ λέξις τὸ αὐτὸ δύναται παθεῖν τῇ ἐμμέτρῳ μενόντων μὲν τῶν ὀνομάτων, ἀλλαττομένης δὲ τῆς συνθέσεως, πάρεστι τῷ βουλομένῳ σκοπεῖν, *Comp.* 4.7). Given all that Dionysius says about the alienating effects of Thucydides's prose and the essential unsociability of his style, the demonstrated awareness of his reader firmly plants Dionysius's flag in Herodotean soil.[76] Dionysius's capacity for topical variety, deployment of varied examples (see e.g., *Comp.* 12–20), and self-conscious comments on digression cohere into an enactment of the very theme he both lionizes in *On Literary Composition* and elsewhere praises in Herodotus.[77] His elevation of ποικιλία (see *Comp.* 16.5)

---

[75] Likewise, when Dionysius feels he has overemphasized a point or digressed beyond expectation, he might register the sort of self-consciousness that readers are likely to find in Herodotus: "When I decided to put together a treatise on this topic, I sought to discover whether anyone before me had said anything about it. . . . But I did not see anywhere a contribution, large or small, to my topic by any author of renown" (ἐγώ γ' οὖν ὅτ' ἔγνων συντάττεσθαι ταύτην τὴν ὑπόθεσιν, ἐζήτουν εἴ τι τοῖς πρότερον εἴρηται περὶ αὐτῆς. . . . οὐδαμῇ δ' οὐδὲν εἰρημένον ὑπ' οὐδενὸς ὁρῶν τῶν γοῦν ὀνόματος ἠξιωμένων οὔτε μεῖζον οὔτ' ἔλαττον εἰς ἣν ἐγὼ προῄρημαι πραγματείαν, *Comp.* 4.19–20). Compare Herodotean narratorial self-consciousness at 1.95.1, 2.65.2, 7.96.1, 7.139.1, 7.171.

[76] For passages in which Herodotus invites his reader into the process of inquiry, even that which extends beyond the results proffered by his text, see, e.g., *Hist.* 1.139: "Their names, which match their physical nature and nobility, all end in the same letter that the Dorians call *san* and the Ionians *sigma*; you will find, if you search (διζήμενος εὑρήσεις), that not some but all Persian names end in this letter"; *Hist.* 2.123 on the Egyptian stories that are "for the benefit of whoever believes such tales" (χράσθω ὅτεῳ τὰ τοιαῦτα πιθανά ἐστι); and *Hist.* 5.54: "If anyone should desire a more exact measurement, I will give him that too" (εἰ δέ τις τὸ ἀτρεκέστερον τούτων ἔτι δίζηται, ἐγὼ καὶ τοῦτο σημανέω). Further examples of Herodotus's engagement with his readers are at 2.146, 5.45, 5.52, and 5.67. See also Dionysius's comment at *Dem.* 41.3, after hailing Herodotus and Plato as exemplary, that anyone "who wishes to consider it may examine this view of mine," opening up judgment to the scrutiny of his reader.

[77] The ostentatious variety of Dionysius's works is also in contrast to the monotony he criticizes in Thucydides (*Pomp.* 3.12).

THE ETHICS OF AUTHORSHIP   69

aligns him with that lauded author of a similarly heterogeneous discourse (πολύμορφος ὁ λόγος, *Comp.* 16.5 ~ ποικίλην ... τὴν γραφήν, *Pomp.* 3.11).

At another point, Dionysius feels the need to justify his project, and in doing so he makes clear the effort he has undertaken to discover his own obligations in light of past critical inquiry. In this case, he defends the need to digress on the treatise that he did *not* write:

> Giving myself to certain speculations, it had seemed to me that I was progressing in my task, when in fact I realized that the road was leading me somewhere altogether different, and not in the direction I had set for myself and in which it was necessary to proceed. So I quit. Perhaps there will be no objection if I touch upon that area of speculation, too, and state the reason why I gave it up. For I wish to avoid the sense that I have passed it over because of ignorance and not by choice. (*Comp.* 4.22–23)

> ἁψάμενος δέ τινων θεωρημάτων καὶ δόξας ὁδῷ μοι τὸ πρᾶγμα χωρεῖν ὡς ἔμαθον ἑτέρωσέ ποι ταύτην ἄγουσαν ἐμὲ τὴν ὁδόν, οὐχ ὅποι προυθέμην καὶ ἀναγκαῖον ἦν ἐλθεῖν, ἀπέστην. κωλύσει δ᾽ οὐδὲν ἴσως κἀκείνης ἅψασθαι τῆς θεωρίας καὶ τὰς αἰτίας εἰπεῖν δι᾽ ἃς ἐξέλιπον αὐτήν, ἵνα μή με δόξῃ τις ἀγνοίᾳ παρελθεῖν αὐτὴν ἀλλὰ προαιρέσει.

Proceeding through his task (ὁδῷ μοι τὸ πρᾶγμα χωρεῖν), Dionysius marks his sense of narrative wandering in Herodotean metaphor (Hdt. 1.5.3), only here in the vulnerable fashion of one who admits at times what he does not know.[78] Yet while Herodotus might anticipate the potential for digressions to seem irrelevant or desultory by ascribing their appearance to the agency of narrative itself (especially at 4.30, προσθήκας γὰρ δή μοι ὁ λόγος ἐξ ἀρχῆς ἐδίζητο), Dionysius announces his averted digression as a matter of deliberate choice (προαιρέσει), in echo of the criterion of narratorial behavior highlighted earlier.[79] An expressed narratorial humility—an

---

[78] Hdt. 1.5.3, προβήσομαι ἐς τὸ πρόσω τοῦ λόγου; cf. *Comp.* 11.5. On the metaphor of narrative as travel in Herodotus, see Wood 2016 passim; see Wood 2016: 15 with n. 10 for the phrase as an imitable Herodotean "trademark." Dionysius reiterates the metaphor a few sections later: "I will now turn to the original subject from which I disembarked into these matters" (ἐπάνειμι δὴ ἐπὶ τὴν ἐξ ἀρχῆς ὑπόθεσιν ἀφ᾽ ἧς εἰς ταῦτ᾽ ἐξέβην, *Comp.* 5.12).

[79] For an example in Herodotus of what we might call his narrative "vulnerability," expressing the limits of his powers even as he assures us of his faithful effort, see, e.g., *Hist.* 5.9: "As for the region which lies north of this land, no one can say with certainty (οὐδεὶς ἔχει φράσαι τὸ ἀτρεκές) what people live there. ... I am able to learn through inquiry (δύναμαι πυθέσθαι) of no people dwelling beyond the Ister." Herodotus indicates here his ignorance, along with that of other men (οὐδεὶς ἔχει

70 HERODOTUS AND IMPERIAL GREEK LITERATURE

acknowledgment of indeterminacy—keeps both Dionysius and Herodotus accountable to their readers.[80] Dionysius's advertised awareness of his reader stems both from the socialized nature of his often epistolary criticism and from the wish to convey a sense of the past by evoking the qualities of its best authors—in this case, the interactive feel of Herodotus.

As a final example, let us briefly return to *On Thucydides*. In the opening paragraphs of the work, Dionysius presents himself as one who anticipates the responses of and engages overtly with his readers.[81] He admits that he was previously cursory in his treatment of Thucydides in *On Imitation*, not because he was lazy or lacked arguments but "because I endeavored to write on a scale appropriate (εὐκαιρίας) to my text" (*Thuc.* 1.3). His decision to expound upon Thucydides grows specifically out of his friend Tubero's request that Dionysius should compose a separate essay on Thucydides, resulting in the advertised self-interruption in the epistolary frame of *On Thucydides*: "Setting aside my work on Demosthenes that I had in hand, I vowed to do as you requested. Here I give you the essay in fulfillment of that promise" (ἀναβαλόμενος τὴν περὶ Δημοσθένους πραγματείαν ἣν εἶχον ἐν χερσίν, ὑπεσχόμην τε ποιήσειν, ὡς προῃροῦ, καὶ τελέσας τὴν ὑπόσχεσιν ἀποδίδωμι, *Thuc.* 1.4). The explicit relational aspect of Dionysius's opening statements—evident in his claim to have made and fulfilled a promise (ὑπεσχόμην . . . τελέσας) and in his answering his interlocutor's request (προῃροῦ) for revision—centers the narrator in an overtly socialized context.[82] The advertisement of Dionysius's correction-in-stride contributes to his self-construction as a responsible author far more evocative of the accessible Herodotean narrator than the Thucydidean persona ostensibly under consideration. Dionysius then offers further self-justifying comments designed to shore up his authority as critic and implicitly to distinguish himself from his subject:

φράσαι τὸ ἀτρεκές), while still intimating the positive act of his own effort at learning by inquiry (πυθέσθαι). Compare Marincola 2016.

[80] Alternative explanation and indeterminacy can also have philosophical resonances: Dionysius's style has an air of non-resolution that would become a hallmark of, for instance, sympotic literature, which obviously also has a social component. On Plutarch and alternative explanation, see König 2012: 68. On Dionysius's social circle, see Rawson 1985: 3–18; Luraghi 2003: 269–70; Hunter and de Jonge 2019b: 8–9; de Jonge 2019: 263.

[81] In Dionysius's case, his attitude is shaped by dependence on the support of prominent Romans: see Weaire 2005: 248–49. On Q. Aelius Tubero specifically, see Bowersock 1965: 130–32.

[82] See also *Amm. I* 1–2.

THE ETHICS OF AUTHORSHIP 71

Concerning myself it will suffice for me to say the following only, that throughout my entire life up to the present I have steered clear of quarrelsomeness, fractiousness, and indiscriminate barking at others. I have never published anything in which I lambaste someone. . . . I would never have attempted . . . to display in a work the ill will which is appropriate neither to a man of open-minded character nor to my own nature. (*Thuc.* 2.3)

περὶ μὲν ἐμαυτοῦ τοσοῦτον ἀρκεσθήσομαι μόνον εἰπὼν ὅτι τὸ φιλόνεικον τοῦτο καὶ δύσερι καὶ προσυλακτοῦν εἰκῇ τισὶν ἐν παντὶ πεφυλαγμένος τῷ βίῳ μέχρι τοῦ παρόντος καὶ οὐδεμίαν ἐκδεδωκὼς γραφὴν ἐν ᾗ κατηγορῶ τινος. . . . οὐκ ἂν ἐπεχείρησα . . . τὴν οὔτ᾽ ἐλευθέροις ἤθεσι πρέπουσαν οὔτ᾽ ἐμαυτῷ συνήθη κακοήθειαν ἐναποδείκνυσθαι.

Dionysius is as conscious of demonstrating his own arguments as he is of "displaying" (ἐναποδείκνυσθαι) his own *ethos* in doing so. His comments about his lack of κακοήθεια carry specific force in the context of a treatise about Thucydides, inasmuch as they conjure Dionysius's supposition that Thucydides was motivated by ill will toward Athens (see *Pomp.* 3.9, 3.15). The nature of the arguments must, moreover, suit the "open-minded character" of the critic (ἐλευθέροις ἤθεσι), in distinction from the grudging choices of Thucydides. The felt need to establish his benevolence reinforces Dionysius's self-alignment with his own view of Herodotus as the ethically self-conscious writer. In forging a connection to the classical past both as a critic and as an imitator, Dionysius ensures a continuum of authorial deportment. He fortifies his own acts of praise, increasing credence in the narrator of the rhetorical treatises—that is, in the Herodotean-sounding narrator who is himself telling us why we should care about Herodotus.

Herodotus's model holds a peculiar power for Dionysius, stretching beyond historiography proper. Dionysius's overt preference for Herodotus allies with his own attempts to build up a dialogic disposition whose tendency is one of narratorial transparency. Dionysius's open-ended hermeneutic style rejects obscure and seemingly inflexible Thucydideanism in favor of Herodotean accessibility. He subscribes to the usefulness of a varied, sometimes digressive style in his own literary criticism and furthermore assures readers of his self-consciously good-natured attitude. Even as he makes pronouncements and inhabits the pose of critic, he repeatedly reveals that he is first a reader, then a critic, and that his critical judgments are informed by his absorption of and response to particular narratorial sensibilities. In the end, Dionysius manages not only to praise Herodotus but also, as an implied imitator, to capture something of Herodotus's narratorial *ethos* in a different generic mode altogether. Through submerged imitation, Herodotus's sensibility is imbricated with Dionysius's own and acts as a critical force in constructing Dionysius's own sense of what it means to be an author. In chapter 2, we shall see how aspects of Dionysius's historical worldview are likewise filtered through Herodotus.

2

Dionysius's Global Herodotus

> The world of history has not always been conceived in terms of the unity of world history. As with Herodotus, for example, it can also be considered a moral phenomenon. As such it offers a larger number of exempla but no unity. What justifies the talk of the unity of world history? (Gadamer 1975 [1960]: 212)

In chapter 1, we saw how Dionysius's consistent approbation of Herodotus goes deeper than unreflective patriotism or preference for stylistic charm. His singular vindication is bound up with a gestalt of authorial virtues, aesthetic and ethical, that he discovers in Herodotus's high-minded deliberate choice for a genial narrative disposition and air of accessibility. Dionysius's readings produce a strong impression of Herodotus's authorial distinctiveness. In turn, Dionysius appropriates elements of this characterization in the effort to cast his own self-portrait in the mold of the admirable Herodotus, vivifying the past and allowing Herodotus to speak through and with him.

In this chapter, I turn to Dionysius's elevation of Herodotus as it relates to aspects of Dionysius's own historical project. I argue that Dionysius has recourse to his predecessor as part of a wider consciousness of imperial ideology and that his assessment of Herodotus should be read in light of the critic-historiographer's own articulation of nascent Roman imperium. Dionysius's acclamation of Herodotus's unified yet variegated narrative, along with his use of what might be termed ethnographic cosmopolitanism, mirrors a rhetoric of empire germane to Dionysius's first-century BCE Roman milieu. Analyzing remarks from the rhetorical treatises alongside comments from his *Roman Antiquities*, I argue for connections between what Dionysius perceives as Herodotus's harmonious, "one-bodied" historiography and Dionysius's reckoning with the polity of Rome, itself gathering up different peoples and lands. To be sure, attention to the *Roman Antiquities* might seem

Herodotus and Imperial Greek Literature. N. Bryant Kirkland, Oxford University Press. © Oxford University Press 2022.
DOI: 10.1093/oso/9780197583517.003.0003

74 HERODOTUS AND IMPERIAL GREEK LITERATURE

to depart from one of the stated purposes of this study, which is to examine the resonances of Herodotus beyond historiography proper. But there are good reasons, as I shall discuss, for seeing the *Roman Antiquities* as part of Dionysius's rhetorical project.[1] In both his preface to *On the Ancient Orators* and various sections of his *Roman Antiquities*, Dionysius creates a framework for understanding literary and world history that encourages us to read his corpus holistically, and an overall coherence emerges in Dionysius's intellectual program. In line with Jeffrey Walker's attempt at a reparative reading of the work's "rhetoricality," I restrict my analysis to the *Roman Antiquities'* prologue and a few select passages, rather than attempting a broad-scale comparison over two vast sides of Dionysius's corpus.[2] Even on a limited scale, however, Dionysius's views on Herodotus will be seen to magnify him through the lens of empire by which the critic's own literary endeavor is shaped, and his appropriations of the *Histories* will contribute to the long tradition of interpreting Herodotus as a global narrator.

As Kadir observes in the essay on world literature quoted in my introduction, Herodotus's text has a particular connection with periods of imperial self-reflexivity. Kadir's image of imperial modulation and cultural complexity offers a framework for considering Dionysius in his Roman context as well:

> Throughout history, Herodotus has been read and remarked most intensely at historical moments of intensified imperial hegemony, as in the Hellenistic era of Alexander the Great and his *razzia* eastward, and during the so-called Age of Discoveries that accompanied the westward transatlantic movement of Europe and its Renaissance. There is a continuity between such imperial ventures and what elicits the inquiries of Herodotus in the fifth century B.C., namely, the cultural complexity that ensues once the supposed homogeneity of Magna Graecia [*sic*] is shattered by the westward reach of Persian imperialism.[3]

---

[1] See Sacks 1983: 74–76 for parallels between the historiographic ideals of *Pomp.* and those expressed in the *Ant. Rom.* By his own account (*Ant. Rom.* 1.7.2, 7.70.2), Dionysius published the first part of the *Roman Antiquities* in 8/7 BCE (Hunter and de Jonge 2019b: 1), but the chronological relation to various rhetorical treatises is not entirely clear (Bonner 1939: 1–3). For text of the *Roman Antiquities*, I follow K. Jacoby's Teubner editions (Jacoby 1885–1905).

[2] Walker 2012: 266–80. On the potential deficiencies of describing Dionysius's view of history as "rhetorical," see also Gabba 1991: 74–75. For a thorough consideration of the classicizing elements of the preface to Dionysius's *Roman Antiquities* especially (with some recourse as well to its early books), see Wiater 2011a: 165–223.

[3] Kadir 2004: 3. Cf. Rood 2020: 24–25 cautioning against anachronistic parallels.

DIONYSIUS'S GLOBAL HERODOTUS 75

As Kadir goes on to ask, "The larger question, of which Herodotus himself becomes symptomatic, is what happens to the locus of the *oikoumene* when it ceases to be tantamount to *the* world and becomes yet another locus *in* the world?"[4] I argue in what follows that Dionysius's *On the Ancient Orators* and *Roman Antiquities* are programmatically intertwined, both registering the author's consciousness (and perhaps celebration) of a transformed *oikoumene*, one in which topographic Greece may have become "yet another locus" in the Roman world but also one in which a cultural idea of Greece comes to occupy a paramount position under Rome—and *as Roman*. I discuss the ideological coherence between Dionysius's rhetorical and historiographic projects before analyzing how Dionysius's ethnography of virtue and ethnographic cosmopolitanism rely on Herodotus. I then turn to Dionysius's ideas of a unified historiography, both in Herodotus and in his own work, followed by analysis of how certain of Dionysius's rhetorical examples may be interpreted in light of the imperial historiography he propounds.

Dionysius's Coherent Corpus

Dionysius's corpus, both his rhetorical criticism and historiography, is marked by an ideological consistency.[5] Put broadly, Dionysius's historiography betrays a set of rhetorical motivations;[6] complementarily, the preface to his rhetorical study is laced, as Thomas Hidber has shown, with historiographic threads.[7] Nor does this exhaust the ways in which one could trace continuity between both projects as they form an interlocking whole. Regarding the rhetorical premises of the *Roman Antiquities*, for instance, Nicolas Wiater has written that the text "implements a political and cultural programme. The aim of Dionysius' work is not to *describe* the history of early Rome, but to *create* it along the lines of Classical Greek past and culture."[8] As Wiater has done much to show, Dionysius's work tells us less about Roman history proper and more about how a Greek intellectual under the nascent principate might reason his way through to an understanding of

---

[4] Kadir 2004: 3. See also Alonso-Núñez 1988 on Herodotus's sense of imperial succession.
[5] A signal contribution of the Hunter and de Jonge volume (2019a) is the integrative view of Dionysius's rhetorical and historiographic works; see, e.g., Hunter and de Jonge 2019b: 2–6.
[6] On the *Roman Antiquities* and the kinds of historical "truth" it tells, see Fox 1993. Compare Wiater 2011a: 110–16.
[7] Hidber 1996: 87.
[8] Wiater 2011a: 165. See also Gabba 1982: 44, 48.

76 HERODOTUS AND IMPERIAL GREEK LITERATURE

Greek identity.[9] Likewise, Dionysius's focus in various rhetorical treatises on the most effective aspects of historiographic writing prompts readers to draw links between his rhetorical treatises and historiographic work. When, for instance, he mentions early in the *Roman Antiquities* his "deliberate choice" as a historian (προαίρεσις, *Ant. Rom.* 1.1.2), his diction recalls his focus on the weighty deliberate choices of previous historians (see *Thuc.* 5.3, 16.4, 24.12; *Pomp.* 4.1) who, according to Dionysius, rendered important decisions on topic, scope, and style. Dionysius's use of the term conveys the sense that he, too, acts on certain prescriptions set forth in the rhetorical works, in which, as Hunter has observed, the concept of προαίρεσις (which Hunter translates in context as "what a writer plans to do") is one of Dionysius's main critical concerns.[10] His own prominent authorial persona on both sides of his corpus marks such linchpins between theory and practice.

Another point of contact between the rhetorical treatises and the rhetorical program of the *Roman Antiquities* involves Dionysius's effort at archaizing for the future. Both the preface to *On the Ancient Orators* and the opening pages of the *Roman Antiquities* stress the usefulness of the past for fashioning good lives in the present and beyond (cf. *Orat. Vett.* 4.1–2 and *Ant. Rom.* 1.6.5), including for Dionysius's goals of producing able public speakers and reconciling the trajectories of Greek and Roman history. As Emilio Gabba once framed it, "Dionysius wrote of Rome's archaic period, but he was intent on imperial Rome."[11] Evocations of his own rhetorical ideas in the early pages of his historical prologue suggest that readers are on the right track when they attempt to identify how the various historiographic presences described in the rhetorical works might factor into Dionysius's own historiographic program—and furthermore how these presences are useful for his present day. Indeed, when Dionysius draws attention in his preface to *On Ancient Orators* to past writers' "deliberate choices both in life and literature" (προαιρέσεις τοῦ τε βίου καὶ τῶν λόγων, *Orat. Vett.* 4.2), the collocation perhaps suggests his desire to extend imitative classicality into his own *lived* present. The literary imitation explored in the treatises enables a connection to antiquity that is redoubled, in turn, in the *Roman Antiquities*, in Dionysius's account of Rome's living continuation of Greek virtue. Finally, yet another correspondence between Dionysius's

---

[9] See esp. Wiater 2011b.
[10] Hunter 2019: 38.
[11] Gabba 1991: 213.

DIONYSIUS'S GLOBAL HERODOTUS   77

historiography and his rhetorical treatises, and one that has particular bearing on his evocation of Herodotus, lies in his express interest in writing a "universal" (κοινή) history (*Ant. Rom.* 1.2.1–3.3). Dionysius's claim echoes his universalist critical purposes (*Orat. Vett.* 4.1–2); together, the two constitute a joint effort at serving all humankind (κοινὴν καὶ φιλάνθρωπον, *Orat. Vett.* 4.1) as part of a project that is itself enabled by the universalizing dominance of Rome (*Orat. Vett.* 4.1).[12]

Dionysius thus provides multiple reasons to believe that the rhetorical program of the *Roman Antiquities*, in establishing continuity between present and past through an imitative focus on virtue, coheres with his idealizing program as enunciated in the preface to *On the Ancient Orators*. Dionysius's historical work and rhetorical-critical ambit are repeatedly projected as intertwined as he delineates a livable classicality. This intermingling involves the recurrent possibility of a Greek classicality as lived out in and *through* Rome—indeed, the possibility that Rome can enact a classical Greek ideal that has not yet been achieved.[13] We are accordingly emboldened to read with an eye to the presence of various protagonists, as it were, from his rhetorical treatises (including the figure of Herodotus) in the ideological shaping of the *Roman Antiquities*.

Ethnographic Cosmopolitanism

In his (re-)creation of Greco-Roman history, Dionysius's historiographic vision broadly recalls the globalism of Herodotus's text in two key ways. The first is that Dionysius's vision is cosmopolitan rather than local, unifying rather than segmenting.[14] As Stephen Oakley has written, "Dionysius states that he intends to record the entire (ὅλον, 1.8.2) life of the city, dealing with both war and politics, in contrast to writers who deal with only one or the other."[15] Dionysius's historical vision will recall Herodotus on precisely one of the grounds he celebrates in his rhetorical treatises: that Herodotus was the first historian to transcend local accounts and to create a harmonious historiographic whole, forging unity despite disparateness (see *Pomp.* 3.3,

---

[12] On Rome's ascendancy as key to Dionysius's claim of a revival in Greek rhetoric, see Gabba 1982: 45, 50; Swain 1996: 21–27, esp. 25–26.

[13] See Wiater 2019.

[14] On this point, see Marincola 1997: 245–46.

[15] Oakley 2019: 137.

78   HERODOTUS AND IMPERIAL GREEK LITERATURE

3.14; *Thuc.* 5.5, all to be discussed).[16] The worldview of the *Roman Antiquities* approaches at some level the breadth of historical vision that Dionysius himself magnifies in Herodotus.

At same time, Dionysius also resembles in this regard both his predecessor Polybius, who had called for a move away from an atomized historiography (κατὰ μέρος; see Polyb. 1.4) in favor of a universalizing project, and such near-contemporaries as Nicolaus of Damascus and Strabo, who in different ways assume in their writings a holistic approach to Roman power.[17] While there are similarities between Dionysius and Polybius especially, one should also observe some important differences—and, indeed, reasons to resist seeing Polybius as the main intellectual anchor for Dionysius.[18] First, the scopes of their universalizing differ, as is well summarized in comments by Wiater:

> the idea of a continuous development of Roman power from the beginnings of Roman history is alien to Polybius' interpretation of Roman rule. . . . Programmatically, Dionysius begins with the beginnings of Roman history, the foundation of Rome and Romulus' constitution: for

[16] See also the remark of Wiater 2011b: 76: "The provocative paradoxicality of this project is further underscored by Dionysius' intimation that his narrative continues the historiographical tradition of Herodotus, whose work and the bipolar world view it represents he praises as the paradigm of classical historiography in his critical writings." See further Wiater 2011b: 62–69.

[17] On Polybius and Dionysius, with the view that the latter wanted his work to be seen as a prequel of his predecessor's *History*, see Delcourt 2005: 50–53, with the detailed treatment of Gozzoli 1976. Cf. Martin 1993. Gabba 1991: 73–79 suggests that the primary influence on Dionysius's idea of universal or comprehensive history is Theopompus, but as Oakley 2019: 137 n. 18 cautions, we do not know enough about Theopompus or very much about Dionysius's views of him, beyond his comments in *Pomp.* 6.1–11. (See, however, Matijašić 2018: 120–22 on Dionysius's Theopompus as an Isocratean corrective foil to Thucydides.) There are important differences between the holistic approaches of Polybius and Dionysius, the chief being Dionysius's repudiation of fortune as an explanatory mechanism. On universal histories, with comments on Polybius and Nicolaus of Damascus, see Fornara 1983: 42–46 and Schmitz and Wiater 2011: 32, on the similarities between Nicolaus and Dionysius (e.g., Nicolaus's comment on Roman protection of Greek and barbarian customs [*FGrHist* 90 F 125]). On universality of scope among historians of the Augustan period, see Clarke 1999b; on systematizing tendencies across genres in the same era, see Most 2011.

[18] See Gabba 1991: 193–94; Wiater 2011a: 194–98; Fox 2011: 106–10. Clarke 1999b: 250 excludes Herodotus and Polybius from her essay, despite what she calls the "commonplace" assumption that both represent universal history. For her, Herodotus is not systematic in attempting to cover the known world, and Polybius starts his account at the 140th Olympiad, thereby limiting his account's universality. One might make a similar point against Dionysius's supposed universalism, insofar as his account reaches down only to Polybius's starting point. But Dionysius's basic stress on ethnic identity transcends particular historical markers. Dionysius co-opts the ethnographic present by portraying Roman history as bound up with the habitual tendencies of the Greek *ethnos*. I do not share Clarke's interpretation of Dionysius's own proclamation to have written the history of "one nation" (Clarke 1999b: 251; cf. *Ant. Rom.* 1.3.6), since the history of that "nation" is effectively grafted onto the history of Greece itself.

DIONYSIUS'S GLOBAL HERODOTUS   79

him the origins of Roman history and the origins of Roman power are the same. . . . Choosing 264 BCE as the *end* of his account, Dionysius contradicts Polybius' assertion that this year is crucial to a proper understanding of Roman hegemony.[19]

When it comes to the question of fortune (τύχη), Polybius for his part also seems to reject it outright (*Hist.* 1.63.9), yet its complex and at times seemingly contradictory roles leave readers in no doubt that it bears weight in Polybius's historical model (compare *Hist.* 1.4.1–2).[20] Polybius describes fortune as leading human affairs to one and the same point (πρὸς ἕνα καὶ τὸν αὐτὸν σκοπόν, 1.4.1) and feels a consequent obligation (δεῖ, 1.4.1) to offer a single historical vision (μίαν σύνοψιν, 1.4.1). But crucial to Dionysius's goal of explaining Roman power according to virtue is a rejection of the idea that fortune takes a leading role in shaping Roman history, as opposed to the ethical deportment of human actors, such as when he cites Rome's "piety, justice, and every other virtue" (εὐσέβειαν δὲ καὶ δικαιοσύνην καὶ τὴν ἄλλην ἀρετήν, *Ant. Rom.* 1.4.2). As Matthew Fox observes, "This [de-emphasis by Dionysius on fortune] is a direct challenge to Polybius: instead of Rome's greatness being the result of a growth in power propelled by good fortune, it is the identity of Romans themselves that is at the root of Rome's success."[21] Dionysius's forceful and consistent downplaying of fortune was thus a polemical move.[22]

Also by way of contrast, Polybius's focus is largely on the externals of political history, rather than on aspects of moral exemplarity, the approach taken by Dionysius.[23] Dionysius's transcendent model of moral behavior permits the earliest stages of Roman history to be soldered onto the continued exercise, even outdoing, of Greek virtue.[24] His work thus recalls Herodotus's

---

[19] Wiater 2011a: 198.

[20] See Walbank 2007, with ample bibliography.

[21] Fox 2011: 108–9.

[22] Further on the rejection of fortune, see Bowersock 1965: 131 n. 5; Ando 1999: 11–12; de Jonge 2008: 61 n. 69 (with bibliography)

[23] On the importance, however, of the constitution and political structures in Dionysius's text, see Oakley 2019: 137–38. Cf. Delcourt 2005: 65.

[24] Gabba 1991: 194. See, e.g., *Ant. Rom.* 2.17.1–4, contrasting early Rome's strength in overcoming various "dangers" (κινδύνοις, 2.17.3) even more impressively than early Greeks, and "not through Fortune's favor" (οὐχ . . . εὐνοίᾳ τύχης, 2.17.3); further, *Ant. Rom.* 2.18.1 on Romulus's "moderation and sense of justice" (σωφροσύνην τε καὶ δικαιοσύνην) and 20.13.2 on Roman censors. See also Fox 2011: 108: "So although it can be argued that a universalizing, proto-Stoic system underlies his [i.e., Polybius's] justification of Roman rule, this does not result in the naïve reduction of all historical events to one kind of event. He [Polybius] is saved from such a fate by his avoidance of early Roman

80 HERODOTUS AND IMPERIAL GREEK LITERATURE

own moralizing and ethnographic focus on the tendencies of Greek (and non-Greek) behavior.[25] Finally, we should note that Dionysius himself vociferously disclaims Polybius on grounds of style (*Comp.* 4). Given the interrelatedness of style, content, and narratorial deportment delineated in chapter 1, Dionysius's dismissal of Polybius's style cannot be regarded as frivolous; rather, style is developed as part of a broader ethical composite. Even to accept the nearer influences of, say, Nicolaus of Damascus or Diodorus Siculus would controvert the very aims of Dionysius's program. Dionysius, after all, consistently urges his readers to engage with older models, an objective that his own submerged imitations variously exemplify. So even as we acknowledge the likely role of nearer influences, we are in better accord with Dionysius's own stated program if we adumbrate the presences of his own harped-upon classical, rather than Hellenistic or contemporary, models.[26]

Dionysius sees Rome as a world power whose historical reach extends both over space and back in time through its connection to the Greeks (*Ant. Rom.* 1.5.1, 1.90.1).[27] He explains Roman power in part through a quasi-ethnographic lens of behavior and custom. Similar to Herodotus, Dionysius is programmatically concerned with the dynamics of collective and ethnic identity. In Herodotus's *Histories*, the Greco-Persian Wars occasion the coalescing of a notional Greekness that, despite various fissures and slippages, existed as a mobile motif tied at times to various ideals (*isonomia, eleutheria, isêgoria*) that putatively functioned as part of a polar opposition to the practices of *barbaroi*.[28] The Persian Wars created a notional Greekness that Imperial Greeks could later invoke, however tendentiously, as a stable instance of Greek identity (e.g., Plutarch, *de Glor. Ath.* 350A), and Dionysius will also rely on a holistic idea of Greekness that explains Roman dominance. Indeed, as is well known, Dionysius's explanation of Roman dominance over Greece (and others) is that Rome's power paradoxically acts as a continuation

---

history, and the consequent necessity of inflecting that history with a teleology that corresponds to his theoretical interests. Dionysius, however, takes up that very challenge."

[25] See Fox 2011: 108 on Dionysius's response to Polybius as focusing "firmly on the question of national identity." On the relationship between ethnography and historical causation in Herodotus, see Lateiner 1989: 145–62; Dewald 1997. On Herodotus's moralizing focus, see Hau 2016: 172–93.

[26] Compare Gabba 1982: 49: "[A]ccording to Dionysius' concept, the ancient civic eloquence (of the fourth century B.C.) is exalted for its extremely lofty moral and political value, for the ideals it maintains, and for the cultural model it offers."

[27] See Luraghi 2003: 277–81.

[28] The idea of these "mirroring" qualities has been most famously propounded by Hartog 1988 [1980]. See also Lincoln 2018: 73–95, complicating the notion of comparison in Herodotus.

of Greek power.[29] This is chiefly expressed in two passages that roughly frame the first book of the *Roman Antiquities*:

> Since I am choosing to remove these errant judgments, as I have called them, from the minds of many, and to replace them with the truth, in this book I will show who the city's founders were and at what points in time they came together, and through what turns of fate they left their countries. By this I undertake to show that they were Greek, and that they came together from neither the smallest nor the least remarkable peoples. (*Ant. Rom.* 1.5.1)

> ταύτας δὴ τὰς πεπλανημένας, ὥσπερ ἔφην, ὑπολήψεις ἐξελέσθαι τῆς διανοίας τῶν πολλῶν προαιρούμενος καὶ ἀντικατασκευάσαι τὰς ἀληθεῖς, περὶ μὲν τῶν οἰκισάντων τὴν πόλιν, οἵτινες ἦσαν καὶ κατὰ τίνας ἕκαστοι καιροὺς συνῆλθον καὶ τίσι τύχαις χρησάμενοι τὰς πατρίους οἰκήσεις ἐξέλιπον, ἐν ταύτῃ δηλώσω τῇ γραφῇ, δι' ἧς Ἕλληνάς τε αὐτοὺς ὄντας ἐπιδείξειν ὑπισχνοῦμαι καὶ οὐκ ἐκ τῶν ἐλαχίστων ἢ φαυλοτάτων ἐθνῶν συνεληλυθότας.

> Let the reader say good-bye to those who would make Rome a haven for barbarians, refugees, and vagabonds, and let the reader boldly aver that it is a Greek city.... (*Ant. Rom.* 1.89.1)

> ὥστε θαρρῶν ἤδη τις ἀποφαινέσθω πολλὰ χαίρειν φράσας τοῖς βαρβάρων καὶ δραπετῶν καὶ ἀνεστίων ἀνθρώπων καταφυγὴν τὴν Ῥώμην ποιοῦσιν Ἑλλάδα πόλιν αὐτήν....

Both passages rely on an ethnic basis for Roman Greekness, and in the latter, Dionysius goes on to catalogue Roman ethnic lineage (*Ant. Rom.* 1.89.2–3), defending it as Greek by tracing it back through the Arcadians and

---

[29] For the elaboration of the idea that Rome matures by enacting a set of Hellenic virtues, see Gabba 1982: 53; Gabba 1991: 200, 203–4; Hidber 1996: 77 n. 322, with references. Compare Martin 1993: 202–5. For the notion that Rome fulfills a classical ideal that the Greeks themselves failed to achieve, see Wiater 2019: 67–68. Dionysius shows Romans undertaking good actions by modeling their behavior on paradigmatic Greek behavior from the past; see *Ant. Rom.* 3.11.4; Wiater 2019: 75. Dionysius's contention that Rome was an extension of Greece also allows him to elaborate an idea of mimesis, since the best examples of Roman virtue are in imitation of (or correction to) Greek deeds of the past; see the example at *Ant. Rom.* 14.6, in which the Romans are presented as outdoing their Greek predecessors in virtue (discussed later).

82 HERODOTUS AND IMPERIAL GREEK LITERATURE

Pelasgians, all the way to the Argives.[30] But what defines an *ethnos* itself for Dionysius? Is the genealogical connection sufficient to demonstrate Rome's Hellenism? After all, Dionysius must acknowledge certain obvious historical changes, including the Romans' intense admixture with various peoples (1.89.3). How can the Romans still be Greek?

On the heels of his genealogical catalogue, Dionysius tips his hand to this anxiety, admitting a potential flaw in his thesis. For, in fact, many Greeks have become "thoroughly barbarized" (ἐξεβαρβαρώθη, 1.89.3). In the course of describing Greeks who, "living among barbarians" (ἐν βαρβάροις οἰκοῦντες), have become detached from their roots, Dionysius adduces a raft of identity markers that barbarized Greeks have forgotten:

> After all, many others who live among barbarians have in short order unlearned Greekness completely, with the result that they no longer speak Greek or practice a Greek way of life. Nor do they heed the same gods or have reasonable laws, the thing that most differentiates Greek nature from that of the barbarian, nor are these people in agreement with anything else at all connected to ordinary Greek life. (*Ant. Rom.* 1.89.4)

> ἐπεὶ ἄλλοι γε συχνοὶ ἐν βαρβάροις οἰκοῦντες ὀλίγου χρόνου διελθόντος ἅπαν τὸ Ἑλληνικὸν ἀπέμαθον, ὡς μήτε φωνὴν Ἑλλάδα φθέγγεσθαι μήτε ἐπιτηδεύμασιν Ἑλλήνων χρῆσθαι, μήτε θεοὺς τοὺς αὐτοὺς νομίζειν, μήτε νόμους τοὺς ἐπιεικεῖς, ᾧ μάλιστα διαλλάσσει φύσις Ἑλλὰς βαρβάρου, μήτε τῶν ἄλλων συμβολαίων μηδ᾽ ὁτιοῦν.

The definition of Greekness shifts here to a decidedly cultural one, notwithstanding the mention of a "Greek nature" (φύσις Ἑλλάς). As many will recognize, Dionysius's catalogue has its basis in a well-known passage from Herodotus, in which the Athenians, in response to Spartans worried about possible Athenian medizing, provide a formulation of Greekness:[31]

---

[30] On the history of the idea of Romans as Greeks, with bibliography, see Peirano 2010: 40 n. 29, and for further passages relevant to this idea in Dionysius, Peirano 2010: 39–43. On the provisionality of Dionysius's ethnic definition, see Fox 2019: 199.

[31] The argument by the Athenians is no doubt tendentious in context. On the ways in which this passage can be taken out of context and can cause readers to overlook the complexities of Hellenism as Herodotus presents them, see Thomas 2013. Dewald 1998: 721 notes of this passage, "It is not clear that before Xerxes' invasion most Greeks would have thought such connections important or would have thought of themselves principally as Greeks rather than as members of an individual tribe or city."

DIONYSIUS'S GLOBAL HERODOTUS   83

There is the matter of our Greekness, being a thing of one name and one language, and having common temples to the gods and common religious rites and the same way of life, to which things it would not behoove the Athenians to turn traitor. (Hdt. 8.144.2)

αὖτις δὲ τὸ Ἑλληνικόν, ἐὸν ὅμαιμόν τε καὶ ὁμόγλωσσον, καὶ θεῶν ἱδρύματά τε κοινὰ καὶ θυσίαι ἤθεά τε ὁμότροπα, τῶν προδότας γενέσθαι Ἀθηναίους οὐκ ἂν εὖ ἔχοι.

Like Herodotus, Dionysius centers Greekness around common language, manner of life, and religious practices: φωνὴν Ἑλλάδα (*Ant. Rom.* 1.89.4) ~ ὁμόγλωσσον (Hdt. 8.144.2); ἐπιτηδεύμασιν Ἑλλήνων χρῆσθαι (*Ant. Rom.* 1.89.4) ~ ἤθεά τε ὁμότροπα (Hdt. 8.144.2); θεοὺς τοὺς αὐτοὺς νομίζειν (*Ant. Rom.* 1.89.4) ~ θεῶν ἱδρύματά τε κοινὰ καὶ θυσίαι (Hdt. 8.144.2). A cultural definition unmoored from place or territory well fits Dionysius's promulgation of the notion that the Greeks live on in a new place under a new dispensation. Thus, although he offers a lengthy genealogy, Dionysius ultimately summons literary genealogy, lifting a page from Herodotus to supply a definition of "the Greek thing" rendered along lines of *nomoi*.

Just as it is evident, however, in the world of Herodotus's text that even *nomoi* can change quickly (see, e.g., the story of the Lydians who change their customs virtually overnight: Hdt. 1.157), so is Dionysius somewhat boxed into a corner when, in the very next breath, he must acknowledge that the Romans obviously no longer speak Greek (1.90.1).[32] The strain of thought that started with *genos*, followed by *nomoi*, now requires yet further redefinition. Since even the other markers of *ethnos* that remain are changeable, it is here that Dionysius hints at a subtler elaboration of Roman Greekness, one based less on shared ethnicity or language and more on a notion of shared virtue. A trace of this has already emerged in the prologue, where Dionysius writes that people mistakenly believe that "Rome in time came to its hegemony over all not through piety, justice, and every other virtue, but rather through some kind of randomness and unjust fortune, which haphazardly dispenses its greatest kindnesses on the least suited" (οὐ δι᾽ εὐσέβειαν

---

[32] Dionysius does, however, develop linguistic arguments to support an idea of Roman Greekness, as de Jonge explains (2008: 60–65). Dionysius describes the Roman tongue as neither "completely barbarous nor wholly Greek, but a mixture, as it were, of both" (οὔτ᾽ ἄκρως βάρβαρον οὔτ᾽ ἀπηρτισμένως Ἑλλάδα φθέγγονται, μικτὴν δέ τινα ἐξ ἀμφοῖν, *Ant. Rom.* 1.90.1). De Jonge understands Dionysius's linguistic arguments as "part of his wider theory on the origin of the Roman people, which is closely related to his interpretation of the bicultural world in which he lived" (2008: 62).

84 HERODOTUS AND IMPERIAL GREEK LITERATURE

δὲ καὶ δικαιοσύνην καὶ τὴν ἄλλην ἀρετὴν ἐπὶ τὴν ἁπάντων ἡγεμονίαν σὺν χρόνῳ παρελθούσης, ἀλλὰ δι' αὐτοματισμόν τινα καὶ τύχην ἄδικον εἰκῇ δωρουμένην τὰ μέγιστα τῶν ἀγαθῶν τοῖς ἀνεπιτηδειοτάτοις, *Ant. Rom.* 1.4.2). Both here and elsewhere (e.g., *Ant. Rom.* 1.6.3, 2.17.3), Dionysius rejects the notion that Roman dominance should be explained as the result of fortune and turns his attention instead to Roman virtue, which the reader will come to understand as Greek virtue.[33]

At the close of his first book, Dionysius adverts again to the connection between Greekness and virtue. Even after he has just noted the ethnic persistence of the Romans' Greekness, Dionysius now turns to matters ethical:

> The Romans did not only just now turn to humane living, since the time when they have known a full flow of good fortune that has taught them the good things of life, nor since the time when they first began yearning to conquer places overseas, after they overthrew the Carthaginian and Macedonian empires: rather, it is completely from the time when they jointly founded their city that they were living a Greek life, and they do not attempt anything more remarkable in the pursuit of virtue now than they did formerly. (*Ant. Rom.* 1.90.1)

> οὐ νῦν πρῶτον ἀρξάμενοι πρὸς φιλίαν ζῆν, ἡνίκα τὴν τύχην πολλὴν καὶ ἀγαθὴν ῥέουσαν διδάσκαλον ἔχουσι τῶν καλῶν οὐδ' ἀφ' οὗ πρῶτον ὠρέχθησαν τῆς διαποντίου τὴν Καρχηδονίων καὶ Μακεδόνων ἀρχὴν καταλύσαντες, ἀλλ' ἐκ παντὸς οὗ συνῳκίσθησαν χρόνου βίον Ἕλληνα ζῶντες καὶ οὐδὲν ἐκπρεπέστερον ἐπιτηδεύοντες πρὸς ἀρετὴν νῦν ἢ πρότερον.

Dionysius's ultimate proof resides in a kind of circularity. The Romans do not now attempt anything more remarkable in the pursuit of virtue (πρὸς ἀρετήν) than they did formerly. The proof of Greekness is that they have *always* pursued virtue (ostentatiously, even: ἐκπρεπέστερον), and their continued Hellenicity is shown in their still doing so now.[34] A certain consonance

---

[33] See Wiater 2011a: 169, emphasizing Dionysius's belief that the moral quality of Greek (read: now Roman) virtue explains Roman power from the very start (εὐθὺς ἐξ ἀρχῆς, *Ant. Rom.* 1.3.4): "The *Antiquitates*... explains Roman power as the result of the Greek moral and political virtues on which Roman society had been based from its very beginnings, i.e., ever since Romulus' constitution." So also Fox 2011: 108 on Dionysius's response to "concrete historical events" in his "insistence that the origins of Rome provide a prehistory to a form of timeless Hellenism."

[34] See Peirano 2010: 42: "What starts as a narrative of Roman superiority thus becomes a demonstration of how Rome is in effect carrying on the Greek cultural project." See similarly Fox 2019: 199.

may even be felt between the ethico-intellectual virtues of Dionysius's preferred Greek authors, including Herodotus, and the idealized form of Hellenic excellence that undergirds the Roman continuation of Greek excellence. Roman dominance emerges not strictly from a genetic or nomothetic connection but from the broader practice of classical (Greek) virtue. The Romans are, in essence, imitative authors of their own virtuous identity, including such identity as was presented in the *Histories*.

Dionysius has, then, moved through a definition supplied by a famous passage from Herodotus (8.144.2), only to tilt at a different kind of universal *nomos* that transcends religious or linguistic difference. He emphasizes a unifying set of ideals that collectively rewrite the ethnographic connection between Greeks and Romans. His ethnography of Rome qua Greek has its basis in behavior, and by this formulation, Dionysius can further refine his ethnic distinctions between Greeks and barbarians:

> I would differentiate Greeks from barbarians not by name, nor on the basis of dialect, but according to intelligence and a predisposition toward decent behavior, especially in not transgressing against others in ways unbecoming of human nature. Accordingly, for as many peoples as the aforementioned good qualities are dominant by nature, these peoples I think ought to be called Greeks—and for as many as the opposites of these qualities prevail, barbarians. (*Ant. Rom.* 14.6.5)

> τὸ γὰρ Ἑλληνικὸν οὐκ ὀνόματι διαφέρειν τοῦ βαρβάρου ἠξίουν οὐδὲ διαλέκτου χάριν, ἀλλὰ συνέσει καὶ χρηστῶν ἐπιτηδευμάτων προαιρέσει, μάλιστα δὲ τῷ μηδὲν τῶν ὑπὲρ τὴν ἀνθρωπίνην φύσιν <εἰς> ἀλλήλους παρανομεῖν. ὅσοις μὲν οὖν ταῦτα ἐπὶ πλεῖον ὑπῆρξεν ἐν τῇ φύσει, τούτους οἶμαι δεῖν λέγειν Ἕλληνας, ὅσοις δὲ τἀναντία βαρβάρους.

The idea of Greek superiority operative in this passage and, one may surmise, throughout the work channels the Herodotean interest in ethnography while also reconfiguring it. Herodotus's *Histories* has often been taken to stress—albeit with complications—a notion that Greek independence from hubristic despots helped secure victory against the Persians, subjugated as they were to the foolhardy ambitions of the Great King.[35] Greek *nomoi*, in this view, offer

---

[35] This binary is complicated by Greek disunity and medizing and by the ways in which Herodotus perturbs the very stereotypes in which his work seems to traffic; see Hartog 1988 [1980]: 212–59; Pelling 1997.

86 HERODOTUS AND IMPERIAL GREEK LITERATURE

a recipe for avoiding disastrous attempts at imperial expansion.[36] Notably, however, the virtues that once *curbed* Greek expansiveness in Herodotus are now attributed by Dionysius to the expanding Romans, in ways that do not directly parallel the defensive posture of the Greeks in their repulse of the Persians. Dionysius appropriates the language of Greek virtuousness but, by applying it to the Romans, somewhat inverts its consequences. If good Greek behavior prevents transgression (παρανομεῖν) beyond human nature (ὑπὲρ τὴν ἀνθρωπίνην φύσιν), such moderation is now paradoxically applied to an imperial entity that, based on how Dionysius elsewhere describes it, enacts its virtue not through a defensive restraint characteristic of Herodotus's fifth-century Greeks but rather through an expanding dynamic more akin to Herodotus's Persians. One consequence, then, of his interest in Herodotus's synoptic scope is that Dionysius can mix and match his parallels, so to speak: the Romans who will be seen to fulfill Xerxes's vision of empire do so, Dionysius would have us understand, on the basis of *Hellenic* norms.

Thus, while playing to a notion of a superior Greekness, Dionysius also points up the flexibility of what defines it, privileging the "deliberate choice for upright behavior" (χρηστῶν ἐπιτηδευμάτων προαιρέσει), again with the loaded term that marks the "writerly life" in the rhetorical treatises. Rather than suggesting that the customs already typical of a people have a hand in determining their success or misfortune, and that Rome was inevitably successful because of its Hellenic roots, Dionysius accords the Romans the *choice to become Greek*, as it were, by choosing to behave justly, by transgressing in no way "outside of human nature" against others.[37] Even as Dionysius floats an essentialist notion that some have it in their own nature (ἐν τῇ φύσει) to behave one way or the other, his radical proposition stands: Greeks and barbarians determine their ethnographic markers not by the bonds of religion, language, or custom but by their capacity for choosing to act decently.

Rome's mimetic enactment of a prevailing Greekness is, then, both retrospective and prospective, since Dionysius wants his readers to regard various events and fine deeds (ἔργων καλῶν, *Ant. Rom.* 11.1.4) in Roman history for their inspiring exemplarity. This should prove especially important for "public men," among whom Dionysius includes philosophical sorts

---

[36] Contrastive notions of imperial ambition and hesitation are brought out in Xerxes's debate with Mardonius and Artabanus (Hdt. 7.8–11) and at the close of the *Histories* (9.122), there in ironic counterpoint to the actions that the Persians *did* actually undertake.

[37] See Langlands 2020: 84–85 with her n. 36, though I find her observation that Dionysius's version of mimesis is "used . . . in the context of literary rather than ethical imitation" (85 n. 36) unduly separates Dionysius's intertwined categories.

DIONYSIUS'S GLOBAL HERODOTUS   87

who regard philosophy as the practice of noble deeds rather than just the use of fine language (τοῖς δὲ πολιτικοῖς ἀνδράσιν, ἐν οἷς ἔγωγε τίθεμαι καὶ τοὺς φιλοσόφους, ὅσοι μὴ λόγων, ἀλλ᾽ ἔργων καλῶν ἄσκησιν ἡγοῦνται τὴν φιλοσοφίαν, *Ant. Rom.* 11.1.4–5). These men, Dionysius asserts, have an interest in common with other humans, namely, "taking delight in the comprehensive observation of the matters related to the main events" (τὸ μὲν ἥδεσθαι τῇ παντελεῖ θεωρίᾳ τῶν παρακολουθούντων τοῖς πράγμασι κοινὸν ὥσπερ καὶ τοῖς ἄλλοις ἀνθρώποις ὑπάρχει, 11.1.4). This focus on philosophical-political virtue allows Dionysius to reiterate the proposed universality (παντελεῖ) of his work: the historical breadth he aims to cover parallels the "universal" (κοινόν) system of belief he credits among political men.[38] That "contemplation" (θεωρία; cf. Hdt. 1.30.2) reiterates the sense in which the inspection of virtue is undertaken through the observations of reading, including, of course, reading the *Histories* or Dionysius's *Roman Antiquities*.

Herodotus's World Model

As a proponent of Atticism, Dionysius articulates his view of rhetoric according to a Greco-barbarian polarity that reasserts in broad form the moral boundaries of Herodotus's universe.[39] This much is evident in the schematic vision of the chaste Attic muse and the Asian harlot that introduces his preface to *On the Ancient Orators* (*Orat. Vett.* 2–3).[40] As with his emphasis on common lineage between Rome and Greece, Dionysius's representation of rhetorical history is a kind of ethnographic history, in which certain tendencies of geographic determinism shape his present day.[41] As Dionysius puts

---

[38] See Gabba 1982: 48.

[39] See Diller 1962 and Hidber 1996: 29–30, citing the influence of Isocrates in solidifying this polarity and its instantiation in rhetoric at least a generation before Dionysius. See also Wiater 2011a: 92–100. On the model of literary history offered in the preface to *On the Ancient Orators*, see Kim 2010b: 472–74, noting the important opposition in Dionysius's critical works between classical authors and the largely disdained Hellenistic authors (473), and, further, Kim 2017a: 215–26. More generally, on the complicated debates of Dionysius's relationship to Atticist circles and influences, see Dihle 1977; Gelzer 1979; Bowersock 1979; Gabba 1982: 47–48; Wisse 1995.

[40] On the feminizing trope of "Asian" rhetoric in the context of first-century and Augustan attitudes toward *mos* and *virtus*, see Spawforth 2012: 20–26, with further bibliography.

[41] See Wiater 2011a: 98: "Modelling the struggle between Classical and Asianist rhetoric after the fight of the Greeks against the Persians in Classical times, Dionysius turns the Hellene-Barbarian antithesis into a pattern of historical interpretation." I am not sure I would go so far as to credit Dionysius with turning this pattern into one of historical interpretation, given its long-standing usefulness as a lens for interpreting history, but at the very least, Dionysius manipulates the motif for his own purposes.

88   HERODOTUS AND IMPERIAL GREEK LITERATURE

it, "The rival Rhetoric, arriving only yesterday or the day before from one of the backwaters of Asia (being some Mysian or Phrygian or some infernal Carian thing), thought herself worthy to inhabit the [Greek] cities after she drove out the original [Attic Muse] from our common life" (ἡ δὲ ἔκ τινων βαράθρων τῆς Ἀσίας ἐχθὲς καὶ πρῴην ἀφικομένη, Μυσὴ ἢ Φρυγία τις ἢ Καρικόν τι κακόν, [ἢ βάρβαρον] Ἑλληνίδας ἠξίου διοικεῖν πόλεις ἀπελάσασα τῶν κοινῶν τὴν ἑτέραν, *Orat. Vett.* 1.7).[42] There is both a wide-ranging eclecticism and a vivid specificity to Dionysius's dismissal of Eastern backwater towns, now gathered up into the redoubtable monolith of Rome (see *Orat. Vett.* 3).[43] While Dionysius's analogy may seem hackneyed, the particulars of its articulation evoke the geographic sweep of Herodotus's history-writing, in the course of an ideological preface already laced with historiographic subtexts. Additionally, they reassert the motif of Eastern invasion along with the ultimate repulse by a Greek foe.[44]

In turn, in the *Roman Antiquities*, although Dionysius seemingly undertakes to write about one world power, his argument for Rome's Greekness inherently encompasses a temporally deep account of the Greeks, too. The grandeur of this move replays both the cosmopolitan breadth of Herodotus's own *Histories* and the sense of continuity between the deep past and the more recent present.[45] Indeed, if Dionysius has an understanding of historical "truth," it is the truth of Greek virtue and the possibilities of excellence enabled by the cooperation and right thinking

[42] De Jonge 2014: 396–98 has rightly drawn attention to the political aspects of Dionysius's muse–harlot framework, including the emphasis on the harlot's corruption of cities and their political offices, where philosophy ought to hold power (ἀλλὰ καὶ τὰς τιμὰς καὶ τὰς προστασίας τῶν πόλεων, ἃς ἔδει τὴν φιλόσοφον ἔχειν, *Orat. Vett.* 1.4). De Jonge does not mention Cleopatra, frequently called a *meretrix* in Roman literature. The possibility (as suggested to me by Kathryn Morgan) that Dionysius's conceit plays to a Roman audience fresh off the banishing of an "Eastern" mistress is certainly intriguing. Aujac 1978: 11–12 floats the suggestion that Dionysius's biography is relevant to the mention of Caria. Citing his contemporary Strabo's denunciation of Halicarnassus for its "softness" (τρυφή, 14.2.16, C656), Aujac speculates that the man from Carian Halicarnassus perhaps defected to Rome for reasons related to his hatred of Asiatic style ("On est frappe, à la lecture des *Opuscules rhétoriques*, de la hargne constante de Denys contre cette forme de style qui a nom asianisme et dont le plus illustre représentant fut Hégésias de Magnésie," 11). Hidber 1996: 111–12 avoids conjecture on the reasons for Dionysius's specific mention of Caria at *Orat. Vett.* 1.7, commenting only on Dionysius's formulation of an "antithetischen Satzbau: Καρικόν τι κακόν steht—(auch syntaktisch) in Antithese zur Ἀττικὴ μοῦσα—als polemische Klimax am Schluss" (112).

[43] The three places mentioned are perhaps a representative triad; Cicero also groups them (*Orator* 25) as locales of the "least refinement" (*minimeque elegantes*). Also relevant is Caecilius of Caleacte's Atticist treatise *Against the Phrygians*; see Swain 1996: 24; de Jonge 2008: 13 (with his n. 52).

[44] See Hidber 1996: 85–87.

[45] Dionysius's recall of Herodotus in the *Roman Antiquities* is ideological and related to worldview, not necessarily to style; see Kim 2010b: 473, with further bibliography, on Dionysius's style in the *Ant. Rom.* as often reminiscent of Polybius and Diodorus.

DIONYSIUS'S GLOBAL HERODOTUS   89

of Hellenic unity.[46] In spelling out Rome's achievement as an extension of Greek achievement, privileging fusion over fission, Dionysius continues to find his footing in Herodotus, whom he lauds as the first great prose expositor of unifying Greek achievement. Dionysius's historical vision in the *Orators* preface and in the *Roman Antiquities* recalls Herodotus on precisely the grounds for which he celebrates him in his rhetorical treatises, namely, that Herodotus was the first historian to transcend local accounts and to create a harmonious historiographic whole, forging unity despite disparateness.

In the *Letter to Gnaeus Pompey*, Dionysius had praised Herodotus's choice of subject, not, in fact, by first pointing to the memorialization of Greek victory but by noting that Herodotus

> brought forth a common history of the doings of Greeks and barbarians, "in order that neither human events become faded, nor their deeds," just as he said: for the proem itself is both the start and end of his history. (*Pomp.* 3.2)

ἐκεῖνος μὲν γὰρ κοινὴν Ἑλληνικῶν τε καὶ βαρβαρικῶν πράξεων ἐξενήνοχεν ἱστορίαν, ὡς μήτε τὰ γενόμενα ἐξ ἀνθρώπων <ἐξίτηλα γένηται> μήτε ἔργα, καθάπερ αὐτὸς εἴρηκε· τὸ γὰρ αὐτὸ προοίμιον καὶ ἀρχὴ καὶ τέλος ἐστὶ τῆς ἱστορίας.

The language of a "common history" (κοινὴν . . . ἱστορίαν), in hyperbaton that itself encompasses Herodotus's broad subject, echoes Dionysius's own project for a universal approach to rhetoric (κοινὴν καὶ φιλάνθρωπον, *Orat. Vett.* 4.1). Dionysius's praise of Herodotus's choice of topic eschews the jingoism of Hellenic glory and points rather to the text's wide embrace of peoples, introducing the theme of Herodotean unity and coherence—his "global" vision—that shortly becomes more explicit (*Pomp.* 3.14). Dionysius recapitulates the sense of Herodotean narrative wholeness in his claim that the proem is both the "start and end" (ἀρχὴ καὶ τέλος) of the work, playing off the resonances of τέλος as "purposive end" and suggesting that the totality of the *Histories* is present already in its inaugural focus on "human

---

[46] See the remarks on Dionysius's proto-formalist idea of historical truth in Fox 1993: 39: "He shapes his history to a preconceived notion of historical goodness, which in no way derives from an objective consideration of the events which he describes." Dionysius himself certainly professes to believe in the goal of truthfulness for historiography; see *Pomp.* 1.3, ἡ γὰρ ἀλήθεια οὕτως εὑρίσκεται μάλιστα, ἧς οὐδὲν χρῆμα τιμιώτερον, and *Thuc.* 8.1.

90 HERODOTUS AND IMPERIAL GREEK LITERATURE

events." The unified coherence of Herodotus's latitude is all in contrast to the Thucydidean account of internecine conflict among Greeks.

Dionysius's broader concern with unified history-writing is more forcefully conveyed in two signal elevations of Herodotus that lay bare the kinds of global, imperial concerns with which Dionysius will also be preoccupied:

> But Herodotus of Halicarnassus, who was born a little before the Persian Wars and survived up to the Peloponnesian War, expanded the scope of history's content toward something greater and more illustrious. For he did not choose to write up an inquiry of one city or one people, but he chose rather to bring together many diverse events from both Europe and Asia within the confines of a single work (in fact, starting his inquiry from the rule of the Lydians, he brought it down through the Persian Wars, encompassing in his one composition every remarkable event that occurred across 240 years among Greeks and barbarians), and he topped it all off by imparting to his style the virtues that had been neglected by prose writers before him. (*Thuc.* 5.5)

> ὁ δ᾽ Ἁλικαρνασεὺς Ἡρόδοτος, γενόμενος ὀλίγῳ πρότερον τῶν Περσικῶν, παρεκτείνας δὲ μέχρι τῶν Πελοποννησιακῶν, τήν τε πραγματικὴν προαίρεσιν ἐπὶ τὸ μεῖζον ἐξήνεγκε καὶ λαμπρότερον, οὔτε πόλεως μιᾶς οὔτ᾽ ἔθνους ἑνὸς ἱστορίαν προελόμενος ἀναγράψαι, πολλὰς δὲ καὶ διαφόρους πράξεις ἔκ τε τῆς Εὐρώπης ἔκ τε τῆς Ἀσίας εἰς μιᾶς περιγραφὴν πραγματείας συναγαγεῖν (ἀρξάμενος οὖν ἀπὸ τῆς τῶν Λυδῶν δυναστείας μέχρι τοῦ Περσικοῦ πολέμου κατεβίβασε τὴν ἱστορίαν, πάσας τὰς ἐν τοῖς τεσσαράκοντα καὶ διακοσίοις ἔτεσι γενομένας πράξεις ἐπιφανεῖς Ἑλλήνων τε καὶ βαρβάρων μιᾷ συντάξει περιλαβών), καὶ τῇ λέξει προσαπέδωκε τὰς παραλειφθείσας ὑπὸ τῶν πρὸ αὐτοῦ συγγραφέων ἀρετάς.

> In narrating his way through the deeds of the Greeks and barbarians over a period of 220 years as they occurred across three continents, and writing his history up to Xerxes' flight, Herodotus did not scatter his narrative. But it happened that while Thucydides took one subject and divided its one body into many parts, Herodotus, making a deliberate choice for many subjects, and those in no way similar to each other, rendered them as one harmonious body. (*Pomp.* 3.14)

> διεξελθών τε πράξεις Ἑλλήνων καὶ βαρβάρων ἔτεσιν ὁμοῦ διακοσίοις καὶ εἴκοσι γενομένας ἐν ταῖς τρισὶν ἠπείροις καὶ παραγράψας τῇ Ξέρξου φυγῇ

τὴν ἱστορίαν, οὐ διέσπασε τὴν διήγησιν· ἀλλὰ συμβέβηκε τῷ μὲν μίαν
ὑπόθεσιν λαβόντι πολλὰ ποιῆσαι μέρη τὸ ἓν σῶμα, τῷ δὲ τὰς πολλὰς καὶ
οὐδὲν ἐοικυίας ὑποθέσεις προελομένῳ σύμφωνον ἓν σῶμα πεποιηκέναι.

In the first passage, Dionysius credits Herodotus with magnificent, sweeping qualities, mirrored in Dionysius's single, broadly encompassing sentence that itself captures the variety of Herodotus's narrative: the diverse events from two continents, the chronological sweep, and the stylistic virtues (ἀρετάς) that bind it all together. Herodotus's text is an empire in its own right, one that widens the scope of what historical writing can do, bringing together in "more illustrious" fashion (λαμπρότερον) both Europe and Asia within the confines of "a single work" (εἰς μιᾶς περιγραφὴν πραγματείας).[47] In the second passage, Dionysius's comprehensive Herodotus is set in motion, as it were, by Dionysius's use of the (Herodotean) historiographic metaphor of "moving through" narration (διεξελθών; cf. Hdt. 1.5.3, ἐπεξιών), as though his extensive account is unified by his journeying among different places and peoples.[48] Herodotus's refusal to "scatter the narrative" (οὐ διέσπασε τὴν διήγησιν), perhaps like some general (Thucydides?) who scatters his troops, reinforces the focus on unity.[49] Herodotus exercises deliberate choice to discipline unrelated (οὐδὲν ἐοικυίας) matter into "one harmonious body." Although Polybius had also underscored the importance of offering something more comprehensive (τὴν δὲ καθόλου καὶ συλλήβδην οἰκονομίαν τῶν γεγονότων, 1.4.3) than accounts of "discrete wars and their attendant events" (τοὺς μὲν κατὰ μέρος πολέμους καί τινας τῶν ἅμα τούτοις πράξεων, 1.4.3), his doing so appears to have been guided by the belief, as Malcolm Heath has argued, that such a comprehensive vision was most appropriate to the period about which he was writing.[50] These passages from Dionysius, however, show that he recognizes history-writing as having the potential for, but

---

[47] Recall also the image of holism at *Imit.* 1.4 seen in chapter 1: "Whatever quality of each young woman was worthy of depiction, these he collected into a single bodily image, and from the selection of many parts he in his skill brought together a complete form" (ὃ δ' ἦν ἄξιον παρ' ἑκάστη γραφῆς, ἐς μίαν ἠθροίσθη σώματος εἰκόνα, κἀκ πολλῶν μερῶν συλλογῆς ἕν τι συνέθηκεν ἡ τέχνη τέλειον [καλὸν] εἶδος).

[48] On narrative as travel, see Greenwood 2018: 164.

[49] See, however, Rood 2020: 31–32 for the good observation that in his account of Thucydides at *Thuc.* 5–6, Dionysius conveys how *both* Herodotus and Thucydides offer "less confined" narratives than the "pre-Herodotean mode of local history."

[50] According to Heath 1989b: 81, Polybius regarded the capacity for integration and unity as peculiar to his own work (citing Polyb. 1.4.1) and to the time period that his *History* covers: "This, clearly, is an observation, not on the correct way to write history, but on the correct way to write the history of the period beginning in 220/16." See Heath 1989b: 80–81 for the use of the "organic analogy" in Polybius, and 83, 85 for the metaphor in Diodorus Siculus, with comparison to *Pomp.* 3.14.

92 HERODOTUS AND IMPERIAL GREEK LITERATURE

not necessarily an inherent predisposition toward, organic unity.[51] No notion of obligation or inevitability seems to inform Dionysius's view of what Herodotus was doing. Rather, he credits Herodotus with actively choosing to render (προελόμενος, προελομένῳ . . . πεποιηκέναι) the many into one and with having the vision to "expand[] the scope of history's content toward something greater" (τήν τε πραγματικὴν προαίρεσιν ἐπὶ τὸ μεῖζον ἐξήνεγκε). It is up to the historian to make of disparate parts "one harmonious body," to create a sense of formal continuity that contains heterogeneity of content. In Herodotus's case, presumed polarities are harnessed and contained: Persia and Greece are brought into narrative whole, paving the way for Dionysius to combine Rome and Greece into one intelligible historiographic weave and to narrate Rome in its "many parts" (*Ant. Rom.* 1.3.3–4).

The notions of heterogeneity-in-unity evident in Dionysius's accounts of Herodotus are assuredly a feature of the discourse of empire.[52] As Pliny the Elder would write, a generation or two after Dionysius, Rome was granted power by the gods (*numine deum electa*) "to collect the scattered powers (*sparsa congregaret imperia*), to tame their customs, and to unite the disparate wild tongues of so many peoples into a common language so they could understand each other, to give civilization to mankind, and in fine to become the one common home of all peoples on the earth" (*breviterque una cunctarum gentium in toto orbe patria fieret, NH* 3.39). Nearer to Dionysius's day, Augustus's *Res Gestae* would proclaim a vision of multitudinous unity, whether through wide Roman colonization (*RGDA* 3), the prayers of the "entirety of the citizens, in private and municipality by municipality, with one accord" (*pr]iva[ti]m etiam et municipatim universi [cives unanimite]r, RGDA* 9.2), the "multitude from all Italy" (*cuncta ex Italia*) assembling for his election as Pontifex Maximus (*RGDA* 10.2), or the peace supposedly effected "throughout the whole domain of the Roman people on land and sea" (*[p]er totum i[mperium po]puli Roma[ni terra marique, RGDA* 13).[53] And already an idea of heterogeneous unity that well matches

---

[51] See Heath 1989b: 81. Unity for Dionysius is a matter of the historian's arrangement of his material; harmony is narrative harmony, rather than being intrinsic to history itself (Heath 1989b: 89). See also Gabba 1991: 63–65, 216.

[52] See, e.g., Ward 2008: 10: "Herodotus, in his writing, points beyond politics to satisfy the imperial desire to make the world one unified whole while also maintaining the diversity of the peoples and their conventions that exist within it."

[53] Text of *RGDA* is that of Cooley 2009. On its language of world conquest, see Cooley 2009: 36–37. For further examples of such imperial discourse, compare "the whole of Italy" (*tota Italia*) pledging allegiance (*RGDA* 25.2) and the expansion of imperial space across provinces and territories (*RGDA* 26–29).

DIONYSIUS'S GLOBAL HERODOTUS 93

Dionysius's descriptions of Herodotus's achievement appears in the prologue to his *Roman Antiquities*:

> Rome rules over every land that is not inaccessible but is in fact settled by humans, and Rome rules over the entire sea, not only within the Pillars of Heracles but also over Ocean, save the part that cannot be sailed. Rome is the first and only ruler of those remembered in all ages to make her boundaries of power the risings and settings of the sun. The duration of her power has not been short, but longer than that of any other city or kingdom. For straightaway, from the start, after her founding, she started to add to herself the multitude of neighboring, martial peoples, and Rome went from strength to strength, always subjugating each rival. (*Ant. Rom.* 1.3.3–4)

> ἡ δὲ Ῥωμαίων πόλις ἁπάσης μὲν ἄρχει γῆς ὅση μὴ ἀνέμβατός ἐστιν, ἀλλ᾽ ὑπ᾽ ἀνθρώπων κατοικεῖται, πάσης δὲ κρατεῖ θαλάσσης, οὐ μόνον τῆς ἐντὸς Ἡρακλείων στηλῶν, ἀλλὰ καὶ τῆς Ὠκεανίτιδος ὅση πλεῖσθαι μὴ ἀδύνατός ἐστι, πρώτη καὶ μόνη τῶν ἐκ τοῦ παντὸς αἰῶνος μνημονευομένων ἀνατολὰς καὶ δύσεις ὅρους ποιησαμένη τῆς δυναστείας· χρόνος τε αὐτῇ τοῦ κράτους οὐ βραχύς, ἀλλ᾽ ὅσος οὐδεμιᾷ τῶν ἄλλων οὔτε πόλεων οὔτε βασιλειῶν. εὐθὺς μὲν γὰρ ἐξ ἀρχῆς μετὰ τὸν οἰκισμὸν τὰ πλησίον ἔθνη πολλὰ καὶ μάχιμα ὄντα προσήγετο καὶ προὔβαινεν ἀεὶ πᾶν δουλουμένη τὸ ἀντίπαλον.

The passages cited earlier concerning Herodotus's narrative achievement, set in relation to Dionysius's proclamation here (and amid the wider context of imperial language in Augustus and Pliny) reveal a discourse of empire running through Dionysius that finds roots and affirmation in his celebrated Herodotus. Herodotus's text brings together "many diverse events from both Europe and Asia within the confines of a single work" (πολλὰς δὲ καὶ διαφόρους πράξεις ἔκ τε τῆς Εὐρώπης ἔκ τε τῆς Ἀσίας εἰς μιᾶς περιγραφὴν πραγματείας συναγαγεῖν, *Thuc.* 5.5), much as Rome now "rules over every land" (ἁπάσης μὲν ἄρχει γῆς) and the "multitude of neighboring peoples" (τὰ πλησίον ἔθνη πολλά).[54] Any area settled by humans (ὑπ᾽ ἀνθρώπων

---

[54] Rood (2020: 32), as part of his argument that the "ethnographic element" plays a small role in ancient criticism of Herodotus, makes the subtle observation that Dionysius (at *Thuc.* 5.5) "focusses on the geographical regions treated by Herodotus rather than on the content of his account of those regions," i.e., on "only events," not the "modes of living in those lands." While this is accurate as a strict interpretation of Dionysius's language at *Thuc.* 5.5 (πολλὰς δὲ καὶ διαφόρους **πράξεις**), I note Dionysius's more expansive phrasing at *Pomp.* 3.14 (πολλὰς καὶ οὐδὲν ἐοικυίας **ὑποθέσεις**). In any

94 HERODOTUS AND IMPERIAL GREEK LITERATURE

κατοικεῖται) is ruled by Rome, echoing Herodotus's textual empire over human events (τὰ γενόμενα ἐξ ἀνθρώπων, *Pomp.* 3.2). Rome "subjugates each rival" (προΰβαινεν ἀεὶ πᾶν δουλουμένη τὸ ἀντίπαλον) into one empire, much as Herodotus's text took "many subjects, and those in no way similar to each other, and rendered them as one harmonious body" (τὰς πολλὰς καὶ οὐδὲν ἐοικυίας ὑποθέσεις προελομένῳ σύμφωνον ἓν σῶμα πεποιηκέναι, *Pomp.* 3.14). Rome's geographic sweep picks up on Herodotus's own focus on events "as they occurred across three continents" (ἐν ταῖς τρισὶν ἠπείροις, *Pomp.* 3.14). And just as Dionysius underscores the coherence of "start and end" in the *Histories* (ἀρχὴ καὶ τέλος, *Pomp.* 3.2), so does Rome, despite its eventual eclecticism, carry out a sense of unitary purpose from the start (εὐθὺς μὲν γὰρ ἐξ ἀρχῆς μετὰ τὸν οἰκισμὸν), always bringing under submission "every" possible rival (ἀεὶ πᾶν δουλουμένη τὸ ἀντίπαλον). While such parallels between textual achievement and imperial ambition might appear to be no more than formal analogues, the interrelations in Dionysius between rhetoric and history—and between authorial choice and the moral weight of events recorded—suggest that such analogies bespeak his deeper sense of the connection between word and world.

I noted that Dionysius's single long sentence at *Thuc.* 5.5 recapitulates the unifying textual empire he ascribes to Herodotus. We might see something similar in Dionysius's analysis of the Herodotean sentence in *On Literary Composition* (at *Comp.* 4.7–11), where his preference for Herodotean style and syntax (in reference to *Hist.* 1.6.1) appears not unrelated to Herodotus's offering a fluid catalogue of Croesus's empire. By contrast, Dionysius's Thucydidean and Hegesian rearrangements of the sentence chop its sweep into slightly disrupted segments.[55] In Dionysius's two reworkings, subtle adjustments to word order (ἁρμονία, *Comp.* 4.8) produce a rougher sense of unifying imperial breadth, compared with that found in the Herodotean original, whose style Dionysius describes as "drawn out" (ὑπαγωγικόν) and "appropriate to history" (ἱστορικόν). I quote the rearrangements here with the translations of Casper de Jonge:

---

case, regardless of Dionysius's particular diction, Herodotus's geographically expansive account of the war obviously includes much attention to ethnographic custom, and whether intended or not, Dionysius's framing of Herodotean capaciousness will for many readers have sparked thought of ethnic variety consonant with ideas of imperial scope.

[55] On this passage, see de Jonge 2005, 476–78.

DIONYSIUS'S GLOBAL HERODOTUS 95

Hdt. 1.6 (in Attic): Κροῖσος ἦν Λυδὸς μὲν γένος, παῖς δ' Ἀλυάττου, τύραννος δ' ἐθνῶν τῶν ἐντὸς Ἅλυος ποταμοῦ· ὃς ῥέων ἀπὸ μεσημβρίας μεταξὺ Σύρων τε καὶ Παφλαγόνων ἐξίησι πρὸς βορέαν ἄνεμον εἰς τὸν Εὔξεινον καλούμενον πόντον. (Croesus was a Lydian by birth and the son of Alyattes. He was king of the nations on this side of the river Halys, which flows from the south between Syria and Paphlagonia and discharges itself into the sea to the north, which is called the Euxine, *Comp.* 4.8)

Dionysian rearrangement no. 1 (à la Thucydides): Κροῖσος ἦν υἱὸς μὲν Ἀλυάττου, γένος δὲ Λυδός, **τύραννος δὲ τῶν ἐντὸς Ἅλυος ποταμοῦ ἐθνῶν·** ὃς ἀπὸ μεσημβρίας ῥέων μεταξὺ Σύρων καὶ Παφλαγόνων εἰς τὸν Εὔξεινον καλούμενον πόντον ἐκδίδωσι πρὸς βορέαν ἄνεμον. (Croesus was the son of Alyattes, and by birth a Lydian. He was king, on this side of the Halys, over nations; which river from the south flowing between Syria and Paphlagonia runs into the sea which is called the Euxine and issues towards the north, *Comp.* 4.9)

Dionysian rearrangement no. 2 (à la Hegesias): Ἀλυάττου μὲν υἱὸς ἦν Κροῖσος, γένος δὲ Λυδός, **τῶν δ' ἐντὸς Ἅλυος ποταμοῦ τύραννος ἐθνῶν·** ὃς ἀπὸ μεσημβρίας ῥέων Σύρων τε καὶ Παφλαγόνων μεταξὺ πρὸς βορέαν ἐξίησιν ἄνεμον εἰς τὸν καλούμενον πόντον Εὔξεινον. (Alyattes' son was Croesus, by birth a Lydian. **King over all nations was he, on this side of the river Halys;** which river from the south flowing between Syria and Paphlagonia discharges itself to the north, into the Euxine-called sea, *Comp.* 4.11)

Between rearrangements no. 1, which Dionysius calls "straightforward" (ὀρθόν), and no. 2, which he labels "finicky" (μικρόκομψον), Dionysius quotes a geographically focused line from Thucydides (1.24.1) notable also for its somewhat halting dispersal of information: "Epidamnus is a city on the right for one sailing into the Ionian Gulf: directly neighboring it are the Taulantii, barbarians, an Illyrian race" (Ἐπίδαμνός ἐστι πόλις ἐν δεξιᾷ εἰσπλέοντι τὸν Ἰόνιον κόλπον· προσοικοῦσι δ' αὐτὴν Ταυλάντιοι βάρβαροι, Ἰλλυρικὸν ἔθνος, *Comp.* 4.10). In both rearrangements and in the Thucydides example, one notices a less-than-fluid syntactical scheme. We shift from "He was king of the nations on this side of the river Halys" to "He was king, on this side of the Halys, over nations" to "King over all nations was he, on this side of the river Halys." Likewise, the river that first "discharges itself into the

96 HERODOTUS AND IMPERIAL GREEK LITERATURE

sea to the north, which is called the Euxine," becomes the river that "runs into the sea which is called the Euxine and issues towards the north" and, in the last instance, the river that "discharges itself to the north, into the Euxine-called sea." The diminished smoothness suggests a consequent diminishment in the grandeur that Herodotus's sentence seems to convey.[56] Rather than the fluid encincturing of Croesus's power as imparted by Herodotus's sentence, the rewritten clauses mince unity into parts, parceling them out in a discrete fashion similar to what Dionysius says of Thucydides at *Pomp.* 3.12: "Thucydides, stretching on through a single war, proceeds without taking a breath, stringing together battle after battle, preparation scene after preparation scene, speech after speech, with the result that he wearies his readers' minds" (Θουκυδίδης δὲ, πόλεμον ἕνα κατατείνας, ἀπνευστὶ διεξέρχεται μάχας ἐπὶ μάχαις καὶ παρασκευὰς ἐπὶ παρασκευαῖς καὶ λόγους ἐπὶ λόγοις συντιθείς, ὥστε μοχθεῖν [μὲν] τὴν διάνοιαν τῶν ἀκρωμένων).[57] As we have seen, Dionysius's sense of unifying imperial rhetoric applies to choice of content at the macro level, but the *On Literary Composition* example hints that even at the micro level—the very placement of words in a sentence—Dionysius has a recurrent interest in the parallels between style and subject, text and documented power.

Hence, at *Ant. Rom.* 1.3.3–4 and other similar passages lies the sense that Dionysius's texts will encompass the kind of imperial sweep for which he praises Herodotean historiography. He reinforces this idea elsewhere in the opening chapters of the *Roman Antiquities*. At *Ant. Rom.* 1.2.1, he mentions dynasties that "acquired the widest rule and displayed the most glorious deeds" (ἀρχήν τε μεγίστην ἐκτήσατο καὶ πράξεις ἀπεδείξατο λαμπροτάτας). He notes (*Ant. Rom.* 1.3.5) Rome's aspiration to "rule all humankind" (ἐπὶ τὴν ἁπάντων . . . ἀρχήν) and says that "there is no nation that disputes Roman rule or is at odds with being ruled by Rome" (ἔθνος δὲ οὐδὲν ὡς εἰπεῖν ἐστιν, ὃ περὶ τῆς κοινῆς ἡγεμονίας ἢ τοῦ μὴ ἄρχεσθαι πρὸς αὐτὴν διαφέρεται). He intimates the extent of his own deep dive at *Ant. Rom.* 1.5.3, promising to start "from the beginning" and to offer "countless" examples of virtue (μυρίας ἤνεγκεν ἀνδρῶν ἀρετὰς εὐθὺς ἐξ ἀρχῆς). The promise is redoubled at *Ant. Rom.* 1.6.2, in a comment on previous historians of Rome who wrote only

---

[56] As de Jonge notes (2005: 477–78), "The reason why the Thucydidean version is described as ὀρθόν is probably that it has a more systematic way of distributing its information than the original. . . . Dionysius' second metathesis of Herodotus 1.6 is a clear example of a defective style, which pays no attention to the systematic distribution of information."

[57] On Dionysius's critique of Thucydides's rhetoric of the "episodic," see Irwin 2015.

DIONYSIUS'S GLOBAL HERODOTUS   97

about contemporary events but did not stretch their accounts into early Roman history (τούτων δὲ τῶν ἀνδρῶν ἑκάτερος, οἷς μὲν αὐτὸς ἔργοις παρεγένετο, διὰ τὴν ἐμπειρίαν ἀκριβῶς ἀνέγραψε, τὰ δὲ ἀρχαῖα τὰ μετὰ τὴν κτίσιν τῆς πόλεως γενόμενα κεφαλαιωδῶς ἐπέδραμεν). Dionysius, with similar promises of amplitude, vows to give "in sum a whole account of the ancient life of the Romans" (συλλήβδην ὅλον ἀποδείκνυμι τὸν ἀρχαῖον βίον τῆς πόλεως, *Ant. Rom.* 1.8.3). He declares his own heterogeneity of narrative style, matching his catholic content: "This work is a combination mixed together of every form: forensic, theoretical, narrative" (ἀλλ᾽ ἐξ ἁπάσης ἰδέας μικτὸν ἐναγωνίου τε καὶ θεωρητικῆς καὶ διηγηματικῆς, *Ant. Rom.* 1.8.3).[58]

In short, his history will possess a latitude worthy of Rome. Rome's expanding power urges a certain kind of account, and there is for Dionysius an implicit connection between and among the narrative enterprise that he attributes to Herodotus, the perceived totalization that was Roman power in his day, and the account of Roman power (qua Greek power) that he himself undertakes. In the end, then, his analysis of Herodotean scale cannot be separated from his own historiographic concerns. We come to recognize that Dionysius is reading—and valorizing—Herodotus *through* the lens of imperium by which his own historiographic endeavor is inflected. Herodotus's virtues as a global writer emerge for Dionysius on the horizon of Rome's global machinations.

Reversing Xerxes, Achieving Empire

Glen Bowersock once noted that "Dionysius gave expression to the fusion of cultures which characterized the Graeco-Roman world."[59] Ideas of ethnographic fusion surface in the prologue to the *Roman Antiquities*, as we have seen. Moreover, Dionysius's sense of imperial documentation shares a lineage with Herodotus, one that Dionysius himself in some sense fashions in his descriptions of the *Histories'* global purview. The connection to Herodotus serves both to confirm Dionysius's place in a literary tradition and to affirm the continuities between Greece and Rome that he propounds. In light of the overlaps and analogues of imperial language described, Dionysius's choice, in one of his few instances of lengthy quotation from Herodotus, to broadcast

[58] καὶ διηγηματικῆς add. Cary.
[59] Bowersock 1965: 131–32.

98 HERODOTUS AND IMPERIAL GREEK LITERATURE

Xerxes's Book 7 speech of imperial ambition acquires arresting resonance. The quotation comes in a portion of the treatise *On Demosthenes*, in a discussion of the "mixed style" (*Dem.* 41.1).[60] Dionysius refracts the theme of fusion from the viewpoint of Xerxes, the ultimately failed bridge-builder between Asia and Europe, and thereby focuses our attention for several pages on an instance of dramatic irony, the confident vision of the Great King who would be greater. Dionysius's choice of Xerxes' speech, perhaps innocuous enough in the context of discussing style, activates again the global vision he sees at the heart of Herodotus's own distinctiveness as a historian. I quote two relevant passages from the speech, with Herodotus's Ionic re-cast in Dionysius's Attic:

I intend after yoking the Hellespont to drive an army through Europe all the way to Greece, in order to exact a punishment against the Athenians commensurate with what they did against us Persians and my father. (*Dem.* 41.5)

μέλλω ζεύξας τὸν Ἑλλήσποντον ἐλαύνειν στρατὸν διὰ τῆς Εὐρώπης ἐπὶ τὴν Ἑλλάδα, ἵνα Ἀθηναίους τιμωρήσωμαι, ὅσα δὴ πεποιήκασι Πέρσας τε καὶ πατέρα τὸν ἐμόν.

If we bring these Greeks and their neighbors into submission . . . we shall show forth the Persian landscape as sharing a border with Zeus's heaven. For the sun will look upon no land that does not border our own, and I shall bring them all together for you into one land, proceeding through all of Europe. And I find it is the case that no city or people among humans will be left that will be able to enter into battle against us once the cities I have mentioned have been destroyed. (*Dem.* 41.5)

εἰ τούτους τε καὶ τοὺς τούτοις πλησιοχώρους καταστρεψόμεθα . . . γῆν [τε] τὴν Περσίδα ἀποδείξομεν τῷ Διὸς αἰθέρι ὅμορον οὖσαν. οὐ γὰρ δὴ χώραν

---

[60] The setup for the passage from Herodotus is that Dionysius is discussing the *charactēr* of different styles (*lexis*) and composition techniques (*harmonia*). Between the "austere" style (*Dem.* 38–39) and the "smooth" or polished style (*Dem.* 40) lies the mixed style (*Dem.* 41.1). Dionysius adduces Herodotus and Plato as the best exemplars of the mixed, from whose styles both "dignity and charm run forth" (καὶ γὰρ καὶ ἀξίωμα καὶ χάρις αὐτῶν ἐπιτρέχει ταῖς ἁρμονίαις, *Dem.* 41.3). Without analyzing in detail what exactly constitutes middle style, Dionysius asks rhetorically who could disagree that the passage he quotes from Herodotus exists halfway between the austere and what he now calls the sweet style (*Dem.* 41.4).

γε οὐδεμίαν κατόψεται ὁ ἥλιος ὅμορον οὖσαν τῇ ἡμετέρᾳ, ἀλλ᾽ αὐτὰς ἁπάσας ἐγὼ ἅμα ὑμῖν μίαν χώραν θήσω, διὰ πάσης ἐξελθὼν τῆς Εὐρώπης. πυνθάνομαι γὰρ ὧδε ἔχειν· οὔτε τινὰ πόλιν αὐτῶν οὐδεμίαν οὔτε ἔθνος ἀνθρώπων οὐδὲν ὑπολείπεσθαι ἡμῖν, ὃ οἷόν τε ἔσται ἐλθεῖν εἰς μάχην, τούτων, ὧν ἔλεξα, ὑπεξῃρημένων.

Xerxes's definition of empire stretches both vertically and horizontally, such that the heavens are reached and no city or nation on earth, envisioned as part of one land, is "left over" to engage Persia in battle. Xerxes's totalizing vision, in bringing together Asia and Europe (even land and sky), reasserts the very copulative gestures that Dionysius claims Herodotus's text to have achieved, with Xerxes's hope to "proceed through" (ἐξελθών) Europe recalling Dionysius's Herodotus as he "moves through" (διεξελθών) his narrative across three continents (*Pomp.* 3.14). Dionysius's focalization of the Persian aspiration to empire as represented by Herodotus is furthermore comparable with one of Dionysius's own better-known pronouncements in the preface to *On the Ancient Orators*:

> I think that the cause and origin of so great a turn of events was almighty Rome, who has made it necessary that all cities turn their attention to her . . . and many other noble works have emerged by both Romans and Greeks, the results of serious effort, and they will in all likelihood continue. (*Orat. Vett.* 3.1–2)

> αἰτία δ᾽ οἶμαι καὶ ἀρχὴ τῆς τοσαύτης μεταβολῆς ἐγένετο ἡ πάντων κρατοῦσα Ῥώμη πρὸς ἑαυτὴν ἀναγκάζουσα τὰς ὅλας πόλεις ἀποβλέπειν . . . ἄλλαι τε πολλαὶ καὶ καλαὶ πραγματεῖαι καὶ Ῥωμαίοις καὶ Ἕλλησιν εὖ μάλα διεσπουδασμέναι προεληλύθασί τε καὶ προελεύσονται κατὰ τὸ εἰκός.

Various similarities link the vision set forth by Xerxes, in his effort to bring different lands together into one entity, and the nature of Roman dominance as characterized by Dionysius. Xerxes's hope is to create one space of all cities (αὐτὰς ἁπάσας ἐγὼ ἅμα ὑμῖν μίαν χώραν θήσω) and to leave no city behind that can become a source of opposition (οὔτε τινὰ πόλιν αὐτῶν οὐδεμίαν οὔτε ἔθνος ἀνθρώπων οὐδὲν ὑπολείπεσθαι ἡμῖν). In Dionysius's account of Rome, in turn, the city has achieved power over all (ἡ πάντων κρατοῦσα) and has created a similar conglomeration of urban totality (τὰς ὅλας πόλεις

100   HERODOTUS AND IMPERIAL GREEK LITERATURE

ἀποβλέπειν).[61] Rome exercises a centripetal power that forces cities to "look upon" it (ἀποβλέπειν), much as Xerxes imagined that the sun would gaze down upon (κατόψεται) an extensive Persian empire. The focus on the panoply of cities all staring at Rome, after the Asian harlot who thought herself worthy to inhabit Greek cities has been banished, also gains in resonance when set beside Dionysius's active praise of Herodotus's synoptic abilities.

Dionysius envisions a new dispensation that nourishes the practice of a virtuous rhetoric. Insofar as he insists in the *Roman Antiquities* that Romans are, in fact, Greek, his enunciation of an ascendant Rome reasserts the Greek victory over Persia, ironically harnessing the vision of Xerxes quoted in his *On Demosthenes* to the positive elaboration of Roman power. Xerxes's would-be empire is now Rome's, and for Dionysius, that means it now belongs as well to the descendants of Greece. His description of Rome's power recasts and successfully embodies the *projected* vision of Xerxes, reshaping a vision of empire already put forth in the pages of his predecessor. Only now it is Herodotus's vision—a textual achievement—that is fused with Xerxes's dream. Rome, Dionysius's extension of Greece, succeeds where Xerxes failed. These various parallels have the effect of reinforcing Dionysius's praise for Herodotus's synoptic history, bringing together as it does the major forces of "global" history into one harmonious body (σύμφωνον ἕν σῶμα, *Pomp.* 3.14), much as Rome has now brought together the local spaces into one peaceable realm in which writers such as Dionysius feel themselves to flourish. Dionysius's Herodotean-tinged globalism thus informs his understanding both of rhetoric *and* of the political dispensations that enable certain kinds of speech.[62]

At the same time, this redoubling of Xerxes's vision presents an irony: Dionysius's Romans enact the vision of Xerxes, which means that *Greeks* have in a certain sense come to enact the vision they supposedly thwarted. Does that mean the Greeks/Hellenized Romans have become the Persians? It might have been sufficient for Dionysius to distinguish, say,

---

[61] Whether Dionysius's essay *On Demosthenes* is the essay on Demosthenes that (would have) appeared in *On the Ancient Orators* is a matter of some debate; see Bonner 1939: 27–31 and Aujac 1988: 7–9, 24–33. It remains the case, however, that a reader familiar with Dionysius's overall purpose in writing about the ancient orators will have encountered, either in that work or in a separate work on Demosthenes, a passage that presents a clear parallel to the kinds of imperial structures that supposedly enable Dionysius's literary undertaking.

[62] The global understanding of rhetoric has specific political dimensions; see Gabba 1982: 48 and Wiater 2011a: 98–100, with his concluding remark that Dionysius "re-interprets *the* crucial event in contemporary *Roman* history, Augustus's principate, as a turning point in the prolonged, *Greek* struggle against the Barbarians" (emphasis in original).

DIONYSIUS'S GLOBAL HERODOTUS   101

Xerxes's vengeful vision of conquest (Ἀθηναίους τιμωρήσωμαι, *Dem.* 41.5) from his apparently more sanguine sense of Herodotus's authorial gestures as the author of a work with imperial purview. But the hauntings of hypotextual activation linger. For Herodotus's preoccupation with the growth of Persia has been interpreted by some as analogous to (and perhaps critical of) the growth of Athens.[63] A precious few references in Herodotus to events and persons closer to the time of his writing are often the cynosure of these discussions. Herodotus declares, for instance, that in the three generations of Darius, Xerxes, and Artaxerxes, "more evils befell Greece" (ἐγένετο πλέω κακὰ τῇ Ἑλλάδι) than in the prior twenty generations, including evils from Persia and from internecine conflict among the leading powers within Greece (ἀπ' αὐτῶν τῶν κορυφαίων περὶ τῆς ἀρχῆς πολεμεόντων, 6.98.2). He mentions Agariste's dream of birthing a lion just before she gives birth to Pericles (6.131.2). And he comments on Sparta's clemency toward Decelea during the Peloponnesian War, despite its otherwise widespread destruction of Attica (9.73.3). In a similar vein, various judgments by the narrator about the role of the Athenians during the Greco-Persian Wars have been interpreted as carrying political resonance in a late-fifth-century context, including Herodotus's comments on the flourishing of Athenian ἰσηγορίη after the expulsion of the tyrants (5.78); his witty remark, in narrating Aristagoras's persuasion of the Athenians to send ships to the Ionians after his failure before King Cleomenes of Sparta, that it is easier to deceive a crowd than to deceive one person (5.97.2); and his offering up what he claims will be his "envy-inducing" (ἐπίφθονον) judgment that the Athenians were the saviors of Greece (7.139.1).[64] In the first set of instances, Herodotus comments directly on matters within his lifetime; in the other set, remarks about past events and actions may have interpretive reverberations in the present.

Much like that of Herodotus, Dionysius's narration of the fairly distant past leaves it mostly up to readers to draw (or not draw) analogies with the present. Indirectly and extradiegetically, Dionysius refers to contemporary and future events and persons.[65] But in general, he is muted when it comes to more recent controversies. Irene Peirano has argued, for instance, that Dionysius's choice to end his historical narrative before the outbreak of the

---

[63] See Moles 1996; Forsdyke 2006; Irwin 2009; Stadter 2012.

[64] On these three passages, see esp. Fornara 1971: 37–58. See the more skeptical approach of Rutherford 2018: 10–13.

[65] See, e.g., *Ant. Rom.* 1.6.5 on future generations and the many comments cited earlier on Rome's rise.

102   HERODOTUS AND IMPERIAL GREEK LITERATURE

Punic Wars "allows him to leave the issue of the causes of Roman decline unresolved."[66] Yet, as Peirano also points out, Dionysius "subtly hints at the consequences of the Roman conquests and expansionism which lie outside his chronological boundaries."[67] If this is almost precisely what some have argued for Herodotus, too, with respect to Athens, one may wonder to what extent Dionysius's appropriation of Herodotus assumes an analogous critical valence. Certainly, Dionysius is not above reproving the Romans, or at least adverting to the fragility of their superior position.[68] Even instances of apparent praise can sport a monitory underbelly. At *Ant. Rom.* 14.6.4–5, for instance, Rome's just treatment of its conquered is contrasted with Athenians' and Spartans' past records of injustice toward their enemies. Dionysius notes that one could cite "countless faults" (μύρια . . . ἡμαρτημένα, 14.6.5) among the Spartans and Athenians. While the passage would seem to highlight the improved moral stature of the Hellenized Romans, any such contrast implicitly hints at the risk that Rome, too, will at some point exhibit the flaws of its forebears. For already, as Wiater has argued in fine detail, Dionysius's classicism does not entail an uncritical exaltation of the past: "Dionysius . . . is fully aware that the 'classical ideal' which he endorses and which he seeks to impart to his readers, is and always has been a culturally and historically contingent construction that was at odds with the reality already at the time of its creation."[69] If his classicality is a contingent work in progress, rather than a perfect prior entity, Dionysius's framework is compatible with the notion that there is always opportunity for improvement, both in relation *to* the classical past (when it offers a superior model) and *upon* the classical past (when it offers a flawed model).

I would submit, finally, that however we interpret the hypotextual potential of Dionysius's imperial language, his deployment of such language betokens an early instance of the *Histories'* reception as a piece of world literature. As characterized by Dionysius, Herodotus's authorial moves produce in textual form the conglomeration of powers under the force of a single

---

[66] Peirano 2010: 51.

[67] Peirano 2010: 52. See also Gabba 1991: 211–13; Wiater 2011b: 70–91; Fox 2011, with his observation that "neither [classical Greece nor early Rome] are in fact idealized, and neither beyond unfavourable criticism" (109).

[68] On Dionysius's critiques of contemporary Roman decadence and moral failures, see Peirano 2010: 45–46, 46 n. 58, citing instances in which Dionysius highlights contemporary Romans' behavior unbecoming of their ancestors: lack of respect for auspices (2.6.2), crimes by slaves (4.24.4), and disrespect for elders (7.47.1). See also Schultze 2019: 167. Compare Gabba 1982: 54–55, 64–65 on tensions between Dionysius's classicist ideals and the new realities of Rome under the principate.

[69] Wiater 2019: 63.

control that is by analogy the model of empire. Dionysius's *Histories* is, in effect, a text both imperial in content and imperializing in its organization. In this regard, Dionysius's own account of the relationship between political power and literary endeavor recapitulates the kind of global kinship posited between Herodotus's encompassing text and the would-be synoptic powers of Persia, had it succeeded. Dionysius's newly liberated rhetoric implicitly moves away from panchoric affiliation (to invoke categories described by Alexander Beecroft) toward a new cosmopolitan literature now possible under Rome.[70] Dionysius's reference in *On Ancient Orators* to the Asian harlot as "being some Mysian or Phrygian or some infernal Carian thing" (*Orat. Vett.* 1.7) denounces an essentially local, minor figure who attempts to "adapt" to "different political niches."[71] The ejection of the Asiatic harlot not only involves the stylistic rejection of flowery rhetoric, but it also marks Dionysius's embrace of Rome's ability to create a cosmos in which sound rhetoric will have a home. Rome subsumes the panchoric catalogue of various places that practice a bastardized rhetoric. Hence, the all-encompassing spectacle (ἀποβλέπειν) of Rome revives Xerxes's failed plan for the same (κατόψεται), while the emphasis on a unified set of lands (αὐτὰς ἀπάσας ἐγὼ ἅμα ὑμῖν μίαν χώραν θήσω [*Dem.* 41] ~ ἡ πάντων κρατοῦσα . . . τὰς ὅλας πόλεις ἀποβλέπειν [*Orat. Vett.* 3.1]) has dimensions both political and literary: world power enables Dionysius's idea of a world literature, in which Asianism has been defeated. Dionysius's long quotation from Xerxes resurrects an imperial vision to which his own corpus offers a riposte, "redefeating" Xerxes through Hellenic Rome. His program is strengthened by such channeling of Herodotus, whose synoptic, global qualities as a chronicler of empire are now made all the more imitable *because* of Roman imperial power (*Orat. Vett.* 3.1).

I have argued that Dionysius's preferences for Herodotus should be connected to his own rhetorical and historiographic motivations. His proclamation of Herodotus's unifying virtues in the rhetorical treatises relates to his interest in an expanding Roman power and the global rhetoric it fosters. He lauds Greek virtue, including as represented in the *Histories*, for enabling, through the Roman descendants of Greece, a kind of (literary) history keyed to his

---

[70] See Beecroft 2008, esp. 93–95. Panchoric literatures are, as Beecroft writes, "literary texts and systems of circulation operating across a range of epichoric communities, united to some degree in language and culture, but generally fragmented politically" (93).
[71] Beecroft 2008: 93.

own political moment. In an ironic convolution, the vision of Xerxes from Herodotus's *Histories* comes to parallel both Herodotus's textual achievement as an author of synoptic imperial scope and Rome's own historical acts as a nascent imperial force. A question that must linger has to do with the scope of hypotextual activation for Dionysius's political moment: how subversive was he willing to let his Herodotus be, if he took Herodotus to have been subversive at all? It seems likely, in any event, that in his apparent enthusiasm for Rome, Dionysius will have looked past some of the potentially darker energies of Herodotus's text. A generation or two later, much like Dionysius of Halicarnassus, Plutarch of Chaeronea will also be concerned with potential models of classicality. But as we shall see in chapter 3, Herodotus becomes in Plutarch's eyes an evident hindrance to a full appreciation of the past's virtues.

3

Parallel Authors

Plutarch's "Life" of Herodotus

As we have seen in chapters 1 and 2, Dionysius of Halicarnassus elaborates the positive ethical aspects of Herodotus's narratorial persona and appropriates that *ethos* to his own aesthetic and ideological concerns, ultimately connecting Herodotus's coverage of a wide *oikoumene* to his own narrative of Rome. Plutarch of Chaeronea, by contrast, cuts a path largely divergent from that of Dionysius. In place of Dionysius's highly celebrated writer, Plutarch's essay *On the Malice of Herodotus*, the focus of this chapter, tells of a fundamentally flawed figure, a man marked by a malign disposition (his so-called κακοήθεια) and guilty not only of having written an inaccurate history but also of deceiving readers about the quality of his character. Dionysius and Plutarch thus present a contrastive diptych in Herodotean reception that itself bespeaks the varied provocations to which Herodotus gave rise.[1] But as with my analysis of Dionysius, my interest in Plutarch often involves a focus on the kinetic possibilities of his reception acts: How does Plutarch play to or against critical orthodoxies about Herodotus, and what is the relationship between what Plutarch says about Herodotus and what he *does* as a critic? How does Plutarch's essay on Herodotus instruct readers in ways of reading (Plutarch) more generally?

Anchoring this chapter in Plutarch's Herodotus essay is not inevitable. Indeed, even if Herodotus were not among the most-quoted authors (behind Plato, Homer, and Euripides) in Plutarch, and even in the absence of the *Malice* essay, Herodotean receptions could still be traced along many lines of Plutarch's massive corpus.[2] One could, for example, examine Herodotean

---

[1] See Marincola 1994: 202, noting the stark disparity between the two critics. Luce 1989: 22 n. 23 raises the possibility that *On the Malice of Herodotus* is a response to the positive reception of Herodotus in Dionysius's *Letter to Gnaeus Pompey*. For the text of *On the Malice of Herodotus* (*dHM*), I follow the Loeb edition of Pearson 1965. Unless otherwise stated, for other *Moralia* texts I follow Loeb editions; for the *Lives* I follow the Teubner editions of Ziegler 1957–1971.

[2] On quotations in Plutarch, see Morgan 1998 (at Table 19) and Helmbold and O'Neil 1959: 34–37. For Plutarch's use of Herodotus in different genres, see Pelling 2007: 155–62; and for a wider survey of Herodotean presences in Plutarch, see Inglese 2003.

Herodotus and Imperial Greek Literature. N. Bryant Kirkland, Oxford University Press. © Oxford University Press 2022. DOI: 10.1093/oso/9780197583517.003.0004

106   HERODOTUS AND IMPERIAL GREEK LITERATURE

overlaps with Plutarch's religious ideas or in the Persian Wars material of his *Lives*.[3] I choose, however, to dilate on Plutarch's Herodotus treatise in part because it cogently frames an act of author-focused reception. While the work is somewhat atypical within Plutarch's corpus in devoting sustained attention to one writer, it nonetheless presents a moment of acute reception in the shaping of an author's afterlife.[4] And despite the bad press it gives Herodotus, the text continues the tradition of distilling Herodotus as a figure worthy of attention in the first place, reifying an idea of Herodotus qua distinctive author, much as Dionysius had done.[5]

All the same, the familiarity (to us) of a single-author focus should not mean that Plutarch's effort can be taken for granted. To the extent that it fixates on Herodotus's unique potential to offer an authoritative account of his subject, for good or ill, Plutarch's essay highlights the very ownership that Herodotus is presumed to exercise over his text and the responsibility he takes for it in the opening pages.[6] The seriousness of Plutarch's jeremiad against Herodotus might not have registered as strongly against an author who had not himself asserted so robust a level of responsibility in bringing forth his work. We should therefore recognize, building on Dionysius's sense of his narratorial character, that it is Herodotus who in some sense predetermines and frames Plutarch's ethical focus: his own forceful narratorial character generates the terms of Plutarch's response. Plutarch's reception act in *On the Malice of Herodotus* is in that regard never entirely his own. Herodotus *acts on* Plutarch, provoking his judgment. Our attention, in turn, to Plutarch's singular handling of Herodotus is an effect created by (or at the very least related to) Plutarch's own focused cathexis.

In what follows, I examine how aspects of Plutarch's essay function as literary criticism, while also placing the work in the wider web of Plutarch's character-focused thought.[7] Rather than studying the various historical

---

[3] On divinity in Herodotus and Plutarch, see Ellis 2015b; Marincola 2015a. On Plutarch's Persian Wars, see Marincola 2010; Marincola 2012a.

[4] Relevant author-focused parallels in Plutarch's *Moralia* include the *Comparison of Aristophanes and Menander* and *Against Colotes*. Author-focused reception was certainly a feature of Imperial Greek literature; see, e.g., Kim 2010a: 175–215 (esp. 206–11) on Homer in the *Heroicus*, where Philostratus's interest in Homer's omissions and biases (209) mirrors some of Plutarch's concerns regarding Herodotus; see later discussion here on the ἴχνη at *dHM* 855B–856D.

[5] It is not uncommon for scholarship treating the essay to acknowledge its odd qualities; see Wardman 1974: 189; Russell 1990c: 306. Cf. Marincola 2015b: 83.

[6] On the distinctive and inventive turns of Herodotus's work, see Goldhill 2002: 11–44 (esp. 11–13 on Herodotus's taking responsibility for his subject and eschewing divine inspiration) and Grethlein 2010: 149–204. For the newfangled role of the narrator, see Dewald 2002.

[7] Van der Stockt 1992, on Plutarch's literary criticism, passes over the *dHM*. Recent studies have demonstrated a range of approaches to the work, but few have studied the text as a literary-critical

PARALLEL AUTHORS 107

corrections that Plutarch offers, my interest lies in the essay's hermeneutic premises, their connections to Plutarch's practical ethics, and their interaction with Plutarch's broader strategies in his biographic corpus.[8] Plutarch uses the Herodotus essay to develop an idea of traditionality from which Herodotus has deviated; in turn, Plutarch's reading of Herodotus helps to construct an image of his *own* way of being an author, in contradistinction to a denounced Herodotean mode of authorship. For Plutarch, Herodotus comes to stand for a nexus of concerns having to do with the disposition of the past and of oneself as author. Plutarch's essay devotes a kind of attention to character contiguous with practices in the *Lives* and thereby encourages our ethical reading not only of Herodotus but also of a more holistic Plutarch.

Characterizing Style

Plutarch's *On the Malice of Herodotus*, a work of unknown date, though likely late, mounts a ferocious blitz against Herodotus that is by turns acid, mordant, and exhausting.[9] While the work's relentless mode of refutation may read like a kind of *controversia*,[10] it would be a mistake to view it as a virtuosic exercise only, unrelated to Plutarch's broader interests. Plutarch aims to persuade readers that the Halicarnassian was not just factually wrong but was also fundamentally flawed in his character.[11] The treatise as a whole is less interested in, or not exclusively interested in, historical correction. Nor does it attempt to promulgate Herodotus's reputation for fabrication; rather,

document in its own right. On the historian's character, see Marincola 1994; Marincola 2015b. On ancient historiographic theory and its concern for both propriety and moral improvement, see Wheeldon 1989. For efforts to read Plutarch's oeuvre synoptically, see the essays in Nikolaidis 2008.

[8] For historiographic focus, including attention to Plutarch's historical corrections, the specific events of the Persian Wars, and questions of historical accuracy, see Pelling 2007 and Marincola 2016, with further bibliography. See also Hershbell 1997 for the essay's reflections on history as a genre.

[9] The text's date is not entirely clear, though Wardman (1974: 189), Lachenaud (1981: 128–29), and Bowen (1992: 2) subscribe to a later date, closer to the time of Plutarch's composition of the *Lives*. See also Pelling 2007: 157 n. 41: "*Malice* probably belongs to the period when the *Lives* were being composed . . . i.e. over a substantial period after 96 . . . not long before his death." The work's dyspeptic tone once inspired doubt about authorship; see, however, Teodorsson 1997, with conclusion at 439: "The old question concerning the authorship of *De Herodoti Malignitate* is now antiquated."

[10] See Seavey 1991; see also Webb 2001: 302–3 on "cast of character" exercises. Compare Trapp 2020: 96 on Plutarch's "controversial works" as "uncompromising in their desire to annihilate their opponents' intellectual credit."

[11] The ethical and historiographic concerns of the essay cohere, as Marincola 1994 rightly emphasizes. For further elaboration, see Marincola 2015b: 89–91, 94–95. See also Roskam 2017: 163–66.

108 HERODOTUS AND IMPERIAL GREEK LITERATURE

it assumes that reputation: "Our argument does not concern the fact of his lies; we confine our examination to his *malicious* lies" (ἀλλ' ὃ μὲν ἔψευσται, λόγος ἡμῖν οὐδείς· ἃ δέ γε **κατέψευσται** μόνον ἐξετάζομεν, 870B).[12] We all know he lies, Plutarch seems to say, but do we reckon with the deeper flaws that dispose him toward doing so?

Plutarch is from the start concerned with reforming our impression of Herodotus's character, suggested by the work's first sentences:

> The style of Herodotus, Alexander, has deceived many, one so smooth and unlabored and gliding easily over his subject; but even more have experienced this deceit with respect to his character. For not only, as Plato says, is it the height of injustice "to seem just when not so"; it is also an act of extreme bad character to escape detection while falsely portraying a good spirit and sincerity. (854E–F)

> πολλοὺς μέν, ὦ Ἀλέξανδρε, τοῦ Ἡροδότου καὶ ἡ λέξις ὡς ἀφελὴς καὶ δίχα πόνου καὶ ῥᾳδίως ἐπιτρέχουσα τοῖς πράγμασιν ἐξηπάτηκε· πλείονες δὲ τοῦτο πρὸς τὸ ἦθος αὐτοῦ πεπόνθασιν. οὐ γὰρ μόνον, ὥς φησιν ὁ Πλάτων, τῆς ἐσχάτης ἀδικίας μὴ ὄντα δοκεῖν εἶναι δίκαιον, ἀλλὰ καὶ κακοηθείας ἄκρας ἔργον εὐκολίαν μιμούμενον καὶ ἁπλότητα δυσφώρατον εἶναι.

Plutarch jump-starts his essay with an odd claim: Herodotus's style is the problem, a negative assertion that tonally echoes other denunciations of Herodotus but in fact defies the conventional wisdom that Herodotus's style constituted one of his virtues.[13] Plutarch also surprises by initially sidestepping an overt attack on Herodotus's fabled mendacity.[14] Instead, he locates the deceptive quality in Herodotus's smooth (literally, "not pebbly") style.[15]

---

[12] Note the lacunae and various proposals: α δε τ + (lac. 3 litt.) + ψεῦσται EB. ‖ ἃ δέ γε κατέψευσται Turnebus: ἃ δὲ κατέψευσται Hansen: ἃ δὲ τῶν Ἑλλήνων κατέψευσται Wyttenbach: ἃ δέ τραγικῶς ἔψευσται Pohlenz: alii alia. Wyttenbach's proposal would reinforce the pro-Greek sentiments of the treatise.

[13] On positive assessments of Herodotean style, see, e.g., Dionysius, *Comp.* 10.5 (with Chapter 1); Demetrius, *Eloc.* 181.

[14] Plutarch takes Herodotus's supposed lies for granted. See *dHM* 854F for the claim that it would take many books to account for all Herodotus's lies and fabrications (ψεύσματα καὶ πλάσματα).

[15] As noted by Lachenaud 1981: 237, this characterization recalls Cicero's statement (*Or.* 39) that "Herodotus flows without any rough spots, like a tranquil river" (*alter enim sine ullis salebris quasi sedatus amnis fluit*). Unlike the showy charms of epideictic orators, who speak for the sake of pleasure (*delectationis causa*, 37), Herodotus and Thucydides are remarkable (*mirabiles*, 39), Cicero claims, for being "a very long way off from such charms, or to put it more strongly, such follies" (*longissime tamen ipsi a talibus deliciis vel potius ineptiis afuerunt*, 39). Cicero's judgment on the *lack*

PARALLEL AUTHORS   109

Herodotus's *lexis* is δίχα πόνου in a double sense, at once not overly elaborated and not requiring, it seems, much work on the reader's part.[16] Herodotus's style was famous, and Plutarch thus offers an effectively arresting gambit in upending expectations of that style's significance. The acknowledgment that Herodotus's style *is* smooth, that of what Plutarch later calls a "writerly" man (γραφικός, 874B), enables the critique of deceit that the smoothness allegedly hides. The historian's deceptive self-presentation implies a gap between Herodotus the narrator, visible on the surface of his text, and Herodotus the person whose ἦθος skulks behind that smooth text.[17]

So despite the initial focus on style, the tilt of the first sentence in fact falls on Herodotus's character, which deceives even "more" (πλείονες) people than his style. Plutarch here invokes the familiar collocation of style and *ethos* only to problematize their conventional relation, even attempting to drive a wedge between the two, the better to magnify Herodotus's threat (if only meretriciously, for the sake of argument).[18] For in asserting that *more* people have fallen victim to his *ethos* than to his style, it is as if Plutarch conceives of a Herodotus who is somehow transcendent to his work, whose reputation precedes him: Plutarch's contrast adumbrates an author whose character has taken on a life of its own. Plutarch's hyperbole intimates Herodotus's *ethos* as a kind of preexisting condition that disposes readers to a set of false views

of pleasure-mongering in Herodotus's style provides some context for appreciating Plutarch's judgment, which affirms the verdict on Herodotus's smooth style (ἀφελὴς καὶ δίχα πόνου καὶ ῥᾳδίως ἐπιτρέχουσα ~ *sine ullis salebris quasi sedatus amnis fluit*) but relocates Herodotus to the realm of potentially deceitful (ἐξηπάτηκε) and pleasurable ornamentation from which Cicero has separated him (see *TLL* s.v. 2. *dēlicia* I B 2 *nugae, lusus*).

[16] A few sections later, Plutarch's opening thoughts are echoed by the admission of Herodotus's "charm and power" (χάριν ἔχοντι καὶ δύναμιν, 855A), and they will again be reinforced by a concession near the essay's conclusion about Herodotus's graceful and sweet style (ἡδὺς ὁ λόγος, καὶ χάρις ἔπεστι, 874B). The deceitfulness of Herodotus's apparently ἀφελής style would appear especially offensive to Plutarch, who in his *Lycurgus* speaks approvingly, in almost verbatim language, of the "smooth and unfussy" style of Spartan music and poetry (ἡ λέξις ἦν ἀφελὴς καὶ ἄθρυπτος, *Lyc.* 21.1). Lachenaud notes the double quality of ἀφελής (1981: 237), "L'adjectif ἀφελής définit aussi bien l'absence de recherche que l'absence de malice." Compare Plutarch, *Amat.* 755D.

[17] The point has been well put by Marincola (1994: 193): "[T]he style of Herodotus, Plutarch says, *seems* simple and effortless, but this is deceptive and in contrast with the author's true character" (emphasis in original).

[18] See Kurke's comment (2011: 385) along similar lines, with reference to his bard comparison (874B–C), that Plutarch is attempting to "pry apart style and authorial *ēthos*." I stress the meretricious aspect of this move because I do not ultimately disagree with Marincola 2015b: 90 n. 18 that Plutarch is "reasserting, against those who tried to separate the work from the author . . . that one's writings really are indicative of character." But Plutarch's method in the *Malice*, however much it will end up affirming the common view of style-as-sign-of-character, nonetheless plays with having things both ways at different times: it initially discounts this connection, the better to highlight the monstrous deceit of Herodotus's style in apparently *not* revealing his character, even if the essay ultimately demonstrates that his style *can* be shown to reveal precisely that character.

110   HERODOTUS AND IMPERIAL GREEK LITERATURE

under which his work is read.[19] Plutarch likely assumes here the generally benign prestige that had come to surround Herodotus, one derived in part from his having written about events that Greeks found uplifting to recall.[20] On this view, Plutarch seems to imply that very many approach Herodotus's work *already presupposing* his character to be good because of his popular association with felicitous material, which then circularly leads to false positives, as it were, in the assessment of his style. The mimetic concern (μιμούμενον, 854F) flagged by Plutarch thus relates to both the representation of content and the self-representation of Herodotus: readers who become enamored of Herodotus's style are less disposed to uncover its deceits, instead taking its pleasantness as confirmation for their preconceptions of the kind of man he was.

Sign Language

To organize his exposition, and perhaps to make his dyspeptic treatise palatable to readers, Plutarch introduces the concept of ἴχνη (855B–856D), variously translatable as "traces," "footprints," or "signs."[21] Plutarch designates these ἴχνη as the features by which readers can hope, with his help, to uncover Herodotus's bad character, his so-called κακοήθεια (a term that I leave

---

[19] The circular contours are not dissimilar to Foucault 1977's discussion of the author: as Wilson 2004 has shown in detail, Foucault at some points in his essay suggests that the author is constructed by the reader but at other times implies that the author creates the conditions of the text (the "plurality of egos") from which the very notion of an author-function arises. As Wilson (359) summarizes, "the 'author-function' variously appear[s] as cause and as effect, as arising from the text and as imposed upon it." A similar notion of Herodotus's reputation for good character as imposed upon his style is afoot here, while at the same time the ultimate truth (Herodotus's bad character) is an effect generated by a careful reading of the *lexis*.

[20] The particular degree, however, to which Plutarch's screed against Herodotus scanned as anomalous or conventional for its time is hard to say. Momigliano (1966 [1958]: 133) reckons that Plutarch's may have been one of many anti-Herodotus tracts dating to the first two centuries CE, of which only titles remain extant; see also Homeyer 1967: 185; Hershbell 1993: 161–62. All the same, Plutarch's attack unavoidably railed against an indispensable source of an important nostalgic tradition for Imperial Greeks; see Ehrhardt 1988: 852; Schmidt 2010: 106. On Herodotus's general reputation, see this book's introduction.

[21] The historiographic principles of the ἴχνη have been central to various treatments of the essay; see the remark of Russell 1966: 182 that the essay "contains in its opening sections one of the most revealing accounts of the principles of ancient historiography that we possess." Compare, however, Bowen 1992: 4, who contends that Plutarch "more or less ignores" the signs after introducing them. Plutarch's method of detective reading comports with stated interests elsewhere; see, e.g., his preference in *Table Talk* for "tracking down the truth" (ἀνιχνεύειν τὴν ἀλήθειαν) rather than uncritically "filling up" (ἀναπίμπλησι) on traditional solutions (πρεσβύτερων ἐπιχειρήματα, 694D).

PARALLEL AUTHORS   111

purposefully untranslated for now).[22] Plutarch proposes the following signs of an author's bad character:

1. Highly unpleasant (δυσχερεστάτοις) language when milder (ἐπιεικεστέρων) language is available (855B).
2. Needless, gleeful (ἡδόμενος) digressions on human misfortune (855C).
3. Omission (παράλειψις) of something good (855D).
4. Choosing the worse (τῷ χείρονι) account when more are available (855E).
5. Choosing the worse interpretation (ὁ πρὸς τὸ χεῖρον εἰκάζων) when facts are clear (855F–856A).
6. Attributing bad motives, for example, success owing to money, not courage (856B).
7. Attacking people (κακῶς λέγουσι), directly or through innuendo (856C).
8. Offering faint praise to magnify criticism (856C–D).

What role do these signs imply for Plutarch as critic? Although Plutarch states that the ἴχνη mark by common consent (κοινῇ, 855B) the signs of an impure narrative, readers may have reason to doubt their "common" workability. After all, some seem to depend upon the critic's psychological sensitivity or insight (e.g., signs 1, 2, 6, 7, 8, and sometimes 5), while others might require the availability of factual knowledge (signs 3, 4, and again sometimes 5). Yet the items in both categories are presented by Plutarch as though they were things readers can spot by themselves. Granted, nothing stops readers from suspecting on their own that Herodotus has chosen a negative interpretation here or attacked a character through innuendo there.[23] But Plutarch makes in his opening claim the crucial point that the dangers of Herodotus's text are hidden beneath the subterfuge of style. This observation goes against the notion that readers will easily, or without Plutarch's guidance, spot the tracks—let alone discern the character of which they are a sign. Herodotus's text, *because* of his deceitful crafting, makes it peculiarly hard to perform the

---

[22] "Malice" is a concise, if inevitably somewhat flattening, translation; see esp. Boake 1975, 109–13 for passing attention to the term in Aristotle and a useful survey of the term's appearances elsewhere in the Plutarchan corpus. See further Lachenaud 1981: 126; Marincola 1994: 192–93; and later discussion here.

[23] Indeed, Herodotus's text may encourage such moves. On Plutarch's recognition of Herodotus's subtlety, see Baragwanath 2008: 10–12, 15–17, citing Wolfgang Iser. On Plutarch's development of his critical reader, see Konstan 2004; Hunter 2009: 171–74; Duff 2011.

112   HERODOTUS AND IMPERIAL GREEK LITERATURE

necessary kind of critical reading; reading Herodotus means engaging in a special kind of hermeneutic task for which Plutarch (we are meant to believe) serves as the proper guide.

Rather than being readily workable in the hands of readers, then, the ἴχνη often carve out a role for Plutarch as a privileged interpreter. In several instances, Plutarch presumes to enact an invasive hermeneutic that reveals the author's psyche, whether through his ability to discern Herodotus's own motivations (sign 6) or to determine just when it is that Herodotus offers praise with ill intent (sign 8). That the ἴχνη presuppose Plutarch's access to Herodotus's own mind is brought out well in the wider context of Plutarch's seventh ἴχνος:

> If they fail to control themselves, it is possible to accuse those who patently slander whom they wish of irritability and brashness, even insanity. But those who make a sidelong attack, releasing their slanderous arrows from an unseen place, then wheeling about and retreating, saying they do not believe what they want others to believe completely—these men, by denying their malice, reveal their servility to it. (856C)

> ἔστι τοίνυν τοῖς ἀπ᾽ εὐθείας οὓς βούλονται κακῶς λέγουσι δυσκολίαν ἐπικαλεῖν καὶ θρασύτητα καὶ μανίαν, ἐὰν μὴ μετριάζωσιν· οἱ δὲ πλαγίως οἷον ἐξ ἀφανοῦς βέλεσι χρώμενοι ταῖς διαβολαῖς, εἶτα περιιόντες ὀπίσω καὶ ἀναδυόμενοι, τῷ φάσκειν ἀπιστεῖν ἃ πάνυ πιστεύεσθαι θέλουσιν, ἀρνούμενοι κακοήθειαν ἀνελευθερίαν τῇ κακοηθείᾳ προσοφλισκάνουσιν.

Plutarch's channeling of authorial intent moves through various levels of mental disturbance (δυσκολία, θρασύτης, μανία) before introducing the more devious threat of κακοήθεια. Direct attack (ἀπ᾽ εὐθείας) has a manifest and possibly dismissible link with madness. Plutarch's contrastive language of concealment (πλαγίως, ἐξ ἀφανοῦς, ἀναδυόμενοι) not only underscores Herodotus's cryptic character and his fostering a disconnect between what he claims to deny and what he wants others to believe (τῷ φάσκειν ... θέλουσιν), but such language also implicitly adverts to Plutarch's ability to detect these subtle distinctions in the first place. The passage, in its ranging set of psychological assumptions, traffics in a kind of cognitive-biographic fantasy, wherein Plutarch's investigation assumes privileged access to Herodotus's thought. Hence it is key to Plutarch's program as a critic that the ἴχνη depend on knowledge not immediately available to the average reader through the text itself. Although the metaphor of ἴχνη implies that detection is possible by means of signs that exist already in the *Histories*, what Plutarch sets forth as "traces" are themselves hidden signs, invisible links between the text and that which lies behind or beyond it.

More than setting up a plan for independent study, then, many of the ἴχνη require or potentially require that readers trust Plutarch to do undercover work in his self-appointed position as endoscopic critic. Yet Plutarch's proximity to Herodotus as a critic should not be confused with a homology of authorial character (in contradistinction from the kind of homology implicitly proposed by Dionysius vis-à-vis Herodotus). Plutarch's Herodotus falls outside a canon of ethical acceptability, but Plutarch, by contrast, in helping readers to recognize Herodotus's deviations, implicitly asserts his own position within the contours of salutary criticism.[24]

The Idea of Κακοήθεια in Plutarch's *Moralia*

Regardless of whether one views the ἴχνη as generalizable (or even practicable) rules for reading, they summon Plutarch's broader ethical focus in the *Moralia*, insofar as they aim to uncover Herodotus's κακοήθεια.[25] Plutarch's invocation of the term invites us to situate the essay within his broader moralizing project and helps to substantiate the contention (as elaborated later in this chapter) that similar to readers' encounters with figures in Plutarch's *Lives*, Plutarch wants us to see Herodotus as a person whose moral constitution can be assessed.[26]

In surveying κακοήθεια and cognate terms in the *Moralia*, some limitations of the standard English translation "malice" become apparent.[27]

---

[24] See Kirkland 2019 for the argument that Plutarch presents himself as a responsible steward of the literary past, not only correcting Herodotus but also demonstrating mastery of Platonic and Aristotelian premises.

[25] See Marincola (2015b: 95) on the non-transferability of the signs: they "cannot be read in isolation as detachable historiographical 'rules.' Because they concern a historian's entire disposition, they all fit together and are employed to show everything is of a piece for a particular type of writer." Cf. Roskam 2017: 164: "the criteria can in principle be applied to every kind of narrative (διήγησις, 855B)."

[26] Chrysanthou 2020 argues for connections between the kinds of readerly judgment that Herodotus encourages in his readers and the sort that Plutarch invites in his *Lives*. My emphasis differs slightly: just as Plutarch provokes us to judge character in the *Lives*, so does he provoke readers to judge the character of Herodotus, too.

[27] The term κακοήθεια and related adjective κακοήθης appear some fifty-four times across the span of Plutarch's *Moralia*. Unsurprisingly, a goodly proportion (33.3 percent) appear in the *Malice* essay, whose instances of such terminology in fact constitute some 25 percent of appearances overall in Plutarch's entire corpus.

114 HERODOTUS AND IMPERIAL GREEK LITERATURE

Inasmuch as that word tends now in English to connote short-lived spite or specific instances of bad intention, it does not always map neatly onto κακοήθεια.[28] The Greek term can sometimes register a more deep-seated dispositional depravity: not a passing mean-spiritedness, then, but the mark of enduringly bad character.[29] The vice lies buried within one's nature, deeply nested in the "folds of soul" (τινὰς διπλόας . . . τῆς ψυχῆς), as described in a passage in *Table Talk* (7.10, 715F) in which Plutarch's brother lauds the unveiling force of wine:

> Wine drives out the apprehensiveness that is the not least impediment to those in deliberation, and it thoroughly drowns many other base and uncharitable emotions. It shakes out badness of spirit and one's hidden enclosures (τὸ κακόηθες καὶ τὸ ὕπουλον)—the folds of the soul, so to speak—and through one's words it brings to the light of day every bit of his character and emotion.

Indeed, more than some other vices or personal qualities, κακοήθεια has to do with ethical legibility. That Plutarch in his Herodotus essay wants us to read for the signs of Herodotus's κακοήθεια squares well with the broader diffusion of the term in the *Moralia*, since κακοήθεια differs from such vices as anger or arrogance principally in its hiddenness. Recognizing κακοήθεια is in some sense a hermeneutic act. Plutarch's examination of Herodotus's bad character thus fits with a wider program of literary interpretation: as κακοήθεια in the practical realm calls for a specific kind of moral literacy, so does Plutarch's charge against Herodotus reflect the need for an *interpretive* bent that reads through the surface of a text. Plutarch's sense of Herodotus as larded with ill will collapses textual and practical ethics, making of reading an act not unlike discerning and measuring the moral qualities of one's acquaintances.

Not only is κακοήθεια a hidden quality, but one must also reckon with the fact that the very attempt to conceal it is symptomatic of affliction. Those

---

[28] See *Oxford English Dictionary* s.v. "malice": I. "malicious intent": 1.a. "the intention or desire to do evil or cause injury to another person," whereas "malicious character" (II) is regarded as "obsolete" (II.3), as is "bad quality, badness; (chiefly in moral sense) wickedness" (II.5).

[29] See Boake 1975: 111–13 for a survey of the term, connecting κακοήθεια with slander and defamation in Plutarch. Already κακοήθεια as a fixed quality of bad character appears in Aristotle, e.g., *History of Animals* 491b22–26: "Common to the eyelid both above and below is a part called the *canthus* (the corner where the lids meet), and there are two of these: one toward the nose, the other toward the temples. If they are long, this is a sign of bad character (κακοηθείας σημεῖον)." See further *Rh.* 1389b15–21, with Kirkland 2019: 496–501.

PARALLEL AUTHORS 115

with bad character thicken the difficulty of detection by making a point to hide it, as conveyed in the *Progress in Virtue* (82B):

> It is just as when someone displays the dirt or stains on his clothes or the hole worn in his shoe but puts on a good face in public, with the insincere affectation of not being bothered (ἀτυφίᾳ κενῇ); or makes some joke about himself as small or hunched and thinks he is showing his youthful swagger, while the inward turpitude of his soul, the shameful bits of his life (τὰ δ' ἐντὸς αἴσχη τῆς ψυχῆς καὶ τὰ περὶ τὸν βίον ἐγχρέμματα)—his pettiness, devotion to pleasure, ill spirit (κακοηθείας), and feelings of envy— all of these he cloaks over and conceals (περιστέλλων καὶ ἀποκρύπτων) as though they were open wounds (ὥσπερ ἕλκη). He permits no one to touch or inspect them for fear of being interrogated (δεδιὼς τὸν ἔλεγχον). Such a man has little share in the progress in virtue—or really no share at all.

Here κακοήθεια is reckoned as part of the "inward turpitude of the soul." Plutarch's biological metaphor also figures it as an open wound that the disordered person "cloaks over and conceals" for fear of critical examination, the formidable Socratic-style *elenchos* that may expose vice. The badly disposed are aware of their own ill will and consequently intent upon masking it.[30] But those who disguise κακοήθεια miss opportunities for being challenged out of their deplorable ways. If this depiction of the malignant man seems somewhat ludicrous—what with the showy insouciance about stained clothes and wisecracks about scoliosis—the sense that the ill in spirit attempt to hide their sick dispositions shows up in more sober contexts, too. Consider the opening anecdote of *The E at Delphi* (384D), where we are told that the person who gives to the rich from scanty means can raise eyebrows and acquire a reputation for κακοήθεια: "As it is not plausible that he gives for no reason, he acquires a reputation for a wayward disposition and for servility" (ἀπιστούμενος δ' ἀντὶ μηδενὸς διδόναι κακοηθείας καὶ ἀνελευθερίας προσλαμβάνει δόξαν). The phrasing recalls that from the *Malice* essay on the general tendency toward concealment and complaisant servility (ἀρνούμενοι κακοήθειαν ἀνελευθερίαν τῇ κακοηθείᾳ προσοφλισκάνουσιν, 856C). Thus, while these examples in the *Moralia* are drawn from the realm of practical ethics, a consistent principle of

---

[30] Compare with this passage Plutarch's recommendation (*How to Profit by One's Enemies* 92B) that people conscious of their own negative disposition should direct it toward their enemies so as not to burden their friends.

116 HERODOTUS AND IMPERIAL GREEK LITERATURE

concealment—generating a need for ethical literacy—reiterates Plutarch's assessment of Herodotus as an author whose "deeds" (see πρᾶγμα, 855D) become textual acts that conceal his turpitude.

The line from *The E at Delphi* leads to a final observation on κακοήθεια and legibility in Plutarch's *Moralia*, namely, that the term is repeatedly associated with ideas of not being straightforward or simple, with a kind of internal crookedness that underlies differences between seeming and being, pretense and action. This notion finds its background in Platonic instantiations and helps Plutarch to characterize Herodotus as essentially deviant, his representation of the Persian Wars flawed from the start.[31] Because κακοήθεια involves a layer of artifice, it constitutes precisely the sort of thing that cannot be tolerated among people for whom mutual trust is essential, whether this means people getting together for a dinner party or, indeed, readers relying on an author.[32] In his essay on *Virtue and Vice* (101A), Plutarch describes τὸ κακόηθες as a latent force awakened in the wee hours by one's general propensity for wickedness:

> During the day, vice (ἡ κακία) looks outward and conforms itself (συσχηματιζομένη) in relation to others. It has a sense of shame and conceals its feelings, and it does not surrender itself wholly to its impulses, instead repeatedly resisting and fighting them. But in the sleeping hours, having fled common opinion and custom and being as far as one can get from fear or shame, vice sets in motion every desire (πᾶσαν ἐπιθυμίαν κινεῖ), and it energizes bad character and licentiousness (ἐπανεγείρει τὸ κακόηθες καὶ ἀκόλαστον).

The image well encapsulates several features that inform Plutarch's analysis in *On the Malice of Herodotus*. The quality of vice that includes τὸ κακόηθες operates deceitfully by day, "conforming itself" politely, all the while concealing its deplorable urges. But when the lights are out—recall the imagery of concealment quoted above (*dHM* 856C)—vice indulges in a shameless free-for-all.

---

[31] See, e.g., Plato, *Resp.* 347e–349b: Thrasymachus has defined justice as a πάνυ γενναία εὐήθεια, "a high-minded simplicity" or "guilelessness," prompting Socrates to ask whether he views *injustice* as a form of κακοήθεια; in context the term scans as waywardness of spirit, a failure of simplicity or straightforwardness. Cf. Roskam 2017: 165.

[32] Plutarch programmatically seeks to expunge κακοήθεια from the convivial table (*QC* 7 *praef.*, 697E).

PARALLEL AUTHORS 117

To see Herodotus clearly, we must learn to see in the dark, to see his muddle and ambiguity. Yet Plutarch would have us believe that Herodotus makes such seeing even more difficult than it should be:[33]

> Just as painters make a painting's bright parts clearer through shading, so does Herodotus intensify his attacks through negations and make his deep-hidden intentions deeper still by means of ambiguous presentations. (863E)

> ὥσπερ οἱ ζωγράφοι τὰ λαμπρὰ τῇ σκιᾷ τρανότερα ποιοῦσιν, οὕτω ταῖς ἀρνήσεσι τὰς διαβολὰς ἐπιτείνοντος αὐτοῦ καὶ τὰς ὑπονοίας ταῖς ἀμφιβολίαις βαθυτέρας ποιοῦντος.

Herodotus's darkness is intensified by a play of *both* light and dark in ταῖς ἀμφιβολίαις.[34] Painters use contrast, but Herodotus uses like upon like, negation upon attack, ambiguous meaning upon concealed thought. Plutarch's simile is therefore composed of its own ambiguity (ἀμφιβολία), in which darkness functions as both the means of contrastive highlighting (in the painter's case) and the very thing obscured (in Herodotus's case). Painters highlight bright things through shadow; but Herodotus only makes his own darkness harder to see, hyperbolizing the sense of hiddenness and soulful ambiguity intimated in Plutarch's charge of κακοήθεια.

Double Mimesis

Several times in the treatise, Plutarch draws comparisons between Herodotus and various kinds of poets: comic, tragic, mock-epic, and, climactically, a deceitful bard.[35] The comparisons to poet figures bolster Plutarch's effort to associate Herodotus with moral ambiguity and form part of Plutarch's traditionalizing critique.[36] For by linking Herodotus with Platonic-style

---

[33] With this passage, compare Plato, *Resp.* 598b–e (with Marušič 2011: 229–30). On the painting motif in Plutarch, see *de glor. Ath.*, 346F–347A (with Van der Stockt 1992: 29).

[34] Cf. Aristotle's discussion of the elderly at *Rh.* 1389b15–21: old people have a tendency to hesitate and qualify (ἀμφισβητοῦντες προστιθέασιν ἀεὶ τὸ ἴσως καὶ τάχα) and are noted for their bad disposition in looking always on the worse side of things (κακοήθεις εἰσίν· ἔστι γὰρ κακοήθεια τὸ ἐπὶ τὸ χεῖρον ὑπολαμβάνειν πάντα).

[35] See *dHM* 855F–856A, 870C, 873F, 874B–C.

[36] See discussion of Plutarch's handling of ambiguous material in Hunter and Russell 2011: 7–8; Lather 2017. Accounting for the development of prose in a separate discussion of Pythian oracles, Plutarch notes (*de Pyth. or.* 407A–B) how people had come to dislike the Pythia's use of riddle and

118 HERODOTUS AND IMPERIAL GREEK LITERATURE

meditations on poetic fraudulence and with the seeming-and-being contrast suggested by the latencies of κακοήθεια, Plutarch sets his attack within a venerable critical pattern.[37] This argumentative strategy may speak to the awareness on Plutarch's part that his broadside risked pitting him against the canonical representative of the Persian Wars and the nostalgic value it held for many Imperial Greeks.[38] The Platonizing strategy of implicating Herodotus's poetic deceits, then, seeks to set Herodotus's character straight along the orthogonals of an ancient literary-critical tradition, potentially allowing Plutarch to curb the eccentricity of his treatise by making it seem as if the thrust of his argument has a recognizable critical stature. Only, a crucial difference exists between Plutarch's attack and the general Platonic ideas on which he relies: Herodotus's deceit cannot owe to a lack of knowledge, as would be the case with Plato's poets.[39] Indeed, Plutarch's focus on Herodotean character introduces an element largely downplayed in Platonic discussions of poetry, which tend to emphasize mediation itself as problematic, rather than the character of the (largely ignorant) poet.[40] Herodotus is indeed like a poet for Plutarch, but a poet who understands, who *knows*. Instead of Plato's noble gods (cf. *Resp.* 380b), Plutarch's treatise provides a sense of Plutarch's noble war: a topic of unassailable moral quality that places high demands on those who write about it.[41]

The mimetic concern of the essay thus inheres not exclusively in the content of the *Histories* but also, as was the case for Dionysius, in the text's capacity to convey its author. Moreover, while the mimetic concern reflects

---

ambiguous statement (on which see Whitmarsh 2006a: 364–65; Lather 2017: 333–34; and Kim 2017b). In a similar vein, Herodotus's poetic and painterly discolorations signify retreat into a polysemous world, of little assistance to the reader's moral judgments.

[37] Compare Plutarch's treatment of poetic passages at *De aud. poet.* 16F, 17B, 17F–18A, with Hunter 2009: 179–88. For a corrective to an overly Platonic interpretation of *De aud. poet.*, see Blank 2011. See further Lamberton 2001: 44–52; Bowie 2014; Xenophontos 2016.

[38] See, e.g., Kurke's observation (2011: 384) that "imperial Greeks wanted a celebratory history of Greek unity and Greek triumph over barbarian invaders." See also Bowie 2013.

[39] See Kirkland 2019: 490–96.

[40] As Said remarks (1983: 132), "After all in the *Phaedrus*, in the *Ion*, and the *Republic* and the *Laws* Plato separates the philosopher from the artist, *the knower from the morally liable performer*, the contemplative from the actor" (emphasis added). See also Langlands 2020: 82–90 for Plutarchan ethical mimesis as different from Platonic notions of mimesis, insofar as an objective of Plutarchan mimesis involves "reaching the same level of being as the model, and even to become as one with the model" (85).

[41] See Barrow 1967: 156–57. Plutarch's Herodotus may put one in mind of other Platonic resonances, for instance, the wise man in *Hippias Minor* who can lie if he wishes (365d–367d) or the person who offers the noble lie (*Resp.* 382c–d, 414c–415d), justified by the goal of making citizens care more for their city (although Herodotus would seem to be the opposite: a compromised man who knowingly distorts a noble topic).

PARALLEL AUTHORS 119

Plutarch's Platonist background, the paramount concern with mimesis of the self also implies the added adjustment (again in contrast to Platonic ideas) that the content of the Persian Wars *is* inherently representable. Herodotus's double misrepresentation of character and style constitutes a special shame in Plutarch's view, given the capacity of the Persian Wars to inspire virtue.[42] As Plutarch states in his *Pericles*: "Virtue in action immediately disposes someone in such a way that he no sooner marvels at the deeds than he emulates their doers" (ἀλλ' ἥ γ' ἀρετὴ ταῖς πράξεσιν εὐθὺς οὕτω διατίθησιν, ὥσθ' ἅμα θαυμάζεσθαι τὰ ἔργα καὶ ζηλοῦσθαι τοὺς εἰργασμένους, *Per.* 2.2). Plutarch here seems to privilege action over representation, not least because of its immediately catalyzing effect in developing one's capacity for προαίρεσις toward the good (*Per.* 2.4).[43] But given other comments on narrative vividness, one comes away with the sense that for Plutarch, history-writing comes closest to depicting "virtuous deeds" fully (τοῖς ἀπ' ἀρετῆς ἔργοις, *de Glor. Ath.* 348A–B): "Among historians, the most powerful is he who uses emotions and characters to make the impression of his narrative resemble a painting" (*de Glor. Ath.* 347A). As Plutarch goes on to say:

> Myth is a false *logos* that wants to resemble the truth. For that reason it stands far apart from reality, if *logos* is a picture and image of reality, and myth is a picture and image of *logos*. So those who write of fictional deeds trail as far behind the historians as the persons who talk about deeds trail behind those who perform them. (*de Glor. Ath.* 348A–B)

> ὁ δὲ μῦθος εἶναι βούλεται λόγος ψευδὴς ἐοικὼς ἀληθινῷ· διὸ καὶ πολὺ τῶν ἔργων ἀφέστηκεν, εἰ λόγος μὲν ἔργου, καὶ λόγου δὲ μῦθος εἰκὼν καὶ εἴδωλόν ἐστι. καὶ τοσοῦτον τῶν ἱστορούντων οἱ πλάττοντες τὰς πράξεις ὑστεροῦσιν, ὅσον ἀπολείπονται τῶν πραττόντων οἱ λέγοντες.

Since historians stand at only one remove from the deeds they describe, Plutarch can accord them a privileged ontological status relative to poets, who engage in doubly removed myth-making. If one cannot orient oneself to the best in reality, the next-best thing is to be "edified in looking" (τρέφηται τῷ θεωρεῖν, *Per.* 1.2) toward good historical accounts.

---

[42] See Roskam 2017: 163 on Plutarch's "concern to obtain a correct, morally appropriable account of this significant period in Greek history."

[43] On the centrality of προαίρεσις in Plutarch's ethical thought, see Wardman 1974: 107–15.

120 HERODOTUS AND IMPERIAL GREEK LITERATURE

Plutarch therefore regards Herodotus as a failed "agent of verisimilitude," to borrow a phrase from Seán Burke.[44] By implying a direct relation between the Persian Wars and the possibilities of their virtuous representation (and the representation of their virtues), Plutarch's essay convicts Herodotus on all sides. Plutarch is in the end interested in a kind of moralizing radiance that, however ineluctably mediated (through words, through images), overcomes the deficiencies of its status *as* mediated by producing the proper ennobling effect.[45] Herodotus departs from the expected enargic representation by writing ambiguously and, in so doing, engenders extra obscurity: for readers such as Plutarch, attempting to "look through" to history by "looking at" Herodotus, the inevitable mediation is rendered all the more turbid.[46] Herodotus reveals in the process his own wavering, hedging his way through history.[47] And the fact that these difficulties of mediation are orchestrated by a man who does not truthfully represent *himself* makes the entire business more dire.

Plutarch provides an image of this thorny entanglement of author and work in the peroration of the Herodotus essay:

> The man can write, and his *logos* is pleasurable. There is grace, intensity and beauty in his narrative. . . . No doubt these things bewitch and attract everybody; but we must be vigilant against his slander and his abuse which, like a beetle in a rose, skulk beneath a smooth and soft appearance. We must be vigilant lest we unwittingly accept bizarre and false views about the greatest and best cities and men of Greece. (874B–C)

> γραφικὸς ἀνήρ, καὶ ἡδὺς ὁ λόγος, καὶ χάρις ἔπεστι καὶ δεινότης καὶ ὥρα τοῖς διηγήμασι . . . ἀμέλει ταῦτα καὶ κηλεῖ καὶ προσάγεται πάντας ἀλλ᾽ ὥσπερ ἐν ῥόδοις δεῖ κανθαρίδα φυλάττεσθαι τὴν βλασφημίαν αὐτοῦ καὶ

---

[44] Burke 1992: 45.

[45] Russell 1979: 114, in a discussion of Dionysius and Longinus, neatly characterizes the "two educational demands—for rhetorical effectiveness and moral acceptability" that "dominate most surviving Greek criticism" of the Imperial era. Plutarch's expectation that even a text composed centuries earlier should embody these moralizing qualities offers no exception.

[46] The terminology of "looking through" and "looking at" is that of Ankersmit 1994 (see 128). See Bassi 2014: 175 on these tropes, relevant to the questions with which Plutarch is concerned: "[L]ooking *at* the historical text means noticing that it is not a transparent window on a set of pre-existing real events, but that events are endowed with historical reality by virtue of the text's mediating practices; transparency is an effect of rhetoric" (emphasis in original). Plutarch's awareness of the pitfalls of "mediating practices" positions him well to detect Herodotus's layered non-transparency.

[47] Compare Aristotle's malicious old man, who can never settle on a firm view (*Rh.* 1389b15–21).

PARALLEL AUTHORS 121

κακολογίαν, λείοις καὶ ἁπαλοῖς σχήμασιν ὑποδεδυκυῖαν, ἵνα μὴ λάθωμεν
ἀτόπους καὶ ψευδεῖς περὶ τῶν ἀρίστων καὶ μεγίστων τῆς Ἑλλάδος
πόλεων καὶ ἀνδρῶν δόξας λαβόντες.

Yet Plutarch cannot simply throw out the rose with the beetle, as it were, for
the problem remains that, just as Dionysius had seen, Herodotus *did* choose
the right topic in Plutarch's eyes. As he solemnly proclaims elsewhere, "At
Salamis, Mycale, and Plataea they established, as though in adamant, the
freedom of Greece, and they handed it down to the rest of humankind" (ἐπί τε
Σαλαμῖνι καὶ Μυκάλῃ καὶ Πλαταιαῖς ὥσπερ ἀδαμαντίνως, στηρίξαντες τὴν
ἐλευθερίαν τῆς Ἑλλάδος παρέδοσαν τοῖς ἄλλοις ἀνθρώποις, *de Glor. Ath.*
350A). The Persian Wars offered Plutarch one of the supreme moments in
Greek history, showcasing "Greece's greatest and best cities and men" (*dHM*
874C). As much as he rails against Herodotus, Plutarch cannot ultimately
dispense with him. Since he must be kept, then, Plutarch makes a virtue of
necessity: if Greeks must still read their Herodotus, they must in doing so
learn to judge his character.

In the remainder of this chapter, then, I argue for some ways in which
Plutarch's Herodotus essay, in delineating a particular idea of authorial *ethos*,
undertakes a critique coextensive with the techniques of Plutarch's late-life
project of *Parallel Lives*. As with the subjects of the *Lives*, Plutarch's *Malice*
wants us to think of Herodotus as an actual person, one with moral capacities
and possible choices for exemplary (and counter-exemplary) behavior. In
Herodotus's case, the subject's deeds are conceived as textual commitments,
though some scant biographic details about Herodotus also arise in the treatise and add texture to Plutarch's assessment. In this sense, the *Malice* differs
in degree, but not always in kind, from certain features of the *Lives*. The
treatise functions in part as a piece of quasi-biography, a text that urges its
readers toward moral judgment of actions—cognitive, historical, textual—
that betray one's nature. In particular, Plutarch's negative attitude toward
Herodotean multifariousness will map onto a network of associations with
foreignness. Accordingly, as we consider how Plutarch's cathexis comports
with select portions of his *Lives*, and with the possibility that character traits
can be discerned through reading, we shall see how Herodotus ultimately
becomes in Plutarch's eyes a vaguely barbaric, non-Greek Greek.[48]

---

[48] On the *Malice* and the *Lives*, see, e.g., Wardman 1974: 189–96; Teodorsson 1997: 443–47;
Ingenkamp 2016: 234–42. See also the suggestions of Chrysanthou 2018: 159–70 on how both the
Herodotus essay and the *Lives* lead toward what Chrysanthou calls "judicial" reading.

122 HERODOTUS AND IMPERIAL GREEK LITERATURE

The *Malice* as Quasi-Biography: Reading for Character

As is often the case for readers of the *Moralia*, readers of Plutarch's *Lives* are urged to think in terms of virtue and vice.[49] If the *Moralia* encourage us to think in terms of practical ethics—the everyday encounters that benefit from the pursuit of good behavior—Plutarch's *Lives* often instruct in virtue and vice more implicitly through a form of displacement, allowing the reader access to the seemingly privileged domain of various outstanding actors in history, sometimes bringing the protagonists from these realms into the ordinary space of "an utterance or some joke" (ῥῆμα καὶ παιδιά τις, *Alex.* 1.2).[50] The "signs of soul" (τὰ τῆς ψυχῆς σημεῖα, *Alex.* 1.3) on display connect readers to figures across time. As signs, these marks avail themselves to readers who are alert to the discerning of character.

Yet the question of what character means in Plutarch's *Lives* persists. As Russell observed:

> Philosophers and teachers of rhetoric . . . classified ἤθη in such a way that the behaviour of an individual, once his type was recognized, could be predicted, and his characteristics turned to good account by those who wished to impose their opinions upon him. The historian or biographer has to perform this process, as it were, in reverse. Generally speaking, what is recorded by tradition of a great man is his πράξεις, and—a subdivision—his public λόγοι. These, together with any significant minutiae that happen to be preserved, form the evidence from which his ἦθος and φύσις must be inferred.[51]

Although describing biography, Russell's comments have a bearing on Plutarch's *Malice* as well, to the extent that Plutarch sets himself the task of inferring the character of Herodotus from his *logoi*, his literary πράξεις, as it were—and, in a few precious instances, from the "significant minutiae" of

---

[49] On moralism in Plutarch's *Lives*, see Martin 1995; Pelling 1995; Stadter 1997; Duff 1999: 52–71; Duff 2007–8: 4–7; Stadter 2000; Stadter 2003–4.

[50] On the purposes of the *Lives*, see Russell 1995; Duff 1999: 13–51 (a subtle reading of the prologues); Duff 2014, esp. 334 with n. 10. On Plutarch's engaging the critical reader, see Duff 2011, with attention to both particular *Lives* (61–75) and the *Moralia* (76–82). See further Nikolaidis 2014 (esp. 353–58, 360–64); Pelling 1988a; Pelling 1990b; with Gill 1983 and Gill 1990 on how the *Lives* create opportunities for judgment of character, rather than evaluation of an individual personality. Using Gill's terminology, we might say that Plutarch's Herodotus has a character type but is not necessarily accorded the status of having a personality (but see the section on "Roundness of Character" later in this chapter).

[51] See Russell 1995: 81–86, quotation at 82.

his life. In one sense, Herodotus provides an ideal subject for a critic such as Plutarch because his frequent narratorial insertions and declarations (and his moments of laissez-faire non-interventionism) all construct an image of an authorial *ego* whose virtues and vices lie open to the reader's assessment. Something of his proffered "character" is palpable from the start. Moreover, the potential convergence of the *Malice* and the *Lives* is reinforced by the likelihood that Plutarch wrote the *Malice* already with some idea of how his own *Lives* functioned or would function, as indicated in the passing comment (*dHM* 866B) that Plutarch intends to correct Herodotus's representation of Leonidas in his own biography of that man.[52] As far as we know, that *Life* never appeared. But the intention indicates, at a minimum, how Plutarch was thinking of Herodotus's material as kindling for his biographies.

It is not only the character of the *Lives*' subjects, as Russell outlines, for which we read; character also applies to readers. Plutarch elaborates this point in some well-known comments from the start to his *Aemilius Paulus*.[53] Although the remarks are presented as germane to the *Lives*, they put an emphasis on history(-writing), notable in this context because Plutarch's comments might be taken to convey the expectations he maintained when reading Herodotus. They may indicate the ideals that Plutarch sought and some of the ways in which Herodotus perhaps disappointed him:

> It was the case that when I first set hand to writing the *Lives* I did it for the sake of others, but as I have remained with the project, I now enjoy spending time with it for my own sake, trying in some manner to use history as though looking into a mirror, to shape my life rightly and to set it in conformity with the virtues of those men. For the event is like nothing other than sharing daily life and associating together, any time I welcome and receive each subject in turn as though he were my guest in my *historia*. . . . But in my case, by spending my time concerned with *historia*, and through constant familiarity with it for the sake of my writing, I prepare myself—by always gathering in my soul recollections of the best and most reputable persons—to drive off and reject anything base, malicious, or ignoble with which my necessary associations may assault me, benevolently and gently turning the focus of my thought away from them toward the noblest of my exempla. (*Aem.* 1.1–2, 1.5)

---

[52] On the consequences of this remark for dating the *Malice*, see Teodorsson 1997: 445–47.

[53] On this passage and others in the *Lives* that encourage the reader's participation in making moral judgments, see Duff 2011: 76–77.

124 HERODOTUS AND IMPERIAL GREEK LITERATURE

ἐμοὶ [μὲν] τῆς τῶν βίων ἅψασθαι μὲν γραφῆς συνέβη δι' ἑτέρους, ἐπιμένειν δὲ καὶ φιλοχωρεῖν ἤδη καὶ δι' ἐμαυτόν, ὥσπερ ἐν ἐσόπτρῳ τῇ ἱστορίᾳ πειρώμενον ἁμῶς γέ πως κοσμεῖν καὶ ἀφομοιοῦν πρὸς τὰς ἐκείνων ἀρετὰς τὸν βίον. οὐδὲν γὰρ ἀλλ' ἢ συνδιαιτήσει καὶ συμβιώσει τὸ γινόμενον ἔοικεν, ὅταν ὥσπερ ἐπιξενούμενον ἕκαστον αὐτῶν ἐν μέρει διὰ τῆς ἱστορίας ὑποδεχόμενοι καὶ παραλαμβάνοντες. . . . ἡμεῖς δὲ τῇ περὶ τὴν ἱστορίαν διατριβῇ καὶ τῆς γραφῆς τῇ συνηθείᾳ παρασκευάζομεν ἑαυτούς, τὰς τῶν ἀρίστων καὶ δοκιμωτάτων μνήμας ὑποδεχομένους ἀεὶ ταῖς ψυχαῖς, εἴ τι φαῦλον ἢ κακόηθες ἢ ἀγεννὲς αἱ τῶν συνόντων ἐξ ἀνάγκης ὁμιλίαι προσβάλλουσιν, ἐκκρούειν καὶ διωθεῖσθαι, πρὸς τὰ κάλλιστα τῶν παραδειγμάτων ἵλεω καὶ πραεῖαν ἀποστρέφοντες τὴν διάνοιαν.

Plutarch's preface lays out a program for using literature to banish vice. He first acknowledges the transition from writing on behalf of others toward his own enjoyment of loitering (φιλοχωρεῖν) in research for his own sake.[54] The two are not mutually exclusive, but the latter implies that Plutarch set out with one purpose and in the process of writing his *Lives* was personally affected. What caused this change? While Duff has commented on Plutarch's apparent self-presentation as "paradigmatic reader of his own *Lives*,"[55] one should note that in describing the effects of looking at history as in a mirror, Plutarch refers to the raw material for composing his *Lives*, rather than the biographies themselves. Plutarch anchors the labor of moral renovation in the historical research he undertakes, not necessarily in reading the works themselves once complete.[56]

The second part of the quotation makes this clear: Plutarch's own efforts at focusing on virtue involve a process of refinement, transacted between the negative things—including mean-spiritedness (κακόηθες)—that the necessary associations (ἐξ ἀνάγκης ὁμιλίαι) of daily life throw one's way (προσβάλλουσιν) and the deliberate (and antithetically gentle) attitude by which he reorients his focus. It is not so much Plutarch's own writing that he "looks into" but rather the sources that inform its fashioning and through which he in turn shapes his life (and *Lives*) in conformity with others' virtue. Writing the *Lives* involves extracting *from history* that which is neither base nor ill disposed, a corrective

[54] On this verb, see Russell 1993: 428; Zadorojnyi 2006: 109.

[55] Thus, Duff 1999: 30–34, esp. 33–34, quotation at 30. See also Desideri 1989: 199–202, 212–13.

[56] As Duff 1999: 33 observes, the use of the word *historia* is ambiguous, since it can refer to the events of history or to the research related to, and ultimately giving expression to, those events. Looking into the mirror of history for Plutarch could then mean delving into his own research process, in effect affirming the self-referentiality of the statement.

act that Plutarch juxtaposes with the potential ugliness of ordinary interaction. While Plutarch does not think of himself as writing history (*Alex.* 1.2), we may nonetheless observe from the *Aemilius Paulus* preface that the careful, appropriately dispositioned (ἀποστρέφοντες) process of *historia* allows him to banish τὸ κακόηθες. This expectation—that the activity of reading and researching history/*historia* both traffics in and creates opportunities to "drive off" moral turpitude—informs our view of Plutarch's assessment of Herodotus, by whom history/*historia* has been vitiated.

Indeed, Plutarch metaphorically extends the idea that his "associations" (ὁμιλίαι) in daily life are relatable to his encounters in "sharing life and association with" historical figures (συνδιαιτήσει καὶ συμβιώσει). Yet it is not only, say, Alcibiades and Themistocles but also in some sense Thucydides and Herodotus, among others, with whom Plutarch shares time in the course of his research. Even as he "welcomes" historical figures "like guests" (ὥσπερ ἐπιξενούμενον ἕκαστον αὐτῶν ἐν μέρει διὰ τῆς ἱστορίας ὑποδεχόμενοι καὶ παραλαμβάνοντες), past authors, too, in their (implicit) presentation of their own characters, necessarily provide Plutarch with fodder for moral contemplation. Hence the process of reading history as a means to his own *historia*—his own inquiry into the past—draws Plutarch into relation with not only the characters about whom he writes but also, of course, the characters of past researchers. Already we have seen something of how Plutarch's *Malice* confronts the character of Herodotus. We might then ask what is *Life*-like about the *Malice*. Of what biographic techniques does it partake in offering us a portrait of Herodotus's corrupt ἦθος? Given the vast scale of Plutarch's *Lives*, I must in what follows restrict the scope of inquiry. I therefore highlight three aspects of Plutarchan biography—psychologizing, attention to counter-exemplarity, and an interest in a certain fullness of character—that affiliate the *Malice* with the *Lives*. In each case, I discuss the *Malice* and the *Lives* interchangeably as suits each topic.

Psychologizing in the *Malice*

Proving malice means proving intent. As we have seen, Plutarch foregrounds his abilities to attribute motive in the opening sections of the Herodotus essay when he itemizes the eight ἴχνη (*dHM* 855B–856D). Plutarch encourages dependency in his reader, since the "signs" frequently mean relying on a critic who presumes to know a writer's intentions. Even if readers can technically

126 HERODOTUS AND IMPERIAL GREEK LITERATURE

interrogate Herodotus's text on their own, the drift of Plutarch's technique urges reliance on his insight.

But what does Plutarch's psychological insight look like, and what latitude does it afford him as critic? Plutarch's sense of the text as a symptom of Herodotus's psyche means that the *Histories* belongs tout court to Herodotus. Any claim therein, even by its characters, can be re-ascribed to the author; Herodotus's mind applies throughout the work, and Plutarch can, accordingly, draw conclusions that might otherwise seem to overreach. Consider, for instance, how Plutarch rebuts the *Histories'* statement that "It is clear that the women would not have been carried off if they were not wanting it" (Hdt. 1.4.2; see *dHM* 856E–857A). Plutarch assumes an ability to detect Herodotus's own thoughts and apparent misogyny in attributing the statement to the author himself: "Herodotus blames the violated women and defends the abductors" (Ἡρόδοτος δὲ κατηγορεῖ τῶν βιασθεισῶν γυναικῶν, ἀπολογούμενος ὑπὲρ τῶν ἁρπασάντων, 857A). On one level, Plutarch's ingenious counterargument, including the reductio ad absurdum that even strong creatures such as lions and leopards are carried off all unwilling, is specious, for Plutarch elides the fact that the statement at *Histories* 1.4.2 is set in the mouth of Persian *logioi*, not the narrator himself; in making Herodotus the subject of the sentence, Plutarch has thus fudged a detail.[57]

Yet on another level, such interpretive sleight of hand does not matter when the interpreter is operating by the premise that what one sees on the page is only a cover for the truth. As Plutarch states:

It seems to me rather a good idea to gather into some kind of general category the many **traces, as it were, and recognizable features** of narrative which commonly mark it as neither pure nor well intentioned, but as emanating from a bad character . . . . (855A–B)

δοκεῖ δέ μοι βέλτιον εἶναι τύπῳ τινὶ λαβόντας ὅσα κοινῇ μὴ καθαρᾶς μηδ᾽ εὐμενοῦς ἐστιν ἀλλὰ κακοήθους **οἷον ἴχνη καὶ γνωρίσματα** διηγήσεως . . . .

---

[57] While such authorial attribution is not uncommon in ancient criticism, it is not inevitable. Compare Longinus, *On the Sublime* 4.7, commenting on the apparent lapse in dignified style in Herodotus's description of women as "grievances for the eyes" (ἀλγηδόνας . . . ὀφθαλμῶν, 5.18.4). Longinus partially excuses the description on the grounds that Herodotus has focalized it from the perspective of the (inebriated) Persians (καίτοιγε ἔχει τινὰ παραμυθίαν, οἱ γὰρ παρ᾽ αὐτῷ ταυτὶ λέγοντές εἰσι[ν οἱ] βάρβαροι καὶ ἐν μέθῃ) but notes all the same that Herodotus displays a "smallness of soul" (μικροψυχίαν) in deploying such a phrase. Notwithstanding Longinus's ultimate criticism here, his offering up an excuse (παραμυθία) on Herodotus's behalf indicates sensitivity to Herodotus's multi-perspectival work whose tones could be adjusted to suit a particular characterization.

PARALLEL AUTHORS 127

In his rearranging *Histories* 1.4.2 and its surrounding context to make the statement emerge as though ex cathedra from Herodotus, we can picture Plutarch like Roland Barthes's reading *scriptor*, wresting control of the text away from the (dead) author as he unveils the ἴχνη, reshaping the *Histories* according to its "traces" and "recognizable features," and in the process displaying his critical acumen.[58]

Another instance of rearranged attribution appears in Plutarch's deprecation of Herodotus's handling of Solon. In a way that anticipates latter-day critics, Plutarch recognizes a congruence of Solonian thought and Herodotean narrative patterning.[59] But in Plutarch's case, the designation of Solon as mouthpiece for Herodotus again foregrounds Plutarch's apparent ability to detect Herodotus's own beliefs. Plutarch introduces this section with the claim that "Herodotus has spoken in revilement of the gods, using Solon as a mouthpiece" (τοῖς δὲ θεοῖς λοιδορούμενος ἐν τῷ Σόλωνος προσωπείῳ ταῦτ' εἴρηκεν, 857F). In particular, Plutarch cites Solon's statement at *Histories* 1.32.1 that the divine is "envious" (φθονερόν) and "prone to confounding human affairs" (ταραχῶδες . . . ἀνθρωπηίων πραγμάτων πέρι). There follows the new attribution: "By inflicting upon Solon what he himself thought about the gods, Herodotus adds to his bad character with his blasphemy" (ἃ γὰρ αὐτὸς ἐφρόνει περὶ τῶν θεῶν τῷ Σόλωνι προστριβόμενος κακοήθειαν τῇ βλασφημίᾳ προστίθησι, 858A).[60] Plutarch finds in Herodotus's text instances of a kind of transference that, for the benefit of his own readers, he redirects back onto its author. Plutarch can read invidiously for Herodotus's submerged spirit, separating the "true" Solon on whom Plutarch himself wrote from the distorted Herodotean version.

A well-known example of general psychologizing in the *Malice* essay— and one that Plutarch likely wished readers to apply more widely to other examples in Herodotus—appears in his charge that Herodotus is φιλοβάρβαρος (857A), a lover of things foreign. In its presumption to know Herodotus's inclination, the charge obviously differs from a more basic accusation of lying or misquotation. Plutarch bases his charge on various bits of evidence. These include Herodotus's apparently favorable judgments toward the Egyptians (evidenced by his belief that they did not attempt to kill

[58] For the *scriptor*, see Barthes 1977 [1967]: 145–47.
[59] On Solon as a vehicle for Herodotean thought, see Moles 1996; Pelling 2006, with further bibliography. Cf. Branscome 2013: 24–53 for the "rivalry" between Herodotus and Solon.
[60] On this passage, see Ellis 2015b. As Pearson notes in his Loeb edition (1965: 29, n. f), "In fact Solon's attitude towards the gods is not unusual and appears constantly in Greek literature." See Harrison 2000: 33–43.

128 HERODOTUS AND IMPERIAL GREEK LITERATURE

Heracles but that they were treated poorly at the hands of Menelaus, 857A–B). Plutarch also decries Herodotus's statement that the Persians learned pederasty from the Greeks (857C). Yet in denouncing it, Plutarch does not exactly contradict the claim, either. Instead, he tries to downplay the notion that the Persians adopted pederasty by insisting that Persians were already given over to the "licentiousness" (ἀκολασία, 857C) of castration well before they encountered the Greeks. Since Persians cannot, accordingly, "owe their education" in turpitude to the Greeks (857C), only someone φιλοβάρβαρος would dare say otherwise. Thus, whatever the flaws in Plutarch's logic, once the assumption of Herodotus's corrupt attitude is taken for granted, any aspect of the *Histories* can be psychologized according to the rubric.[61] It is not so much that Herodotus makes historical mistakes; it is more that he has particular *cognitive commitments* of which readers should be wary. From Plutarch we might conclude that nothing in Herodotus's work lacks motive—often nasty motive—and that the simplest of factual assertions cannot be read innocently, in much the way that passing details from Plutarch's *Lives* can be illustrative of more encompassing judgments of character.

A Philobarbaric *Life?*

The description of Herodotus as φιλοβάρβαρος may in fact have a deeper connection to Plutarch's idea of bad character than appears at first glance, and here we should refer to Plutarch's use of κακοήθεια terminology in one of his *Lives*. In the *Alcibiades*, a work with four instances of such phrasing, Plutarch seems to match the oscillations of Alcibiades's behavior with shifting applications of the term.[62] At one point, the narrator describes "some insult or maliciousness" (διαβολή τις ἢ κακοήθεια, 12.1) on Alcibiades's part that generated much gossip (πλείονα λόγον παρέσχε, 12.1), namely, his promising to purchase a chariot for his friend Diomedes to use at Olympia, only then to list the chariot under his own name. Later the term shifts to Alcibiades's perception of the proposal by the Athenian *demos* to allow him to venture forth

---

[61] See Marincola 1994: 202 for a similar point about Plutarch's stress on the utter pervasiveness of Herodotus's bad character. See also Plutarch's bald assertion regarding the malicious spirit of delight, even schadenfreude (ἐπιχαιρεκακία, 858B), that Herodotus assumes toward his characters' misfortunes. Such schadenfreude is elsewhere more generally grouped with envy and ill spirit (*On Being a Busybody* 518C).

[62] With its four references, the *Alcibiades* has the highest number of occurrences of such κακοήθεια terminology among all the *Lives*: *Alc.* 12.1, 19.7, 24.5, 41.1 (= *synk.* 2.1).

PARALLEL AUTHORS 129

on the Sicilian Expedition but stand trial upon his return: "The ill will behind their delay did not escape Alcibiades" (οὐκ ἐλάνθανε μὲν οὖν ἡ κακοήθεια τῆς ἀναβολῆς τὸν Ἀλκιβιάδην, 19.7). Plutarch's use of the term in this context to describe Alcibiades's view of the people's lack of good faith balances the earlier characterization of the popular talk of Alcibiades's ill will.[63]

But the climactic use of such language, and the most relevant here for purposes of comparison, comes later in the *Alcibiades*, when the protagonist, on the heels of the failure of the Sicilian Expedition and increasingly loathed at Sparta (24.2), seeks asylum among the Persians. By now, readers will recognize how carefully Plutarch has crafted the *Life* so as to make Alcibiades's reception among the Persians seem like the inevitable result of his own fickleness and propensity for luxury. In this context, the appearance of κακοήθης is pointed:

By all means possible he avoided coming into the hands of the Spartans, but for his own safety gave himself up to Tissaphernes, satrap of the King, and was soon enough in preeminent and preferred position with him. For it was the case that this barbarian marveled at his versatility and the remarkable nature of his cleverness, for Tissaphernes himself was not a plain dealer but an ill-spirited man, and a friend to the wicked. (*Alc.* 24.4–5)

τὸ δ᾽ εἰς χεῖρας ἰέναι παντάπασιν ἔφευγε, Τισσαφέρνῃ δὲ τῷ βασιλέως σατράπῃ δοὺς ἑαυτὸν ὑπὲρ ἀσφαλείας, εὐθὺς ἦν παρ᾽ αὐτῷ πρῶτος καὶ μέγιστος. τὸ μὲν γὰρ πολύτροπον καὶ περιττὸν αὐτοῦ τῆς δεινότητος, οὐκ ὢν ἁπλοῦς, ἀλλὰ κακοήθης καὶ φιλοπόνηρος, ἐθαύμαζεν ὁ βάρβαρος.

Tissaphernes recognizes in his new friend a kindred spirit. Plutarch goes on (24.6) to highlight the fact that Tissaphernes, "although in every other way uncouth and most vociferous in his hatred of Greeks, so thoroughly gave himself over to the flatteries of Alcibiades as to surpass him in reciprocal flattery."[64] At this juncture in the *Life*, the person with whom Alcibiades feels most comfortable is a man noted for being "not a plain dealer" but rather "an

---

[63] The capacity of this *Life* in particular to present equivocal material and to require of the reader various instances of reanalysis in light of what has come earlier has been noted; see Duff 1999: 229–40; Duff 2011: 71–72.

[64] τἆλλα γοῦν ὠμὸς ὢν καὶ μισέλλην ἐν τοῖς μάλιστα Περσῶν ὁ Τισσαφέρνης οὕτως ἐνεδίδου τῷ Ἀλκιβιάδῃ κολακευόμενος, ὥσθ᾽ ὑπερβάλλειν αὐτὸς ἀντικολακεύων ἐκεῖνον.

130   HERODOTUS AND IMPERIAL GREEK LITERATURE

ill-spirited man, and a friend to the wicked."[65] Tissaphernes seems to recognize in Alcibiades's polytropic ways someone equally lacking in straightforwardness. Furthermore, the pointed reuse of the κακοήθης term, echoing its initial appearance in describing Alcibiades, now links the label with clichés of Persian waywardness, after first associating it with one of the more ambivalent figures in Plutarch's *Lives*. It confirms the term's use in the *Alcibiades* as relating to problems of seeming versus being, to the failure of simplicity and a lack of plain dealing.[66] Finally, in a gesture of stereotypical orientalizing, Plutarch furthers this association of κακοήθεια and non-simplicity by conveying at some length Tissaphernes's opulence—evident in his elaborately decked (περιττῶς) garden named "Alcibiades" (24.5). He is indeed not a simple man (οὐκ ὢν ἁπλοῦς) in more ways than one.

That the character of this explicitly labeled "barbarian" is complicated in all the wrong ways can be looped back to Plutarch's assessment of Herodotus. Plutarch's indictment of Herodotean complication, his only *seeming* to be straightforward (ἀφελής . . . μιμούμενον καὶ ἁπλότητα, 854E), indicates in this wider context his own barbarism, playing off the stereotype of the simple Greeks and the luxury-loving Persians.[67] Likewise, Plutarch's remark on Herodotus's servility (ἀνελευθερίαν, 856C) to his bad character vaguely replays the stereotype of "free" Greeks and "servile" Persians. The Halicarnassian's bad character not only disposes him poorly toward Greek achievement, but his lack of simplicity and freedom actually renders him less Greek, more (*philo*)*barbaros*.

Psychologizing in the *Lives*

Among the features distinguishing Plutarchan biography from its ancient parallels is Plutarch's tendency to enter his subjects' minds.[68] While overt

---

[65] Compare *Alc.* 41.1/*synk.* 2.1 for the characterization of Alcibiades's malice in contrast to Marcius Coriolanus's being a "straightforward" man (ἁπλοῦς). Compare Plutarch's use of this term to describe Antony (24.9), with Pelling 1988b. ad loc., noting that ἁπλοῦς is "not pejorative (it is not 'simple-mindedness')."

[66] See Plato, *Resp.* 347e–349b.

[67] On Plutarch's own multifaceted attitudes toward non-Greek peoples of the East, see Pelling 2016: 48: "Foreigners and foreign culture offer him a repertoire of possibilities and thought-prompts, and the issue should not be reduced to a single, monolithic 'what Plutarch thinks.'"

[68] This claim is not without controversy, and the extent to which the *Lives* psychologize their subjects (or whether they do so at all) forms a topic of debate; see Nikolaidis 2014: 353–54, with bibliography. Compare Jones 1982: 963, who concludes that Plutarch "in some ways . . . anticipates not so much objective biography of the eighteenth and nineteenth centuries as the psychological biography

PARALLEL AUTHORS 131

psychologizing features less prominently than seemingly "straight" narrative, narrative choices themselves carry psychological implication. Moreover, various irruptions of psychologizing assumption on the part of the Plutarchan narrator (and of internal characters) encourage the reader to supply motives where none is clearly articulated.[69]

Let us take two examples in which Plutarch appears to enter characters' minds. In a passage from *Alexander* devoted to the protagonist's personal traits (*Alex.* 42), part of a longer digression (38–42) on Alexander's nature (φύσις, 39), Plutarch interrupts the chronological flow to offer general remarks. Most of Plutarch's observations in this section depend upon an action Alexander has taken or a comment he has made, which is then used to substantiate a claim about Alexander's nature. But Plutarch looks to the future, using the pause to indicate, proleptically, a negative shift in Alexander's behavior:

> But later the many accusations coarsened him and caused him to give credence to the false ones because so many were true. And especially when he was spoken of badly, he lost his cool and was cruel and implacable, since (ἄτε) he had a love for glory more than for life or his kingdom. (*Alex.* 42.3–4)[70]

The conjunction ἄτε typically indicates the speaker's avowal of the stated cause. This gives the concluding remark extra punch. Plutarch, in the midst of a series of comments about characteristics he can tie to action or word,

---

of the twentieth." On the whole, I stand by Russell's claim that Plutarchan biography is more psychologically ambitious than many of its sources and antecedents; see Russell 1995: 87: "Two types of modification [from Plutarch's source material, especially history-writing] seem to be specially significant. One is the attribution of motives of an emotional kind, where the historian deals rather in expediency and rational calculation. . . . The other is the attribution of public or communal action to the hero's own initiative." See further Russell 1963: 23 on Plutarchan retrojecting, with Pelling 1990b, esp. 226–35, with an eye to Plutarch's psychological attribution (thus, "inferring," 226), even if, as Pelling concedes, Plutarch cannot be said to be interested in "psychological *understanding*" (229, emphasis in original) of "characters [who] are clearly very different from the more complex figures which modern writers like to develop" (237). For background on ancient and modern assumptions of (biographic) character, see Dihle 1956: 76–81; Halliwell 1986: 149–52.

[69] On rendering moral judgments in the *Lives*, a task often reliant on a perception of psychological insight, see Duff 2011, esp. 64–65 on direct narratorial intervention to make a moral point, 66–67 on internal characters' moral judgements, 68–75 for the reader's moral judgment.

[70] ἀλλ᾿ ὕστερόν γ᾿ αὐτὸν ἐξετράχυναν αἱ πολλαὶ διαβολαί, διὰ τῶν ἀληθῶν πάροδον <καὶ> πίστιν ἐπὶ τὰ ψευδῆ λαβοῦσαι, καὶ μάλιστα κακῶς ἀκούων ἐξίστατο τοῦ φρονεῖν καὶ χαλεπὸς ἦν καὶ ἀπαραίτητος, ἄτε δὴ τὴν δόξαν ἀντὶ τοῦ ζῆν καὶ τῆς βασιλείας ἠγαπηκώς. The passage at 42 perhaps brings back to our attention Plutarch's original stated interest in "the signs of the soul" (τὰ τῆς ψυχῆς σημεῖα, *Alex.* 1.3) mentioned in the work's prologue, on which see Duff 1999: 14–22; Duff 2014: 339–40.

132   HERODOTUS AND IMPERIAL GREEK LITERATURE

appears to sneak in a deduction that speaks to Alexander's broader character.[71] On one level, Plutarch's analysis of Alexander, coming as it does so late in the *Life*, allows for a retroactive kind of reading by which the audience is invited, based on the evidence he has given, to affirm his conclusion.[72] At the same time, the statement offers a thesis for which the rest of the *Life* may provide proof, the same kind of "routine" generalization in which Plutarch's hand has been recognized and for which the details of various *Lives* may or may not offer satisfactory support.[73] Plutarch has shown us the *sort* of character Alexander may have been (e.g., μεγαλοδωρότατος, 39, among other things), as represented through various actions. But the fact that Plutarch explicitly psychologizes about his "love" (ἠγαπηκώς) for reputation marks a departure from descriptions of external action and connects the hermeneutic tactics of this *Life* with those we have seen in the *Malice*, in which apparently external facts become keys to psychological insight.

But the topic of character remains slippery. As Stephen Halliwell notes, in a discussion of ἦθος in the *Poetics*, Aristotle does not present an idea of psychological inwardness and concealment, which Halliwell describes as features of the modern novel. Character, at least in the *Poetics* (though Halliwell makes the case for its being consistent in Aristotle), is always "a specific moral factor in relation to action, not a vague or pervasive notion equivalent to modern ideas of personality or individuality." Furthermore, character must involve "the *manifestation* of moral choice in word or action ([*Poet.*] 50b 8, 54a 18)."[74] At *Alex.* 42, we see a form of "manifestation" (e.g., when maligned, Alexander became cruel), but we also get something slightly more in the ἅτε clause: a

---

[71] Compare Pelling 1990b: 228 on Plutarch's treatment of *Coriolanus* at 4.5–8, where Plutarch's psychological intervention vis-à-vis his Dionysian source leads Pelling to conclude, "[I]s Plutarch not really trying *to get inside Coriolanus' skin*, to work out why he acted in a way which was so distinctive, and to relate it to what was individual in his personal background?" (emphasis added). See also the remark of Duff 2011: 65 n. 18: "where we might expect Plutarch to make a comment on an *action*, he often speaks in terms of *character*: so, when Perseus surrenders to the Romans Plutarch comments, 'At that time he made it clear that his love of life was a more ignoble evil in him than his love of money' (*Aem.* 26.7)" (emphasis in original). See also *Cam.* 1.4 and *Aem.* 2.6, with Duff 2011: 65.

[72] See Wilamowitz's comment (1995 [1922]: 70) contrasting Plutarch with Hellenistic biography: "This is one of Plutarch's positive features, that he does not try to label his characters with one description or another, but even so he does not even consider the possibility of tracing their development" (70). The latter half of this statement is too strong: the passage from *Alexander* explicitly points to a shift in character, and while still perhaps falling short of "tracing" the "development" of his behavior, it nonetheless does not quite fit Wilamowitz's assertion. For the sense that readers *can* trace development in Alexander, and are encouraged to read critically, see Duff 2011: 70, contrasting *Alex.* 14.6–7 with the preceding material at *Alex.* 11–13.

[73] The phrasing is that of Pelling 1990b: 227.

[74] Halliwell 1986: 149–52, quotations at 151–52, emphasis in original. For continuity of ἦθος in Aristotle, see Halliwell 1986: 152 and his n. 21.

PARALLEL AUTHORS 133

"pervasive notion" in the general psychologizing claim that Alexander "loved his reputation more than his life or his kingdom." Should this count as an idea of personality or individual identity? Perhaps not, since many people can prioritize reputation, and personality ought to be more specific and distinctive. Yet Plutarch's comment here is used to *explicate* the characteristic reaction to being maligned: Alexander was cruel in response to criticism *because* he had a love of glory. While this may still not measure up to a modern idea of a complex personality, it nonetheless seems that Plutarch is working with some notion of psychological inwardness, a predisposition that is in fact "vague" and "pervasive" enough to manifest itself in a variety of ways. It is not merely in actions but also in their being narrativized by Plutarch's biographies that these predispositions become manifest. Biography is the site of potentially generalizable psychological insight, in which actions are explained according to suppositions of ἦθος.

Before returning to Plutarch's sense of Herodotus's ἦθος and how it becomes manifest, let us consider one further example of Plutarch's psychologizing, this time from a passage in his *Aristides* in which he mixes historical and psychological assertions:

> Aristides kept to himself just as he kept to his own path, as it were, in politics. First of all, he did not want to join with his colleagues in unjust action, nor did he want to irritate them by refusing to show them favor. Moreover, since he saw that power emanating from friends incited not a few toward wrongdoing, he guarded himself against it, holding the belief that the good citizen should feel confidence only in doing and saying what is serviceable and just. (*Aristides* 2.5)[75]

Plutarch again makes telling choices in presuming to speak for what Aristides did or did not want (βουλόμενος) or what he perceived and believed (ἰδών, ἀξιῶν; see also *Arist.* 3.2, ἡγούμενος). To be sure, the statements here are rather anodyne ascriptions of uprightness. But the mechanism of attribution exemplifies Plutarch's psychologizing propensity, not only in deducing character from deeds but also in proposing broader insights into his protagonist's point of view, offering readers a code by which deeds not

---

[75] Ἀριστείδης δὲ καθ' ἑαυτὸν ὥσπερ ὁδὸν ἰδίαν ἐβάδιζε διὰ τῆς πολιτείας, πρῶτον μὲν οὐ βουλόμενος συναδικεῖν τοῖς ἑταίροις ἢ λυπηρὸς εἶναι μὴ χαριζόμενος, ἔπειτα τὴν ἀπὸ τῶν φίλων δύναμιν οὐκ ὀλίγους ἰδὼν ἐπαίρουσαν ἀδικεῖν, ἐφυλάττετο, μόνῳ τῷ χρηστὰ καὶ δίκαια πράσσειν καὶ λέγειν ἀξιῶν θαρρεῖν τὸν ἀγαθὸν πολίτην.

134   HERODOTUS AND IMPERIAL GREEK LITERATURE

explicitly commented on by the narrator may still be tested. Plutarch gives us the example here of how we might interpret a particular action: he explains Aristides's just behavior in relation to that man's "observation" (ἰδών) about the nature of power that issues from friends. This is not a historical act or a recordable deed but rather an ascription of belief based on Aristides's own acts.

In both the *Alexander* and *Aristides* passages, then, Plutarch practices before (and encourages in) his reader habits of inference in line with the reading principles of the *Malice*. In turn, in the Herodotus essay, Plutarch sets up Herodotus as a character to be judged from his textual actions, as it were, transmuting to the realm of literary activity a notion of character as a manifestation of προαίρεσις in dramatic action. As in the *Lives*, where Plutarch surmises the disposition that informs his subjects' actions, Plutarch considers Herodotus's textual deeds as an avenue to his thoughts:[76]

> It would have been possible to enumerate even more characteristics of his bad character: but these suffice to give a mental impression of the man's purposeful choice and manner. (*dHM* 856D)

> ἦν δὲ καὶ πλείονας καταριθμεῖσθαι τῶν χαρακτήρων· ἀρκοῦσι δ᾽ οὗτοι κατανόησιν τἀνθρώπου τῆς προαιρέσεως καὶ τοῦ τρόπου παρασχεῖν.

The mention of Herodotus's προαίρεσις, his deliberate choice, elides into one realm the man's intellectual disposition and the corollary actions on which the reader may judge him.[77] As Halliwell states, regarding the concept of προαίρεσις, it "is not a casual ingredient in anything that people do or say, but a carefully delimited matter of conscious desire and intention, based on dispositions which are those of virtue and vice."[78] Moreover, as Halliwell goes on to say, "Ideally, of course, character and action go closely together. . . . But to make the firmest moral judgments we must be able to be sure of *prohairesis*."[79] Herodotus is accorded a kind of "writerly life" (see chapter 1) in which his own decision-making becomes manifest in (literary) deed.

Now, for Aristotle, not only is ἦθος linked to action in a seemingly linear fashion, but also (at *Poetics* 1450b8–9) ἦθος "makes clear" (δηλοῖ) the

---

[76] On this passage, see Roskam 2017: 166, who draws comparison to *Nicias* 1.5 (κατανόησιν ἤθους καὶ τρόπου).

[77] For the notion of writing as an elaboration of character, compare *Dem.* 8.3–4.

[78] Halliwell 1986: 151. See my chapter 1 on the concept in Dionysius.

[79] Halliwell 1986: 152 n. 21.

προαίρεσις behind the action (ἔστιν δὲ ἦθος μὲν τὸ τοιοῦτον ὃ δηλοῖ τὴν προαίρεσιν). But for Plutarch, Herodotus's manifestations of character are not readily transparent, and the assumption in Aristotle and the *Lives* about the capacity or necessity for ἦθος to be readable in action proves troubling for Plutarch's take on Herodotus. Some of Plutarch's metaphors early in the *Malice* reinforce the need for psychologizing in the dark. Plutarch likens κακοήθεια specifically to those making a guerrilla assault, "releasing their slanderous arrows from an unseen place" (ἐξ ἀφανοῦς βέλεσι χρώμενοι, *dHM* 856C). The ethical concern in the *Malice* involves psychologizing, to be sure, but the metaphors imply that an extra layer of penetration is required, too. Oblique (πλαγίως) arrows shot from the unseen (ἐξ ἀφανοῦς) imperil because they fail to play by the rules and instead show up sidelong, just as Plutarch says that Herodotus's wicked spirit resembles a wind that secretly slips through a narrow crack (ὥσπερ οἱ κρύφα διὰ στενοῦ παραπνέοντες ἄνεμοι, 855A)—not easily noticed, if noticed at all. Hence, rather than the revelation of character that the *Lives* propose through the narrativizing of deeds, Plutarch's *Malice* essay, although likewise giving an impression of Herodotus's general intellectual manner (κατανόησιν τἀνθρώπου τῆς προαιρέσεως καὶ τοῦ τρόπου παρασχεῖν, *dHM* 856D), must upend the usual interpretive game by seeing through an extra layer of deceit.

Finally, in connection with Plutarch's mention of Herodotus's προαίρεσις, we might refer to a passage from Plutarch's *Pericles*:[80]

> The good motivates activity toward itself and right away embeds an active urge, forming the spectator's character not through proper representation, but through his inquiry into the work it creates opportunity for deliberate choice. (*Per.* 2.4)

τὸ γὰρ καλὸν ἐφ᾽ αὑτὸ πρακτικῶς κινεῖ καὶ πρακτικὴν εὐθὺς ὁρμὴν ἐντίθησιν, ἠθοποιοῦν οὐ τῇ μιμήσει τὸν θεατήν, ἀλλὰ τῇ ἱστορίᾳ τοῦ ἔργου τὴν προαίρεσιν παρεχόμενον.

---

[80] See the comments of Duff 2011: 77 on this passage: "What Plutarch calls ἱστορία here probably refers both to the author's research and narrative and to the reader's own thoughtful analysis and reflection." The passage has also caused some difficulty of interpretation: see Duff 1999: 37–42; Van der Stockt 1992: 32–37. Nikolaidis 2014: 355 translates *proairesis* as "moral principle or choice" and construes as follows: "noble actions do produce an eagerness for imitation, but what molds and improves the character of the observer are the moral criteria he acquires, namely a determining *proairesis*, through the examination of these actions."

136 HERODOTUS AND IMPERIAL GREEK LITERATURE

Investigating the work of the good—especially the virtuous deeds depicted in the *Lives*—develops the observer's own προαίρεσις, that capacity for purposeful choice, much as Plutarch relates the banishment of bad character to the process of *historia* for his *Lives* (*Aem.* 1). Study of Herodotus's moral sensibility and the choices that issue from that sensibility should inform one's general disposition toward (narrating) the past. Plutarch's supposedly noble intervention enables comprehension (κατανόησις, 856D) of the man's deliberate choice, and it is implied that the readers of the *Malice*, as with those of the *Lives*, should accordingly develop their own moral sensibility in relation to the figure under examination.

Behavior beyond the Text

In the *Lives*, readers are urged toward judging deeds as manifestations of virtue and vice, while in the *Malice*, Herodotus's intellectual actions become his deeds. But is Herodotus responsible for other kinds of actions for which readers might judge him? In fact, the *Malice* provides two brief glimpses of Herodotean biographic behavior, specifically two charges of bribery.[81] According to the first, Herodotus received ten talents from the Athenians to flatter them: "That Herodotus accepted ten talents as a gift from the Athenians, on the decree of Anytus, comes from the writings of Diyllus, an Athenian man, whom people do not disregard with respect to his *historia*" (ὅτι μέντοι δέκα τάλαντα δωρεὰν ἔλαβεν ἐξ Ἀθηνῶν Ἀνύτου τὸ ψήφισμα γράψαντος, ἀνὴρ Ἀθηναῖος, οὐ τῶν παρημελημένων ἐν ἱστορίᾳ, Δίυλλος εἴρηκεν, 862B).[82] This charge of an activity unrelated to the textual "tokens of recognition" (γνωρίσματα, 855B) adds dimension to the more endoscopic assertions in Plutarch's treatise, while at the same time setting up a link between the act of bribery and Herodotus's otherwise more invisible intellectual operations.

As a consequence of the bribe, Herodotus is said to have given the Spartans an unfavorable write-up by emphasizing their lateness to Marathon.[83] The event of bribery generates a string of *adunata* dramatically addressed to the

---

[81] See Chrysanthou 2015: 34, who also notes Plutarch's charge of Herodotus's possible flattery of the wealthy Hipponicus (863B).

[82] See Beloe 1812: 7: "The citizens of Athens, not satisfied with heaping praises upon him, presented him with ten talents, which gift was solemnly ratified by a decree of the people." Beloe offers no citation, but it is probable he takes this from Eusebius, *Chronicle* 83.4. See also Bowen 1992 ad loc. 862B; Priestley 2014: 47, with her n. 114.

[83] See also [Dio] *Orations* 37.7 on Herodotus's alleged demand of a bribe from the Corinthians.

second-person Herodotus: "You move the full moon from the middle of the month to the beginning, throwing into confusion the heavens and its days and everything else; and you do all this while announcing that you write the history of Greece so that it shall not lack fame."[84] On the heels of the bribery charge, Plutarch's deployment of the second person and his subsequent hyperbolic description both focus and exaggerate the range of Herodotean misdeed. Herodotus takes bribes, but the depth of his venality has larger consequences: he can move the moon.[85]

Bribery recurs a few sections later. Here Plutarch cites Aristophanes of Boeotia for the detail that Herodotus solicits a bribe from the Thebans, only to be refused (864C–D), and for the story that Theban officials prevent him from conversing with Theban youth, supposedly "on account of their rusticity and anti-intellectualism" (δι' ἀγροικίαν αὐτῶν καὶ μισολογίαν, 864D). But Plutarch also notes that while "no further proof" for the rumors exists (ἄλλο μὲν οὐδέν ἐστι τεκμήριον, 864D), Herodotus himself bears witness (μεμαρτύρηκε) to the story in his false stories about and hostile treatment of the Thebans. In short, Plutarch does not need corroboration because the consequences of the rebuffed bribe and refused meeting with Theban youth are traceable within Herodotus's own text.[86] So while we again find a putative element of Herodotean biography informing Plutarch's literary-critical interpretation, we also see how in this instance, Plutarch can simultaneously cast evidentiary doubt on the tale while reinforcing it through his reading of the *Histories*.

All the same, "real-life" deeds of (attempted) bribery add texture to the broader set of accusations, in which malicious writing functions as Herodotus's primary (mis)deed.[87] Such negative exemplarity has its uses, too. Here we might invoke the biographer's prologue to *Demetrius*, one of the

---

[84] σὺ δὲ μεταφέρεις τὴν πανσέληνον εἰς ἀρχὴν μηνὸς ἐκ διχομηνίας, καὶ τὸν οὐρανὸν ὁμοῦ καὶ τὰς ἡμέρας καὶ πάντα πράγματα συνταράσσεις. καὶ τὰ τῆς Ἑλλάδος ἐπαγγελλόμενος γράφειν <ὡς μὴ ἀκλεᾶ γένηται> (861F–862A) ‖ ὡς μὴ ἀκλεᾶ γένηται add. Pearson ex Hdt.: lac. c. 20 litt. EB. See Bowen 1992: 101.

[85] Plutarch's use of the second person to address Herodotus picks up on a feature of Herodotean narrative (e.g., *Hist.* 1.139) to which Longinus was alert and which constituted an element of his sublimity, namely, Herodotus's apparent incorporation of the reader (see *De Subl.* 26.2, quoted in chapter 1). Cf. Trapp 2020: 99–100 on Aristides's apostrophizing of Plato.

[86] One wonders if Plutarch was himself uncomfortable with the *Histories'* own preoccupation with bribery (see, e.g., Hdt. 3.56 on Polycrates's alleged bribery of would-be Spartan invaders, the Euboeans' bribe of Themistocles at 8.4, and the Alcmaeonid bribery of the Delphic oracle in order to persuade the Spartans to overthrow the Peisistratids at Athens at 5.63 and 5.90) and responded by stressing Herodotus's place in the unsavory universe of subornation. I owe this point to Emily Greenwood.

[87] Recall that Plutarch describes Herodotus's omission of good and creditable material as an act (πρᾶγμα) in his list of *ichnê* (855D).

138 HERODOTUS AND IMPERIAL GREEK LITERATURE

more explicitly negative figures in Plutarch's *Lives*, and whose value Plutarch explicitly ties to counter-exemplarity:

> The arts that by use of reason proceed toward the purposeful choice and adoption of what is theirs, and toward avoidance and rejection of what is alien, contemplate some things for their own sake and purposefully, but other things incidentally, with the intent of avoiding them. (*Demetr.* 1.3)

> αἱ δὲ τέχναι μετὰ λόγου συνεστῶσαι πρὸς αἵρεσιν καὶ λῆψιν οἰκείου τινός, φυγὴν δὲ καὶ διάκρουσιν ἀλλοτρίου, τὰ μὲν ἀφ᾽ αὑτῶν καὶ προηγουμένως, τὰ δὲ ὑπὲρ τοῦ φυλάξασθαι κατὰ συμβεβηκὸς ἐπιθεωροῦσι.

The contrast between intent and randomness allows Plutarch to make the point that under the influence of reason (and thus in ideal circumstances), readers purposefully seek the good and incidentally (κατὰ συμβεβηκός) encounter what they ought to avoid.[88] Plutarch's writing the *Demetrius* indicates a belief in not suppressing the negative but rather using it to exemplify the good by contrast.[89] As he goes on to say:

> When men have conducted themselves without considered reflection, and have become visible for being no good in their exercise of power and great deeds, perhaps it is not for the worse if I introduce a couple of them into the examples of my *Lives*. . . . So it seems to me that we also will more eagerly wish to be observers and imitators of the better lives if we are not left devoid of inquiry into the base and blameworthy. (*Demetr.* 1.5–6)

> τῶν δὲ κεχρημένων ἀσκεπτότερον αὑτοῖς καὶ γεγονότων ἐν ἐξουσίαις καὶ πράγμασι μεγάλοις ἐπιφανῶν εἰς κακίαν, οὐ χεῖρον ἴσως ἐστὶ συζυγίαν μίαν ἢ δύο παρεμβαλεῖν εἰς τὰ παραδείγματα τῶν βίων. . . . οὕτω μοι δοκοῦμεν καὶ ἡμεῖς προθυμότεροι τῶν βελτιόνων ἔσεσθαι καὶ θεαταὶ καὶ μιμηταὶ βίων εἰ μηδὲ τῶν φαύλων καὶ ψεγομένων ἀνιστορήτως ἔχοιμεν.[90]

---

[88] On the prologue to the *Demetrius* specifically, see Duff 1999: 45–51.

[89] On the uses of negative material, see *How to Study Poetry* 18B. There the student must become accustomed, Plutarch argues, to praising not the deed represented but rather the *technē* of the representation, so long as it conveys adequately the subject at hand (εἰ μεμίμηται προσηκόντως τὸ ὑποκείμενον). On Plutarch's pedagogical and ethical approach to literature more broadly, see Van der Stockt 1992: 123–42, esp. 128–32; Morgan 1998: 147–49, 262–65; Cribiore 2001; Hunter and Russell 2011; Bowie 2014; Xenophontos 2016; Roskam 2017.

[90] Cf. *dHM* 854F, 855B, 856C, 872A for Herodotus's deployment of χράομαι. A public person can conduct a bad life, and a writer can conduct himself well or poorly.

PARALLEL AUTHORS   139

Plutarch proposes adding unfavorable instances into the "examples of my *Lives*" in order to increase his readers' zeal for imitating better ones. He proceeds to write a *bios* in which the protagonist manifests increasing corruption but is never wholly or uninterestingly bad. Again, the polyvalent use of a cognate of *historia* (ἀνιστορήτως) implies both that the morally informed should make inquiry into that which seems ignoble and that Plutarch's work as a critic and biographer can serve the writing of such narratives. In the case of the *Malice*, Herodotus's choice of subject is the exemplary deed, while his behavior on the page becomes coextensive with his life off the page. His bad character in both realms informs his counter-exemplary deeds, the incidental "other things" (*Demetr.* 1.5) that readers must contemplate as part of their reckoning with the larger good of the Persian Wars. Contemplation of the past thus requires multiple types of critical alertness.

Roundness of Character

Christopher Gill's definition of personality as individuation within a type, part of his wider appraisal of the tendency in antiquity to view character in moral terms, has been an influential (though not entirely uncontroversial) heuristic for understanding aspects of Plutarch's *Lives*.[91] Plutarch may openly declare that Demetrius, for instance, was "lustful, boozy, war-mongering, lavish" (*Demetr.* 1.7), but Demetrius's individual way of inhabiting these traits differs from the manner in which Antony, his *comparandum*, embodies these same traits.[92] His depravity is of a kind, but his way of living out that depravity is individual. Given the individual combination, where "lustful" (ἐρωτικοί) and "lavish" (μεγαλόδωροι) can mingle, Plutarch's depiction of Demetrius, though largely negative, nonetheless forms part of a decidedly mixed life, a matter to which he alludes in his quotation of the Platonic comment that "great natures show forth great vices just as they do great virtues" (καὶ κακίας μεγάλας, ὥσπερ ἀρετάς, αἱ μεγάλαι φύσεις ἐκφέρουσι, *Demetr.* 1.7).[93] The negative exemplum does not tell the whole story, and a reader's

---

[91] Gill 1983: 470–72; Gill 1990: 2–3. Gill distinguishes between modern biographies written from a "personality viewpoint" and Plutarch's "character viewpoint" (1983: 473). Compare Pelling 1990b, esp. 228–29, defending, pace Gill, a notion of personality in Plutarch's *Lives*. See also Pelling 1989: 231.

[92] On the issue of individuality and personality in the *Lives*, see the discussion of Nikolaidis 2014: 362–65.

[93] Compare *Ant.* 24.10 for Plutarch's description of Antony's decidedly mixed character, which seemed immoderate (ὑπερβάλλειν τὸ μέτριον) more for granting favors (χαριζόμενος) than for punishing people (κολάζων). See also Wardman 1974: 132–40 on character.

140 HERODOTUS AND IMPERIAL GREEK LITERATURE

deciding against vice is conducted in the context of a mixed *Life*. A clear statement in defense of representing admixture appears near the beginning of Plutarch's *Cimon*, in his discussion of Lucullus's statue:[94]

> In the same way, since it is difficult, or perhaps really impossible, to display a man's life as blameless and pure, writers must in the better parts round out the truth and as it were form a likeness of the man. Those errors and faults that either from some passion or from political necessity course along a man's career, these we should consider as moments of coming up short in some particular virtue rather than as the base products of some vice. We should not with excessive eagerness or with especial interest point them out in narrative, but we should act in a sense respectfully toward human nature, given that it provides no character whose excellence is unmixed or who in the category of virtue is completely without blame. (*Cim.* 2.4–5)

> οὕτως ἐπεὶ χαλεπόν ἐστι, μᾶλλον δ᾽ ἴσως ἀμήχανον, ἀμεμφῆ καὶ καθαρὸν ἀνδρὸς ἐπιδεῖξαι βίον, ἐν τοῖς καλοῖς ἀναπληρωτέον ὥσπερ ὁμοιότητα τὴν ἀλήθειαν. τὰς δ᾽ ἐκ πάθους τινὸς ἢ πολιτικῆς ἀνάγκης ἐπιτρεχούσας ταῖς πράξεσιν ἁμαρτίας καὶ κῆρας ἐλλείμματα μᾶλλον ἀρετῆς τινος ἢ κακίας πονηρεύματα νομίζοντας οὐ δεῖ πάνυ προθύμως ἐναποσημαίνειν τῇ ἱστορίᾳ καὶ περιττῶς, ἀλλ᾽ ὥσπερ αἰδουμένους ὑπὲρ τῆς ἀνθρωπίνης φύσεως, εἰ καλὸν οὐδὲν εἰλικρινὲς οὐδ᾽ ἀναμφισβήτητον εἰς ἀρετὴν ἦθος γεγονὸς ἀποδίδωσιν.

The exhortations here correspond to the faults for which Herodotus is blamed in some of the ἴχνη, including his gleeful (ἡδόμενος) digressions on human misfortune (855C) or his choosing an unfavorable account when more are available (855E). Herodotus could be said to dilate with "excessive eagerness" on the apparent "errors and faults" of various actors. But given Plutarch's own withering assessment of Herodotus, what are we to make of his apparently

---

[94] On the prologue to *Cimon*, see Duff 1999: 16, with bibliography; Duff 2014: 339. Jones 1971: 88 cites this passage and makes specific reference to the *Malice*: "In his essay on Herodotus, he [Plutarch] expounds a doctrine of historiography that preferred lenience to severity, patriotism to impartiality, optimism to pessimism." I disagree with Jones's next comments: "The *Lives* show the application of these principles. Faced with a fault in his hero, the biographer should treat it as an artist treated a blemish in his sitter's face, drawing as little attention to it as truth allowed" (88). Jones's view here diminishes the extent to which the *Lives* take a broad-minded approach to both the virtues and vices of their subjects. For a different view, compare Nikolaidis 2014: 357, 364–65: "His heroes are taken from real life, and therefore are not black or white personalities but display a mixture of qualities, good and bad." See also Stadter 2003–4: 90.

admirable reticence before the complicated quality of human nature? Does the *Malice* allow any room for thinking that Plutarch regarded Herodotus as not altogether "unmixed" (οὐδὲν εἰλικρινές), his vices not completely devoid of some saving grace?

At first glance, despite Plutarch's acknowledgment of human complexity and its mixture of good and bad, his concept of character seems rather more limited when it comes to his assessment of Herodotus. As Chris Pelling has written, describing Plutarch's "integrated" conception of character in the *Lives*:

> the differing elements of a character are regularly brought into some sort of relationship with one another, reconciled: not exactly unified, for a character cannot be described with a single word or category, is not a stereotype; but one element at least goes closely with another, and each element predicts the next.[95]

The rhetorical strategy of the *Malice*, however, must downplay readers' sense that Herodotus was possessed of a complex, individuated personality: he registers as but an extreme example of a *type*. Whatever complexity Plutarch allows him seemingly has to do with the variety of mechanisms by which he deceives. His lack of simplicity (ἁπλότης, 854E) inheres in his deceitful dexterity, much like the many-sided flatterer who is "neither simple nor 'one' but manifold and dappled" (οὐχ ἁπλοῦς οὐδ' εἷς ἀλλὰ παντοδαπός ἐστι καὶ ποικίλος, *De Am. et Ad.* 52B).

At the same time, although Herodotus is much reduced to a stock type, there passingly flashes a hint of something else. While portraying Herodotus in seeming monochrome, Plutarch tips his hand to the potential complexity of Herodotus's motives and fills out (ἀναπληρωτέον, *Cim.* 2.4) a possible reason for Herodotus's inconsistencies. As we have seen, Plutarch takes issue with Herodotus's moral equivocation in the *Histories*. Herodotus is accused of representing individuals and groups one way at one time and another way at another time. Per the apparently consistent Plutarch, Herodotus is inconsistent in his own moral assessments.[96] Such critique may appear at odds with the broader backdrop of Plutarch's own mixed presentation of problematic characters. In

---

[95] Pelling 1990b: 235. See, however, his point at 239, that it would be a "mistake to think that this was Plutarch's *reason* for the integration ... to make the extraction of morals more straightforward."
[96] See *dHM* 861A, 863E, 864A, 872A, with Baragwanath 2008: 9–33; Roskam 2017: 171–72 ("harmony is the work of virtue," 172); Kirkland 2019: 499–501.

142 HERODOTUS AND IMPERIAL GREEK LITERATURE

the *Lives*, implicit praise and blame are more changeable, while in the *Malice*, Plutarch seems to call for a rhetorically pristine history in which praise and blame are consistent and fair. But in one brief instance, we see Plutarch's alertness to the influence of Herodotus's biography and to the fact that it may not be exclusively ill will that generates Herodotus's varied presentations:

> He ought not to have stomped so hard on the Greeks who medized: after all, although he is thought by many to be Thurian, he has an attachment to Halicarnassus, whose people are Dorians. The people of Halicarnassus joined the march against the Greeks—and brought along their harem. (*dHM* 868A)

> ἔδει μὲν οὖν μηδὲ τοῖς μηδίσασιν Ἑλλήνων ἄγαν ἐπεμβαίνειν, καὶ ταῦτα Θούριον μὲν ὑπὸ τῶν ἄλλων νομιζόμενον αὐτὸν δὲ Ἁλικαρνασέων περιεχόμενον, οἳ Δωριεῖς ὄντες μετὰ τῆς γυναικωνίτιδος ἐπὶ τοὺς Ἕλληνας ἐστράτευσαν.

Plutarch alludes to Herodotus's potentially equivocal motivations. On one view, Herodotus can perhaps be thought to have a weakened sense of the pressures on Eastern Greeks who medized because his allegiances were to Thurii—that is, he was a non-participatory Western Greek of Athenian colonizing extraction. But Plutarch wants to reorient our view of Herodotus as, once again, a kind of liminal Greek, a φιλοβάρβαρος, if not an outright βάρβαρος. For his original attachment was to Halicarnassus, and hence to a city under the Persian rule that threatened Greece. The insult about the harem surely anticipates what from Plutarch's standpoint are Herodotus's inappropriately laudatory remarks on his "fellow citizen" Artemisia (πολῖτιν, 869F) and her actions in the war against the Greeks. While the feminizing, orientalist portraiture is reductive, shrinking Herodotus's motivations to those of geographic determinism, the mention of Thurii at the very least nods to Herodotus's other possible allegiances and motivations. Hence, in this quasi-biographical move, Plutarch manages to explain Herodotus as a writer who could both praise Athens (his views perhaps shaped as a member of an Athenian *apoikia*) and marvel at Artemisia's actions (as a Halicarnassian/compromised Greek/φιλοβάρβαρος). Compared with the charge of κακοήθεια, these explanations lend color to Plutarch's often undifferentiated venom. Even as Plutarch harangues Herodotus for his morally compromised, inconsistent treatment of particular cities and persons,

PARALLEL AUTHORS   143

attention to Herodotus's roving biography means acknowledging his potentially ambivalent fealties.

This one comment about Herodotus's personal background and its connection to his political allegiances says something about Herodotus's ability to slip between categories.[97] Herodotus is faulted, from Plutarch's chronological vantage, for failing to represent Greek unity. He fails to convey a consistency to Greek identity in the fashion Plutarch apparently thought to have existed during the Persian Wars—or needed to believe to have existed.[98] At the same time, notions of Greekness during Herodotus's time were, of course, no less constructed or fungible than at other times.[99] Herodotus's *Histories* captures a sense of flux more than a set of fixed allegiances and unities. In no small way, the work *creates* the unified sense of victory to which it gives witness. Although flux was no less true of Plutarch's time, the politics of projecting Greek unity had assumed new form. In some sense, even as Plutarch faults Herodotus for failing to square with the ideological necessities of his time, his passing comment on Herodotus's background acknowledges that Herodotus's own political situation was tangled. More than malice must have been at work in Herodotus's political worldview. This biographic detail nods en passant to a complex and rounder identity. Indeed, allowing for the role Herodotus's background may have played, in fact, creates a weird symmetry between Herodotus and Plutarch, whose own motives in the treatise are confessedly local ones in defending the Boeotians (854E) and whose own identity as a Greek living under Roman rule shaped his views of history's purposes.[100]

The Implicit *Synkrisis*

We read Plutarch's treatment of Herodotus already conditioned by Herodotus's proclamations of his narratorial responsibilities, and in our

---

[97] Pelling 2007: 155 indicates a different kind of Herodotean versatility when, in a separate line of argument, he writes that "Herodotus should seem much more than a simple 'source' for Plutarch's *Life* [of Themistocles]: he offers a *repertoire of possibilities*, one which Plutarch knew extraordinarily well, and assumed his audience knew well too; and an author whose themes and subtleties he thoroughly understood" (emphasis in original).

[98] On the complexities of commemorating the Persian Wars, see generally Yates 2019.

[99] On Plutarch's shaping of the past relation to his Roman present, see Swain 1996: 135–86. On Greekness and issues of Athenian identity and Herodotus and more broadly, see Connor 1993; Hall 1997; Allen 2003; Sourvinou-Inwood 2003; Thomas 2000; Thomas 2001a.

[100] On the extent to which Plutarch's views on Greek history, particularly the Persian Wars, may be relatable to his views of Rome, see generally Jones 1971; Gabba 1982. On Plutarch's Boeotian allegiances, see Ingenkamp 2016. Cf. Roskam 2017: 166–69.

144 HERODOTUS AND IMPERIAL GREEK LITERATURE

assessment of Plutarch, we evaluate *him* as ourselves conditioned by his moves in the essay: much as he felt entitled to take on Herodotus, so do we measure his authorial character vis-à-vis his own estimation of Herodotus. Against Herodotus's bad behavior Plutarch pits his own noble actions as critic. The two figures stand in constant, if implicit, contrast throughout the *Malice* essay. This falls in line with Plutarch's tendencies elsewhere to encourage his readers toward comparison and contrast in assessing different persons.[101] The contrast need not be announced, since the reader's work of making moral judgments, of deciding for and against, between and among, recurs as a defining feature of his corpus, as Timothy Duff has argued:

> This is exactly the sort of reader Plutarch expects in the *Lives*: engaged, reflective, critical. . . . They are also alert to complexities, subtleties and contradictions, as well as to allusions and references to earlier literature. When faced with morally or intellectually challenging material, they see this as an opportunity to flex their critical muscles.[102]

While there are times when Plutarch's Herodotus treatise crosses into the scurrilous, one surmises another way he may have wished his attacks to have been interpreted: as a close, thorough, scholarly engagement with Herodotus's text.[103] Earlier it was seen how Plutarch in fact engages in some clever footwork in misattributing characters' lines to Herodotus. Plutarch nonetheless wishes to convey the impression that he is steeped in Herodotus's text, and this emerges not only in his historical corrections but also in a series of sardonic appropriations by which Plutarch advances his critique, at times by redeploying Herodotus's own language and imagery.

In addition to the factual corrections, Plutarch demonstrates his careful absorption of the *Histories* and his (ostensibly) responsible acts of reading. Plutarch's tactics involve more than simply cut-and-paste quotation. Instead,

---

[101] On such comparison in the *Lives*, see Stadter 2000: 500–505, 507–9; Stadter 2003–4: 91–94; Duff 2011: 72–75. On taking sides in texts that present differing or equivocal views, see Duff 1999: 203–4, 268–69, 282–83; Pelling 2002b: 274–75; Duff 2011: 75. On Plutarch's authorial persona, see Pelling 1995: 207; Pelling 2002b: 277–78.

[102] Duff 2011: 81. Although Duff pinpoints the *Lives* in this quotation, the full context of his chapter derives a part of its argument from the *Moralia* as well (76–81), since Duff sees the kinds of readerly judgments called for in the *Lives* as of a piece with those of the *Moralia* (and vice versa).

[103] One may also consider the possibility that the extremism of Plutarch's argument implicitly calls on the active reader to supply an opposing viewpoint; see Duff 2011: 79–80, describing such a hypothetical procedure for *On the Fortune of Alexander* and *Were the Athenians More Glorious in War or in Wisdom?* See also Duff 1999: 245–48 for further instances in the *Moralia* where opposing arguments or exclusively one-sided presentations may be felt to provoke the reader's reflection.

he trains certain passages of Herodotus back upon his subject. While writers such as Lucian outwardly parody Herodotus for the outlandish, apparently fabulous aspects of his text, Plutarch's main frustration lies with Herodotus's account of the Persian Wars, rather than with his ethnographic eccentricities. But in the effort to show himself an alert reader of Herodotus, he can adapt such ethnographic details that otherwise do not bulk large in his treatise:

> Is it not possible to have Herodotus say the very thing that he has his Ethiopian say? Responding to the offer of perfume and purple clothing he is made to say: "Full of deceit are the Persian oils and full of deceit are the Persian clothes." So could one say to him: "Full of deceit are your sentences and full of deceit is the whole structure of Herodotus's *logoi*" . . . . (*dHM* 863D–E)

> ἆρ' οὖν οὐχ, ὅπερ αὐτὸς τὸν Αἰθίοπά φησι πρὸς τὰ μύρα καὶ τὴν πορφύραν εἰπεῖν, ὡς δολερὰ μὲν τὰ χρίματα δολερὰ δὲ τὰ εἵματα τῶν Περσέων ἐστί, τοῦτ' ἄν τις εἴποι πρὸς αὐτόν, ὡς δολερὰ μὲν τὰ ῥήματα δολερὰ δὲ τὰ σχήματα τῶν Ἡροδότου λόγων . . . .

Plutarch turns Herodotus's own language back on him to link a character suspicious of the Persians to Plutarch's own suspicion of the Persian-loving Herodotus.[104] That he effects his mordant joke with a passing detail of cross-cultural encounter from the *Histories* suits his purported authority as a reader of Herodotus: Plutarch can correct not just the big stories of the climactic battles but the apparently lesser details, too. A similar gesture appears in Plutarch's comment on Herodotus's (supposedly mendacious) treatment of Leonidas: "It is as though, just like Hippocleides standing upside-down on the table, kicking his legs in the air, Herodotus would 'dance away the truth' and say: 'Herodotus doesn't care!'" (καθάπερ Ἱπποκλείδης ὁ τοῖς σκέλεσι χειρονομῶν ἐπὶ τῆς τραπέζης, εἰπεῖν ἂν ἐξορχούμενος τὴν ἀλήθειαν· οὐ φροντὶς Ἡροδότῳ, 867B). Herodotus himself had reported (6.129.4) that "Hippocleides doesn't care" became a well-known phrase (ἀπὸ τούτου μὲν τοῦτο ὀνομάζεται). Plutarch makes a remark at Herodotus's expense by using the memorable phrase, and in so doing, he also flags his own engagement with Herodotus's claim at *Histories* 6.129.4: here is the catch-phrase, turned back on its source.

---

[104] See Irwin 2014: 27–42 for the ways in which the internal character of the Ethiopian king only apparently functions as a positive analogue for the inquiring/suspicious reader.

146   HERODOTUS AND IMPERIAL GREEK LITERATURE

Finally, in what may constitute another carefully layered joke at Herodotus's expense, Plutarch makes reference to the possible existence of "antipodean peoples," who "as some say . . . dwell on the other side of the world" (869C) and who, Plutarch quips, must have heard of Themistocles: "If there really are people on the other side of the world, as some say, living on the bottom of the world, I am certain that even they have heard of Themistocles and Themistocles's battle plan . . ." (869C).[105] Since it has been contended that Herodotus subscribed to a symmetrical theory of geography and possibly believed in the existence of Hyperboreans and Hypernotians, Plutarch's conditional about unseen peoples on opposite poles of the earth may coyly indict such gullibility.[106] That Plutarch's statement is written as a conditional likely forms part of the joke, echoing as it does *Histories* 4.36: "If there are Hyperborean people, there are others, too, who are Hypernotian." Even the improbable peoples on the far side of the earth, in whom Herodotus may have believed, have heard his false account. Plutarch thus intimates the foolishness of such quixotic beliefs in far-off peoples while also conveying an idea of himself as a sensitive reader, replaying through submerged imitation one of the Halicarnassian's more dubious comments.

The Ethical Reader, the Ethical Canon

Plutarch was surely aware that his attack on Herodotus had the potential to come off the wrong way, and early in the essay he invites readers to view his intervention positively, as that of a man standing up for his ancestors and for the truth (οἶμαι προσήκειν ἡμῖν, ἀμυνομένοις ὑπὲρ τῶν προγόνων ἅμα καὶ τῆς ἀληθείας, 854F). Plutarch sets out to restore dignity to what he sees as the Greeks' finest hour—their victory over the Persians centuries before—and to defend the local efforts that he believes Herodotus omitted or maligned.[107]

---

[105] εἰ γάρ εἰσιν ἀντίποδες ἡμῶν, ὥσπερ ἔνιοι λέγουσι, τῆς γῆς τὰ κάτω περιοικοῦντες, οἶμαι μηδ' ἐκείνους ἀνηκόους εἶναι Θεμιστοκλέους καὶ τοῦ Θεμιστοκλέους βουλεύματος. . . .

[106] On Hyperboreans and Hypernotians in Herodotus (and his later Hellenistic critics), see Priestley 2014: 111–18, esp. 113–14. See also Romm 1989. Both Priestley and Romm discuss the comment of Herodotus at 4.36. For Priestley, the passage at Herodotus 4.32–35 "suggest[s] he entertained the possibility of their [Hyperborean] existence" (114).

[107] On the importance of local elements in the essay and the defense of Boeotia's role in Persian Wars, see Wardman 1974: 192; Marincola 1994: 202; Ingenkamp 2016. As evidence of local pride in the Greek victory over Persia, see Fornara 1977: 58, doc. 59, the text of the "serpent-column" at Delphi denominating various groups by whom "the [Persian] war was fought." One group, the Tenians, was added at a

PARALLEL AUTHORS 147

These lofty aspirations aside, Plutarch's readers will have been provoked to read critically into Plutarch's own techniques, to locate them on a plane of acceptable hermeneutics. Is Plutarch not out of line in turning Hippocleides on his head again, in taking Herodotus to be a trickster-poet, in turning him into the very barbarian whom the Greeks had repelled? If the reader is to affirm the soundness of Plutarch's intentions, it seems necessary that a noble Plutarch be detected beneath his own text's harsh verbal surface. The ancient critical concern with the historian's character puts a special burden on the critic himself to project a good image by contrast.[108] The hermeneutics of the κακοήθεια essay fundamentally require readers to trust Plutarch and to connect the essay's principles of character discernment to those of Plutarch's *Lives*, thereby rendering the treatise of a piece with Plutarch's larger ethical program and tempering its vitriol.

Plutarch's implicit self-portrait as a trustworthy critic contributes to his wider invitation to join his cause. His attack on Herodotus goes against a man whom some regarded (ἀξιοῦσι) as the "panegyrist of Greece" (ὑφ᾽ οὗ κεκοσμῆσθαί τινες ἀξιοῦσι τὴν Ἑλλάδα, 867C). In passing through the text to its dark side, as it were, Plutarch's communal call to arms appeals directly to his readers in protecting not merely an aesthetic canon but also an ethical one: "Especially since Herodotus has abused Boeotians and Corinthians— while not checking himself from attacking anyone else—it falls upon us, in my view, to come to the rescue on behalf of both our ancestors and the truth" (μάλιστα πρός τε Βοιωτοὺς καὶ Κορινθίους κέχρηται μηδὲ τῶν ἄλλων τινὸς ἀπεσχημένος, οἶμαι προσήκειν ἡμῖν, ἀμυνομένοις ὑπὲρ τῶν προγόνων ἅμα καὶ τῆς ἀληθείας, 854F). The first-person plural is not simply a throwaway.[109] The reader and Plutarch are together called to an act of heroic exegesis, latent in the epic diction of the verb ἀμύνειν, in defending both forebears and the truth. Just as Herodotus had an ethical duty to record

---

later date, indicating that name recognition mattered and that various groups could revise the inscription; see further Yates 2019: 29–60. Plutarch's *Malice* similarly offers a kind of editorial on the past.

[108] Recall Dionysius's defense of his right to criticize Thucydides in his attempt to cast himself as lacking the κακοήθεια unsuited to a man of open-minded character (*Thuc.* 2.3). For discussions of Plutarch's balance between self-advertisement and self-effacement, see König 2011: 184, 187–95 (on Plutarch's *Table Talk*). See also Russell 1993: 436: "I would conclude that, both in Plutarch and in Horace, self-disclosure is in general an aspect of the teaching function of literature. . . . Only the hope of being useful justifies self-advertisement."

[109] Compare Duff 2014: 340, who notes that in the *Lives* prologues, "frequent use of first-person plurals . . . construct the readers as likewise learned, curious, and philosophically minded, sharing the same goals and attitudes as Plutarch." See Duff 2014: 339 on the importance of Plutarch's local connection to Chaeronea.

148 HERODOTUS AND IMPERIAL GREEK LITERATURE

accurately the events of the Persian Wars, so do Plutarch and his readers have an obligation to guard the canon of Greek history. But in the case of Herodotus, his canonicity cannot so much be denied as chastened and corrected. Indeed, Plutarch would have his reader believe that the canon's exemplarity function does not apply tout court to the authors whose works that canon embraces.[110] Plutarch's essay has the effect of putting an asterisk after Herodotus's name, marking him as special, his character and work an opportunity to guide readers through an instance of what Hunter has called Plutarch's "directed reading."[111]

Plutarch in essence summons his audience to help him reconstitute Greek history. In this process of calling on readers and establishing a reading community, he indirectly points to one of his own virtues: philanthropy for the reader, who without Plutarch—so his argument goes—would be hoodwinked by Herodotus.[112] For Herodotus "destroys" (διέλυσε) and "abuses" (διελυμήνατο, 861A) Greek accomplishments and "tosses everything into disarray" (πάντα πράγματα συνταράσσεις, 861F). Herodotus "darkens the deed" (ἠμαύρωκε πρᾶξιν, 866A) of heroic action and "robs Sparta of her wonderful victory and highly lauded success at Plataea" (ἀφείλετο τὴν ἀοίδιμον νίκην καὶ τὸ περιβόητον Πλαταιᾶσι κατόρθωμα τῆς πόλεως, 871E). These flourishes show that Herodotus does not simply write about but rather actually *affects* history by distorting memory.

The notion that Herodotus has so misrepresented the wars as to strip them of their archetypal moral fiber comes to a head at the very end of the essay:

What, in the end, remains from these contests that is glorious or great for the Greeks, if . . . Herodotus alone knows the truth, while all other humans, anyone who has ever heard tell of the Greeks, has been deceived by the tradition that these rightly accomplished events are outstanding achievements? (874A–B)

τί οὖν περίεστιν ἔνδοξον ἢ μέγα τοῖς Ἕλλησιν ἀπ' ἐκείνων τῶν ἀγώνων, εἰ . . . μόνος δὲ τἀληθὲς Ἡρόδοτος ἔγνω, τοὺς δ' ἄλλους ἅπαντας

---

[110] On this point, I am grateful for a conversation with Emily Greenwood.
[111] Hunter 2009: 190.
[112] See Pelling 2007: 151, with n. 26 on Plutarch's tendency to "generat[e] a sort of genial complicity with his audience."

PARALLEL AUTHORS 149

ἀνθρώπους, ὅσοι λόγον Ἑλλήνων ἔχουσιν, ἐξηπάτηκεν ἡ φήμη τῶν τότε κατορθωμάτων, ὡς ὑπερφυῶν γενομένων;

The tradition of achievements marks the common consensus from which Herodotus has deviated. Plutarch accuses Herodotus of intellectual self-isolation. So thoroughly idiosyncratic a view of Greek history—what for Plutarch (and for his reassured readers) ought to be a known and incontrovertible reality—means that Herodotus has placed himself outside the canon of which he is nominally a part. Herodotus may be part of an aesthetic canon (recall the concession to his smooth style in the work's first sentence), but he is emphatically not a member of Plutarch's ethical canon, a belief that Plutarch expresses with his own aesthetic flourish:

> No doubt, these things [i.e., charm of narrative, sweetness of style] both bewitch and mislead everyone, but as in roses we must mind the rose-beetle, so must we guard against Herodotus's slander and abuse, cloaked as they are in smooth and soft appearances . . . . (874B–C)

> ἀμέλει ταῦτα καὶ κηλεῖ καὶ προσάγεται πάντας, ἀλλ᾽ ὥσπερ ἐν ῥόδοις δεῖ κανθαρίδα φυλάττεσθαι τὴν βλασφημίαν αὐτοῦ καὶ κακολογίαν, λείοις καὶ ἁπαλοῖς σχήμασιν ὑποδεδυκυῖαν . . . .

Note the irony that Plutarch, now as his own γραφικὸς ἀνήρ (cf. 874B), here criticizes another by means of a stylish metaphor.[113] For all of Plutarch's criticism of Herodotus's charm, seductive prose likewise supplies Plutarch with one of his own persuasive powers. But the reader's encounter with Plutarch is meant to encourage the assumption that, in his case at least, the aesthetic sonorities correspond to an ethical wholeness. In *On the Malice of Herodotus*, Plutarch is both the bee attracted to the rose for what he can *usefully* extract from it and the astute gardener who eliminates the beetle.

In an oration on Homer, Plutarch's contemporary Dio Chrysostom contrasts the relative degree of narratorial presence with that of other authors. Homer "does not refer to himself in his poetry" (μηδὲ ἐν τῇ

---

[113] On this passage, see Van der Stockt 1992: 132, with n. 44 on Plutarch's tendency to "compare literature with flowers." See also Morgan 1998: 262–64, esp. 263: "They [bees] suggest that not only should he [the educated reader] be busy, useful and virtuous; he should also direct his activity at the common good and live in harmony with his society."

150 HERODOTUS AND IMPERIAL GREEK LITERATURE

ποιήσει αὐτοῦ μνησθῆναι, *Or.* 53.9), in stark contrast to all other writers (τῶν ἄλλων ἁπάντων, 53.9), in particular Hecataeus, Herodotus, and Thucydides (53.10). For his part, Homer was so "broad-minded and intellectually generous as never to be obvious in referring to himself" (οὕτως ἄρα ἐλευθέριος ἦν καὶ μεγαλόφρων ὥστε οὐδαμοῦ φανήσεται τῆς ποιήσεως αὐτοῦ μεμνημένος, 53.10), speaking instead "from the invisible" (ἐξ ἀφανοῦς, 53.10). This last phrase, ἐξ ἀφανοῦς, marking in Dio a virtuous space associated with prophets and gods, takes us right back to where we began this chapter, with Plutarch's detective operation against the hidden Herodotus, who operates from the shadows (ἐξ ἀφανοῦς, 856C). What in Dio marks Homer's modesty and self-deprecation designates for Plutarch the very tactic by which Herodotus deceives. The apparent (φανήσεται) self-assertiveness by which Dio characterizes authors such as Herodotus and Thucydides ironically turns out to be the problem for Plutarch, who sees Herodotus's overt narratorial presence as a ruse. Herodotus is manifest but also hidden. Dio states that Homer's life deserves more praise than his poetry (τὸν βίον ἐπαινέσαι τις ἂν τοῦ ἀνδρὸς πολὺ μᾶλλον τῆς ποιήσεως, 53.9), but for Plutarch's Herodotus, the issue turns out contrariwise: the life hidden in the work merits censure.

I have argued that Plutarch's *On the Malice of Herodotus* functions as part of Plutarch's larger ethico-literary program. Like a *Life*, the work focuses its audience on the perception of Herodotus's character. It psychologizes his actions. It seeks to typify him according to certain categories of behavior. And, however superficially, it glances at the mixed motivations that Herodotus's own background may have engendered. In some sense, then, the *Malice* inclines readers to accept the Herodotean narrator's success at conveying an idea of himself. His irrepressible presence becomes that which Plutarch wishes to repress—or, rather, to hyperbolize, all the better to serve his own self-differentiation. For in the end, Plutarch's kinetic reception treats Herodotus appropriatively: it constructs Herodotus's character negatively against a canvas of critical expectation, but it does so ultimately to demonstrate Plutarch's own sound *ethos*. Plutarch's act of criticism rings antiphonally with the life he harangues, refracting through contrast his own alert probity in unveiling the hidden Herodotus. By showing how Herodotus fails to represent character, especially his own—and by associating his multiplicity of character with stereotypes of barbaric non-simplicity—Plutarch allows parallel visions of authorship to emerge: Herodotus is figured negatively as an ambiguous and morally dubious fabricator, while Plutarch is seen as an author who responsibly transmits and preserves tradition. And yet, however clear Plutarch wishes it to be, that tradition is not without its opacities. In fact, as we shall see in chapter 4, Plutarch's aforementioned contemporary Dio makes rich use of Herodotean ambiguity in his own activation of the past's filterings into the present.

4

Hellenism in the Distance

Herodotean Fringes in Dio Chrysostom's *Borystheniticus*

In previous chapters, we have seen how Dionysius and Plutarch fixate overtly on the character of Herodotus. In this chapter, I turn to Dio Chrysostom, a writer who conducts a rather different, more implicit mode of reception, in which reference to Herodotus is largely oblique. Dio's lone direct remark on Herodotus comes from a letter on public speaking (*Or.* 18), in which, surveying ancient models, he sounds a programmatic grace note on Herodotean ambiguity:[1]

> Now on to Herodotus: if ever you are in need of good cheer, you will read him with much contentment. For the relaxed quality and charm of his narrative will leave you with the suspicion that his composition is more story than history. (*Or.* 18.10)

> Ἡροδότῳ μὲν οὖν, εἴ ποτε εὐφροσύνης σοι <δεῖ>, μετὰ πολλῆς ἡσυχίας ἐντεύξῃ. τὸ γὰρ ἀνειμένον καὶ τὸ γλυκὺ τῆς ἀπαγγελίας ὑπόνοιαν παρέξει μυθῶδες μᾶλλον ἢ ἱστορικὸν τὸ σύγγραμμα εἶναι.[2]

Dio's passing comment offers an aperçu onto Herodotean slipperiness: does reading Herodotus lead to the suspicion (ὑπόνοια) that a putatively serious work is actually just so much fabulism (μυθῶδες)? Or is Dio saying that one acquires from Herodotus the impression (taking the word ὑπόνοια differently) of an author who writes about serious things but in a manner so

---

[1] Ancient critics routinely offered what were effectively annotated syllabuses of worthy authors in various genres; compare, e.g., Cicero's *Brutus*, Dionysius of Halicarnassus's *Letter to Gnaeus Pompey*, Quintilian's *Institutio Oratoria* Book 10. See also the comment of Dio's Loeb editor J. W. Cohoon (1939: 209) on the relatively stable canon of names: "The fact that there are no great divergences in these lists gives the impression that there was general agreement in the ancient schools as to which were the best authors for students." On Dio's general belief in the morally improving effects of reading history, including its capacity to curb arrogance and to enable the bearing of misfortune, see *Or.* 18.9, with Hau 2016: 1–2.

[2] For Dio's text, I follow von Arnim 1962 [1893–1896], unless otherwise indicated.

Herodotus and Imperial Greek Literature. N. Bryant Kirkland, Oxford University Press. © Oxford University Press 2022.
DOI: 10.1093/oso/9780197583517.003.0005

HELLENISM IN THE DISTANCE 153

disarmingly pleasant (τὸ γὰρ ἀνειμένον καὶ τὸ γλυκύ) as to slip his own grav-
itas under the radar? Are we, in other words, reading storytelling disguised
as something serious or something serious dressed up as storytelling? Either
way, the fact that the author in question provides good cheer and content-
ment may cloud one's judgment. The ambivalence generated by Herodotus
will, as this chapter attempts to show, prove useful to Dio in one of his most
virtuosic and allusively Herodotean orations, the so-called *Borystheniticus*
(*Or.* 36). In his reception of Herodotus, the author who generates ὑπόνοια,
Dio will emerge as both an imitator of tradition and a continuator of its
ambiguities.

Dionic Masks

But before turning to *Borystheniticus*, it may be helpful to note some features
of Dio's literary persona more generally, especially as they connect to his
Herodoteanism. Dio's solitary observation on Herodotus could well apply
to himself, as the golden-mouthed orator has long been recognized as a
deft narrator whose moral seriousness comes swathed in smooth prose not
without its own sweetness.[3] As with Dio's Herodotus, the Prusan is sometimes a writer easier to read than to interpret.[4] Given his own ability to say
potentially serious and weighty things under a patina of smoothness, then, it
should not surprise us to find the strong presence of Herodotus inflecting his
corpus. Indeed, at the level of language and syntax, Dio's Herodoteanism has
seemed patent to some; witness C. G. Cobet's assertion that "Dio studied no
other writer more carefully than Herodotus, traces of whom are everywhere
in his corpus."[5] Similarly, at a more granular level, Daniel Penick concluded
that Dio's use of "coordinate clauses joined by coordinate particles, especially

---

[3] See Whitmarsh 2001b: 216: "[E]lusiveness and tricksiness are the central components of the
Hellenic tradition he affects to emblematize." On Dio as a kind of fraud who peddled a misleading
public persona, see Moles 1978; Moles 1995: 192. For an overview of Dio's interpretation and reception, see Swain 2000b: 16–48. Already for Philostratus, Dio was a conundrum, his undecidability well
conveyed in the memorable quip put into the mouth of Trajan, who, addressing Dio, declares, "I do
not understand what you say, but I love you as I love myself" (τί μὲν λέγεις, οὐκ οἶδα, φιλῶ δὲ σε ὡς
ἐμαυτόν, *VS* 488 = 8.19); see Whitmarsh 1998: 206–10.

[4] See Porter 2001: 88: "Dio's own sympathies, and the identity he broadcasts and performs, are as
elusive as those he describes."

[5] Cobet 1877: 98: *nullum alium scriptorem Dio diligentius lectitavit quam Herodotum, cuius ubique
apud eum sunt vestigia.*

154 HERODOTUS AND IMPERIAL GREEK LITERATURE

in narrative passages, is due to the influence of the one master in such prose composition, Herodotos."[6]

This seemingly cosmetic effect of sounding like the past, in fact, constitutes part of a deeper effort at connection with both Herodotus and other writers.[7] Indeed, as is typical of other Imperial authors, Dio's habit inclines toward what one might call celebrity sourcing: even if aspects of Herodotus reach Dio already mediated through, say, an Onesicritus or a Strabo, the imitative culture regnant among Imperial Greeks accorded cachet to returning to (and sounding like) an original authorial *Quelle*, as intimated in Cobet's comments on Dio's language.[8] If the passage at *Or.* 18.10 is any guide, Dio's own overt encouragement to study Homer, Herodotus, Plato, and others means that we do well to measure the effects of various, specifically classical intertextual presences in his corpus, even as we are bound to acknowledge epigonal transmission. Dio's concern with celebrity sourcing relates to audience, too, to the "cognitive import of imitation," as Gadamer calls it:

> When a person imitates something, he allows that he knows it to exist and to exist in the way he knows it. . . . He intends that what he represents should exist, and if something is to be guessed, then this is it. We are supposed to recognize what it "is."[9]

Dio will have wanted to layer his works with the texts that readers were likely to have "guessed" and to have "recognized," playing to what Aristotle famously describes as the pleasure of such recognition (*Poetics* 1448 b16–18): "For this reason they enjoy seeing the likenesses, since it happens that as they look they learn and surmise what each is, for example, 'This is thus-and-such.' "[10] Similar to what I will characterize in chapter 5 as Lucian's projected reification as a new Herodotus, fantasized through a theatrical moment of recognition, Dio's allusive art depends on gambits of legitimation that

---

[6] Penick 1902: 9. On Dio's Herodotean vocabulary and syntax, including a close analysis of Dio, *Or.* 77/78.32, see Penick 1902: 8–10. Although language is not under the interpretive microscope of this chapter, what Cobet and Penick both recognized in Dio's consistent evocation of the Herodotean linguistic surface puts us on solid ground for tracking other Herodotean *vestigia*.

[7] Compare, e.g., Dio's engagement with Plato, in both style and substance; see Trapp 2000.

[8] On this type of imitation, see Anderson 1993: 69–85, 103–5. Compare Most 2011: 168 on Nicolaus of Damascus's reliance upon "a few older authoritative historians belonging (more or less) to the fifth and fourth centuries as sources rather than upon the numerous more recent and accurate ones."

[9] Gadamer 1975 [1960]: 117–18.

[10] διὰ γὰρ τοῦτο χαίρουσι τὰς εἰκόνας ὁρῶντες, ὅτι συμβαίνει θεωροῦντας μανθάνειν καὶ συλλογίζεσθαι τί ἕκαστον, οἷον ὅτι οὗτος ἐκεῖνος. Cited also by Gadamer 1975 [1960]: 170 n. 18.

HELLENISM IN THE DISTANCE   155

demand recognition from the listener/reader who senses when "this is that" (οὗτος ἐκεῖνος).[11] To read Dio and his audience along the presumed horizon of expectations to which each of them was playing, we must take seriously that Dio encourages his readers to engage with certain past writers because *he* had. Alongside his intertextual layering stands the fact that, as John Moles concluded on more than one occasion, Dio's autobiographic strategies, so to speak, are often sublimated to form, his "life" evocative of (if also subtly different from) various philosophical precursors.[12] Dio wanted to be seen as a type, whether as an Odysseus (*Orr.* 13.4, 40.12; Philostr., *VS* 488 O = 8.6–13), a Socrates (*Orr.* 13.9, 47.7), or an Aristotle (*Or.* 47.9–11). In this sense, Dio through typology registers as familiar.

At the same time, Dio often angles himself as an outsider, again in ways that may recall Herodotus. If in general terms the ethnographic gaze involves the "characterization of 'other peoples' particularly with reference to their customs, practices, and the behavior that typifies them and/or their lands," to quote Emma Dench, we often find Dio in his urban orations adopting and adapting a type of ethnographic position, describing the behaviors and customs of various places—often directly to the inhabitants themselves.[13] In his *Alexandrian* (*Or.* 32), for instance, Dio harangues the Alexandrians for their obsession with theater and describes how various other peoples— Ethiopians, Arabs, Bactrians, Scythians, Persians—visit Alexandria and observe its odd habits, as though these people were joining Dio in his own autopsy of the Alexandrians' questionable behavior.[14] Likewise, in the *First Tarsian* (*Or.* 33), Dio's attack on the supposedly dissolute city catalogues the ξύμβολα of Tarsian misbehavior (52), including gait, posture, gestures, and haircuts, as if offering an ethnographic description. Finally, in *Or.* 35 in Phrygian Celaenae, Dio deploys a utopian pseudo-ethnographic account

---

[11] See my chapter 5, discussing Lucian, *Hdt.* 2: οὗτος ἐκεῖνος Ἡρόδοτός ἐστιν.

[12] Moles 1978 (esp. 96–100); Moles 2005: 125–27. See also Whitmarsh 1998: 206–7; Whitmarsh 2001b: 215: "What matters to Dio is the construction and dramatization of a philosophical persona for himself, for (on the present interpretation) he is not so much attempting to communicate dogma as competing for public validation in the highly charged, highly agonistic space of sophistic performance. Dio is ever the man of masks."

[13] See Dench 2007: 494. Dio's rhetoric frequently partakes of the "barbarian repertoire" as described by Vlassopoulos 2013: 30–31. On Dio's depictions of barbarians as revealing his openmindedness ("grande ouverture d'esprit face aux barbares") and "solidarity" ("solidarité") with non-Greeks, see Schmidt 2010: 106–15, esp. 114 (source of quotations).

[14] See Dio 32.41, with Trapp 1995: 170, 174–75; Gangloff 2007: 70 n. 17 (noting Dio's recall of Herodotus's description of Persian horsemanship). For treatments of Herodotus's own ideological uses of the ends of the earth, see Romm 1992 (esp. 32–41, 54–60); Nesselrath 1995; Bichler 2000; Bichler 2006; Gagné 2019.

156 HERODOTUS AND IMPERIAL GREEK LITERATURE

of India (18–24) to critique Celaenian mercantilism. In such works, Dio presents himself as an outsider looking in, a rhetor who fuses ethnographic and philosophical perspectives.

One might therefore characterize Dio as sometimes playing what sociologist Georg Simmel once called "the stranger," an outsider "not bound by roots to the particular constituents and partisan dispositions of the group" he addresses:[15]

> For a stranger to the country, the city, the race, and so on, what is stressed is again nothing individual, but alien origin, a quality which he has, or could have, in common with many other strangers. For this reason strangers are not really perceived as individuals, but as strangers of a certain type. Their remoteness is no less general than their nearness.[16]

Dio's masks and intertextual anchors allow him to display his having connection to "many other strangers . . . of a certain type" and thus the capacity to (re)enact estrangement and the critical authority it endows. As a dimension of his traditionalizing mode of playing the stranger, Dio at times adopts an autoptic, Herodotean persona to help render his narrator as a kind of philosophical ethnographer, documenting not only a city's physical features and customs but also its failings and foibles. Additionally, Dio may use his city speeches to get audiences thinking not just about their own city but also about different and other places beyond their physical environs. Dio often draws in the edges of the known *oikoumene* to inspire self-reflection among his Greek audiences.[17] He jolts audiences precisely through the suggestion that there are other places superior in whatever way: more morally upright, better at managing resources, more favored in the eyes of the gods.[18] Such comparative possibilities play a salient role in the oration to which we now turn.

[15] Simmel 1971 [1908]: 145.

[16] Simmel 1971 [1908]: 148.

[17] Compare Montiglio 2005: 203, with her n. 69 on Dio as inquirer at *Orr.* 1.51 and 12.21 and his uses of geography at *Orr.* 5.8–9, 6.2–4, and 32.36. See also Dench 2007: 494, commenting on one of the uses of ancient ethnographic writing: " 'Other peoples' could also be called upon to comment on, correct, or give a new perspective on Greek morals, accounts, or world views." On the ethical or didactic side of ethnography, see Dench 2007: 501.

[18] In this regard, aspects of Dio's work slot into what Romm and others have denoted as the inverse or negative ethnocentric scheme, one that "envisions foreigners growing not less but more virtuous in proportion to their distance from the Greek center" (1992: 47, discussing Strabo 7.3.7). See Romm 1992: 45–49, with Momigliano 1975; Karttunen 2002: 459–60.

Dio at the Edge: The *Borystheniticus*

With this background in mind, let us examine Dio's *Borystheniticus*, arguably his most richly Herodotean oration, in which his self-presentation as a roving moral ethnographer weds historiographic-style travelogue to philosophical ends.[19] The oration first recounts Dio's arrival in Olbia, which he calls by its old-fashioned name of Borysthenes. Dio gives a snapshot topographic and historical description (1–6). He then recounts interactions with some of the locals (7–17), including exchanges on the uses of poetry, and he offers up a speech on the nature of the earthly city (18–28). Finally, and grandiloquently, Dio offers, at the request of a Borysthenite local, a second and longer speech, in two parts, on the nature of the true cosmic city, the first part clearly indebted to Stoic ideas (29–38), the other purportedly a Zoroastrian myth sung by the Persian Magi but also, it turns out, demonstrably Stoic (39–61).[20]

At a structural level, the *Borystheniticus* is a formidably complex work. The oration's main narrative, as just summarized, takes place in Pontic Olbia, where Dio functions as a character (a stranger arriving among the Borysthenites, to whom he delivers two speeches). Yet in the manuscript tradition, the work is labeled as having been delivered before his native city of Prusa. Dio thus occupies two roles, as it were: as the narrative's protagonist in Olbia and as the narrator before a Prusan audience of his own fellow citizens, who hear Dio deliver an oration that not only narrates his time at Borysthenes but also quotes two speeches (effectively, inset speeches) that he supposedly delivered before the Borysthenites.[21] The duality of audiences (Borysthenes and Prusa) contributes to the work's narratological intricacy, as Michael Trapp has observed, noting that "just as the Borysthenites within the speech were invited to contrast with that of another [the Magi of Persia], so the Prusan audience (and any subsequent audience and readers) are invited

---

[19] The text has attracted much attention: see von Arnim 1898: 306–8, 482–92; Bidez and Cumont 1938: Vol. I, 91–97; Treu 1961; Jones 1978: 61–64; Desideri 1978: 318–27; Salmeri 1982: 107–10; Schofield 1991: 57–92; Russell 1992: 19–23, 211–47; Anderson 1993: 216–20; Moles 1995: 184–92; Trapp 1995: 165–67; Veyne 1999: 538–39; Anderson 2000: 157–58; Salmeri 2000: 85–86; Porter 2001: 85–90; Billault 2005; Kim 2010a: 93–94, 198–99; Bost-Pouderon 2011; Hunter 2018: 28–41.

[20] On the Stoicism of the first half (29–38), see above all Schofield 1991: 57–92, esp. 57–63, 84–92. On the pseudo-Zoroastrianism of the second speech, see (pace Bidez and Cumont 1938: Vol. I, 91–97) de Jong 2003.

[21] The work's structure is dizzying and disjointed (see Porter 2001: 87), and even the clearest pieces of scholarship on the oration (including, to my mind, Trapp 1995 and Moles 1995) cannot help but reproduce something of its opacity and density.

158   HERODOTUS AND IMPERIAL GREEK LITERATURE

to compare themselves with both Magi and Borysthenites."[22] The fact of internal and external audiences results in a complicated mirroring effect: in the *Borystheniticus*, it is not the otherworldly Scythians who are reflected back to the Greeks but rather the ostensibly "authentic" Borysthenite Greeks, themselves intermingled with Scythians, who reflect for a different audience of Greeks (i.e., Dio's Prusans) a complicated, alloyed Hellenism. That all of this elaborate narrative structuring is cast by Dio as the side product of a Herodotean-style journey in search of the Getae (§ 1) contributes to the literary stratigraphy of a complicated composition.

Scholars have traced various other influences on Dio's text, chief among them Plato.[23] The work's culminating intertextual debt to Plato, both stylistically and substantively, is strongly felt in the speech on the cosmic city (and its dramatic framing) as well as in the lead-up to the speech on the earthly city.[24] Inasmuch as the speech on the cosmic city, however, represents the climax of the oration, the earlier portions of the text have received relatively less attention.[25] These earlier sections—the less patently philosophical portions of the work—not only unmistakably activate Herodotus but also set up the reader's understanding of what is to come. In the remainder of this chapter, I examine the interpretive consequences of Dio's Herodotean evocations to argue that the Herodotean intertextual presence serves as more than mere window dressing. To the extent that the setup of the oration matters for understanding its latter sequence, including the climactic "Magian" hymn, the work's early topographic and ethnographic sections prove foundational to its structure and meaning. The Herodotean aura of the work's early chapters imbues the speech with a programmatic atmosphere of seeming otherworldliness, integral to the work's ambiguous effects. At the same time, the myth of the Magi that *seemingly* transcends worldly polities and affairs will be seen to recapitulate notions of historical cyclicality. Dio's allusions enable a kinetic reception of Herodotus, playing to his inherited authority while also reworking aspects of the Herodotean backdrop for his own intricate philosophical oration.

---

[22] Trapp 1995: 165. Compare Trapp 2012: 137. See also Moles 2005: 130, noting how Dio in this speech (and elsewhere) "disconcertingly plays internal and external audiences off against each other."

[23] See Trapp 1990: 148–55; Trapp 2000: 214–19. See also Nesselrath 2003: 18–22.

[24] Both the framing and the cosmic speech evoke the *Phaedrus*; for the parallels and echoes, see Trapp 2000: 216–18. On the *Cratylus*-style lead-up (18–21) to the speech on the earthly city, see Porter 2001: 89.

[25] The studies of Bäbler and Braund offer important exceptions, bringing out aspects of Dio's literary and rhetorical purposes in his (sometimes distorted or inaccurate) representation of Olbia: Bäbler 2002: 321–25, esp. 324–25; Bäbler 2003; Bäbler 2007; Braund 2007.

HELLENISM IN THE DISTANCE 159

Stranger in a Strange Land: Dio's Scythian Recall

In the opening of the *Borystheniticus*, Dio makes a bid both to inhabit the Herodotean persona and to upstage the claim to autoptic authority.[26] Dio evokes Herodotus in several ways at the outset, and observing the Herodotean details is essential to recognizing the overall coherence of Dio's text as it proceeds:

> I happened to be in Borysthenes during the summer, since I had sailed there [after my exile] wanting, if possible, to make my way through Scythia to the Getae, in order to conduct observation on what sort of conditions prevailed there. In this particular instance, I was taking a stroll by the River Hypanis round about market hour. Although the city has taken its name from the River Borysthenes because of its beauty and great size, the current city, like its predecessor, is in fact situated on the Hypanis, just above the so-called Cape Hippolaus on the opposite shore. This part of the land, around where the two rivers meet, is as sharp and solid as the beak of a ship. (36.1–2)

> ἐτύγχανον μὲν ἐπιδημῶν ἐν Βορυσθένει τὸ θέρος, ὡς τότε εἰσέπλευσα [μετὰ τὴν φυγήν], βουλόμενος ἐλθεῖν, ἐὰν δύνωμαι, διὰ Σκυθῶν εἰς Γέτας, ὅπως θεάσωμαι τἀκεῖ πράγματα ὁποῖά ἐστι. καὶ δὴ καὶ περιεπάτουν περὶ πλήθουσαν ἀγορὰν παρὰ τὸν Ὕπανιν. ἡ γὰρ πόλις τὸ μὲν ὄνομα εἴληφεν ἀπὸ τοῦ Βορυσθένους διὰ τὸ κάλλος καὶ τὸ μέγεθος τοῦ ποταμοῦ, κεῖται δὲ πρὸς τῷ Ὑπάνιδι ἥ τε νῦν καὶ ἡ πρότερον οὕτως ᾠκεῖτο, οὐ πολὺ ἄνωθεν τῆς Ἱππολάου καλουμένης ἄκρας ἐν τῷ κατ' ἀντικρύ. τοῦτο δέ ἐστι τῆς χώρας ὀξὺ καὶ στερεὸν ὥσπερ ἔμβολον, περὶ ὃ συμπίπτουσιν οἱ ποταμοί.[27]

Dio's first words indicate that his will be an embodied account: not launching a work of paradoxography or armchair geography, he begins with the notice that he "happened to be in Borysthenes during the summer," situating

---

[26] On the Herodotean presences, see Bäbler 2003: 126: "Herodots Bedeutung wurde bereits mehrfach erwähnt; für Dion war Herodots Beschreibung von Olbia zweifellos das hervorragende Exemplum, dem es nachzueifern galt." See also Russell 1992: ad loc. §§ 1, 2, 3, 7; Bichler 2000: 69–71. The Herodotean qualities are also flagged by Trapp 2005 (in a brief review of Nesselrath 2003), who laments the fact that Nesselrath's introduction "says less about the Herodotean elements [of the speech] and their ramifications" than it might have (78). On Dio's representation of the Scythians, see Gangloff 2007: 72–75. There hovers some uncertainty around Herodotus's *logos* of Olbia: his autopsy (4.81.2) of a site four days' journey upriver from Olbia may imply that his description of Olbia, too, derived from more than hearsay, but readers cannot be sure; see West 2007: 80–81.

[27] For text of *Oration* 36, I follow that printed in Russell 1992.

160 HERODOTUS AND IMPERIAL GREEK LITERATURE

himself in the tradition of the traveling reporter, and specifically in the mode of Herodotus, who remained the major reportorial source on that region before Dio, as will have been obvious to Dio's learned listener.[28] One senses a neat coincidence of text and journey, as though copy were generated simply by Dio's happening to be in a particular place (ἐτύγχανον μὲν ἐπιδημῶν ἐν Βορυσθένει). This spontaneous opening, however, also offers something of a feint, conveyed in the participle ἐπιδημῶν, a word that can mean both "to be at home" and "to come to stay in a foreign city" (LSJ s.v. ἐπιδημέω, A and A.III). Given the ways in which Borysthenes will come to seem both outlandish (3) and resolutely Hellenic (9, 16), the ἐπιδημῶν adds ambiguous sheen to the start of a text delivered at his hometown but nominally concerned with visiting another town.[29]

Readers are prompted to think of Herodotus, whose "direct" influence Anne Gangloff has called "undeniable," at several turns in this initial paragraph.[30] In the reference to the Scythians (cf. *Histories* Book 4 passim), in the proposed ethnographic trip to "conduct observation" (θεάσωμαι) on what life is like among the Getae (cf. Hdt. 4.93–96, 118), and in the naming of Borysthenes itself, both the town and the river (cf. Hdt. 4.53), Dio repeatedly recalls his predecessor.[31] Even the notion of making one's way "through Scythia" (διὰ Σκυθῶν) is perhaps a recherché intertextual joke, since Scythia is figured in the *Histories* as a pathless, plan-defeating space for the outsider.[32] Dio's use of the archaizing name Borysthenes, despite his surely knowing that the town was properly called Olbia (evident in contemporary inscriptions), firmly plants his flag in Herodotean territory.[33] As West has observed:

---

[28] The most thorough literary treatment of the region was that of Herodotus, and in the succeeding centuries, as West (2007: 81) notes, Dio is the only extant ancient Greek author who claims actually to have visited Olbia.

[29] The through-line of the text—Dio's delivering a speech to one city, itself quoting a speech to another city—is in some sense redoubled by the fact that the speeches of the inset narrative are precisely pieces of wisdom *about* cities. As Trapp (2012: 137) has put it eloquently, characterizing the later portions of the work, when Dio addresses the Borysthenites, "it is a complicated play of perceptions that Dio sets in motion, as we readers look at the citizens of Prusa looking at the people of Borysthenes looking at Dio, with each frame offering its own angle of view on Dio's ability and talents vis-à-vis those of his audience(s)."

[30] Gangloff 2007: 74 n. 26: "Une influence directe est indéniable."

[31] See further Hdt. 4.17, 4.18, 4.24, 4.78–79. For Dio's lost work on the Getae, see the fragments (*FGrHist* 707), esp. *BNJ* 707 F1 for the emphasis on an idea of alien wisdom. See also references at *Or.* 12.16–20 to his visits among the Getae. On Dio's ethnographic gaze in the opening parts of the *Borystheniticus*, see Gangloff 2007: 73–74.

[32] See Hartog 1988 [1980]: 57–60.

[33] On the name's archaism, see Treu 1961: 140; Jones 1978: 62 (mentioning inscriptions); Porter 2001: 86. On the Herodotean evocation, see Bäbler 2002: 315; Gangloff 2007: 74. Compare, however, a later tradition (see, e.g., Steph. Byz. s.v. Βορυσθένης) holding that locals called the city Olbia and

HELLENISM IN THE DISTANCE   161

He [Herodotus] does not even use the name Olbia, though he tells us that the Greeks who live on the Hypanis (Bug) call themselves Olbiopolitai. To refer to their town he uses various expressions: τὸ Βορυσθενειτέων ἄστυ (78.3) (the Borysthenites' city), Βορυσθένης (78.5) (Borysthenes), Βορυσθενειτέων ἡ πόλις (79.2) (the Borysthenites' city), perhaps also τὸ Βορυσθενειτέων ἐμπόριον (17.1) (the Borysthenites' trading centre). This toponymic informality, avoiding the "official" name used by the citizens themselves, suggests that he did not overestimate Olbia's importance.[34]

Dio's emphasis on rivers further locates his programmatic intertextuality in Herodotus, who had devoted several chapters to Scythian rivers (4.82) and the Black Sea (4.85.2), claiming these as the sole wonders of Scythia, aside from the footprint of Heracles. And Dio rounds off the Herodotean flourish of his opening with a reference both to Cape Hippolaus and to the metaphorical ἔμβολον, echoing details found elsewhere only in Herodotus: "Near the Black Sea, the Borysthenes River mixes with the flow of the Hypanis, together debouching into the same marshland. The area between the two rivers is a beak of land called Hippolaus's Point, on which there is set a sanctuary for Demeter. On the far side of the sanctuary, on the Hypanis River, lies the Borysthenes settlement" (Hdt. 4.53.5–6).[35]

Given this Herodotean framing, it will be instructive to glance at some of Herodotus's wider account of the area, especially as that account conjures a sense of allure and mystery on which Dio's capitalizes. In Herodotus's telling (principally, the long chapter at *Hist.* 4.53), the River Borysthenes is first described with a sense of majesty and wonder. Herodotus calls it the most productive of all rivers, not just of those in Scythia but of all the world's rivers, outside of the Nile (πολυαρκέστατος κατὰ γνώμας τὰς ἡμετέρας οὔτι μοῦνον τῶν Σκυθικῶν ποταμῶν ἀλλὰ καὶ τῶν ἄλλων πάντων, πλὴν Νείλου τοῦ Αἰγυπτίου, 4.53.1). The Borysthenes produces "the most beautiful and most fecund pastureland" (νομάς τε καλλίστας καὶ εὐκομιδεστάτας κτήνεσι παρέχεται) and "eminently the best fish, in huge amounts" (ἰχθῦς τε ἀρίστους

outsiders called it Borysthenes. Cf. also Strabo 7.3.17 and Pseudo-Scymnus 806–7. I owe my awareness of these references to William Hutton.

[34] West 2007: 80.

[35] ἀγχοῦ τε δὴ θαλάσσης ὁ Βορυσθένης ῥέων γίνεται καί οἱ συμμίσγεται ὁ Ὕπανις ἐς τὠυτὸ ἕλος ἐκδιδούς. τὸ δὲ μεταξὺ τῶν ποταμῶν τούτων ἐὸν ἔμβολον τῆς χώρης Ἱππόλεω ἄκρη καλέεται, ἐν δὲ αὐτῷ ἱρὸν Δήμητρος ἐνίδρυται· πέρην δὲ τοῦ ἱροῦ ἐπὶ τῷ Ὑπάνι Βορυσθενεῖται κατοίκηνται. The echo of ἔμβολον is noted by Russell 1992: ad loc. § 2 and Bäbler 2002: 315.

162   HERODOTUS AND IMPERIAL GREEK LITERATURE

διακριδὸν καὶ πλείστους, 4.53.2). The water is clear, the nearby crops superb (ἄριστος), and the river yields invertebrate fish called *antakaioi* (which the Scythians preserve through salting), along with "very many creatures worthy of wonder" (πολλὰ θωμάσαι ἄξια, 4.53.3).[36] At the same time, Herodotus's description of this exceptional place is tied in with inexplicability, as indicated, for instance, by the uncertainty of what lies at its northernmost reaches (τὸ δὲ κατύπερθε δι᾽ ὧν ῥέει ἀνθρώπων **οὐδεὶς ἔχει φράσαι**) and by his inability—indeed, the inability of "any Greek"—to report on the origins of the River Borysthenes (μούνου δὲ τούτου τοῦ ποταμοῦ καὶ Νείλου **οὐκ ἔχω φράσαι** τὰς πηγάς, δοκέω δέ, **οὐδὲ οὐδεὶς** Ἑλλήνων, 4.53.4).

Already there lurks, then, in Dio's intertextual recall the more general atmosphere of strangeness that wafts from the Herodotean context, sustained more broadly in a stretch of Herodotus's narrative focused on Scythian oddity and intrigue. Herodotus evokes a liminal zone suspended between known and unknown, conjured by journeys physical and intellectual to the world's *eschatiai*.[37] Indeed, the segment of Herodotean narrative that Dio evokes is marked by what one might call the Herodotean uncertainty principle.[38] By this I mean the constantly provisional knowledge on display, evident in narratorial and intradiegetic expressions (from sources) of not knowing what lies beyond a certain point as well as in the consequent analytic adjustments readers must practice in grappling with Herodotus's (or internal reporters') oscillations between certitude and doubt.[39] The statement at 4.53.4 on not knowing what lies beyond the far north of the river, for instance, echoes similar statements from earlier in Herodotus's fourth book. At 4.18.3, for example, Herodotus remarks on the northernmost reaches of Scythia, a site of "true desolation, where no human race dwells as far anyone knows" (τὸ δὲ τούτων κατύπερθε ἔρημος ἤδη ἀληθέως καὶ ἔθνος ἀνθρώπων οὐδέν, ὅσον ἡμεῖς ἴδμεν). And again, at 4.20.2, after mentioning the so-called Blackcloaks (Μελάγχλαινοι), whose trademark garb will appear in Dio's oration (7), Herodotus says that "beyond the Blackcloaks are lakes and an empty space devoid of humans, as far as anyone knows" (Μελαγχλαίνων δὲ τὸ κατύπερθε λίμναι καὶ ἔρημός ἐστι ἀνθρώπων, κατ᾽ ὅσον ἡμεῖς ἴδμεν).

---

[36] Dio echoes the detail of the salted fish at *Or.* 36.3.

[37] See Karttunen 2002: 460–66 on aspects of both the "anarchy" (460) and the "just and peaceful" (464) ways of Herodotus's fringe peoples.

[38] I use the phrase conscious of John Gould's use of the same phrase with reference to Greek religion (see Gould 1994: 94).

[39] See Nesselrath 1995: 23–24 on the inconsistencies of what is presented as plausible in Herodotus Books 3 and 4 and what readers are accordingly asked to believe.

HELLENISM IN THE DISTANCE 163

Nor do the people themselves living within this part of the world know much. The Black Sea region is filled with what Herodotus calls the world's "most ignorant people" (ἔθνεα ἀμαθέστατα, 4.46.1), the Scythians excepted. That group, in its praiseworthy nomadic life, has found the wisest solution to what Herodotus grandly declares "the single most important matter in human affairs" (ἓν μὲν τὸ μέγιστον τῶν ἀνθρωπηίων πρηγμάτων σοφώτατα πάντων ἐξεύρηται τῶν ἡμεῖς ἴδμεν, 4.46.2).[40] Yet given their nomadic ways, Herodotus asks rhetorically how the Scythians could be anything but "elusive" (ἄποροι, 4.46.3), a word whose connotations would only seem to recapitulate Scythia's "waylessness"—and the Scythians' interpretive inaccessibility. Herodotus goes on all the same to spell out how the Scythians' "discovery" (ἐξεύρηται) is made "in alliance with" their landscape and their rivers (ἐξεύρηται δέ σφι ταῦτα τῆς τε γῆς ἐούσης ἐπιτηδέης καὶ τῶν ποταμῶν ἐόντων σφι συμμάχων, 4.47.1), thereby asserting a strong if paradoxical link between the essential placelessness of the Scythians and the physical affordances of Scythia as place.

In short, Herodotus's *logoi* of the Black Sea region and the Scythian rivers, the specific sections of the *Histories* that Dio's text recalls, form part of Herodotus's ranging *logos* of the nomadic, elusive Scythians, spread across a sweeping, recursive, and itself almost mimetically "nomadic" stretch of narrative.[41] From the very start, then, Dio's Herodotean evocations only seem straightforward. Only *apparently* tidy is Dio's harking back to a well-known text at the start of his own work that will itself move toward describing something of an ambered-in-time, primitive Greek populace at Borysthenes. Rather, Dio has with the mention of old Borysthenes, the Scythian rivers, and the Olbian "beak" of land opened a can of intertextual worms, transporting his audience to the very place that Herodotus had stamped as one of the world's "aporetic" zones, in an account set amid his capaciously uncertain canvas of Scythia. While Renaud Gagné has argued that the Herodotean over-north is a place at once evocative of past inexplicability and mythic attribution but also, in the hands of Herodotus, "the ultimate frontier for

---

[40] For discussion of this passage, see chapter 6 on Anacharsis.

[41] Even a casual glance at an outline of Book 4 (as at Asheri, Lloyd, and Corcella 2007: 571–72) is enough to sense the disrupted and complicated structure of Herodotus's Scythian *logos*: Herodotus's *logos* on the Scythians themselves (4.46–82) contains a lengthy excursus on Scythian rivers (4.47.2–58), only to be followed later by a description of the Scythian landmass (4.99–101), which itself picks up on an earlier discussion of Scythian origins and geographic limits (4.5–45). The details on Scythian customs (concentrated at 4.46–47.1, 4.59–75) weave in the stories of Anacharsis and Scyles (4.76–80) and are implicitly contrasted with the ethnographies that Herodotus later offers (4.103–17) of Scythian neighbors.

164   HERODOTUS AND IMPERIAL GREEK LITERATURE

the demonstration of *historia*," I cannot help but believe that Herodotus's sprawling narrative of the region will have left many ancient readers with the continued impression of its difficulty, both as terrain and as a site of intelligibility.[42] Likewise, Dio's Prusan listeners will have experienced a sense of wariness at the prospect of his account of these nebulous regions. Dio's initial signal to his reader that the city of Borysthenes does not actually sit on the eponymous river (1) programmatically marks it as a space that can throw off the novice. His oration, moreover, by inaugurating itself through reference to a "classic" treatment, also touches upon questions of frontier knowledge that Herodotus's work had already provoked, in turn imbuing his own text with an air of suspense. What sort of weird place *did* Dio see? What did he learn there, and what are we (Prusans or latter-day readers) to learn from him?

"As Is the Custom of the Borysthenites"

Dio's conjuring of the Herodotean presence establishes a certain authoritativeness.[43] Yet, as we have just seen, that "authority" comes freighted with the baggage of uncertainty and not-knowing: recalling Herodotus on Scythia means recalling a voice at the edge of its assertive abilities. The question of what Dio, channeling Herodotus, can say confidently of this far-off place thus adumbrates the oration from the get-go. As Dio journeys on in the speech and into the area of Borysthenes, an initially eerie and at times disorienting atmosphere prevails. Unlike Herodotus's glowing description of the riverbanks, Dio's presentation is more restrained, noting how the confluence of the rivers "forms a pool" (λιμνάζουσι, 2), marked by lagoons and a sense of calm (τέναγος καὶ γαλήνη), the sort of calm that settles upon a windless harbor (ταῖς εὐδίαις ὥσπερ ἐν λίμνῃ γίγνεται σταθερά, 2).[44] The area presents a "marshy shore, shaggy with reeds and trees" (τὸ δὲ λοιπὸν ἠών ἐστιν ἐλώδης καὶ δασεῖα καλάμῳ καὶ δένδροις, 3). These trees, Dio says, confound the inexperienced traveler, who cannot distinguish land from sea: "Many of the trees appear in the middle of the marsh and so resemble the masts of ships. Already some of the more inexperienced have lost

---

[42] Gagné 2019: 95. See also Nesselrath 1995: 29–30 on Herodotus's use of Greek and non-Greek sources in Book 4, which perhaps has the effect of making otherwise implausible accounts seem at least worthy of record (i.e., to the extent that independent traditions testify to them).

[43] See Whitmarsh 2001b: 215–16 on Dio's adapting himself to different rhetorical situations.

[44] Reiske's proposed emendation of σταθερᾷ to produce "stagnant harbor" would contribute to the less uplifting sense of calm conveyed by other parts of this passage.

HELLENISM IN THE DISTANCE   165

their way, moving toward them as though they were boats" (φαίνεται δὲ τῶν δένδρων πολλὰ καὶ ἐν μέσῃ τῇ λίμνῃ, ὡς ἱστοῖς προσεοικέναι, καὶ ἤδη τινὲς τῶν ἀπειροτέρων διήμαρτον, ὡς ἐπὶ πλοῖα ἐπέχοντες, 3). Borysthenes proves a place of hazy visual sensations, a quality echoed a few sections later when Dio notes how the ruins of towers outside the now-inhabited city might mislead one into thinking that they had not once belonged to the same city (τῶν δὲ πύργων εἰσί τινες πολὺ ἀφεστῶτες τοῦ νῦν οἰκουμένου, ὥστε μηδ' εἰκάσαι ὅτι μιᾶς ἦσαν πόλεως, 6). The ensuing mention of salt works, in echo of Herodotus (4.53.3), continues to locate Dio's text on a recognizable literary map, even as the land he describes produces disorientation and errant judgments for the inexperienced (ἀπειροτέρων).

In the passages that follow, the washy impressionism of Dio's description begins to seep into his presentation of the history and culture of Borysthenes, a place where simple distinctions between "Greek" and "barbarian" are confounded. Dio first underscores, in solemn Herodotean fashion, that Borysthenes was once a great city but has, over time, become small:[45]

> The size of the city of the Borysthenites does not correspond to its ancient glory, owing to constant seizures and wars. For since it has been settled for so long in the midst of barbarians—and nearly the most bellicose barbarians at that—there has always been war, and the city has repeatedly been captured. . . . But after they were taken that time [i.e., by the Getae, some 150 years before Dio's report], the Borysthenites once again founded a community with, it seems to me, the wishes of the Scythians, since they needed the commerce and traffic of the Greeks. The Greeks, in fact, had ceased sailing into port at Borysthenes after the city's leveling, since there was no one there to receive them who spoke their language. Nor did the Scythians think it a good idea—or know how—to set up their own emporium in the manner of the Greeks. (36.4–5)

> ἡ δὲ πόλις ἡ τῶν Βορυσθενιτῶν τὸ μέγεθός ἐστιν οὐ πρὸς τὴν παλαιὰν δόξαν διὰ τὰς συνεχεῖς ἁλώσεις καὶ τοὺς πολέμους. ἅτε γὰρ ἐν μέσοις οἰκοῦσα τοῖς βαρβάροις τοσοῦτον ἤδη χρόνον, καὶ τούτοις σχεδόν τι τοῖς πολεμικωτάτοις, ἀεὶ μὲν πολεμεῖται, πολλάκις δὲ καὶ ἑάλωκεν. . . . ἁλόντες δὲ τότε οἱ Βορυσθενῖται πάλιν συνῴκησαν, ἐθελόντων ἐμοὶ δοκεῖν τῶν Σκυθῶν διὰ τὸ δεῖσθαι τῆς ἐμπορίας καὶ τοῦ κατάπλου τῶν Ἑλλήνων.

---

[45] On the history and archaeology of the site, see Bäbler 2002: 313–14.

166 HERODOTUS AND IMPERIAL GREEK LITERATURE

ἐπαύσαντο γὰρ εἰσπλέοντες ἀναστάτου τῆς πόλεως γενομένης, ἅτε οὐκ ἔχοντες ὁμοφώνους τοὺς ὑποδεχομένους οὐδὲ τῶν Σκυθῶν ἀξιούντων οὐδὲ ἐπισταμένων ἐμπόριον αὐτῶν κατασκευάσασθαι τὸν Ἑλληνικὸν τρόπον.

Dio captures the vagaries of urban fortune, that imperishable Herodotean topos of fall-and-rise. Alongside the sense of constant trouble, Dio hints at a renewal for the city through the willingness (ἐθελόντων) of their Scythian neighbors.[46] Indeed, as Bäbler has noted, Dio captures something of the genuinely mixed life of Greeks and others at Borysthenes.[47] This nod to the Scythians as cooperating with the Greeks after "not thinking it a good idea—or knowing how" to run an emporium would seem to endorse one of the balder ethnographic assertions by Herodotus, who had commented that the Scythians as a people "categorically avoid the adoption of foreign customs, particularly the customs of the Greeks" (ξεινικοῖσι δὲ νομαίοισι καὶ οὗτοι αἰνῶς χρᾶσθαι φεύγουσι, μήτε τεῶν ἄλλων, Ἑλληνικοῖσι δὲ καὶ ἥκιστα, 4.76.1). In Dio's case, we have something in between rejection and adoption. The harmony of the cosmic, universal city that Dio will later describe (39–61) is hinted at here, as Dio modulates both the programmatic Herodotean fixation on the rise and fall of cities (τὸ μέγεθός ἐστιν οὐ πρὸς τὴν παλαιὰν δόξαν διὰ τὰς συνεχεῖς ἁλώσεις) and the traditional polarity of Greeks and Scythians into something new, in the service of a work that defies expectations of where one finds "Greekness" and what that Greekness looks like.[48]

Indeed, the narrator's first personal encounter with a Borysthenite raises further questions about the outward appearance of "Greekness" in these far-off spaces:

Anyway, as I was saying, I happened to be walking outside the city when some of the Borysthenites came out from within their walls and approached me, as is their custom. At first Callistratus rode by on horseback, driving in from somewhere beyond, and after he had driven a bit beyond me, he got off the horse and gave it to the charge of one of his attendants. He approached me in full decorous fashion, tucking his arm under his cloak. On his belt

---

[46] Compare Porter 2001: 86–87 on this passage, and see his 89 n. 102 on Pausanias's distanced references to the "Greeks," similar to Dio's here.

[47] Bäbler 2007: 151.

[48] Compare already Herodotus 4.17.1 on the Callipidae, described as "Greek Scythians" (Ἕλληνες Σκύθαι) yet whose customs Herodotus describes as mostly Scythian, diet aside.

HELLENISM IN THE DISTANCE 167

was hung a large cavalry sword, and he was wearing trousers and all other trappings of Scythian dress, surmounted at the shoulders by a small black cape, made of slender fabric, as is the custom of the Borysthenites. Indeed, for the rest of their clothing they wear mostly black, something they took from the Scythian group called the Blackcloaks, it seems to me, a group given that name by the Greeks for this very reason. (36.7)

ὅπερ οὖν ἔφην, ἔτυχον περιπατῶν πρὸ τῆς πόλεως, καί τινες ἐξῄεσαν ἔνδοθεν τῶν Βορυσθενιτῶν πρὸς ἐμέ, ὥσπερ εἰώθεσαν· ἔπειτα Καλλίστρατος ἐφ᾽ ἵππου τὸ μὲν πρῶτον παρίππευσεν ἡμᾶς ἔξωθεν προσελαύνων, παρελθὼν δὲ ὀλίγον κατέβη, καὶ τὸν ἵππον τῷ ἀκολούθῳ παραδοὺς αὐτὸς πάνυ κοσμίως προσῆλθεν ὑπὸ τὸ ἱμάτιον τὴν χεῖρα ὑποστείλας. παρέζωστο δὲ μάχαιραν μεγάλην τῶν ἱππικῶν καὶ ἀναξυρίδας εἶχε καὶ τὴν ἄλλην στολὴν Σκυθικήν, ἄνωθεν δὲ τῶν ὤμων ἱμάτιον μικρὸν μέλαν, λεπτόν, ὥσπερ εἰώθασιν οἱ Βορυσθενῖται. χρῶνται δὲ καὶ τῇ ἄλλῃ ἐσθῆτι μελαίνῃ ὡς τὸ πολὺ ἀπὸ γένους τινὸς Σκυθῶν τῶν Μελαγχλαίνων, ὡς ἐμοὶ δοκοῦσι, κατὰ τοῦτο ὀνομασθέντων ὑπὸ τῶν Ἑλλήνων.

Dio's ethnography of the Borysthenites operates both by basic description of group behavior as they emerge from the city (ὥσπερ εἰώθεσαν) and by synecdoche, offering up Callistratus as an example of the broader customs of the group (ὥσπερ εἰώθασιν οἱ Βορυσθενῖται). Yet the claim to resume the narrative thread from the supposed historical and topographic digression (ὅπερ οὖν ἔφην, ἔτυχον περιπατῶν) is a ruse: for the hazy and mixed sensations of those foregoing sections are now revealed as preparatory to, rather than a divagation from, this description of the Borysthenites, whose "customs" include, for instance, the explicitly non-Greek dressing habits of the Blackcloaks. Seeing the connections to the beginning of the speech, Trapp has illuminated the thematic importance of Dio's original geographical introduction: "Thus at the outset, the reader is confronted by a place of confluence, where boundaries—between earth and water, freshwater and salt, and nature and human artefact—become blurred. This prepares for the presentation of city and its inhabitants, as a place and a people on the uncertain boundaries of civilization."[49] Here the Borysthenite Callistratus extends the "uncertain boundaries" by cutting a curious figure, decked out in trousers and "all other trappings of Scythian dress" (τὴν ἄλλην στολὴν

[49] Trapp 1995: 166.

168   HERODOTUS AND IMPERIAL GREEK LITERATURE

Σκυθικήν)—topped by a Blackcloak cape (potentially adding to the sartorial syncretism for any listener who recalls that the Blackcloaks are supposedly *not* Scythian: Hdt. 4.20.2).[50] Nor is Dio's focus on Callistratus's clothing incidental. Fixating on such outward details recalls one of the key markers of Greek "passing" that the Scythian Scyles had adopted, amply recounted in Herodotus's *logos* on Scyles (Hdt. 4.78.4–5), in which to actualize Greekness, the Scythian first needed to look like one. In Herodotus, the attempted cultural mingling produces unfortunate results, leading to his conclusion that the Scythians are so "wrapped up in"—the word περιστέλλουσι (4.80.5) can also mean "to cover with clothing"—their own customs as to treat harshly those who adopt foreign manners.[51]

After presenting Callistratus as cosmetically Scythian, Dio goes on to describe him in the following chapter as having an Ionian mien, an enthusiasm for philosophy and rhetoric (8), and a love for Homer (φιλόμηρον, 9)—awareness of which fact on the narrator's part (εἰδώς, 9) is never fully explained but is declared as characteristic of the Borysthenites generally (9). Thus, the degree to which Dio stresses the Hellenic credentials of the Borysthenites is tempered for his Prusan audience by mixed messaging: the people of Borysthenes, "nearly all of whom have a zeal for Homer" (σχεδὸν δὲ καὶ πάντες οἱ Βορυσθενῖται περὶ τὸν ποιητὴν ἐσπουδάκασιν, 9), are also first represented in the text by a man who dresses as Scythian. This hybrid Hellenism is increased by the fact that the Borysthenites have two temples to Achilles and nearly all know the *Iliad* by heart (ὀλίγου πάντες ἴσασιν ἀπὸ στόματος, 9) but can "no longer speak Greek clearly because they dwell in the midst of barbarians" (οὐκέτι σαφῶς ἑλληνίζοντες διὰ τὸ ἐν μέσοις οἰκεῖν τοῖς βαρβάροις, 9).[52] In an oration that will come to be preoccupied with transcendent ideas of the true city, told through a supposedly Persian (but actually Greek) myth, we see the narrator in these early chapters inculcating his audience into the difficulties of parsing the cultural mélange of the frontier world. For even before Dio's Prusans hear his descriptions of the Hellenic credentials of the Borysthenites, that audience has been primed,

---

[50] On the Blackcloaks, see further Hdt. 4.20, 4.100–102, 4.107, 4.119, 4.125.

[51] See Gangloff 2007: 74, commenting on Dio's apparent "inversion" of the Herodotean material related to Scyles ("Dion semble avoir opéré une inversion par rapport aux données hérodotéennes"). Insofar as Scyles had been punished by the Scythians for adopting Greek ways, the cultural melding of Callistratus (both Greek and Scythian) presents, by contrast, a rather more hybridized image. Such hybridity is complicated, however, by Dio's references to the continued war between Greeks and Scythians.

[52] On the senses in which Borysthenes both is and is not Greek, see Kim 2010a: 93–94. Porter 2001: 86–87 also notices the ironies of this "ethnic hodgepodge" (87).

HELLENISM IN THE DISTANCE   169

both through Dio's summoning of Herodotean uncertainty and through the programmatically hybrid image of the Borysthenites, to view these Greeks through a set of heterogeneous cultural signifiers.

A further twist in all this deserves mention, namely, Dio's comment on sexual practices among the Borysthenites. Following on from his remarks on Callistratus's eagerness for philosophy and rhetoric, and his willingness to "sail off" (ἐκπλεῦσαι, 8) with him, the narrator seems to confirm the Greekness of the Borysthenites by referring to Callistratus's many lovers and the fact of Borysthenitic same-sex relationships, a practice they have continued from their mother-city of Miletus (εἶχε πολλοὺς ἐραστάς. πάνυ γὰρ δὴ τοῦτο ἐμμεμένηκεν αὐτοῖς ἀπὸ τῆς μητροπόλεως, τὸ περὶ τοὺς ἔρωτας τοὺς τῶν ἀρρένων, 8).[53] Dio goes on to say that they "risk persuading some of the barbarians to take it up, and not with good effect, but rather as those men would tend to take on such a practice: in a non-Greek way, and with hubris" (ὥστε κινδυνεύουσιν ἀναπείθειν καὶ τῶν βαρβάρων ἐνίους οὐκ ἐπ' ἀγαθῷ σχεδόν, ἀλλ' ὡς ἂν ἐκεῖνοι τὸ τοιοῦτον ἀποδέξαιντο, βαρβαρικῶς καὶ οὐκ ἄνευ ὕβρεως, 8).[54] Dio's distant Greeks, who love Homer and who maintain a cultural connection to their Greek mother-city through the practice of same-sex relations, now "risk teaching" an aspect of their culture to barbarians, who would only vitiate the custom, Dio warns. Yet already Dio has presented us with cross-cultural mingling, in the Scythian wish for a common marketplace (ἐμπόριον, 5) and in Callistratus's Scythian clothing, making his anxiety here about Greek persuasion of barbarians rather hard to interpret. What kind of cultural emporium is being imagined?

To be sure, the stereotype of the luxurious non-Greek has deep roots and is already evident, for instance, in Herodotus's comments on the "manifold comforts" (εὐπαθείας τε παντοδαπάς) of the Persians, including their adoption of Greek pederasty (Hdt. 1.135). So we may be dealing in Dio's case with an age-old stereotype of the Eastern exaggeration of Greek practices.[55] But it seems also that a somewhat warped mirror is being held up to the Prusans: the authentic fringe-world Greeks, devoted to Homer but poor speakers of Greek

[53] On the evocations of Plato in this passage, see Trapp 1990: 150–52; Trapp 2000: 217–18. On Callistratus's exceptional beauty, compare Herodotus 3.106.1 on the edges of the earth as containing τὰ κάλλιστα.

[54] On this passage, see Houser 2002: 344–45, arguing against the notion that it betrays a negative attitude on Dio's part toward same-sex relations. Rather, Houser makes the narrower claim that the comment only reveals a (stereotypical) view about a non-Greek lack of moderation (βαρβαρικῶς καὶ οὐκ ἄνευ ὕβρεως). See also Russell 1992: ad loc. § 8.

[55] See Russell 1992: ad loc.: "[W]hen βάρβαροι learn these practices, they naturally implement them βαβαρικῶς."

170 HERODOTUS AND IMPERIAL GREEK LITERATURE

and who indeed hold their city in part because of Scythian cooperation, maintain vaguely Old World same-sex relations that neighboring non-Greeks have not yet taken up. The Prusan audience may wonder: is the Borysthenites' archaic Greekness to be admired? Is it compromised by the infiltration of Scythian habits and commerce? Or is Dio already, well before his speech "philosophizes" formally about it, presenting an unexpected kind of harmony between putatively different peoples, perched on the distant horizons of the Prusans' known world, a place kept in balance by good behavior, devoid of hubris (and thus offering a model to his Prusan audience)?[56] In any event, Dio has manipulated the Herodotean backdrop to prompt thought of cities and the cooperation of their inhabitants well before he formally expounds upon themes of civic justice and righteousness.[57]

The text proceeds to a complex discussion on Homer (9–14), which begins with Dio asking Callistratus in jest (προσπαίζων, 10) whether Homer is really the superior (ἀμείνων) poet compared with Phocylides—of whom Callistratus laughingly claims never to have heard.[58] One detail in particular extends the Herodotean evocations that I have thus far documented and amplifies the sense in which the oration's later, more overtly philosophical sections are anticipated by these earlier chapters. In this case, the detail again has to do with Dio's focus on the idea of the city. Dio encourages Callistratus to consider the merits of Phocylides based on a small sample (δεῖγμα ἐν βραχεῖ, 11), using the analogy of how a Borysthenite might test a visiting sea merchant's wares before buying.[59] The loosely Callimachean aesthetic here (see § 12, comparing Homer's "long and continuous poem" [μακράν τινα καὶ συνεχῆ ποίησιν] with Phocylides's brevity) seems to feed into the very content of the Phocylides poem that Dio quotes:

> Do you not think Phocylides was right to put his name on a judgment and statement such as this?

---

[56] In this regard, Dio's presentation may connect with his emphasis elsewhere on concord as a means to minimizing Imperial intervention; see Jones 1978: 83–94; Veyne 1999: 554–56.

[57] Moreover, that these hybrid and harmonized images come on the far side of what Dio describes as the constant warfare (ἀεὶ μὲν πολεμεῖται, 4) of the region between the Greeks and the "essentially the most warlike" barbarians (σχεδόν τι τοῖς πολεμικωτάτοις, 4) shows him playing up a vague kind of "end-of-history" image that will be both echoed and, I suggest, undone in the Magian myth's tale of cosmic destruction and renewal.

[58] See Hunter 2018: 28–41 for an illuminating analysis of this sequence of the oration.

[59] One may hear a vague echo of Herodotus's opening story in Dio's analogy (appropriately preparatory to the Phocylides poem that itself hints at Hdt. 1.5.3–4): κἂν ἄλλο τι **φορτίον** ἄγῃ, δεῖγμα λαβόντες, **ἐὰν μὲν ἀρέσῃ ὑμᾶς, ὠνεῖσθε**, εἰ δὲ μή, ἐᾶτε (*Or.* 36.11) ~ ταύτας στάσας κατὰ πρύμνην τῆς νεὸς **ὠνέεσθαι τῶν φορτίων τῶν σφι ἦν θυμὸς** μάλιστα (*Hist.* 1.1.4).

HELLENISM IN THE DISTANCE 171

This from Phocylides: the well-ordered city set on a high rock, though small, is mightier than Nineveh out-of-its-mind.

Come now, when compared with the entire *Iliad* and *Odyssey*, these lines are no sideshow for those who attend to them, are they? Or is it more advantageous for you to hear about the leapings and rushings of Achilles, and about his voice, how only by crying out he turned back the Trojans? Are those things more beneficial for you to learn by heart than what I just recited, that a small city set on a rough rock is more powerful and more fortunate, if it is well ordered, than a great city on a smooth and wide plain, if indeed that city is run in a disorganized and lawless fashion by foolish men? (36.13)

ἢ οὐ δοκεῖ σοι εἰκότως προσθεῖναι Φωκυλίδης τῇ τοιαύτῃ γνώμῃ καὶ ἀποφάσει,

κaὶ τόδε Φωκυλίδου· πόλις ἐν σκοπέλῳ κατὰ κόσμον
οἰκεῦσα σμικρὴ κρέσσων Νίνου ἀφραινούσης.

ἀλλ’ οὐ πρὸς ὅλην Ἰλιάδα καὶ Ὀδύσσειαν ταῦτα τὰ ἔπη ἐστὶ τοῖς μὴ παρέργως ἀκροωμένοις; ἢ μᾶλλον ὑμῖν ἀκούειν συνέφερε περὶ τῶν τοῦ Ἀχιλλέως πηδήσεών τε καὶ ὀρούσεων καὶ τῆς φωνῆς, ὅτι μόνον φθεγξάμενος ἔτρεπε τοὺς Τρῶας, ταῦτα μᾶλλον ὠφελεῖ ὑμᾶς ἐκμανθάνοντας ἢ ἐκεῖνο, ὅτι ἡ σμικρὰ πόλις ἐν τραχεῖ σκοπέλῳ κειμένη κρείττων ἐστὶ καὶ εὐτυχεστέρα κατὰ κόσμον οἰκοῦσα ἢ μεγάλη ἐν λείῳ καὶ πλατεῖ πεδίῳ, ἐάνπερ ἀκόσμως καὶ ἀνόμως ὑπὸ ἀνθρώπων ἀφρόνων οἰκῆται;

The emphasis on cities now does something to differentiate the Borysthenitic Greeks from their Scythian neighbors, if Dio's audience at all has in mind the old notion that Scythians lack cities (cf. Hdt. 4.46.3: τοῖσι γὰρ <ἂν> μήτε ἄστεα). On the heels of the decidedly mixed picture I have described, Dio now directs the conversation toward one of the very things that would seem to separate the (Borysthenitic) Greeks out from their city-less neighbors. The emphasis here will recur a few chapters later, when Dio, launching into his first disquisition on the nature of the earthly city, tells the Borysthenites that they "do well, as people inhabiting an ancient and Greek city, in wanting to hear about a city" (εἶπον ὅτι δοκοῦσί μοι ὀρθῶς ποιεῖν, πόλιν οἰκοῦντες ἀρχαίαν καὶ Ἑλληνίδα, 18). Yet it is another irony of the oration that Dio's

172   HERODOTUS AND IMPERIAL GREEK LITERATURE

focus on the rationally ordered city as "harmonizing the human race with the divine" (ξυναρμόσαι τῷ θείῳ τὸ ἀνθρώπειον γένος, 31) will attempt to transcend the "national" and notional differences between (citied) Greeks and (city-less) Scythians.

The very attention to cities, and on their contrasting size—and, further, on the difficulty of discerning the moral quality of a place from its size or physical features—again summons one of the programmatic concerns of the *Histories*.[60] Dio's own shift recalls that of Herodotus 1.5.3–4, where the narrator not only changes the topic from the explanations of the Persian *logioi* but also alters the focus from individuals exclusively to the more expansive scope on collectivities in the form of towns both great and small (σμικρὰ καὶ μεγάλα ἄστεα, Hdt. 1.5.3 ~ σμικρὰ πόλις, *Or*. 36.13). The focus on cities in the *Histories* and in this text is not inevitable, and in both cases it represents an authoritative move on the narrator's part to alter the direction of the narrative. In *Oration* 36, Dio's literary fusion weds the Callimachean aesthetic (smaller is better) with the Herodotean paradox: smaller is better both for poetry and possibly for the polis itself. Indeed, Phocylides's sentiment amplifies the *Histories*' through-line interest on small as equal in importance to big (Hdt. 1.5.3: ὁμοίως σμικρὰ καὶ μεγάλα) for purposes of historical consideration. Small can be advantageous, as Artabanus reminds Xerxes in a well-known analogy, telling him that large animals get struck by lightning, while small beings do not "chafe against" (κνίζει) the god (ὁρᾷς τὰ ὑπερέχοντα ζῷα ὡς κεραυνοῖ ὁ θεὸς οὐδὲ ἐᾷ φαντάζεσθαι, τὰ δὲ σμικρὰ οὐδέν μιν κνίζει, 7.10.ε). Furthermore, in his summary rehashing of the Phocylides poem, Dio modifies the sense (not strictly present in the language of the poem itself) of a city set on a "a **rough** rock" (ἐν **τραχεῖ** σκοπέλῳ), adding an adjective that underscores the notion that rugged lands may breed more virtuous people. This tendentious adjustment sustains the Herodotean echo in the passage (compare, e.g., the *Histories*' conclusion, 9.122.3).[61] Dio's allusive turn to ideas of the city and to the moral qualities of measurable space gives thematic continuity (via the sustained Herodotean intertext) to the first third of this oration, and by previewing the topics to come, such intertextual ballast contributes to the overall plan of the speech.

---

[60] On the complicated relationship in Herodotus between the apparent power indicated by a place's scale and changes wrought on scale through time, see Greenwood 2018.

[61] The quotation also presents an implicit challenge to Dio's Prusan audience, as Moles 1995: 186 observes: the Prusans may be prompted to reckon with the question of whether the relatively smaller Borysthenes is superior to their city, already itself small.

HELLENISM IN THE DISTANCE   173

The Herodotean substrate, to this point in the text, has provoked questions about the relative Greekness or barbarism of the place visited—and more fundamentally about the "knowability" of these far-off societies, notwithstanding Dio's autopsy. The Prusans' ability (or our ability) to "read" the Borysthenites as Greeks continues to waver. The constant warfare that Dio had earlier mentioned (4) as endemic to the region stands, we learn, only temporarily at a lull. For when Callistratus agrees to hear Dio expound further upon Phocylides and the idea of the city, he acknowledges that despite the desire to listen, he and his fellow Borysthenites are in "a hardly unperturbed state of mind" (καίτοι οὐ σφόδρα ἀθορύβως ἔχοντας, 15), owing to the continued threat (and reality) of war with the Scythians.[62] Yet this city under threat will nonetheless pause, "under arms" (ἐν τοῖς ὅπλοις, 16), to listen to Dio discourse on the true city, leading him to describe the Borythenites as "such zealous listeners, and so thoroughly Greek in character" (οὕτως ἦσαν φιλήκοοι καὶ τῷ τρόπῳ Ἕλληνες, 16). Following his earlier ethnographic-style observations about the watered-down Greekness of the Borysthenites (7, 9), the narrator now oscillates toward underscoring their thoroughgoing Hellenism, precisely because they are willing, in the midst of their (Greek-credentialing?) war with the Scythians, to gather before the Temple of Zeus (17) and hear Dio out.[63] The mirror that Dio holds up to his Prusan audience continues to change reflective angle, while the passing remark on the attentiveness of the Borysthenites reinforces (temporarily, at least) for his Prusan audience the idea that by the very act of paying attention to Dio, they are reconstituting Hellenicity. To gather as a city to listen to Dio talk about the city is one way of being a Greek city. But it is something superior to and rather strangely beyond any one city that Dio, in fact, goes on to describe.

Cities Earthly and Cosmic

Let us turn, then, to the latter portion of the *Borystheniticus*, the speech on the cosmic city, a stretch of the work that has received much attention

[62] See §§ 15–16 on the recent Scythian raid, including the slaughter of some Greeks, the city gates shut in defense, and the Borysthenites' hoisted ensigns.

[63] The continued warfare with Scythia seems on the one hand to confirm Borysthenite Greekness but on the other, as Gangloff 2007: 74 notes, to make them look barbaric in their un-Greek, uncivil behavior: "Les habitants de Borysthène sont donc plongés dans la contradiction: leur préférence marquée pour un hellénisme archaïque et fermé les fait basculer dans la barbarie, puisqu'ils ignorent que la concorde est l'une des principales valeurs civiques."

174 HERODOTUS AND IMPERIAL GREEK LITERATURE

and inspired some interpretive conundrum.[64] I concentrate here on some of the ways in which the latter stretch of the text completes the work's early Herodotean evocations, even as the work coalesces around a vision that transcends the binary polarity of Greek-and-barbarian casually evoked by the *Histories*. In particular, the Magian hymn (39–61) achieves its cosmic transcendence precisely through its earthly specificity as "alien wisdom" (however specious Dio's claim that it is a composite of Persian ideas). That is, more than simply impressing the Borysthenites or the Prusans with a defamiliarizing turn in delivering the oration's summa of wisdom, Dio's lofty transfer to the Persians, a putative bogeyman in Greek (literary) history— and specifically his handing over his speech to the Magi, a group often cast by Herodotus in a poor light—*enacts* the very cosmic cooperation the hymn purports to describe.

Following his provocations about Homer and Phocylides, Dio pledges that he and Callistratus can praise Homer on another occasion (ποτε ἐπαινεσόμεθα Ἀχιλλέα τε καὶ Ὅμηρον, 14). Instead, he persists with the obligation to "examine" (σκεπτέον) Phocylides, on the grounds that "he speaks, in my view, quite nobly on the subject of the city" (ὡς ἐμοὶ δοκεῖ σφόδρα καλῶς λέγειν ὑπὲρ τῆς πόλεως, 15). Once mooted, the focus on cities, and eventually on the philosophical notion of the true divine city, occupies the rest of the oration. I have suggested above that this city focus is a reverberation of Herodotus's own opening gestures, that narrator, of course, echoing the start of the *Odyssey*. Dio, by means of an intertextual double play, now chooses to center a work in which he has already cast himself in Odyssean and Herodotean roles on that very subject of cities, too.[65] Malcolm Schofield has noticed the elegance of Dio's transition: "The precarious hold Borysthenes has on the status of city and on Hellenism makes a visit to it an appropriate occasion to raise the philosophical question: what is a city?"[66] Dio's *Borystheniticus* reveals that there is more than an incidental connection between the (intertextually enhanced) "setting" and the topic at hand. His artistry is at once to weave together topic and setting, intertext and topos.

But even as different aspects of the oration appear to converge, continued complexities arise. As Dio begins his disquisition on the city, he variously talks about the differences between a well-ordered and a poorly ruled place

[64] See Schofield 1991; Porter 2001: 85–90; and in particular Moles 1995, to whose reading my own is much indebted.
[65] Compare Trapp 1995: 166.
[66] Schofield 1991: 58–59.

(21), the absence of perfect cities on earth (22), and the perfection of the divinely ruled city (23). The Borysthenite Hieroson then interrupts, apologizing for his "rustic and barbaric manner" (ἄγροικον μηδὲ βαβαρικόν, 24), to ask that Dio focus on precisely this last topic; postpone talk of the mortal city, Hieroson implores, and carry on discoursing on the divine city (26–27). Now, it should be noted that the Dionian narrator laces his characterization of Hieroson's request for loftiness with no small irony. For not only does Hieroson importune Dio to carry on in the very fashion that Dio's disquisition had already begun to assume (23), but Hieroson also couches his plea for a "more exact" (ἀκριβεστέρας, 26) and ultimately philosophical lecture by emphasizing aspects of the Borysthenites' *unrefined* ways. Hieroson indicates, for instance, that Borysthenes has not been a crossroads for learned Greeks: the usual visitors are "Greeks in name but are in truth more barbarous than we are" (δεῦρο ἀφικνοῦνται ὀνόματι Ἕλληνες, τῇ δὲ ἀληθείᾳ βαρβαρώτεροι ἡμῶν, 25). Yet, while living in this backwater, Hieroson tells Dio that in addition to being huge Homer fans, the Borysthenites love Plato, too. Hieroson himself is a devotee, a fact that he says may seem "strange" (ἄτοπον, 26, a playfully Socratic formulation)—namely, that a man "who speaks the worst Greek of all the people of Borysthenes should take delight in and keep company with the 'most Hellenic' and wisest man" (βαρβαρίζοντα τῶν πολιτῶν μάλιστα τῷ ἑλληνικωτάτῳ καὶ σοφωτάτῳ χαίρειν καὶ ξυνεῖναι, 26). That each of these statements—about barbaric visitors, about being poor Greek speakers—echoes narratorial remarks from earlier in the work (see §§ 5 and 9, quoted earlier) complicates the sense in which Hieroson registers as "rustic and barbaric": the style of his request, in fact, recalls the (distinctly not rustic) narrator of *Oration* 36 and thus resurrects as well the Herodotean theme of indeterminate identity from its earlier chapters.[67]

The style of Hieroson's request helps to effect the transition into the final sequence of the work. Hieroson concludes by assuring Dio that the Borysthenites are prepared to hear a recondite speech on the divine city because "even if we understand nothing else, we understand Plato's voice from our long acquaintanceship with it. We know that Plato speaks not inconsequentially, and not far off from Homer" (εἰ γὰρ μηδενὸς ἄλλου, τῆς γε φωνῆς ξυνίεμεν ὑπὸ συνηθείας ὅτι οὐ σμικρὸν οὐδὲ πόρρω τοῦ Ὁμήρου φθέγγεται, 27). Hieroson's ironically sophisticated speech emphasizing Borysthenitic

---

[67] Porter (2001: 89) is right to see that the "play of identities in the speech [*Or.* 36 generally] is rampant, and in fact no identities seem finally certain."

176 HERODOTUS AND IMPERIAL GREEK LITERATURE

unsophistication has neatly paved the way for Dio's next move. As Schofield notes, there is a smooth connection between Hieroson's self-conscious "barbarism" and the responsive tack Dio will pursue in his disquisition on the city: "It is accordingly a nice touch when Dio concludes his *logos* by clothing Stoic cosmological theory in a myth he attributes to Zoroaster and the Magi (§§ 39–61) and describes as a 'barbarian song'—apologizing for not offering something 'Greek and graceful' (§ 43)."[68] Hieroson's speech channels Dio's remarks from earlier in the work (§§ 5 and 9), and Dio's final Magian/"barbarian" hymn in turn channels the "barbaric" Hieroson.

Dio's speech on the divine city (29–61) divides into two parts that have received much comment, especially because what Trapp has called the "weird and wonderful myth of the Magi" seems, prima facie, rather different in tone and style from the "fairly sober exposition of standard Stoic doctrine" that precedes it.[69] Nor are the seemingly disjointed segments of the long speech the result of a taxonomy imposed by scholars. Dio, in fact, marks them himself, promising initially to offer a *logos* (28) on the divine city, only to pause with an ostensibly concluding statement a few chapters later (ὅδε μὲν οὖν ὁ τῶν φιλοσόφων λόγος, 38). The dangling μέν is answered in the next chapter by the δέ that brings something new: "There is a different myth that inspires wonder, one sung in secret rites by the Magi, who hymn this god as the perfect and first charioteer of the most perfect chariot" (ἕτερος δὲ μῦθος ἐν ἀπορρήτοις τελεταῖς ὑπὸ μάγων ἀνδρῶν ᾄδεται θαυμαζόμενος, οἳ τὸν θεὸν τοῦτον ὑμνοῦσιν ὡς τέλειόν τε καὶ πρῶτον ἡνίοχον τοῦ τελειοτάτου ἅρματος, 39). This irruptive, *thauma*-inspiring myth presents various difficulties of interpretation, not the least of which involves how to understand its story (and its own two apparently irreconcilable parts) in relation to what has come before. As James Porter has observed:

> the connection between the myths [of the Magi] and what precedes them is casually bridged over (ἕτερος δὲ μῦθος, 39) and then lost in near-parallels. Dio's discourse threatens to fall apart into a series of non sequiturs. He does little to lift the cloud of confusion and everything, it seems, to foster it. Perhaps his discourse is not about harmoniousness in the cosmos, though it wants to be this (55–57), but about its very own oscillation.[70]

[68] Schofield 1991: 58.
[69] Trapp 2000: 215.
[70] Porter 2001: 87. See also Russell 1992: 231–33.

But does the speech's seeming "cloud of confusion" and apparent representation of "oscillation" over the "harmoniousness of the cosmos" in fact depart from what has come before? Both Porter and, along somewhat different lines, Moles have proposed ways of integrating the myth into the oration. For Porter, the myth's tale of melting horses, who become part of "one nature" (εἰς μίαν ἅπαντα συνέλθῃ φύσιν, 51), contributes to a political allegory of hybridization and "hybrid identities that Dio has been highlighting throughout the speech. . . . The metaphors recall nothing so much as imperial expansion."[71] Moles, too, recognizes in Dio's Magian myth the possibility that its "hybrid nature seems to suggest the ultimate harmony of Greek and barbarian peoples within the universe," though he also emphasizes that Dio's myth offers a "higher vision" than outright political allegory and that in both "space and time this vision dwarfs and transcends" the Roman Empire.[72]

I also propose an integrative reading compatible with such arguments. Dio's adoption of a supposedly Magian myth lends, on the one hand, continuity to a work that has repeatedly situated itself in the realm of the "barbaric," the faraway, the heterogeneously Herodotean. On the other hand, in his summons to his internal Borysthenitic and external Prusan audiences to digest supposedly Eastern wisdom, Dio makes good on the broader provocations of a work that invites intellectual flexibility about potentially crude binaries of identity and relation.[73] I would stress, however, a few further interpretive consequences that issue from Dio's "barbarian" myth and would argue that it sustains the work's Herodotean energies at its close—indeed, fusing a rhetoric of historical cyclicality with one of philosophical transcendence.

---

[71] Porter 2001: 88.

[72] Moles 1995: 190–91. Moles also teases out, with admirable lucidity, the intricate subtleties of Dio's rhetorical positioning vis-à-vis his internal and external audiences: "Dio's 'apology' for 'out-of-place' Magian material interacts with Hieroson's preconceptions in contradictory ways. Qua apology, it acknowledges Hieroson's request for impeccably Hellenic material. But Dio provides Hieroson with formally non-Hellenic material. Yet this formally non-Hellenic material is actually not non-Hellenic. Yet, in turn, the rhetorical effect of providing formally non-Hellenic material is not erased, especially for the Borysthenites, who cannot penetrate the philosophical disguise. For them it remains both disconcerting and educative to receive the highest truths about the universe wrapped up in the teachings of their Iranian enemies" (190).

[73] See also Momigliano 1975: 141–43 on the relationship between Plato and Magi and on the Academy as influenced by Zoroastrianism, and 146–47 on the Magian myth as "Dio's own creation": "What mattered was the total impression of the dependence of Greek culture on barbarian wisdom."

178   HERODOTUS AND IMPERIAL GREEK LITERATURE

The Magian Perspective

Dio's myth represents a sort of referendum on the status of the Magi more generally, about whom there existed a welter of negative characterizations in Greek literature.[74] Such stereotyping lies in the background of Dio's barbed comment that Zoroaster associated not with all men (συγγίγνεσθαί τε μετὰ ταῦτα οὐχ ἅπασιν) but specifically with people described as

> most naturally gifted with respect to the truth and best able to understand the god, whom the Persians call Magi, the people who know how to cultivate the divine power, not like the Greeks who, in their ignorance of the term, use it to describe men as wizards. (36.41)

> ἀλλὰ τοῖς ἄριστα πρὸς ἀλήθειαν πεφυκόσι καὶ τοῦ θεοῦ ξυνιέναι δυναμένοις, οὓς Πέρσαι μάγους ἐκάλεσαν, ἐπισταμένους θεραπεύειν τὸ δαιμόνιον, οὐχ ὡς Ἕλληνες ἀγνοίᾳ τοῦ ὀνόματος οὕτως ὀνομάζουσιν ἀνθρώπους γόητας.

Dio's challenge to his two audiences involves revising the negative views by which readers of various sources may have come to regard the Magi—a provocation made deeply ironic by the fact that the lauded Magian "wisdom" here is only so much Greek material (see later discussion). On a surface level, Dio's response to the self-proclaimed "barbarism" of Hieroson is to disclaim, by reciting a "Magian" myth, the already largely negative image of the Magi derived from the very *Histories* that Dio's *Oration* 36 repeatedly activates.

For to any members of Dio's audience sensitive by this point to his intertextual sparks, the turn toward the Magi in an oration anchored in Herodotus confirms Dio's ability to defy expectation. The Magi of the *Histories* had repeatedly been cast as intellectual failures and, ultimately, as feckless arms of the Persian invasion of Greece. Programmatically, they appear in the story of Astyages's attempt to thwart the rise of Cyrus (see Hdt. 1.107–8, 1.120). Their crucial misinterpretation of Astyages's dream spells their doom, as they are impaled for their bad hermeneutics (1.128). Elsewhere we get images of the Magi as lethally intolerant of everything except humans or dogs, killing with their own hands, and making a "great game of it" (ἀγώνισμα μέγα),

---

[74] See, e.g., Eur., *Or.* 1497; Soph., *OT* 387; Aeschin., *Against Ctesiphon* 137; Pl., *Resp.* 572e4; Lucian, *Demonax* 23, 25, and *Philopseudes* 14, 15.

HELLENISM IN THE DISTANCE 179

anything that "crawls or flies" (1.140.3). Later they make a spectacular failure of an attempted political rebellion against the rule of the Persians (3.61–79). Finally, in Herodotus's account of Xerxes's plot against and eventual invasion of Greece, the Magi are shown again erring with respect to (or perhaps fawningly misinterpreting) dreams and omens (7.19.2, 7.37.2–3) in service to the Great King and, in their final two cameos, performing sacrifices on what will be a losing campaign (7.113, 7.191).

Dio drops hints of his anxiety in relying on the Magi, whose very mention likely recalls their unprepossessing reputation. Dio's pointedly alien wisdom is conditioned by his supposed embarrassment in telling their story in the first place:

> What comes next, concerning horses and the driving of them, I am ashamed to utter in the way the Magi say it when setting forth their tale, since they are not altogether minded to present a consistent picture. For I will perhaps seem out of place chanting a barbarian song in contrast to the charming Greek songs. But all the same I must try. (36.43)

> τὸ δὴ μετὰ τοῦτο αἰσχύνομαι φράζειν τῶν ἵππων πέρι καὶ τῆς ἡνιοχήσεως, ὅπως ἐξηγούμενοι λέγουσιν, οὐ πάνυ τι φροντίζοντες ὅμοιόν σφισι γίγνεσθαι πανταχῇ τὸ τῆς εἰκόνος. ἴσως γὰρ ἂν φαινοίμην ἄτοπος παρὰ Ἑλληνικά τε καὶ χαρίεντα ᾄσματα βαρβαρικὸν ᾆσμα ἐπάδων· ὅμως δὲ τολμητέον.

Yet the embarrassment must ultimately be Dio's and that of the Greeks, since the myth is really theirs, along with the myth's (and the oration's) own inconsistencies.[75] Courtesy of Dio, the Magi (or, to acknowledge the level of invention, the "Magi"), so often degraded in the Greek literary tradition, offer their philosophical riposte to that Greek tradition.

For all the abstraction of the myth that follows, I suggest that the authority by which the Magi transmit their wisdom rests to some degree on their adopting a *historiographic* perspective. When, for instance, the Magi insist that the movement of the universe goes on "without pause and in unceasing cycles of time" (ἄπαυστον ἐν ἀπαύστοις αἰῶνος περιόδοις, 42), the

---

[75] In addition to the Magian myth's Platonic footing in the *Phaedrus* (see Trapp 2000), Dio employs many echoes of *Timaeus* 22b–d, itself a clever reworking of Herodotean material, with Solon positioned as learning from the Egyptian priests. I am grateful to Kathryn Morgan on this point.

180 HERODOTUS AND IMPERIAL GREEK LITERATURE

image recalls the historical patterns of conquest and recovery, destruction and renewal, that Dio had earlier described as characteristic of Borysthenes and that still endure.[76] Moreover, the Magi describe how the Greeks mistakenly apprehend as unique an event that only appears to be such: "The Magi say that the Greeks, remembering this [a conflagration of the universe] as a one-time occurrence, link it with Phaethon" (τοῦτο δὲ τὸ πάθος ἅπαξ Ἕλληνας μνημονεύοντάς φασι Φαέθοντι προσάπτειν, 48). The Magi furthermore call out the Greeks for their "youthful ignorance and weak memory" (ὑπὸ νεότητός τε καὶ μνήμης ἀσθενοῦς, 49) in likewise supposing the deluge of the earth to be singular, as told in the story of Deucalion.[77] The Magian μῦθος thus corrects Greek myth and rebukes the limitations of Greek historical understanding. The Magi, as if taking on the perspective of the historian over the longue durée, recognize what the Greeks supposedly do not: that these periodic events (σπανίως ξυμβαίνοντα, 50) occur according to the reason and order of the universe (κατὰ λόγον . . . μετέχειν τῆς τοῦ παντὸς τάξεως, 50). Even when the spreading of seed across the universe reaches a point of perfection (55), it does so only to "long for" a prior life (ἐπόθησε τὸν ἐξ ἀρχῆς βίον, 55). That the perfected seed immediately (εὐθύς, 55) pines for an earlier state and undergoes purifying conflagration (56) reiterates the fluctuation that the Magian myth posits.[78] The cosmos so described moves not toward static equilibrium but rather through a continual cycle of renewal and destruction.

The Magi, then, provide a kind of historical perspective that takes account "over a long space of time and in many revolutions" (ἐν μήκει χρόνου καὶ πολλαῖς περιόδοις, 47). This cyclicality echoes the fluctuations articulated in the oration concerning Borysthenes itself (§§ 4, 15), whose cycles of destruction and rebuilding reiterate the reciprocal cycles of conflict that themselves recall Herodotus's Histories. Indeed, in light of the oration's evocative Herodotean intertextuality, the Magian sense of long temporal spans and patterned cycles may also put one in mind of Herodotus's Solon and his comment on what one may see "in a long period of time" (ἐν . . . τῷ μακρῷ χρόνῳ, 1.32.2) or Herodotus's Croesus as he describes the constant "cycle of human affairs" (κύκλος τῶν ἀνθρωπηίων ἐστὶ πρηγμάτων . . . αἰεί, 1.207.2). Or one

---

[76] See § 4 for the constant and repeated wars (συνεχεῖς . . . ἀεὶ μὲν πολεμεῖται, πολλάκις δὲ καὶ ἑάλωκεν) and § 15 on the continuing warfare.

[77] Compare Pl. Tim. 22b. On Or. 36.48–49 in relation to other representations of memory among Imperial Greeks, see Porter 2001: 89–90.

[78] See Porter 2001: 88 on §§ 51–53 and § 55, with attention to fluctuation.

HELLENISM IN THE DISTANCE   181

may recall Herodotus's own programmatic enunciation of the inconstancy of human fortune (εὐδαιμονίην οὐδαμὰ ἐν τὠυτῷ μένουσαν, 1.5.4) or his later remark that "anything can happen over a long period of time" (γένοιτο δ' ἂν πᾶν ἐν τῷ μακρῷ χρόνῳ, 5.9.3). In taking the long view, then, the Magi reprove Greek myth by speaking commandingly from the pages of *historia*. They do so no longer as the mistaken hermeneuts from Herodotus but rather with self-assured authority (αὐθαδῶς, 42), ironically enabled by the wider historiographic perspective that itself recalls Herodotus.

Dio's ascription of the Magian authority thus adds to the work's historiographic texture. Although he offers up their description as a μῦθος, he reports on the Magian effort to rise above poetry and to speak, rather, in a manner that differs from that of prophets. The Magi further adopt the rhetoric of *historia* in their use of the verb ἐξηγέομαι ("explain"), activating the sound of Herodotean inquiry: "They **explain** their myth not in the style of our prophets of the Muses, who declare each thing with much persuasiveness, but rather **according to their own conviction**" (ἐξηγοῦνται δὲ τὸν μῦθον οὐχ ὥσπερ οἱ παρ' ἡμῖν προφῆται τῶν Μουσῶν ἕκαστα φράζουσι μετὰ πολλῆς πειθοῦς, ἀλλὰ μάλα **αὐθαδῶς**, 42).[79] One recognizes in this pivotal distinction a self-conscious transition from the realm of poetic prophecy, with its reliance on the Muses for persuasion (τῶν Μουσῶν . . . πειθοῦς), to the arena of independently authoritative (αὐθαδῶς) declaration that distinguishes both historiographic (including Herodotean) prose and the sophist's posture of authority in the Imperial era.[80] Dio's kinetic reception channels the Herodotean hypotext but recasts one of its own dubious sources of authority (the Magi) as the authoritative voice of a recondite myth, the recounting of which represents the pinnacle of Dio's own authority in the *Borystheniticus*.

In addition, then, to the Stoic and Platonic basis of what Dio claims to be Zoroastrian, one senses in the myth of the Magi undercurrents of both the content (reciprocal cycles of violence) and the rhetoric (authoritative explanation and understanding derived from taking the long view) of the very *Histories* wherein the Magi once made many an appearance. Yet Dio's gambit of allusive Greekness-as-Zoroastrianism leaves us still with questions about what he is up to in this oration, and whether his hybridizing gestures have turned out to be merely specious, only reaffirming (through the disguised

---

[79] For the verb, compare Hdt. 2.3.2, 2.113.3, 2.115.3, 3.72.1.

[80] Some irony underlies this apparent contrast, however, insofar as Dio claims to be "chanting" (ἐπᾴδων, 43) a myth sung (ᾄδεται, 39) by the Magi, giving his authoritative, historiographically inflected speech a poetic flair.

182   HERODOTUS AND IMPERIAL GREEK LITERATURE

Greek narrative passed off as Magian) a kind of Greek cultural chauvinism.[81] Does Dio hoodwink his Borysthenite audience, who in their backwater, confused Greekness cannot see through his rhetorical tricks, falsely presenting Greek wisdom as Persian? Likewise, one may speculate about the Prusan audience's percipience of Dio's elaborate masking in hearing Dio flatter these far-off Greeks. One could press further, as we have just seen. Do the Magian depictions of recurrent cosmic renewal, in fact, "transcend" earthly, imperial time, as Moles would have them do?[82] Or do they merely recall by analogy endless (ἀεί, 4) cycles of warfare between the Greeks and non-Greeks that are the historical backdrop for the speech, the Magi now "recruited" rhetorically in that back-and-forth between Greek and barbarian? Or, in fine, has Dio's text, in moving from Homer to Phocylides to Plato, all cast against the backdrop of the murky Herodotean border-world, attempted somehow to move through and encapsulate literary history, offering up a cosmic μῦθος at once Greek *and* "barbarian"—showcasing the speech of a Greek whose own wisdom supposedly derives from and tries to exalt (δυνατὸν ἐπᾶραι, 60) barbarian wisdom, even as it falls back on Greek allusions?

Much of this remains suspended. Dio's own final comments leave matters unresolved, as uncertainty and irony linger:

If the form of the *logos* has turned out to be entirely lofty and indistinct— just as the experts in augury say about the bird that advances too high and, hiding itself in the clouds, makes the act of divination incomplete—well, it is not right to hold me responsible. Rather, the Borysthenites are guilty, since on that occasion it was they who ordered me to speak. (36.61)

εἰ δὲ ἀτεχνῶς ὑψηλόν τε καὶ ἐξίτηλον ἀπέβη τὸ τοῦ λόγου σχῆμα, ὥσπερ οἱ δεινοὶ περὶ τοὺς ὄρνιθάς φασι τὸν σφόδρα ἄνω χωρήσαντα καὶ τοῖς νέφεσιν ἐγκρύψαντα αὑτὸν ἀτελῆ τὴν μαντείαν ποιεῖν, οὐκ ἐμὲ ἄξιον αἰτιᾶσθαι, τὴν δὲ Βορυσθενιτῶν ἀξίωσιν, ὡς τότε ἐκεῖνοι λέγειν προσέταξαν.

The Magian μῦθος (39) is now subordinated to the entirety of the λόγος, "blurring the distinction" Dio had earlier made, as Moles notes (see §§ 29,

---

[81] See Gangloff 2007: 75: "But the Persian elements seem, in the final analysis, to be part of the Greek view of alien wisdom. Ought we to conclude, then, that there is no real curiosity about this wisdom?" ("Mais les éléments iraniens semblent, en dernière analyse, relever du regard grec posé sur la sagesse étrangère. Faut-il pour autant en conclure un manque de curiosité réelle pour cette sagesse?").
[82] Moles 1995: 188.

38).[83] Dio admits that his account risks being overly lofty (ὑψηλόν) and indistinct (ἐξίτηλον), the latter a pointedly Herodotean term, recalling the anxiety about deeds and events that may fade with time (Hdt. *proem*). It is as if in delivering this complex oration on the hazy outer edges of the Greek world, where Hellenism becomes hard to define, Dio's own language has crossed over into the indistinctness of his topic. The would-be ethnography of the Getae, interrupted by the journey among the partly Greek, partly barbarian Borysthenites, yields to a vision of "foreign" (but actually) Greek wisdom that in its disguise only points up the manipulability of categories. And further blurring the distinctions at the speech's end comes the difficulty of discerning clearly whom Dio addresses. The temporally distant, third-person reference to the Borysthenites (τότε ἐκεῖνοι) implies a metaleptic jump. The Magian speech that began as addressed to the Borysthenites has without announcement shifted to the external audience of the Prusans. Such confounding, finally, only adds to the reader's sense that definitive "divination" on the various issues raised in the *Borystheniticus*—on identity, on the nature of the city, on the cycles of (cosmic) history, on where wisdom comes from—proves elusive, "hiding itself in the clouds" (τοῖς νέφεσιν ἐγκρύψαντα αὐτόν). Dio has conjured the ambiguating effects of distant inquiry into the far-flung, kinetically mooting Herodotus's opacities only to appropriate them for himself. He has transdiscursively soldered the Herodotean uncertainty principle onto philosophy's aporia.

In his 1965 essay "Hermeneutics and Historicism," Gadamer at one moment refers to the "generic" differences between "ontic" and "historical" modes and the importance of recognizing "the so-called subject in the mode of being of historicity that is appropriate to it."[84] He goes on:

> It is true that the historical writing of, say, Herodotus, even of Plutarch, is able to describe very well the ebb and flow of human history, as a great variety of moral exempla, without reflecting on the historicity of their own present and on the historicity of human life in general. The model of the

---

[83] Moles 1995: 188. Compare Pl. *Tim.* 22c–d: "This tale as told has the form of *mythos*, but its truth inheres in the movement of heavenly bodies around the earth and, over long intervals, destruction of things on earth through great fire" (τοῦτο μύθου μὲν σχῆμα ἔχον λέγεται, τὸ δὲ ἀληθές ἐστι τῶν περὶ γῆν κατ᾽ οὐρανὸν ἰόντων παράλλαξις καὶ διὰ μακρῶν χρόνων γιγνομένη τῶν ἐπὶ γῆς πυρὶ πολλῷ φθορά).
[84] Gadamer 1965: 550.

cosmic order, in which everything that is divergent and opposed to the norm passes quickly away, as it is ironed out in the great harmonizing process of a natural cycle, can also be used as a description of human affairs. The best order of things, the ideal state, is in conception just as permanent an order as the cosmos, and even if an ideal realization of it does not endure, but is superseded by the new confusion and disorder that we call history, this is the result of an error in calculation by human reason, which knows what the right thing is. The right order has no history. History is always a history of disintegration and, sometimes, of the restoration of the right order.[85]

In bringing this chapter to a close, I draw attention to Gadamer's remarks because they seem to capture some of the Herodotean features and tensions in Dio's *Borystheniticus*. Like Gadamer's Herodotus, Dio is often preoccupied with a variety of moral exempla, and the "ebb and flow of human history" become in his city speeches a vast repository for bringing the edges of the earth to the center of various rhetorical situations, simultaneously allowing for a kind of flattery of cities—they are often worldly, much-trafficked sites—and for a critical judgment by that outer world. It is the "new confusion and disorder that we call history" that avails Dio of various exempla—in the *Borystheniticus* specifically, the Scythians, the peculiar Borysthenites, and the Magi—that feature in speeches often concerned either implicitly or explicitly with the "model of cosmic order." On that particular note, as I have argued with regard to the *Borystheniticus*, the cosmic and historical orders reflect each other, and "the great harmonizing process" of the Magian myth can also be used for a "description of human affairs," as the (*historia*-evoking) Magi tell the story of the universe in a way that reiterates a "history of disintegration and . . . restoration," cosmic conflagration paralleling human cycles of conflict. Dio's oration may, in fact, move beyond Gadamer's Herodotus by provoking reflection for his audience(s) on the "historicity" of their own present and the "historicity of human life in general," as Dio revolves his audience from specific to universal, from physical earth to heights beyond the clouds, in an oration inaugurated by and subtly bookended with Herodotean detail.

[85] Gadamer 1965: 550.

The precariousness of the ethnographic encounter in *Oration* 36 and the questions raised about the stability of identity would in the next generation become central to Lucian of Samosata's reception of Herodotus. However different in tone Dio might seem from Lucian, the Prusan anticipated some of the very questions of consistency and identity that become prominent in Lucian, and it is to the latter's Herodotean refractions that we turn next.

5

Removable Eyes

Lucian and the Truths of Herodotus

Across Herodotus's *Histories*, nothing seems certain except uncertainty and change.[1] A quality of instability applies not only to the fortunes of the work's many actors but also to the reader's experience in negotiating chronological jumps, shifts in topic, and apparent digressions. Herodotus's sprawling text has a formal variety that recapitulates thematic focus: instability inheres in both the work's documentation of the "circle of human affairs" (1.207.2) and the reader's effort to reduce diffuseness to one clear pattern, amid analepses, prolepses, and diverting *logoi* that can make reading itself feel destabilizing. And if instability in Herodotus has narratological dimensions that mirror its content, it is also the case that Herodotus's thematic focus on instability encompasses more than just the rise and fall of various places. As scholars have shown, the *Histories* has the capacity to unseat an easy sense of fixed identity, too.[2] The work's ethnographic features may lure readers into a sense of patterned fixity—"Greeks behave this way, Persians that way," and so on— but such would-be patterns inevitably belie the complexity of Herodotus's world.[3]

Relatively early on in the work, for instance, Herodotus gives readers cause to doubt ethnographic essentialism when he describes how the

---

[1] See Węcowski 2004: 156–57: "The true contents of this [i.e., Herodotus's] special type of knowledge are no doubt fluctuations of human fate, implied already in the notion of oblivion threatening great human achievements (*incipit*)."

[2] On Herodotus's flexible presentation of (national) stereotypes, see esp. Pelling 1997. For deconstructions of the Greek/barbarian polarity, see Hall 1989: 201–24; Gruen 2011: 25–39; McWilliams 2013. See Thomas 2000: 78, 96, 112, 200–201, against strict versions of Herodotean schematism. Compare Harrison's remarks (2020: 142) on Herodotus's "multiple, overlapping polarities" along with his further comments on the "explorations, undercuttings, inversions" of polarity (pp. 144–45), with, finally, his critique of what he calls the "balance-sheet" approach to analyzing Herodotus's representations of non-Greeks: "As post-colonial writers have recognized, positive and negative stereotypes are frequently part of the same complex of ideas" (146).

[3] On cultural admixture at the "center" of Herodotus's world, see Redfield 1985: 110–11: "The center of Herodotus's historical map is Ionia, where the natural mixture is most delicately balanced." See Rutherford 2018: 14 on Herodotus's own background as shaping his worldly perspective.

Herodotus and Imperial Greek Literature. N. Bryant Kirkland, Oxford University Press. © Oxford University Press 2022.
DOI: 10.1093/oso/9780197583517.003.0006

Lydians, seemingly overnight, undertook a complete change in lifestyle (τὴν πᾶσαν δίαιταν τῆς ζόης μετέβαλον) by adopting new clothes, surrendering weapons, teaching their sons to be salesmen, and taking up the cithara and harp (1.157.2). Typical markers of ethnographic enumeration—clothes, customs, familial relations—factor here as evidence of willed change, not unbroken tradition. As W. R. Connor has written, "Being Ionian (or Dorian, or Aeolian) . . . was a decision, conscious or unconscious, not an automatic inheritance from one's ancestors."[4] Other instances of altered names, newly adopted allegiances, and deviations from expected custom only amplify this sense that change in Herodotus is not restricted to shifts up and down in fortune but can, in fact, embrace fundamental reconfigurations of identity. Compare Herodotus's expressions of uncertainty in discussing the Caunians:

> The Caunians I myself believe to be natives of the land, but according to their own account they came originally from Crete. Concerning dialect, they have come to sound like the Carians—or the Carians have come to sound like them. I cannot say for sure which way round it should be. In their way of life they differ greatly from other humans and from the Carians. (1.172.1)

> Οἱ δὲ Καύνιοι αὐτόχθονες δοκέειν ἐμοί εἰσι, αὐτοὶ μέντοι ἐκ Κρήτης φασὶ εἶναι. προσκεχωρήκασι δὲ γλῶσσαν μὲν πρὸς τὸ Καρικὸν ἔθνος, ἢ οἱ Κᾶρες πρὸς τὸ Καυνικόν (τοῦτο γὰρ οὐκ ἔχω ἀτρεκέως διακρῖναι), νόμοισι δὲ χρέωνται κεχωρισμένοισι πολλὸν τῶν τε ἄλλων ἀνθρώπων καὶ Καρῶν.

The narrator's inability to flag the direction of change is perhaps less a confession of his inadequacy and rather more a nod to the complexity of hybrid identities that structures the world he describes.[5]

Questions of hybridity and mixed identity often come to the fore in the works of Lucian of Samosata, in whose large corpus Herodotus himself bulks large.[6] At the fundamental level of quotation and citation, Herodotus appears

---

[4] Connor 1993: 198. With Connor's comment on non-essentialist identity, compare the Athenians' remark (Hdt. 9.27.4), in their speech before Plataea, on historical fluctuations in different groups' characters; the instability of identity cited acts as (a tendentious) grounds for their dismissing the value of historical examples.

[5] For other hybrid ethnographies or genealogies in Herodotus, see his account of Athenians and Pelasgians (1.56; cf. 2.51 and 6.136–40, with McInerney 2014 and Sourvinou-Inwood 2003) and of the Termilae/Lycians (1.172–73).

[6] On Herodotus in Lucian, see Jones 1986: 152; Macleod 1991: 286–88; Avery 1997. For Lucian's use of Herodotus in texts not directly treated in this chapter, see Anderson 1976c: 2–5, 13–21, 27,

188 HERODOTUS AND IMPERIAL GREEK LITERATURE

throughout Lucian.[7] But what *kind* of Herodotus informs Lucian, and how are we to trace the polymorphic Herodotus through the multifaceted Lucian, himself a multipronged writer defiant of orthodoxies? What kind of reader of Herodotus was Lucian? What motivated his readings, and how should we ourselves read Lucian reading Herodotus?[8] In what follows, I build on Lucian's evident allusiveness to Herodotus to plumb the intellectual symbiosis that he shares with his predecessor.[9] For the aura of Herodotus's intertextual ambience supersedes specific allusions. Lucian's reception of Herodotus, even in the seemingly jocular *True Histories*, harks to serious themes of instability and fluidity of identity, mediated through Lucian's extended replay of the ethnographic encounter.[10] His engagement with Herodotus zooms in repeatedly on a notion of flux. Lucian's own peripatetic experience of the Roman world under which his curious Hellenism took shape inflects a literary corpus rife with foreign encounter and an accosting sense of otherness.[11] In this regard, Lucian's extended historiographic riffs contained in

with critique of Anderson's allusion-hunting at Free 2015: 126 n. 105. For Lucian's texts, I follow Macleod's Oxford Classical Text (1972–1987).

[7] Among the prose authors whom Lucian cites or quotes, Herodotus ranks second only to Plato. For statistics on allusions, quotations, and citations in Lucian, see Householder 1941: 15, 38, 41, 44, 53, with the critique of Anderson 1976b, citing Penick 1902: 16–41, that with respect to both Herodotus and Plato, "Householder's lists should be expanded considerably" (67). As Anderson 1976b shows, Lucian's "short cuts" to the past often raise more questions than they settle (thus, at 59: "Householder himself did not devote attention to the content or context of the citations"). On Lucian's direct relation to Herodotus, rather than having Herodotean interests as mediated through Theopompus or Ephorus, see Penick 1902: 1–4. On Lucian's quotations, see also Bompaire 1958: 382–404; for a discussion of sources, see von Möllendorff 2000: 12–23.

[8] See Whitmarsh 2006b: 106–9 on the polyvocality of a *Rezeptionsgeschichte* that allows for "polygonal relationships with intermediary interpreters" (108), such as ours with Lucian as he interprets Herodotus.

[9] The large size of Lucian's corpus restricts the number of texts that this chapter and the next can treat. I do not focus on Lucian's *How to Write History*, for which see Homeyer 1965; Tamiolaki 2015; and Free 2015, with Free's particular argument (168) for the independence, rather than interdependence, of *Hist. conscr.* and *True Histories* (cf. Georgiadou and Larmour 1994).

[10] On Lucian's seriousness, see Reardon 1971: 180 and Smith 2009, the latter cautioning against a view of his satires as "comedies of nihilism" (Whitmarsh 2001b: 252): "The self-canceling of Lucian's satire does not altogether invalidate ethical and moral positions that may be found within the text" (Smith 2009: 80 n. 4). I share Smith's view, which also contrasts with the relatively dismissive slant offered by Anderson 1982 (e.g., 64: "[H]e must be judged on the comic results rather than the moral pose"; 74: "The almost oppressive complexity of his borrowings, and the simplicity of their results, have long been a cause of impatience").

[11] See Jones 1986: 6–14; Smith 2009. See generally Pretzler 2007a on travel and *paideia* and her point (136–37, citing Philostratus, *VS* 625) that travel in the Imperial era offered a way to construct oneself as a Greek *pepaideumenos* relative to the (traditionally, if not truly) sedentary self-construction of the Romans. One should be wary, however, of reducing Lucian's corpus to a biographic reflection; it remains an intellectual construct; see Richter 2011: 146–47 on Lucian's Syrians as "not self-evident records of Lucian's own struggles" (147). For an attempt to trace an idea of biographic coherence in Lucian's corpus see, e.g., Swain 1996: 298–329, arguing for Lucian's attitudes toward Rome. Pace Swain, see Richter 2017: 327–28, arguing against biographic coherence and a consistent Weltanschauung, with further bibliography.

the *True Histories*, despite the cosmetic difference of genre, make manifest the romping variety of cosmopolitan encounter, the "drunkenness of things being various," in the phrase of poet Louis MacNeice.[12] It will be seen that for Lucian, Herodotus can be reduced neither to being simply a liar nor to being a memorial shorthand for the Persian Wars.[13] Lucian's reframing readings of Herodotus unmoor the Halicarnassian from the nostalgic jingoism of the Persian Wars tradition. Indeed, we may doubt the appeal such a tradition will have held for Lucian, whose Hellenism is never straightforward. For all his ability to showcase his fine-tuned *paideia*,[14] an outsider sense of non-Greekness and marginal identity persists in his work. In reading Lucian as he reads Herodotus, it emerges that Lucian was himself already alive to the porousness of identity that Herodotus captures. His engagements with Herodotus do not so much improvise upon the Greek past as they uncover certain latent energies, activating margins that were already there.

Recognizing "Herodotus" in the *Herodotus and Aëtion*

But let us start somewhat off-kilter, as he might have wished, with Lucian's brief *prolalia* called *Herodotus and Aëtion*, a work that directly summons questions of reception.[15] This tripartite text casts Herodotus as a public performer, introduces a digression on the painter Aëtion (to whom Herodotus is implicitly compared), and finally reintroduces the performing Herodotus, whom the narrator says he wishes to emulate. The work thus focuses readers on Herodotus as an acute figure in Lucian's activation of the literary past.

Lucian opens the *Herodotus* with a cascade of conventional imitative possibilities, only to dismiss them as unattainable. He cites the "beauty of

---

[12] From MacNeice's "Snow." I owe awareness of MacNeice's poem to Thomas Harrison, who quoted it in an SCS lecture (San Francisco, 2016) when describing Herodotean variety.

[13] Compare Tatum 1997: 30, discussing Lucian's take on Ctesias: Lucian is less captivated, it seems, by the outright liar than by the uncanny truth teller.

[14] See Bompaire 1958: 158 on Lucian's mimesis as "une imitation médiate qui ruse avec son objet et le metamorphose"; see also Whitmarsh 2001b: 247–94; Andrade 2013: 261–313.

[15] The work has been generally ignored as trifling: see, e.g., Anderson 1976c: 36, 73, in passing, and his more general comment (1977: 313) that Lucian's *prolaliae* belong to "the slightest trifles among the vast amount of ephemera produced by the Second Sophistic." (A more recent study, Baumbach and von Möllendorff 2017, does not mention the work at all.) Pace Anderson, see Branham 1985; Nesselrath 1990 (esp. 111–17 for general remarks and 117–22 for comments on the *Herodotus and Aëtion*); ní Mheallaigh 2014: 1–2. Scholarship has focused on this particular *prolalia* as evidence for Herodotus's public performances: Jacoby 1913: 274; Munson 2001: 15 n. 38; Evans 2008. See also Free 2015: 125–38 (esp. 126–29 for specific comments on the *Herodotus and Aëtion*), who recognizes the value of the *prolaliae* as articulations of Lucian's rhetorical identity.

190 HERODOTUS AND IMPERIAL GREEK LITERATURE

Herodotus's *logoi* or the way he joined them together, the idiosyncrasy and appropriateness of his Ionic, and the remarkable nature of his thought," all adduced as "beyond hope of imitation" (πέρα τῆς εἰς μίμησιν ἐλπίδος, *Hdt.* 1).[16] From the beginning, the narrator thus exposes the selectivity of reception. His opening μέν-clause lists particular literary charms that one might imitate, only to alter the focus to performance in the ensuing δέ-clause: "But what he did on behalf of his writings and, in a brief span, how he became a figure of great worth among all Greeks, this is something you and I and someone else could imitate" (ἃ δὲ ἐποίησεν ἐπὶ τοῖς συγγράμμασιν καὶ ὡς πολλοῦ ἄξιος τοῖς Ἕλλησιν ἅπασιν ἐν βραχεῖ κατέστη, καὶ ἐγὼ καὶ σὺ καὶ ἄλλος ἂν μιμησαίμεθα, 1). Lucian both does and does not provide his audience with the Herodotus they might expect. For even as he includes certain critical *topoi* concerning Herodotus, he magnifies the author in an unconventional way by shifting emphasis from his style to his performance:

> The idea of giving readings now at Corinth or Argos or in turn at Sparta he thought a considerable task that would prove a not negligible waste of time in the effort. He certainly did not think it a good idea to spread out his task and little by little, through such division, cobble together and compile his reputation. He wanted, if it should prove possible, to capture all the Greeks somehow as one body. The great Olympic Games were at hand, and Herodotus supposed that the right moment had arrived that he was longing for. He took care that the gathering was at its fullest and waited until it was full of the best selection of people from every place; then he appeared in the temple hall, presenting himself not as an onlooker, but as one vying for an Olympic victory of his own. Singing his *Histories*, he beguiled those present, to the point that each book was named after one of the Muses, whose number they matched. (*Hdt.* 1)

> νῦν δὲ Κορινθίοις ἀναγινώσκειν ἢ Ἀργείοις ἢ Λακεδαιμονίοις ἐν τῷ μέρει, ἐργῶδες καὶ μακρὸν ἡγεῖτο εἶναι καὶ τριβὴν οὐ μικρὰν ἐν τῷ τοιούτῳ ἔσεσθαι. οὔκουν ἠξίου διασπᾶν τὸ πρᾶγμα οὐδὲ κατὰ διαίρεσιν οὕτω κατ' ὀλίγον ἀγείρειν καὶ συλλέγειν τὴν γνῶσιν, ἐπεβούλευε δέ, εἰ δυνατὸν εἴη, ἀθρόους που λαβεῖν τοὺς Ἕλληνας ἅπαντας. ἐνίσταται οὖν Ὀλύμπια

---

[16] Ἡροδότου εἴθε μὲν καὶ τὰ ἄλλα μιμήσασθαι δυνατὸν ἦν. οὐ πάντα φημὶ ὅσα προσῆν αὐτῷ (μεῖζον γὰρ εὐχῆς τοῦτό γε) ἀλλὰ κἂν ἓν ἐκ τῶν ἁπάντων—οἷον ἢ κάλλος τῶν λόγων ἢ ἁρμονίαν αὐτῶν ἢ τὸ οἰκεῖον τῇ Ἰωνίᾳ καὶ προσφυὲς ἢ τῆς γνώμης τὸ περιττὸν ἢ ὅσα μυρία καλὰ ἐκεῖνος ἅμα πάντα συλλαβὼν ἔχει πέρα τῆς εἰς μίμησιν ἐλπίδος.

τὰ μεγάλα, καὶ ὁ Ἡρόδοτος τοῦτ᾽ ἐκεῖνο ἥκειν οἱ νομίσας τὸν καιρόν, οὗ μάλιστα ἐγλίχετο, πλήθουσαν τηρήσας τὴν πανήγυριν, ἀπανταχόθεν ἤδη τῶν ἀρίστων συνειλεγμένων, παρελθὼν ἐς τὸν ὀπισθόδομον οὐ θεατήν, ἀλλ᾽ ἀγωνιστὴν Ὀλυμπίων παρεῖχεν ἑαυτὸν ᾄδων τὰς ἱστορίας καὶ κηλῶν τοὺς παρόντας, ἄχρι τοῦ καὶ Μούσας κληθῆναι τὰς βίβλους αὐτοῦ, ἐννέα καὶ αὐτὰς οὔσας.

Relocating the exemplary achievement from Herodotus's textual unification of the Greeks and barbarians to his unification *through performance* of the best of the Greeks (ἀπανταχόθεν ἤδη τῶν ἀρίστων συνειλεγμένων, 1), Lucian casts that performance as the attractive imitative possibility (ἂν μιμησαίμεθα). Readers therefore encounter a double reception move: Lucian switches the expected focus on stylistic imitation to imitation of Herodotus's self-promulgation, and he maps the critical insight about Herodotus's unifying historical structure onto the unifying *effect* of his performance.[17] Lucian has Herodotus imitate himself, as it were, as if paralleling his Panhellenic performance to his globally encompassing content.

Hence, already in the first part of the *prolalia*, the narrator differentiates one version of Herodotean reception from other possible versions. For Lucian, Herodotus's achievement inheres in his chosen moment of self-presentation. His "singing" the *Histories* at Olympia obviates a piecemeal approach and allows him "to catch, somehow, all the Greeks together." He is depicted as sensing his *kairos* and achieving the plenitude of literary reification, not only with respect to his audience (πλήθουσαν . . . ἀπανταχόθεν) but also with respect to his work. The moment of performance is coterminous with (ἄχρι, "to the point at which") his books' quasi-apotheosis as the Muses. Lucian therefore marks the shift from Herodotus the θεατής, the man whose *Histories* stressed his own autopsy, to Herodotus ἀγωνιστής, conscious of winning literary fame.[18] A programmatic distinction is thereby imparted between the received Herodotus of popular tradition and Lucian's own "Herodotus," an agent of literary self-actualization and self-promotion.[19]

---

[17] For the critical perception of Herodotus's unified content, see Dionysius *Thuc.* 5.5 and *Pomp.* 3.14, with discussion in chapter 2.

[18] On the Olympic Games as a rhetorical performance space in the second century CE, see Free 2015: 128 n. 117, with further references. Cf. Dio, *Or.* 12.

[19] See Free 2015: 128 for discussion of Lucian's emphasis on Herodotus "als umherziender Redner" and for the link between Lucian's image of Herodotus as sophist and the author's own projected self-image.

192   HERODOTUS AND IMPERIAL GREEK LITERATURE

Lucian has converted Herodotus into a fellow practitioner of self-conscious literary spectacle—a fellow sophist, as it were.

Lucian complicates this introduction, however, by proceeding to do some of what he initially disclaims as impossible. For in the middle sections of the *prolalia*, Lucian indeed imitates Herodotus the "marvelous writer" (συγγραφέα θαυμαστόν, 7) by means of a Herodotean-style digression centered on a *thauma* (5).[20] Lucian connects the work's main topic to the digression on Aëtion through a verbal echo linking Herodotus's writings (συγγράμματια, 1) with Aëtion's painting (συγγράψαντα, 4). This perceptual blending—Herodotus as akin to the painter—assimilates Herodotus to Aëtion and unites them in particular through their acts of public display. We are led to ask what separates Herodotus the display artist from Aëtion, or for that matter from Lucian, who himself displays (δεῖξαι, 7) his own skill in the Herodotean ekphrastic digression on the *thauma*. The marvelous painting that Lucian curates through Herodotean autopsy (κἀγὼ εἶδον ὥστε καὶ σοὶ ἂν εἰπεῖν ἔχοιμι, 5) loops back to Herodotus the "marvelous writer" (συγγραφέα θαυμαστόν, 7), whom Lucian has "shown us" in varying acts of display (διεξιόντα . . . διεξῆλθεν, 7).

Lucian's wonder-writing, in focusing readers on the spectacle of Aëtion's painting, also recalls the visual allure of Herodotus himself from earlier in the work. There we are told that Herodotus need only appear (εἴ πού γε φανείη μόνον) for spectators to point their fingers and "indicate" him (ἐδείκνυτο ἂν τῷ δακτύλῳ, 2). In this context, one mode of "reading" Herodotus can be done iconically, with his visual presence sufficient to inspire a particular kind of (un)critical response. But in the audience's pointing, a meta-literary operation is at work. By offering a new version of Herodotus—a figure who is more important for his performance itself rather than strictly for his content (the Greco-Persian Wars)—a tension is again established between the Herodotus whom Lucian's audience expects and the one whom Lucian aims to describe. The short work's accumulation of assimilative echoes suggests that Herodotus is not really offering a πάρεργον (8) at the Olympic Games, the view held by what Lucian calls the "jumbled mob" (συρφετώδης ὄχλος,

---

[20] Lucian seems to invoke Aëtion's painting as a *thauma* to justify his digression, much as Herodotus justifies potentially diverting material based on its wondrousness (see, e.g., *Hist.* 2.35, 4.30). On Herodotus's well-known interest in wonders, see Hunzinger 1995; Thomas 2000: 134–67; Munson 2001, esp. 259–65 (with my chapter 8). See further Popescu 2014: 39–40 on how Lucian's *prolaliae* move audiences from "bewilderment to aesthetic enthrallment" (40).

8).[21] Rather, in Lucian's eyes, Herodotus (or *his* Herodotus) constitutes, in fact, the *ergon* itself. He produces the authorial event that the Imperial author hopes to emulate. As his own self-conscious text shows, Lucian is keen to complicate the received Herodotus, the one to whom people might point the finger and utter, "This is that Herodotus who wrote the story of the Persian Wars in Ionic, who hymned our victories" (οὗτος ἐκεῖνος Ἡρόδοτός ἐστιν ὁ τὰς μάχας τὰς Περσικὰς Ἰαστὶ συγγεγραφώς, ὁ τὰς νίκας ἡμῶν ὑμνήσας, 2). In this brief work, then, Lucian scrambles straightforward indexicality. For even as Lucian expresses his desire for recognizing himself in Herodotus (*Hdt.* 1, 7), the implied parallels of the text invite us to recognize the (performing) Herodotus in him. The pointing crowd sees one version of Herodotus; Lucian provokes us to see the other—the transdiscursive Herodotus *in Lucian* who himself performs before an audience (7–8).

And yet, to observe one last wrinkle, even if Lucian seeks to model himself on Herodotus qua performer, this aspect cannot be read as completely straightforward either, since Lucian's Herodotean imitation in the work's middle section abuts his professed *inabilities* of imitation (1). Lucian thereby demonstrates a meta-critical sensibility and capacity for kinetic reception: he alludes to reputation only to give it a twist. Lucian writes a work that "receives" (a version of) Herodotus and that is also fundamentally *about* receiving Herodotus. As Michel Riffaterre once wrote, discussing intertextuality, "We simultaneously decipher the text that is before our eyes and the one that comes back to our memory. . . . It is as if the [text] that we are reading has already been tested and approved, since we can recognize another [text] in it."[22] Lucian's perceptual blurring in the *Herodotus and Aëtion* provides such double vision. The short work is "tested and approved" by its Herodotean resonances. Although Lucian seems to broadcast one version of Herodotus— the traveling performer in the unquestionably Greek space of Olympia—he nonetheless tampers with our ability to "point the finger" at Herodotus alone through his act of self-likening. It is Herodotus's very indexicality that Lucian has queried.[23] Lucian converts Herodotus's canonical reception, centered on

---

[21] While the reference to the "mob" seems to jibe well with Lucian's intended differentiation of his Herodotus from the crowd's clichéd version, Nesselrath (1990: 118) sees an essential incongruity between the elite mentioned in § 1 (ἀπανταχόθεν ἤδη τῶν ἀρίστων συνειλεγμένων) and the ὄχλος mentioned here. But it is not hard to imagine that the diverse audience included all different types.

[22] Riffaterre 1983: 250. See also Genette 1997 [1982]: 4.

[23] Compare Mark Poster's concepts of "analog" and "digital" authorship (2002: 490). The former posits a close proximity between author and text, "as an expression of . . . style, mind, or feelings," whereas the "digital" author "connotes a greater alterity between the text and the author." Lucian's

194　HERODOTUS AND IMPERIAL GREEK LITERATURE

stylistic mimicry or evocation of the Persian Wars, into a newly inhabitable performance position. Subverting the mob that "points at" Herodotus, Lucian implies that readers should be wary of accepting a crowd-sourced, reflexive Herodotus.[24] Instead, we find Lucian's "Herodotus" present in the essay not only as the topic of discussion but as a quasi-authorial force, shading into the ostensible presence of the authorial Lucian. Pointing the finger at Herodotus means also pointing at Lucian—that is, at the *Herodotean* Lucian.

Lucian's *True Histories* and the Truths of *Historia*

Lucian's moves as a reception artist in the *Herodotus and Aëtion* condition our encounter with another complex text reliant on Herodotus, Lucian's *True Histories*, his masterpiece of allusion and portmanteau creativity. The work is saturated with past presences, among which that of Herodotus is again anything but minuscule.[25] With what has appeared to many an emphatic playfulness, the work's (pseudo-)ethnographic content, professed reliance on autopsy, and travelogue narrative style all generate consistent surface correspondences with Herodotus.[26] But as seen in the last section, the nature of Herodotean influence and presence in Lucian—the "Herodotus" to whom Lucian would have us point—is not always obvious, and the playfulness is not without serious intent. If an aspect of Lucian's challenge in the *Herodotus and Aëtion* is to reorient our perception of Herodotus, and in turn to flout attempts at drawing a firm line between himself and his "Herodotus," then the *True Histories* will only intensify this reorienting of perception, urging readers to look beyond cosmetically recognizable allusions in sensing the aura of the past.

finger-pointing mob ironically flags the "analog" Herodotus as an index of the Persian Wars victory, his image onstage evoking that signification. Lucian's "digital" Herodotus subtly posits an "alterity between the text and the author" by reformulating signification: Herodotus's value rests not so much in his text as in his enviable capacity to *perform* it.

[24] See, however, Anderson 1993: 54 for the point that Lucian's text flatters his learned audience of rhetors, historians, and sophists (*Hdt.* 8), implying that the internal audience is not wholly composed of the spectacle-focused hoi polloi who are likely to miss Lucian's subtlety.

[25] On its allusive nature, see Rütten 1997; Georgiadou and Larmour 1998; von Möllendorff 2000. See generally Baumbach and von Möllendorff 2017: 80–85 for comments on the work's "border-crossings" (*Grenzüberschreitungen*). For the programmatic importance of Herodotus, see, e.g., Lucian's allusion to a passage from *Histories* Book 2 in the opening of the *True Histories*' internal narrative, with a meta-critical comment on Ocean at *VH* 1.5, in addition to the historiographic language at 1.1–4 (see later here).

[26] See Georgiadou and Larmour 1998: 28–40.

Studies of the *True Histories* that reckon specifically with its historio-graphic resonances have often emphasized how the work's parodic inversions offer a counterexample of what historians should do.[27] On this view, the text functions as so much exaggeration of sober historiography.[28] To a certain extent, this approach must assume a consistent polar relationship between "real" history-writing and Lucian's fictive "true" history. Lucian's *How to Write History*, not treated in detail here, would seem the obvious counter-point to *True Histories*, but in fact, that work might itself confound attempts to be taken seriously. Lucian compares himself, in writing the treatise amid so much contemporary history-writing, to Diogenes rolling his barrel up the hill, the better to look busy during war preparations (*Hist. conscr.* 3).[29] The sense of needing to throw his hat into the ring perhaps explains some of the rather hackneyed advice given in the treatise: Lucian is showing that he knows the discursive lingo. Despite the familiar proclamations later in the treatise (esp. at §§ 39–41) on the need for truth in history-writing (e.g., § 50 on having a mind like a mirror; see later), Lucian's humorous tone at the outset may inspire readers to question how it is that future audiences (see 40, 61) will actually come to know "how it happened" (ὡς ἐπράχθη, 39) and accordingly be able to judge the usefulness (τὸ χρήσιμον, 42) of his-torical writing. The emphasis on truth-telling is never squared with future audiences' (in)ability to judge that truth, and thus the potential for deceit by historians remains unresolved, a deceit echoed by the "disarming ambiva-lence" of Lucian's introduction.[30]

While *True Histories* clearly presents falsehoods that defy conventional historiographic expectations, its evocations of Herodotus are more complex than the ostensibly "straight" treatise that extols the paramount importance of truth.[31] For the Herodotean features of the *True Histories* are complicated

---

[27] See above all Saïd 1994, with Georgiadou and Larmour 1994; Porod 2009; Free 2015 (and his 160–68 on the *True Histories*); Tamiolaki 2015, 2016, and 2017. That Lucian had a ready audience for thinking about the purposes of historiography is implied in the opening pages of *Hist. conscr.*, where he compares the spate of historical accounts of the Parthian Wars to a plague that has gone viral among his contemporaries (1).

[28] See esp. Tamiolaki 2013.

[29] I share Bracht Branham's view that however "serious" the arguments of *How to Write History*, Lucian gives us good reason at the start to doubt the work's seriousness. Branham 1989: 56–57: "[Lucian] begins by suggesting that his advice bears the same relationship to the historians' endeavors as Diogenes' did to the Corinthians': a vain reproof to idle efforts." Lucian takes part in war, he says, from a position of safety (ἀνέξω ἐμαυτὸν εὖ ποιῶν, *Hist. conscr.* 4), and this ironic distance also helps to convey the work's tone.

[30] Branham 1989: 57.

[31] One further reason I eschew setting *Hist. conscr.* in relation to the *VH* has to do with the former's emphasis on avoiding flattery: while the *VH* is fantastical and riffs on ethnographic outlandishness, it

196   HERODOTUS AND IMPERIAL GREEK LITERATURE

by the fact that the earlier writer's own text, by preceding, initiating, and in some cases failing to conform to what would come to count as "standard" for historiography, already itself colored outside the lines.[32] The *Histories* forces readers to grapple with the interrelation of truth, myth, narratorial subjectivity, the reportage of others, and the effects of operating at what Hartog has called the "limits of the sayable."[33] In encountering Lucian's amplifications of Herodotus, we are compelled to adjust our focus, to shift away from the surface falsities of Lucian's text and to ask, instead, how the *True Histories* in fact conveys certain truths about both the historiographic process and the experience of historiographic reading—especially the experience of reading Herodotus.[34] Put differently, rather than regarding the *True Histories* as the antonym of genuine historiography, we might ask how it creates a reading experience that coheres with—even illuminates aspects of—reading real historiography, compelling readers to ponder anew the quandaries of "truth" that pervade the Herodotean reading experience.[35]

To focus my discussion of Lucian's sizable text, I examine several of Lucian's Herodotean-style ethnographic encounters. Even if part of a putatively false work, they raise questions about the narrator's subjective positioning vis-à-vis his subject matter and about the possibilities of self-reflection generated by ethnographic inquiry into the lives of others.[36] The *True Histories* allows readers to question the definitional fixity of the categories of inquirer

is not a work that clearly flatters anyone. The *VH*'s way of engaging readers already conditioned to expect certain things from historiography has more to do with creating a sensation of realness around obviously absurd matters than with exaggerating historiography's admixture with panegyric.

[32] See Lateiner 1989: 212 on Herodotus's "peculiar isolation" in the genre of historiography; on his ex post facto labeling as historian, see Schepens 2007: 40–41; Marincola 2007b: 55–56.

[33] Hartog 2013 [1979]: 247.

[34] On the complexity of defining truth and falsehood, see Wiseman 1993 and esp. Morgan 1993. On some of the difficulties of parsing ideas of accuracy, truth, and falsehood in Herodotus (with attention to Book 2), see Marincola 2007b: 51–57. With attention to Lucian, see Georgiadou and Larmour 1994 and 1998: 38 n. 103, with further references.

[35] I follow an expansive view of historiographic discourse whose essential definition is flexibility around a set of practices that can manifest across genre; see Marincola 1999. An inquiry into the historiographic seriousness of the *VH* in part draws inspiration from scholarship that has approached the work's capacious idea of philosophical discourse, affording increased appreciation of the work's sophistications; see Laird 2003; ní Mheallaigh 2005, 2009, and 2014: 171–85, 207–60; Popescu 2014; Maciver 2016.

[36] It is by now well recognized in Herodotean scholarship that Herodotus, too, engaged such questions; see, e.g., Irwin 2014: 26, with general comments on the relationship between inquirer and subject in Herodotus's Ethiopian *logos* (3.17–26). See also Saïd 1994: 163, arguing that Lucian demonstrates "que l'étrangeté est une notion toute relative" and that Lucian "s'amuse à inverser les rôles et à transformer le spectateur en spectacle et l'indigène en ethnographe"; see generally 153–63, including a brief summary (153–54) of Herodotus's ethnographic method in Egypt, with later discussion here.

and other.[37] By pushing us to re-evaluate the nature of those encounters in Herodotus, I show that Lucian's Herodotean activations focus us on the quasi-philosophic suppositions upon which Herodotus's own text is premised, including the role of the historiographic narrator as simultaneously external and internal and the role of the ethnographic self in relation to those about whom inquiry is made. As Steven Smith has put it, in an essay on subject formation in the *True Histories*, "Even *writing* about the weird and wonderful out there requires a serious exploration of the self."[38] Lucian evokes the ethnographic Herodotus less to articulate a sure notion of identity (Hellenic, educated, or otherwise) and more to convey the uncertain stance of perceiving identity in the first place.[39] The fantastic element of the *True Histories* will be seen to inhere in its paradoxically realistic depiction of the subjective "hesitations" (in the phrasing of Tzvetan Todorov) that attend one's effort at attaining truth.[40]

Herodotus Explicit and Implicit: The Ocean of Herodotus in the *True Histories*

Lucian's *True Histories* adverts to Herodotus from its very start. The work begins with a brief parable on the need for pleasurable relaxation in contrast to a life of constant seriousness, a point made through analogy of the taut and loosened bow. The analogy recalls King Amasis of Egypt's words in Herodotus (*VH* 1.1 ~ Hdt. 2.173) and thus provides our first signal that *Histories* Book 2 will play an integral role in the intertextual weave of the *True Histories*.[41] The Herodotean allusion is supported by the explicit and repeated

---

[37] Lucian's Herodotean reversals in the *True Histories*, including what I call the "self-othering" of the narrator, harmonize with the recognition that Lucian's literary persona is one of performed flexibility; see Richter 2005; Fields 2013; Richter 2017: 328.

[38] Smith 2009: 90 (emphasis in original); compare 82 on "paradoxography as an ironic means of self-awareness."

[39] Ideas of identity construction have been central to scholarship on Imperial Greek literature; see Dench 2017, with further citations, and fundamentally Woolf 1994, Goldhill 2001, and Whitmarsh 2001b. Yet the concept of identity itself is flexible and is worth interrogating; see Brubaker and Cooper 2000; Whitmarsh 2001a (esp. 300–304); Connolly 2007a: 28–32.

[40] Todorov 1973 [1970]: 103: "[I]n the universe evoked by the text, an event—an action—occurs which proceeds from the supernatural (or from the pseudo-supernatural); this action then provokes a reaction from the implicit reader (and generally in the hero of the story). It is this reaction which we describe as 'hesitation,' and the texts which generate it, as fantastic."

[41] Compare Genette's concept of meta-textuality, which "unites a given text to another, of which it speaks without necessarily citing it (without summoning it), in fact sometimes even without naming it" (1997 [1982]: 4). The ensuing encouragement to the reader to spot the allusions in Lucian's source

198 HERODOTUS AND IMPERIAL GREEK LITERATURE

cognates of *historia* that crop up in the following sections (ἱστορουμένων, 1.2; ἱστοροῦντες, 1.3; ἱστορεῖν, 1.4). Lucian's tricky business of false eyewitness and supposedly truthful reportage of things never seen only thickens the Herodotean atmosphere.[42] But it has less often been noted that as the prologue shifts from the narrator's programmatic start to the protagonist's homodiegetic tale, the transition between the two, in fact, clinches the primacy of Herodotus, when the protagonist states that his journey's motivation is grounded in the wish to "understand what the border of Ocean is and what people dwell beyond it" (μαθεῖν τί τὸ τέλος ἐστὶν τοῦ ὠκεανοῦ καὶ τίνες οἱ πέραν κατοικοῦντες ἄνθρωποι, 1.5).[43] This comment, echoed by the protagonist's later claim to have "seen the Ocean clearly" (τὸν ὠκεανὸν ἤδη σαφῶς ἑωρῶμεν, 1.29), signals another activation of, and in this case provocative riposte to, Herodotus's *Histories* Book 2:

> The person who spoke about "the Ocean" has carried his story into the invisible where it admits of no disproof. I certainly do not know of any river "Ocean," and it seems to me that Homer or some other early poet invented the name and introduced it into poetry. (Hdt. 2.23)

> ὁ δὲ περὶ τοῦ Ὠκεανοῦ λέξας ἐς ἀφανὲς τὸν μῦθον ἀνενείκας οὐκ ἔχει ἔλεγχον· οὐ γάρ τινα ἔγωγε οἶδα ποταμὸν Ὠκεανὸν ἐόντα, Ὅμηρον δὲ ἤ τινα τῶν πρότερον γενομένων ποιητέων δοκέω τοὔνομα εὑρόντα ἐς ποίησιν ἐσενείκασθαι.

Lucian's going beyond (πέραν) Ocean has an obvious a meta-literary function, a bid to go "beyond" the doubting Herodotus into the cognitive realm of

---

material, however unrelaxing a reading program it might promise, perhaps leaves readers feeling justified in clocking the Amasis allusion. Cf. Whitmarsh 2006b, who sees the real joke of *True Histories* as its constant receding from interpretability (109–15, esp. 112–13); and Maciver 2016: 246–47 on the text as "anti-teleological." If the opening of the *VH* is a kind of false-start move, as Whitmarsh sees it, such a move may mirror the false-start narratives of Herodotus Books 1 and 2; see Węcowski 2004: 150 n. 41, citing Vannicelli 2001: 213–14. See also ní Mheallaigh 2014: 207–60, arguing that Lucian, in fact, privileges the fake over the real and that the marvel of the work's synthetic qualities is precisely what readers are encouraged to enjoy, something at which Lucian himself hints (ἐπαγωγὸν ἔσται αὐτοῖς, 1.2).

[42] On the prologue, see Laird 2003; Whitmarsh 2006b; Kim 2010a: 144–46.

[43] The inset narrative is apparently distinguishable from the prologue (1.1–4), and has for some implied a distinction between external narrator and internal protagonist. On the differentiated levels of "reality" between narrator Lucian and the internal character of apparently the same name, see Sciolla 1988: 59; Ligota 2007: 66–67; Popescu 2014: 54–55. The distinction is smudged by the appearance of Lucian's name in the intradiegetic inscription (*VH* 2.28).

invisibility which for Herodotus had foreclosed meaningful disputation (ἐς ἀφανές . . . οὐκ ἔχει ἔλεγχον). Moreover, the fact that Herodotus in his comment on Ocean adverts to Homer's error in "introducing the name Ocean" means that Lucian now not only "corrects" Herodotus but also plants for his reader a mile-marker on the long road of reception.[44] Lucian picks up on Herodotus exactly where Herodotus had picked up on Homer, and as with the *Herodotus and Aëtion*, he makes clear his awareness of being positioned to enact reception.

The twin evocations of Herodotus Book 2 at the start of the prologue and inset narrative connect what will become Lucian's own thaumastic, "ethnographic" text to one of the most *thauma*-rich, ethnographically dense stretches of Herodotus's *Histories*, a matter that Herodotus himself had underscored: "I shall proceed to dilate upon my account of Egypt because it has the greatest abundance of wondrous material (more than every other land), and again compared with all other lands it has monuments beyond description (λόγου μέζω): for these reasons there will be more that I say about it" (2.35). Lucian's early activations point to a somewhat offbeat, though not entirely unpopular, part of the *Histories*.[45] Lucian's programmatic Herodotean allusions echo the spirit described earlier in the *Herodotus and Aëtion* by highlighting an unexpected Herodotus, at least when compared with the version of Herodotus we saw in Dionysius and Plutarch. Closer to Dio's Herodotus, Lucian's is not Herodotus the Persian Wars chronicler but rather Herodotus the curious traveler to spaces of potentially edifying oddity, whose narrations will often show the Greeks up for their relative cultural youth, even wrongheadedness (see, e.g., 2.2.5, 2.4.1, and 2.119, on

[44] On the centrality of Homer to Lucian's *True Histories*, see Kim 2010a: 140–74; Maciver 2016 (esp. 239–47).

[45] Book 2 certainly inspired response in antiquity (see Priestley 2014: 118–37 on Hellenistic engagements with Herodotus's account of the Nile), but as West 2011: 71 notes, "Book 1 comes top by a long way"; see the papyri in Chambers et al. 1981: 22–73, with West 2011: 71: "Almost half our papyri (19) come from Book 1; Books 2 and 5 achieve quite a respectable score (six each). Book 8 has four; Book 7 three; Books 3 and 4 two each. Book 6 is not attested at all." See also Ehrhardt 1988: 858 on the plurality of ancient citations from Book 1. There does not appear to be strong ancient evidence for the view that Book 2 was separate from, or an anomalous precursor to, other portions of the work, as described by Jacoby's developmental model (see Fornara 1971: 1–23, who asserts that Herodotus's "every reader has . . . sensed the relative independence of his account of Egypt in Book II" [3]). Compare Harrison 2003: 147 and, for a more integrationist reading, Bowie 2018. At the very least, Lucian's choice to point to Book 2 activates one of the more supposedly doubtful stretches of the *Histories* according to ancient views, at least judging from various bits of evidence such as Aristotle's dismissal of Herodotus's "foolish" account of Egyptian fish (*Gen. An.* 3.5.755b6; see my introduction), attempts to outdo Herodotean accounts of the Nile, or the corrective account by the Egyptian priest Manetho (see Momigliano 1966 [1958]: 133; Murray 1972: 209–10, who observes that Manetho's attack was against not Herodotus's mendacity but his ignorance: ὑπ' ἀγνοίας ἐψευσμένον).

200   HERODOTUS AND IMPERIAL GREEK LITERATURE

the misbehavior of Menelaus in Egypt).[46] As Alan Lloyd says of Herodotus, "[T]here is a readiness to admit Egyptian superiority which could, at times, disturb a Greek audience."[47] The *True Histories*, which do much to decenter the reader's experience of truth, thus begins by grounding itself in (even as it implicitly claims to pass "beyond") Herodotus's own decentering operations in Egypt. Via an unexpected byway into the Greek literary canon, Lucian drives on the shoulder, not the road.

The Author as Actor: Ambiguity in Herodotus's *Histories* Book 2

"Die Erfahrung des Wandels, der Veränderung, des Anders-Seins führt zu methodologischen und epistemologischen Konsequenzen: 'the experience of change, of alteration, of being different, leads to methodological and epistemological consequences.'" This sentence of H. A. Weber expresses well the "experience of otherness" (and alteration) that is at the base of Herodotus's research. (Corcella 2013 [1984]: 55)

Before proceeding with analysis of the *True Histories*, however, we should consider more carefully the relevance of certain narrative aspects of *Histories* Book 2 in Lucian's reception act.[48] What is special about this book of Herodotus that would move Lucian to summon two of its passages at the start of the *True Histories*? I suggest that the connections between *True Histories* and *Histories* Book 2 have much to do with the ambiguities that arise amid the recalibration of the perception of self and other and with affirming these

[46] Compare, however, Harrison 2003: 153 on Egypt's own "insularity, indeed their 'Egyptocentrism,'" and 154, with Harrison 2020: 147, for the reminder that underlying Herodotus's positive presentation of Egypt's long period of stability is the awareness that its good fortune has come to an end.

[47] Lloyd 1990: 231, citing Plutarch, *dHM* 857A–B. See also Lloyd 1975: 154–55; Moyer 2002; Moyer 2011: 59. Compare Richter 2011: 182 for provocative questions about the place of Egypt in the sphere of Imperial Greece: "Why would an educated Roman on the Grand Tour stop off in Athens rather than heading right to the source of knowledge in Egypt?" See also Chamberlain 2001: 11–12, discussing Herodotus 4.27.1 and the formulation of referring to himself as part of "we the others" (ἡμεῖς οἱ ἄλλοι): "'We' are now simply those people who don't speak Scythian—which makes for an ironic twist on the Greeks' conventional way of defining the foreigner (the other) as the *barbaros*, the babbler who does not speak Greek. This kind of ironic reflection, it must be said, seems to be part and parcel of Herodotus' heterological game."

[48] Patently, both works concern narrators/protagonists who travel. On Herodotus's travels in Book 2, see Lloyd 1975: 61–76 and Marincola 1987, with Brown 1988: 67–75.

REMOVABLE EYES 201

as narratological (in addition to ethnographic) categories, susceptible to reversal and manipulation.[49]

Herodotus's Egyptian *logos* sublimates a series of subjective encounters. As Carolyn Dewald has observed:

> Herodotus' quasi-autobiographical comments about his own efforts as an investigator provide his most explicitly personal and engaged expressions as a *histōr*. In Book Two especially, Herodotus presents himself in his own text almost as an actor, certainly as the initiator, guide, and discoverer of information.[50]

There is indeed a blurriness hard to articulate about Herodotus Book 2, captured well in Dewald's phrase "almost as an actor." Where exactly are we to locate the Herodotus of this book? At times, we feel him to be an outsider, a narrator who filters Egypt through an *interpretatio Graeca*—Redfield's "tourist"—but at other times, his presence registers as that of an insider, the protagonist of his own quest for knowledge, undertaking an improbably ambitious physical and intellectual journey.[51] An effect of reading both *Histories* Book 2 and the *True Histories* is a kind of je-ne-sais-quoi regarding the narrator: who is this person, how does he know what he knows, can I believe it, and what does it do to a reader's cultural positioning, especially for a Greek?[52] The marked wondrousness of Egypt puts Herodotus in the position of playing up his authority in the very midst of telling his readers about dubious matters they might not otherwise swallow—save on good authority.[53]

---

[49] See Chamberlain 2001: 12: "Though Herodotus' use of the first person plural is impossible to pin down ethnographically (as referring to a group that can be represented and defined *in* the text, that is), it is narratologically constant: 'we' are always the observers, the interpreters, the readers and representers of the other group; and we achieve all this through the defining mediation of language."

[50] Dewald 2002: 278; see also 279, relevant to considering of the roles of "narrator" and "protagonist" in *VH*: "We should note that this part of Herodotus' authorial voice, the critical *histōr*, often cannot be completely separated from his voice as a narrator, editing and assessing *logoi*." Compare passing remarks of Andrade 2013: 279, with slightly different emphasis, on the historian as "no less an actor than a poet or an orator."

[51] On Herodotus's intellectual habits in Book 2, see Lloyd 1975: 141–70, with particular attention to schematization at 149–53, arguments from likelihood at 162–63, and arguments from analogy at 164–65.

[52] See Marincola 2007b: 57–59 for good discussion of the Herodotean "I" in Book 2. There is, of course, the larger positivist debate about whether Herodotus actually visited Egypt and interviewed the Egyptian priests, for which see, skeptically, Armayor 1978, Fehling 1989 [1971], West 1991; contra, Pritchett 1993, Rhodes 1994, Lloyd 1995. For my purposes, the veracity of his (possible) visits matters less than the manner of narration.

[53] See Marincola 1987: 121 and his appendix (137) on the authorizing markers that appear in *Histories* Book 2, the preponderant site of their concentration (e.g., 2.29.1, αὐτόπτης ἐλθών, τὸ δ' ἀπὸ

202 HERODOTUS AND IMPERIAL GREEK LITERATURE

Let us consider a representative passage from Book 2, one that encapsulates recurrent ambiguities regarding truth, the value of Greekness, and the role of the narrator. Late in this book, the reader is permitted to tag along with Herodotus in a kind of virtual-reality ride through the labyrinth near the so-called City of Crocodiles.[54] Already, the name of the city, after the curious creature Herodotus has described at some length (2.68–69), designates the place as special. The reader is permitted a sense of the autoptic access Herodotus has achieved there, but the passage also runs up against Herodotus's limits, at times giving itself over to the pall of astonishment, a narratorial vertigo. The passage deserves full quotation:

> They thought it best to leave behind a public monument, and after reaching this decision they constructed a labyrinth, just beyond Lake Moeris, right near the town called the City of Crocodiles, surpassing description among the things I have ever seen. For if someone were to gather together and display the fortifications and works of the Greeks, it would be clear that they were constructed with less labor and expense than this labyrinth—despite how remarkable, I concede, are the temples at Ephesus and Samos. The pyramids surely surpass description, and each is the equivalent of several massive Greek structures. But this labyrinth actually eclipses even the pyramids.
>
> There are twelve roofed courtyards situated opposite each other, six to the north, and six lined up directly opposite to the south. A single outside wall girds them. The labyrinth has a double set of dwelling spaces—some on the lower level and some on the upper level atop those—with a total of three thousand rooms, fifteen hundred on each level. Now the upper stories I myself saw: I walked through them and can speak about them because I actually saw them.[55] But the lower level I learned about from others'

τούτου ἀκοῇ ἤδη ἱστορέων, and 2.123.1, ἐμοὶ δὲ παρὰ πάντα τὸν λόγον ὑπόκειται ὅτι τὰ λεγόμενα ὑπ' ἑκάστων ἀκοῇ γράφω). Marincola links Herodotus's abundant self-disclosure in Book 2 to the author's aim of correcting or displacing past statements by Hecataeus and/or Ionian researchers. Further treatments of Herodotean autopsy and narrative technique include Nenci 1951: 14–46; Schepens 1980: 14–26; Darbo-Peschanski 1987: 84–189; Dewald 1987: 155–59; Lateiner 1989: 55–108; Shrimpton 1997: 229–65; Dewald 2002; Dewald 2009: 117–28.

[54] The existence of the labyrinth has been questioned; see Armayor 1985; contra, Lloyd 1995.
[55] For the translation of the first-person plural in this context as singular, see Chamberlain 2001, esp. at 17: "'We measured' a pyramid, for instance (2.127.1); 'we can give the names of the tribes of Libya' (4.197.1); 'we classify' (*diaireomen*, 2.6.1); 'we recognize' (2.16.1); 'we see' (2.131.3); and so on. This is not the activity of an audience or of a projected readership; it is the activity of a *histor*." See 17 n. 39 for the citation of the passage at 2.148.

accounts. The Egyptian guards absolutely refused to show them, asserting that there are situated the tombs of the kings who first built the labyrinth and the tombs of the sacred crocodiles. So about the lower chambers I report what I have been told, while the upper portion that we ourselves saw, this surpasses human works. For the corridors in and out of the chambers and the winding passageways through the halls are so complicated as to produce endless astonishment for me, as I made my way from courtyard to chamber, from chamber to colonnade, and then into further courtyards from the colonnades and into other courtyards from other chambers.

The roof of the entire edifice is of stone, as are the walls; the walls are filled with figured carvings, and each colonnaded courtyard is constructed with specially joined-together blocks of white stone. At the edge where the labyrinth ends stands a pyramid forty fathoms tall, with large lifelike creatures carved on it. The entrance into the pyramid has been constructed underground. But there is a wonder still greater than this labyrinth—Lake Moeris, beside which the labyrinth was constructed. (2.148–149.1)

καὶ δή σφι μνημόσυνα ἔδοξε λιπέσθαι κοινῇ· δόξαν δέ σφι ἐποιήσαντο λαβύρινθον, ὀλίγον ὑπὲρ τῆς λίμνης τῆς Μοίριος κατὰ <τὴν> Κροκοδείλων καλεομένην πόλιν μάλιστά κη κείμενον, τῶν ἐγὼ ἤδη εἶδον λόγου μέζω <ἐόντα>.[56] [2] εἰ γάρ τις τὰ ἐξ Ἑλλήνων τείχεά τε καὶ ἔργων ἀπόδεξιν συλλογίσαιτο, ἐλάσσονος πόνου τε ἂν καὶ δαπάνης φανείη ἐόντα τοῦ λαβυρίνθου τούτου· καίτοι ἀξιόλογός γε καὶ ὁ ἐν Ἐφέσῳ ἐστὶ νηὸς καὶ ὁ ἐν Σάμῳ. [3] ἦσαν μὲν νυν καὶ αἱ πυραμίδες λόγου μέζονες καὶ πολλῶν ἑκάστη αὐτέων ἑλληνικῶν ἔργων καὶ μεγάλων ἀνταξίη· ὁ δὲ δὴ λαβύρινθος καὶ τὰς πυραμίδας ὑπερβάλλει.

[4] τοῦ γὰρ δυώδεκα μέν εἰσι αὐλαὶ κατάστεγοι, ἀντίπυλοι ἀλλήλῃσι, ἓξ μὲν πρὸς βορέω, ἓξ δὲ πρὸς νότον τετραμμέναι, συνεχέες· τοῖχος δὲ ἔξωθεν ὁ αὐτός σφεας περιέργει. οἰκήματα δ' ἔνεστι διπλά, τὰ μὲν ὑπόγαια, τὰ δὲ μετέωρα ἐπ' ἐκείνοισι, τρισχίλια ἀριθμόν, πεντακοσίων καὶ χιλίων ἑκάτερα. [5] τὰ μὲν νυν μετέωρα τῶν οἰκημάτων αὐτοί τε ὡρῶμεν διεξιόντες καὶ αὐτοὶ θηησάμενοι λέγομεν, τὰ δὲ αὐτῶν ὑπόγαια λόγοισι ἐπυνθανόμεθα· οἱ γὰρ ἐπεστεῶτες τῶν Αἰγυπτίων δεικνύναι αὐτὰ οὐδαμῶς ἤθελον, φάμενοι θήκας αὐτόθι εἶναι τῶν τε ἀρχὴν τὸν λαβύρινθον τοῦτον οἰκοδομησαμένων βασιλέων καὶ τῶν ἱρῶν κροκοδείλων. [6] οὕτω τῶν μὲν κάτω πέρι

---

[56] See Wilson 2015: 42–43 for an explanation of this reading, departing from Hude's OCT (τὸν ἐγὼ ἤδη εἶδον λόγου μέζω, itself following Powell's emendation of τὸν for the manuscripts' τῶν).

204 HERODOTUS AND IMPERIAL GREEK LITERATURE

οἰκημάτων ἀκοῇ παραλαβόντες λέγομεν, τὰ δὲ ἄνω μέζονα ἀνθρωπηίων ἔργων αὐτοὶ ὡρῶμεν. αἵ τε γὰρ διέξοδοι διὰ τῶν στεγέων καὶ οἱ εἵλιγμοὶ διὰ τῶν αὐλέων ἐόντες ποικιλώτατοι θῶμα μυρίον παρείχοντο ἐξ αὐλῆς τε ἐς τὰ οἰκήματα διεξιοῦσι καὶ ἐκ τῶν οἰκημάτων ἐς παστάδας, ἐς στέγας τε ἄλλας ἐκ τῶν παστάδων καὶ ἐς αὐλὰς ἄλλας ἐκ τῶν οἰκημάτων.

[7] ὀροφὴ δὲ πάντων τούτων λιθίνη κατά περ οἱ τοῖχοι, οἱ δὲ τοῖχοι τύπων ἐγγεγλυμμένων πλέοι, αὐλὴ δὲ ἑκάστη περίστυλος λίθου λευκοῦ ἁρμοσμένου τὰ μάλιστα. τῆς δὲ γωνίης τελευτῶντος τοῦ λαβυρίνθου ἔχεται πυραμὶς τεσσερακοντόργυιος, ἐν τῇ ζῷα μεγάλα ἐγγέγλυπται· ὁδὸς δ᾽ ἐς αὐτὴν ὑπὸ γῆν πεποίηται. τοῦ δὲ λαβυρίνθου τούτου ἐόντος τοιούτου θῶμα ἔτι μέζον παρέχεται ἡ Μοίριος καλεομένη λίμνη, παρ᾽ ἣν ὁ λαβύρινθος οὗτος οἰκοδόμηται.

To be sure, one could cite many examples of outlandish description in Herodotus Book 2: the crocodile with earrings (2.69), the cats who leap into house fires (2.66), or the improbable multitiered account offered by the Cyreneans concerning the sources of the Nile, including a journey among wizards (2.32–33). But I choose this example because it hovers, in a way that seems representative for many parts of Book 2, between plausible and implausible. One sees Herodotus operating between precise articulation and discursive limit. As with his programmatic description of Egypt's wondrousness (ἔργα λόγου μέζω, 2.35.1), Herodotus finds his task with the labyrinth "greater than words" (λόγου μέζω, 2.148.1) yet goes on to spill many words in the effort to make visible the astonishing site that surpasses the buildings of the Greeks and indeed all human works (μέζονα ἀνθρωπηίων ἔργων). After detailed enumeration of courts and rooms, a moment of rupture comes, voiced unusually in the first-person plural: "Now the upper stories I myself saw: I walked through them and can speak about them because I actually saw them. But the lower level I learned about from others' accounts."[57] The guides refuse (οὐδαμῶς ἤθελον) to show the lower level, so the reader's belief in the coffins of kings and crocodiles itself depends on Herodotus's own trust in the reports he heard. The description then gives way to a dizzying, concatenated account, marked by a rapid movement of directional prepositions (**ἐξ** αὐλῆς τε **ἐς** τὰ οἰκήματα διεξιοῦσι καὶ **ἐκ** τῶν οἰκημάτων **ἐς** παστάδας, **ἐς** στέγας τε ἄλλας **ἐκ** τῶν παστάδων καὶ **ἐς** αὐλὰς ἄλλας **ἐκ** τῶν οἰκημάτων), replicating

---

[57] Here Herodotus's departure from his usual penchant for statements in the first-person singular may suggest the presence of a personal guide or companion, socializing outward to the viewer what was already a non-solo effort to capture the labyrinth in words.

REMOVABLE EYES   205

in syntax the structure's elaboration (ποικιλώτατοι), itself inducing in Herodotus "endless astonishment" (θῶμα μυρίον).

Then, after all this, about something that has been proclaimed greater than words and other human works, Herodotus finds it in himself to describe "an even greater marvel" (θῶμα ἔτι μέζον). The reader, already offered a manifestation of the visible (the upper story) and the katabatic unseen (the lower story), must again readjust, for the putative majesty of the labyrinth is now demoted by the "still greater marvel" of Lake Moeris. Attaining to a sense of truth in Herodotus's account is inflected by the narrator's own capacity to announce the limits of his ability—and then to force the reader's recalibration by unproblematically describing "something still greater." Thus, long before we encounter the uncanny world of Lucian's *True Histories*, we see supposedly true history fashioning its own strange effects. Is the labyrinth really greater than words? What makes it a more stupendous achievement than anything in Greece? And how much of what we are reading is a reliable and fair report, as opposed to Herodotus's gushing in the face of the sublime?

One way of negotiating strangeness is through analogy, Herodotus's use of the so-called *interpretatio Graeca*.[58] When confronted with something strange, Herodotus often attempts to mediate that strangeness, rather than merely present without analogy or comment, as would become the mode of paradoxography.[59] Herodotus may draw a comparison to something familiar within a Greek reader's cultural idiom and appeal to what is "reasonable" or "probable" in assessing a strange claim or in explaining something ostensibly wondrous.[60] This is especially germane to Book 2, with its proliferation of Herodotus's autoptic claims.[61] Autopsy and assertions of *oikos* go together

---

[58] On Herodotus's use of analogy, see Corcella 2013 [1984]. See also Itkonen 2005: 1–15.

[59] On the general lack of rationalization among paradoxographers, see Gabba 1981: 54; Popescu 2014: 48.

[60] On the language of probability in Herodotus, see Thomas 2000: 168 n. 1, 190 n. 51, with further references. Thomas points out (190 n. 51) that *oikos* appears forty times in Herodotus's text. In the entirety of the *Histories*, five of the twelve instances in which the narrator (rather than an intradiegetic character) comments on what is or is not *oikos* occur in Book 2. The likely etymology of the word ἔοικα as connected to proto-Indo-European *weik-, and thus to the noun εἰκών ("image"), suggests origins for the idea of analogy in a process of visual comparison. For instances of Herodotus's analogizing, see, e.g., 2.24, 2.27, 2.56, 2.93, 2.104, 2.125.

[61] See Marincola 1997: 63–86, including 82 for a discussion of autopsy as a "voucher for a marvel or wonder" (citing Ctesias, *FGrHist* 688 F 45b and 45dβ). I differ somewhat from Marincola at 80, where he identifies Thucydides as the writer who "set the precedent for contemporary historiography with the one basic claim made at the outset, and this is the standard (so to speak) form, the claim of autopsy and inquiry from those who know or were eyewitnesses." Thucydides's statement (1.22.1–3) of autopsy is indeed a forceful one, but given the relatively infrequent references to autopsy in the *History*, it seems more reasonable to highlight the prominent role of autopsy in Herodotus, regardless

206 HERODOTUS AND IMPERIAL GREEK LITERATURE

both etymologically and practically, and it comes as little surprise that the language of likening arises when Herodotus is faced with his presentation of Egypt's inversions.[62]

In this process of rationalizing and likening, Herodotus strives to mark his critical distance, subjecting his material to a series of cognitive procedures that stamp his information as critically processed, rather than merely transferred. Yet the nature of these procedures, in relation to the information given, inspires questions about just how "clean" is the transfer between what was seen/heard and how it gets reported.[63] When, for instance, Herodotus cites his own personal impressions in affirmation of information he has been provided, the reader may still wonder by which procedure—direct report from a source, personal judgment, or both—he chooses to report it to us: "Much of the land I am talking about is the acquisition of the Egyptians, according to what the priests were saying, and this seemed to me, too, to be the case" (ταύτης ὦν τῆς χώρης τῆς εἰρημένης ἡ πολλή, κατά περ οἱ ἱρέες ἔλεγον, ἐδόκεε καὶ αὐτῷ μοι εἶναι ἐπίκτητος Αἰγυπτίοισι, 2.10.1). This combination of reportorial proximity and subjective scrutiny recurs often, as when Herodotus gives credence to the things said about Egypt because he has himself confirmed through autopsy what others have said (τὰ περὶ Αἴγυπτον ὦν καὶ τοῖσι λέγουσι αὐτὰ πείθομαι καὶ αὐτὸς οὕτω κάρτα δοκέω εἶναι, ἰδών, 2.12.1).[64] Likewise, Herodotus asserts his own verifying role when he makes the explicit remark, in a comment on Egypt's size, that an oracle affirmed his own judgment *after* he had already come to his own view about Egypt (τὸ ἐγὼ τῆς ἐμεωυτοῦ γνώμης ὕστερον περὶ Αἴγυπτον ἐπυθόμην, 2.18.1). There is in Book 2 an interplay of information and cognition that repeatedly blurs the line between basic categories of objectivity and subjectivity.[65] It is a blur that Lucian's narrator/protagonist will manipulate.

---

of whether it was accompanied by a precedent-setting statement. The density of autoptic remarks in Herodotus and the explicit references to travel offer a more direct parallel to the *True Histories*.

[62] Vasunia 2001: 75–109 (esp. 92–100) analyzes the various kinds of inversion on display in Herodotus Book 2. See also Redfield 1985: 103–4: "In Egypt both nature and culture are upside down—that is, opposite to what a Greek would expect" (103).

[63] On this front, see the comment of Schepens 2007: 44: "Whereas current handbooks of historical method define evidence as the objective material medium between the historian and past reality and tend to formally exclude as subjective means the various capabilities and activities of the researcher, Greek theory—as far as it can be reconstructed from the most representative pronouncements of the historians—appears to focus precisely on those 'subjective means.'"

[64] On the uses of the verb δοκεῖν in Herodotus, see Marincola 1989: 218–19.

[65] See Dewald 2002, esp. 272–73. Even when Herodotus seems to shift gears, it is notable that he does not let go of the cognitive processes; see 2.99, where the apparent passivity of telling what he was told (κατὰ τὰ ἤκουον) is immediately undercut by the active proposal to supplement with

REMOVABLE EYES 207

Adding to the blurriness of the author's role(s) is the fact that at other times, readers are implicitly summoned to work with Herodotus, to act as an affirming force for the ethnographic self he projects into the text. In his theorization about the Nile, for instance, Herodotus invites the reader into the process of reasoning. When he dismisses the notion that the Nile comes from melted snow as unlikely (οὐδὲ οἰκός, 2.22.2), he does so in the eyes of "anyone able to reason about the truth of such things" (ἀνδρί γε λογίζεσθαι τοιούτων πέρι οἵῳ τε ἐόντι, 2.22.2). Where physical travel and autopsy may separate Herodotus from his reader, the reader and narrator may nonetheless be joined by a common process of λογίζεσθαι based on a presumed knowledge of what constitutes οἰκός. For the reader to whom Herodotus's *logos* seems outlandish, the possibility of shared intellection bridges the possibility of joint inquiry.[66]

Yet even as analogizing to an inverted world bespeaks Herodotus's critical distance, it likely also codes for an anxiety about how the relative truthfulness of his descriptions will be perceived.[67] Herodotus's appeals to a common sense of οἰκός in describing the outlandish may mark points of worry about his persuasiveness; thus, the more visibly "rationalizing" portions of his account may carry a whiff of the suspect. The potentially somewhat anxious process of analogy and the overt presentation of a judging ethnographic self are both related to my final consideration before we return to the *True Histories*, and this has to do with the fact of Herodotus's *embodied* narration in Book 2. Herodotus famously characterizes himself as subordinated to "observation, judgment, and inquiry" (ὄψις, γνώμη, ἱστορίη), which, he says in

what he has seen (τῆς ἐμῆς ὄψιος). Compare also Herodotus's handling of a detail about Egyptian fish: "Where these probably come from, I believe that I can guess" (κόθεν δὲ οἰκὸς αὐτοὺς γίνεσθαι, ἐγώ μοι δοκέω κατανοέειν τοῦτο, 2.93.6), and an explanation follows. In such passages, seemingly straight-up reportage mixes with the disclosure of *how* the narrator can reason or suppose based on what is likely; his presentation explicitly, not just implicitly, refracts the seemingly odd through a prism of that which is mutually intelligible between his perspective and that of his reader.

[66] See, e.g., Herodotus's reference to the distance between the Altar of the Twelve Gods in Athens and the Temple of Olympian Zeus in Pisa, as an analogy for the distance between the Egyptian coast and Heliopolis (2.7.1). Here the analogy is clearly "local" for a putative Athenian audience. See Clarke 2018: 86–87 on Herodotus's mention of journeying distances "to draw the reader into not only the action but also the physical context of his narrative" (87).

[67] Complementary to the tendency in Book 2 to be explicit about his research activities, and part of the self-authorizing technique, is Herodotus's mentioning things for which he cannot vouch, as noted by Griffiths 1999: 179: "[T]here are regular verbal cues to signal such transitions from the plane of the main narrative to areas where less strict standards of verisimilitude apply"; see 179 n. 36 for examples.

208 HERODOTUS AND IMPERIAL GREEK LITERATURE

an arresting formulation, "do the talking" (ταῦτα λέγουσά ἐστι, 2.99.1).[68] Herodotus's mechanization of these processes and his making them the subject of the periphrastic abet the tendency to think of Herodotean methods as critical methods only, rather than methods that are specifically related to the spatial movement of a human body. But Herodotus's research compelled him physically, and in anticipation of the Lucianic protagonist's depiction of the bodily journey through ethnographic wonders, I highlight the fact that the processes denominated by Herodotus, while certainly cognitive, encourage us to visualize the body that enacted them.[69] As he writes early in his account of Egypt:

> Further, I heard other things in Memphis, where I came into conversation with the priests of Hephaestus. And indeed because of what they said I took myself to Thebes and Heliopolis, because I wanted to know whether they would agree with the reports from Memphis. (2.3.1)

> ἤκουσα δὲ καὶ ἄλλα ἐν Μέμφι, ἐλθὼν ἐς λόγους τοῖσι ἱρεῦσι τοῦ Ἡφαίστου· καὶ δὴ καὶ ἐς Θήβας τε καὶ ἐς Ἡλίου πόλιν αὐτῶν τούτων εἵνεκεν ἐτραπόμην, ἐθέλων εἰδέναι εἰ συμβήσονται τοῖσι λόγοισι τοῖσι ἐν Μέμφι.

Movement leads to information (ἐλθὼν ἐς λόγους), and information leads to movement (ἐτραπόμην). The repeated emphasis on autopsy suffuses the atmosphere of this book, even where autopsy goes unmentioned.[70] Herodotus's own body is subsumed into a process of constructing a *logos*, joining and comparing its parts. Irruptions of his narratorial presence remind the reader that even the most "objectively" described passages nonetheless are ensconced within the *histōr*'s overarching schema, parts of which

---

[68] "Up to this point my observation and judgment and inquiry have done the talking, but from this point forward I shall proceed by telling the Egyptian *logoi* according to the things I was hearing: and I shall add to them something from my own observation, too" (μέχρι μὲν τούτου ὄψις τε ἐμὴ καὶ γνώμη καὶ ἱστορίη ταῦτα λέγουσά ἐστι, τὸ δὲ ἀπὸ τοῦδε αἰγυπτίους ἔρχομαι λόγους ἐρέων κατὰ τὰ ἤκουον· προσέσται δέ τι αὐτοῖσι καὶ τῆς ἐμῆς ὄψιος, 2.99.1). See Schepens 1975: 261 n. 15; Schepens 2007: 44.

[69] See Schepens 2007: 45: "It is significant that the majority of those places where Herodotus speaks *in propria persona* refer to his role as an inquirer, inspecting sites or monuments, interviewing witnesses or locals, evaluating stories."

[70] Even instances in which Herodotus does not call attention to his movements may still imply movement and provoke the reader to supply Herodotus's bodily presence, as when he reports on the gulf of the Red Sea: "There is in Arabia, not far from Egypt, a gulf extending out from the Red Sea, as long and as narrow as I shall now set out to describe" (2.11.1). Did Herodotus see this himself? Whether he did or not is made harder to determine by its juxtaposition with passages in which Herodotus forthrightly calls attention to his own eyewitness.

REMOVABLE EYES 209

required movement from place to place. Autopsy is not just a research technique; it is a machination of the eyes in an itinerant body. The point may seem rudimentary. But there is surely something lost in failing to sense the physical travails that made his eyewitness and hearsay possible. His body, for which eyewitness and hearsay function as synecdoche, becomes an implicit part of Herodotus's *Beglaubigungsapparat*.

Recognizing Herodotus's embodiment returns us to one of the questions raised in discussion of the labyrinth passage, namely, whose narrative, exactly, we are getting. Herodotus is, of course, at a certain level, a heterodiegetic narrator who tells other people's *logoi*. He did not fight in the Persian Wars or march over the Hellespont under Xerxes's whip.[71] But much of Book 2 (and indeed Books 1–4 generally) constitutes an overarching *logos* that belongs, as it were, to Herodotus.[72] That the result, the *display* of his inquiry, involves his own bodily movement would seem to complicate any easy sense with which we might assert that Herodotus is purely heterodiegetic. As Marco Dorati writes, the "polyphonic and dialogic nature of the social reality, which is the object of ethnographical discourse—and also of the intellectual operations aiming at its interpretation—may be turned into a monological and authorial voice, which sublimates its original nature." Dorati goes on:

> In this translation process, the present tense, as stressed by Johannes Fabian, identifies not a "time," but an "epistemological position" and the "ethos of detached observation" facing an external, ahistorical reality, conceived as a given object; similarly, the transition from the first to the third person expresses the ethnographer's desire to make himself invisible through the construction of a depersonalized and aseptic "seeing eye" . . . by removing any subjective element of the experience, ethnographical writing tries to engender the illusion of an immediate perception of reality.[73]

Herodotus's *logos* is often acquired through, and affirmed by, a series of physical actions that become part of the narrative, which, as Dorati further

---

[71] See Dorati 2011: 274, "Herodotus' work lacks any truly autobiographical dimension: as Jacoby stressed, his λόγοι are not *Reiseberichte*; more generally, as Carolyn Dewald warns, his voice is a 'profoundly non-autobiographical voice'" (citing Jacoby 1913: 248 and Dewald 2002: 268). See also Chamberlain 2001: 30: "Herodotus' *we* . . . does not operate as part of the text's historical content."

[72] See Dewald 2002: 277–86, discussing Herodotus as *histōr*.

[73] Dorati 2011: 278–79. See another representative passage from Dorati's study, on the Ethiopian *logos*: "Herodotus' text does not *reproduce* the 'historical' point of view of any individual witness (distinct from the κατάσκοποι), it creates the virtual point of view of a hypothetical observer at the Ethiopian court on the basis of the envoys' experience" (294).

210   HERODOTUS AND IMPERIAL GREEK LITERATURE

reminds us, is a "*consequence* of a journey":[74] Herodotus's own witness of places and peoples, his own sense-perception of a living story preserved up to the present, and his tendency to note that something remains visible—still physically extant and available for one's own bodily encounter in his time. Where explicitly marked, and where implied, autopsy is both a means to information and a piece *of* the information Herodotus conveys. Herodotus's creation is therefore one with which his own bodily labors and movements and, by implication, his own personal details (what he ate, whom he met, physical encumbrances during his journey) are all bound up. As Dewald puts it, "[W]hile the Thucydides narrator remains 'extradiegetic' for the most part (not intruding himself overtly into his narrated account), the Herodotus narrator is 'intradiegetic', taking an active part qua narrator throughout the narrative (he is, however, extradiegetic to the logoi his text includes)."[75] Yet I stress that the sensation of reading Herodotus as an involved, autoptic narrator squiggles these distinctions, making his reports so much his own that we cannot experience them as purely extradiegetic. Herodotus may be a narrator positioned outside his story, but he is nonetheless embedded in the means of its production. The blur of objective and subjective reporting in Book 2, which I have argued engenders some of its uncanny qualities, centers on precisely this "almost as an actor" quality to which Dewald has alerted us. The slippery contours of this blurring are part of what Lucian energizes in his own quasi-historiographic representation of truth—and the true experience of the varieties of subjective encounter.

What's True about the *True Histories*?

Although Lucian's *True Histories* retails untrue "facts," at a broader level it traffics in ideas of the subjective encounter that inform Herodotus's Book 2. Lucian's text represents a "true history" insofar as it is true to the act of *historia*: the work reflects on how *historia* entails a process of investigation and subjective judgment, along with the potential to see oneself from the perspective of another.[76] Put differently, we might say the *True Histories*

---

[74] Dorati 2011: 275 (emphasis in original). See also Chamberlain 2001: 16–17, noting the self-inscription of Herodotus's own historical (and historicized) voice into his work.

[75] See Dewald 2009: 117–18 (quotation at n. 7).

[76] For Lucian's ability to manipulate stereotypes of self and other, see Elsner 2001a; Richter 2011: 147–76, 235–42; Andrade 2013: 261–313, esp. 289 ("While eliciting such complexities, the text also marks the shiftiness of cultural positioning and the incoherence of binary cultural categories")

REMOVABLE EYES 211

posits a level of meta-inquiry, inquiring implicitly into the position of the inquirer, as if philosophizing the process of *historia*. The work's absurd bits of ethnography—people with feet of cork, penis sailors, vulture riders, and so on—distract from the more fundamental mystery of the narrator-protagonist: how readers are to understand his cultural positioning, the nature of his authority, his relation to the framing narrator, and the meaning of his Greekness (if, in fact, he is meant to be thought of as Greek at all).[77] No origin for the speaker is given; no home is named. Where the protagonist comes from and what it would mean for him to return remain unsaid. Rather than providing easy answers, Lucian imbues his text with a sense of uncertainty and ambiguity about the very self at its center, an ambiguity worthy of his signal intertextual forebear in Herodotus. In the remainder of this chapter, I trace out various Herodotean ambiguities through a series of close readings.

Greek Solipsism and the Vine-Women

At the start of the crew's disembarkation (1.7), signs of Greekness guide Lucian's narrator and his men. They discover a Greek inscription, faded and worn (ἀμυδροῖς δὲ καὶ ἐκτετριμμένοις, 1.7), alerting them to how far Heracles and Dionysus had traveled.[78] In turn, the river they happen upon flows with a liquid "very similar" to (ὁμοιότατον μάλιστα) Chian wine, offering further signs (σημεῖα) of Dionysus's presence. The men, far from home, soon become drunk. The inscription and wine function as ties to a Greek place, never identified, from which they have come. Already, then, at the start of the work, origins are semiotic rather than specific: the men are in a general realm of Hellenicity, but, as suggested by the intoxication, connection to the past can prove disabling.

and 295 ("Lucian's narrator stages himself as a single body constituted by this Greek subject and its barbarian other, as viewer and spectacle").

[77] On the transition between "authorial"/framing Lucian and "character"/protagonist Lucian in the *True Histories*, see Laird 2003: 125–27, with further bibliography, and his point (126) about the "phenomenological slippage" of Lucian's denominating two actual writers along with a fictional character (Odysseus) in the prologue's citation of the writer's various forebears.

[78] On the meta-literary aspects of this passage, see ní Mheallaigh 2014: 209–10; Baumbach and von Möllendorff 2017: 84.

212 HERODOTUS AND IMPERIAL GREEK LITERATURE

Later, meeting with the Vine-Women—half Greek women, half grapevine—some of the crew engage in sex, only to become physically stuck to the viny alloys. The monstrous hybridity is marked as one of processual transformation, the women being like Daphne "in the process of becoming a tree" (ἀποδενδρουμένην, 1.8). The participle's hint of an incomplete transformation previews the possible transformations of identity that will become available to Lucian and his men. The narrator's first ethnographic encounter in the work is hence not with fixity but with fluctuation. The Vine-Women somatize the confusion of boundaries dissolved and the unreliability of posing a static Greek self against a stable other, when the latter both does and does not reflect the self. Indeed, the Vine-Women embody, in a fashion that becomes programmatic for the work, the difference between what Brubaker and Cooper have called "identity" and "identification": the former denotes a reification, a static condition, while the latter "calls attention to the complex (and often ambivalent) *processes*" of shaping identity.[79] The Vine-Women at first seem to reflect a recognizably Greek presence, especially in their ability to speak Greek (1.8). They desire sex with the Greek men (αἱ δὲ καὶ μίγνυσθαι ἡμῖν ἐπεθύμουν, 1.8), but hybridity results in a literal impasse of physical commingling. The physicality reinforces the sense of an intellectual journey enacted through the spatial movement of the body: Lucian presents the experience of reckoning with the past, and with some notion of truth, as embodied, recalling Herodotus's own emphasis on physical travel.[80]

Only here, early in the *True Histories*, one sees that Lucian's riff on Herodotean-style ethnography intimates the instability of its putative categories. Lucian evokes ethnographic activity only to subvert the power of the fixed point of view: the men who become trapped fail to inquire into whether what they reckon as familiarly Greek actually is. They misread the women's nature and, perversely, their attraction to their own cultural presumptions, in a solipsistic ethnographic folding. Lucian represents the experienced subjectivity of truth by playing up the porousness between encountered presence and encountering subject.

---

[79] Brubaker and Cooper 2000: 17 (emphasis in original). Compare Appiah 2005: 66, in a similar formulation: "[I]*dentification*, the process through which individuals shape their projects—including their plans for their own lives and their conceptions of the good life—by reference to available labels, available identities" (emphasis in original).

[80] See Booth 2013 on the concept of "embodied mind," relevant to *VH*'s conceit of intellectual transformation through physical journeying. Compare ní Mheallaigh 2014: 30 on Lucian's "insistence on fiction as an embodied, sensory and psychological experience."

A Move to the Moon

In classic Herodotean ethnographic mode, the protagonist who arrives on the moon describes its exotica by means of comparison. The features of the vegetable-plumed birds are like leaves of lettuce (1.13); vultures on which cavalrymen ride have wings longer and thicker than ship masts (1.11); clouds reddened by the Vulture Cavalry blood are likened to sunsets (1.17). The protagonist suggests that his descriptions issue only from autopsy, as when he comments on the Crane Cavalry: "I did not see these because they never arrived. For this reason, I have not dared to write up their natures. Let me tell you: the things said about them are monstrous (τεράστια) and not to be believed" (1.13).[81] The ability to offer ethnographic comments is enhanced by Lucian's embedding his protagonist among the fighting forces of the Selenites, at war with the Heliots. The protagonist therefore combines two postures, that of historical observer and active participant in the action described.[82] Joining their war, the protagonist participates in the local action, and he and his men even help set up the victory trophies (1.18). It is this participation in the war that occasions sketches of both battle and ethnography (1.14–17); joining in the Selenite war at once lends credibility to the ethnographic "information" delivered while altering the expected narrative stance of the inquirer.[83]

Narratorial participation narrows the distance between self and other, observer and interlocutor, and may even permit the distance to collapse.[84] For King Endymion implies that the moon may become the new home for both the protagonist and his men, stating that if he wins his war against the Heliots, the crew "will enjoy living the happiest life possible with me" (ἁπάντων εὐδαιμονέστατα παρ' ἐμοὶ καταβιώσεσθε, 1.12). The possibility of permanent relocation heightens the degree of possible autopsy—the reporter may

---

[81] For other Herodotean echoes on Lucian's moon, see Tamiolaki 2013: 155, with nn. 47–52.

[82] Compare Andrade 2013: 293 on how the narrator of *On the Syrian Goddess* "emerges as an actor occupying strategic positions in the spectacle that he observes."

[83] See Redfield 1985: 100–101 on how the "ethnographer tries to overcome it [cultural superiority] by participant observation, which means abandoning power and throwing oneself on the mercy of the natives. Only in this way can the ethnographer begin to see the culture as the native sees it, from the inside, not as a collection of oddities but as a meaningful, livable, complex whole." Compare Clarke 2018: 30–32 on Herodotus's combination of the Odyssean/hodological viewpoint (citing Marincola 2007b) and "other, more distanced perspectives" (31).

[84] On Lucian's moon as a liminal "Thirdspace" (borrowing from Homi Bhabha), see ní Mheallaigh 2020: 235–40.

214   HERODOTUS AND IMPERIAL GREEK LITERATURE

become resident.[85] If, in effect, Lucian's narrator has temporarily become a Selenite, a physical partisan in the war, is the "credibility" of his ethnographic report automatically enhanced? While a fundamental difference between the protagonist and the bizarre Selenites can be presumed, the opportunity to stay on the moon invites the possibility of adopting Selenite customs, such as eating barbecued frogs or using perfume derived from onions (1.23). The protagonist thus hints at the possibility of becoming a cultural Selenite, if obviously not an anatomical one. Although Endymion's invitation is not accepted (1.27), the ostensible differences between the protagonist's unnamed (but presumably Greek) identity and that of the Selenites are narrowed by the possibility of joining their society.

Adding to the sense of the Selenite other as a category collapsible into the (Greek) self is the fact that King Endymion himself describes how he, who had once been a human (ἄνθρωπος), was transferred in his sleep from "our land" (ἀπὸ τῆς ἡμετέρας γῆς) to the moon and became its king (1.11). The Selenite king is revealed as an emigrant from a previously shared land. So while the bizarre ethnography of the Selenites casts them as fundamentally different from Greeks (see 1.22–25), their ruler exemplifies a particular liminality. Rather than merely presenting aspects of moon life as odd, Lucian uses them to imply possibilities of a negotiable identity.[86] In so doing, he amplifies the porousness of identity that informed Herodotus's account in Book 2, where certain aspects of Greek culture were said to derive from or be related to Egyptian customs, including various religious customs (2.49–53, 2.57.3, 2.81, 2.171), the practice of geometry (2.109.3), and one of the laws of Solon (2.177.2). Lucian, for his part, amplifies the sense of cultural borrowing and crossover.

This process of self-othering—of seeing oneself as either derived from or transformable into another initially imagined as different—might be elucidated in the parlance of the twentieth-century sociologist George Herbert Mead. For Mead, formation of the self involves a social process, constituted through a series of reflections of the "generalized other." One's self does not exist apart from or precede social interaction; rather, it becomes manifest only in and through society.[87] In his discussion of the internalization of the other,

---

[85] Marincola 1987 distinguishes between Book 2, for instance, of Herodotus's *Histories* and Books 7–9, in which participation on the narrator's part is necessarily limited. Here Lucian seems to combine both aspects of the Herodotean narrator: the embodied ethnographer and the war chronicler.

[86] Compare Smith 2009: 85 on Endymion as the "narrator's second-self."

[87] Mead 1982: 85. See also Mead 2015 [1934]: 223.

Mead saw the self as potentially multi-perspectival: "It is here that mental life arises—with this continual passing from one system to another, with the occupation of both in passage and with the systematic structures that each involves. It is the realm of continual emergence."[88] The notion of a "continual passing from one system to another" maps well onto Lucian's journeying in the *True Histories*, in which the protagonist has a series of encounters that create reflective possibilities for experiencing himself as other. "Continual emergence" arises from recognizing the flexible articulations of the identity within a social system. As Mead notes, "Sociality is the capability of being several things at once," and any sense of unity of self is reified in relation to "the generalized other."[89] As is already clear from the *True Histories*, and as will continue to unfold, it is the protagonist's encounters with the generalized other and the possibility of "being several things at once"—including the invitation to join battle, to reside permanently as a member of the Selenite life, and, as we shall see, to view the earth from a critical distance—that produce a sense of the self as object. Lucian stages an externalized process of reflection, susceptible of what Jean-Paul Sartre called "The Look," which fixes the self as the object of another's scrutiny.[90]

Moon with a View

Herodotean analogizing helps establish not only the novelty of the lunar world for the protagonist and Lucian's reader, but its use also marks the protagonist's own estrangement from home. Early in this episode, the protagonist is depicted in the role of "supposing" that what he sees from afar is, in fact, earth. In a lunar realm explicitly marked as one of novelty and strangeness (καινὰ καὶ παράδοξα, 1.22), Lucian's language of likeness will upend the Herodotean technique of accounting for foreign variables through a Greek perspective, by training that perspective back on the very things normally reckoned as the control:

---

[88] On Mead, see Aboulafia 1986: 3–26; Callero 2003; Burke and Skowroński 2013.

[89] Quotations from Mead 1982: 49 and 2015 [1934]: 154, respectively.

[90] Sartre 1956: 259–60. See Aboulafia 1986: 27–44 (esp. 37–40): "By experiencing this transformation of myself under the gaze of others, I am convinced that there must be others" (42); further, Aboulafia 1986: 45–61 for a comparison of Mead and Sartre.

216 HERODOTUS AND IMPERIAL GREEK LITERATURE

Seven days and seven nights we ran on the air. On the eighth day, we spied out a large tract of land suspended in the air like an island, gleaming, spherical, awash with light. Docking there we threw anchor and disembarked, and as we observed the countryside, we found it inhabited and cultivated. Now, by day we could see nothing from there. But when night was upon us, many other islands nearby came into our view, some bigger, some smaller, in color like fire. And another piece of land below came into view, with cities on it, rivers, seas, woods, and mountains. This, we supposed, was the land we inhabited. We decided to press on even further.... (1.10–11)

ἑπτὰ δὲ ἡμέρας καὶ τὰς ἴσας νύκτας ἀεροδρομήσαντες, ὀγδόῃ καθορῶμεν γῆν τινα μεγάλην ἐν τῷ ἀέρι καθάπερ νῆσον, λαμπρὰν καὶ σφαιροειδῆ καὶ φωτὶ μεγάλῳ καταλαμπομένην· προσενεχθέντες δὲ αὐτῇ καὶ ὁρμισάμενοι ἀπέβημεν, ἐπισκοποῦντες δὲ τὴν χώραν εὑρίσκομεν οἰκουμένην τε καὶ γεωργουμένην. ἡμέρας μὲν οὖν οὐδὲν αὐτόθεν ἑωρῶμεν, νυκτὸς δὲ ἐπιγενομένης ἐφαίνοντο ἡμῖν καὶ ἄλλαι πολλαὶ νῆσοι πλησίον, αἱ μὲν μείζους, αἱ δὲ μικρότεραι, πυρὶ τὴν χρόαν προσεοικυῖαι, καὶ ἄλλη δέ τις γῆ κάτω, καὶ πόλεις ἐν αὐτῇ καὶ ποταμοὺς ἔχουσα καὶ πελάγη καὶ ὕλας καὶ ὄρη. ταύτην οὖν τὴν καθ' ἡμᾶς οἰκουμένην εἰκάζομεν. δόξαν δὲ ἡμῖν καὶ ἔτι πορρωτέρω προελθεῖν....

The narrator recognizes the literal outlandishness of his own home and engages in an act of self-distancing.[91] The linguistic and analogical choices bespeak the protagonist's hesitation in properly describing his experience.[92] The compact ἀεροδρομήσαντες points to a peculiar, uncertain synthesis of activities (running and flying), while the strangeness evoked is in turn softened by the hedging markers of analogy. Yet the analogies slide subtly from comparison to apparent fact. Note, for instance, how land that is at first "just like an island" (καθάπερ νῆσον) is subsequently described as being surrounded by "many islands" (πολλαὶ νῆσοι); this second mention of islands is rendered in straight terms, with no suggestion that the lands are *like* islands. Through such slippage, the likening now operates as fact, and the *comparandum* of island overtakes the unnamed thing to which it is adduced as comparison.

[91] Compare discussions of Lucian's ability to create situations of "enstrangement," borrowing a term from Viktor Shklovsky (see Branham 1985: 242 with n. 7). See also Popescu 2014: 52 and, on this passage's philosophical resonances, von Möllendorff 2000: 99–101.
[92] On characters' "hesitations" that arise in fantastical texts, see Todorov 1973 [1970]: 32, 155–56 (on self and other, citing Martin Buber), 167–68.

This description culminates with the explicit moment of supposition about the protagonist's home space (ταύτην οὖν τὴν καθ' ἡμᾶς οἰκουμένην εἰκάζομεν). On the one hand, such guessing registers that the men are so far from home that they can only surmise, in effect, where they started. But the guess also hits upon a certain profundity, for the protagonist's identification of home has now become the object of supposition rather than knowledge. The protagonist can thus mark the initially sought-after novelty of his travels (πραγμάτων καινῶν ἐπιθυμία, 1.5) not strictly by accounting for the oddities of a new place but also by emphasizing the cognitive disorientation of having to guess at one's home. Lucian here puts his hand to the Herodotean toolbox but uses analogizing to invert the objects of knowledge and supposition. That the wondrous can become the source of knowledge and that one's putative origin can become the object of guessing together constitute a form of subjective flexibility, seeing oneself or one's origins from a new perspective. The moment is rooted in ethnographic rhetoric but trains the prism of curiosity back onto the self.

Removable Eyes

In Lucian's encounter with the Selenites, the shifts in perspective find thematic reinforcement when he highlights a detail that gives meta-reflective attention to some of the concerns discussed so far:

> Concerning the kinds of eyes they have, I hesitate to say, lest someone suppose me a liar because of the unbelievable nature of my account. Nevertheless, I will state it: they have removable eyes, and anyone who wishes can remove his own eyes and guard them until he needs to see again. When he puts them in, he sees: and many who have lost their own eyes see by using the eyes of others. (1.25)

> περὶ μέντοι τῶν ὀφθαλμῶν, οἵους ἔχουσιν, ὀκνῶ μὲν εἰπεῖν, μή τίς με νομίσῃ ψεύδεσθαι διὰ τὸ ἄπιστον τοῦ λόγου. ὅμως δὲ καὶ τοῦτο ἐρῶ· τοὺς ὀφθαλμοὺς περιαιρετοὺς ἔχουσι, καὶ ὁ βουλόμενος ἐξελὼν τοὺς αὑτοῦ φυλάττει ἔστ' ἂν δεηθῇ ἰδεῖν· οὕτω δὲ ἐνθέμενος ὁρᾷ· καὶ πολλοὶ τοὺς σφετέρους ἀπολέσαντες παρ' ἄλλων χρησάμενοι ὁρῶσιν.

By according special attention to the Selenites' choosable, removable eyes, Lucian comically literalizes the cognitive processes of autopsy and cultural

218 HERODOTUS AND IMPERIAL GREEK LITERATURE

positioning so clearly associated with Herodotus. Indeed, Lucian elsewhere in his corpus explicitly cites Herodotus in making the claim that the eye is the most trustworthy sense organ.[93] Lucian's image of interchangeable eyeballs provides metonymy for the very process of perspectival fluidity that the work sets in motion, one in which the putative gazing subject (the protagonist) has already been forced to see his home from a distance, to feel himself under the gaze of a generalized other, and, in revising his view of Homer (see 1.17), to interrogate the literary past that constructs the educated Greek self. For readers of Herodotus and Lucian, the ethnographic encounter always raises the specter of comparison, of asking whether another people's customs are superior to those of one's own (famously brought to the fore at *Hist.* 3.38 on the potential, if ultimately unwanted, interchangeability of customs). Here, while the removable eyes are an aspect of Selenite anatomy, using someone else's eyes connotes the perspectival shifts enabled by foreign encounter.

Mirror on the Moon

One of the plumpest episodes of ethnographic inversion in the moon sequence comes during the protagonist's encounter with the weird mirror.[94] Lucian casts the mirror experience in Herodotean terms as a "further wonder" (ἄλλο θαῦμα):

> And I saw a further wonder in the moon king's palace: a very large mirror
> is set over a not terribly deep well. Whoever goes down into the well hears
> everything being said among us on the earth. If he looks into the mirror,
> he sees every city and every people as if he were standing next to each
> one. At that time I saw my family and the entirety of my native land, but
> whether they, too, were looking at me, I am no longer able to say for certain.

---

[93] See, e.g., *Dom.* 20, *Hist. conscr.* 29, and *Salt.* 78. See also the programmatic importance of seeing's superiority to hearing at Hdt. 1.8.2. Compare Schepens 2007: 42–48, esp. 42 for the remark that "it was by the methodically conscious application of this principle [of autopsy] to a new field of inquiry—research about human affairs in the past—that Herodotus established the authority of an enterprise that was entirely his own" (42). Note as well the Todorovian moment of hesitation in Lucian's ὀκνῶ μὲν εἰπεῖν.

[94] On this passage, see von Möllendorff 2000: 182–88, and see esp. ní Mheallaigh 2014: 216–27 and ní Mheallaigh 2020: 254–59, with further bibliography. Cf. *Hist. conscr.* 50, where the historian is encouraged to have a mind "like a mirror," accurately reflecting reality. The *True Histories* reminds readers that mirrors can just as easily distort as accurately reflect.

Whoever does not believe these things to be so, if ever he reaches that point himself, will know that I speak the truth. (1.26)

καὶ μὴν καὶ ἄλλο θαῦμα ἐν τοῖς βασιλείοις ἐθεασάμην· κάτοπτρον μέγιστον κεῖται ὑπὲρ φρέατος οὐ πάνυ βαθέος. ἂν μὲν οὖν εἰς τὸ φρέαρ καταβῇ τις, ἀκούει πάντων τῶν παρ' ἡμῖν ἐν τῇ γῇ λεγομένων, ἐὰν δὲ εἰς τὸ κάτοπτρον ἀποβλέψῃ, πάσας μὲν πόλεις, πάντα δὲ ἔθνη ὁρᾷ ὥσπερ ἐφεστὼς ἑκάστοις· τότε καὶ τοὺς οἰκείους ἐγὼ ἐθεασάμην καὶ πᾶσαν τὴν πατρίδα, εἰ δὲ κἀκεῖνοι ἐμὲ ἑώρων, οὐκέτι ἔχω τὸ ἀσφαλὲς εἰπεῖν. ὅστις δὲ ταῦτα μὴ πιστεύει οὕτως ἔχειν, ἄν ποτε καὶ αὐτὸς ἐκεῖσε ἀφίκηται, εἴσεται ὡς ἀληθῆ λέγω.

Lucian continues to navigate Herodotean concepts of wondrousness and autopsy, but what, precisely, constitutes the "further wonder" that the protagonist sees? The wonder offered, it turns out, is not the mirror itself but rather the particular kind of panoptic, pan-acoustic (re-)encounter with earth that it provides. The protagonist is here given only illusory access to the "real" world from the vantage point of the putatively reflective, mimetically inferior world of the moon.[95] Yet this earth, the foil against which all the oddities of the moon are counterpoised, becomes its own seemingly unreal place, where one's image appears with uncertain perceptibility (οὐκέτι . . . ἀσφαλές). The view of earth is mediated, seen through a mirror, and not, as earlier (1.10), witnessed directly through autopsy. The protagonist thus sees "**as if** standing next to" (ὥσπερ ἐφεστώς) others. Though aware of the possibility that he is gazed back upon by others, he cannot be sure.

In this Herodotean territory of wonder and foreign description, the narrator has now become the object of his *own* gaze. Sartre talks of how the self can "bestow[] an outside on its own eyes" and how through "The Look" of another, one becomes an object in the eyes of someone else.[96] Here the roving, ethnographic narrator gives himself "The Look." The ability to see differently arises in a moment that returns Lucian to the earth, but that same ability confirms him, ironically, as a Selenite: although anatomically not a lunar person, it is as if the protagonist has now seen with removable eyes. This solo descent into the well and the "reflection" it occasions therefore lead instantly to a peculiar re-socialization on earth, in which one's own autopsy becomes a way of seeing (a reflection

---

[95] See ní Mheallaigh 2014: 216–21 for ancient philosophical considerations of the moon's nature, with an emphasis on the moon as a mirror-world of the earth.

[96] See Sartre 1956: 170; on "The Look," 259–60.

220   HERODOTUS AND IMPERIAL GREEK LITERATURE

of) oneself from the outside. The mirror recapitulates the self-othering that the text has enacted, through which Lucian's ethnographic protagonist comes to see himself as an object. Although Lucian's autopsy is now mediated by the mirror, it is nevertheless autopsy that is hailed as dispositive for doubters, should they get "there" (ἐκεῖσε) and see for themselves, harking to a characteristic move by Herodotus to assert the power of autopsy in doubtful stretches.[97]

In short, the swirl of questions raised, themselves capped by the Herodotean expression of uncertainty (οὐκέτι ἔχω τὸ ἀσφαλὲς εἰπεῖν ~ Hdt. 1.57, 1.160, 1.172, 7.60, 9.84), imbues the entire passage with doubt. The usual vector of ethnographic ambivalence is reversed: wonder and hesitation apply not to (or not exclusively to) the difficulties of understanding foreign or lunar material but rather to the narrator's experience with an image of himself in the mirror. Far from home, he is given illusory access to it. The encounter with earth, seen through a mirror "as if" standing upon its reflected image, marks a fitting climax for this episode, in which the narrator's participation among the Selenites permits special autopsy but also confirms his distance from his own land. His fatherland has become a reflection, his presence there part of the mirror's trompe l'oeil.

A Reminder of Home in Lamptown

Journeying on, the protagonist and his crew arrive at Lamptown (1.29), a sequence that in this instance involves allusion to a passage from Herodotus (2.62).[98] Beyond the surface similarities of the two passages, congruities of narrative effect emerge, centered on narratorial positioning and the pretense to truth. These effects blur the reader's ability to parse the veridical expectations that attend to either. Lucian's fantastic story is couched in the "realistic" terms according to which truthful history is composed, but Herodotus's passage also reveals that "real" history can itself be given over to seemingly fantastical narrative stretches.

---

[97] In addition to the examples cited earlier, compare Herodotus's inviting "anyone with understanding" simply to use his eyes, even if he has not heard reports, to affirm that Egyptian topography is not what it once was: δῆλα γὰρ δὴ καὶ μὴ προακούσαντι, ἰδόντι δέ, ὅστις γε σύνεσιν ἔχει, ὅτι <ἡ> Αἴγυπτος ἐς τὴν Ἕλληνες ναυτίλλονται ἐστὶ Αἰγυπτίοισι ἐπίκτητός τε γῆ καὶ δῶρον τοῦ ποταμοῦ (2.5).

[98] See Jerram 1991 [1879]: ad loc. 1.29.

REMOVABLE EYES 221

In his account of Egypt, Herodotus describes the worship of Neith (whom he likens to Athena, 2.59.3) in the Egyptian town of Saïs, part of his broader description of festivals in Egypt (see generally 2.58–63):

> When they gather together in the town of Saïs on the night of the sacrifice, they all burn lamps in a circle outside their houses. The lamps are saucers filled with salt and oil, on which the wick is positioned and which burns all night. The name of this festival is the Lamplight. The Egyptians who do not attend this festival are nonetheless all careful during the night of the sacrifice to burn their own lamps, and thus there is lamplight not at Saïs alone but throughout the whole of Egypt. As to why light and the night itself have acquired this honor, there is a sacred tale told about it. (2.62)

> ἐς Σάϊν δὲ πόλιν ἐπεὰν συλλεχθέωσι τῆς θυσίης ἐν τῇ νυκτὶ λύχνα καίουσι πάντες πολλὰ ὑπαίθρια περὶ τὰ δώματα κύκλῳ. τὰ δὲ λύχνα ἐστὶ ἐμβάφια ἔμπλεα ἁλὸς καὶ ἐλαίου, ἐπιπολῆς δὲ ἔπεστι αὐτὸ τὸ ἐλλύχνιον, καὶ τοῦτο καίεται παννύχιον. καὶ τῇ ὁρτῇ οὔνομα κεῖται Λυχνοκαΐη. οἳ δ' ἂν μὴ ἔλθωσι τῶν Αἰγυπτίων ἐς τὴν πανήγυριν ταύτην, φυλάσσοντες τὴν νύκτα τῆς θυσίης καίουσι καὶ αὐτοὶ πάντες τὰ λύχνα, καὶ οὕτω οὐκ ἐν Σάϊ μούνῃ καίεται ἀλλὰ καὶ ἀνὰ πᾶσαν Αἴγυπτον. ὅτευ δὲ εἵνεκα φῶς ἔλαχε καὶ τιμὴν ἡ νὺξ αὕτη, ἔστι ἱρὸς περὶ αὐτοῦ λόγος λεγόμενος.

How does Herodotus's voice work in this passage? Where ought the reader to locate the narrator? The passage includes details both broad and minute, down to component parts of the lamps, leaving the reader to speculate about whether Herodotus has seen the lamps or simply heard them described. The narrator does not resolve his own role, autoptic or otherwise, in acquiring such knowledge. Was he witness to the lamplight as it burned "throughout the whole of Egypt"? The passage ends abruptly with the mention of the undisclosed sacred tale, and this closural tidbit tantalizes. Herodotus has apparently told us everything he knows about the festival but ends by alerting us that he will not or cannot tell us one final detail about the story behind the festival.[99] Depending on where the reader locates him, the narrator can seem to exist inside the narrative—as eyewitness reporter—or just outside it, at

[99] In reference to this passage, von Möllendorff 2014: 527 calls this last line "Herodotus' solution of the dilemma . . . an inaccessible ἱρὸς λόγος." Herodotus's "solution" does not necessarily resolve the readerly dilemma regarding the state of Herodotus's knowledge. Cf. Harrison 2000: 182–207.

222 HERODOTUS AND IMPERIAL GREEK LITERATURE

the end of a chain of hearsay.[100] The final comment on the λόγος λεγόμενος offers a glimpse into something unseen: a moment of subjectivity and hesitation and ultimately Herodotus's decision *not* to tell the tale.

Lucian conjures the Herodotus passage on lamps with amusing adjustments of narratorial function:

> We sailed the following night and day and around evening arrived at Lamptown, as it is called. Upon arrival we did not find any humans, but instead we found many lamps running around in the agora and loitering around the harbor. Some of the lamps were small and poor, so to speak, but a few, of the great and powerful sort, were altogether brilliant and conspicuous. They have houses, and each has his own private sconce. They have names just like humans, and we heard them talking. In no way did they do us harm but rather welcomed us hospitably. But we were nonetheless fearful, and not one of us dared to eat with them or fall asleep. In the center of their city a town hall has been built, where the whole night long their archon presides, calling each of them by name. Whoever does not answer the summons is sentenced to die on the charge of deserting ranks. Death is by snuffing out. We were present to witness the proceedings and to hear as well the lamps defending themselves and stating the reasons why they were late. There I recognized my own lamp, and speaking with him I inquired how matters were at home. He gave me a full account of those matters. (1.29)

> πλεύσαντες δὲ τὴν ἐπιοῦσαν νύκτα καὶ ἡμέραν, περὶ ἑσπέραν ἀφικόμεθα ἐς τὴν Λυχνόπολιν καλουμένην ἀποβάντες δὲ ἄνθρωπον μὲν οὐδένα εὕρομεν, λύχνους δὲ πολλοὺς περιθέοντας καὶ ἐν τῇ ἀγορᾷ καὶ περὶ τὸν λιμένα διατρίβοντας, τοὺς μὲν μικροὺς καὶ ὥσπερ πένητας, ὀλίγους δὲ τῶν μεγάλων καὶ δυνατῶν πάνυ λαμπροὺς καὶ περιφανεῖς. οἰκήσεις δὲ αὐτοῖς καὶ λυχνεῶνες ἰδίᾳ ἑκάστῳ πεποίηντο, καὶ αὐτοὶ ὀνόματα εἶχον, ὥσπερ οἱ ἄνθρωποι, καὶ φωνὴν προϊεμένων ἠκούομεν, καὶ οὐδὲν ἡμᾶς ἠδίκουν, ἀλλὰ καὶ ἐπὶ ξένια ἐκάλουν· ἡμεῖς δὲ ὅμως ἐφοβούμεθα, καὶ οὔτε δειπνῆσαι οὔτε ὑπνῶσαί τις ἡμῶν ἐτόλμησεν. ἀρχεῖα δὲ αὐτοῖς ἐν μέσῃ τῇ πόλει πεποίηται,

---

[100] Compare again Dewald 2002: 272, complicating the apparently binary divide between narrator and narrated *logoi* that Herodotus often seems to present: "But if one instead broadens the notion of authorial presence to include not only the overt first-person pronouns and verbs but also all of the places where the authorial 'I' is effectively present as a tacit register of authoritative control over what is being recounted, as narratology has taught us now to do, the picture one forms of Herodotus' authorial interventions is more complex than this initial binary separation into narrator and focalized *logoi* suggests."

ἔνθα ὁ ἄρχων αὐτῶν διὰ νυκτὸς ὅλης κάθηται ὀνομαστὶ καλῶν ἕκαστον· ὃς δ᾽ ἂν μὴ ὑπακούσῃ, καταδικάζεται ἀποθανεῖν ὡς λιπὼν τὴν τάξιν· ὁ δὲ θάνατός ἐστι σβεσθῆναι. παρεστῶτες δὲ ἡμεῖς ἑωρῶμεν τὰ γινόμενα καὶ ἠκούομεν ἅμα τῶν λύχνων ἀπολογουμένων καὶ τὰς αἰτίας λεγόντων δι᾽ ἃς ἐβράδυνον. ἔνθα καὶ τὸν ἡμέτερον λύχνον ἐγνώρισα, καὶ προσειπὼν αὐτὸν περὶ τῶν κατ᾽ οἶκον ἐπυνθανόμην ὅπως ἔχοιεν· ὁ δέ μοι ἅπαντα ἐκεῖνα διηγήσατο.

Von Möllendorff has noted some of the patent intertextual overlaps with Herodotus 2.62, where the lamp activities described also last all night and apparently require or inspire complete participation.[101] But these and other surface details do not exhaust the intertextual energy between Herodotus's lamps and Lucian's Lamptown. Lucian's narrator not only describes his actions but also explicitly positions himself and his men in relation to them (**παρεστῶτες** δὲ ἡμεῖς **ἑωρῶμεν** τὰ γινόμενα καὶ **ἠκούομεν**). In Lucian's Lamptown, the role of the inquirer, sublimated in the Herodotus passage, is transformed into a more explicit participation with the forces encountered. In the private exchange, the protagonist recognizes (ἐγνώρισα) his own lamp and acquires knowledge—not of a foreign land, à la Herodotus, but rather of how matters fare at home (κατ᾽ οἶκον). Ostensible ethnographic inquiry thus boomerangs back to the protagonist's origin (compare Herodotus's analogizing of Neith to Athena, 2.59). The Lucianic protagonist's inquiry (ἐπυνθανόμην) becomes a mode of self-inquiry, rather than discovery of something new.

So when Lucian foregrounds his protagonist's (self-interested) inquiry, manifest in his question to the lamp about his own home, he emphasizes some of the lurking energies of Herodotus's text, where inquiry can be assumed but is not always stated. Lucian conjures in his Lamptown passage *both* Herodotus's discussion of religious ritual *and* the implied slippages of reportorial distance that inform the passage. And while both passages are concerned, to varying degrees, with narratorial subjectivity, the Lucian passage introduces a new element of subjectivity in making the *object*, the lamp, come alive. In foregrounding the ludic intersubjectivity made available through the conversation between the protagonist and the sentient lamp,

---

[101] Von Möllendorff 2014: 526–27, commenting on Lucian's "combinatory mimesis." His mimesis is not an end in itself, however, and should not obscure the extent to which his combinations draw on aspects both explicit (lamps) and implicit (epistemic possibilities) from prior sources.

224 HERODOTUS AND IMPERIAL GREEK LITERATURE

Lucian again collapses the difference between subject and object.[102] The narrator's recognition of a personal object and his subsequent inquiry not only showcase his "participation" in an intersubjective experience, but they also reflect one way in which the lamp is folded back into the life of the protagonist, allowing the external, ethnographic material to "participate" in that life.[103] Lucian's transformation highlights the inherent self-interestedness of ethnographic inquiry and underscores, albeit by playfully animating a domestic object, the subjectivity of the interrogated other.

Hence, the ostensible differences between the two writers do not derive strictly from putative differences between the realm of "straight" truth-telling in historiography and the exaggerations of fantasy, or whatever generic mode we classify Lucian's *True Histories*.[104] Indeed, pointing to differences of genre is perhaps circular. Rather, the effect of Lucian's passage is to jolt any reader who spots the allusion into the realization that a quality of the fantastical is already present in the *Histories*: not necessarily in the neon signage of wonder but in the relay of (potentially questionable) information, mediated by the narrator's now-present, now-invisible hand. The fantasy of historiography is that of having consistent and reliable knowledge. Even with his Egyptian sources, Herodotus must acknowledge their inability to explain, for instance, the Nile itself.[105] Nor are the Greek theories any better (οὐδ᾽ ἀξιῶ μνησθῆναι, 2.20.1). And in a moment when the narrator's own experience seems to burst through the text's heterodiegetic facade, Herodotus admits to thinking absurd the man who claimed to have an explanation of the Nile's source, when no one else in conversation could offer up information (ἐς λόγους οὐδεὶς ὑπέσχετο εἰδέναι, 2.28.1): "This man seemed to be pulling my leg when he said he had precise knowledge" (οὗτος δ᾽ ἔμοιγε παίζειν ἐδόκεε, φάμενος εἰδέναι ἀτρεκέως, 2.28.2). In turn, Lucian raises questions about the kind of "straightness" one might expect from *historia*, if its slips in objectivity can so easily allow readers to *feel* as though they are traipsing into some other realm. What is the phenomenological difference in reading experience,

---

[102] Compare Smith 2009: 82, citing Julia Kristeva's notion of "passivation": "Rather than functioning as a means of objectification and therefore control, paradoxography will instead become a mechanism whereby, encountering and documenting the abject, the imperial subject undergoes a process of passivation, acquiring the ability to put himself in the position of the imperial subject."

[103] Compare Todorov 1973 [1970]: 120 on the "fragility of the limit between matter and mind."

[104] See ní Mheallaigh 2014: 256 n. 150. Lucian lampoons various instances of absurdity in history writing at *Hist. conscr.* 11–28, esp. at 29 on the historian who describes Parthian ensigns in the shape of serpents as actual snakes.

[105] See 2.19.3: "Concerning these things I was unable to obtain any information from the Egyptians" (τούτων ὦν περὶ οὐδενὸς οὐδὲν οἷός τε ἐγενόμεν παραλαβεῖν {παρὰ} τῶν Αἰγυπτίων).

REMOVABLE EYES 225

Lucian seems to ask, between readers of the *Histories* who have never been to Egypt, have never seen the lamps on which Herodotus reports, and certainly have never heard the "tale told" about them and readers of the *True Histories*, who have likely never seen a talking lamp?

Uncertain Selves inside the Whale

The protagonist and his companions are later swallowed by a whale (1.31). The recognizably Greek world discovered therein, including a temple to Poseidon, would at first seem to counteract the text's running theme of physical and cognitive disorientation, returning readers to a stable pastiche of ethnographic encounter that, in this instance, results in the protagonist's restoration to a recognizably Hellenic world, in echo of the first foray among the Vine-Women.[106] Despite, however, the initial reiteration of Greek life, a sinister quality lurks in the whale episode, tipped off by the foreshadowing reference to an ἀρχὴ κακῶν, evoking both Homer (*Il.* 5.63) and Herodotus (5.97.3): "A change for the better seems often to become the start of greater evils" (ἔοικε δὲ ἀρχὴ κακῶν μειζόνων γίνεσθαι πολλάκις ἡ πρὸς τὸ βέλτιον μεταβολή, 1.30). That Herodotus's use of the phrase, in reference to the Athenian ships sent to assist the incipient Ionian Revolt, itself recalls Homer's reference to the "evil-starting" (ἀρχέκακος) ships that came for Helen renders Lucian's use here a double play, the Samosatan channeling Herodotus channeling Homer—a set of layered literary references that seemingly reinforce the ostensible "Greekness" to prevail in the whale. But as we shall see shortly, Lucian continues to use Herodotean mechanisms in the whale scene to fashion a particular kind of inquiring experience, in which encounters with foreign material convert the traveling subject into object, the "I" into a "me," in the language of Mead.[107] For while the whale episode

---

[106] On the microcosmic aspects of this episode, in which the narrator's familiar world is gradually reconstituted, see Rütten 1997: 87–91. For this scene as a rewriting of Plato's allegory of the cave, see Georgiadou and Larmour 1998: 156–60 and ad loc. 1.31; ní Mheallaigh 2014: 227–30, with bibliography. Compare Todorov 1973 [1970]: 73–74 on the limits of allegorical readings of fantastical literature.

[107] See Mead 2015 [1934]: 178 on the "I" as the subject who through encounters with the generalized other becomes the objective "me." See also Rütten 1997: 91, "Durch diese Veränderungen der Positionen und Perspektiven verschwimmen abermals die Grenzen zwischen den Welten: Inmitten einer phantastischen Abenteuerwelt, die sich von seiner Lebenswirklichkeit fundamental unterscheidet, wird der Held in einen abgeschlossenen Mikrokosmos entführt, der nun wiederum ganz und gar seiner Heimatwelt entspricht."

226   HERODOTUS AND IMPERIAL GREEK LITERATURE

has been interpreted along allegorical and philosophical lines, it also centers on issues of identification, likeness, and assimilation that evoke aspects of historiographic narration and the notion of a porous self whose Herodotean filtering I have wanted to accentuate. In the whale, the Lucianic protagonist registers a psychological bond with the displaced community he finds, marking the episode with both the ethnographic observations of an outsider and the subjective experience of an insider.

The world inside the whale, initially dark and shadowy (τὸ μὲν πρῶτον σκότος ἦν καὶ οὐδὲν ἑωρῶμεν, 1.31), gradually gives way to a site that appears to have been cultivated (ἐῴκει πάντα ἐξειργασμένοις, 1.31). The protagonist's processual reckoning (ἐμοὶ δοκεῖν, 1.31) of a discernible space congeals when he recognizes the interior's Hellenic credentials upon seeing a temple to Poseidon.[108] But the discovery of the temple alone does not assure the reader that the whale's interior space lacks strangeness. Rather, it is the historiographic verification offered by the phrase "as the inscription made clear" (ὡς ἐδήλου ἡ ἐπιγραφή, 1.32) that confirms the soundness of Greek intelligibility. Lucian domesticates the whale's interior not merely through recognition of Hellenic realia, but by referring to the inscription, he also enunciates the *process* of recognition, the means of discernment, in a move meant to solidify his authority and that juxtaposes the generic imprimatur of historiography with this unreal place.

When the protagonist encounters two figures living in the whale, an old man and a youth, a moment of intersubjectivity and mutual recognition occurs:

> With simultaneous pleasure and fear we stood there: and they seemed to be experiencing the same thing as we, standing near us, speechless. After some time the old man spoke: "Well, strangers, who are you? Are you of the stock of sea gods, or are you unfortunate mortals like us? We, who were humans and were dwelling on the earth, now have become sea people, and we swim around in this beast that encompasses us, and we do not know precisely what it is we are experiencing: for we suppose ourselves dead, but we put trust in being alive." (1.33)

---

[108] See ní Mheallaigh 2014: 229: "[T]he fake world inside the whale, with its conspicuous tokens of human and Hellenic civilization (agriculture and irrigation, a temple, tombs, a domicile), is *closer* to the reader's 'reality' than the fantasy world outside."

ἠσθέντες οὖν ἅμα καὶ φοβηθέντες ἔστημεν· κἀκεῖνοι δὲ ταὐτὸ ἡμῖν ὡς
τὸ εἰκὸς παθόντες ἄναυδοι παρειστήκεσαν· χρόνῳ δὲ ὁ πρεσβύτης ἔφη,
τίνες ὑμεῖς ἄρα ἐστέ, ὦ ξένοι; πότερον τῶν ἐναλίων δαιμόνων ἢ ἄνθρωποι
δυστυχεῖς ἡμῖν παραπλήσιοι; καὶ γὰρ ἡμεῖς ἄνθρωποι ὄντες καὶ ἐν γῇ
τραφέντες νῦν θαλάττιοι γεγόναμεν καὶ συννηχόμεθα τῷ περιέχοντι τούτῳ
θηρίῳ, οὐδ' ὃ πάσχομεν ἀκριβῶς εἰδότες· τεθνάναι μὲν γὰρ εἰκάζομεν, ζῆν
δὲ πιστεύομεν.

The passage forces the reader to pause, to stand still with the protagonist
(ἔστημεν) and contemplate a simultaneity (ἅμα) of sensations. The protagonist, meeting someone unknown, presumes a commonality of sensation (ταὐτό), again in the language of supposition (ταὐτὸ ἡμῖν **ὡς τὸ εἰκὸς
παθόντες**). But the supposition does not rationalize away the men's strangeness. Rather, the protagonist infers an affective bond between himself and the
men, who appear to be experiencing the same impasse of uncertain emotion.
Lucian inverts the presumed dynamic of ethnographic inquiry and replays
the inquiry of Endymion to Lucian: the visited makes inquiry of the visitor,
proffering possible identities (πότερον . . . ἤ).

Although evoking the techniques of inquiry and observation, Lucian, by
reversing the direction, firmly puts the inquiring subject into the position of
object. Moreover, despite having earlier alerted the reader to the possibility
of Greek community inside the whale, the protagonist, in fact, comes face
to face with men who are uncertain of their own existential situation, in a
dissolving of the stable basis of any ethnographic inquiry. In anticipated answer to the visitor's own question about who the whale-dwellers might be,
the inhabitants offer the claim that they have "become sea people" and that
they do not know precisely what it is they are experiencing: "For we suppose
ourselves dead, but we put trust in being alive." Uncertainty again inflects
self-perception. Instead of the ethnographer who encounters a foreign group
and must find ways of describing them, by analogy or otherwise, Lucian's
protagonist meets with a pair so ontologically disoriented as to know not
whether they are alive or dead.

In the whale, then, as in the moon sequence, an element of the uncanny
arises in this moment of existential hesitation, which in Todorov's view
marks fantastical literature.[109] Yet it would underserve Lucian's text to describe it as merely fantastical. For, as we have seen, the seemingly bizarre

---

[109] Todorov 1973 [1970]: 31–33.

228   HERODOTUS AND IMPERIAL GREEK LITERATURE

details of various encounters nevertheless touch upon questions of identity, self-perception, and the attainment of truth. Lucian's riffing on Herodotus is not merely a ludic maneuver on historiography; rather, it engages a nexus of serious questions already latent in Herodotus. Lucian's protagonist demonstrates a repeated performance of becoming, not a static assertion of being. The protagonist might have stayed on the moon. He might have remained imprisoned in the whale. But the text insists on iteration and, consequently, reiteration of identity claims in relation to others encountered. In the final portion of this chapter, I ask how the work's closing evocations of Herodotus solidify these interests.

Estrangement on the Isle of the Blessed

Although sometimes treated only briefly, given his classification of Herodotus with Ctesias in the "usual suspect" category of liars (2.31),[110] Lucian's creative iterations of Herodotus in the Isle of the Blessed episode both frame the entire sequence and extend the historiographic through-line of the *True Histories*. Lucian deploys the Isle of the Blessed episode to mock conventional wisdom that had accrued around particular literary figures. His acknowledgment and seeming acceptance of conventional literary opinion about Herodotus at 2.31 stand oddly next to his own Herodotean literary methods. Lucian only appears to bow to the conventional wisdom on Herodotus; in fact, the usefulness of Herodotus's slippery relation to the truth again proves irresistible to Lucian's kinetic reception, his simultaneously rejecting and incorporating Herodotus.

When the protagonist and his crew reach the place that Lawrence Kim has called a fulfillment of "the ultimate fantasy of the educated Imperial Greek," they are condemned by one of Hades's judges for their "restlessness and for leaving home" (τῆς μὲν φιλοπραγμοσύνης καὶ τῆς ἀποδημίας) and are told they can remain only for a fixed period (χρόνον μείναντας, 2.10).[111] Unlike previous stints on the moon and in the whale, where permanent participation appears to be an option, the protagonist is restricted from living forever on the Isle of the Blessed. He is made an object, put into the passive position of being judged. Indeed, the climax of reaching the Isle of the Blessed thus

---

[110] See Kim 2010a: 145 with n. 23 and 148–50 with n. 41. Kim calls the reference to Herodotus "customary" (150).

[111] Kim 2010a: 158.

REMOVABLE EYES 229

comes as an anticlimax, like the repetition of the literary past encountered there, where the marks of glory have become a broken record whose recital is a kind of punishment.[112] The intellectual impetus toward restlessness and flight from home has led the protagonist to a place among the heroes, but it turns out there is a price to pay.

It is none other than Herodotus whom Lucian uses to frame his work's (anti)climax. Indeed, a rare moment of outright reference to Herodotus, one of only two in the work (and the only explicit citation of a passage), initiates the long stretch of narrative covering the Isle of the Blessed and the Isle of the Wicked (2.5–32).[113] As the protagonist nears the isles and perceives a whiff of their pleasures, he states, "We were already very near when a wondrous breeze blew around us, pleasant and fragrant, the sort of breeze Herodotus the historian says blows off rich Arabia" (ἤδη δὲ πλησίον ἦμεν, καὶ θαυμαστή τις αὖρα περιέπνευσεν ἡμᾶς, ἡδεῖα καὶ εὐώδης, οἵαν φησὶν ὁ συγγραφεὺς Ἡρόδοτος ἀπόζειν τῆς εὐδαίμονος Ἀραβίας, 2.5). The citation perhaps unsurprisingly summons Herodotus to comment on something wondrous (θαυμαστή). Subtler, however, is the hint that Lucian is referring not only to Herodotus but also to the *critical tradition* concerning him. For the language of sweetness and pleasantness (ἡδεῖα καὶ εὐώδης . . . τὸ ἡδὺ . . . ἡσθέντες, 2.5) conjures critical commonplaces concerning Herodotus's style.[114] Considering the use of the Ocean reference that activates Herodotus at the start of the *True Histories* (1.5), the reappearance of Herodotus at 2.5 offers a quiet proem-in-the-middle, whereby the Isle of the Blessed episode, on which the text's second half dilates, is also inaugurated by reference to Herodotus.

The reference holds significance not only as an index of the questionable veracity of the account that follows (had Herodotus made it to Arabia?) but also because the critical metaphors, referring meta-critically to the *reception* of Herodotus, inaugurate a stretch of Lucian's narrative that is itself

---

[112] See Zeitlin 2001: 245 on the "twilight" quality of Lucian's ethnography on the Isle of the Blessed; Kim 2010a: 157 on the characters as "frozen in time"; ní Mheallaigh 2014: 240–50 on the narrator's fighting against the tedium of tradition.

[113] That this is the only explicit citation is so noted by Georgiadou and Larmour 1998: 185.

[114] See, e.g., Dionysius, *On Literary Composition* 10.5 (with my chapter 1); Demetrius *On Style* 181: "the charm of sweetness" (ἡδονῆς χάρις); Hermogenes *On Style* 330–36 Rabe, esp. 2.4 "On Sweetness," lines 30–31: "His form possesses pleasure and sweetness of thought" (εἶδός ἐστιν ἡδονὴν ἔχον καὶ γλυκύτητα ἐννοιῶν); and Menander Rhetor 2.3.5: "The *Histories* of Herodotus are filled with sweet narratives (γλυκέων διηγημάτων) that contribute pleasure of every sort (ἡδονὴ παντοδαπής) to the writing." See Priestley 2014: 198; Tribulato 2016: 178. These various links of Herodotus with pleasure make it likely that Lucian has him in the crosshairs at *Hist. conscr.* 9–10, when he privileges useful history over pleasurable history.

230　HERODOTUS AND IMPERIAL GREEK LITERATURE

explicitly concerned with the reception of classical authors. Lucian caps his description with the same word—"bewitched" (κηλούμενοι, 2.6)—that he uses in describing Herodotus's abilities in the *Herodotus and Aëtion* (κηλῶν, 1).[115] At the height of his work, then, just as Lucian proceeds into a bravura display of Greek *paideia* and literary virtuosity, he adverts to Herodotus both with the very terms that literary criticism had attached to his style and with reference to the literary effect Lucian elsewhere claims Herodotus exercised on his own audiences and that Lucian wishes to emulate in bewitching his own. The Herodotean passage (3.113) that Lucian summons derives from one of the Halicarnassian's more far-fetched ethnographic sweeps, moving outward from Arabia to Ethiopia and eventually into Asia; both the far-off locale and the questionable truth-value of Herodotus's assertion weigh on this portion of Lucian's narrative. Hence, even before Lucian and his men enter the realm of the isle and receive their condemnatory sentence, Lucian suggestively cites an author who had described the seductive qualities of a place he had perhaps not visited; Lucian's own move is to hint that the seductive entrance to the isle, and to permanent literary stature, is also a mirage.

This mirage-like quality of the *True Histories* presents, in the Isle of the Blessed episode especially, an ontological conundrum. The reader must recategorize figures normally aligned along different planes, as when, for example, the fictional Odysseus defends the actual poet Homer in court (2.20).[116] Moreover, the controlling voice that retails this material, suspended between real and unreal, is the voice of the ethnographic observer, whose own authoritativeness appears to vouch for implausibility. The "real," time-bound authors exist as part of a timeless zone (2.12). The strange details are registered in a clinical, ethnographic air. He notes (2.12) that the literary figures "have no bodies themselves, but are intangible and without flesh" (ἀναφεῖς καὶ ἄσαρκοί), "manifesting only shape and form" (μορφὴν δὲ καὶ ἰδέαν μόνην ἐμφαίνουσιν) and having "the semblance of a body" (τὴν τοῦ σώματος ὁμοιότητα). But a method of verification exists: "In truth, unless someone should touch them, he would not deduce that what he saw was not a body" (εἰ γοῦν μὴ ἄψαιτό τις, οὐκ ἂν ἐξελέγξειε μὴ εἶναι σῶμα τὸ ὁρώμενον):

---

[115] The concept of Herodotus's bewitching qualities was already alive in Plutarch (see *dHM* 874F, with my chapter 3).

[116] On the "real-life" status of Odysseus in the *True Histories*, see Laird 2003: 126–27.

For they are like standing shadows, but not dark. No one grows old, but each remains the same age he was on arrival. There is not quite night among them and day is not altogether bright: rather the light that prevails in this land is like the sort of grayness toward dawn, before the sun has yet risen. (2.12)

εἰσὶ γὰρ ὥσπερ σκιαὶ ὀρθαί, οὐ μέλαιναι. γηράσκει δὲ οὐδείς, ἀλλ᾽ ἐφ᾽ ἧς ἂν ἡλικίας ἔλθῃ παραμένει. οὐ μὴν οὐδὲ νὺξ παρ᾽ αὐτοῖς γίνεται, οὐδὲ ἡμέρα πάνυ λαμπρά· καθάπερ δὲ τὸ λυκαυγὲς ἤδη πρὸς ἕω, μηδέπω ἀνατείλαντος ἡλίου, τοιοῦτο φῶς ἐπέχει τὴν γῆν.

On the one hand, seeing familiar figures should supply the least otherworldly scene of the *True Histories*, in comparison with other places visited. But this pinnacle moment of literary interface between present and past is cast in the language of ethnographic distance.[117] Lucian renders this climactic experience in terms that bespeak estrangement and the protagonist's inability to participate: even as he and his men advance to meet their literary lights, the overriding sense is of their hazy, otherworldly, allo-somatic qualities. The islanders' non-corporeality (αὐτοὶ δὲ σώματα μὲν οὐκ ἔχουσιν, 2.12) connotes the *otherness* of Lucian and his men, weighed down bodily in the space they have transgressed. Finally, Lucian defies the ethnographic expectation that sight is the foremost tool, since here autopsy might deceive: unless one should *touch* the figures, one would not know that they are bodiless. A landscape in which even the usual authority of (Herodotean) autopsy must yield to touch is indeed not a land of black-and-white intelligibility but rather like a land of shadows (ὥσπερ σκιαί), where senses overlap with each other. The Herodotean autoptic tool par excellence does not suffice.[118] The blended moments of intersubjectivity that have arisen already in the text now yield to a scene of greater uncertainty, in which literary luminaries exist in and as shadow.

Still, a hope for collapse between self and other is underscored by Lucian's hope to stay on the island—if not in deed, then at least in word:

So at that time I was getting things ready to sail. When the time was right, I dined with them. And on the next day I went to the poet Homer and asked

---

[117] See Georgiadou and Larmour 1998: 183; von Möllendorff 2000: 328–35.

[118] Cf. Purves 2013, however, on the importance of touch as part of the historiographer's experience in the *Histories*.

232   HERODOTUS AND IMPERIAL GREEK LITERATURE

him to write a two-line epigram for me. And when he had done it, I set up a beryl stele near the harbor and inscribed the distich, which read as follows:

Lucian, dear to the blessed gods, saw all these things
And came again into his dear native land. (2.28)

τότε μὲν οὖν τὰ περὶ τὸν πλοῦν παρεσκευασάμην, καὶ ἐπεὶ καιρὸς ἦν, συνειστιώμην αὐτοῖς. τῇ δὲ ἐπιούσῃ ἐλθὼν πρὸς Ὅμηρον τὸν ποιητὴν ἐδεήθην αὐτοῦ ποιῆσαί μοι δίστιχον ἐπίγραμμα· καὶ ἐπειδὴ ἐποίησεν, στήλην βηρύλλου λίθου ἀναστήσας ἐπέγραψα πρὸς τῷ λιμένι. τὸ δὲ ἐπίγραμμα ἦν τοιόνδε·

Λουκιανὸς τάδε πάντα φίλος μακάρεσσι θεοῖσιν
εἶδέ τε καὶ πάλιν ἦλθε φίλην ἐς πατρίδα γαῖαν.

Following the previous "readings" of inscriptions that have informed the text (*VH* 1.7, 1.32, 2.3), Lucian now sets up the inscription of himself to be read by others and performs his own first "reading" of it.[119] The incorporation of the inscription into the narrative manufactures both historical "evidence" and an element of historiographic "text" that might in a future time be subsumed into another's account of the isle. The simultaneous presence of his name and impending absence of his body imbues "Lucian" with a ghostly presence on the isle, inscribed by Homer's hand but at Lucian's command, as if Lucian were turning back time to have Homer incorporate his own name into literary history ab initio. The inscription reifies the double location with which Lucian played in the mirror episode; now, rather than appearing to be on earth while actually on the moon, "Lucian" can be found on the Isle of the Blessed, even as encountering him there through the inscription is to encounter his having moved on, his absence. "Lucian" is splayed across space, the beryl-stone marking a point of both contact and departure. The process of composition is double, involving Homer as author and the protagonist as inscriber (ἐπέγραψα). The reiteration of autopsy (εἶδε) attests to the very activity by which the first historiographer claims to have crafted his account, but the inscription marks a proleptic and, textually at least, unfulfilled promise to reach an unnamed home (ἐς πατρίδα γαῖαν).[120] Since Lucian's

---

[119] See von Möllendorff 2000: 412–25; ní Mheallaigh 2009; Kim 2010a: 172–73. See ní Mheallaigh 2014: 254–58 on the inscription as bound up with the work's problematization of authorship: "The fact that the inscription is attributed explicitly to *Homer* further reinforces the disjunctivity between the *Loukianos* in the text and the 'real' author" (257–58).

[120] On this point, see ní Mheallaigh 2008: 421–22.

REMOVABLE EYES 233

character does not reach home in the work intradiegetically, the inscription becomes preemptive and potentially untrue, at least based on the "evidence" of the rest of the work.[121]

All the same, the inscription, however misleading, by granting his name a place on the isle confirms Lucian's ability to imitate the past, to be included among its prototypes, as a *true* ability. That is, Lucian's inclusion among the literary greats, even if playfully self-nominated, speaks to the fact that his successful imitation of the past—his ability to seem like various authors—de facto ensures a place on the canonical isle.[122] If Lucian's intertextual density makes it difficult for the reader to distinguish aspects of his work from those of various authors already included on the isle, why should he not have a place there? The persistent intertextuality of the *True Histories*, including its Herodoteanism, belies its surface falsehoods, for although patently false in content, the *True Histories* showcases its ability to inhabit "accurately" a system of citation, allusion, and intertext. The constituent components of pastiche, inasmuch as they derive from actual authors and works, make of Lucian's hybrid something false in sum but "truthful" as a set of itemized parts.

What is more, although on one level false, the inscription also conveys another "truth" of the *True Histories* having to do with a notion of a split self. Already, readers wrestle with the paradox of the narrator who in the prologue tells us that he has neither seen nor experienced anything that follows—only to have his protagonist inscribed by Homer as having "seen" the very things that the narrator disclaims (cf. 1.4 and 2.28). So the speaking *ego* of the prologue who disclaims the account that follows nonetheless includes "Lucian" in that account. The question raised in an earlier part of this chapter, about the extent to which Herodotus as ethnographer is a narrator inside or outside his *logos*, thus resurfaces, as Lucian/"Lucian" straddles a line between external narrator and internal protagonist. In the scene between Herodotus and the Egyptian priests (2.143), Herodotus patently refuses, unlike Hecataeus, to give his own genealogy, in a well-known demarcation of keeping himself outside his story.[123] But, as we have seen, readers encounter ambivalent moments in which the Herodotean narrator's presence, whether

---

[121] Laird 2003: 125 makes a similar point about the apparent falsity of the inscription.

[122] This is reinforced by the fact that Lucian's description of the isle itself has imitated Herodotean-style ethnographic discourse (2.12, 14–15).

[123] On this scene, see West 1991, esp. 147–51, more focused on historicity than literary effect, for which see Dewald 2002: 267–68, with comments at 276–77 on other people's *logoi* as objects, "themselves part of the phenomenal world."

234 HERODOTUS AND IMPERIAL GREEK LITERATURE

concealed or adverted to, can be felt to affect the *logos*, to be somehow inextricable from and nearly inside it. Lucian has presented his readers here with a similar puzzle: how are we to understand Lucian the author and "Lucian" the inscribed protagonist? The self that previously has viewed itself as object, or that has sensed the sympathetic subjectivity of the other, now places a version of itself in literary eternity.

Lucian closes this multisensual excursus on the Isle of the Blessed with one further reference to Herodotus—specifically, to his afterlife on the Isle of the Wicked:

> The worst punishments of all were reserved for those who had lied in some way all their lives and those who had not written the truth, among whom were Ctesias of Cnidus and Herodotus, and many others. Looking upon these men I had good hope for the future: for I knew myself to be someone who had spoken no falsehoods. (2.31)

> καὶ μεγίστας ἁπασῶν τιμωρίας ὑπέμενον οἱ ψευσάμενοί τι παρὰ τὸν βίον καὶ οἱ μὴ τὰ ἀληθῆ συγγεγραφότες, ἐν οἷς καὶ Κτησίας ὁ Κνίδιος ἦν καὶ Ἡρόδοτος καὶ ἄλλοι πολλοί. τούτους οὖν ὁρῶν ἐγὼ χρηστὰς εἶχον εἰς τοὐπιὸν τὰς ἐλπίδας· οὐδὲν γὰρ ἐμαυτῷ ψεῦδος εἰπόντι συνηπιστάμην.

The narrator alludes to the conventional wisdom on Herodotus while also, of course, alluding to his own deceptiveness, since this is the same figure who earlier claimed that his only statement of truth is that he does not tell the truth (1.4). In addition to the ironic contradiction with Lucian's statement from the prologue, Lucian's condemnation of Herodotus as a liar marks the climax of an episode to which Herodotus's own name (2.5) and techniques have lent narratorial authority. Lucian's kinetic reception has set in tension the overt reputation of Herodotus as a liar alongside his own consistent evocation of him; the nominally dismissed force is also a thoroughgoing presence. Lucian's contorted interplay with Herodotus culminates with the historian's exile on the Isle of the Wicked, even as Lucian—a great Herodotean imitator—senses his own exile from the blessed past. Problematic figures who dwell on the Isle of the Wicked nonetheless live in the overarching credit of eternity. But Lucian arrives late to the party. If we take seriously his overlaps with Herodotus, we must also recognize that his way in among the literati is, ironically, in the company of the exiled and damned.

In this chapter, we have seen how Lucian carries out a complex reception of Herodotus. Already in *Herodotus and Aëtion*, he foregrounds his own version of a performing Herodotus and renders him a metonym for reception, focusing on his afterlife to project his *own* afterlife. We saw how Lucian also disclaims certain modes of narrative imitation, even as the work exhibits them. In turn, in the *True Histories*, Lucian engages ambiguities of Herodotean narrative technique, and the Herodotean background contributes to the work's elaboration of the potential otherness of oneself as seen from another's point of view. In that regard, the historiographic and Herodotean foundations of Lucian's *True Histories* run deeper than merely ludic evocations of ethnography. Lucian's reconfigurable "I" is no escapist fantasy; rather, such iterability points to Lucian's awareness of the contingencies of perspective. In working out these contingencies, Lucian evokes some of the very indeterminacies of Herodotus, a writer who both set forth and complicated a world of "Greeks and barbarians," a writer who trafficked in multivalence and crossover, and a writer whose Book 2 especially (the specific portion of the work initially summoned by Lucian) raises questions about the narrator-inquirer's perspectival role in relation to his material. Lucian's *True Histories* is, accordingly, sensitive to slippages beneath the surface of Herodotus's *logos*. Activating the *Histories* as he does, Lucian engages a text that seems to instantiate identity but, in fact, draws out its underlying instability, revealing the very interchangeability of self and other that it appears to concretize. Similar notions of changeable identity will arise in Lucian's handling of the Anacharsis tradition, the subject of chapter 6. And as with the *True Histories*, Lucian's reception acts energize ambiguities of representation already latent in the source text.

6

Anacharsis at Border Control

A borderland is a vague and undetermined place created by the emotional residue of an unnatural boundary. It is in a constant state of transition. The prohibited and forbidden are its inhabitants. *Los atravesados* live here: the squint-eyed, the perverse, the queer, the troublesome, the mongrel, the *mulato*, the half-breed, the half dead; in short, those who cross over, pass over, or go through the confines of the "normal." (Anzaldúa 2007 [1987]: 25)

In chapter 5, we saw how Lucian explored the paradoxes of Herodotus's canonicity as both a source of authority and a magnet for aspersion. Lucian's improvisation on the ethnographic Herodotus in the *True Histories* activates ostensibly marginal elements of Herodotus's text and presents an alternative to the Imperial standby of revivifying Marathon or Salamis or other such nostalgic topoi.[1] Lucian avoids easy appropriation of a stable idea of Greekness and resists the notion that any such uncomplicated totality exists. Yet the waywardness of the *True Histories* offers an intellectual journey by means of alterity *and* canonicity. Its exotica are paradoxically corralled, for an educated Greek reader, at least, by Lucian's mimetic commitments to familiar sources. For Lucian, then, the way to weirdness is through such authors as Herodotus. His defamiliarizing use of the Halicarnassian is a strategy of slipping sideways into the canon while also, by impersonating an ancient author, making that sideways entry on familiar terms.

In this chapter, I explore how for Lucian the oddities of Greek literary culture need no concoction and how the past, so exalted among Lucian's contemporaries, already offers its own "alternative" voices through which Lucian can ponder its value. My focus falls on Lucian's mediations of the

---

[1] See Bowie 2013 on the Imperial reuse of Marathon. On Lucian's manipulations of Hellenism vis-à-vis Roman rule, see generally Jones 1986: 59–77; Swain 1996: 312–29.

Herodotus and Imperial Greek Literature. N. Bryant Kirkland, Oxford University Press. © Oxford University Press 2022.
DOI: 10.1093/oso/9780197583517.003.0007

Scythian wise man Anacharsis in two works, the *prolalia* called *Scythian* and the dialogue *Anacharsis*. I explore how both texts, by engaging the Anacharsis tradition, necessarily engage with Herodotus's *Histories*.[2] While Lucian's capacity for relativism and obliqueness is well recognized,[3] I wish to tease out aspects of the Herodotean intellectual thrust of this capacity. Lucian's transactions with Herodotus will reveal how the first prose writer (of whom we know) to represent Anacharsis did so already in a fundamentally ambiguous way, one that complicates readers' ability to parse Herodotus's cultural valuations and indeed lays the groundwork for Lucian's ambiguities. Herodotus's acclamation of Scythian nomadism and the exceptional figure of Anacharsis implies admiration for those who defy the "rustic uncatholicity" of parochialism, to lift a phrase from Rabindranath Tagore.[4] Even as Herodotus identifies Scythia as xenophobic and backward (4.46), his interest in Anacharsis as exceptional leaves dangling an allusive opportunity for Lucian, in whose hands Anacharsis becomes a border-crossing avatar who escapes the limitations of the local.

Anacharsis in Herodotus

Anacharsis first appears in extant Greek literature in the fourth book of Herodotus's *Histories* as part of his Scythian *logos*.[5] Herodotus presents Anacharsis in his debut already as an ambiguous figure about whom differing stories are told and whose grisly end caps a somewhat perplexing miniature biography. In the context of his wider treatment of Scythia, Herodotus presents two versions of the Anacharsis story (4.76–77). In both, Anacharsis is murdered for his apparent adoption of Greek customs. Inasmuch as the full strangeness of Anacharsis in Herodotus comes to light partly through the two stories' juxtaposition, I recount them both as background to Lucian's eventual manipulations.

---

[2] While Anacharsis appears recurrently in classical, Hellenistic, and Imperial Greek sources (see Kindstrand 1981: 6–82; Ungefehr-Kortus 1996), one observes a notable uptick among Imperial authors (Kindstrand 1981: 3).

[3] Lucian's Anacharsis texts interrogate the value of Greek cultural practices and complicate the image of Athens as the center of Hellenism; on Lucian's subversions of Greek practices in the *Anacharsis*, see König 2005: 45–96; on his decentering of Athens in the *Scythian*, see Richter 2011: 171–72, with later discussion here.

[4] Tagore 2001 [1907]: 150.

[5] Kindstrand 1981: 3.

238 HERODOTUS AND IMPERIAL GREEK LITERATURE

Herodotus first presents the story that he will later claim to prefer (see 4.77.2, with discussion here), apparently as proof that Scythians spurn the adoption of foreign customs.[6] Anacharsis is the exception who proves the rule:

These people [the Scythians], too, categorically avoid the adoption of foreign customs, particularly the customs of the Greeks, as the stories of Anacharsis and later Skyles demonstrate.[7] Once Anacharsis had contemplated the wide world and had appropriated (ἀποδεξάμενος) a great deal of wisdom throughout, he tried importing it among the Scythian people . . . . (4.76.1–2)[8]

ξεινικοῖσι δὲ νομαίοισι καὶ οὗτοι αἰνῶς χρᾶσθαι φεύγουσι, μήτε τεῶν ἄλλων, Ἑλληνικοῖσι δὲ καὶ ἥκιστα, ὡς διέδεξαν Ἀνάχαρσίς τε καὶ δεύτερα αὖτις Σκύλης. τοῦτο μὲν γὰρ Ἀνάχαρσις ἐπείτε γῆν πολλὴν θεωρήσας καὶ ἀποδεξάμενος κατ᾽ αὐτὴν σοφίην πολλὴν ἐκομίζετο ἐς ἤθεα τὰ Σκυθέων . . . .

Anacharsis comes to Greece as a practitioner of *theôria*, observation of a more critical sort than mere sightseeing.[9] After stopping at Cyzicus on his return voyage, where he vows to the Mother of the Gods to practice her rites if she grants him safe return, Anacharsis gets home, goes out to the Hylaia to worship the Mother, and, upon being discovered practicing supposedly foreign ways, is killed by the Scythian king Saulius (4.76.3–5).[10] Anacharsis's perceived flirtation with foreign customs dooms him both in life and in death, since Herodotus indicates that Scythians later pretend never to have

---

[6] Kindstrand 1981: 13–14 notes that Herodotus appears already to have heard of Anacharsis but seeks to verify his historicity from his source, one Tymnes (a name of Carian origin; compare Hdt. 5.37 and 7.98). On historical aspects of Herodotus's Scythian accounts, see Ivantchik 1999 and Ivantchik 2011, and for analysis of the comparative mode implicit in Herodotus's approach, see Lincoln 2018: 73–77, 84–94, 100–104, 107–9.

[7] As West 2007: 88 notes, the emphatic καί suggests that Herodotus has in mind his similar comment (2.91.1) on the Egyptians' reluctance to adopt foreign customs: "In his own mind the distance between the passages might have seemed rather less" (88).

[8] The participle ἀποδεξάμενος presents a challenge of translation that I will discuss. I translate with the contranym "appropriate" under advisement, intending to convey two meanings: both "to take for oneself" and "to dispense to others."

[9] On *theôria*, see Nightingale 2004: 63–71 and passim. See also Redfield 1985: 98 on the *theôria* of customs.

[10] I say "supposedly" because Hylaia, Cyzicus, and the Mother of the Gods map onto categories of Greek and foreign in ambiguous ways, as Hartog has shown; see Hartog 1988 [1980]: 67–70, 75, 80–82 (with n. 84 for further bibliography). See also Borgeaud 2004 [1996]: 23–26, 31–32.

heard of him: "And now if anyone mentions Anacharsis, the Scythians say they don't know him, all because he traveled abroad to Greece and took up foreign ways" (καὶ νῦν ἤν τις εἴρηται περὶ Ἀναχάρσιος, οὔ φασί μιν Σκύθαι γινώσκειν, διὰ τοῦτο ὅτι ἐξεδήμησέ τε ἐς τὴν Ἑλλάδα καὶ ξεινικοῖσι ἔθεσι διεχρήσατο, 4.76.5).

Anacharsis's bad end fits with Herodotus's remark many chapters earlier, in which he singles out the Scythians, and in turn Anacharsis, from his essentializing narrative of the Black Sea peoples (4.46.1):[11]

The Black Sea . . . is inhabited everywhere by the most ignorant of peoples, not counting the Scythians: for there is neither a race on the Sea to whom we could in any way ascribe wisdom except the Scythian people, nor we do know of there being a man of learning (ἄνδρα λόγιον), except Anacharsis.[12]

Ὁ δὲ Πόντος ὁ Εὔξεινος . . . χωρέων πασέων παρέχεται ἔξω τοῦ Σκυθικοῦ ἔθνεα ἀμαθέστατα· οὔτε γὰρ ἔθνος τῶν ἐντὸς τοῦ Πόντου οὐδὲν ἔχομεν προβαλέσθαι σοφίης πέρι οὔτε ἄνδρα λόγιον οἴδαμεν γενόμενον, πάρεξ τοῦ Σκυθικοῦ ἔθνεος καὶ Ἀναχάρσιος.

Herodotus goes on to admit that he is unimpressed by Scythian customs (τὰ μέντοι ἄλλα οὐκ ἄγαμαι), save their discovery of the virtues of nomadism, which he describes as "the wisest solution to the most important issue of human affairs" (τὸ μέγιστον τῶν ἀνθρωπηίων πρηγμάτων σοφώτατα πάντων ἐξεύρηται, 4.46.2). This statement would seem to carry particular resonance in a work that not only emphasizes the various movements of peoples and the changes they undergo but also emphasizes, both in metaphor (e.g., προβήσομαι ἐς τὸ πρόσω τοῦ λόγου, Hdt. 1.5.3) and in factual account (esp. in Book 2), the movement of the narrator himself. Thus, when Herodotus introduces the Anacharsis story to demonstrate his claim that Scythians categorically avoid adopting foreign ways (4.76.1), his prior approbation of nomadism, in fact, accords Anacharsis a certain narratological privilege: he is the nomad who journeys beyond his own borders for wisdom, a wanderer par excellence, perhaps implicitly worthy of Herodotus's admiration. Indeed, Herodotus and later Lucian thematize movement in their works through the

---

[11] For the consistency in Greek literature of representing the Scythians as living at the far ends of the earth and as nomads, see Mestre 2003: 304–5 with further references.

[12] On the word λόγιος, see Luraghi 2009, with reference to Anacharsis at 444–45, 455–56. For the textual variants and the suitability of *logios* over *logimos*, see Wilson 2015: 77.

240 HERODOTUS AND IMPERIAL GREEK LITERATURE

implicit adoption of mobile alter egos (Solon for Herodotus, Anacharsis for Lucian). If the Scythians are defined by the blank spaces of their wandering habitation and the borderlessness of open land, yet make a virtue of movement, then Anacharsis simultaneously functions as a reprobate Scythian who adopts foreign ways and, qua wanderer, as an *exemplary* Scythian, too.[13]

Further ambiguities color Herodotus's account. In the second story (4.77), Herodotus offers another version he heard from Peloponnesians (ἤκουσα λόγον ἄλλον ὑπὸ Πελοποννησίων λεγόμενον, 4.77.1), to the effect that Anacharsis was sent by the Scythian king specifically to become "a student of Greece" (τῆς Ἑλλάδος μαθητὴς γένοιτο, 4.77.1). Upon his return, he reports that "all Greeks are preoccupied with every kind of wisdom, except Lacedaemonians, but that these alone speak and listen in a sensible manner" (Ἕλληνας πάντας ἀσχόλους εἶναι ἐς πᾶσαν σοφίην πλὴν Λακεδαιμονίων, τούτοισι δὲ εἶναι μούνοισι σωφρόνως δοῦναί τε καὶ δέξασθαι λόγον, 4.77.1). In their lauded simplicity, the Spartans are tacitly likened to the unrefined but potentially wise Scythian. But Herodotus has little time for this tale: "This story has anyway been invented by the Greeks themselves, and Anacharsis met his bad end exactly as was said earlier" (ἀλλ' οὗτος μὲν ὁ λόγος ἄλλως πέπαισται ὑπ' αὐτῶν Ἑλλήνων, ὁ δ' ὢν ἀνὴρ ὥσπερ πρότερον εἰρέθη διεφθάρη, 4.77.2).[14] Even as he dismisses the *logos* and reiterates his thesis about Anacharsis, the image of the Scythian is marked by certain obscurities. Why was Anacharsis in Greece after all? What was he learning or teaching? Who killed him, and who tells the true story?

Herodotus offers a passing indication of Anacharsis's overall elusiveness early on. His initial description carries trace elements that imply Anacharsis's ambivalent moral status as a wise man and traveler—a man who adopts foreign customs while also rendering judgment on them (as at 4.77.1). First, as others have noted, Herodotus's phrasing invites readers to connect Anacharsis with Solon: "Once Anacharsis had **contemplated the wide world** and appropriated a great deal of wisdom throughout, he

[13] To be sure, while Anacharsis appears to be "simply fulfilling his innate Scythian nomadism" (Clarke 2018: 84) in traveling to Greece (4.76), one should note that Herodotus praises Scythian nomadism as a military strategy, not as a tool of intellectual inquiry (4.46.2–3). On the virtues of Scythian movement, see Hartog 1988 [1980]: 12–33. On tensions between Scythian stability and mobility, see Clarke 2018: 277–79. See Branham 1989: 84–85 for the connection between Anacharsis's "Januslike" (85) roles as naive barbarian and Hellenized wise man in Lucian and Herodotus (similarly, Ungefehr-Kortus 1996: 36–52, esp. 50–52, on Anacharsis as "Janus-headed" [*janusköpfig*]).

[14] The detail of the king's command would suggest that Anacharsis does not represent the exception to Scythian ignorance as much as he is the ambassador of a more general spirit of curiosity—all obviously contra Herodotus's preferred view that Anacharsis marks the (ultimately tragic) exception to Scythian benightedness.

ANACHARSIS AT BORDER CONTROL   241

was returning to Scythian territory" (τοῦτο μὲν γὰρ Ἀνάχαρσις ἐπείτε γῆν πολλὴν θεωρήσας καὶ ἀποδεξάμενος κατ' αὐτὴν σοφίην πολλὴν ἐκομίζετο ἐς ἤθεα τὰ Σκυθέων, 4.76.1–2). The wording directly recalls Croesus's address to Solon: "My Athenian guest, we have heard a lot about you: you are famous for your learning and travels. We hear that you love knowledge and have journeyed far and wide, **to see the world**" (ξεῖνε Ἀθηναῖε, παρ' ἡμέας γὰρ περὶ σέο λόγος ἀπῖκται πολλὸς καὶ σοφίης εἵνεκεν τῆς σῆς καὶ πλάνης, ὡς φιλοσοφέων γῆν πολλὴν θεωρίης εἵνεκεν ἐπελήλυθας, 1.30.2).[15] The shared expression suggests two figures committed to a similar quest for knowledge and inspired to travel widely for its sake.[16] Croesus's comment to Solon about his *theôria* implies a connection between Solon's travels and his knowledge, and the echo several books later suggests an obvious kinship between knowledge and travel for Anacharsis, too, whether self-directed or commanded by the Scythian king.[17] Moreover, Herodotus's participle distills something of Anacharsis's ambiguity as both a student and a teacher, as a man who "appropriated" wisdom (ἀποδεξάμενος), both acquiring it and/or doling it out. Since the Ionic form can come from either ἀποδέχομαι ("to receive") or ἀποδείκνυμι ("to display"), Anacharsis is marked from the start by liminality.[18] Translating the participle with an emphasis on display would

[15] On the connections between the two figures, see Hartog 1988 [1980]: 64; Montiglio 2005: 128–34 (to whom the parallels between Solon and Anacharsis suggest more contrast than similarity). See also Plutarch, *Solon* 5 for a version of the meeting between the two figures.

[16] Of course, both were later counted among the so-called Seven Sages (see Strabo 7.3, C303, citing Ephorus, on Anacharsis as a wise man): the various members are seemingly not so classed earlier than Plato; see Schubert 2010: 69–75. While Herodotus does not specifically refer to a concept of the Seven Sages, he does include scattered accounts or references to five others who became part of the group: Pittacus (1.27), Periander (1.20, 1.23–24, 3.48–53, 5.92, 95), Thales (1.74–75), Chilon (1.59, 7.235), and Bias (1.27, 1.170). See the comments of Ungefehr-Kortus 1996: 51: "Einen Kreis von Sieben Weisen erwähnt Herodot nicht, aber er berichtet von sechs Weisen, die in späterer Zeit fest zu dieser Gruppe gehörten. . . . Anacharsis hingegen wird weder mit ihnen in Verbindung gebracht, noch äußert sich seine Weisheit in dieser Art." On Anacharsis's eventual inclusion, see Kindstrand 1981: 36–39. See Mestre 2003: 313–14 for the vagaries of the list of sages and Anacharsis's place in it. The fact that in Herodotus's time Anacharsis had not been enrolled on the roster of Seven makes the parallel to Solon more notable, if only for the fact that such a link was perhaps not yet axiomatic.

[17] The link that Herodotus intimates between Anacharsis and Solon encourages my reading, in which details of the Solon–Croesus exchange are shown to inform Lucian's *Anacharsis*.

[18] Published translations differ. Godley 1921 has "after having seen much of the world in his travels and given many examples of his wisdom," perhaps in the footsteps of Macaulay 1890: "after having visited many lands and displayed in them much wisdom." Waterfield 1998 hedges: "[H]e visited many countries all over the world and became known for his great wisdom wherever he went." Grene 1987 rather wonderfully prints, "He traveled over much of the world, sight-seeing, **and showed that he had gained** great wisdom in the course of his travels," while, finally, Mensch 2014 translates, "Anacharsis, after he had traveled widely and given many proofs of his wisdom, was on his way home to Scythia." See Schubert 2010: 148–49 for similar observations about the ambiguity of the participle. The phrasing links Anacharsis to Herodotus's proem (ἀπόδεξις, ἀποδεχθέντα) and to Odysseus (πλάνης . . . γῆν πολλὴν θεωρίης ~ πλάγχθη . . . πολλῶν δ' ἀνθρώπων ἴδεν ἄστεα καὶ νόον ἔγνω, / πολλά, *Od.* 1.1–4).

242   HERODOTUS AND IMPERIAL GREEK LITERATURE

seem better to suit the intended contrast between the two stories on offer—
Anacharsis as a traveling wise man or Anacharsis as a disciple of Greece—but
this seems too neat in the context of other ambiguities. Why should we see
Anacharsis as only dispensing wisdom, if part of the ultimate issue depends
on his adopting new customs?

In the context of his presentation of Scythia, then, the clues about
Anacharsis offered by Herodotus encourage us to draw connections between
travel and knowledge, nomadic wandering and wisdom. Anacharsis is rendered liminally, both barbarian and not.[19] His similarity to Solon reduces his
potential alterity (from a Greek perspective), as does his exceptionalism vis-
à-vis the otherwise strange Scythians. At the same time, Herodotus's second
story reminds readers that *logoi* about foreigners can be colonized from
one's own perspective: the tale told by the Peloponnesians and "invented"
(πέπαισται) by Greeks has Anacharsis casting the Spartans (and perhaps all
Greeks) in a pleasant light. It is a marker of Herodotus's intellectual largesse—
one likely informed by his own wide traveling—to dismiss the smallness of
this story, to leave room for alien wisdom, and to lay a foundation for the
flexible intellectual nomadism that Lucian's Anacharsis will exhibit.

Anacharsis in Lucian: The *Scythian*

> The human soul has a natural disposition to know itself among
> others. (Tagore 2001 [1907]: 140)

Anacharsis occupies center stage in two works by Lucian: the *Scythian* and
Anacharsis. In analyzing both works, my claim is that Lucian scrambles,
inverts, and otherwise refashions elements of the Anacharsis tradition as they
relate to Herodotus, while at the same time activating some of the opacities
that originally appear in Herodotus's account.[20] The result of these hypotextual

---

[19] On Anacharsis's ambiguous roles in Herodotus, see Ungefehr-Kortus 1996: 46–49. Note also
Hartog 1988 [1980]: 71 n. 35 on Hdt. 4.77: "This is the first time that Anacharsis is represented as
having set out to learn from the Greeks, and it is worth noting that Herodotus does not himself claim
to vouch for this version of the adventures of Anacharsis."

[20] That educated readers will have relied on Herodotus for understanding Lucian's text is pointed
out by Sidwell 2004: 397–98 n. 8: "The *locus classicus* for Lucian's audience's knowledge of Scythia
was Book 4 of Herodotus' *Histories*." Lucian's engagement with Zamolxis—e.g., commenting that
the Athenian heroization of Toxaris proves that it is not only Scythians who immortalize humans
and "send them to Zamolxis" (οὐ Σκύθαις μόνον ἐπιχώριον ὂν ἀπαθανατίζειν καὶ πέμπειν παρὰ
τὸν Ζάμολξιν, *Scyth.* 2)—suggests further Herodotean intertextuality. See Sidwell 2004: 397–98
n. 8 for remarks on Lucian's various references to Zamolxis and his particular remarks with respect

mobilizations reveals both the enduring range of signification issuing from Herodotus's version and their broad manipulability as exploited by Lucian.

In the *Scythian*, Anacharsis arrives in Athens confused and overwhelmed, only to be recognized by the Scythian Toxaris, who has preceded him there. Toxaris has been completely transformed and is now unrecognizable, so thorough is his Hellenization.[21] Held in high esteem by the Athenians for his medical skills, Toxaris has been memorialized on a stele marking his successful entrée into Greek society. Upon discovering his fellow Scythian, Toxaris reassures Anacharsis that he knows a "short-cut" (ἐπίτομόν τινα, 7) into Greek culture by means of meeting Solon, who has "all of Greece" within him: "Know that you would have all of Greece in meeting Solon, and you would know the acme of good things found there" (πᾶσαν νόμιζε τὴν Ἑλλάδα ἐν αὐτῷ ἔχειν καὶ τὸ κεφάλαιον ἤδη ἂν εἰδέναι τῶν τῇδε ἀγαθῶν, 5). Toxaris brokers the introduction, and all goes apparently smoothly: Anacharsis never leaves Solon's side and returns to Scythia only after Solon dies. The work then switches to Lucian's first-person voice, as he likens himself to Anacharsis as a fellow newcomer to Greece who seeks the patronage and support of locals.[22]

Lucian undoes the primacy of Anacharsis as found in Herodotus: "Anacharsis was not the first who left Scythia for Athens with a desire for Greek learning, but one Toxaris preceded him, a wise man, a lover of beauty, and eager student of the best customs" (οὐ πρῶτος Ἀνάχαρσις ἀφίκετο ἐκ Σκυθίας Ἀθήναζε παιδείας ἐπιθυμίᾳ τῆς Ἑλληνικῆς, ἀλλὰ καὶ Τόξαρις πρὸ αὐτοῦ, σοφὸς μὲν καὶ φιλόκαλος ἀνὴρ καὶ ἐπιτηδευμάτων φιλομαθὴς τῶν ἀρίστων, *Scyth.* 1). Toxaris is now foregrounded as the original Scythian wise man and student of Athens.[23] His precedence inspires mimetic desire on the part of Anacharsis: "Know that I've become your student and a seeker of the passion you have fallen into—to see Greece" (μαθητήν σου ἴσθι με γεγενημένον καὶ ζηλωτὴν τοῦ ἔρωτος ὃν ἠράσθης, ἰδεῖν τὴν Ἑλλάδα, 4).

to Herodotus Book 4: "The use of a similar word for 'immortalize' and the same for 'send . . . to Zamolxis' *strongly suggests* that Lucian has this passage in mind" (emphasis added).

[21] For analysis, see Kindstrand 1981: 29; Ungefehr-Kortus 1996: 187–207; Gangloff 2007: 82–84; Richter 2011: 168–73.

[22] Lucian, however, presents himself as performing in Macedonia; see Richter 2011: 171–72.

[23] Ungefehr-Kortus 1996: 191 also notes Lucian's shifting the initiative from Anacharsis to Toxaris, in contrast to other sources on Anacharsis (including Diogenes Laertius 1.104). On class issues in this text, by which Lucian renders entry into Greek culture a matter not of royal birthright but of upward mobility, see Richter 2011: 172.

244 HERODOTUS AND IMPERIAL GREEK LITERATURE

The frame of the work takes us to the author's present day, for we are told that Toxaris's legacy in Athens was such that the Athenians honored him with a carved image that "even now" (καὶ νῦν) one can see, albeit in faded remains. The image of Toxaris holding a bow and a book risks erasure: "The upper part of the stele and the face—these time had already defaced, I suppose" (τὰ δὲ ἄνω τῆς στήλης καὶ τὸ πρόσωπον ὁ χρόνος ἤδη ἐλυμήνατό που, 2). The description accords Toxaris a sense of the ambiguous balance between Scythian-ness (the bow) and Hellenization (the book) that harks back to the double nature of Herodotus's Anacharsis.[24] The *prolalia* hovers over this ambivalence in the encounter between the now-unrecognizable Toxaris, so thoroughly Hellenized as to be "truly one of the autochthonous Athenians" (αὐτῶν τῶν Ἀττικῶν ἕνα τῶν αὐτοχθόνων, 3), and the bewildered, out-of-place Anacharsis.[25]

Yet Lucian's staging effects an ironic reverse recognition, in which the Scythian-become-Greek grandee now inculcates the Scythian *barbaros* into Greekness, code-switching between his Hellenized self and his barbarian origins to put the foreigner (and his quasi-duplicate) at ease ("Only take heart," πλὴν ἀλλὰ θάρρει, 5). Even Solon as presented in the work is both native and not, the ur-Athenian and the man whose very wisdom derives from having spent time away from Athens: "There is a wise man here, **a native Athenian, but one who has traveled widely** in Asia and Egypt and has mixed with the best of humankind" (ἔστι σοφὸς ἀνὴρ ἐνταῦθα, **ἐπιχώριος μέν, ἀποδημήσας δὲ μάλα πολλὰ** ἔς τε Ἀσίαν καὶ ἐς Αἴγυπτον καὶ τοῖς ἀρίστοις τῶν ἀνθρώπων συγγενόμενος, 5). Recall Herodotus's observation that "Somehow the extremities of the inhabited world happen to have the things of the greatest beauty" (αἱ δ' ἐσχατιαί κως τῆς οἰκεομένης τὰ κάλλιστα ἔλαχον, 3.106.1). In seeking out Solon as a "shortcut" (ἐπίτομόν τινα, 7) to Greek culture, Toxaris trains Anacharsis's energy on a man who has journeyed variously to the edges of the world but who also himself embodies and recenters Herodotus's phraseology.[26] Athens and Solon are now positioned as the cynosure for the undefined κάλλιστα that, for Herodotus, had been projected onto the outer bounds of the known world.[27] Moreover,

---

[24] See Ungefehr-Kortus 1996: 188 n. 4 for a similar remark, in passing: "Schon in der frühesten Quelle, bei Herodot, ist diese Ambiguität festzustellen."

[25] The motif of the bewildered foreigner is common in Lucian; see Anderson 1976a: 19, 37, 45, 82; Anderson 1976c: 14.

[26] Compare τὰ κάλλιστα (Hdt. 3.106.1 ~ *Scyth.* 4, 7) and διδάσκων τὰ κάλλιστα (*Scyth.* 8).

[27] Complications to the Atheno-centrism will arise, however, as we note later.

that Toxaris has become "truly one of the autochthonous Athenians" recalls something of Herodotus's own take on the self-serving flexibility of Athenian self-representation, especially in relation to Athenian origins.[28] As Rosalind Thomas has put it, "While Athenian myth-making used the remote past to explain and define the present in an image of ever enduring stability, Herodotus seems willing to go far in his image of ethnic and polis character as unstable."[29] The Herodotus who indicates the fictions of Athenian autochthony is the same writer who extols the Scythians for their ability to excel at a lifestyle based on its opposite. In the *Scythian*, Lucian seems to heighten the illusion of autochthony: Toxaris can, after all, *acculturate* himself into ethnic lineage.[30]

Lucian's Anacharsis, meanwhile, rather than presenting the exception to the rule of Scythian benightedness—and showcasing a fate that, in the end, only confirms Scythian xenophobia—apparently offers a way out of being *barbaros*.[31] When Toxaris comments on his surprise that he is still remembered in Scythia (4), Lucian again implicitly adverts to Herodotus's version, where we are told that the Scythians intentionally forgot Anacharsis, in a passage seen earlier: "And now if anyone mentions Anacharsis, the Scythians say they don't know him, all because he traveled abroad to Greece and took up foreign ways" (4.76.5). Lucian's Anacharsis further reverses the trajectory of Herodotus's version because, although the *Scythian* is Atheno-centric, Anacharsis's arrival in Athens is emphatically not motivated by any apparent intellectual intentionality. Indeed, he is confused and discombobulated by Athens (οὐ μετρίως τεταραγμένος . . . πάντα ἀγνοῶν), its novelty and noises (ψοφοδεὴς πρὸς τὰ πολλά), leaving him bewildered

---

[28] On Athenian Pelasgianism, see Sourvinou-Inwood 2003. See in particular 139–40 for the important distinction between the Pelasgians mentioned at Hdt. 1.56 and the Pelasgians discussed at Hdt. 2.51. See further Blösel 2013 and McInerney 2014, including the general remarks at 25–6, quoting Myres 1907, who recognized Greeks' "vague cycle of memories" in the sixth and fifth centuries and the "connotative usage of the name [Pelasgian]" (Myres 1907: 222, quoted at McInerney 2014: 26).

[29] Thomas 2000: 121; see further 117–22 on Herodotus's treatment of Athenian claims to autochthony. See also Hall 1997: 52–56; Pelling 2009: 474, 482; Strasburger 2013 [1955]: 297–98. The exposure of Athens's contradictory self-definitions is perhaps an aspect of Herodotus's (debated) critical program toward Athens; for the evidence that Herodotus could admire Athens without being blind to its faults, see, among others, Wells 1923: 145–68; Fornara 1971: 56, 81; Moles 2002.

[30] On Lucian's criticisms of Athenian autochthony, see also Gangloff 2007: 81–82: "En critiquant l'origine autochtone des habitants d'Athènes, Lucien se démarque de l'attitude générale depuis la création par Hadrien du Panhellénion: les cités cherchaient à valoriser (ou à s'inventer) une origine grecque, notamment grâce aux mythes de fondation."

[31] Lucian avoids mention of Anacharsis's murder. All the same, the optimism of *Scythian* flattens out in *Anacharsis*: the former shows a reliance on semiotic cultural markers that become in the latter the focus of dispute.

246 HERODOTUS AND IMPERIAL GREEK LITERATURE

about everything—except the fact that he is being laughed at (οὐκ ἔχων ὅ τι χρήσαιτο ἑαυτῷ. καὶ γὰρ συνίει καταγελώμενος ὑπὸ τῶν ὁρώντων ἐπὶ τῇ σκευῇ, 3). Rather than being the pioneering Scythian defector or zealot for Greek culture, Lucian's Anacharsis progresses toward Hellenization by copying a fellow Scythian.

Lucian's description of Toxaris's transformed identity comes after his amicable accosting of Anacharsis, and it is perhaps the case that Anacharsis's desire to be like Toxaris is fed by his seeing *through* the outward appearance to the countryman who might otherwise have been indistinguishable:

> What first drew Toxaris's attention to Anacharsis was that he was clad in Scythian clothing. . . . But how could Anacharsis have ever recognized Toxaris as being a fellow Scythian, tricked out as he was in Greek style, his hair and beard cropped short, without belt or sword, already a blabbermouth—truly one of the autochthonous Athenians! So thoroughly had he been transformed by time. (*Scyth.* 3)

> καὶ τὸ μὲν πρῶτον ἡ στολὴ αὐτὸν ἐπεσπάσατο πατριῶτις οὖσα. . . . ὁ Ἀνάχαρσις δὲ πόθεν ἂν ἐκεῖνον ἔγνω ὁμοεθνῆ ὄντα, Ἑλληνιστὶ ἐσταλμένον, ἐν χρῷ κεκαρμένον τὸ γένειον, ἄζωστον, ἀσίδηρον, ἤδη στωμύλον, αὐτῶν τῶν Ἀττικῶν ἕνα τῶν αὐτοχθόνων; οὕτω μετεπεποίητο ὑπὸ τοῦ χρόνου.

Hence, the eroticized desire for Greek acculturation (ζηλωτὴν τοῦ **ἔρωτος** ὃν **ἠράσθης**, ἰδεῖν τὴν Ἑλλάδα, 4) is mediated through attraction to one's fellow countryman who outwardly presents as Greek but who, in hailing Anacharsis, is reconstituted as Scythian. In Lucian's reworking, the attraction to the foreign is at a fundamental level an attraction to/through the known. The erotics of acculturation are later replayed in Solon's pedagogy toward the younger Anacharsis, which vaguely recalls Athenian pederastic relations.[32] Anacharsis's eros for Hellenic culture is quelled through Solon's educative companionship.[33] Lucian's self-comparison to Anacharsis, finally, reinscribes mimetic desire: Anacharsis's desire for Toxaris is now echoed by Lucian's for Anacharsis, who himself has access to the central figure of Solon.

---

[32] See *Scyth.* 8 for the eroticized accent on exchange and companionship: "Solon delighted in the gift. . . . They kept company for a long time" (ἥσθη ὁ Σόλων τῷ δώρῳ. . . . τὸ λοιπὸν συνῆσαν).

[33] "The teacher instructing in the best things . . . making Anacharsis a friend to all" (ὁ μὲν παιδεύων καὶ διδάσκων τὰ κάλλιστα . . . φίλον ἅπασι ποιῶν τὸν Ἀνάχαρσιν, *Scyth.* 8).

ANACHARSIS AT BORDER CONTROL 247

A longing for the center is thus kindled at the margins through a series of "self"-recognitions in another.

That Lucian's declaration of analogy to Anacharsis should occur in Macedonia (9) recalls the narrator's wish, likewise expressed in a performative context in Macedonia (*Hdt.* 7), to follow in the footsteps of Herodotus.[34] Thus, while reconfiguring aspects of Herodotus's Anacharsis, Lucian also brings the *Scythian* to a close in ways that affirm the narrator's own wish to trace the itinerant trajectory of Herodotus himself. Herodotus's Anacharsis offers Lucian an avatar for his own oblique Hellenism and simultaneously, by virtue of his being singled out by Herodotus, the sturdy image of an "insider," an already canonical figure whose experience precedes and validates the postulant narrator of Lucian's *Scythian*.[35] Anacharsis's befuddlement in Athens, which may suggest an irreverence before the supposedly venerable place, subtly introduces the relativizing mode that will dominate the *Anacharsis* dialogue. Athens and Greek culture are not a given, a fixed marquee glowing in the distance. As we turn to the eponymous dialogue, we shall see how the dynamics of Anacharsis's would-be Hellenism become altogether less stable.

The Double Inversions of the *Anacharsis*

A meeting between Solon and Anacharsis, mooted at *Scyth.* 8, forms the centerpiece of Lucian's *Anacharsis*, making this work something of a sequel or companion to the *Scythian*.[36] To be sure, the convening of various sages, including the encounter between Solon and Anacharsis, recurs in ancient literature.[37] Nor are the criticisms that Lucian's Anacharsis launches against athletic practices unknown in the wider tradition.[38] But the specifics

---

[34] One wonders if Lucian knew of the biographic tradition that placed Herodotus in Macedonia, specifically Pella; see Priestley 2014: 34–42.

[35] It is instructive to compare Lucian's identifications with Anacharsis, explicit in the *Scythian* and implicit in *Anacharsis*, with Plutarch's inclusions of the character in *Dinner of the Seven Sages*, on which see Kindstrand 1981: 44–48. While Plutarch's Anacharsis seems to figure as a foil to other wise men (see *Septem* 148C, 150D–E, 155F–156A), Kindstrand passingly notes (47–48) how Plutarch uses Anacharsis to voice some of his own philosophical views.

[36] See Bompaire 1958: 679, who dates the *Anacharsis* after *Scythian*. For a different dating scheme, compare Hirzel 1895: Vol. 2, 286 n. 2. For analysis, see Bompaire 1958: 679–82; Anderson 1976a: 154 and n. 12; Kindstrand 1981: 65–67; Branham 1989: 81–104; Ungefehr-Kortus 1996: 207–33; Mestre 2003; König 2005: 45–96 (esp. 72–96); Schubert 2010: 21, 24; Konstan 2010.

[37] See in general Kindstrand 1981: 33–50, but esp. 39–40 for the meeting with Solon, with reference to Anacharsis, *Ep.* 2 (Hermippus fr. 9 Wehrli Suppl. 1), and Plutarch, *Solon* 5.1–3. See also Diogenes Laertius 1.101–5.

[38] Compare Diogenes Laertius 1.103–4; Dio, *Or.* 32.44.

248 HERODOTUS AND IMPERIAL GREEK LITERATURE

of Lucian's work, in his choice to stage the dialogue between the inquiring visitor Anacharsis and the confident Solon, is not elsewhere similarly elaborated in the Anacharsis tradition.[39] In this section, rather than analyzing Solon's and Anacharsis's various arguments for and against Greek custom, I show how the hypotextual activations of the *Anacharsis* inhere not only in Herodotus's nebulous presentation of Anacharsis as barbarian outsider and Hellenizing wise man but also in aspects of his programmatic exchange between Solon and Croesus.[40] This intertextual watermark serves as implicit background to Lucian's extending the inversions already on display in the *Scythian*.[41]

While Herodotus's exchange between Solon and Croesus is itself a fictional interchange, its structure—a powerful figure has his assumptions challenged— proves useful for Lucian.[42] Like Herodotus, Lucian manipulates the exchange in order to portray an irruptive outsider capable of destabilizing entrenched perspectives. And like Herodotus, Lucian imputes intellectual potency to the traveling inquirer. In Herodotus, Croesus had believed that his (literally) estimable, as in countable, wealth speaks for itself, only to have Solon puncture that notion. In Lucian's dialogue, in turn, Anacharsis in effect becomes the new Solon, the ironic arriviste who leaves the confident native flummoxed and at pains to explain himself. In much the way that Herodotus's Croesus does not know the depth of his ignorance, Lucian's ambiguous dialogue leaves readers tantalized by the ways in which Anacharsis often emerges as the more philosophically trenchant figure.[43]

As we shall see, Lucian's Solon seems to think that Greek cultural practices speak for themselves—or at the very least that they can be explained

---

[39] The nearest approximation would be the brief scene in Plutarch, *Solon* 5, in which, as in Lucian's dialogue, Anacharsis shows himself a match for Solon with his own "sharp wit" (ἀγχίνοια, 5.3). Anacharsis mocks (καταγελᾶν, 5.4) Solon for thinking that he could write laws that would stop the excesses of human behavior. Despite Solon's self-defense, Plutarch states, without further explanation, that Solon's laws "turned out rather more as Anacharsis supposed than according to Solon's wishes" (ἀλλὰ ταῦτα μὲν ὡς Ἀνάχαρσις εἴκαζεν ἀπέβη μᾶλλον ἢ κατ' ἐλπίδα τοῦ Σόλωνος, 5.6).

[40] Herodotus's Solon–Croesus exchange is possibly echoed as well by the detail that Anacharsis sought a meeting with Croesus: Diogenes Laertius 1.105.

[41] Branham 1989: 81–104 offers a sensitive treatment of Lucian's dialogue (to which my own reading is much indebted), focused on Platonic resonances but certainly leaving room for detecting other influences. See also Reardon 1971: 172–77 on the bookish allusivity of Lucianic comic dialogue.

[42] On the historicity of Herodotus's *logos*, see Asheri, Lloyd, and Corcella 2007 ad loc. 1.29: esp. 99, with bibliography. On Solon's thematic roles in Herodotus, see Moles 1996; Shapiro 1996; Ker 2000; Pelling 2006; Branscome 2013: 24–53.

[43] While I share the view of König 2005: 80 (in line with Branham 1989: 101–2) that neither side of the dialogue emerges as the clear victor, I note also the dialogue's generally undecidable qualities, brought out well by König 2005: 81: "Is Solon a true representative of the Greek tradition? Or is the Scythian Anacharsis paradoxically more Hellenic and more admirable precisely through his skeptical, interrogatory attitude to received custom?"

according to an idiom that will persuade the skeptical Anacharsis. But Anacharsis flummoxes Solon's confidence in his own views.[44] The upshot of the exchange, and that of its structural model between Solon and Croesus, is an off-kiltering whereby the visiting traveler perplexes the visited. Such off-kiltering is not uncommon in various meetings between wise men and rulers, as Kindstrand has observed.[45] But the notion that this motif structures Lucian's *Anacharsis* is not usually given much weight, since the work itself is sometimes seen as ephemeral, "purely rhetorical."[46] Insofar as Lucian's inversion at once "flips" Herodotus's Solon while also rearticulating a Herodotean framework central to the *Histories*, in which reversal of expectations pervades, the *Anacharsis* performs a kind of double inversion. On the one hand, Anacharsis's challenge to Solon offers analogy for Lucian's own style of comic flipping; the "establishment of excluded, neglected, or alien perspectives" is "fundamental to Lucian's satiric strategies," as Branham observes.[47] But given that "uprootings" and reversals form a structuring force in Herodotus generally (see Hdt. 1.33, 1.207.2, 3.40.3, 7.10.ε, 7.46.2), Lucian maneuvers at once "against" the Herodotean intertext and *in echo* of that text's pattern of reversals.

Rather more than simply Kindstrand's *jeu d'esprit*, then, the *Anacharsis*, drawing on this underlying template, highlights the force of the foreign visitor's "estranging" ability to confound assumptions of putative power.[48] While Lucian in the *Anacharsis* avoids the explicit self-identification he offers in the *Scythian*, Anacharsis's nomadic deracination nonetheless redoubles Lucian's perspective as an outsider, capable of lampooning the very cultural practices about which Anacharsis claims he is eager to learn.[49] As Branham

[44] This intellectual unbalancing replays both a central aspect of the Solon–Croesus exchange and a wider feature of wisdom literature, including other stories about Anacharsis himself in which the Scythian is put in the awkward position of not getting the answer he wants, as from an oracle when inquiring into his own supposed wisdom; see Diod. Sic. 9.6.1, where Anacharsis's inquiry about who of the Greeks is "wiser" than he (σοφώτερος) yields the surprising answer of Myson, a Malian with a mountain home in a small village called Chenae. The unexpected answer recalls the manner in which Solon produces names of relative nobodies in response to Croesus's inquiries about happiness. On Anacharsis and Myson, see Kindstrand 1981: 40–42.

[45] Kindstrand 1981: 42.

[46] See Kindstrand 1981: 66–67 (quotation at 67).

[47] Branham 1989: 90.

[48] See Branham 1989: 88 for "estranging." For the view that Anacharsis's provocations are more than simply playful, see also Gangloff 2007: 82 (contra Ungefehr-Kortus 1996: 187–203): "Lucien est bien conscient des consequences."

[49] Since neither side clearly trounces, there has been some debate about which figure in the work should be seen as "voicing" Lucian's view; Kindstrand 1981: 66 n. 60, with detailed bibliography. Read together with Lucian's procedures in the *Scythian*, however, there seems little impediment to the assumption that Lucian takes a sympathetic approach to Anacharsis's skepticism (cf. Kindstrand 1981: 67 on Lucian's "mixture of humour and sympathy").

250 HERODOTUS AND IMPERIAL GREEK LITERATURE

has observed, in terms that rightly caution against seeing Lucian's dialogue as unambiguously favoring one side or the other: "Lucian's technique is not to persuade us of the truth of one of two opposed dogmas but to generate comically disorienting contrasts between traditional 'truths,' and thereby to reveal both the kind of validity that inhabits a tradition and why that validity is merely partial."[50] If claiming one side as fully bettering the other proves reductive, Lucian nonetheless imparts the strong impression that his own critical energy lies behind Anacharsis's "comically disorienting" Solon. After all, it is none other than the nomadic wise man with whom Lucian elsewhere explicitly identifies who sets Solon on his back foot.[51]

"I Will Be Taught Anew"

The *Anacharsis* begins somewhat abruptly with the eponymous character's description of Greeks choking each other and wallowing like pigs, leaving us to construe the gymnastic setting from his focalization. While the text will eventually (14) suggest that Anacharsis had sought out Solon all along, the education Anacharsis pursues is from the start antagonistic, querulous, and skeptical.[52] The *Anacharsis* elaborates the title character's skepticism principally toward Greek gymnastic training, which he describes as an apparent form of mania (ὡς ἔμοιγε μανίᾳ μᾶλλον ἐοικέναι δοκεῖ τὸ πρᾶγμα, 5).[53] By the end of the dialogue, the skepticism seems to fall on Solon himself: if in the *Scythian* Solon was figured as the quintessence of Greece (*Scyth.* 5), by the close of the *Anacharsis* his ability to embody that quintessence and to persuade others of its value has come under fire.[54] All the same, seemingly in harmony with the other text, Solon is initially put on a pedestal by Anacharsis (however fulsomely):

---

[50] Branham 1989: 101–2, quotation at 102.

[51] See Martin 1996: 150; Mestre 2003: 315.

[52] Ungefehr-Kortus (1996: 208) notes the shift in tone between the *Scythian* and this work: "Folgt in *Skythes* ein glücklicher Zufall auf den nächsten und endet die Legende in einer vollkommenden Harmonie dreier Freunde, *gerät hier die anfängliche Harmonie ins Wanken*" (emphasis added). See also Mestre 2003: 315–16 on differences between the works.

[53] For the specifics of Anacharsis's critique against the historical backdrop of athletic practices and views on the gymnasium among Imperial Greeks, see Ungefehr-Kortus 1996: 212–17 and esp. König 2005: 72–96. Anacharsis's position would seem to align him somewhat with Herodotus's Cambyses and his mad mockery of foreign custom (Hdt. 3.38.1–2), but see discussion later on the ways in which the dialogue's conclusion undoes any easy sense of Solon as rational, Anacharsis as crazed.

[54] For the work as an inquiry in cultural valuation, see Branham 1989: 102: "The dialogue centers on the problem of locating, describing, and authenticating value and the difficulty in communicating value when a common frame of reference is missing."

ANACHARSIS AT BORDER CONTROL   251

I mean it, Solon, when I say that I came to you from Scythia, traveling over so much land and sailing over the huge, stormy Black Sea, for no other purpose than to learn about Greek customs, to contemplate your practices, and to get acquainted with the best aspects of your political life. Consequently, I chose you out of all the Athenians, considering your reputation, as my friend and host, since I myself have heard that you are an author of laws, an inventor of the best customs, a leader in introducing beneficial practices—to sum it all up, the shaper of this polity. Please do not delay in teaching me and making me your student. I would happily go without food or drink just to sit next to you and listen eagerly as you discuss government and law. (*Anacharsis* 14)

καὶ μήν, ὦ Σόλων, κατ᾽ οὐδὲν ἄλλο ἀπὸ τῆς Σκυθίας ἥκω παρ᾽ ὑμᾶς τοσαύτην μὲν γῆν διοδεύσας, μέγαν δὲ τὸν Εὔξεινον καὶ δυσχείμερον περαιωθείς, ἢ ὅπως νόμους τε τοὺς Ἑλλήνων ἐκμάθοιμι καὶ ἔθη τὰ παρ᾽ ὑμῖν κατανοήσαιμι καὶ πολιτείαν τὴν ἀρίστην ἐκμελετήσαιμι. διὸ καὶ σὲ μάλιστα φίλον ἐξ ἁπάντων Ἀθηναίων καὶ ξένον προειλόμην κατὰ κλέος, ἐπείπερ ἤκουον νόμων τε συγγραφέα τινὰ εἶναι σε καὶ ἐθῶν τῶν ἀρίστων εὑρετὴν καὶ ἐπιτηδευμάτων ὠφελίμων εἰσηγητήν, καὶ ὅλως πολιτείας τινὸς συναρμοστήν. ὥστε οὐκ ἂν φθάνοις διδάσκων με καὶ μαθητὴν ποιούμενος· ὡς ἔγωγε ἡδέως ἂν ἄσιτός σοι καὶ ἄποτος παρακαθεζόμενος, εἰς ὅσον ἂν αὐτὸς διαρκοίης λέγων, κεχηνὼς ἐπακούοιμι περὶ πολιτείας τε καὶ νόμων διεξιόντος.

The work initially installs Solon in a lofty position. Yet, like the Solon of Herodotus's Solon–Croesus exchange, it is Anacharsis who emerges here as a man of wide travel (τοσαύτην μὲν γῆν διοδεύσας, μέγαν δὲ τὸν Εὔξεινον καὶ δυσχείμερον περαιωθείς ~ αὐτῶν δὴ ὦν τούτων καὶ τῆς θεωρίης ἐκδημήσας ὁ Σόλων εἵνεκεν ἐς <τε> Αἴγυπτον ἀπίκετο παρὰ Ἄμασιν καὶ δὴ καὶ ἐς Σάρδις παρὰ Κροῖσον, Hdt. 1.30.1). Likewise, Anacharsis is depicted as participant in a guest friendship (ξένον ~ ξεῖνε Ἀθηναῖε, Hdt. 1.30.2) and is interpellated into a position of cultural observation at the behest of his host (θεάσαιο, *Anacharsis* 37 ~ θεησάμενον . . . καὶ σκεψάμενον, Hdt. 1.30.2).

Much as Croesus in the Herodotus exchange invites Solon to enter into dialogue about the perceived meaning of his riches (Hdt. 1.30.2), so it is Solon who in Lucian's dialogue encourages dialogic expatiation. Take, for instance, his cautioning Anacharsis against the idea of acquiring knowledge of Greece easily, in a passage that, in fact, resists the very notion of the "shortcut" (ἐπίτομόν τινα, 7) endorsed by Toxaris in *Scythian*:

252 HERODOTUS AND IMPERIAL GREEK LITERATURE

It is not easy, my friend, to describe everything in brief, but if you go little by little you will learn each thing: what we believe about the gods, about our ancestors, about marriage, and all the rest. (*Anacharsis* 15)

τὰ μὲν πάντα οὐ ῥᾴδιον, ὦ ἑταῖρε, διελθεῖν ἐν βραχεῖ, ἀλλὰ κατὰ μέρη ἐπιὼν εἴσῃ ἕκαστα, οἷα μὲν περὶ θεῶν, οἷα δὲ περὶ γονέων ἢ περὶ γάμων ἢ τῶν ἄλλων δοκεῖ ἡμῖν.

Whereas in Herodotus's account of Solon and Croesus the latter conditioned his conversation on having shown Solon "everything rich and magnificent" (πάντα ἐόντα μεγάλα τε καὶ ὄλβια, 1.30.1), here Lucian's Solon reverses this somewhat by *disclaiming* the ability to demonstrate "everything." Throughout the *Anacharsis*, the debate is one of semiotics. Solon's caution points to the way in which the characters in Lucian's dialogue are not speaking on equal terms. When Anacharsis derides athletes who compete for prizes apparently as insignificant as parsley or pine wreaths, Solon responds that it is the symbols of victory (σημεῖα τῆς νίκης, 10), and not victory's ephemeral artifacts, that matter.[55] It thus seems, at first, that Solon is providing an important corrective to the crude ethnography voiced by Anacharsis, who describes the athletes as behaving like animals and as suffering from madness. And yet, a few sections later, Anacharsis amps up his critique not only against athletic activities but also against the idea that people would leave behind "the things that matter (τἀναγκαῖα) and fritter away their time" (σχολάζουσιν, 11). Solon's response is striking: "Not by speaking (οὐ ... λέγων) could someone persuade you of the delights accomplished in the gymnasium, if you do not see it for yourself, sitting in the middle of the spectators" (οὐ γὰρ οὕτω λέγων ἄν τις προσβιβάσειέν σε τῇ ἡδονῇ τῶν ἐκεῖ δρωμένων, ὡς εἰ καθεζόμενος αὐτὸς ἐν μέσοις τοῖς θεαταῖς βλέποις, 12).[56] Solon, Herodotus's agent of *theôria*, now urges upon Anacharsis a relatively more primitive mode of visual activity: Anacharsis's naive ethnographic observations have led to his uncomprehending critique, yet the solution, says Solon, is not with words but rather with *further* looking.[57] If only Anacharsis could join the *theatai*, who

[55] See Branham 1989: 90–91 for the dialogue's focus on "intangibles." With Anacharsis's criticism of victory wreaths, compare at Hdt. 8.26.2–3 the Persian Tritantaechmes's positive remark about Olympic prizes, which in his view show the Greeks' preference for virtue over money.

[56] Montiglio (2005: 118–46, esp. 132–36), reacting to Konstan 1987, pushes for a rather fine distinction between *theôrein* and *theâsthai*: the latter, she suggests, carries a more superficial connotation than the former.

[57] The deflating picture of Solon in the dialogue fits well with what Konstan 2010 has emphasized about *both* characters' failure to look beyond the limited perspective each offers; see esp. 186–87 and

never tire of "praising and shouting and applauding" (ἐπαινῶν καὶ ἐπιβοῶν καὶ ἐπικροτῶν, 12). Rather like Croesus in Herodotus's first book, who gives a tour of his wealth expecting its semiotics to be clear, Lucian's Solon tries to forestall further critical inquiry by suggesting that observation leads to self-evident, immediate truth. Although he had stressed mediation (σημεῖα, 10), Lucian's Solon now endorses visual immediacy.

As with the Herodotean exchange, the *Anacharsis* thus turns upon the different interpretive frameworks of its interlocutors.[58] The characters believe at different points that one or the other is, in effect, misreading reality, and readers may toggle between seeing Anacharsis as naive or wise, Solon as worldly or chauvinistic.[59] Hence, an aspect of the work's provocation arises not simply from the questions posed by Anacharsis but from the reader's difficulty at different points in deciding how to view them—stunted or sophisticated, clueless or trenchant.[60] Solon, seemingly in a state of confidence that his views will not be challenged by the man whom he ironically calls his "blessed" friend (μακάριος, 34), openly invites Anacharsis's critique, permitting the possibility of a "worlding" of Athenian values. By encouraging dialogue with a foreigner, Solon appears initially the open-mannered opposite of Herodotus's xenophobic Scythians (see Hdt. 4.76.1, quoted earlier). But through interrogation, Greek custom grows vulnerable to Anacharsis's inquisition, and the invitation dangles the possibility that Anacharsis will have something substantive to say. As Solon states:

Now be sure not to take what I say to you as law or to trust it in every regard. If I seem to you to say something amiss, challenge me on it right away and straighten out my argument. In one way or another we might not entirely fail: either you will be firmly persuaded, after you have objected to all the

---

his comment in conclusion at 189: "Neither the archaic Greek nor the wise Scythian manages to understand what sports really are."

[58] See König 2005: 90–91 for the view that Anacharsis's perspective offers a stand-in for the impression many Romans had of Greek practices. For some qualifications of König's view, see Konstan 2010: 185–86. See also Gangloff 2007: 83: "C'est une remise en question sérieuse d'un élément important de l'hellénisme traditionnel, par un regard étranger."

[59] See Branham 1989: 83 on Anacharsis's cultural authority as combining "conflicting" ideas of barbarism and Hellenic wisdom and further remarks on the "perspicacious outsider" (84): "Anacharsis is one of those paradoxical figures, like Demonax or Socrates, whose peculiar perspective sets him at odds with the norm while giving rise to an equally eccentric form of insight and authority."

[60] See Ungefehr-Kortus 1996: 210: "Das Pikante dieser Anekdoten beruht auf der Ambivalenz einer naiven Unverständigkeit und einer provokativen Uneinsichtigkeit" and her further comments (210–11) on the shifts of register in both the *Anacharsis* and Plutarch's *Dinner of the Seven Sages*.

254 HERODOTUS AND IMPERIAL GREEK LITERATURE

matters that you think must be contradicted, or I will be taught anew that I do not rightly know about these topics. (*Anacharsis* 17)

καὶ ὅπως μὴ καθάπερ νόμοις προσέξεις οἷς ἂν λέγω πρὸς σέ, ὡς ἐξ ἅπαντος πιστεύειν αὐτοῖς, ἀλλ᾽ ἔνθα ἄν σοι μὴ ὀρθῶς τι λέγεσθαι δοκῇ, ἀντιλέγειν εὐθὺς καὶ διευθύνειν τὸν λόγον. δυοῖν γὰρ θατέρου πάντως οὐκ ἂν ἁμάρτοιμεν, ἢ σὲ βεβαίως πεισθῆναι ἐκχέαντα ὁπόσα οἴει ἀντιλεκτέα εἶναι ἢ ἐμὲ ἀναδιδαχθῆναι ὡς οὐκ ὀρθῶς γιγνώσκω περὶ αὐτῶν.

Playing on the ambiguity of *nomos*, Lucian has Solon discourage Anacharsis from regarding his discussion of Greek customs as law. On the far side of a thorough exchange lies the supposed promise of deeper knowledge for either party, including the (tongue-in-cheek) suggestion that Solon, the custodian of Athenian customs, will be re-educated. Later in the same chapter, Solon goes on to describe a scenario in which he, with the support of Athens, would publicly install a laudatory image of Anacharsis in Athens and magnify his contributions to the city, should the foreigner prove Solon wrong. Only a few chapters later, Anacharsis takes Solon up on this proffered freedom for critique (see §§ 21–23). But in his effort to show where Solon has gone astray, Anacharsis only confirms the naivete that Solon implicitly suspects and upon which his openness to critique was offered—an openness that from Solon's perspective never fully entertains the possibility that Anacharsis will offer meaningful insight. The fact that by the end of the dialogue Anacharsis's "acute observations continually catch him out," as Francesca Mestre puts it, doubles Solon's intellectual embarrassment: it is not merely his explanations that fail to persuade; it is also his original self-assurance that is challenged.[61]

Further on, Anacharsis apparently mistakes the value of Athenian theatrical practices, remarking on the "weighty high boots, clothing decorated with gold belts, absurd headgear with huge gawking mouths" (ὑποδήματα μὲν βαρέα καὶ ὑψηλὰ ὑποδεδεμένοι, χρυσαῖς δὲ ταινίαις τὴν ἐσθῆτα πεποικιλμένοι, κράνη δὲ ἐπικείμενοι παγγέλοια κεχηνότα παμμέγεθες, 23) and the dangerously wide strides that actors take in such clothing and footgear. Anacharsis's volley of "misreadings," which, in fact, have the effect of showing up the relativistic valuation of (Greek) cultural idiom, inspires one final long-winded speech from Solon, on the value of athletic training

---

[61] Mestre 2003: 315.

ANACHARSIS AT BORDER CONTROL   255

for military purposes.[62] Solon's consistent, static argumentative pose is countered by Anacharsis's nomadic leaps in logic, which themselves seem to create anxiety for Solon's sense of his own ability to stay on topic. Anacharsis's leaps come to a head in his ingenious syllogism that if the Athenians want to inspire fear in their enemies, they should send into battle their tragic actors with wide-mouthed masks and high boots:

> If a foray presents itself, you can don those big-mouthed headpieces to inspire fear and scare off your opponents, and you can obviously wear those high boots. They will be light in retreat, if necessary, and hard for the enemy to escape if you pursue them with such great strides. (*Anacharsis* 32)

> ἢν προτεθῇ ὑμῖν ἔξοδος, ἐκεῖνα τὰ κράνη περιθήσεσθε τὰ κεχηνότα, ὡς φοβερώτεροι εἴητε τοῖς ἐναντίοις μορμολυττόμενοι αὐτούς, καὶ ὑποδήσεσθε τὰ ὑψηλὰ ἐκεῖνα δηλαδή· φεύγουσί τε γάρ, ἢν δέῃ, κοῦφα, καὶ ἢν διώκητε, ἄφυκτα τοῖς πολεμίοις ἔσται, ὑμῶν οὕτω μεγάλα διαβαινόντων ἐπ᾽ αὐτούς.

The actors' high shoes will make for easy flight, and, conversely, their long strides will make an enemy retreat impossible.[63] Anacharsis connects two areas of Greek culture that Solon has tried strenuously to defend—athletics as a military preparation, theater as moral education—and, in the new combination (theatrics as a military tactic), produces an absurdity. For the reader of Lucian's time, for whom the glory days of Greek military achievement had vanished,[64] such critical inquiry into the past was more than rhetorical. Anacharsis's query is a reminder that, rather than something settled or fixed, Greek practices could have their meaning evacuated by time. But the point is made in the context of a traditionalizing literary move: for Anacharsis's tactic of reductio ad absurdum again has a precursor in the

---

[62] See Branham 1989: 88–91.

[63] Ewald 2004: 262 notes, with reference to Hölscher 2003: 7, how the dialogue here "ironically reverses famous Greek stories of athletic warriors' bodies striking fear in the minds of their non-Greek enemies."

[64] See, e.g., Veyne's (1999: 528) passing remark on the frustration Greeks might have felt, following Nero's proclaimed liberation of Achaea, for "an independence that had not been acquired at the price of insurrection or anarchy" ("Au-delà de leurs divergences et de leur acquiescement à la *pax Romana*, tous les Grecs pouvaient n'éprouver que des regrets pour une indépendance qui n'avait pas été acquise au prix de l'insurrection et de l'anarchie"). Compare, however, his comments at 540–41 (with his n. 146) on Greeks as "warriors and voluntary combatants" ("des guerriers, des combattants volontaires," 540) and allies of the emperor.

256 HERODOTUS AND IMPERIAL GREEK LITERATURE

Solon–Croesus exchange. Recall that after Solon has offered counterintuitive answers to Croesus's question about who is the happiest (ὀλβιώτατος) of men, Solon peppers his more general remarks about human happiness with a long-winded and somewhat droll disquisition on the average length of a person's life (1.32.3–4). Much like Anacharsis in the later dialogue, the Solon of the *Histories* adopts his interlocutor's metrics, only to flip them in offering a novel assessment of value. Herodotus's Solon reveals the absurdity of measuring happiness by Croesus's numbers (total wealth) through a different kind of reckoning (total days), while Lucian's Anacharsis reveals the risible significance of various cultural practices by literal extension of one cultural practice (dressing for theater) into another (dressing for battle).[65] Each deflates his interlocutor's putatively high-minded examples. The latter reductio is accompanied by Anacharsis's threat that he could pull out his Scythian dagger and take over the gym without a problem. Theater and athletics may be components of military prowess, Anacharsis implies, but their collective power could not withstand one armed Scythian.

Croesus was a powerful figure who eventually lost his empire, but that is intradiegetically unknown at the end of Herodotus's dialogue. In the analogy Lucian intimates between Solon-meets-Croesus and Anacharsis-meets-Solon, no decisive "loss" for Solon is adduced, but he is nonetheless seen grasping at rhetorical straws to preserve his view of Athenian custom. His final moments are indicative of the extent to which Anacharsis has rattled his own semiotic system. In his initial critique of athletics, Anacharsis had unfavorably compared the gymnasts to cocks when they stir up dust (ἀλεκτρυόνων δίκην, 2). Now, some thirty-five OCT sections later, Solon adopts the same comparison, although here in an attempted *defense* of the athletes. The image of brutality and violence becomes an inspiration, Solon argues, for the athletes:

> How would you feel if you were to witness quail-fights and cockfights among us and observed that we had no small interest in them? You would laugh, of course. . . . But this is not ridiculous: our soldiers' souls are affected deeply by an urge toward dangers, lest they seem less noble and courageous than the cocks . . . . (*Anacharsis* 37)

---

[65] Branham 1989: 93 locates much of the humor in the dialogue in Lucian's ability to riff on the caricature of Solon's bloviated (but here ineffectual) speech-making: "Indeed, much of the dialogue's humor derives from the fact that Solon's speeches have precisely the opposite of their intended perlocutionary effect." See further (93) on Solon's defense of "social constructs . . . lacking any inalienable claim to value independent of the social context in which they evolved."

καίτοι τί ἂν πάθοις, εἰ θεάσαιο καὶ ὀρτύγων καὶ ἀλεκτρυόνων ἀγῶνας παρ᾽
ἡμῖν καὶ σπουδὴν ἐπὶ τούτοις οὐ μικράν; ἢ γελάσῃ δῆλον.... ἀλλ᾽ οὐδὲ τοῦτο
γελοῖον· ὑποδύεται γάρ τις ἠρέμα ταῖς ψυχαῖς ὁρμὴ εἰς τοὺς κινδύνους, ὡς
μὴ ἀγεννέστεροι καὶ ἀτολμότεροι φαίνοιντο τῶν ἀλεκτρυόνων....

Such imagery obviously differs from the more traditional ideals of Greek education that Solon has previously adduced.[66] Cornered by the relentlessness of Anacharsis's arguments, Solon ultimately debases his rhetoric to the same *comparandum* that Anacharsis had himself first used in his comments against athletes, as the image of the cock returns, ironically, to function as an icon for military inspiration. Rather, then, than being a work that "peters out," as Kindstrand puts it, the text generates a curious symmetry between its two interlocutors by returning to this image, revealing the extent to which Solon's arguments have reached a desperate nadir.[67] Solon's echo of Anacharsis's image of the cock plays out against worries voiced earlier about going astray argumentatively, in language that ironically aligned Solon with the nomadic Anacharsis. For Solon had commented about not wishing to "wander" from his argument (ἀποπλανᾶν οὐ βούλομαι τὸν λόγον, 21), echoing an earlier remark that Anacharsis should watch out lest Solon's speech "wanders at random somewhere far from its flow" (πόρρω ποι ἀποπλανᾶσθαι εἰκῇ ῥέων, 19). Such comments play off Anacharsis's own self-designation as "a nomad and wandering man" (ἐγὼ νομὰς καὶ πλάνης ἄνθρωπος, 18); if readers already had sensed some ludic slippage between Solon who fears "wandering" in his argument and his wandering interlocutor, the closing portions of the dialogue will only confirm the feeling that Solon has become more "Scythian" through his exchange with Anacharsis.

In his last-ditch attempt to defend his own views, Solon turns from Athenian examples altogether to comment instead on Spartan whipping

---

[66] Compare Solon's loftier framing at *Anacharsis* 14: "If it ever concerns you to know how a city might best be managed and how its citizens might become excellent, you will then laud these exercises and the ambition with which we strive over them, and you will understand what benefits they possess, mixed in with their pains, even if now you think we exert ourselves in vain" (ἢν δέ σοι μελήσῃ ποτὲ εἰδέναι ὅπως ἂν τὰ κάλλιστα οἰκηθείη πόλις καὶ ὅπως ἂν ἄριστοι γένοιντο οἱ πολῖται αὐτῆς, ἐπαινέσῃ τότε καὶ τὰς ἀσκήσεις ταύτας καὶ τὴν φιλοτιμίαν ἣν φιλοτιμούμεθα περὶ αὐτάς, καὶ εἴσῃ ὅτι πολὺ τὸ χρήσιμον ἔχουσιν ἐγκαταμεμιγμένον τοῖς πόνοις, εἰ καὶ νῦν μάτην σπουδάζεσθαι δοκοῦσιν).

[67] Quotation at Kindstrand 1981: 66, who also notes the difficulty of deciding which side of the dialogue advances the Cynic argument in the text, ultimately landing on the conclusion that the work's outcome is "neutral" (67). The animal comparisons may be part of this light-touch Cynic influence in the work; see Ungefehr-Kortus 1996: 220 (with wider remarks on the animal comparisons at 217–23). On the use of Anacharsis by the Cynics, see Martin 1996 and Mestre 2003: 311–13.

258   HERODOTUS AND IMPERIAL GREEK LITERATURE

practices.[68] Solon claims they are not the practices of madmen, again using language that recalls Anacharsis's from much earlier (μήτε μαίνεσθαι ὑπολάβῃς, 38 ~ μανίᾳ, 5). Yet Solon does not offer a genuine defense; instead, he defers to Lycurgus. This appeal to Sparta marks the rhetorical lockjaw in which Solon finds himself. As Branham comments, "The choice of topic hardly seems designed to strengthen our confidence in Solon's position; rather, it returns us to the original focus of the dialogue—the apparent madness (*mania*: 5, *mainesthai*: 38) of other peoples' customs—and to sharpen that focus."[69] Unable to champion Athenian customs satisfactorily, the paragon of Athenian culture must turn to the base imagery of cockfights and bloody Spartan whipping.

Even more emblematic of Solon's faltering is the statement with which he caps the exchange. For when Anacharsis next asks whether Lycurgus himself undergoes such whipping, and further why Athens has not adopted it, if it is as salutary for military strengthening as Solon claims, he offers this reply: "Because our athletic practices, these local practices, are sufficient for us, Anacharsis. We do not think it is at all right to emulate foreign customs" (ὅτι ἡμῖν ἱκανά, ὦ Ἀνάχαρσι, ταῦτα τὰ γυμνάσια οἰκεῖα ὄντα· ζηλοῦν δὲ τὰ ξενικὰ οὐ πάνυ ἀξιοῦμεν, 38). The response seals the work's gestures of reversal by rendering *Solon* as one of Herodotus's Scythians, those people who spurn the adoption of foreign customs (Hdt. 4.76.1). Scythians flee foreign ways like the nomads they are, just as Solon figuratively retreats from the expected cultural boundaries he is supposedly poised to defend. The Athenian is now the Scythian, thinking it in no way right to adopt foreign ways (ζηλοῦν δὲ τὰ ξενικὰ οὐ πάνυ ἀξιοῦμεν ~ ξεινικοῖσι δὲ νομαίοισι καὶ οὗτοι αἰνῶς χρᾶσθαι φεύγουσι, Hdt. 4.76.1).

Solon's earlier remarks in the dialogue concerning the nature of Athenian citizenship similarly conjure an image that could well map onto Herodotus's description of the city-less nomad culture of Scythia:[70]

Well then, I must first briefly describe to you the things that seem best to us with respect to the city and its citizens. For we do not take the city to be the built environment, such as its walls, temples, or docks. These make up a stable, unmovable body, as it were, for the support and protection of

---

[68] This is perhaps meant to appeal to Anacharsis as a rustic sort, one who might approve of Spartan practices, as at Hdt. 4.77.

[69] Branham 1989: 99.

[70] On this aspect of Scythia, see Hdt. 4.11, 4.123, 4.127, with Hartog 1988 [1980]: 12–19, 193–206.

ANACHARSIS AT BORDER CONTROL 259

people who live here. But we place supreme importance in the citizens, for it is they who supply, enact, and bring to fruition all things; and they guard their accomplishments. They are something like the soul that exists in each person. (*Anacharsis* 20)

Οὐκοῦν διὰ βραχέων προακοῦσαι χρή σε ἃ περὶ πόλεως καὶ πολιτῶν ἡμῖν δοκεῖ. πόλιν γὰρ ἡμεῖς οὐ τὰ οἰκοδομήματα ἡγούμεθα εἶναι, οἶον τείχη καὶ ἱερὰ καὶ νεωσοίκους, ἀλλὰ ταῦτα μὲν ὥσπερ σῶμά τι ἑδραῖον καὶ ἀκίνητον ὑπάρχειν εἰς ὑποδοχὴν καὶ ἀσφάλειαν τῶν πολιτευομένων, τὸ δὲ πᾶν κῦρος ἐν τοῖς πολίταις τιθέμεθα· τούτους γὰρ εἶναι τοὺς ἀναπληροῦντας καὶ διατάττοντας καὶ ἐπιτελοῦντας ἕκαστα καὶ φυλάττοντας, οἷόν τι ἐν ἡμῖν ἑκάστῳ ἐστὶν ἡ ψυχή.

This emphasis on the unimportance of the physical locale and building blocks of the city is on the one hand harmonious with other Athenian expressions about the city being a collectivity of humans, not structures (e.g., Thuc. 7.77.7). But in the context of this dialogue, the comment contributes to the parallels between the Athenian and the nomad, between the supposedly rooted autochthonous figure and the free man of the steppe.[71] Indeed, Lucian's choice to close the work with an appeal to Sparta throws into doubt the dialogue's entire defense of Athenian athletic practice.[72] Lucian has again exploited Herodotus's own originally ambiguous semiotics, succinctly conveyed by that crucial participle ἀποδεξάμενος. In Lucian's dialogue, Anacharsis has ostensibly visited Athens to acquire wisdom, but by the end, however rambunctiously or heedlessly, he has *displayed* his own, leading Solon into aporia. Rooted in the Solon–Croesus exchange, in which the limitations of the Lydian king hinder his ability to digest the substance of Solon's wisdom, the relativity of values and unexpected vectors of wisdom are evoked anew in Lucian's dialogue.

[71] For the connection between Scythian nomadism and moments in Athenian history that mobilize the idea of a nomadic, movable people, see Herodotus 7.140–43 and Payen 1997: 300–302.

[72] Thus, König 2005: 93. Branham 1989: 103 has put the matter well, with the hint that something of Lucian's own perspective is echoed by Anacharsis: "Thus, while neither figure is given Socratic authority by the author, it is Solon's baroque celebration of Athenian cultural superiority that is made the more suspiciously ludicrous; the effect of humor is not to refute Solon, but to suggest a subtle appreciation of the relativity of cultural values, a point of view that we might well expect a Hellenized 'barbarian' sophist to share."

260 HERODOTUS AND IMPERIAL GREEK LITERATURE

Lucian's *Anacharsis* thus recognizes and exploits the special parallel Herodotus had contrived between Solon and Anacharsis. Both men cross borders in the *Histories* on quests for knowledge. Both are, in their way, exemplary figures. Solon voices a recurrent principle of Herodotus's work, that only in the end, with hindsight (and only that of others who still live), can a life's value be measured. Anacharsis exemplifies another recurrent motif—the potential dangers of crossing borders (cultural and geographic)—but also the virtues of nomadism and itinerant reinvention. Although there lurks in the *Histories* the essentializing suggestion that certain peoples are bound to behave in certain ways, as would seem to be the case for the Scythians (4.46), Herodotus's readers have repeatedly detected cross-currents to such essentializing. It remains an open question how one is to reconcile Herodotus's principle of historical flux with apparent national stereotypes: if what defines a people can change, how are actors' behaviors to be predicted, historical patterns to be discerned?

I have argued that in certain works by Lucian, we see an author who had already discovered various Herodotean layers of subtlety. Lucian recognizes in Herodotus a style of ambiguity that made of his literary predecessor a companion in inquiry, someone with and through whom to question the value of the past. By revivifying—but also by reworking—different elements of Herodotus's Anacharsis, Lucian reveals how his own sophisticated elusiveness precedes him, how his ambiguously irreverent imitation of the past summons and exploits that which was already strange. Through Herodotus, he interacts with an author who had himself explored the pliability of truth. The undecidable Anacharsis and the relativizing debate between him and Solon are mediated, then, *through* the backdrop of a relativizing Herodotus. In the end, Lucian's reception act showcases just part of the *Histories*' capacity to provoke response. Lucian's appropriations help us to read Herodotus more openly, to see his work loosened from the bonds of ethnographic fixity and cultural chauvinism, summoning instead a Herodotus who is varied, protean, alert to a world in motion. If Lucian's Herodotus is one who already possesses a certain degree of irreverence, the work of Pausanias, the final author we shall examine, reasserts the reverent Herodotus, although one not altogether devoid of ambivalent effect.

7

Acts of God

Pausanias Divines Herodotus

If Lucian's responses to Herodotus afforded him opportunity to locate his own ironies as already present in the past, the reception acts of Pausanias present a rather different picture. His profound literary kinship with Herodotus—in phraseology, method, and scope—has long been recognized.[1] On one view, Pausanias's imitation would seem to confirm Mario Segre's passing observation that imitating Herodotus was "nearly a norm" for writers of the second century CE.[2] Yet this "norm" came potentially freighted. Taking account of the "criticism and ridicule of Herodotos and Herodotean writing" among Imperial authors, William Hutton has astutely asked, "Would an author who wished his work to be taken seriously tread so obviously and deliberately in Herodotos' footsteps?"[3] Depending on one's perspective, the imitative Pausanias may be viewed as either a conformist or a certain kind of risk-taker. Or he may be taken to represent multiple and not fully reconcilable qualities, at once refraining from overattachment to Herodotus (by, say, not adopting his dialect) while also manifestly resurrecting Herodotus in phrase and pattern of thought. Such tension is that of kinetic reception, in which conventional reputation and idiosyncratic appropriation interact. As we have seen throughout this book, such reception is multifarious, and the contours of Herodotean imitation can be complex, inasmuch as they may partake of both his canonical authority and his status as problematic. How does Pausanias place Herodotus, and where should we place Pausanias?

---

[1] See Pfundtner 1866; Gurlitt 1890: 15–20; Ambaglio 1991; Meadows 1995: 94–96; Akujärvi 2005: 28–30; Hutton 2005b: 191, 195–213; Hogan 2014: xiii–xiv; Hawes 2016; Schreyer 2017. The text of Pausanias follows the Teubner editions of Spiro.

[2] Segre 2004 [1927]: 207–9 ("quasi un canone," 207) = 2004: 40–45. Cf. Ehrhardt 1988: 855 for the observation that Pausanias was among the Imperial authors who directly "consulted Herodotus for their own particular concerns" ("die H. für ihre besonderen Anliegen nachschlugen"), rather than relying on indirect knowledge.

[3] Hutton 2005b: 204. See similarly Elsner 2001a: 128.

Herodotus and Imperial Greek Literature. N. Bryant Kirkland, Oxford University Press. © Oxford University Press 2022.
DOI: 10.1093/oso/9780197583517.003.0008

262   HERODOTUS AND IMPERIAL GREEK LITERATURE

Pausanias's literary artistry has received sympathetic reappraisal in recent decades, and in light of renewed attention to his narrative craftsmanship, the final two chapters of this book consider anew how and why Pausanias channels Herodotus.[4] As Hutton has noted of Pausanias's engagement with the Halicarnassian, "Pausanias' nuanced Herodotism demonstrates the possibility of a serious, complex mimetic creativity that takes something different from Atticism as its foundation. . . . Pausanias is not trying to replicate Herodotos in his work; he is trying to recall Herodotos."[5] Accordingly, we might ask what it means that Pausanias repeatedly recalls Herodotus as he does—indeed, so consistently as to lend his *Periegesis* a pervasive Herodotean atmosphere that is hard to characterize.[6] Especially in places where one might be tempted to write off Herodotean resonances as simply "conventional," the role of such putative conventionality in Pausanias begs for analysis.[7] In the words of Greta Hawes, "Pausanias' evocation of Herodotus secures his place within a particular literary genealogy, but this strategy should not be understood as *merely* rhetorical."[8] The tag of conventionality should not arrest inquiry into its effects or purposes. Moreover, Pausanias's repurposing of what to modern lights might seem some of the more naive or simplistic aspects of Herodotean narrative can inspire reflection on how such "conventional" reception of Herodotus has unduly contributed to how *we* receive Pausanias.

As part of his many-dimensional and allusive project, Pausanias's cognitive landscapes play to Greek collective memory. His textual landscape makes pointed allusion not just to the past but to the literary past, summoning events recorded as well as the earlier textures of their recording.[9] Pausanias evokes the charged meanings of the Greek natural and built landscapes, and

---

[4] For recent attention to Pausanias, see Bingen 1996; Alcock, Cherry, and Elsner 2001; Hutton 2005b; Akujärvi 2005; Pretzler 2007b.

[5] Hutton 2005b: 213.

[6] See Hawes 2016: 340–41 on the "vague language" of characterizing Pausanias's relation to Herodotus. Further, see Bowie 2001: 25 for "impressions" of Herodotean influence, and Hutton 2017: 364–66 on Pausanias's Herodotean self-modeling and the "ambiguities" (366) generated. See, e.g., the slipperiness evident in Pausanias's evocation of Herodotean non-commitment around conflicting stories (e.g., Pausanias 6.3.8 and 2.17.4 echoing Herodotus 2.123.1 and 7.152.3), with Hawes 2016: "Pausanias' emulation of Herodotus makes this slipperiness a virtue" (339–40).

[7] Hawes 2016 rightly states that Pausanias's Herodoteanism is "no superficial patina" (323) but is rather a "necessary strategy" (323) for shaping the *Periegesis*. Compare Jones 2004: 18 on Pausanias's account of the Gallic invasion of 279 BCE (10.19.5, 12): "[B]ecause Pausanias imitates Herodotos, it does not follow that he is being 'insincere' or 'artificial': rather, he gives significance to the event by dressing it in Herodotean colors."

[8] Hawes 2016: 340 (emphasis in original).

[9] See Meadows 1995: 113.

ACTS OF GOD   263

his *Periegesis* can be said to do the same for the literary artifacts that themselves helped to shape those landscapes, including the *Histories*. Pausanias's literary filiation recalls Herodotus in phraseology and lexical pattern, but such soundings resonate as more than fading echoes.[10] Rather, Pausanias structures his *Periegesis* on distinctly Herodotean patterns of thought. The periegete not only takes as his frequent focus various ancient objects and spaces, but he also focuses them through a Herodotean, and often archaizing, worldview.[11] Pausanias looks to Herodotus for guidance not only on what constitutes Greece but also for how to think about Greece.[12]

In this chapter, I focus largely on Pausanias's attention to the role(s) of divinity in history, a characteristic that forges a clear connection between his literary persona and that of Herodotus, who himself repeatedly works the divine into his narrative, albeit in complicated ways.[13] For as Pelling has observed, Herodotus's narrative reminds us that the gods are "very difficult to know about," and while he may advert to the divine element in historical explanation, "the focus and the interest so regularly remain on the human level."[14] Pelling emphasizes the irreducible admixture of divine and human in historical explanation—indeed, stressing "explanation, not justification."[15] Yet for all its complexity, Herodotean narrative generates meaning through thematic repetition and patterns of intratextuality, and the repeated incorporation of the

[10] Pausanias's syntax, as Strid has documented, recalls many rhetorical features characteristic of Herodotus; see Strid 1976: 22–23, 78–80, 99. See also Bowie 2001: 25–27; Jones 2001: 34–35; Lightfoot 2003: 95; Hutton 2005b: 175–77, 218, 194–95 on the "numerous" similarities between Pausanias and Herodotus, from "the overall structure of their works down to their choice of individual words" (194).

[11] Pausanias's tendency to ignore more recently built structures has been noted: see, e.g., Stewart 2013: 244. See Porter 2001: 70–71, with n. 32, and further 67–76; Pretzler 2007b: 75–76, 91–104. Cf. Hutton 2005b: 16.

[12] For a parallel to Pausanias's taking intellectual cues from Herodotus, see Harloe 2010 on Winckelmann's reading Pausanias not only as a source of "information about lost artworks, but also as a source of what he called 'Denkweise': of the appropriate attitudes by which to contemplate and interpret the history of Greece" (180). Compare Stewart 2013: 232 on Pausanias's shaping of later interests: "Perhaps more than any other author, Pausanias has governed the way both past and contemporary scholars have conceptualized the archaeology of Classical Greece."

[13] On the common divine terminology between the two writers, see Pfundtner 1866: 10–14. See Bowie 2001: 25, remarking en passant on Pausanias's Herodotean-style comments on "the gods' punishment of human wickedness." The scholarship on divinity in Herodotus is ample; see Harrison 2000, esp. 158–81; Harrison 2009; Pelling 2019: 146–62, with further bibliography. See Ellis 2015b: 17–40 on the relationship between Herodotean theodicy and narrative shape. Cf. Harrison's caution (2009: 111–12) against detecting "any simple, over-arching theological design to his work" (111) (echoing Harrison 2000: 114–16), but also the strong statement at Harrison 2009: 101: "Herodotus believes that certain actions will inevitably receive retribution from the gods."

[14] See Pelling 2019: 146–62, quotations at 161. Cf. Lateiner 1989: 214 on Herodotus as having "transcended myth but not god."

[15] Pelling 2019: 161.

264 HERODOTUS AND IMPERIAL GREEK LITERATURE

divine no doubt contributes to this.[16] When Thomas Harrison declares that "The moral of divine retribution is a moral of the *Histories* as a whole," the sense of asseveration is hard to separate from the narrative's own repetitions that seem to suggest as much.[17] Pausanias likewise structures his own narrative through thematic intratextual repetitions, a point that has not always been the dominant view of what some have taken to be a disorganized work.[18] In turn, such intratextual structures may themselves be interpreted *inter*textually in relation to Herodotus.[19] While it will not be the case that Pausanias mimics all the various nuances of Herodotean thought on divinity, we will find instances of a Pausanian theology that derives a certain authoritativeness from sounding Herodotean and from recalling his narrative patterns. But Pausanias does not simply stare nostalgically backward. Rather, in mobilizing a Herodotean-style configuration of beliefs on divine justice and human fortune, Pausanias also directs his work toward the present and the future.[20] In its capacity to speak authoritatively about divine intervention in human affairs, Pausanias's text adumbrates patterns of interpretation that may hold for a future time as well, beyond the period of the work's documentation. The divine may well overturn, upend, or renew the world to which the *Periegesis* gives witness.

Divine Detections in Herodotus

Both in Herodotus and in Pausanias, physical features (and disasters related to them) can inspire theological meditation and create opportunity

[16] See Immerwahr 1966: 148 on pattern in Herodotus: "The form [of the *Histories*] is not an arbitrary creation, but the arrangement of the work embodies Herodotus' perception of repetition, patterning, and structure in the sequence of historical events: history becomes intelligible only when individual happenings are viewed together as parts of an orderly process." Compare Lateiner 1989: 165–66, 215: "Above all, he [Herodotus's reader] finds verbal and situational echoes and oblique cross-references to events past and future. These implicit analogies give coherence to the multitude of otherwise apparently unrelated happenings." See also Bowra 1966: 169–71.

[17] Harrison 2009: 105.

[18] Hutton (2005b: 55–126 and again 2010: 424–29, 442–48) has argued convincingly for the text's overall organization as both "synoptic" and "sequential." See Akujärvi 2005: 61–64 on Pausanias's many cross-references.

[19] Compare Rood 2009: 150 on Thucydides's intertextual links with Herodotus as building on Herodotus's own ability to "forge[] links between the wars he describes." Compare Baragwanath 2017: 155–57 for a general discussion of the kinds of plural truths communicated by intertextuality.

[20] Compare Bowie 1996: 213–16 on the juxtaposition of past and present. See Sidebottom 2002: 496 for examples; see further Schreyer 2017: 58–61 for discussion of the relationship between past and present in Pausanias, with an emphasis on Pausanias's "account of the myth-historical past as of unbroken validity" and his predominant focus on "an unbroken continuity between past and present" (quotations at 59).

ACTS OF GOD   265

for ratiocination. The peaceful functioning of the Nile River, for instance, presents Herodotus with the chance to display his speculative abilities.[21] But already in his work, rationalizing discussions involve a mixture of registers and data, ranging from the symbolic thought-world of dreams, oracles, and omens to the narrator's more ostensibly dispassionate accounts of landscape and topography. Where, then, does the idea of a natural disaster fit within the Herodotean worldview, and how does Herodotus position such events between naturally explicable and divinely inspired?

Among the most well-known natural events Herodotus recounts is the supposed earthquake at Delos:

> After Datis set sail from there, Delos was rocked by an earthquake, the first and last time, as the Delians say, that Delos shook up to my time. This was perhaps a portent manifested by the god of the evils that were to ensue. For in the time of Darius, son of Hystaspes, and of Xerxes, son of Darius, and of Artaxerxes, son of Xerxes, three generations in a row, more evils befell Greece than in the entirety of the twenty generations prior to Darius. Some of these evils arose from the Persians, but others from the leading groups in Greece who were fighting for supremacy. So it was not altogether out of line that Delos shook, though it had not shaken before. Moreover, there had been written an oracle: "I shall move Delos unmoved before-time." (6.98.1–3)

> μετὰ δὲ τοῦτον ἐνθεῦτεν ἐξαναχθέντα Δῆλος ἐκινήθη, ὡς ἔλεγον Δήλιοι, καὶ πρῶτα καὶ ὕστατα μέχρι ἐμεῦ σεισθεῖσα. καὶ τοῦτο μέν κου τέρας ἀνθρώποισι τῶν μελλόντων ἔσεσθαι κακῶν ἔφηνε ὁ θεός. ἐπὶ γὰρ Δαρείου τοῦ Ὑστάσπεος καὶ Ξέρξεω τοῦ Δαρείου καὶ Ἀρτοξέρξεω τοῦ Ξέρξεω, τριῶν τουτέων ἐπεξῆς γενεέων, ἐγένετο πλέω κακὰ τῇ Ἑλλάδι ἢ ἐπὶ εἴκοσι ἄλλας γενεὰς τὰς πρὸ Δαρείου γενομένας, τὰ μὲν ἀπὸ τῶν Περσέων αὐτῇ γενόμενα, τὰ δὲ ἀπ᾽ αὐτῶν τῶν κορυφαίων περὶ τῆς ἀρχῆς πολεμεόντων. οὕτως οὐδὲν ἦν ἀεικὲς κινηθῆναι Δῆλον τὸ πρὶν ἐοῦσαν ἀκίνητον. καὶ ἐν χρησμῷ ἦν γεγραμμένον περὶ αὐτῆς ὧδε· κινήσω καὶ Δῆλον ἀκίνητόν περ ἐοῦσαν.

---

[21] Indeed, as was noted in chapter 5, much of Herodotus's account of Egypt is taken up with analogy, probable reasoning, and the attempt to harness apparently outlandish aspects of Egyptian life under the control of Greek knowledge; see Lloyd 1975; Thomas 2000: 168–212; Pelling 2019: 62–65, 146–47.

266 HERODOTUS AND IMPERIAL GREEK LITERATURE

Jeffrey Rusten has well shown the timing of this "event" to be a fabrication that Thucydides would also later manipulate for literary effect: "The Delian earthquake is less a seismic event, than a semiotic one."[22] But the event as presented by Herodotus is layered, teetering between affirmation of a divine plan and Herodotus's own penchant for skeptical inquiry. Even as Herodotus shifts the story to a chronologically and semiotically convenient place, he nonetheless demonstrates that supposition (κου) of divine presence can accompany his methods of reasoning. Indeed, as Fowler has argued, Herodotus moves the figure of supreme god from "predicate to subject," that is, from the presumed active force behind things to the object of inquiry itself.[23] Herodotus is seen discovering divine workings through an advertised process of inference.[24]

Indeed, Herodotus's comments on the Delian temblor offer the patina of ratiocination. Herodotus foregrounds his reasoning process in his remark— subsequent to his hindsight deductions about the earthquake's meaning— that there is nothing "strange" or even "unseemly" (ἀεικές) about believing there to have been an earthquake where there had never been one before or since. Divinity may be present, but such presence is not unambiguously clear.[25] Rather, Herodotus exposes the *methods* by which divinity may be presumed or ascertained.[26] The conjunctive γάρ binds the event itself and Herodotus's inference. The eccentrically high number of evils to befall Greece in three generations is thus prefigured by the unwonted earthquake: while the omen portends evils to strike Greece from the outside, Herodotus also emphasizes internecine Hellenic struggles, the woes of its own making that afflict Greece.[27] Hence, if we aver that Herodotus manipulated the chronology of this "event" to augur the oncoming war between Greeks and Persians, we recognize more fully his interest in using narrative to suggest a

---

[22] Rusten 2013: 142.

[23] Fowler 2010, esp. 322–23. Further examples of Herodotus's pronouncements on the divine are listed at Harrison 2000: 231–32 and n. 22 and Pelling 2019: 146.

[24] See Smolin 2018: 34–35.

[25] See Pelling's (2019: 146 n. 2) comment that the word "supernatural" is not ideal, "especially as for Herodotus and his audience divine activity could be regarded as a perceptible phenomenon within 'natural' human experience; but it is hard to find a better one to capture the range of phenomena that baffled explanation without gods or fate or *daimones*." See also Harrison 2009: 110–11.

[26] I am not the first to make this point; in addition to Fowler 2010, see Harrison 2000: 103; Harrison 2009: 103–4 (with his n. 14). One might still observe, however, that Herodotus consciously manipulates his material here not only for the semiotic convenience but also to harmonize this story with other images of divine plan in his work.

[27] The tie between divine justice as an outside punishment and self-inflicted internal discord is a theme that resurfaces in Pausanias, too. Yet as Akujärvi (2005: 231) notes, part of what constituted

divine plan. What is more, the passage's faint echo of Herodotus's own proem suggests a role in his overall conception of history:

τὰ μὲν ἀπὸ τῶν Περσέων αὐτῇ γενόμενα, τὰ δὲ ἀπ᾽ αὐτῶν τῶν κορυφαίων περὶ τῆς ἀρχῆς πολεμεόντων. (6.98.2)

~

τὰ γενόμενα . . . τὰ μὲν Ἕλλησι, τὰ δὲ βαρβάροισι. . . . (*Proem*)

Herodotus recapitulates, in solemn fashion, the earthquake's semiotic magnitude for the overall structuring events of his *Histories*. The echo of his own proem suggests the broader salience of (a kind of) theological reasoning to Herodotus's narrative structure.[28] He is willing to manipulate chronology and subscribe to events that may not have occurred for the purposes of making divine justice cohere with narrative.

Similarly, in Herodotus's passage on the Peneus gorge in Thessaly, the narrator's heuristic abilities recur in conjunction with divine explication:

Now the Thessalians for their part say that Poseidon created the channel through which the Peneus flows, a reasonable enough assertion. For whoever believes that Poseidon shakes the earth and that the ruptures of earthquakes are the work of the god, that person, looking at this, would say that Poseidon did it. It is indeed the action of an earthquake, as it appears to me, this split in the mountains. (7.129.4)

αὐτοὶ μέν νυν Θεσσαλοί φασι Ποσειδέωνα ποιῆσαι τὸν αὐλῶνα δι᾽ οὗ ῥέει ὁ Πηνειός, οἰκότα λέγοντες· ὅστις γὰρ νομίζει Ποσειδέωνα τὴν γῆν σείειν καὶ τὰ διεστεῶτα ὑπὸ σεισμοῦ τοῦ θεοῦ τούτου ἔργα εἶναι, καὶ ἂν ἐκεῖνο ἰδὼν φαίη Ποσειδέωνα ποιῆσαι· ἔστι γὰρ σεισμοῦ ἔργον, ὡς ἐμοὶ ἐφαίνετο εἶναι, ἡ διάστασις τῶν ὀρέων.

Herodotus is not necessarily saying that *he* believes the earthquake and the gorge it created to be Poseidon's handiwork. Instead, for someone who believes

independence in the Greek world, per Pausanias, was "the freedom to fight one another in order to enhance one's own position at others' expense, and avoid subjection to others." See 9.13.11 and 10.9.11 for instances of internal discord alluded to by Pausanias.

[28] See Fornara 1990: 27, 45, calling Herodotus a "theological historian"; and Smolin 2018: 26, noting that Herodotus's skepticism "does not extend, it seems, to the operation of divinity" in history. See also Asheri, Lloyd, and Corcella 2007 ad loc. 3.108.2 on the phrase τοῦ θείου ἡ προνοίη.

268 HERODOTUS AND IMPERIAL GREEK LITERATURE

in a connection between earthquakes and Poseidon, such an assumption is "reasonable" (οἰκότα). He does not rule out divine intervention here (nor does he seem to have much interest in endorsing it: note the emphatic placement of the verb ἔστι).[29] The coolness of tone helps to make passages such as that on the Delos earthquake stand out all the more; the unwillingness to make a firm pronouncement about divinity when the opportunity exists underscores those places where Herodotus *does* offer pronouncement. Since Herodotus affirms from his own perspective (ὡς ἐμοὶ ἐφαίνετο εἶναι) that the gorge results from an earthquake (σεισμοῦ ἔργον) and since he says the Thessalians speak reasonably when they claim that the passage is the work of Poseidon, Herodotus in fact affirms the *congruence* of the two statements: through a kind of referential opacity, "Poseidon" and "earthquake" emerge as not mutually exclusive. The passage thus demonstrates again the ease with which Herodotus suggests a harmony between belief in divine causation and the inquirer's ability to draw logical inferences about the same.[30]

In the passage on the gorge encountered on Xerxes's invasion of Greece, then, and more pointedly in the passage on the Delian earthquake, we witness Herodotus's ability to invoke divine explanation in commenting on events of his own time. It is not altogether impossible that Herodotus knew such admixture of inquiry and divination, as it were, to be controversial. As Fowler observes, concerning the incorporation of the divine into Herodotus, Herodotus emerged in the age of sophists and skeptical intellectual activity, and his decision to charge his work with the gods is a significant distinguishing feature of his text.[31] Indeed, when he claims early in his work "to point to" (σημήνας, 1.5.3) the man he knew to be the first cause of hostilities between Greece and the East, he does so in the semantics ascribed by Heraclitus to the Delphic oracle, who neither speaks nor conceals but rather "indicates" (ὁ ἄναξ, οὗ τὸ μαντεῖόν ἐστι τὸ ἐν Δελφοῖς, οὔτε λέγει οὔτε κρύπτει ἀλλὰ σημαίνει, Heraclitus DK 22 B 93).[32] Later, in a passage about a roof falling in on schoolboys in Chios (6.27), part of his narration of the Ionian Revolt, Herodotus observes how the god "loves to indicate somehow in advance" (φιλέει δέ κως προσημαίνειν, 6.27.1). The relationship between the historiographer's own quasi-mantic position and the god's ability to

---

[29] See Gould 1994: 94 on the "uncertainty principle" in Greek religion.

[30] My reading is indebted to that of Harrison 2000: 95–97, who offers convincing rebuttal to the notion that Herodotus is rejecting divine explanation.

[31] Fowler 2010: 318–19, 334.

[32] See Hartog 1988 [1980]: 355 n. 140.

provide signs casts the narrator in a powerful role.[33] His analysis of the past speaks to the present and the future. Pointing to "the god" is a way of enabling his inquiry to speak beyond its own time. Herodotus's natural disasters and the language of divine indication emplot history along some kind of (potentially) discernible pattern, urging readers to navigate the ambiguities of materialist knowledge alongside the stirrings of the divine. These features of Herodotean narrative will also inform Pausanias's strategies in the *Periegesis*.

Divine Detections in Pausanias

Pausanias often shapes his narrative patterning around the supposed intentions of the divine, and, like Herodotus, he has an interest in enunciating instances of its presence. Pausanias likewise places these stories of divine intervention carefully. All the same, some have found it easy to pass over aspects of Pausanias's Herodotean echoes as merely the continuity of tradition. Christian Habicht noted some decades ago that "Pausanias's beliefs [on divine punishment] are conventional; they do not differ from, for instance, those of Herodotus, writing six hundred years earlier."[34] The "for instance" is telling: Habicht cites Herodotus as potentially one among many. Yet when it comes to authors identified with the genre of historiography, Herodotus's "conventional" beliefs about divine punishment obviously differ from, say, the non-theological Thucydides.[35] Moreover, if the style and methods of Thucydides would come in the succeeding centuries to seem more compatible with generic notions of historiographic principle, one may question the extent to which Herodotus's divinely infused narrative offered Pausanias a fully "conventional" option.[36] Even if Pausanias is following a convention, his doing so—insofar as it reinforces his alignment unmistakably with Herodotus—summons the ambivalences of his model, as noted at the outset of this chapter.[37]

---

[33] See generally Hollmann 2011; Kindt 2006: 35: "The authoritative voice of oracles, seers, and omens in many ways corresponds to the authoritative voice of the historian in his role as the researcher and narrator of the history he tells."

[34] Habicht 1985: 154; see also 106–9, 152–54; Swain 1996: 341.

[35] On the downplaying of the religious dimension in Thucydides, see Hornblower 2011. On Herodotus's theological ideas as themselves complex, neither "unexamined [n]or reflexive," see Smolin 2018: 25–39, quotation at 34–35.

[36] See, e.g., Lucian's promulgation of Thucydidean principles, seemingly the more conventional stance for historical narrative; Tamiolaki 2016.

[37] See Hutton 2005b: 204, quoted earlier.

270 HERODOTUS AND IMPERIAL GREEK LITERATURE

In what follows, I take an interconnected set of examples from Pausanias's seventh book—the accounts of Aegium, Helike, and the wrath of Talthybius—as a case study that reveals how his religious fixation enables readers to detect a sense of coherence not only from the past (as history) but also from the *literary* past (as a narrated tradition). In particular, Pausanias's allusion to Talthybius (7.24.1) evokes a memorable story of divine justice told by Herodotus (7.134–37). In Pausanias's case, however, the recall is part of a wider program steering the reader to appreciate the narrative of disaster that he will describe for the city of Helike. The Herodotean activations help to forge a connection between Pausanias and the written past but also implicitly instruct readers in the dynamics of interpreting events.

The story of the disaster at Helike forms part of Pausanias's broader periegetic movement outward from the town of Aegium in Achaea. Aegium and Helike are geographically adjacent as well as textually adjacent in the *Periegesis*, but their narrative proximity is not an inevitability of geography. As Daniel Stewart has noted:

> It is commonly argued that the order in which these *theoremata* [sights] are introduced is topographically determined. . . . There are, of course, many exceptions to this general rule within the *Periegesis*, and Pausanias is just as likely to abandon topographical order for a *thematically determined* discussion of monuments.[38]

The contrast in tone between, and the kinds of thematic impressions conveyed by, the stories Pausanias tells about these two places should be kept in mind. Speaking generally of Pausanias's narratorial interventions, Whitmarsh has observed that the author has the ability to build up "referential density—associating a particular place with a theme, an era, or a personage—or . . . because he wishes to draw attention to jarring disjunction."[39] Pausanias, that is, can move both topographically and with a sense of thematic counterpoint.

Initially, in his account of Aegium, Pausanias chooses to highlight a variety of tonally positive images: he offers description of Eileithuia, goddess of childbirth (7.23.5); he mentions Asclepius and Health (7.23.7); he notices the beardless image of a young Dionysus (7.23.9); and he notes Zeus the

---

[38] Stewart 2013: 239 (emphasis added).
[39] Whitmarsh 2015: 54.

ACTS OF GOD 271

Savior (7.23.9). Further on, he amplifies the mostly sanguine tone evoked by Aegium with notices of its pleasant water, "inexhaustible" and "pleasing both to the eye and to the taste" (ὕδωρ ἄφθονον θεάσασθαί τε καὶ πιεῖν ἐκ πηγῆς ἡδύ, 7.24.3). He extends the positive description with the mention of the sanctuary of Safety (Σωτηρίας ἱερόν, 7.24.3) before noting the bronze images of boy Zeus and the beardless Heracles, in whose priestly service was traditionally chosen a boy who had "won the prize for beauty" (ὁ νικῶν κάλλει, 7.24.4). Childhood, health, youth, safety, beauty of nature and body—collectively, these compose the bright hues in which Pausanias paints Aegium.[40]

By a kind of chiaroscuro, however, his account of Helike is one of doom, rooted in the Herodotean realm of divine justice. Indeed, Pausanias presages the Helike theme in a dark and directly Herodotean tone with a passing remark on Talthybius's grave, since the herald is traditionally reckoned to have died at Aegium (7.24.1). Mention of Talthybius summons for Pausanias's alert reader a figure who had already received brief glances in Homer but whose most memorable account arises in Herodotus's complex narration of his so-called wrath (μῆνις).[41] Pausanias's mention of Talthybius, while obviously relevant to a topographical description of the city in which he is buried, has the added effect of putting his reader in mind of the Herodotean tale, in which the narrator's role in excavating a sense of divine justice will also adumbrate Pausanias's Helike *logos*.

To recall, Herodotus refers proleptically to the wrath of Talthybius (7.134) before detailing the story of how the Spartans sent two ambassadors to Xerxes as compensatory sacrifices for Persian heralds whom the Spartans had earlier killed (7.132–33). Xerxes refrains from murdering them, uttering a high-minded comment, with what Herodotus calls "greatness of spirit" (μεγαλοφροσύνη), that he would not wish to behave like the Spartans. But divine justice cannot be thwarted, and in the following generation, the Spartan heralds' sons—Nicolas and Aneristus—are betrayed to the Athenians en route to Persia, and the Athenians put them to death. Herodotus concludes

---

[40] On the "grammar" of Pausanias's site descriptions, see Stewart 2013: 238–40, with Pretzler 2007b: 6–14.

[41] See Hdt. 7.132–37 (with Smolin 2018: 13–14) and *Il.* 1.320, 3.118, 4.192, 7.276, 19.196, 19.250, 19.267, 23.897. Compare Frazer 1898 on Pausanias ad loc., who mentions only Herodotus, not Homer. See Irwin 2013 on the pointedness of Herodotus's reference to Talthybius and the possible implications for understanding his attitude toward late-fifth-century Athens. On Pausanias's attitudes toward Athens, see Hogan 2017, with 189 n. 5 for bibliography on the political structures of Pausanias's own day.

272 HERODOTUS AND IMPERIAL GREEK LITERATURE

the tale with one of his more unvarnished narratorial comments about divine punishment:

> This above all seems to me to be most clearly the work of the divine. For the fact that the wrath of Talthybius fell upon messengers and did not let up until it had run its course is the working out of justice. Yet the fact that it fell upon the children of those men who had gone to Susa and into the presence of the King, upon Nicolas, the son of Bulis, and on Aneristus, the son of Sperthias. . . . **This is the thing that makes it clear in my eyes that it was a divine deed, arising from his wrath.** (7.137.1–2)

> τοῦτό μοι ἐν τοῖσι θειότατον φαίνεται γενέσθαι. ὅτι μὲν γὰρ κατέσκηψε ἐς ἀγγέλους ἡ Ταλθυβίου μῆνις οὐδὲ ἐπαύσατο πρὶν ἢ ἐξῆλθε, τὸ δίκαιον οὕτω ἔφερε· τὸ δὲ συμπεσεῖν ἐς τοὺς παῖδας τῶν ἀνδρῶν τούτων τῶν ἀναβάντων πρὸς βασιλέα διὰ τὴν μῆνιν, ἐς Νικόλαν τε τὸν Βούλιος καὶ ἐς Ἀνήριστον τὸν Σπερθίεω. . . . **δῆλον ὦν μοι ὅτι θεῖον ἐγένετο τὸ πρῆγμα ἐκ τῆς μήνιος.**

Compared with certain other instances (cf. 6.98 and 7.129, noted earlier) in which Herodotus appears at least superficially more guarded about comments related to the divine, the narrator is relatively unbridled here.[42] The inability to see the outcome of justice within a lived framework is superseded by the author's bird's-eye historical view, viewing the wrath as it leapfrogs over a generation.

In turn, Pausanias's story of Helike elicits a similarly unchecked narratorial comment on divine retribution. Pausanias's Helike *logos* replays elements of the Herodotean aura in both its rhetoric of inquiry and its ultimate pronouncement on divine judgment. Although Pausanias's version of Helike likely relies on Strabo's description of the town's destruction (*Geography* 8.7.1, C384–85), his rendition is hardly a cut-and-paste from the geographer, at least in terms of style and sensibility. For Pausanias, more than just the fact of Helike's disappearance requires description; rather, he devotes his account to the meaning of that disappearance.[43]

---

[42] See Pelling 2019: 147: "Generally, it is true, Herodotus is careful to introduce his more supernatural stories with 'it is said that,' and sometimes to make it clear who does the saying."

[43] Contrast Strabo's measured description (8.7.2), devoid of authorial assertion about the divine, and Diodorus's account (15.48), which explicitly distinguishes divine and materialist explanations (and thus shows that it is *not* always anachronistic to invoke the distinction; cf. Smolin 2018: 27–29).

He initiates his *logos* with the statement that the Helike at which one arrives when moving further from Aigeum (ἰόντι δὲ ἐς τὸ πρόσω) exists no more. In the same breath, he refers to the divine source of destruction: "Here the city of Helike was formerly inhabited, in the place where the Ionians had a supremely sacred sanctuary for Heliconian Poseidon" (ἐνταῦθα ᾤκητο Ἑλίκη πόλις καὶ Ἴωσιν ἱερὸν ἁγιώτατον Ποσειδῶνος ἦν Ἑλικωνίου, 7.24.5).[44] The long narrative of Helike then becomes a set piece for display of others' speculative pondering (see οἱ φροντίσαντες, 7.24.9). As with Herodotus, Pausanias's assertions of divine presence are accompanied by the opportunity for "proof-telling."[45] So, on the one hand, Pausanias tells us right away, with Herodotean assertiveness, that the "wrath of Poseidon" (τὸ μήνιμα ἐκ τοῦ Ποσειδῶνος, 7.24.6) fell upon the Achaeans after their expulsion and slaughter of suppliants at the sanctuary of Heliconian Poseidon. On the other hand, Pausanias launches into a Herodotean-style excursus on the nature of earthquakes, before looping back to his primary assertion many sections later:

> Some are inclined to liken the most destructive type of earthquake to the breath of a person suffering from continuous fever, breath that comes in quick succession and is afflicted with heaviness. (Symptoms of this condition are indicated at various parts of the body, but especially at the wrist of each hand.) They claim that in the same exact fashion an earthquake plunges directly beneath buildings and rattles their foundations, just as molehills pop up from the earth's core. **It is alone this type of tremor that leaves on the earth no trace that humans once lived there**. It was precisely this type of earthquake, then, that shook Helike to its foundations, and they say that a further disaster accompanied it in the season of winter. For the sea inundated a great part of the land at Helike and covered it over, and indeed so deep was the tide in Poseidon's grove that merely the treetops were visible. With the god's sudden earthquake and the accompanying swell of the sea, the wave overwhelmed Helike to a man. . . . **The situation at Helike furnishes proof, as in many other places, that the wrath of the god of suppliants is unavoidable.** (7.24.11–12, 7.25.1)

---

[44] On Heliconian Poseidon, see Herodotus 1.145, 1.148.
[45] Compare Herodotus 9.100.2: "There are many signs/proofs (τεκμήρια) of divinity among human affairs." See Thomas 2000: 190–200.

274 HERODOTUS AND IMPERIAL GREEK LITERATURE

τὸν δὲ αὐτῶν ὀλεθριώτατον τοιῷδέ τινι ἐθέλουσιν εἰκάζειν, τὸ ἐντὸς τοῦ ἀνθρώπου πνεῦμα εἰ συνεχεῖ πυρετῷ πυκνότερόν τε καὶ ὑπὸ πολλῆς ἄνω τῆς βίας <ὠθοῖτο>· τοῦτο δὲ ἀλλαχοῦ τε τοῦ σώματος ἐπισημαίνει καὶ ἐν ταῖς χερσὶν ὑπὸ ἑκάτερον μάλιστα τὸν καρπόν. κατὰ ταὐτὰ οὖν καὶ τὸν σεισμὸν [εἴτ'] εὐθὺ ὑποδύεσθαι τῶν οἰκοδομημάτων καὶ θεμέλια ἀναπάλλειν φασὶν αὐτόν, καθότι καὶ τὰ ἔργα τῶν σφαλάκων ἐκ μυχοῦ τῆς γῆς ἀναπέμπεται· **μόνη τε ἡ τοιαύτη κίνησις οὐδὲ τοῦ οἰκισθῆναί ποτε ὑπολείπει σημεῖα ἐν τῇ γῇ.** τότε δὲ ἰδέαν μὲν ταύτην ἐπὶ τῇ Ἑλίκῃ τοῦ σεισμοῦ τὴν ἐς τὸ ἔδαφος ἀνακινοῦσαν, σὺν δὲ αὐτῇ καὶ ἄλλο πῆμα τοιόνδε οἱ ἐπιγενέσθαι φασὶν ὥρᾳ χειμῶνος. ἐπῆλθε γάρ σφισιν ἐπὶ πολὺ τῆς χώρας ἡ θάλασσα καὶ τὴν Ἑλίκην περιέλαβεν ἐν κύκλῳ πᾶσαν· καὶ δὴ καὶ τὸ ἄλσος τοῦ Ποσειδῶνος ἐπὶ τοσοῦτον ἐπέσχεν ὁ κλύδων ὡς τὰ ἄκρα τῶν δένδρων σύνοπτα εἶναι μόνον. σείσαντος δὲ ἐξαίφνης τοῦ θεοῦ καὶ ὁμοῦ τῷ σεισμῷ τῆς θαλάσσης ἀναδραμούσης, καθείλκυσεν αὔτανδρον τὸ κῦμα τὴν Ἑλίκην. . . . **τὸ δὲ τοῦ Ἱκεσίου μήνιμα πάρεστι μὲν τοῖς ἐς τὴν Ἑλίκην, πάρεστι δὲ καὶ ἄλλοις διδαχθῆναι πολλοῖς ὡς ἔστιν ἀπαραίτητον.**

Although Pausanias ostensibly relies on expert speculation regarding earthquakes, such testimony is subordinated to this initial claim (7.24.6) that the "wrath of Poseidon visited them without delay; an earthquake promptly struck their land and swallowed up, without leaving a trace for posterity to see, both the buildings and the very site on which the city stood."[46] The expert-style excursus on earthquakes, rendered in fine detail (see generally 7.24.7–11), leads to the conclusion already given, allowing Pausanias to vindicate his own initial assertion about divine wrath, only now under the guise of rationalizing inquiry. The original pronouncement harmonizes with the knowledge of οἱ φροντίσαντες ("those who ponder, give heed to") and their students who study earthquakes (οἱ φροντίσαντες τὰ τοιαῦτα ἐξ ἀρχῆς καὶ οἱ παρ' ἐκείνων διδαχθέντες ἰδέας καταμαθεῖν ἐδυνήθησαν τοσάσδε ἐπὶ τοῖς σεισμοῖς, 7.24.9). Moreover, Pausanias's medical analogy of the feverish body, as if the earth were ill, contrasts with the predominant images of health just presented in his Aegium *logos* and thus reinforces the marked tonal shift from one *logos* to another. His asseveration on the divine combined with medicalizing analysis replays, albeit with some difference, Herodotean strategies outlined above with regard to natural events, in turn rooting

---

[46] οὐκ ἐμέλλησε τὸ μήνιμα ἐκ τοῦ Ποσειδῶνος, ἀλλὰ σεισμὸς ἐς τὴν χώραν σφίσιν αὐτίκα κατασκήψας τῶν τε οἰκοδομημάτων τὴν κατασκευὴν καὶ ὁμοῦ τῇ κατασκευῇ καὶ αὐτὸ τῆς πόλεως τὸ ἔδαφος ἀφανὲς ἐς τοὺς ἔπειτα ἐποίησε.

ACTS OF GOD   275

Pausanias's assertions in the doubly authoritative fold both of those who consider earthquakes and of the Herodotean voice.[47]

These overlaps and intertextual connections coalesce finally in a stark statement in clear thematic echo of Herodotus: "The situation at Helike furnishes proof, as it does in many other places, that the wrath of the god of the suppliants is unavoidable" (7.25.1). Pausanias's utterance is a full-throttle declaration of divine presence expressed in the language of proof. The statement recalls in tone and thought, although not directly in language, Herodotus's comment on divine justice from the Talthybius story (τοῦτό μοι ἐν τοῖσι θειότατον φαίνεται γενέσθαι, Hdt. 7.137.2). Pausanias thereby completes a sustained engagement within a particular Herodotean pattern, initiated by his own preemptive reference to Talthybius. His solemn final pronouncement, on the heels of so much proof-telling, closes a section of his narrative in which the possibilities of learned display mingle with the narrator's sense of divine historical shaping.[48] Pausanias's Herodoteanism is thus seen to possess an additional dimension, beyond those usually noted. For atop his many phraseological echoes, Pausanias imbues his narrated landscape with elements of the Herodotean thoughtscape.[49] His strongly Herodotean assertion registers his work's own continuity with the past, conjoining his second-century CE visit to Helike to the long stretch of time that had intervened between its destruction and his present day. He avoids both a bare factual recall and a strongly materialist explanation and chooses, rather, to account for the past in the voice of the past.[50]

Accordingly, the Helike story by way of Talthybius becomes an instance in which Pausanias's intertextuality with Herodotus includes the further facet of referring to Herodotus's own *intra*textuality. For when Pausanias refers to a passage from Herodotus whose significance depends, in part, on its own atypicality vis-à-vis other, more cautious pronouncements on divinity by Herodotus, Pausanias's intertextual connection partakes of the target passage's

---

[47] Elsewhere Pausanias grapples with the interrelation of divine intent and natural occurrence, as in his discussion of Apollo and the eradication of locusts (1.24.8) and in his pointing out the "long-ago" (πάλαι) tendency of dangerous beasts to be sent as agents of divine justice (1.27.9).
[48] Compare Hawes 2016: 332: "By highlighting the role of the authoritative travelling narrator, it [the *Periegesis*] puts experiential subjectivity centre-stage, and demonstrates a way of converting the complexities of the world into a comprehensible, manageable account which nonetheless reflects the messy dynamics of knowledge and dispute."
[49] Compare Pelling 2019: 47–55 on Herodotus's "narrative codes," though he is careful to show some of the ways in which reading Herodotus complicates an easy sense of such codes' consistency.
[50] Compare Pretzler 2007b: 87: "Echoes of Herodotus' style and approach are particularly common in the *Periegesis*, and this can lend a certain archaic weight to events that might otherwise seem less conspicuous."

276 HERODOTUS AND IMPERIAL GREEK LITERATURE

own original intratextual distinctiveness. Pausanias's allusion, then, subsumes the subtleties of the hypotext partly by tapping into patterns latent within the *Histories*, highlighting what was already an outlier remark. At the same time, an overriding sense of continuity, transcendent to historical particulars, comes through. Harry Sidebottom has put it well: "The stability of the human condition [per Pausanias] has implications for a reading of the text's construction of Greekness. The reader is encouraged to think of contemporary Greeks as not much different from those of the ancient past."[51] Not only are the events not terribly different, but the possibilities of their signification also endure.

The Limits of Happiness

Scholars have stressed the extent to which Pausanias's *Periegesis* offers more than a guide to topographical or physical space (if it can be taken to give practical guidance in navigating physical space at all).[52] In Pausanias's text, physical spaces provoke different kinds of contemplation, including on occasion the narrator's moral reflection. In some instances, these reflections can feel disjunctive to the journeylike quality of the work. As Johanna Akujärvi observes, "[W]hile in other Greek narratives descriptions interrupt the main narrative, in Pausanias it is the other way around: narratives interrupt description."[53] It is by means of such reflections that Pausanias deepens the import of particular spaces. Charged landscapes afford Pausanias the chance to de-temporalize a site, as it were, elevating its significance to the level of moralizing truth. Since I have already suggested that this mode of cogitation interacts with Herodotus, let us turn to another instance of narratorial reflection tinged with specifically Herodotean coloring.

The story concerns the narration of Arcadia from Book 8. Pausanias first provides a description of the city of Psophis (8.24), starting with an etymological history of the city's name (8.24.1–3), before remarking on certain natural features (8.24.4–5) and proceeding finally to detail some of Psophis's sacred spaces and edifices (8.24.6–7). Among these, mention of Alcmaeon's tomb (μνῆμα) leads the narrator to the story of that man's flight from Argos, following the murder of his mother (8.24.8–10). Later, Alcmaeon falls victim to murder himself, during his attempt to reacquire his mother's

---

[51] Sidebottom 2002: 494.
[52] See, e.g., Hutton 2005b: 25; Stewart 2013: 231–45; chapter 8 here.
[53] Akujärvi 2012a: 249.

ACTS OF GOD 277

necklace. Pausanias lingers in this digression with comments about topography (8.24.11–12) before drawing to his conclusion:

> In Psophis the account I heard about a Psophidian named Aglaüs, a coeval of Croesus the Lydian, namely that he was happy for the entire span of his life—this account I did not believe. Sure, one may receive fewer evils for himself compared with his fellow men, just as one ship may be buffeted by fewer storms than another. But a man always standing outside misfortune or a ship always caressed by a favoring wind—it is impossible that we shall be able to find this . . . . (8.24.13–14)

> ὃν δὲ ἤκουσα ἐν Ψωφῖδι ἐπὶ Ἀγλαῷ λόγον ἀνδρὶ Ψωφιδίῳ κατὰ Κροῖσον τὸν Λυδὸν ὄντι ἡλικίαν, ὡς ὁ Ἀγλαὸς τὸν χρόνον τοῦ βίου πάντα γένοιτο εὐδαίμων, οὔ με ἔπειθεν ὁ λόγος. ἀλλὰ ἀνθρώπων μὲν τῶν ἐφ᾽ ἑαυτοῦ κακὰ ἄν τις ἐλάσσονα ἀναδέξαιτο, καθὰ καὶ ναῦς ἧσσον ἂν χειμασθείη νεὼς ἄλλης· ἄνδρα δὲ συμφορῶν ἀεὶ στάντα ἐκτὸς ἢ τὰ πάντα οὐρίῳ ναῦν χρησαμένην πνεύματι οὐκ ἔστιν ὅπως δυνησόμεθα ἐξευρεῖν . . . .

What begins, like so many stretches of Pausanias, as a description of place suddenly vaults onto a higher plane of reflection. His comment may at first seem incidental to the description of Psophis, as if a reader is just catching by chance a remark that Pausanias himself overheard (ἤκουσα) while visiting. What does the passing comment on Aglaüs have to do with Psophis? Aglaüs has no apparent connection to the buildings or religious monuments or even more generally to the political history of Psophis. Perhaps the decision to cement the Psophis narrative with this more general set of remarks recapitulates a theme set forth in his earlier telling of Alcmaeon's story, where Pausanias pronounces, also in generalizing tones, that "many men run aground on heedless desires, and even more women" (ἐς ἐπιθυμίας δὲ ἀνοήτους πολλοὶ μὲν ἄνδρες, γυναῖκες δὲ ἔτι πλέον ἐξοκέλλουσιν, 8.24.9).[54] But why Aglaüs, and why now?

The focus turns on the subject of human happiness, and Pausanias's syntax has a kind of quiet drama here that subtly reasserts the theme to which he speaks. He first foregrounds the incorporated relative clause and its subordinate statement in indirect speech (that Aglaüs experienced complete happiness: ὡς ὁ Ἀγλαὸς τὸν χρόνον τοῦ βίου πάντα γένοιτο εὐδαίμων) and

---

[54] On Pausanias's asseverations on love, see Hutton 2009.

278 HERODOTUS AND IMPERIAL GREEK LITERATURE

thereby emphatically delays his own expression of disbelief (οὔ με ἔπειθεν ὁ λόγος), as if striking down the notion of happiness first mooted. In this regard, the fact that Pausanias passingly describes Aglaüs as a contemporary of Croesus has some significance. For by putting readers in mind of the fragility of happiness described by Solon to Croesus (Hdt. 1.29–32) in the midst of a sentence that undercuts a notion of full happiness through its own dramatic syntax, Pausanias's seemingly gratuitous reference preemptively conjures the notions that will follow about the mixed nature of happiness. In fact, Pausanias comes to sound Solonian himself, in his comment that "one may receive fewer evils for himself compared with his fellow men, just as one ship may be buffeted by fewer storms than another."[55] In its modest relativizing logic, the assertion recalls the statement by Herodotus's Solon that no two days in a human life bring exactly the same thing (1.32.4). What is more, Pausanias's simile harks to the comment from Solon that no mortal enjoys all good fortune at one time, just as countries fail to enjoy unmitigated blessing:

> It is not possible for one who is mortal to have all these good things all at once, just as there is no one country sufficient in its own right to provide all good things; but one has one thing while it lacks another, and the country that has the most is best. (Hdt. 1.32.8)

> τὰ πάντα μέν νυν ταῦτα συλλαβεῖν ἄνθρωπον ἐόντα ἀδύνατόν ἐστι· <ἀλλ᾽> ὥσπερ χώρη οὐδεμία καταρκέει πάντα αὐτὴ παρέχουσα, ἀλλὰ ἄλλο μὲν ἔχει ἑτέρου δὲ ἐπιδέεται· ἣ δὲ ἂν τὰ πλεῖστα ἔχῃ, αὕτη ἀρίστη.

Pausanias's language affirms Solon's, and as many have understood by implication, Herodotus's "vulnerability ethic," along with the impossibility of finding an exception to the rule (οὐκ ἔστιν ὅπως δυνησόμεθα ἐξευρεῖν, Paus. 8.24.14 ~ ἀδύνατόν ἐστι, Hdt. 1.32.8).[56] While some might again dismiss such statements as "conventional," the link between Aglaüs and Croesus appears not to have been so conventional. As Frazer observed, "Pliny [*Natural History* 7.151] and Valerius Maximus [7.1.2] represent Aglaüs as a contemporary of

---

[55] Pausanias's allusions to Herodotus are elsewhere similarly indirect: compare Habicht 1985: 98 on what he calls a "hidden reference to Herodotus" (with n. 9 on Hdt. 7.154). See also Pausanias 5.25.11 with reference to Herodotus 7.164.1 (what Robert calls "latente Herodot-Anspielungen," 1909: 98 n. 3.). Other comparable pairs include Paus. 9.32.10 ~ Hdt. 1.137, Paus. 6.3.8 ~ Hdt. 7.152.3. See Segre 2004 [1927]: 44.

[56] See Aicher 2013 for Herodotus's "vulnerability ethic."

ACTS OF GOD   279

Gyges, whereas Pausanias makes him a contemporary of Croesus."[57] Pausanias has adjusted the chronology to produce a richer literary (and Herodotean) savor. Chronologically aligning Aglaüs with Croesus more readily summons Solon for the alert reader, and such synchronization renders more intricate Pausanias's allusion to Solon's own pronouncements on divinity's grudging and disruptive nature (1.32.1), along with the inscrutability of human fate (1.32.9). Even Pausanias's comment on the impossibility of finding "a man always standing outside misfortune" (ἄνδρα δὲ συμφορῶν ἀεὶ στάντα ἐκτός) recalls the striking phrase of Herodotus's Solon that a "person is entirely what happens to him" (πᾶσά ἐστι ἄνθρωπος συμφορή, 1.32.4). The connection of Aglaüs to Croesus, tacked as passing apposition to a prepositional phrase, thus lends extra thematic weight to the entire passage.

One may connect with statements on divine justice the prominent role Pausanias accords fortune.[58] Take, for example, Pausanias's conclusion to his long account of the Messenian War (4.4–29), where he ostensibly changes topic: "Up to this point my account has covered the many sufferings (παθήματα) of the Messenians and how the god (ὁ δαίμων) bestrewed them to the ends of the earth, far away from the Peloponnese, and later restored them safely to their own land. From this point let us now turn to a description of the land and cities" (4.29.13).[59] This change of topic is cosmetic, for only a few paragraphs later, in the midst of describing the city of Pharae, divinity's role in human affairs resurfaces:

> There is also a Temple of Fortune and an ancient statue among the people of Pharae. The first of those whom I know to have made mention of Fortune in his poems was Homer.... He said nothing further about **this goddess as the greatest of gods among human matters and as maintaining the greatest might**, though in the *Iliad* at least he sets up Athena and Enyo as having authority in war, Artemis as a fearful force in child-bearing, and Aphrodite

---

[57] Frazer 1898 ad loc. 8.24.13. Pausanias and Herodotus alter chronology: Pausanias updates Aglaüs, while Herodotus likely does the same in having Solon meet with Croesus. On the historicity of Herodotus's *logos*, see Asheri, Lloyd, and Corcella 2007 ad loc. 1.29, esp. 99, with bibliography.

[58] See Porter 2001: 73–74: "The workings of fortune are in some sense the true subject of his ten books, as the sheer frequency and prominence of his descriptions of sanctuaries to Tyche throughout Greece might suggest alone."

[59] ἄχρι μὲν δὴ τοῦδε ὁ λόγος ἐπῆλθέ μοι Μεσσηνίων τὰ πολλὰ παθήματα, καὶ ὡς ὁ δαίμων σφᾶς ἐπί τε γῆς τὰ ἔσχατα καὶ ἐπὶ τὰ πορρώτατα Πελοποννήσου σκεδάσας ὕστερον χρόνῳ καὶ ἐς τὴν οἰκείαν ἀνέσωσε· τὸ δὲ ἀπὸ τούτου τῆς χώρας καὶ πόλεων τραπώμεθα ἐς ἀφήγησιν. For a sensitive reading of Pausanias's "authorial agenda" (Alcock 2001: 143) in narrating Messenian history, with attention to how his chronological telescoping and relative reticence on *theoremata* have influenced later archaeology of the region, see Alcock 2001.

280   HERODOTUS AND IMPERIAL GREEK LITERATURE

as concerned with marital matters. But of Fortune he made no further comment. Now Bupalus, an accomplished sculptor in temple construction and statuary, made the statue of Fortune at Smyrna. He is the first of those whom we know who sculpted her with a sphere upon her head and in her hand what the Greeks call the horn of Amaltheia, revealing her works as far as they extend. Later Pindar sang other aspects of Fortune, and he called her Supporter of the City (4.30.3; 5–6).

ἔστι δὲ καὶ Τύχης ναὸς Φαραιάταις καὶ ἄγαλμα ἀρχαῖον. πρῶτος δὲ ὧν οἶδα ἐποιήσατο ἐν τοῖς ἔπεσιν Ὅμηρος Τύχης μνήμην . . . . πέρα δὲ ἐδήλωσεν οὐδὲν ἔτι, ὡς ἡ θεός ἐστιν αὕτη μεγίστη θεῶν ἐν τοῖς ἀνθρωπίνοις πράγμασι καὶ ἰσχὺν παρέχεται πλείστην, ὥσπερ γε ἐν Ἰλιάδι ἐποίησεν Ἀθηνᾶν μὲν καὶ Ἐνυὼ πολεμούντων ἡγεμονίαν ἔχειν, Ἄρτεμιν δὲ γυναικῶν ὠδῖσιν εἶναι φοβεράν, Ἀφροδίτῃ δὲ τὰ ἔργα μέλειν τῶν γάμων. ἀλλ᾽ οὗτος μὲν οὐδὲν ἄλλο ἐποίησεν ἐς τὴν Τύχην· Βούπαλος δέ, ναούς τε οἰκοδομήσασθαι καὶ ζῷα ἀνὴρ ἀγαθὸς πλάσαι, Σμυρναίοις ἄγαλμα ἐργαζόμενος Τύχης πρῶτος ἐποίησεν ὧν ἴσμεν πόλον τε ἔχουσαν ἐπὶ τῇ κεφαλῇ καὶ τῇ ἑτέρᾳ χειρὶ τὸ καλούμενον Ἀμαλθείας κέρας ὑπὸ Ἑλλήνων. οὗτος μὲν ἐπὶ τοσοῦτο ἐδήλωσε τῆς θεοῦ τὰ ἔργα· ᾖσε δὲ καὶ ὕστερον Πίνδαρος ἄλλα τε ἐς τὴν Τύχην καὶ δὴ καὶ Φερέπολιν ἀνεκάλεσεν αὐτήν.

Pausanias's account blooms outward, from a physical artifact at Pharae, the Temple of Fortune, into a wider discussion of the goddess's cult. As we have seen, the move from physical object to generalizing comment is not untypical, but the tendency to generalizing remark is here heightened by the kind of superlative qualities (μεγίστη, πλείστην) of Pausanias's utterance. Following the narration of the ill-fated Messenians under the direction of ὁ δαίμων, Pausanias's superlatives give peculiar spotlight to the goddess Fortune (ἡ θεός).[60] Even the attention to iconographic aspects evokes both the breadth of her supremacy and the unpredictability of her behavior. Pausanias might have left off his comments about Fortune as the supplement to Homer. But he builds on earlier figures, Homer and Bupalus, who each "first . . . made" (πρῶτος . . . ἐποιήσατο . . . πρῶτος ἐποίησεν) mention or image of Fortune. He also connects himself, in his "primatist" language, to Herodotus.[61] In

[60] On the overlapping indefiniteness of terms such as δαίμων and τύχη in Herodotus, see Harrison 2000: 169: "'According to some daimon' (κατὰ δαίμονα, 1.111.1) seems no different in meaning, for example, from 'by divine chance' (θείῃ τύχῃ, e.g. 5.92.γ3)."

[61] On Herodotus's use of the phrase "the first of whom we know" and similar expressions, see Chamberlain 2001.

ACTS OF GOD   281

echoing Pindar in his conclusion that Fortune is the "Supporter of the City," Pausanias ties his praise to the very heuristic evident in Herodotus's collocation of cyclical human happiness, measured in the rise and fall of cities (Hdt. 1.5.3). Hence, even as Pausanias claims to transition from the story of human suffering to the description of lands and cities (4.29.13), he cannot help but give airtime to his perception that Homer had understressed the overriding characteristic of the goddess: that she is supreme and that cities may rise or fall by her hand. The emphasis on the instability of human habitations not only reinforces the preceding narrative of the Messenians, but it also implicitly corrects Homer and recapitulates the ongoing sense that the presence of Herodotus is a constituent part of meaning-making in the *Periegesis*.

The Destiny of Bad Ends: The Case of Sulla

Both Herodotus's and Pausanias's narratives attend to reversals of fortune and the workings of divinity.[62] Indeed, it is by now nearly an axiom of Herodotean studies that the encounter between Solon and Croesus offers fundamental clues to interpreting Herodotus's text.[63] Downfalls and disastrous bad ends pervade the *Histories*, yet the theme of reversal appears so consistently that readers make take its presence for granted.[64] A sustained reading of the work may convey the sense that one of its primary meanings inheres in this pattern. Starting with his sweeping enunciation that human happiness does not linger in any one place over time, Herodotus's text wastes no time in elaborating on the notion with the story of Candaules, followed by the story of Croesus (see especially his bad end, 1.91). The theme repeats in the *logoi* of Apries of Egypt (2.161), Polycrates of Samos (3.40–43, 120–26), the Scythian king Skyles (4.79), the doomed invasion of Greece by Persia that "had to happen" (τὸ χρεὸν γενέσθαι, 7.17.2), and finally the evils that "needed" (ἔδεε) to occur for Xerxes's mistress and her family (9.109.2).[65]

Pausanias likewise replays this theme in his presentation of a Greece at once splendid and doomed, its physical state both wondrous and ever on the edge of demise. The motif of characters and cities coming to bad ends

[62] For the typicality of this theme in Herodotus, see Lachenaud 1978: 96; Mikalson 2003: 148.
[63] See, e.g., Lattimore 1939; Chiasson 1986.
[64] See Fornara 1971: 76–80.
[65] There are further instantiations of the theme (and often similar phrasing) at 1.8.3, 2.161.3, 5.33, 5.92.δ.1, 6.64, 6.135.3, and 7.6.4; see Hohti 1975; Gould 1989: 73–85. See also the epic word πόρω and its connection to fate at Hdt. 1.91 and 3.64.

282 HERODOTUS AND IMPERIAL GREEK LITERATURE

shapes emplotment, such as it is, in the *Periegesis*. In tracing out this feature of Pausanias's text, I next draw attention to the Roman leader Sulla among the various figures in the *Periegesis* who come to bad ends. Sulla's presence early and late in the work helps Pausanias to articulate a pattern for blasphemous figures while also imparting, with respect to the fortunes of Athens, a monitory tone potentially evocative of Herodotus's views toward that city. Sulla is thus looped into Pausanias's (Herodotean) views with regard to both the fragility of individual human success and, at the larger level, the success of cities and empire.[66]

Sulla shows up early in Pausanias's text: "Built near the sanctuary of Dionysus and the theater is a structure said to be a model of Xerxes's tent. It has been rebuilt, for the Roman general Sulla burned the old structure when he took Athens" (1.20.4).[67] Sulla's first cameo is as a destroyer, obliterating an object that itself marks a previous destroyer of Athens, the Persian king Xerxes.[68] The simulacrum of Xerxes's tent metonymically incorporates into the cityscape the man who had sought to conquer Greece; Sulla's action, in turn, at once destroys the symbol and enacts a version of Xerxes's own destructiveness. But Pausanias has the privilege of the long view, knowing that the tent was made again. Consequently, for the viewer of Pausanias's day, the spot conjures the repulse of Xerxes and the eventual sunset on Sulla's power, too, as the Athens of Pausanias's day was enjoying the fruits of the happier dispensation of Hadrian:[69]

When Sulla did not relent in his anger at the Athenians, some men made a secret escape to Delphi. There they inquired whether it was already the time when fate would leave Athens desolate, and they received in answer

---

[66] On Pausanias's possible attitudes toward Rome, see Swain 1996: 330–56 (with 343–44 on Sulla); Elsner 1997; Alcock 1996: 268–76; Veyne 1999: 516–17; Hutton 2005b: 30–53; Hutton 2008 (esp. 623 on the difficulty of generalization); Pirenne-Delforge 2008: 142–73; Ursin 2019: 191–210. Compare Akujärvi 2005: 292 (discussing Paus. 1.20.7), 265–95, including her comment that "Asking the *Periegesis* for an answer in that matter [of Roman sympathies] is to ask for information it cannot convey to the reader" (291). Compare the cautionary remark of Bowie 1996: 218: "Pausanias criticises individual Romans, but never to my knowledge explicitly or even implicitly criticises either Romans as a whole or aspects of the Roman character." (Compare the equivocal results of efforts to distill Herodotus's attitudes toward Athens, with the remarks of Rutherford 2018: 10–13.)

[67] ἔστι δὲ πλησίον τοῦ τε ἱεροῦ τοῦ Διονύσου καὶ τοῦ θεάτρου κατασκεύασμα, ποιηθῆναι δὲ τῆς σκηνῆς αὐτὸ ἐς μίμησιν τῆς Ξέρξου λέγεται· ἐποιήθη δὲ καὶ δεύτερον, τὸ γὰρ ἀρχαῖον στρατηγὸς Ῥωμαίων ἐνέπρησε Σύλλας Ἀθήνας ἑλών.

[68] For Pausanias's emphasis on Sulla's destructiveness, see Habicht 1985: 121. Compare Arafat 1996: 99–105 and Bowie 1996: 220–21.

[69] Compare Anderson's discussion (1993: 7) on Pausanias 8.43.1, analogizing Antoninus Pius to Cyrus the Elder: "The nuance is subtle: Antoninus is the best type of barbarian, and the present is being neatly translated into terms of the past."

from the Pythia the response about the wineskin. Later, Sulla was struck with a disease—the same, as I found out, as seized Pherecydes the Syrian. Now, while Sulla did things to the Athenian people so savage as to be unbecoming of a Roman, I do not think that this was the source of his misfortune. Rather it was the divine retribution of the Lord of Suppliants, since Sulla had pulled Aristion from the sanctuary of Athena, where Aristion had claimed refuge, and killed him. Thus was Athens beset by the war with Rome, only to flourish again when Hadrian was emperor. (1.20.7)

Σύλλου δὲ οὐκ ἀνιέντος ἐς Ἀθηναίους τοῦ θυμοῦ λαθόντες ἐκδιδράσκουσιν ἄνδρες ἐς Δελφούς· ἐρομένοις δέ σφισιν, εἰ καταλαμβάνοι τὸ χρεὼν ἤδη καὶ τὰς Ἀθήνας ἐρημωθῆναι, τούτοις ἔχρησεν ἡ Πυθία τὰ ἐς τὸν ἀσκὸν ἔχοντα. Σύλλᾳ δὲ ὕστερον τούτων ἐνέπεσεν ἡ νόσος, ᾗ καὶ τὸν Σύριον Φερεκύδην ἁλῶναι πυνθάνομαι. Σύλλᾳ δὲ ἔστι μὲν καὶ τὰ ἐς τοὺς πολλοὺς Ἀθηναίων ἀγριώτερα ἢ ὡς ἄνδρα εἰκὸς ἦν ἐργάσασθαι Ῥωμαῖον· ἀλλὰ γὰρ οὐ ταῦτα δὴ αἰτίαν γενέσθαι οἱ δοκῶ τῆς συμφορᾶς, Ἱκεσίου δὲ μήνιμα, ὅτι καταφυγόντα ἐς τὸ τῆς Ἀθηνᾶς ἱερὸν ἀπέκτεινεν ἀποσπάσας Ἀριστίωνα. Ἀθῆναι μὲν οὕτως ὑπὸ τοῦ πολέμου κακωθεῖσαι τοῦ Ῥωμαίων αὖθις Ἀδριανοῦ βασιλεύοντος ἤνθησαν.

Pausanias establishes his Herodotean thoughtscape in multiple ways. First, in this initial book, he draws the reader's attention to the fate of Athens. While the rise and decline of cities braids the *Histories*, Herodotus's attention to Athens and his potentially latent warnings about its fate allow us to align Pausanias's concerns with its fortunes to those of Herodotus.[70] In this case, the Athenians who escape to Delphi frame the issue in terms of fate (χρεών). They ask whether the time was "already" at hand for Athens to fall. Viewed from Pausanias's longue-durée perspective, however, the question of Athens's fall is historicized in the larger framework of its successive misfortunes and fortunes. For, as Pausanias observes, the Athens of his day, though at one time "harmed" (κακωθεῖσαι) by Rome, has flowered (ἤνθησαν) again under Hadrian. In the space of a few lines, then, Pausanias depicts the vicissitudes of one place.[71]

[70] On Herodotus and Athens, see Strasburger 2013 [1955]; Fornara 1971 (esp. 37–58); Moles 1996; Raaflaub 2002 (esp. p. 29); Irwin 2013.
[71] See Whitmarsh 2015: 51 on the tensions inherent in Pausanias's presentation of Athens as a site both of memory and of potential renewal under Rome.

284 HERODOTUS AND IMPERIAL GREEK LITERATURE

Much further on, in Book 9, again treating of Sulla, Pausanias continues to shape narrative coherence according to tendencies of Herodotean emplotment. The first reference to Sulla in Book 1 introduces his death by divine punishment, while the final substantive reference to Sulla reiterates his death and lends a ring composition to his appearances.[72] This Book 9 passage echoes that of Book 1 while also deepening its range:

> Alalcomenae is a village of no great size lying at the base of a mountain that is itself not very high. . . . Sulla acted in his treatment of the Athenians savagely, contrary to the character of the Romans, but nonetheless consistently with his treatment of the Thebans and the people of Orchomenus. Even at Alalcomenae he added to his crimes when he stole the very statue of Athena. Following this and other demented acts against the cities of Greece and their gods, the harshest of all diseases seized him. He blossomed with lice, and what had earlier been considered his good fortune now came to such an end. (9.33.5–6)

> Ἀλαλκομεναὶ δὲ κώμη μέν ἐστιν οὐ μεγάλη, κεῖται δὲ ὄρους οὐκ ἄγαν ὑψηλοῦ πρὸς τοῖς ποσὶν ἐσχάτοις. . . . Σύλλα δὲ ἔστι μὲν καὶ τὰ ἐς Ἀθηναίους ἀνήμερα καὶ ἤθους ἀλλότρια τοῦ Ῥωμαίων, ἐοικότα δὲ τούτοις καὶ τὰ ἐς Θηβαίους τε καὶ Ὀρχομενίους· προσεξειργάσατο δὲ καὶ ἐν ταῖς Ἀλαλκομεναῖς, τῆς Ἀθηνᾶς τὸ ἄγαλμα αὐτὸ συλήσας. τοῦτον μὲν τοιαῦτα ἔς τε Ἑλληνίδας πόλεις καὶ θεοὺς τοὺς Ἑλλήνων ἐκμανέντα ἐπέλαβεν ἀχαριστοτάτη νόσος πασῶν· φθειρῶν γὰρ ἤνθησεν, ἥ τε πρότερον εὐτυχία δοκοῦσα ἐς τοιοῦτο περιῆλθεν αὐτῷ τέλος.

Pausanias closes the life of Sulla with Solonian grandeur, focused on the reversal of good fortune (εὐτυχία) and death's end (τέλος).[73] In fact, so laden is the passage with Herodotean evocations that one might miss that it fails to square fully with Pausanias's earlier remarks on Sulla's death. For the reader now finds Pausanias having matters both ways. In Book 1, Pausanias had tied

---

[72] The last actual reference to Sulla, at 9.40.7, refers to Roman victory trophies in the countryside of Chaeronea and thus neatly recalls a theme of Greek loss, just as Pausanias's account linking Sulla and Xerxes conjures the latter's destruction of Athens.

[73] Pausanias's closing comments on Sulla also recall Herodotus's account (4.205) of the divine retribution visited upon Cyrenaean queen Pheretime, who after avenging her son's death comes to a bad end (ἀπέθανε κακῶς), breaking out in a wormy skin disease (ζῶσα γὰρ εὐλέων ἐξέζεε) that Herodotus ties to divine envy (ὡς ἄρα ἀνθρώποισι αἱ λίην ἰσχυραὶ τιμωρίαι πρὸς θεῶν ἐπίφθονοι γίνονται). Hutton 2005b: 194 notes Pausanias's repurposing of the Pheretime material for his description of Antiope (9.17.6). My thanks to Emily Baragwanath on this point.

ACTS OF GOD 285

Sulla's death specifically to a crime at Athens: the murder of the suppliant Aristion in the sanctuary of Athena (1.20.5).[74] The Book 9 passage, however, although retelling Sulla's death, correlates his death generally with insane outrages against the Greek cities and their gods (τοιαῦτα ἔς τε Ἑλληνίδας πόλεις καὶ θεοὺς τοὺς Ἑλλήνων), and in the context of this *logos*, the death is linked narratologically to the theft of Athena's statue at Alalcomenae.[75] Moreover, observe that Pausanias introduces this passage with the mention of the "not great" (οὐ μεγάλη) size of the village, ostensibly to highlight Sulla's bad behavior not only in the more temptingly rich places such as Thebes but also in the relative backwaters—"even at Alalcomenae" (καὶ ἐν ταῖς Ἀλαλκομεναῖς). The passing detail helps Pausanias to frame his Solonian evocation of Sulla's fleeting good fortune (εὐτυχία ~ see Hdt. 1.32) within Herodotus's own interest in places both great and small.

Pausanias's reader may therefore collate the two Sulla passages under the Herodotean foci of divine retribution and the transitory nature of human happiness.[76] The great city of Athens was brought low at 1.20, just as the insignificant place of Alalcomenae is plundered here. Likewise, the good fortune of Sulla disappears, and lice "flower" on his body. This unique use of the verb ἀνθέω secures the link between the passage at 9.33 and that of Sulla's death at 1.20.[77] For in Book 1, in the generations after his death, Athens "flowered" again under Hadrian (Ἀθῆναι μὲν οὕτως ὑπὸ τοῦ πολέμου κακωθεῖσαι τοῦ Ῥωμαίων αὖθις Ἀδριανοῦ βασιλεύοντος ἤνθησαν, 1.20.7). As suggested earlier, the tone of Pausanias's text overall intimates the instability of this resurgence. In this second *logos* on Sulla's death, the Herodotean thoughtscape of fortune's cycle takes hold: "Once deprived of the goddess, the sanctuary at Alalcomenae was then neglected (ἠμελήθη). And in my day a further event contributed to the ruin of the temple, which was that a tall and strong ivy tree grew over the shrine. It shook loose the stones from their

---

[74] Cf. Arafat 1996: 104–5.

[75] On Sulla's impiety, see also Paus. 9.30.1; on the omens that preceded his attacks upon Greece, compare 9.6.2. Description of Sulla's "demented" (ἐκμανέντα) behavior recalls Cambyses and Cleomenes, noted by Frazer 1898 ad loc.: compare Pausanias's τοῦτον μὲν τοιαῦτα ἔς τε Ἑλληνίδας πόλεις καὶ θεοὺς τοὺς Ἑλλήνων ἐκμανέντα and Herodotus's comments on the madness of Cambyses: ταῦτα μὲν ἐς τοὺς οἰκηιοτάτους ὁ Καμβύσης ἐξεμάνη (3.33), ὁ μὲν δὴ τοιαῦτα πολλὰ ἐς Πέρσας τε καὶ τοὺς συμμάχους ἐξεμαίνετο (3.37).

[76] See Mikalson 2003: 150–51, 163–65, for the "Solonian cycle of fortune" (165) in Herodotus; compare Harrison 2009: 110 on "amoral" and "moral" explanations.

[77] Aside from Aeschylus's reference to the sea's "flowering with corpses" (*Ag.* 659), Pausanias's use of ἀνθέω is the only metaphorical use of the word to indicate something ugly or repulsive; LSJ s.v. ἀνθέω II.5.

286 HERODOTUS AND IMPERIAL GREEK LITERATURE

joints (διέλυσεν ἐκ τῶν ἁρμονιῶν) and scattered (διέσπα) them in different directions" (9.33.6–7).[78]

Cities Great and Small: The Case of Megalopolis

The typological pinnacle of this cyclical patterning occurs in Pausanias's treatment of the city of Megalopolis, in what is arguably one of the most Herodotean passages in the entire *Periegesis*.[79] In contrast to some other treatments of this passage, I want to stress that the baroque account of Megalopolis does not emerge as an exception to the otherwise supposedly plodding quality of Pausanias's work. Rather, in line with the patterns we have already traced, the Megalopolis passage represents an elaboration of the leitmotif of mutability that pervades Pausanias. The author presents Megalopolis as a universalizing archetype of the destiny that applies to any place. Indeed, as he pronounces early in his work, in his account of Corinth, even surpassing architectural feats are subject to oblivion: "There is a shrine to Athena that Epopeus dedicated with finer decoration than the other shrines of those days. But in time this also was fated to disappear from memory. The god with thunderbolts burned it up . . . " (2.11.1).[80] Pausanias repeatedly shows sensitivity to loss and fragmentation, and this reaches an acme in his account of Megalopolis.

Leading up to the passage, Pausanias provides a detailed catalogue (8.27) that assembles before the reader's eye, much like Herodotus's catalogue of Xerxes's forces (7.61–100), a remarkable array of names and data, whose careful tabulation renders all the more poignant the doom that overtakes them. The catalogue emphasizes the massive undertaking entailed in founding the Great City. While Pausanias had already mentioned in passing the seizure of Megalopolis by the Spartan Cleomenes (4.29.7), he now repeats mention of that fact (8.27.16) and thereby prepares his reader for his grandiloquent comments on the loss of Megalopolis in his description of the city (8.30.2–8.32.5), which becomes predominantly a

---

[78] <τὸ> ἐν ταῖς Ἀλαλκομεναῖς ἠμελήθη τὸ ἀπὸ τοῦδε ἅτε ἠρημωμένον τῆς θεοῦ. ἐγένετο δὲ καὶ ἄλλο ἐπ' ἐμοῦ τοιόνδε ἐς κατάλυσιν τοῦ ναοῦ· κισσός οἱ προσπεφυκὼς μέγας καὶ ἰσχυρὸς διέλυσεν ἐκ τῶν ἁρμονιῶν καὶ διέσπα τοὺς λίθους ἀπ' ἀλλήλων.

[79] The passage is a magnet for comment: Habicht 1985: 119–20; Hartog 2001: 140–44; Akujärvi 2005: 76–89; Jost 2007: 112–13; Hutton 2005b: 193; Ursin 2019: 159–61.

[80] ναός ἐστιν Ἀθηνᾶς, ὃν Ἐπωπεύς ποτε ἀνέθηκε μεγέθει καὶ κόσμῳ τοὺς τότε ὑπερβεβλημένον. ἔδει δὲ ἄρα χρόνῳ καὶ τοῦδε ἀφανισθῆναι τὴν μνήμην· κεραυνοῖς θεὸς αὐτὸν <κατέκαυσε> . . . .

description of ruins.[81] Narratologically, the tension in Pausanias's account of the Great City is thus steadily increased, only to have its full power climactically unleashed in the extended comment on its demise:

That Megalopolis, a city founded by the Arcadians with full fervent zeal, and a cynosure of great hope among the Greeks, has been deprived of all its beauty and ancient happiness, and in my time is largely a site of ruin— I am in no way astonished by this. I know that divinity is always at work on something novel, and that fortune is transforming all things, both strong and weak alike, things coming into being and things in abeyance, driving them on with forcible necessity according to her own caprice. The city of Mycenae, preeminent among the Greeks during the Trojan War, and the city of Nineveh, where once stood the kingly palace of the Assyrians, and Boeotian Thebes, at one time worthily regarded as outstanding within Greece, these are now places of utter desolation and ruin. The name "Thebes" applies to its acropolis alone and its few residents. As for ancient places distinguished by their wealth—Egyptian Thebes, Minyan Orchomenus, and Delos, the common market of Greece—they are now, in regard to prosperity, more in need of wealth's power than a private citizen of moderate means, while Delos in particular, except for people sent by the Athenians to guard the sanctuary, is devoid of Delians. In Babylon the Sanctuary of Bel remains, but of that Babylon that was the greatest city of its time under the sun's gaze, there is nothing but a wall, just as with Tiryns in the Argolid. Indeed, the god has made these places into nothing. Meanwhile, the city of Egyptian Alexandria and the Seleucid city on the Orontes, both founded only yesterday or the day before, have attained to their current size and prosperity because fortune favors them. But the following shows that the power of fortune is greater and more astonishing than can be judged by the disasters and good fortunes of cities. Not far by boat from Lemnos was once the island called Chryse, where people say Philoctetes had his misfortune with the water-snake. But the sea utterly overtook this island, and Chryse sank down and vanished under the deep.

---

[81] Porter 2001: 73 seems to ascribe Strabo's refusal (8.8.1, C388) to linger on the site of Megalopolis instead to Pausanias, remarking on his "unusual refusal to describe the site" of Megalopolis. In fact, Pausanias offers a highly detailed description of Megalopolis (8.30.2–8.32.5), building on the long catalogue (8.27) of cities that were abandoned in order to build the Great City. Examples of Megalopolis ruins: Temple of the Mother of Gods, of which only columns remain (8.30.4); lack of human figures in front of the temple, only pedestals where figures once stood (8.30.5).

288 HERODOTUS AND IMPERIAL GREEK LITERATURE

Another island called Hiera *** at this time. Such is the momentary and altogether unstable fortune of humans. (8.33.1–4)

εἰ δὲ ἡ Μεγάλη πόλις προθυμίᾳ τε τῇ πάσῃ συνοικισθεῖσα ὑπὸ Ἀρκάδων καὶ ἐπὶ μεγίσταις τῶν Ἑλλήνων ἐλπίσιν ἐς αὐτὴν κόσμον τὸν ἅπαντα καὶ εὐδαιμονίαν τὴν ἀρχαίαν ἀφῄρηται καὶ τὰ πολλά ἐστιν αὐτῆς ἐρείπια ἐφ᾽ ἡμῶν, θαῦμα οὐδὲν ἐποιησάμην, εἰδὼς τὸ δαιμόνιον νεώτερα ἀεί τινα ἐθέλον ἐργάζεσθαι, καὶ ὁμοίως τὰ πάντα τά τε ἐχυρὰ καὶ τὰ ἀσθενῆ καὶ τὰ γινόμενά τε καὶ ὁπόσα ἀπόλλυνται μεταβάλλουσαν τὴν τύχην, καὶ ὅπως ἂν αὐτῇ παριστῆται μετὰ ἰσχυρᾶς ἀνάγκης ἄγουσαν. Μυκῆναι μέν γε, τοῦ πρὸς Ἰλίῳ πολέμου τοῖς Ἕλλησιν ἡγησαμένη, καὶ Νῖνος, ἔνθα ἦν Ἀσσυρίοις βασίλεια, καὶ Βοιώτιαι Θῆβαι προστῆναι τοῦ Ἑλληνικοῦ ποτε ἀξιωθεῖσαι, αἱ μὲν ἠρήμωνται πανώλεθροι, τὸ δὲ ὄνομα τῶν Θηβῶν ἐς ἀκρόπολιν μόνην καὶ οἰκήτορας καταβέβηκεν οὐ πολλούς. τὰ δὲ ὑπερηρκότα πλούτῳ τὸ ἀρχαῖον, Θῆβαί τε αἱ Αἰγύπτιοι καὶ ὁ Μινύης Ὀρχομενὸς καὶ ἡ Δῆλος τὸ κοινὸν Ἑλλήνων ἐμπόριον, αἱ μὲν ἀνδρὸς ἰδιώτου μέσου δυνάμει χρημάτων καταδέουσιν ἐς εὐδαιμονίαν, ἡ Δῆλος δέ, ἀφελόντι τοὺς ἀφικνουμένους παρ᾽ Ἀθηναίων ἐς τοῦ ἱεροῦ τὴν φρουράν, Δηλίων γε ἕνεκα ἔρημός ἐστιν ἀνθρώπων. Βαβυλῶνος δὲ τοῦ μὲν Βήλου τὸ ἱερὸν λείπεται, Βαβυλῶνος δὲ ταύτης, ἥντινα εἶδε πόλεων τῶν τότε μεγίστην ἥλιος, οὐδὲν ἔτι ἦν εἰ μὴ τεῖχος, καθὰ καὶ Τίρυνθος τῆς ἐν τῇ Ἀργολίδι. ταῦτα μὲν δὴ ἐποίησεν ὁ δαίμων εἶναι τὸ μηδέν· ἡ δὲ Ἀλεξάνδρου πόλις ἐν Αἰγύπτῳ καὶ ἡ Σελεύκου παρὰ τῷ Ὀρόντῃ χθές τε ᾠκισμέναι καὶ πρῴην ἐς τοσοῦτο ἐπιδεδώκασι μεγέθους καὶ εὐδαιμονίας, ὅτι σφᾶς ἡ τύχη δεξιοῦται. ἐπιδείκνυται δὲ καὶ ἐν τῷδε ἔτι τὴν ἰσχὺν μείζονα καὶ θαύματος πλείονος ἢ κατὰ συμφορὰς καὶ εὐπραγίας πόλεων· Λήμνου γὰρ πλοῦν ἀπεῖχεν οὐ πολὺν Χρύση νῆσος, ἐν ᾗ καὶ τῷ Φιλοκτήτῃ γενέσθαι συμφορὰν ἐκ τοῦ ὕδρου φασί· ταύτην κατέλαβεν ὁ κλύδων πᾶσαν, καὶ κατέδυ τε ἡ Χρύση καὶ ἠφάνισται κατὰ τοῦ βυθοῦ. νῆσον δὲ ἄλλην καλουμένην Ἱερὰν * * * τόνδε οὐκ ἦν χρόνον. οὕτω μὲν τὰ ἀνθρώπινα πρόσκαιρά τε καὶ οὐδαμῶς ἐστιν ἐχυρά.

This is the *Periegesis*'s supreme aria of desolation, voiced in unmistakably Herodotean tones.[82] While Hartog stresses loss and ruin—what he calls the "one-way change" from greatness to nothingness—one should also recognize that Pausanias embeds his Megalopolis observations within a wider weave

---

[82] See Hartog 2001: 140–44, esp. 143; Hutton 2005b: 193–4.

ACTS OF GOD   289

of fortunes reversed, fortunes both good and bad.[83] This Pausanian oscillation preserves the possibility of renewal.[84] The fluctuation tracks with what Hutton has rightly noted as the passage's anchoring in a famous programmatic moment of the *Histories*.[85] The original Herodotean observation on cyclicality is notable, among other things, for its quality of abruptness:

> Now, this is what the Persians and the Phoenicians say. But I for my part am not about to state, concerning these things, that they happened this way or somehow in some other way. Rather, the one I myself know to have originated unjust acts against the Greeks, by indicating this man I shall advance into the forward part of my narrative, passing through small and great towns alike. For of the towns that used to be great long ago, many have become small, and the ones that were in my time great earlier used to be small. As someone who understands that human well-being in no way lingers in the same place, I shall make mention of both small and great alike. (Hdt. 1.5.3–4)

> ταῦτα μέν νυν Πέρσαι τε καὶ Φοίνικες λέγουσι. ἐγὼ δὲ περὶ μὲν τούτων οὐκ ἔρχομαι ἐρέων ὡς οὕτως ἢ ἄλλως κως ταῦτα ἐγένετο, τὸν δὲ οἶδα αὐτὸς πρῶτον ὑπάρξαντα ἀδίκων ἔργων ἐς τοὺς Ἕλληνας, τοῦτον σημήνας προβήσομαι ἐς τὸ πρόσω τοῦ λόγου, ὁμοίως σμικρὰ καὶ μεγάλα ἄστεα ἀνθρώπων ἐπεξιών. τὰ γὰρ τὸ πάλαι μεγάλα ἦν, τὰ πολλὰ αὐτῶν σμικρὰ γέγονε, τὰ δὲ ἐπ' ἐμεῦ ἦν μεγάλα, πρότερον ἦν σμικρά. τὴν ἀνθρωπηίην ὦν ἐπιστάμενος εὐδαιμονίην οὐδαμὰ ἐν τὠυτῷ μένουσαν ἐπιμνήσομαι ἀμφοτέρων ὁμοίως.

What motivates Herodotus's sudden change from a focus on an individual (τόν . . . τοῦτον) to larger collectivities of humans, moving to the "forward part" of his narrative and "passing through" small and great towns alike? The switch in stride from individual to collective forms part of the polemical distantiation from the accounts of the *logioi* that Herodotus brackets. It is not simply that others have cast about incorrectly for the cause (or blame).[86] It is that their entire heuristic is too limited: although Herodotus *seems* to share

---

[83] Hartog 2001: 144. Albeit in reference to a different Pausanian context, compare Hutton 2010: 442: "Just as the erotic stories Pausanias tells in Book VII hold out the hope that even a destructive ἔρως can ultimately confer blessings on those who suffer from it, the downfall brought about by the ἔρως of the Achaean leaders may yet be redeemed by the course of events."

[84] See also Pausanias 4.29.8–9, with later discussion here.

[85] Hutton 2005b: 193.

[86] On the interrelation of causality and blame in Herodotus, see Pelling 2019: 22–39.

290 HERODOTUS AND IMPERIAL GREEK LITERATURE

their interest in pinpointing an individual, his comment implies that a wider truth inheres in the broader perspective afforded by the fortunes of human collectivities. The accent indeed falls on *human* happiness—as in grouped, peopled happiness—and hence on the cities upon which Herodotus widens his inquiring lens. Indeed, Pausanias's phrase "utter desolation and ruin" (αἱ μὲν ἠρήμωνται πανώλεθροι) picks up on the "utter destruction" (πανωλεθρίη) Herodotus overtly ascribes to the work of divine vengeance at the city of Troy (2.120.5).[87] That Pausanias should root one of his work's most profound meditations in the concept of cities thus seems an unmistakable move both to ensconce his narrative within the Herodotean thoughtscape and to activate its original sweeping force: no one individual—for Pausanias no one Sulla, just as for Herodotus no one Io or Medea (1.1–2)—fully embodies the overriding vagaries of historical change, things coming into being and things moving into abeyance (τὰ γινόμενά τε καὶ ὁπόσα ἀπόλλυνται).[88] One must look to broader patterns of growth and decline.

In a work so self-consciously Herodotean, it matters that Pausanias teases out the lesson of vicissitude precisely in relation to a city whose very name encodes the Herodotean sense that greatness is feeble and that it inspires the envy of the gods.[89] Pausanias might have chosen any number of cities as an illustration of this principle, but in fact he chooses a city whose name makes his point all the more illustrative. Herodotus claims to have been concerned equally (ὁμοίως) with towns both small and great (σμικρὰ καὶ μεγάλα ἄστεα, 1.5.3). So although other sites of desecration and decay punctuate his work, Pausanias's choosing Megalopolis (ἡ μεγάλη πόλις) directly echoes the fundamental Herodotean concern with cities while also latching on to the onomastic power of the "Great City."[90] His use of εὐδαιμονία recalls the focal point not only from Herodotus 1.5 on the instability of human happiness but also from the discussion between Solon and Croesus (1.32.1), whose relevance to Pausanias we have elsewhere seen.[91] These echoes acquire further

---

[87] Compare Thucydides's recall (7.87.6) of Herodotus on the "utter destruction" (πανωλεθρίᾳ) of Athenian forces in Sicily; see Rood 2009: 171, with further bibliography.

[88] Compare Hdt. proem, τὰ γενόμενα ἐξ ἀνθρώπων.

[89] With Hdt. 1.5.3 and 1.32 compare Artabanus's discouragement of Xerxes's desired invasion of Greece (7.10): lightning strikes the biggest (μέγιστα) homes and trees (7.10.ε) because small things (σμικρά) do not provoke (κνίζει) the gods.

[90] Symbolism availed itself: compare Strabo's quotation (8.8.1, C388; repeated at 16.1.5, C738) of the acid remark, ascribed to an unknown poet, that "the Great City is now a Great Desert" (ἐρημία μεγάλη ᾿στὶν ἡ Μεγάλη πόλις).

[91] Σόλων μὲν δὴ **εὐδαιμονίης** δευτερεῖα ἔνεμε τούτοισι, Κροῖσος δὲ σπερχθεὶς εἶπε· Ὦ ξεῖνε Ἀθηναῖε, ἡ δ᾽ ἡμετέρη **εὐδαιμονίη**. Hutton 2005b: 193–94 also draws the connection to Hdt. 1.32.1 but with reference to divine jealousy rather than happiness.

ACTS OF GOD 291

resonance in the Pausanias passage, where the city of Megalopolis is figured in terms of human desire and hope (προθυμίᾳ τε τῇ πάσῃ . . . καὶ ἐπὶ μεγίσταις τῶν Ἑλλήνων ἐλπίσιν), and the fall of Megalopolis is thus squared with the pattern of human overreach against which the Solon–Croesus story constitutes a warning. Pausanias had professed his aim of accounting for all things Greek (πάντα ὁμοίως ἐπεξιόντα τὰ Ἑλληνικά, 1.26.4), but the Megalopolis passages shows Pausanias operating with a wide spectrum. The geographic range is supplemented by the temporal dimension: the unique (for Pausanias) use of the collocation χθές τε ᾠκισμέναι καὶ πρῴην recalls Herodotus's own single use of a variant of that phrase (πρῴην τε καὶ χθές, 2.53.1), in his discussion of the recent knowledge of the gods among Greeks, relative to the Egyptians.[92] If Herodotus 2.53.1 is making a bold claim about the relative novelty of the Greek pantheon, Pausanias's isolated use of the phrase enriches the Herodotean savor of his passage and reinforces the assertive breadth of his own observation, that the waxing and waning of cities according to fortune applies not simply to the cities "of old" (τὸ ἀρχαῖον) but also to relatively more recent places. The implications extend into the present and the future.

Pausanias's capacious reflection thus recalls Herodotus's global, cosmopolitan scope.[93] It projects a universalizing view, embracing not only Greek cities but also "barbarian" cities such as Nineveh and Babylon, and not only ancient cities but modern ones, too. These places the god has turned to nothing (ταῦτα μὲν δὴ ἐποίησεν ὁ δαίμων εἶναι τὸ μηδέν), giving ballast to Pausanias's own written memorial in the absence of physical remains. For Pausanias, nothing should prove astonishing (θαῦμα οὐδὲν ἐποιησάμην) about Megalopolis's demise. Herodotus had promised to write on the "great and wondrous deeds" (ἔργα μεγάλα τε καὶ θωμαστά) of mortals, but for Pausanias the very mortality of human cities should leave one unfazed.[94] Herodotus is evoked, but the sense of the marvelous is emptied out in this instance. Perhaps somewhat unexpectedly, the Herodotean breadth of the Pausanias passage is adduced as evidence for the *inappropriateness* of wonder. Decline is the way of the world.

---

[92] This phrase is common enough in Greek literature, but one should distinguish between literal uses (e.g., Thuc. 3.113.4; Plut. *De tranq. an.* 473E) and more figurative uses of understatement such as those of Herodotus and Pausanias; compare Pl., *Leges* 677d6; Dem., *Or.* 18.130.

[93] See Rood 2012: 126–27 on cosmic space in Herodotus.

[94] To be sure, Herodotean wondering can issue from a sense of *un*predictability; Pelling 2019: 49–50. On wonder, see my chapter 8.

292 HERODOTUS AND IMPERIAL GREEK LITERATURE

For anyone reading Pausanias in long stretches, then, the Megalopolis passage, however florid, grows naturally within the melancholy field of his thought. At the same time, as Hutton has commented, in Arcadia (Book 8), Pausanias "manifests his new level of insight in a series of declarations on matters religious, cultural, and political that are largely unparalleled elsewhere in the text."[95] This is confirmed by its final section, where Pausanias again assumes the Herodotean tenor: "But the following shows that the power of fortune is greater and more astonishing than can be judged by the disasters and good fortunes of cities" (ἐπιδείκνυται δὲ καὶ ἐν τῷδε ἔτι τὴν ἰσχὺν μείζονα καὶ θαύματος πλείονος ἢ κατὰ συμφορὰς καὶ εὐπραγίας πόλεων, 8.33.4). If Herodotus's universal image of human fluctuation resides in the growth and decline of cities, Pausanias's universalism one-ups this by turning to the even more unpredictable realm of nature. He adduces the example of Chryse: "The sea utterly overtook it, and Chryse sank down and vanished under the deep" (ταύτην κατέλαβεν ὁ κλύδων πᾶσαν, καὶ κατέδυ τε ἡ Χρύση καὶ ἠφάνισται κατὰ τοῦ βυθοῦ).[96] The turn to this exemplum is an inward textual turn, on the one hand, as readers may recall Pausanias's story of Helike in Book 7. Even as Pausanias draws intertextual connections with Herodotus, and to the intratextual patterns within the *Histories*, he also reveals the intratextual patterning of his own work. Despite losing the catalogue of other possible examples (including Hiera) in transmission, readers may sense that Pausanias at 8.33 merely collates that which is consistent about his work.[97] As Pausanias writes in his prior book's account of Achaea, after the defeat by the Romans at Corinth, "Greece fell thoroughly at that time into a state of total weakness, already having suffered indignity bit by bit and destruction from the beginning at the hands of the god" (ἐς ἅπαν δὲ ἀσθενείας τότε μάλιστα κατῆλθεν ἡ Ἑλλάς, λυμανθεῖσα κατὰ μέρη καὶ διαπορθηθεῖσα ἐξ ἀρχῆς ὑπὸ τοῦ δαίμονος, 7.17.1). The Great City exemplifies aspects of Herodotean fluctuation, but it also provokes Pausanias to further thought on the *absolute* disappearance of places that, unlike the Great City, leave no trace at all, no visible ruin. Helike and Chryse allow Pausanias to contribute to the grammar of the Herodotean thoughtscape, where the visible world can register as an index

---

[95] Hutton 2010: 444. See also Pirenne-Delforge 2008: 337–41.

[96] Although there is a lexical switch in 8.33 from ὁ δαίμων and ἡ τύχη, it is not clear that Pausanias means to distinguish their roles: Chryse is yet another city brought low, just like those cited earlier in the passage.

[97] As Levi (1971: 455 n. 242) notes, "All these examples are mentioned again elsewhere by Pausanias, though never in such a torrent."

of loss.[98] For Pausanias, the visible world of ruins is hardly a site for wonder. Rather, the greater wonder (θαύματος πλείονος) lies in the fact that certain places have so thoroughly disappeared as to leave no trace at all.[99]

And yet it is not completely clear, as I have already suggested in passing, that Pausanias subscribes to the irreversible downward slope of human fortune. Just as he had nodded to the resurgence of Athens's fortunes, so does he offer some clues that Megalopolis need not entirely signify futility. Much earlier in his work, Pausanias gives at least one hint to a belief that human fortunes are not destined always for bad ends:

> Some Arcadians who were trapped there were killed in the destruction, but Philopoimen, the son of Kraugis, and the people who fled with him (over two-thirds of the Megalopolites were refugees with him) were welcomed by the Messenians. . . . **There is something endemic, surely, in human affairs that turns matters completely around**, given that the god enabled the Messenians to save the Arcadians in turn and, even more unlikely, to capture Sparta. (4.29.8–9)

> τῶν δὲ οἱ καταληφθέντες οἱ μὲν ἀπώλοντο ὑπὸ τὴν ἅλωσιν, Φιλοποίμενα δὲ τὸν Κραύγιδος καὶ ὅσοι μετὰ Φιλοποίμενος ἀπεχώρησαν—γενέσθαι δὲ τῶν Μεγαλοπολιτῶν τὸ διαφυγὸν καὶ ὑπὲρ τὰς δύο μοίρας λέγουσι—τούτους ὑπεδέξαντο οἱ Μεσσήνιοι. . . . **πέφυκε δὲ ἄρα ὡς ἐπίπαν μεταπίπτειν τὰ ἀνθρώπινα**, εἰ δὴ Μεσσηνίοις Ἀρκάδας τε ἀντισῶσαι καὶ τὸ ἀδοκητότερον ἔτι ἑλεῖν Σπάρτην ὁ δαίμων ἔδωκεν.

On the far side of entropy resides the possibility that human affairs can once again be reversed and that all against expectation the relatively weak Messenians may not only take in the Arcadians but also take on Sparta. While the Megalopolis passage pays homage to Herodotus, Pausanias's text finds ways to resist the sense of inevitability that such intertextuality might imply. Room exists in the intertextual cartography for Pausanias's own thoughtscape.

---

[98] See Bassi 2014 (esp. at 184) on the chronological meeting point of an object's appearance in Herodotus's narrative (an object that itself bespeaks a temporality that precedes Herodotus's own encounter with it) and Herodotus's own time-marked encounter.

[99] In the sense that these cities have vanished and leave virtually nothing behind, the "ruins" of Helike and Chryse represent an intensification of Pausanias's more general interest in visible ruins; see Ursin 2019: 159 and his n. 335 for examples.

294 HERODOTUS AND IMPERIAL GREEK LITERATURE

What many have identified as the religious element of Pausanias's text cannot be disconnected from his vivification of Herodotus. Perhaps more than any potential historiographic influence, Herodotus's work is replete with attention to matters divine, and as we have seen, Pausanias shares with the *Histories* a quality of narratorial pronouncement on such matters. This is not to say that Pausanias lacks Thucydidean qualities, including at the level of syntax.[100] But, as I have argued, Pausanias's overt attention to divinity lands him clearly in the imitative realm of Herodotus. Pausanias puts us in mind of Herodotus not only because of his statements of autopsy and adjudication between possibilities or because his language picks up on Herodotean patterns, but also because, like the Halicarnassian's, his own narrative is infused with a sense that the divine intersects with human history and that its workings can be pondered in narrative.

We have seen that Pausanias consistently activates the Herodotean thoughtscape around divine justice, shifts in fortune, and the cycle of urban rise and decline. It remains to posit why we should care. I would suggest that one reason has to do with what we might call the Pausanian naive. It is no secret that Pausanias has attracted an army of detractors, who have variously dismissed him as unreliable, unimaginative, or simply boring.[101] Yet in a certain sense, it is hard to disentangle criticism of Pausanias from certain presentist expectations: his failure to measure up to latter-day standards of archaeological specificity; his failure to surmount postclassical ideas of originality; or, in this case, his potentially simplistic recourse to divinity. How could a writer so many centuries after Herodotus return to so "archaic" an understanding of human affairs? The verdict of Pausanias's seeming naivete—his "conventional" revivification of a hoary worldview—is perhaps that of a readership that has accepted a certain kind of (Thucydidean) supersessionism and for whom Pausanias registers as a man out of time. His tendency toward tradition has doomed him not necessarily because the effects of his conventionality have been weighed in context and found wanting, but more likely because Pausanias's conventions are not those of many later generations who no longer speak of divine wrath in history. Pausanias's reception of Herodotus in this regard may thus predetermine reception of Pausanias.

---

[100] See Strid 1976: 78, 99. See, however, Hutton 2005b: 219–20 on Pausanias's Thucydidean echoes as paling in comparison with his Herodoteanism.
[101] See Habicht 1985: 161 with n. 82, 165–75.

ACTS OF GOD   295

A further potential ramification of Pausanias's Herodotean theodicy has to do with the monitory resonances of both his and Herodotus's works. That Pausanias's capacity for solemn pronouncement about divine justice should contribute to the moral *ambiguity* of his text is perhaps unsurprising, since the potential significations of his model Herodotus's text depend in part on the obscure threat of cyclicality: not so much the question of whether the past—with its bad actors, blind kings, and moments of occasional justice— will repeat itself as the question of *when*.[102] Owing to their mutual concern with the actions of the divine in human history, both Herodotus and Pausanias suggest possibilities for how the past they (re)present becomes a means for interpreting the present and the future.[103] It is not just that the religious aspects of the Herodotean worldview allow Pausanias to connect his work to the past. They also, by dint of their ambiguity, create uncertainty about what is to come: when will divine retribution descend, and upon whom? Asseveration about the divine offers an oblique mode of commenting without commenting, of warning without specificity, about how things are now and how they may at some point turn out. Pausanias implies continuity with the past without ever needing to assert clearly the justice or injustice of Roman rule. To invoke the presence of the divine, even in instances of strong narratorial assertion, is also to invoke that which is apophatic and beyond definitive assertion.

---

[102] See Harrison 2009: 105–6; see also 112–14 on the ambiguity of "descriptive" moral observation as against "prescriptive" moralizing.

[103] Scholars have contended—for both Herodotus and Pausanias—that each writer does or does not engage his present political circumstances in pointed or meaningful ways. On Herodotus, see, e.g., Raaflaub 1987; Forsdyke 2006; Irwin 2009; more skeptically, Pelling 2011. On Pausanias, see, e.g., Habicht 1985: 117–21; Arafat 1996; Akujärvi 2005: 265–95; Hutton 2008; and Hutton 2010: 436– 37. For both authors, arguments about political suggestiveness hinge on a small number of highly contested passages; for Herodotus, these include 5.78, 5.97, 6.98, 6.131, 9.73, 9.120–21 and, to a lesser extent, the exchange between Solon and Croesus at 1.29–32 (with Moles 1996); for Pausanias, some of the principal passages, among others, include 1.3.2, 1.20.7, 7.17.1–3 (on which see Hutton 2010: 441), 9.7.5–6, 10.7.1, and, above all, 8.27.1, on which see Hutton 2008 passim, with 622 n. 1 and 623 n. 6, with further bibliography.

8

Pausanias in Wonderland

In chapter 7, we saw how Pausanias's activation of Herodotean ideas of divinity and fortune empowers his narrative to speak commandingly, if also ambiguously. There my focus fell on an apparently conventional, traditionalizing element of Pausanias's text, albeit one that does not necessarily blunt (and indeed may aid) his text's potential suggestiveness for the present and the future. In this chapter, I turn to certain ways in which Pausanias both plays to and reworks elements of Herodotus in further enacting a kinetic reception, one that both receives and transforms. For alongside Pausanias's orientation toward the past, one finds certain efforts at innovation and renewal, using Herodotus both as a mirror and as a point for self-separation. In the first part of this chapter, I analyze aspects of Pausanias's articulation of space— physical, geographic, and textual—as he traces an intellectual journey reflective of Herodotus but also expressive of certain differences. In the second half, we shall see how Pausanias's interest in vivifying the Greek landscape involves an appropriation of the Herodotean rhetoric of wonder. Pausanias's origin in Asia Minor (likely Lydia, specifically Magnesia ad Sipylum), which Karim Arafat has called "arguably the most significant fact for understanding him and his work," helps to forge analogy with Herodotus, as Pausanias surveys Greece in the mode of traveling narrator.[1] Writing in some sense as "un *xénos* venu d'ailleurs," in the phrasing of Christian Jacob, Pausanias frames the Greek mainland as a source of marvel; he (re)orients from his own Lydian perspective the vector of interest that Herodotus had more typically trained on matters non-Greek, in the process vivifying Greece's splendor through the voice of the past.[2]

---

[1] Arafat 1996: 8 (contra Elsner 1992: 7, 9, on 9.36.5). See Jones 2004: 15–18 on Pausanias's Lydian background, part of his contention that Imperial literature often reveals "a much more complex web of attachments and loyalties than can be attributed to 'Greekness' or 'Hellenicity'" (20). Cf. Frateantonio 2009: 157–60 and further Gurlitt 1890: 56–57; Habicht 1985: 13–17; Hutton 2005b: 9–10.

[2] Jacob 1980–81: 44.

Herodotus and Imperial Greek Literature. N. Bryant Kirkland, Oxford University Press. © Oxford University Press 2022.
DOI: 10.1093/oso/9780197583517.003.0009

Space between Herodotus and Pausanias

The term *psychogeography* appeared in the late twentieth century and is usually imbued with radical political associations admittedly alien to the study of two ancient authors. Consistently, however, the term has referred to the paired activities of urban walking and investigative writing, and, among its more recent practitioners, psychogeography has been closely tied to antiquarian and occult interests.[3] As Merlin Coverley notes, the mode of writing is characterized by an "obsession with the occult . . . allied to an antiquarianism that views the present through the prism of the past and which lends itself to psychogeographical research that increasingly contrasts a horizontal movement across the topography of the city with a vertical descent through its past."[4]

The relation of horizontal movement and vertical historicization marks a fundamental axis of meaning for both Herodotus and Pausanias.[5] Both narratives articulate signification between visible surfaces (monuments, buildings, statues) and the vertical depths of time that they hold, producing what Susan Stewart has referred to in a different context as "temporal poignancy," by which time's invisible depth is juxtaposed with the topographic motion of the narrator.[6] Already in antiquity, as noted in chapter 1, the author of *On the Sublime* recognized Herodotus's own journeying motion as an alluring feature of narrative, one by which he renders *akoê* visible: "Do you see, reader, how when he carries your spirit with him he leads you across places and makes hearing into sight?" (ὁρᾷς, ὦ ἑταῖρε, ὡς παραλαβών σου τὴν ψυχὴν διὰ τῶν τόπων ἄγει τὴν ἀκοὴν ὄψιν ποιῶν; *Subl.* 26.2). Indeed, Longinus accentuates what some have later come to recognize as the distinctive manner in which Herodotus's text often functions as a kind of hodology, a path of *logos* that metaphorically mirrors some of the actual journeying undertaken by the Halicarnassian. In her reading of Herodotean space, for

---

[3] Coverley 2006: 14.

[4] Coverley 2006: 14.

[5] The bibliography on space in Herodotus is ample, but see esp. Rood 2012; Clarke 2018: 21–26, offering a critical survey. On space in Pausanias, see Akujärvi 2012a; Akujärvi 2012b: 42–47. The radiation of narrative as triggered by a particular locale can move both backward in time and outward in space; see Akujärvi 2005: 181–205; Akujärvi 2012a: 238–40. Compare Whitmarsh 2015 (esp. 51–56) on the "mnemological" space of Pausanias's text. See also Pretzler 2007b: 57–72.

[6] See Stewart 2020: 151, discussing imagery of ruins in Renaissance painting and printmaking. Compare Bassi 2016: 106–43, citing Alois Riegl's (1982 [1903]) distinction between a work's "historical value" in a particular time and place and its "age value" as perceived by the later viewer (Bassi 2016: 108–9).

298 HERODOTUS AND IMPERIAL GREEK LITERATURE

instance, Alex Purves argues that Herodotus eschews internal characters' attempts to render space cartographic (the bird's-eye perspective) and instead emphasizes the authoritativeness of his own hodological, road-based movement.[7] Along similar lines, Emily Greenwood has written that "As readers of the *Histories* we retrace Herodotus' steps (ἐπεξιών, 1.5.3)—both his physical steps, which lie on the other side of the text and are irretrievable to us, and the diegetic steps and conceptual moves of his narrative, which structure the text as we have it."[8] Herodotus's itinerant text furnishes an impression of horizontal movement based in some instances on the narrator's actual journeys or those of various actors.[9] Yet, as suggested by the spatio-temporal axis of psychogeography, these physical and diegetic steps occur in coordination with vertical knowledge, "extensive travels informed by a historical perspective."[10]

The spatiotemporal framework has application to Pausanias, too, as Akujärvi has observed:

> [T]he organisation of the *Periegesis* is not chronological but spatial or topographical. This arrangement along a spatial axis allows for the juxtaposition of events from disparate periods and for a discontinuous and anachronic exploration of the Greek past and present through its monuments and remains.[11]

The *Periegesis* fashions a cognitive space neither strictly hodological nor chronologically predictable; historical detail is tied to space but is also shaped by the idiosyncrasies of Pausanias's focused memorialization. The psychogeography that Pausanias creates is thus tied to the particulars of

---

[7] See Purves 2010: 118–58, esp. 145–47, citing the terminology of Pietro Janni.

[8] Greenwood 2018: 164; see also 167: "Herodotus has to have seen or studied multiple cities in order to make this claim [i.e., about their rise and fall, Hdt. 1.5] and this is reflected in the figuration of the narrative as a physical journey, including the reference to the 'interior' of his *logos* (*to proso*) and the fact that he will go through (*epexion*) small and great cities alike." The metaphor of the "path of *logos*" is recurrent in Herodotus and creates a parallel between the movement of the text and that of the traveling author; see, e.g., Hdt. 1.95.1, 1.117.2 ("the road of lies"), 2.20.1. Compare Paus. 1.26.4 (δεῖ δέ με ἀφικέσθαι τοῦ λόγου **πρόσω**, πάντα ὁμοίως **ἐπεξιόντα** τὰ Ἑλληνικά), with later discussion here.

[9] See Greenwood 2018: 167: "The geographical programme of Herodotus' work is inseparable from the forward-moving historical trajectory which charts the expanding hegemony of the Persian Empire and, in the latter books, its surprising set-backs at the hands of an ill-knit coalition of small Greek states."

[10] Greenwood 2018: 167.

[11] Akujärvi 2012a: 238. See Habicht 1985: 19–20 on the "hub-and-spoke" model at work in the *Periegesis*, by which Pausanias begins at the center of a district and moves outward and back in different directions from that initial center, until he replaces that center with a new center.

PAUSANIAS IN WONDERLAND   299

place but also participates in a more ethereal activation of the literary past by means of intertext, allusion, and stylization.[12] Herodotus functions as both an ever-present scrim and a pliant force that Pausanias can wield. Pausanias's recall partakes of both that narrator's authoritative hodology *and* a carto-graphic mode of bird's-eye geography.[13] While a sense of motion is integral to his work, Pausanias often gives readers the impression of a snapshot, one that pedestals the cartographic authority of his perspective, albeit seemingly grounded in the road-based viewpoint of anyone wandering through Greece, seeing the things Pausanias sees.[14] In what follows, I consider Pausanias's re-ception of Herodotus with attention to three phenomena: Pausanias's rend-ering of physical space into text; his subtle articulation of the space *between* texts, or the points of difference between himself and the past; and, tracing but in some sense also repositioning a major Herodotean vertebra, Pausanias's ex-pression of the wondrous, a quality that seems to edge toward sublimity.

Approaching from the Herodotean Angle

The *Periegesis* is remarkable for its apparent lack of proem, in which the nar-rator might have named himself or explicitly stated the plan of his work.[15] Pausanias's downplaying of himself ab initio perhaps has the effect of con-centrating our focus away from the author and onto the topic at hand.[16] Still, Pausanias's opening provokes questions of literary filiation and perspective, including the physical and cultural vantages from which he sees Greece:

> On the Greek mainland toward the Cyclades and the Aegean Sea the cape
> of Sunium projects forth from the Attic land. When you sail around the
> headland there are a harbor and a temple to Athena at Sunium on the top
> of the cape. If you sail on farther there is Laurium, where the Athenians

[12] See Pretzler 2004 on the ways in which Pausanias's narrative of "travel into text" resists the frag-mentation and decay that it often documents. Cf. Whitmarsh 2010b: 14–15 on local knowledge in Pausanias.

[13] See Rood 2012: 132–35 (esp. 134–35), arguing (pace Purves 2010: 132–38, 144–50) that Herodotus is not hostile to the cartographic or panoramic viewpoint. On Pausanias's invocations of Herodotean authority, see Elsner 2001b: 7–8; Hutton 2005b: 190–93; Pretzler 2007b: 44–56.

[14] On this point, see also Pretzler 2007b: 70.

[15] Some have wondered whether a preface is missing from the start of Pausanias's work: see Gurlitt 1890: 2–3; Habicht 1985: 9, 18; Pritchett 1999: 162–67; Bowie 2001: 27–28. See also Hogan 2017: 188 on Pausanias 1.39.3: "From the start my *logos* has chosen from the multitude of things those that are worthy to record" (ἀπέκρινε δὲ ἀπὸ τῶν πολλῶν ἐξ ἀρχῆς ὁ λόγος μοι τὰ ἐς συγγραφὴν ἀνήκοντα).

[16] On Pausanias's modest profile, see Habicht 1985: 139–40. Cf. Jones 2001: 33.

300 HERODOTUS AND IMPERIAL GREEK LITERATURE

once had silver mines, and an island of no great size, uninhabited, called the Island of Patroclus. It is so named because a fortification and palisade were constructed on it by Patroclus, the admiral in charge of the Egyptian fighters dispatched by Ptolemy, son of Ptolemy, son of Lagus, to aid the Athenians when Antigonus, son of Demetrius, was plundering their land, which he had invaded with an army and was at the same time blockading at sea with ships. (1.1.1)

τῆς ἠπείρου τῆς Ἑλληνικῆς κατὰ νήσους τὰς Κυκλάδας καὶ πέλαγος τὸ Αἰγαῖον ἄκρα Σούνιον πρόκειται γῆς τῆς Ἀττικῆς· καὶ λιμήν τε παραπλεύσαντι τὴν ἄκραν ἐστὶ καὶ ναὸς Ἀθηνᾶς Σουνιάδος ἐπὶ κορυφῇ τῆς ἄκρας. πλέοντι δὲ ἐς τὸ πρόσω Λαύριόν τέ ἐστιν, ἔνθα ποτὲ Ἀθηναίοις ἦν ἀργύρου μέταλλα, καὶ νῆσος ἔρημος οὐ μεγάλη Πατρόκλου καλουμένη· τεῖχος γὰρ ᾠκοδομήσατο ἐν αὐτῇ καὶ χάρακα ἐβάλετο Πάτροκλος, ὃς τριήρεσιν ὑπέπλει ναύαρχος Αἰγυπτίαις, ἃς Πτολεμαῖος ὁ <Πτολεμαίου> τοῦ Λάγου τιμωρεῖν ἔστειλεν Ἀθηναίοις, ὅτε σφίσιν Ἀντίγονος ὁ Δημητρίου στρατιᾷ τε αὐτὸς ἐσβεβληκὼς ἔφθειρε τὴν χώραν καὶ ναυσὶν ἅμα ἐκ θαλάσσης κατεῖργεν.

This opening is perhaps less abrupt than it first appears.[17] After all, Pausanias's project will cover the Greek mainland, moving in a roughly counterclockwise fashion from Attica to Corinth, Corinth to Laconia, and so forth;[18] the initial genitive phrase "on the Greek mainland" thus neatly encinctures the subject of the *Periegesis*. The opening also exhibits shifts in perspective that programmatically prefigure other instances in which Pausanias switches point of view, in ways that establish his authoritative ability to see both hodologically and from a cartographic, bird's-eye vantage.[19] In this instance, readers might take the first line to convey a point of view oriented outward toward (κατά) the Cyclades and the Aegean, as though the speaker were situated on the promontory at Sunium as it projects forth. But the viewpoint

[17] See Hutton 2005b: 175 for the view that the opening, in fact, "broadcasts the author's intentions in a manner that is subtly assertive" and 176–77 for the observation that the opening announces certain Herodotean affinities, even as it moves away from outright imitation, toward a work "not . . . so easily categorized" (176).

[18] See Pretzler 2007b: 5, figure 3.

[19] See Hawes 2016: 335–36 for astute observations about the difficult-to-translate shifts in verbal person and 337 for a comparison to Herodotus 2.29–31. See also Akujärvi 2012a: 250: "Here one of the points of vagueness of the *Periegesis* becomes evident: the direction of the movement is not specified." On Pausanias's different roles as embedded traveling persona and "ego" who discusses his text, see Akujärvi 2005, esp. 34–64, 131–78.

PAUSANIAS IN WONDERLAND   301

jumps to a perspective at sea, for one sailing around (παραπλεύσαντι) the headland, looking upward toward the top of the cape (ἐπὶ κορυφῇ τῆς ἄκρας) and the Temple of Athena at Sunium, before moving again toward Laurium and the Island of Patroclus. Inasmuch as Laurium does not lie on the southwest coast along which the traveler appears to sail, its mention represents a rupture from the implied movement of the narrative.[20] For many readers, Laurium's invocation will spark thought of Themistocles's famous command in Herodotus to repurpose silver wealth for building a navy, which would become integral to the Greek repulse of Persia.[21] That invasion seems itself typologically adumbrated in Pausanias's successive mention of Antigonus's (successful) destruction and naval blockade of Athens. In a few lines, then, Pausanias establishes his narrative's ability to move cartographically and non-contiguously and to juxtapose historical references carrying potentially different tonal resonances (i.e., Themistocles's successful naval operation juxtaposed to the Athenian destruction by Antigonus).

As Peter Levi once noted in passing, the initial phrasing of Pausanias's first sentence recalls phrasing from *Histories* 4.99, a geographic excursus within Herodotus's wider account of Darius's campaign in Scythia: τῆς ἠπείρου τῆς Ἑλληνικῆς κατὰ νήσους τὰς Κυκλάδας καὶ πέλαγος τὸ Αἰγαῖον ἄκρα Σούνιον πρόκειται γῆς τῆς Ἀττικῆς (Paus. 1.1.1) ~ τῆς δὲ Σκυθικῆς γῆς ἡ Θρηίκη τὸ ἐς θάλασσαν πρόκειται (Hdt. 4.99.1).[22] Although the Herodotus line may seem a peculiar or only minor intertextual launching point for Pausanias's work, it appropriately inaugurates a text that will become marked by steady recall of Herodotean phraseology.[23] Moreover, a closer look at *Histories* 4.99 reveals further connections with *Periegesis* 1.1.1, beyond phraseology, that may indicate something about Pausanias's conception of his own authorial role and the perspective he will bring to his description of Greece:

> Thrace projects farther into the sea than the Scythian land. Where a gulf forms in Thrace, there Scythia begins and the Ister issues out, with its

---

[20] See Levi 1971: Vol. 1, 9 n. 2: Laurium lies northeast of Sunium, "but Pausanias is certainly sailing west."

[21] Hdt. 7.144.

[22] Levi 1977: 179: "Ove Strid misses the formal origins of the very odd first sentence of Pausanias in Herodotus (4.99)." See also Asheri, Lloyd, and Corcella 2007 ad loc. 4.99.1 for the echo. See Strid 1976: 78–79 on Pausanias's prolific use of the noun-article-attributive arrangement, which he identifies as Herodotean (as in χερσονήσου τῆς τρηχέης καλεομένης, Hdt. 4.99.3). Pausanias's first chapter contains three instances of the arrangement (noted by Hutton 2005b: 176). My thanks to Ewen Bowie on this point.

[23] See Strid 1976: 99–103, with later discussion here, on Pausanias's language.

302   HERODOTUS AND IMPERIAL GREEK LITERATURE

mouth facing southeast. Starting from the Ister, I am going to indicate the coastline of Scythia itself and its size. Ancient Scythia starts from the Ister, facing toward the south and the south wind, as far as the city called Carcinitis. From here the land going along the same sea is hilly and projects into the Pontus, and the Tauric people inhabit it up to what is called the Rough Peninsula, which stretches to the sea toward the east. For there are two parts of Scythia's boundaries that reach a sea, the part to the south and to the east, just like Attica. The Tauri inhabit a part of Scythia similar to Attica, as if some other people, and not the Athenians, were to inhabit the heights of Sunium from Thoricus to the deme of Anaphlystus (if Sunium reached farther into the sea). I speak, of course, comparing small things with great. Such is the Tauric land. But for anyone who has not sailed along these places in Attica, I will clarify in a different way: it is as if in Iapygia some people other than the Iapygians were to be isolated off and inhabit the promontory from Brundisium harbor to Tarentum. I mention these two lands, but there are many others of a similar sort that Tauris resembles. (Hdt. 4.99)

τῆς δὲ Σκυθικῆς γῆς ἡ Θρηίκη τὸ ἐς θάλασσαν πρόκειται. κόλπου δὲ ἀγομένου τῆς γῆς ταύτης ἡ Σκυθική τε ἐκδέκεται καὶ ὁ Ἴστρος ἐκδιδοῖ ἐς αὐτόν, πρὸς εὖρον ἄνεμον τὸ στόμα τετραμμένος. τὸ δὲ ἀπὸ Ἴστρου ἔρχομαι σημανέων τὸ πρὸς θάλασσαν αὐτῆς τῆς Σκυθικῆς χώρης ἐς μέτρησιν. ἀπὸ Ἴστρου αὕτη ἤδη <ἡ> ἀρχαίη Σκυθίη ἐστί, πρὸς μεσαμβρίην τε καὶ νότον ἄνεμον κειμένη, μέχρι πόλιος Καρκινίτιδος καλεομένης. τὸ δὲ ἀπὸ ταύτης τὴν μὲν ἐπὶ θάλασσαν τὴν αὐτὴν φέρουσαν, ἐοῦσαν ὀρεινήν τε χώρην καὶ προκειμένην τὸ ἐς Πόντον, νέμεται τὸ Ταυρικὸν ἔθνος μέχρι χερσονήσου τῆς τρηχέης καλεομένης· αὕτη δὲ ἐς θάλασσαν τὴν πρὸς ἀπηλιώτην ἄνεμον κατήκει. ἔστι γὰρ τῆς Σκυθικῆς τὰ δύο μέρεα τῶν οὔρων ἐς θάλασσαν φέροντα, τήν τε πρὸς μεσαμβρίην καὶ τὴν πρὸς τὴν ἠῶ, κατά περ τῆς Ἀττικῆς χώρης· καὶ παραπλήσια ταύτῃ καὶ οἱ Ταῦροι νέμονται τῆς Σκυθικῆς, ὡς εἰ τῆς Ἀττικῆς ἄλλο ἔθνος καὶ μὴ Ἀθηναῖοι νεμοίατο τὸν γουνὸν τὸν Σουνιακόν, μᾶλλον ἐς τὸν πόντον {τὴν ἄκρην} ἀνέχοντα, τὸν ἀπὸ Θορικοῦ μέχρι Ἀναφλύστου δήμου. λέγω δὲ ὡς εἶναι ταῦτα σμικρὰ μεγάλοισι συμβαλεῖν. τοιοῦτον ἡ Ταυρική ἐστι. ὃς δὲ τῆς Ἀττικῆς ταῦτα μὴ παραπέπλωκε, ἐγὼ δὲ ἄλλως δηλώσω· ὡς εἰ τῆς Ἰηπυγίης ἄλλο ἔθνος καὶ μὴ Ἰήπυγες ἀρξάμενοι ἐκ Βρεντεσίου λιμένος ἀποταμοίατο μέχρι Τάραντος καὶ νεμοίατο τὴν ἄκρην. δύο δὲ λέγων ταῦτα πολλὰ ἔχω παρόμοια τοῖσι ἄλλοισι οἶκε ἡ Ταυρική.

PAUSANIAS IN WONDERLAND   303

In evoking this geographic digression from the *Histories*, Pausanias allusively supplements his exordium's angle of approach. Like Herodotus, who
indicates or outlines (σημανέων) Scythia, Pausanias figures his narrator as
something of a mobile outsider, homing in on Attica from the sea, much as
Herodotus's narrative treks along the coastline (τὸ πρὸς θάλασσαν), from
Thrace into less familiar foreign territory.[24] But Herodotus also moves by
analogy (κατά περ), from Scythia to Attica, then again to southern Italy. The
Herodotean hypotheticals (ὡς εἰ . . . ὡς εἰ), "comparing small things with
great," afford different audiences with different levels of knowledge the opportunity to visualize Tauris, first by comparing with Sunium, then a specific section of the Iapygian promontory, while also displaying a cartographic
sweep beyond any particular place where his work happens to be narratively
situated (in this case, Scythia).

Herodotus's alternative comparison with Italy helps to show why
Pausanias's recall extends even beyond the two passages' obvious overlapping details of content, such as their common references to the maritime
perspective (παραπλεύσαντι τὴν ἄκραν ~ παραπέπλωκε) or indeed the coincidence of Sunium in both. For as Katherine Clarke notes, while granting
that Herodotus's readers may be no more familiar with the Italian peninsula
than with Attica, Herodotus's reference to Iapygia may "reflect[] his own
links to southern Italy, where he was a resident of the Athenian colony at
Thurii from 444 BC."[25] Herodotus, that is, speaks from and to his own situated perspective (while also demonstrating, as Clarke states, his expert
knowledge). In such a passage, then, Herodotus speaks both hodologically
and cartographically—even if the cartographic jump to Italy encompasses
a biographical (and thus necessarily hodological) detail from Herodotus's
own movement. As we shall see, Pausanias's own occasional tendency to contextualize information about the Greek mainland by comparative reference
to his native Asia Minor replicates something of the Herodotean narratorial gestures at *Histories* 4.99 and elsewhere.[26] Offering his audience different
vantages, Pausanias not only articulates his cartographic authority but also
subtly reminds readers of his viewpoint as a figure apart, not from the land
his narrative primarily describes.[27]

---

[24] Asheri, Lloyd, and Corcella 2007 ad loc. 4.99.2 note that Herodotus's description "follow[s] the
course of an actual *periplus*, from west to east." See Rood 2012: 135.

[25] Clarke 2018: 76.

[26] See also Hdt. 2.10, 2.33, with Lloyd 1975: 164–65.

[27] See, e.g., Paus. 1.21.3 (with later discussion here), 1.24.8, 2.22.3, 3.22.4, 5.13.7, 5.27.5–6, 6.22.1,
7.24.13, 7.27.12, 8.2.7, 8.17.3, 8.38.10, 9.22.4, and 10.4.6, all with reference to Lydia.

304 HERODOTUS AND IMPERIAL GREEK LITERATURE

Pausanias's incipit thus permits him to collate an array of programmatic features: referring both to landscape and to history, while potentially juxtaposing historical incidents, and seeing from perspectives both grounded and elevated, Pausanias adumbrates his intertextual connection to the literary past by inaugurating his work through allusion to Herodotus. To look at the Greek landscape is to see the past, and to describe it is to speak through the past's voices. Pausanias thus begins by subtly attempting to reproduce something of the Herodotean narrator's physical acts of observation while also hinting at his own cultural positioning as an outsider approaching Greece.[28] While it may not appear to be a formal proem, the opening of the *Periegesis* nonetheless, by dint of adverting to the *Histories*, marks that text as one of the primary palimpsestic layers onto which Pausanias inscribes his own project and identity.

Moving In and Out of Attica

In the ensuing sections on Athens that follow his opening, Pausanias continues to toggle between hodological and cartographic perspectives, imbuing his linear movements with a synoptic feel. When, for instance, Pausanias proceeds up the road from the Piraeus toward Athens, his movement appears straightforward enough, trekking inland from the harbor. But once in Athens, his movement often defies clear traceability and proceeds, rather, by means of an idiosyncratic psychogeography. After describing aspects of the Stoa Poikile and having mentioned the statues of Solon and Seleucus that stand before it, Pausanias expounds:

> In the Athenian agora there is among the objects not so well known an altar to Mercy, who, although in truth among all divinities the most useful to human life with its vicissitudes of fortune, receives honors from the Athenians alone among Greeks. And they stand out not only for their humanity but also for their devotion to the gods . . . . (1.17.1)

Ἀθηναίοις δὲ ἐν τῇ ἀγορᾷ καὶ ἄλλα ἐστὶν οὐκ ἐς ἅπαντας ἐπίσημα καὶ Ἐλέου βωμός, ᾧ μάλιστα θεῶν ἐς ἀνθρώπινον βίον καὶ μεταβολὰς πραγμάτων ὄντι ὠφελίμῳ μόνοι τιμὰς Ἑλλήνων νέμουσιν Ἀθηναῖοι. τούτοις δὲ οὐ τὰ

---

[28] See Whitmarsh 2010b: 14 on Pausanias's (and the reader's) "approach[ing] Greece from without." On Pausanias's extensive travels, see Pritchett 1999: 17–36; Hutton 2005b: 18–19; Akujärvi 2005: 28–29.

ἐς φιλανθρωπίαν μόνον καθέστηκεν, ἀλλὰ καὶ θεοὺς εὐσεβοῦσιν ἄλλων πλέον. . . .

The location of the altar to Mercy is only vaguely specified as "in the agora." Given that Pausanias thinks it is not well known (οὐκ ἐς ἅπαντας ἐπίσημα), a reader may wonder about its precise location. As Daniel Stewart has observed, attempts to follow Pausanias's steps have often tendentiously "reified the notion that Pausanias was writing about an actual journey rather than creating a pastiche."[29] Instead, after various indications in Book 1 of proximity and direction, conveyed especially by prepositions, Pausanias elides the specifics of his hodology and indicates, rather, a psychic cartography in which knowledge about Athenian piety becomes paramount. One floats, as it were, above the agora and glides with Pausanias to a site that one might otherwise miss. Cartographic, synoptic movement is reinforced by the narrator's generalizing comment on Athenian devotion that bids to encompass all Athenians in one prism. For Pausanias, the coordinates in the agora may not matter, since any Athenian space might testify to their "devotion to the gods."

All the same, within this cartographic space of Athenian piety, Pausanias will continue to operate with reference to (sometimes vague) hodological markers and to make use of shifting perspectives and jumps on the map, as we saw with regard to Sunium. A telling example comes from the lead-up to and eventual description of the image of Niobe above the Theater of Dionysus. At first, a series of proximal terms (πλησίον, 1.18.3, 1.18.5; μετά, 1.19.1) punctuates Pausanias's movement from the Prytaneion to the Temple of Olympian Zeus. He then refers to the road (ὁδός, 1.20.1) leading from the Prytaneion to the place of the Tripods. Across a few sections, the reader is given directional information, followed by reference to a road that suggests a linear route. Still further markers of proximity follow (πλησίον, 1.20.2, 1.20.4; πρὸς τῷ θεάτρῳ, 1.20.3). Yet the ambiguity of terms such as πλησίον and μετά also suggests the flexibility of Pausanias's hodology. What does he omit? What other things are "nearby"? As Stewart notes, he "creates a *sense* of place rather than a definition of place."[30] Even as he points to a physical road,

---

[29] Stewart 2013: 241; with specific reference to this section of Pausanias's work, see 240–43 on the problems of attempting to reconstruct a path using Pausanias's account. For another instance in Book 1 in which movement in Athens leaps in an unspecified direction, see the abrupt beginning of 1.18, on the sanctuary of the Dioscuri. How one reaches the sanctuary and how it relates to what Pausanias has previously been describing remain unclear. Compare Rood 2012: 127 n. 17 on dative generalizing participles in Herodotus.

[30] Stewart 2013: 232 (emphasis added).

306 HERODOTUS AND IMPERIAL GREEK LITERATURE

Pausanias also grants his readers, many of whom will not have traveled as widely as he, latitude to construct their own psychogeographic paths.[31]

One sometimes has glimpses into Pausanias's own experience, as when details of place from his native Lydia are subsumed into his cartographic authority. We have just seen that while the opening lines of the *Periegesis* apparently fail to offer an overt *sphragis*, they nonetheless conjure an instance of place-based authority in Herodotus. Continuing on in Athens, Pausanias appropriates the Herodotean comparative move:

> At the theater's top is a cave in the rocks beneath the Acropolis. A tripod stands over it, in which Apollo and Artemis are killing the children of Niobe. This Niobe I saw myself when I ascended Mount Sipylus. Up close she is a rock and stream, not even closely resembling a woman in grief or otherwise; but if you go further away you seem to see a woman crying and downcast. (1.21.3)

> ἐν δὲ τῇ κορυφῇ τοῦ θεάτρου σπήλαιόν ἐστιν ἐν ταῖς πέτραις ὑπὸ τὴν ἀκρόπολιν· τρίπους δὲ ἔπεστι καὶ τούτῳ· Ἀπόλλων δὲ ἐν αὐτῷ καὶ Ἄρτεμις τοὺς παῖδάς εἰσιν ἀναιροῦντες τοὺς Νιόβης. ταύτην τὴν Νιόβην καὶ αὐτὸς εἶδον ἀνελθὼν ἐς τὸν Σίπυλον τὸ ὄρος· ἡ δὲ πλησίον μὲν πέτρα καὶ κρημνός ἐστιν οὐδὲν παρόντι σχῆμα παρεχόμενος γυναικὸς οὔτε ἄλλως οὔτε πενθούσης· εἰ δέ γε πορρωτέρω γένοιο, δεδακρυμένην δόξεις ὁρᾶν καὶ κατηφῆ γυναῖκα.

The passage is at first focalized from an Athenian onlooker's perspective, as one looks from the ground upward.[32] Pausanias has just mentioned the so-called South Wall of the Acropolis that faces the theater (1.21.3), and from there he positions the reader's eye upward toward the top (κορυφῇ) of the theater. The perspective then jumps radically in geography, to a different vantage altogether, when we learn that Pausanias has personally seen (αὐτὸς εἶδον) "the same Niobe" (ταύτην τὴν Νιόβην) when he climbed Mount Sipylus near (his probable hometown of) Lydian Magnesia. Suddenly, Pausanias incorporates the hodological encounter of the theater in Athens into the cartographic sphere of his knowledge of Asia Minor, all conjoined by

---

[31] On Pausanias's addressees, including the likelihood of those from his native Asia Minor, see Arafat 1996: 33–36.

[32] See Akujärvi (2005: 140) on the narrator's "manoeuvring" and, on focalization, Akujärvi 2012a: 254–55.

PAUSANIAS IN WONDERLAND   307

the double act of autopsy of having seen both places.[33] Pausanias's description thereby mixes objective and subjective qualities that fit what Gilhuly and Worman have described as the relationship between space and place, the latter being "performative accretions of local meanings."[34] Quoting Andrew Merrifield, who "understands the interaction between [space and place] as a constant negotiation," they relate Merrifield's point that "space and place 'are different aspects of a unity,' and the distinction between the two exists 'only insofar as it represents different "moments" of a contradictory and conflictual process.'"[35] Pausanias's comments on Niobe suggest the linkage of one physical space (in Athens) to another (in Asia Minor), rendering them "different aspects of a unity," a psychogeographic unity of Greek culture that encompasses particular local instantiations. But I stress Pausanias's individual angle here. His reference does not rely on some incidental fragment of common *paideia* but in fact privileges his own personal, local experience.[36] Moreover, as Christopher Jones has shown, Pausanias gives us good reason to doubt that he was always enamored of all things Greek.[37] The sense of encompassing Hellenism implied by the Niobe passage elides to some degree the extent to which Pausanias's comment is a locally specific, potentially patriotic remark as much as a testimony to the diffusion of Greek culture.

The Herodotean autoptic act of seeing Niobe on Mount Sipylus not only reveals a subjectivity of perspective based on the happenstance of origin and experience, but it also bespeaks a kind of art-critical subjectivity that arises in the act of viewing, which may have consequences for the Athenian viewers of Niobe. Up close (πλησίον), Niobe on Mount Sipylus would in no way resemble a woman. But autopsy from only one angle does not suffice. Multiple vantages produce different results: the image's σχῆμα is captured through renegotiated points of view (εἰ δέ γε πορρωτέρω γένοιο). Even then, one will only think one sees (δόξεις ὁρᾶν) a woman in tears. Instead, the distanced perspective, negotiated in relation to the clarity of up-close viewing, exposes the σχῆμα for what it is objectively—sheer rock (πέτρα καὶ κρημνός)—while also highlighting the subjectivity that accords such a rock religious meaning. If Pausanias's Niobe

---

[33] On autoptic authority in Pausanias, see Arafat 1996: 17–18; Pretzler 2007a: 132.

[34] Gilhuly and Worman 2014: 6.

[35] Gilhuly and Worman 2014: 7, quoting Merrifield 1993: 527.

[36] Compare Whitmarsh 2010b: 14–15 for remarks on Pausanias as mediator between the "translocal umbrella" of Greek culture and "diverse locales," though focused on his use of local lore from the Greek mainland (rather than, as here, on Lydia). See also Arafat 1996: 11 and Stewart 2013: 233 on Pausanias's "reference to proxies or stand-ins drawn from personal experience."

[37] Jones 2004: 15–18, with conclusion at 18: "[T]his supposed 'hierophant of all things Greek' has sympathies and interests that are distinctly un-Greek."

308   HERODOTUS AND IMPERIAL GREEK LITERATURE

in Athens is also, recalling the deictic, "this Niobe" he has seen closer to his own home—a Niobe who from one angle is "sheer rock"—his autoptic act in Lydia not only broadens his authoritative witness of the Athenian Niobe but also points to a fundamental constructedness of meaning.

Pausanias, then, only appears to be consistently hodological. Rather, he produces a textual cartography that at once recalls Herodotus's hodological footsteps while *also* summoning that author's overriding, extra-diegetic authority.[38] Pausanias's text frequently constructs its psychogeographic realm by means of authoritative, non-repeatable, only ostensibly hodological movements, supervened by a broader form of narrative power. Akujärvi notes that "As always, the control remains with the narrator. It is he who stages the movement of the 'you,' and he can step in for explanations and narrations at any time."[39] Both Herodotus's and Pausanias's texts involve the movement of a narrator through space, but each also allows for the superimposition of unique knowledge, gained through inquiry and autopsy, in which no reader can have a fully equal share. Such transcendent cartography is not, however, a wholly isolating or hubristic move. Rather, the non-repeatability of Pausanias's journey and his ability to burnish it into narrative separate it from the very material it encompasses. While the stones along the road will fall out of place and buildings collapse, the cartographic superiority of Pausanias's account, itself tied to that of a literary predecessor, has the potential to outlast its historical moment.

(Do Not) Repeat after Me

Pausanias evokes Herodotus by being a traveling narrator and, as suggested earlier, conjoins Herodotus's hodological and autoptic authority to his own cartographic expertise.[40] In some sense, Pausanias's vivification of the mobile narrator is characterized by relative sobriety. As Hawes observes, "Although writing at a time in which a travel narrative might as easily be a fantastic journey designed to entertain, as in his contemporary Lucian, Pausanias' invocation of the Halicarnassian is notably 'straight.'"[41] Hawes's description

[38] See Hawes 2016: 336–37.
[39] Akujärvi 2012a: 251.
[40] Pausanias recalls the blurry boundary in Herodotus between nearly intradiegetic mover and extradiegetic presence (as discussed in chapter 5).
[41] Hawes 2016: 332.

PAUSANIAS IN WONDERLAND   309

obtains on several fronts, such as Pausanias's seemingly "straight" evocation of Herodotean religious aspects of historical patterning described in chapter 7. But in other areas, readers will also discover a more enigmatic inhabitation of the Herodotean identity.[42]

Take Pausanias's unusual linguistic and syntactic style. Among other issues, scholars have puzzled over how best to understand Pausanias's relatively limited Atticizing (compared with that of his contemporaries) as well as his possible imitation of the "Asiatic" stylist Hegesias of Magnesia (third century BCE).[43] In a comprehensive study, Ove Strid rejected the idea that Pausanias's convoluted word order should be explained as the influence of Hegesias, arguing instead that Pausanias's striking use of *hyperbaton* (not to mention many other figures) has good classical precedents in Herodotus and Thucydides especially.[44] At the same time, even as Pausanias's Greek exhibits pervasive Herodotean imitation in phraseological recall and word order, it nonetheless avoids other Herodotean features such as the Ionicizing evident in particular works by Arrian and Lucian.[45] Bowie, following Strid, hypothesizes that Pausanias eschews various Asiatic tics, including "contrived images, short cola, and rhythmical clausulae," because of his sense that a fifth-century style better suited "celebrating the monuments and deeds of a past which entered a new and less distinguished era with the battle of Chaeronea."[46] Finally, Hutton cuts somewhat against this binary and develops a case for Hegesias as a potential model, though certainly not a thoroughgoing one.[47] To be sure, Hutton concedes that Pausanias's clausulae resemble those of classical writers, including Herodotus and Thucydides, and of such exemplars of Attic style as Demosthenes.[48] He moots the

---

[42] Pausanias in various ways distances himself from too close an association with his (potentially controversial) forebear. This has been well discussed by Hutton (2005b: 190–213), with summary remarks (234–35) on Pausanias's ambivalent recollection of Herodotus, characterized by a "deliberate disjunction . . . at the same time that he was doing him homage" (234). See also Hutton 2005b: 51–53 and Hutton 2017: 359, 365, on the peculiarities of Pausanias's persona vis-à-vis other Imperial Greeks, despite his relatively conventional focus on the classical past.

[43] On Pausanias's language and syntax, see Szelest 1953; Strid 1976; Bowie 2001: 25–27; Hutton 2005b: 181–240, esp. 191–200 for Pausanias's relatively modest use of Atticizing vocabulary and orthography.

[44] On Herodotean echoes, see Strid 1976: 22–23, 54, 78–80 and passim, with conclusions at 99–103; cf. Hutton 2005b: 218.

[45] On Pausanias's avoidance of Ionic, see Jones 2001: 35 ("[H]e might have felt that such a choice would have been stylistically flamboyant in his own day, a distraction from the air of studiousness and sincerity that he wished to convey"); Hutton 2005b: 211–12.

[46] See Bowie 2001: 26–27, quotations at 27.

[47] Hutton 2005b: 222–33.

[48] Hutton 2005b: 229, citing Szelest 1953.

310 HERODOTUS AND IMPERIAL GREEK LITERATURE

possibility that Pausanias's unusual word order may recall Hegesias as a way of channeling something of Pausanias's Lydian identity.[49] Now, in the earlier analysis of Pausanias's recall of *Histories* 4.99, we noted the sense in which Pausanias's text "approaches" Greece through the focalization of one moving toward Attica at sea and as a figure from Asia Minor knowledgeable of Greek traditions, on analogy with Herodotus.[50] Pausanias is both an outsider from elsewhere, like his forebear, and via imitation an "insider," insofar as he speaks with the Herodotean voice. With regard to his syntax, then, we also might view matters as not entirely either/or. Rather than seeing Pausanias in stark terms, styling his sentences on either Herodotus or Hegesias, we might accept the fundamentals of Strid's analysis while also allowing, after Hutton, the possibility that his style does two things at once: it clearly resounds with Herodotean flourishes while also potentially paying homage to local influence in burnishing his Lydian identity. For our purposes, such potential hybridity of literary mannerism seems of a piece with Pausanias's larger set of ambivalences and indeed marks his own version of kinetic reception, at once playing to and defying inherited expectations: Pausanias both engages and differentiates himself from Herodotus; he Atticizes (moderately) but flouts the mania for hyper-Atticism; and he presents himself as both steeped in Greek lore and a son of Asia Minor.

Such kinetic evocation of the past links up with Pausanias's repeated articulation of his attempt to avoid duplication, instead working to supplement Herodotus (and others) in the narrativization of Greek antiquity.[51] Others have noted how Pausanias appears conscious, even as his work engages and affirms both the *Histories* and other sources, of not wanting to replicate them. Sidebottom, for instance, has commented on Pausanias's " 'completing' Homer's coverage of the Trojan war" (10.25.1–27.4), and Hutton, too, has observed that Pausanias often avoids providing historical detail if it already exists in the *Histories*, tending instead to send his reader back to the source.[52] Pausanias participates in the Herodotean tradition through imitation, but

---

[49] Hutton 2005b: 233: "Of all the many factors and choices that went into creating Pausanias's style, this one [his possible recall of Hegesias] would be perhaps the most expressive of his personal identity as a native of Magnesia on Sipylos."

[50] See Musti and Beschi 1982: xx–xxi, speculating on Pausanias's emulation of Herodotus as part of the cult of personality Herodotus enjoyed in Asia Minor (see my introduction). Recall also the added layer that the Herodotus of *Hist.* 4.99 appears as another sort of outsider, trekking along the Scythian coast.

[51] See, however, Moggi 1996: 83–87 on Pausanias's account of Ionia in Book 7.

[52] Sidebottom 2002: 498; Hutton 2005b: 195.

PAUSANIAS IN WONDERLAND 311

his construction of psychogeographic space requires addition, rather than repetition.

So while there may have been among Pausanias's readers the expectation that a writer so manifestly fond of Herodotean phraseology and tone would replicate aspects of Herodotus's content, too, such overlap is precisely part of what Pausanias affects to avoid, as when he writes very early in his first book: "The man who established ten tribes instead of four and exchanged their old names for new ones—these things are reported by Herodotus" (ὅστις δὲ κατεστήσατο δέκα ἀντὶ τεσσάρων φυλὰς εἶναι καὶ μετέθετό σφισι τὰ ὀνόματα ἀντὶ τῶν ἀρχαίων, Ἡροδότῳ καὶ ταῦτά ἐστιν εἰρημένα, 1.5.1). Pausanias here and elsewhere assumes his readers' good familiarity with his predecessor.[53] In general, Pausanias attends to what his readers likely know and shapes his narrative accordingly.[54] Often he need not dilate on things already told, as indicated in his first book, in language reminiscent of Herodotus's hodological metaphor:[55] "My narrative must move forward" (δεῖ δέ με ἀφικέσθαι τοῦ λόγου πρόσω, 1.26.4). Yet Pausanias *does* allow his narrative to loiter when he feels compelled to tell something new. Compare his account of the fact that Hippias tortured Leaena: "I speak of things not earlier having come into writing, but otherwise believed among many of the Athenians" (λέγω δὲ οὐκ ἐς συγγραφὴν πρότερον ἥκοντα, πιστὰ δὲ ἄλλως Ἀθηναίων τοῖς πολλοῖς, 1.23.2).

So an operative principle of Pausanias's work is to avoid overly repeating the (written) past.[56] Instead, Pausanias can at times contribute and supplement, as if offering a new accretive layer. Consider the following:

> Since the matters concerning Auxesia and Damia—how the god did not give rain to the Epidaurians, how following the oracle they had these wooden images made from olive they took from the Athenians, how the Epidaurians did not pay the Athenians what they had agreed to pay since

[53] All the same, Pausanias is aware of historical repetitions and the inevitability of repeating the past. On the issue of time repeating itself, compare the invasion of the Gauls in Book 10 (a repeat perhaps of Book 1) as typological repetition of the Persian Wars; see Nachtergael 1977: 19–22, 147–50 (compare Sidebottom 2002: 498). See also Alcock 1996: 256–60.

[54] See, e.g., 2.30.9: "I am not writing up the matters regarding Theseus, grandson of Pittheus, since readers know his story, though I must elucidate one aspect still" (τὰ δὲ ἐς Θησέα θυγατριδοῦν Πιτθέως εἰδόσι τὰ ἐς αὐτὸν οὐ γράφω, δεῖ δέ με τοσόνδε ἔτι δηλῶσαι).

[55] Musti 1996: 35–39 discusses the Herodotean echoes of Pausanias 1.26.4: δεῖ δέ με **ἀφικέσθαι** τοῦ λόγου **πρόσω**, πάντα ὁμοίως **ἐπεξιόντα** τὰ Ἑλληνικά ~ τοῦτον σημήνας **προβήσομαι** ἐς τὸ **πρόσω** τοῦ λόγου, ὁμοίως σμικρὰ καὶ μεγάλα ἄστεα ἀνθρώπων **ἐπεξιών** (Hdt. 1.5.3).

[56] See also Paus. 1.23.10, 2.15.4, 2.30.4, 2.30.9, and 3.17.7 for instances of consciously avoiding repetition. On this point, see Swain 1996: 332, with n. 9.

312 HERODOTUS AND IMPERIAL GREEK LITERATURE

the Aeginetans still had the statues, how the Athenians who crossed over to Aegina to retrieve them died—these matters have been described accurately and in detail by Herodotus, and I have no intention to write up what has been well described, other than to say that I have seen the statues and offered sacrifice to them in the same manner as is customary for sacrifices at Eleusis. (2.30.4)

τὰ δὲ ἐς τὴν Αὐξησίαν καὶ Δαμίαν, ὡς οὐχ ὕεν ὁ θεὸς Ἐπιδαυρίοις, ὡς τὰ ξόανα ταῦτα ἐκ μαντείας ἐποιήσαντο ἐλαίας παρ᾽ Ἀθηναίων λαβόντες, ὡς Ἐπιδαύριοι μὲν οὐκ ἀπέφερον ἔτι Ἀθηναίοις ἃ ἐτάξαντο οἷα Αἰγινητῶν ἐχόντων τὰ ἀγάλματα, Ἀθηναίων δὲ ἀπώλοντο οἱ διαβάντες διὰ ταῦτα ἐς Αἴγιναν, ταῦτα εἰπόντος Ἡροδότου καθ᾽ ἕκαστον αὐτῶν ἐπ᾽ ἀκριβὲς οὔ μοι γράφειν κατὰ γνώμην ἦν εὖ προειρημένα, πλὴν τοσοῦτό γε ὅτι εἶδόν τε τὰ ἀγάλματα καὶ ἔθυσά σφισι κατὰ τὰ αὐτὰ καθὰ δὴ καὶ Ἐλευσῖνι θύειν νομίζουσιν.

Pausanias's reference to Herodotus's story offers detailed lack of detail: even as he says that the story has already been well told, he lists the story's pertinent parts by means of three ὡς clauses and the διὰ ταῦτα clause. He siphons his reader off onto Herodotus's story, but he also touches upon the parts that apparently matter to him before doing so. Both accuracy (ἀκριβές) and narrative quality (εὖ προειρημένα) decide Pausanias against repetition (οὔ μοι γράφειν). At the same time, Pausanias's claim to autopsy (εἶδόν τε τὰ ἀγάλματα)—a claim not made by Herodotus—here has the effect of *completing* and reauthorizing Herodotus's account (5.83–87). His adverting to Herodotus refers the reader to an authoritative text, but his claim to autopsy refers, in turn, to his own.

In a different sort of subtle reauthorization, Pausanias can allude to issues in Herodotus without definitively adjudicating on them. When he refers to Aristeas of Proconnesus's discussion of griffins, for instance, he skillfully adverts to Herodotus (4.14–16), who had dismissed Aristeas's account:

Aristeas of Proconnesus says in his poetry that these griffins spar over the gold with the Arimaspi who dwell beyond the Issedones. He says that the gold that the griffins guard comes out of the earth. The Arimaspi are all one-eyed from birth, while griffins are creatures similar to lions, but with an eagle's wings and beak. Concerning griffins let these several details suffice. (1.24.6)

τούτους τοὺς γρῦπας ἐν τοῖς ἔπεσιν Ἀριστέας ὁ Προκοννήσιος μάχεσθαι περὶ τοῦ χρυσοῦ φησιν Ἀριμασποῖς <τοῖς> ὑπὲρ Ἰσσηδόνων· τὸν δὲ χρυσόν, ὃν φυλάσσουσιν οἱ γρῦπες, ἀνιέναι τὴν γῆν· εἶναι δὲ Ἀριμασποὺς μὲν ἄνδρας μονοφθάλμους πάντας ἐκ γενετῆς, γρῦπας δὲ θηρία λέουσιν εἰκασμένα, πτερὰ δὲ ἔχειν καὶ στόμα ἀετοῦ. καὶ γρυπῶν μὲν πέρι τοσαῦτα εἰρήσθω.

Pausanias embeds his remarks about Aristeas in indirect statement, suitable to the outlandish material, before signing off with the Herodotean tag (καὶ γρυπῶν μὲν πέρι τοσαῦτα εἰρήσθω).[57] Now, Herodotus himself had told a curious, possibly Pythagorean story of Aristeas's vanishing and reappearance (4.14–16). He presented Aristeas at once sympathetically, as someone similarly unable to access the nether regions beyond Scythia, and skeptically, as a figure whose poetry and life are associated with the implausible.[58] Pausanias, for his part, carefully skirts the issues that the reference to Aristeas may have raised. He neither explicitly affirms nor denies belief in griffins, but his use of indirect statement and his unwillingness to linger on the topics raised by Aristeas allow him simultaneously to reveal his *paideia*, knowledgeable as he is of *both* Aristeas and Herodotus. In other words, Pausanias can at one and the same time refer to Aristeas and to Herodotus's own mediation of Aristeas. By neither affirming nor denying Herodotus's take, he refuses to interfere with Herodotus's presentation. His seemingly incidental mention, however, of one-eyed men summons Herodotus's own two references to these people (3.116, 4.13.1), while delicately passing over Herodotus's dismissal. Pausanias's reception channels Herodotus and his skeptical attitude without explicitly echoing or copying it.

A final instance of Pausanias's subtly kinetic reception, complementing Herodotus through simultaneous evocation and distancing, appears in a comment about Homer and Hesiod. Remarking on an image of Hesiod that he encounters in Boeotia, Pausanias writes:

Concerning the age of Hesiod and Homer, although I have busily conducted the most accurate research into the matter, I do not enjoy writing about it, knowing as I do the quarrelsome nature of those who make up the school of epic criticism in my time. (9.30.3)

---

[57] Compare, e.g., Hdt. 6.55: καὶ ταῦτα μέν νυν περὶ τούτων **εἰρήσθω**.
[58] On Herodotus's inquiry in the nether regions beyond Scythia, see Gagné 2019.

314 HERODOTUS AND IMPERIAL GREEK LITERATURE

περὶ δὲ Ἡσιόδου τε ἡλικίας καὶ Ὁμήρου πολυπραγμονήσαντι ἐς τὸ ἀκριβέστατον οὔ μοι γράφειν ἡδὺ ἦν, ἐπισταμένῳ τὸ φιλαίτιον ἄλλων τε καὶ οὐχ ἥκιστα ὅσοι κατ' ἐμὲ ἐπὶ ποιήσει τῶν ἐπῶν καθεστήκεσαν.

This passage offers another combination of Herodotean echo and Pausanian self-differentiation. His statement seems to follow an ethic of journalistic obligation contrary to Herodotus's ethic, as Akujärvi observes: "This statement of the narrator of the *Periegesis* is the opposite of the Herodotean declaration (7.139.1) not to withhold the truth, irrespective of the fact that it is odious in the eyes of most people."[59] Yet whatever programmatic quality such a view holds is perhaps lessened by the presence of other instances in which Pausanias directly echoes Herodotus's declarations about the obligations of reportage.[60] Instead, rather more pointed is the Herodoteanism of Pausanias's commenting on the age of Homer and Hesiod in the first place. To recall, Herodotus writes:

> Whence each of the gods came into existence, or whether they all always existed, and the sort of form they had, these details were not known until the day before yesterday, as it were: for I think Hesiod and Homer existed four hundred years before my time—and no more. These two created for the Greeks their theogony; it is they who gave to the gods the particular names for their genealogy and apportioned among them their honors, arts, and forms. And those who are called poets before Homer and Hesiod were, in my view, born later. (2.53.1–3)

Pausanias says he has done "very precise" (ἀκριβέστατον) research on the question. But after resurrecting the issue, he demurs from diving into this contentious topic. Already Herodotus has alluded to its difficulty in his self-conscious phrasing: "it seems to me" (δοκέω . . . ἔμοιγε δοκέειν), "so-called" (λεγόμενοι), and "I assert" (ἐγὼ λέγω). In some sense, the project of the *Periegesis* involves the very activities that Herodotus assigns Homer and Hesiod: describing what gods look like (τὰ εἴδεα), giving them their names, remarking on their honors. Pausanias continues and works toward

---

[59] Akujärvi 2005: 58 n. 99.

[60] Compare Pausanias 6.3.8, "I am compelled to report the things that are told by the Greeks, but I am not obligated to believe them all" (ἐμοὶ μὲν οὖν <u>λέγειν μὲν τὰ ὑπὸ Ἑλλήνων λεγόμενα</u> ἀνάγκη, <u>πείθεσθαι</u> δὲ <u>πᾶσιν</u> οὐκέτι ἀνάγκη), with Hdt. 7.152.3, "I am obligated to record the things I am told, but I am certainly not required to believe them" (ἐγὼ δὲ ὀφείλω <u>λέγειν τὰ λεγόμενα</u>, <u>πείθεσθαί</u> γε μὲν οὐ <u>παντάπασιν</u> ὀφείλω).

the completion of the task of giving nomenclature and structure to the Greek pantheon. Yet, while he also undertakes, like Herodotus, the job of sorting out the dates of Homer and Hesiod, he ultimately bypasses the activity of reckoning them publicly on the grounds that it is unpleasant (οὐ . . . ἡδύ). Pausanias thus fashions himself at once in the mold of Herodotus, replicating aspects of his thoughtscape, syntax, diction, and general manner, while also carefully articulating his wish to avoid repetition. The strangeness of Pausanias's work inheres, in part, in its fixation on the sights of the past narrated in conscious imitation of past writers but rendered in unusual syntax that attempts to avoid repeating other narratives. Pausanias lives both inside and outside the expectations of genre and tradition. In his labor for novelty and in offering a certain literary freshness, he aspires toward something distinctive that will hold his readers' attention. In this regard, his text's focus on wonder, the final topic to which I turn, conspires with his effort to revitalize a view of Greece.

Make It New: Greece as Wonder

How does Pausanias's dogged focus on the past square with his evident aim to avoid overlap with or repetition of past accounts? One strategy has to do with tone. While a focus on the past was common among Pausanias's near-contemporaries—think of Plutarch's *Parallel Lives* or any number of Lucian's dialogues that vivify past personages—Pausanias tends to avoid triumphalist or overly sanitized visions of a bygone Greek glory.[61] Rather than exalt or satirize, Pausanias is often thought to document with an eye toward decline. Indeed, Hutton has suggested that one of Pausanias's purposes may have been to correct "overly idealized notions of Hellenism by portraying accurately, and with eyewitness authority, the contemporary (and often parlous) state of physical symbols of Hellenic tradition."[62] Even Pausanias's perspective on Greek history is often pessimistic, as Akujärvi has observed:

---

[61] On the preoccupation with the past as a feature of ancient Greek literature generally, see Porter 2001: 91–92: "The mythemes of decline, nostalgia, and irretrievable loss, and the fetishization of the traces of the past at the expense of the present, are not only a persistent feature of Greek writing but arguably one of its least recognized *conventions*" (91, emphasis in original).

[62] Hutton 2005b: 37.

316 HERODOTUS AND IMPERIAL GREEK LITERATURE

The *Periegesis* betrays no difficulty in believing that the Greeks were not able to set their differences aside, that they did not fight the foes to a man or that some chose to join the other side. Though not the best moment in the history of some communities, absence from the battles of the Persian war or even siding with the other side was believable. Plutarch does not accept the Herodotean account as easily as Pausanias does. . . . [Pausanias] reacts against the myth of all Greeks united in the fight against Trojans, Persians, Macedonians, and Gauls.[63]

Pausanias's and Herodotus's convergently realistic viewpoints render all the more intriguing the last of the Herodotean qualities of the *Periegesis* that I wish to discuss, namely, Pausanias's interest in the topos of wonder.[64] Although perhaps counterintuitive when set against the work's sometimes melancholic tone, Pausanias's not insignificant emphasis on wonder and marvels functions as a strategy of attentiveness and novelty. By encouraging his audience to see thaumastically, as it were, Pausanias both registers the remarkable persistence of the Greek world that remains in his time and, less overtly, imparts an appreciation of reality qua marvelous. For by infusing his Greek landscape with wonder, Pausanias frequently (though not exclusively) locates wonder in actual, visitable objects and spaces, vouching through his own autopsy for a series of marvels that are themselves realizable, as it were, through one's own potential visitation.[65] Pausanias thus offers a kind of wonder-writing that differs from the cataloguing of incredible or absurd matters of hearsay.[66] His observation invites readers to experience their own. Wonder, after all, ruptures; it invites in the perspective of others, as if implicitly asking, "Can you make sense of this?" Wonder encourages pause and often marks a limit.[67] In the midst of all that risks erasure, Pausanias's text encourages readers toward their own experience of awe.

[63] Akujärvi 2005: 63–64. On the topic of Greek unity in the past generally, see Alcock 1996: 251–60; Swain 1996: 333–38; Habicht 1985: 105–8; Hutton 2005b: 63–64, 302–3; Pretzler 2007b: 78–90.
[64] A Herodotean feature noted by Hutton 2005b: 191.
[65] To be sure, Pausanias's text countenances marvels that scan as more traditionally paradoxographic. Commenting on the sanctuary of Demeter at Boeotian Mykalessus, for instance, Pausanias writes, "There is displayed the following sort of marvel: before the feet of her statue they set fruits harvested in autumn, but these remain ripe through all the year" (δείκνυται δὲ αὐτόθι καὶ θαῦμα τοιόνδε· πρὸ τοῦ ἀγάλματος τῶν ποδῶν τιθέασιν ὅσα ἐν ὀπώρᾳ πέφυκε γίνεσθαι, ταῦτα δὲ διὰ παντὸς μένει τεθηλότα τοῦ ἔτους, 9.19.5). See ní Mheallaigh 2014: 262–64 for other instances of Pausanian engagement in paradoxography.
[66] Imperial paradoxography did not, however, eschew strategies of authentication; see, e.g., Shannon-Henderson 2020: 166–74 on Phlegon of Tralles's claimed autopsy of marvels. See ní Mheallaigh 2014: 264–65 for Imperial-era exhibitions of wonders.
[67] See Shannon-Henderson 2020: 161.

PAUSANIAS IN WONDERLAND   317

Varieties of Wonder

The topos of wonder in Herodotus has received much attention.[68] Remarks on the wondrous pervade the *Histories*, and its rhetoric surely constitutes an aspect of Herodotus's ancient reception.[69] Ninety-three different instances of θῶμα- cognates are scattered across Herodotus, including the programmatic use of θωμαστά that announces his focus on the "great and wondrous." As Christine Hunzinger has shown, the idea of wonder in Herodotus applies widely: edifices, occurrences, animals, utterances—all can generate amazement (or stated lack thereof: e.g., 6.121.1, 6.123.1) on the part of the narrator or intradiegetic characters. Rosaria Munson has emphasized how the narrator's remarks on wonder can act as discursive events that themselves inspire wonder among readers, who might not previously have considered something marvelous:

> mention of the wonder response [by the narrator] may create, from the point of view of the recipient, a wondrous discourse event, something that surprises primarily within the discourse. . . . In cases of this sort [the leather boats of the Assyrians, Hdt. 1.194], the phenomenon itself perhaps causes less wonder than the text's injunction that we, along with the narrator, should wonder (θῶμα μέγιστον μοι).[70]

Herodotus's generation of wonder as a discursive event produces an effect relevant to Pausanias, namely, that wonder need not always imply gaping astonishment or stupefaction but can, in fact, bespeak a certain kind of understanding.[71] Wonder may arise, and may provoke the same in others, not merely from a *lack* of comprehension but also from amazement that emerges *in* comprehending that something is distinctive. It can materialize on the far side of intellection, rather than always being its incipient driver.[72] When Herodotus describes, for instance, how he "marvels especially" (μάλιστα

---

[68] See Barth 1968; Dewald 1987: 154–55, 165; Hartog 1988 [1980]: 230–37; Hunzinger 1995; Payen 1997: 117–28; Munson 2001: 232–65.

[69] See Priestley 2014: 55–108. On the topos as going back to at least Herodotus, see Elsner 1994: 245. Compare Jacoby 1913: 331–32 on wonder and ancient ethnography. See further Prier 1989; Hunzinger 2015.

[70] Munson 2001: 232–33; see also 251.

[71] See Priestley 2014: 68–75 on wonder as an instigation to understanding in Aristotle; see also Nightingale 2004: 253–56 on the afterlife of this conception through the eighteenth century.

[72] Compare Nightingale 2004: 256–61 on Platonic wonder, "which occurs at the end, rather than the beginning, of the philosophic quest" (256).

θαυμάζω, 2.175.3) at Amasis's chamber carved from a single block, he does so acknowledging other works of Amasis (2.175.1–2) against which this chamber stands out. To recognize its wondrousness is not necessarily to find it beyond explanation but instead to contextualize its distinctiveness vis-à-vis other objects.[73] Similarly, when describing Queen Nitocris's embankment on the Euphrates as "worthy of wonder" (ἄξιον θώματος, 1.185.3), Herodotus invites us to marvel at the work in the context of his already having noted her intelligence (συνετωτέρη, 1.185.1), observant understanding (ὁρῶσα, 1.185.1), and precaution (προεφυλάξατο, 1.185.1) in undertaking engineering projects for anticipatory defense against the Median empire. The wonder of her works acts as a subtly transferred epithet for Herodotus's acclaiming her marvelous insight.[74] Or, to give one further example, mentioned in passing in chapter 5: when Herodotus calls Lake Moeris a wonder (θῶμα ἔτι μέζον, 2.149.1), it is again relationally, this time in comparison with the already supremely marvelous labyrinth, on which Herodotus has lavished much attention as both beyond description (λόγου μέζω, 2.148.1) and capable of inspiring his detailed catalogue (2.148.1–7).[75] The narrator's remarks on wonder, then, may occasion further puzzling or pondering, but they can also arise in contexts in which the designation of wonder itself marks Herodotus's relativized understanding and recognition of something as unusual.

While this feature of wonder as designating the distinctive, rather than the merely confounding, will sometimes obtain also in Pausanias, one important difference lies in how each narrator *locates* wonder. For wonder in Herodotus often has to do with recognition of something non-Greek. Of Herodotus's ninety-three instances of θῶμα- cognates, forty-four are narratorial remarks of one sort or the other (rather than internal instances of wonder on the part of the text's characters).[76] If we isolate among the narratorial remarks

---

[73] Nor should Herodotus's marveling at Egyptian buildings be taken for granted; as Harrison 2003: 148 notes, "There was, already by the time of his writing, a Greek tradition of belittling (in some instances quite literally) such Egyptian achievements: this can be seen, for example, in the original meaning of a number of Greek terms for unfamiliar Egyptian phenomena, the obelisk (a roasting spit or skewer), pyramid (a variety of cake), or crocodile (a lizard; cf. Herodotus II.69.3)."

[74] Compare Herodotus on Artemisia's taking part in the campaign against the Greeks (μάλιστα θῶμα ποιεῦμαι, 7.99.1), ostensibly commenting on the presence of a woman in the expedition but encouraging the reader to view her distinguishing behavior, not simply her mere presence, as wondrous.

[75] See chapter 5.

[76] The narrator's remarks include varied instances of his calling something wondrous, whether an engineering feat (1.185.3, 2.148.6), an explanatory hypothesis (2.21), a cultural practice (3.111.1), or an extraordinary situation (7.99.1). Narratorial expressions also include instances in which the

PAUSANIAS IN WONDERLAND 319

those instances in which he comments on a matter, space, person, or event either non-Greek, physically outside of Greece, or somehow understood (in the context of the narrative) to be non-Greek, then of the forty-four narratorial comments, fully twenty-seven (or 61 percent) apply to declarations of wonder related to non-Greeks or to events occurring to or among non-Greeks.[77] These statistics bring out the fact that in his own expressions of marveling, the Herodotean narrator is often inclined to wonder at things that exist or occur among the groups his text has marked as *barbaros*, whether commenting on the gold dust from Mount Tmolus in Lydia (1.93.1), Arabian rock-rose resin (3.112), Arabian sheep (3.113.1), or Scythian fish (4.53.3).[78] This pattern produces a sustained association between narratorial wonder and matters non-Greek.[79] The fact that many of the internal statements of wonder by characters apply also to the "behaviors, utterances, or appearances of foreigners" only reinforces the association between wonder and non-Greekness effected by the narrator.[80]

Pausanias's text, by contrast, refocuses attention on largely Hellenic wonders and often associates them with religious matters that ultimately supersede comprehension. The *Periegesis* has by my count seventy-two different instances of θαῦμα- cognates, often directed toward aspects of Greece itself,

---

narrator verbally acknowledges that he himself marvels at something (2.175.3, 4.30.1, 4.42.1, 9.65.2), rather than simply specifying it is as "worthy of wonder," "wondrous," etc.

[77] The criterion of "non-Greek" is sometimes ambiguous. Does, for instance, the improbable story of the Persian defector Scyllias diving into the sea and surfacing only at Artemisium, a story that inspires the narrator's wonder (θωμάζω δὲ εἰ τὰ λεγόμενά ἐστι ἀληθέα, 8.8.2), count as a foreign marvel because it involves a Persian? I think not, and I do not count it. It is the *tale* that sparks wonder, not anything exclusively related to the identities of the figures mentioned.

[78] Further examples that appear in non-Greek spaces or occur among or to non-Greeks (in addition to the aforementioned Nitocris's embankment on the Euphrates [1.185.3], the labyrinth in Egypt [2.148.6], Lake Moeris [2.149.1], and the Egyptian monument carved from a single stone [2.175.3, echoing similar comments at 2.155.3 and 2.156.1]): the style of Assyrian boats (1.194.1), Amasis's gateway (2.175.1), the littered bones of Persians and Egyptians (3.12.1), Amasis's breastplate (3.47.3), Scythian rivers and the footprint of Heracles in Scythia (4.82), the wondrous nature of the Black Sea (4.85.2), donkeys when heard by Scythian horses (4.129.1), three harvests in Cyrene (4.199.1), the non-surprise of the Persians' drinking rivers dry (7.187.1), the miraculous movement of the sacred weapons at Delphi (8.37.2), thunderbolts appearing to the Persians as they approach the Temple of Athena Pronaia (8.37.2), and Persians dying outside the consecrated area of the grove of Demeter (9.65.2).

[79] I disagree with Munson's conclusion (2001: 233) that "[m]etanarrative *thoma* is rarely used to describe either the activities of foreign peoples in the ethnographies or those of foreigners in the history." While Munson is correct that Herodotus does not often marvel at foreign "activities" or customs, this should not obnubilate the fact that Herodotean narratorial marveling is preponderantly concentrated on accomplishments, monuments, animals, etc., that appear outside of or among non-Greeks within his narrative.

[80] Quotation at Munson 2001: 233.

320 HERODOTUS AND IMPERIAL GREEK LITERATURE

a trend of a piece with what Domenico Musti has described as Pausanias's "centripetal" ethnographic focus, in contrast to Herodotus's centrifugal, edge-oriented ethnographies.[81] Of the seventy-two statements of wonder, sixty-three are narratorial (rather than focalized through or applied by an internal character), and of those sixty-three narratorial remarks, the vast majority (fully fifty instances, or 79 percent) apply to Greek matters.[82] The fact of Pausanias's Hellenic focus perhaps does not surprise prima facie, given the almost relentlessly Greek content of his intended ambit (see τὰ Ἑλληνικά, 1.26.4). Yet an emphasis on Greek wonders does not constitute an inevitability. As noted previously, Pausanias often does have occasion to mention matters not directly within the Greek mainland. These include the aforementioned reference to Mount Sipylus (1.21.3); the catalogue of the various colors of water he has seen (ἰδόντι, 4.35.11) in different places, including Jaffa, Atarneus, and outer Rome, all of which "amaze" him (θαῦμά τι ἦν, 4.35.9–11); the catalogue of foreign cities in the Megalopolis passage (8.33), in which his reflection embraces a wide array of places, Greek and non-Greek; and his scattered comments on Roman matters, including some that inspire wonder: snow-white deer (8.17.4), a statue of Triton (9.21.1), and the Roman forum (10.5.11). Since the majority of narratorial remarks, however, refer to Greece, I shall spotlight a few instances that specifically position Greece as a site of thaumastic revelation.

Wondering at Greece

As Guido Schepens has shown, the tradition of Hellenistic paradoxography, itself in the lineage of the Herodotean wonder tradition, often focused on foreign or temporally distant material.[83] So it is significant that when wonder

---

[81] Musti 1984.

[82] Similar to such appearances in Herodotus, Pausanias's markers of wonder have a wide coverage of topic and temporality, embracing historical and mythological figures, events, animals, natural phenomena, monuments, and edifices. Examples: historical and mythological figures (Pyrrhus, 1.12.2; the Aeacidae, 1.13.9; Iphicrates, 1.24.7); events (e.g., the revelation of Geryon's bones, 1.35.7; the loss of Messenian luck at the Olympic games, 6.2.10); animals and natural phenomena (e.g., the kites at Olympia, 5.14.1; various rivers, 5.14.3; the water of the Maeander, 8.7.3; the blackbirds of Cyllene in Arcadia, 8.17.3); and artifacts, monuments, and edifices (e.g., the marble stadium of Herodes Atticus, 1.19.6). In one instance, noting the curious fact of the impregnation of Elean mares by donkeys outside Elean territory (5.5.2), Pausanias directly recalls an issue discussed by Herodotus (4.30).

[83] See Schepens and Delcroix 1996: 381 on choosing a particular country's wonders to catalogue (e.g., Philo of Heracleia's Περὶ θαυμασίων ἐν Σκύθαις) and 401–2 on the relationship between the geographical horizons of the Hellenistic world and the proliferation of paradoxography. Writers of

appears in the *Periegesis*, it is far less often for jaw dropping at a far-flung marvel and rather more often to register the marvels that exist within Greek spaces. Moreover, in contrast to the sometimes hyperbolic culture of Imperial paradoxography, Pausanias often issues rather straightforward declarations of wonder about real things, and even where he does indulge in paradoxography, a recurrent energy in his wonder language animates the wondrous realia of the Greek world.[84] Of the pair of Dioscuri statues on the island of Pephnos, Pausanias states simply, "They are indeed a wonder" (τοῦτό τε δὴ θαῦμά ἐστι, 3.26.3). But, as with Herodotus, Pausanian wonder can denote a contextually marked sense of distinctiveness. Concerning the Temple of Hera on Samos and the Temple of Athena at Phocaea, both fated "to have been burned by the Persians" (ὑπὸ Περσῶν κατακαυθῆναι), he writes that they were "wonders all the same" (θαῦμα δὲ ὅμως ἦσαν, 7.5.4), their marvelousness made perhaps all the more special for their having been grazed by destruction.[85] On the bronze statue of Pergamene Apollo, he asserts that "Among bronzes, it is especially a marvel for its size and craftsmanship" (θαῦμα ἐν τοῖς μάλιστα μεγέθους τε ἕνεκα καὶ ἐπὶ τῇ τέχνῃ, 8.42.7), situating it thereby among other bronzes and highlighting the specific criteria of its excellence. Even small matters register for Pausanias. He notes that it is "worthy of wonder" (θαυμάσαι δὲ ἄξιον) that swallows neither lay nor hatch eggs in Daulis (10.4.9).

For all their precise noticing, however, the relatively straightforward declarative style of these passages lends, through implicit contrast, a certain grandeur to his other more elaborated expressions. For not all wonders are created equal for Pausanias, and in some instances, he seems to underscore in bolder detail the wondrous nature or quality of a certain fact, person, object, or place. Some of these instances allow the narrator to model for his readers the openness to astonishment that his wider text encourages. He writes, for instance, in the earliest example of his expressing wonder, how in reading over the less famous (οὐκ ἐπιφανέσιν) accounts of Pyrrhus, he became "tremendously astonished at his daring" (ταῦτα ἐπιλεγομένῳ μοι μάλιστα ἐπῆλθε θαυμάσαι Πύρρου τόλμαν, 1.12.2), indicating a reflective

---

paradoxography were rarely mobile forces à la Herodotus or Pausanias, as Schepens and Delcroix note (388–89). See also Dench 2007: 497; Shannon-Henderson 2020: 163–64.

[84] On Imperial *Wunderkultur* and paradoxography, see ní Mheallaigh 2014: 261–77; Shannon-Henderson 2020, with further bibliography.

[85] Compare Porter 2001: 81 on sublimity and "ruptured wholes."

322 HERODOTUS AND IMPERIAL GREEK LITERATURE

wonder that issues from historical rumination. Wondrous awe is not, in this sense, isolated to the visual encounter with, say, the white marble of the stadium at Athens (1.19.6), mentioned just a few chapters after the comment on Pyrrhus, but manifestly includes the feeling that comes over (ἐπῆλθε) a person comprehending a set of obscure texts.

Later, near the midpoint of his ten-book work, amid his extended description of Olympia (stretching across Books 5 and 6, which, in Elsner's words, "act[] as a grand metonym for all of Pausanias' Greece"),[86] Pausanias declares that "one can indeed see and hear many things in Greece that are worthy of wonder, but especially with the Eleusinian Mysteries and the Olympic Games there is a share of the divine intention" (πολλὰ μὲν δὴ καὶ ἄλλα ἴδοι τις ἂν ἐν Ἕλλησι, τὰ δὲ καὶ ἀκοῦσαι θαύματος ἄξια· μάλιστα δὲ τοῖς Ἐλευσῖνι δρωμένοις καὶ ἀγῶνι τῷ ἐν Ὀλυμπίᾳ μέτεστιν ἐκ θεοῦ φροντίδος, 5.10.1).[87] The reader is invited both to ponder, at the heart of Pausanias's own text, the multisensory (ἴδοι, ἀκοῦσαι) panoply of Greek wonders named and unnamed (πολλά . . . καὶ ἄλλα) and to regard, as though entering into a sacred share (μέτεστιν) of the divine mind (ἐκ θεοῦ φροντίδος), the mystical quality that attaches to the matters Pausanias describes. Wonder here relates to numinous elements that infuse the sacred monuments and spaces Pausanias encounters. Indeed, in the slew of examples that immediately ensue—the sacred grove, the temple, and finally the statue of Zeus at Olympia (5.10.2–11.10)—the narrator ultimately bows before the descriptive incommensurability of facts and figures: "The measurements given are somehow a long way off from the glory that overtakes those who see the statue" (τὰ εἰρημένα αὐτοῖς μέτρα πολύ τι ἀποδέοντά ἐστιν ἢ τοῖς ἰδοῦσι παρέστηκεν ἐς τὸ ἄγαλμα δόξα, 5.11.9).[88] Even the god is invoked as testimonial to the power of the image (his own, no less): "And they report that the god himself was witness to Phidias's skill" (καὶ αὐτὸν τὸν θεὸν μάρτυρα ἐς τοῦ Φειδίου τὴν τέχνην γενέσθαι λέγουσιν, 5.11.9). By such moves—dissolving description into doxology (δόξα) and quoting a local bit of folklore—Pausanias puts readers in mind, on the one hand, of the awed Herodotean narrator bedazzled by the Egyptian labyrinth "surpassing description" (λόγου μέζω, 2.148.1), whose manifold convolutions produce myriad wonders (οἱ εἱλιγμοὶ διὰ τῶν αὐλέων ἐόντες ποικιλώτατοι θῶμα μυρίον παρείχοντο, 2.148.6). But on the other

[86] Elsner 2001b: 17.

[87] For the same collocation, focalized from the "outsider" perspective of the Persians, see Chariton 5.4.4.

[88] Compare Pausanias's Herodotean chariness of disclosing religious details; Bowie 2001: 25; Hawes 2016: 339 (with n. 46).

PAUSANIAS IN WONDERLAND   323

hand, Pausanias delivers his dispatch from the center of Greece, beckoning readers, amid all that is fractured and dilapidated, toward an experience of humbled awe through meditation on a Hellenic sacred site.

Such narratorial gestures conspire toward highlighting the specialness of Greece and toward offering a kind of ruminative pause for his readers. In his account of the River Styx in Arcadia, the periegete brings into focus something in nature that in other literary representations is depicted in the province of the dead:

> As you travel westward from Pheneüs, the road on the left goes to the city called Cleitor, and on the right is the road to Nonacris and the water of the Styx. Long ago Nonacris was an Arcadian settlement that took its name from the wife of Lycaon. In my time it was in ruins, but many of these were not easy to see. Not far from the ruins there is a high cliff. I know of no other cliff rising to such a height. Water trickles down the cliff, which the Greeks call the Styx. . . . Homer in particular introduced the name of the Styx into poetry. . . . He made the Styx a river in Hades. . . . It is said that at one time the river was lethal for the goats who first drank from its water. Other properties attaching to the water also became known that fell into the category of "marvel." (8.17.6, 8.18.2, 8.18.3, 8.18.4)

ἐκ Φενεοῦ δὲ ἰόντι ἐπὶ [τὴν] ἑσπέρας καὶ ἡλίου δυσμῶν ἡ μὲν ἀριστερὰ τῶν ὁδῶν ἐς πόλιν ἄγει Κλείτορα, ἐν δεξιᾷ δὲ ἐπὶ Νώνακριν καὶ τὸ ὕδωρ τῆς Στυγός. τὸ μὲν δὴ ἀρχαῖον ἡ Νώνακρις πόλισμα ἦν Ἀρκάδων καὶ ἀπὸ τῆς Λυκάονος γυναικὸς τὸ ὄνομα εἰλήφει· τὰ δὲ ἐφ᾽ ἡμῶν ἐρείπια ἦν, οὐδὲ τούτων τὰ πολλὰ ἔτι δῆλα. τῶν δὲ ἐρειπίων οὐ πόρρω κρημνός ἐστιν ὑψηλός, οὐχ ἕτερον δ᾽ ἐς τοσοῦτον ἀνήκοντα ὕψους οἶδα· καὶ ὕδωρ κατὰ τοῦ κρημνοῦ στάζει, καλοῦσι δὲ Ἕλληνες αὐτὸ ὕδωρ Στυγός. . . . μάλιστα δὲ τῆς Στυγὸς τὸ ὄνομα ἐς τὴν ποίησιν ἐπεισηγάγετο Ὅμηρος. . . . ἐποίησε δὲ καὶ ἐν Ἅιδου ὕδωρ εἶναι . . . . λέγεται δὲ ὅτι γένοιτό ποτε ὄλεθρος ἀπ᾽ αὐτοῦ καὶ αἰξίν, αἳ τοῦ ὕδατος ἔπιον πρῶτον· χρόνῳ δὲ ὕστερον ἐγνώσθη καὶ εἰ δή τι ἄλλο πρόσεστι τῷ ὕδατι τῶν ἐς θαῦμα ἡκόντων.

The psychogeographic movement in this passage commands attention. The ruins of the site are in Pausanias's day "not easy to see" (οὐδὲ . . . ἔτι δῆλα), their faintness nearly belying a vertical depth of time (τὸ μὲν δὴ ἀρχαῖον). In contrast to the unclear ruins stands the cliff "not far off" (οὐ πόρρω), the height of which renders it unmissable. Its trickling water produces the Styx,

324 HERODOTUS AND IMPERIAL GREEK LITERATURE

which Pausanias bilocates in the tradition as part of another realm (Hades), even as here it is part of the present life acquiring the lore of marvel (ἐς θαῦμα). Pausanias orients one's view from the invisible underworld to the visible life of earth. He goes on to describe various properties, including the water's ability to dissolve or corrode glass, crystal, horn, bone, and so forth (8.18.5), before concluding with a general statement:

> Thus has the god apportioned to the lowliest things mastery over things thought to be far more exalted. Pearls are dissolved by vinegar, and diamonds, hardest of stones, melt in the blood of a goat. The only thing capable of withstanding the Styx's water is the hoof of a horse . . . . (8.18.6)

> ἔδωκε δὲ ἄρα ὁ θεὸς τοῖς μάλιστα ἀπερριμμένοις κρατεῖν τῶν ὑπερηρκότων τῇ δόξῃ. τοῦτο μὲν γὰρ τὰ μάργαρα ἀπόλλυσθαι πέφυκεν ὑπὸ τοῦ ὄξους, τοῦτο δὲ τὸν ἀδάμαντα λίθων ὄντα ἰσχυρότατον τοῦ τράγου κατατήκει τὸ αἷμα· καὶ δὴ καὶ τὸ ὕδωρ οὐ δύναται τῆς Στυγὸς ὁπλὴν ἵππου βιάσασθαι μόνην . . . .

Even as he "relocates" the Styx to the earth, Pausanias underscores its distinctiveness and inflects the passage with a flickering sense of liminality between life and death.[89] Nor is the move incidental, for he ultimately imparts a link between the marvelous nature of the river and the divine assurance that mighty things are subject to surprising reversals. Indeed, returning us to the theme of Herodotean divine leveling, Pausanias's notion of Greece qua wonder frequently connects to his text's broader sense of divine presence. In this regard, it is perhaps not surprising that his Book 8, on Arcadia, exhibits a higher concentration of narrator-designated wonders (eight instances, the highest single-book concentration, tied with Book 1). As Hutton has pointed out, Book 8 appears to have a special quality: "Pausanias presents his experience with the heart of Greece [in Book 8] as something of a transformative one, one that gives him insight into the nature of Greek culture that he did not possess before."[90] The Greek world, described as one pervaded by the gods in Pausanias's long account, exercises an enthralling pull. The powers of the Styx are the powers of the god, who can accomplish things contrary to expectation (κρατεῖν τῶν ὑπερηρκότων τῇ δόξῃ, 8.18.5). Acknowledging

---

[89] See 8.18.4: "This water brings death to all, to both every human and animal" (θάνατον δὲ τὸ ὕδωρ φέρει τοῦτο καὶ ἀνθρώπῳ καὶ ἄλλῳ ζῴῳ παντί).
[90] Hutton 2010: 443.

PAUSANIAS IN WONDERLAND 325

wonder becomes part of the effort in Pausanias to countenance shifts in fortune and the overriding sense of divine ordering, discussed in chapter 7.

Pausanias thus leads readers not only up the heights of mountains or by the flow of rivers but also into a space of contemplation. While he is prone to scientific detail and autopsy, he also has an interest in the unsolvable. His narrative renders Greece mysterious and unaccountable in its own way. In his description of the *temenos* of Lycaean Zeus in Arcadia, it is not entirely clear if the *temenos* itself or the activity associated with it constitutes the θαῦμα:

> As for marvels, Mount Lycaeus furnishes this one especially. There is a precinct sacred to Lycaean Zeus where human entrance is forbidden. Anyone overlooking the law and going in will by necessity live no more than a year. And beyond this is the story that everything within the precinct, human or animal, casts no shadow. It is for this reason that if a creature takes refuge in the precinct a hunter will not wish to follow it in but will remain outside, seeing the beast but not its shadow. So long as the sun is in the constellation of the Crab, no tree or living being has a shadow in Syene just near Ethiopia. But at the Mount Lycaeus precinct it is always the case that there are no shadows in any season. (8.38.6)

> τὸ δὲ ὄρος παρέχεται τὸ Λύκαιον καὶ ἄλλα ἐς θαῦμα καὶ μάλιστα τόδε. τέμενός ἐστιν ἐν αὐτῷ Λυκαίου Διός, ἔσοδος δὲ οὐκ ἔστιν ἐς αὐτὸ ἀνθρώποις· ὑπεριδόντα δὲ τοῦ νόμου καὶ ἐσελθόντα ἀνάγκη πᾶσα αὐτὸν ἐνιαυτοῦ πρόσω μὴ βιῶναι. καὶ τάδε ἔτι ἐλέγετο, τὰ ἐντὸς τοῦ τεμένους γενόμενα ὁμοίως πάντα καὶ θηρία καὶ ἀνθρώπους οὐ παρέχεσθαι σκιάν· καὶ διὰ τοῦτο ἐς τὸ τέμενος θηρίου καταφεύγοντος οὐκ ἐθέλει οἱ συνεσπίπτειν ὁ κυνηγέτης, ἀλλὰ ὑπομένων ἐκτὸς καὶ ὁρῶν τὸ θηρίον οὐδεμίαν ἀπ' αὐτοῦ θεᾶται σκιάν. χρόνον μὲν δὴ τὸν ἴσον ἔπεισί τε ὁ ἥλιος τὸν ἐν τῷ οὐρανῷ καρκίνον καὶ ἐν Συήνῃ τῇ πρὸ Αἰθιοπίας οὔτε ἀπὸ δένδρων οὔτε ἀπὸ τῶν ζῴων γενέσθαι σκιὰν ἔστι· τὸ δὲ ἐν τῷ Λυκαίῳ τέμενος τὸ αὐτὸ ἐς τὰς σκιὰς ἀεί τε καὶ ἐπὶ πασῶν πέπονθε τῶν ὡρῶν.

Pausanias's description "enters" the shrine that humans are forbidden to enter.[91] He reports on something nearly ineffable, since any human observation of what occurs in the precinct is technically forbidden. It would seem that what determines the thaumastic quality of the shrine is not the architecture

---

[91] On this passage, see Elsner 1995: 148.

326　HERODOTUS AND IMPERIAL GREEK LITERATURE

but rather the aura of holiness that swirls about the place, told through legend that itself bespeaks a kind of violation, traversing the impenetrable. Indeed, as if collecting into a larger thesis his own repeated insistence on the marvels of Hellas, Pausanias declares late in his text a core element of his wonder-writing. Shortly before describing the treasury of Minyas in Boeotia as one of the great wonders in Greece and indeed of the world (θησαυρὸς δὲ ὁ Μινύου, θαῦμα ὂν τῶν ἐν Ἑλλάδι αὐτῇ καὶ τῶν ἑτέρωθι οὐδενὸς ὕστερον, 9.38.2), Pausanias overtly refers to the phenomenon of Greeks placing their sense of wonder elsewhere:

> The Greeks appear keen to hold in greater wonder sights foreign compared with sights domestic. For while distinguished writers have described the pyramids of Egypt down to the most accurate detail, they have not made the briefest mention of the treasury of Minyas or the walls of Tiryns, although these are in no way less marvelous. (9.36.5)

> Ἕλληνες δὲ ἄρα εἰσὶ δεινοὶ τὰ ὑπερόρια ἐν θαύματι τίθεσθαι μείζονι ἢ τὰ οἰκεῖα, ὁπότε γε ἀνδράσιν ἐπιφανέσιν ἐς συγγραφὴν πυραμίδας μὲν τὰς παρὰ Αἰγυπτίοις ἐπῆλθεν ἐξηγήσασθαι πρὸς <τὸ> ἀκριβέστατον, θησαυρὸν δὲ τὸν Μινύου καὶ τὰ τείχη τὰ ἐν Τίρυνθι οὐδὲ ἐπὶ βραχὺ ἤγαγον μνήμης, οὐδὲν ὄντα ἐλάττονος θαύματος.

A polemical edge prevails. Greeks have followed the lead of "distinguished writers" in imputing to foreign sites greater wonder. But Pausanias's interest has been to turn his reader's eye away from the exotica of foreign places and instead toward the lambent beauties of Greece.[92]

Connected with this focus on wonder, much has been made of Pausanias's apparently pilgrim-like journey.[93] One of the best-known passages often cited in this line of inquiry may say something not only about Pausanias's perspective on divinity but also about his text's mediation of Herodotean wonder and how Pausanias's appropriation serves less as an explication of Greece and more as a way into the numinous world of its past:

---

[92] See Arafat 1996: 35–36 and Pretzler 2007a: 132 on Pausanias's audiences.

[93] On Pausanias's religious sensibilities, see Habicht 1985: 156–59; Veyne 1988: 11–12, 95–102; Heer 1979: 250–54; Elsner 1992 (with overlaps at Elsner 1995: 125–55); Hutton 2005a; Hutton 2005b: 303–11. Cf. Swain 1996: 342–43. I favor Stewart's term (2013: 231) of "intellectual pilgrimage," which, as he notes, "emphasizes both the intellectual and religious elements of his travels." See further Jost 2007: 119 on Pausanias's "cultural tourism," with her view that Pausanias's "geographical and cultural horizon is wider than that of a pilgrim."

PAUSANIAS IN WONDERLAND 327

When I started writing this account I rather took these legends as so much **foolishness**, but on **reaching as far as Arcadia** I came to have a more thoughtful view of them, which is as follows. Long ago the **Greeks thought to be wise spoke their stories not outright but in riddles**. Thus the legends about Cronus I reckoned to be this sort of Greek wisdom. So when it comes to things about the divine I will employ the tradition handed down. (8.8.3)

τούτοις Ἑλλήνων ἐγὼ τοῖς λόγοις ἀρχόμενος μὲν τῆς συγγραφῆς **εὐηθίας** ἔνεμον πλέον, ἐς δὲ **τὰ Ἀρκάδων προεληλυθὼς** πρόνοιαν περὶ αὐτῶν τοιάνδε ἐλάμβανον· Ἑλλήνων τοὺς νομιζομένους σοφοὺς δι' **αἰνιγμάτων πάλαι καὶ οὐκ ἐκ τοῦ εὐθέος λέγειν τοὺς λόγους**, καὶ τὰ εἰρημένα οὖν ἐς τὸν Κρόνον σοφίαν εἶναί τινα εἴκαζον Ἑλλήνων. τῶν μὲν δὴ ἐς τὸ θεῖον ἡκόντων τοῖς εἰρημένοις χρησόμεθα.

Conjoining his narrative to his physical journey, and its associated intellectual journey, he admits a change of perspective (πρόνοιαν περὶ αὐτῶν τοιάνδε ἐλάμβανον). Pausanias does not speak literally of entering Arcadia but rather of entering into the "things" or "matters" of the Arcadians (ἐς δὲ τὰ Ἀρκάδων). The participle προεληλυθώς thus does double duty as a verb both of physical motion—Pausanias actually went to Arcadia—and of intellectual, psychogeographic motion, entering into matters unseen and unknown *until* he went there. The homophony of εὐηθίας and εὐθέος may suggest that the clearer, more straightforward explanation is in fact the more absurd. For the religious preoccupations of Pausanias's text suggest that the enigmatic aspects of his encounters, not immediately accessible, hold greater explanatory power. Moreover, Pausanias's use of the word εὐηθία with regard to "what the Greeks say" about religion will put readers in mind of Herodotus's own single, pointed use of the word εὐήθης, also in a passage about religion: "The Greeks tell any number of stories uncritically, one of the most absurd being the tale of how Heracles came to Egypt. . . . And may the gods and heroes show me forbearance for talking as I have about these matters" (2.45.1, 3).[94] Herodotus corrects the Greek view of what happened and says the "silly" story only proves how ignorant the Greeks are of Egyptian customs (2.45.2).[95] His own journeying and acquisition of knowledge lead

---

[94] λέγουσι δὲ πολλὰ καὶ ἄλλα ἀνεπισκέπτως οἱ Ἕλληνες· εὐήθης δὲ αὐτῶν καὶ ὅδε ὁ μῦθός ἐστι τὸν περὶ τοῦ Ἡρακλέος λέγουσι, ὡς αὐτὸν ἀπικόμενον ἐς Αἴγυπτον. . . . καὶ περὶ μὲν τούτων τοσαῦτα ἡμῖν εἰποῦσι καὶ παρὰ τῶν θεῶν καὶ παρὰ τῶν ἡρώων εὐμένεια εἴη.

[95] See Harrison 2000: 188.

328   HERODOTUS AND IMPERIAL GREEK LITERATURE

to a correction of the absurd Greek idea. Geographic movement leads to psychogeographic alteration.

But matters differ slightly for Pausanias. His movement through Greece leads not toward a demystification of absurd Greek beliefs but, rather, toward a respect for the tradition of mystification itself, even a kind of near-sublimity.[96] The Greeks of old (πάλαι) who were thought to be wise spoke through riddles (δι᾽ αἰνιγμάτων) and not straightforwardly (οὐκ ἐκ τοῦ εὐθέος λέγειν). The cryptic things held to be wise by locals are not silly things to be dismissed but rather the stories Pausanias will use for encounters with the sacred. What Pausanias describes here is an openness to ancient suppositions about what had been regarded as wise. His work, recording the sites of Greece, both natural and built, embraces the local, even where local idiom surpasses understanding. He is willing to reform, or at least to suspend, his own thinking in favor of prior accounts, particularly as they apply to "the divine" (τῶν μὲν δὴ ἐς τὸ θεῖον ἡκόντων τοῖς εἰρημένοις χρησόμεθα). In encouraging his readers to regard Greece as a surpassing site of wonder, Pausanias encourages them toward a reckoning with the strangeness of Greece, "the goddess of 'Hellenism' itself."[97]

Pausanias thus evokes Herodotus's thaumatizing position as an outsider but retrains his globalizing perspective onto Greece as a cosmos of authentic wonder. The repurposed topos, celebrating the extant marvels of Greece rather than illusory oddities, accords with Pausanias's vision of the fragility of *ta Hellenika* and likely derives from the fact that Greece was not his homeland.[98] Pausanias registers his own such reckoning with the enigmas of the Greek past. Wondrous features such as the River Styx and the Temple of Lycaean Zeus speak to a world charged with divine presence, at some remove

[96] Compare the frequent language of wonder, in cognates of θαῦμα, in Longinus, *On the Sublime* (e.g., 1.4, 7.1, 7.4, 9.2, 9.3, 10.3, 30.1, 35.4–5, 36.3, 39.3, 39.4, 44.1, 44.8), with that of Pausanias, and see generally Porter 2001 for ideas of Longinian sublimity in Pausanias, with comments about wonder at 66–67. See also Porter 2016: 173–77, 382–83 (and generally 382–536) on the materiality of the sublime, relevant to Pausanias's focus on physical artifacts. I here tentatively suggest a correlation between Pausanias's syntax and his work's potential to activate an idea of sublimity, since hyperbaton factors as a component of the Longinian sublime, conveying "vivid emotion" (ἐναγωνίου πάθους, 22.1). Pausanias's syntax well exemplifies the defamiliarization of natural word order that Longinus highlights as a marker of the sublime. On this view, Pausanias's text potentially evokes sublimity not only in the ways Porter has described—through its focus on fragmentary and disappearing objects— but in the very ruptures of traditional syntactic pattern.

[97] Hutton 2010: 448.

[98] Such acclamation is perhaps of a piece with Pausanias's seemingly distanced way of talking about the Greeks; see Porter 2001: 89, commenting on this "curious and alienating tactic of presenting Greek history for Greeks, but from the Roman perspective of what 'the Greeks' are and do," and 89 n. 102, citing Paus. 2.16.4 and 10.17.13.

PAUSANIAS IN WONDERLAND 329

from immediate human cognition. In line with his view of Greece and its realia as subject to decay and oblivion, Pausanias's multifarious attestation of Greece's marvelous qualities contributes to his memorializing act in the *Periegesis*, adding to the sense that his work carries a restorative function as "a text of revelation and discovery" for its Greek readers.[99] In Pausanias's literary crafting, the Herodotean energy of distant, exoticizing wonder is felt anew—for Greece itself.

In this chapter, we have seen how Pausanias recalls Herodotus in his specific negotiation of movement through space as a means to narrativization. He appropriates Herodotus's hodological style but also engages, like his predecessor, in forms of cartographic knowledge that supervene the view from the ground. At the same time, he conveys a sense of wanting to supplement and prolong the past, rather than repeat it, finding ways to mark his text as different and new. Alongside his own efforts at novelty, and against a sense of staleness and decline, pulses the energy of Greece's continued wondrousness. Pausanias's Herodotean openness to marveling extends to his readers an open-ended sense of incompleteness and invites them to form their own impressions. Wonder lures readers to join in contemplation. Ultimately, Pausanias reifies an idea of Greece as both an enduring monument and an ambiguous, uncontainable collection of fragments. His text likewise exhibits both the perceived monumentality of Herodotean authority and the ongoing, unfinishable documentation of τὰ Ἑλληνικά (1.26.4).

---

[99] The phrase is that of Hutton 2010: 453. The line of argument in Hutton is rather intricate and depends in some sense on accepting correspondences between Pausanias Book 4 and Book 10: "To the extent that we, following Sidebottom [2002: 498–99], see Anyte's text [Paus. 10.38] as an allegory for Pausanias's own work, Pausanias seems to be claiming that his text of revelation and discovery can help restore something that the Greeks have lost: a clear vision of their rightful place in a world where they have become gradually more peripheral and unexceptional" (453).

Epilogue

Herodotus without End

"Everyone wants to have the end in view" (τὸ γὰρ τέλος πάντες βούλονται καθορᾶν). (Aristotle, *Rhetoric* 3.9.1, 1409a31–32)

To read the first-century CE treatise *On the Sublime* is to be struck by sublimity's range. The concept and sensation are capacious, both in descriptor and in thing described.[1] This generates part of the attraction. The allure of the sublime connects to a sense of transcendence. Sublimity seems to rise above historical particular. Encountering Longinus's view that, for instance, something wondrous dwells in Sappho's poetry (*Subl.* 10) tempts us to subscribe to an idea of the transhistorical; even this often abstruse critic, one feels, recognized that Sappho is astonishing. Yet the wish to see a connection also constitutes a version of what Quentin Skinner once called the "mythology of prolepsis," that belief that something from earlier anticipates a later manifestation.[2] Indeed, other instances of aesthetic response in Longinus point up such questionable prolepsis. When listing his five sources of sublimity, Longinus writes that the first and most important is "the conception of great thoughts" (τὸ περὶ τὰς νοήσεις ἀδρεπήβολον, *Subl.* 8.1) and claims to have defined this elsewhere in a work on Xenophon. If many readers will feel comfortable with Longinus's exaltation of Sappho, what to make of his attention to the arguably less ecstasy-inducing Athenian historian and general? We might make excuses. Is it Xenophon himself who had "great thoughts" or Socrates as voiced through Xenophon? Or does Xenophon's sublimity reside in his continuation of a "sublime" Thucydides? Even as we (and who are the "we"?) might believe that Longinus "shares" "our" Sappho (or at least "our"

---

[1] See Porter 2016: 57–177.
[2] Skinner 1969: 22.

332 EPILOGUE

fr. 31), the Xenophon comment reminds us of a certain arbitrariness: had we Longinus's lost work, perhaps we would know a Xenophon different from the one we today are unlikely to name among authors who induce sublime transport.

These Longinian glimpses reiterate the contingencies of reception. We accept that we read because others have read and often because of how they have read. But what of the occasions when readers read the "wrong" things or read them the "wrong" way? In this book, I have explored some of the ways in which various ancient authors, not all of them (or all of their works) always highly favored by later audiences, engaged with yet another author who, especially in the early days of his afterlife, inspired both praise and distrust, adulation and denigration. I have wanted to argue that assumptions of critical continuity can blind us to the particulars of interpretive appropriation by these Imperial writers, and that reading for surface affirmations of reputation is not the same as sounding out the depths of reception. I have tried to take seriously a set of writers in the context of their own agendas and to suggest that critical continuity lies less in the content of conclusions reached and rather more in the very fact of motivated reading, even as motivations change. I have shown that among the Imperial Greek writers here studied, there occurs an interplay of not always reconcilable energies. Multiple readings of Herodotus are possible in their hands. If these writers knew how to play down Herodotus, submerging their imitation, touting the conventional wisdom of his mendacity or slipperiness, they also knew how to play him up, in their kinetic imitations, hypotextual activations, and explorations of his transdiscursive thought.

We might ask, all the same, what we are to make of the instances when ancient readers *do* appear to confirm some intuition or insight we believe *we* now hold regarding Herodotus. Is prolepsis always a myth? The fact of apparent continuity raises questions about our own critical largesse as readers. What do we grant previous readers in interpretive ingenuity? How do beliefs in continuity cause us to overlook the details and motivations of ancient readings? We may think, for instance, that we already know Herodotus to be a complex narrator, a writer whose self-presentation has consequences for how we judge his role in (and the truth of) his narrative. Many modern studies have shown this to be a feature any reader of Herodotus must confront. But already both Dionysius and Plutarch, in rather different ways, were onto something similar. Reading them, we recognize that a strong notion of authorship—of a person who creates a work and has an ethical role in molding it—mattered to their own sense of identity as authors and could (in Dionysius's case) inspire a critical geniality or (in Plutarch's case) generate a test of character by which the critic attempts to outclass the author. These writers shape an idea of Herodotus as a force of authorial integrity, one that we might now reflexively take for granted. But they also move us to consider accessibility, the question of who "knows" how to read: the affable Dionysius, with his likable Herodotus, or Plutarch, with his deceptive author who requires *his* elucidation. They do not simply affirm later views, then. The cases of Dionysius and Plutarch also urge us to weigh the question of whom we grant the authority of interpretation.

Likewise, in the case of Lucian, we might believe we already know Herodotus to be a kind of relativist or ironist. Lucian's maneuvers, however, inspire us to wonder how we are to read the original "serious" hypotext without the intervention of Lucian, who turns the serious and straight on their sides. Lucian's *historia* is not a pure fantasy of moon dwellers and whale worlds. It does not simply "weird" Herodotus; instead, his *True Histories* and his Anacharsis dialogues point us to the uncanny that already exists in the midst of the serious. Lucian's refractions of the subjective experience of reading "straight" historiography mean that we cannot reread Herodotus, after Lucian, without also sensing Herodotus's own original strangeness. Likewise, in relatively "straight" authors such as Dio and Pausanias, various questions that seem removed or academic enter into a lived ambiguity. Dio sparks audiences to consider wisdom from various sources and to sense the fragility of what marks their own earthly greatness or distinctiveness. The apparatus of cultural difference that on one reading of Herodotus seems to structure various thrusts of history yields in Dio's hands to a slippery indistinctness of attenuated Hellenism. Where shall wisdom be found? In one learned man, in the voices of the *barbaroi* and Magi, among fringe Greeks of dubious Hellenicity? That Dio mediates these questions by activating Herodotus summons the murkiness to which the already brindled world of the *Histories* could give rise. Pausanias, finally, anchors his project in long-standing questions about the value of the past and cycles of historical meaning. He, too, loops these questions through Herodotus, but not always in a mood of triumphalism. Rather, the opacities of divinity, memory, and wonder produce the sense that the past is not always a zone of glory but often one of loss and mystery. Yet the consistent mooring of the *Periegesis*

334 EPILOGUE

to the *Histories* allows it to share in the survival of the past—Herodotean hauntings attest to the enduring presence of that which has vanished—and make of Herodotus's own achievement a work to which Pausanias himself contributes.

Herodotus's manifold import is thus realized across a range of texts that alternately conjure him explicitly and channel him implicitly. The acts of reception studied throughout this book complicate any straightforward reading of his reputation in antiquity. They suggest that reputation is only part of a complex reception of ideas on authorship and character, globalism and historical cyclicality, selfhood and foreignness, divinity and wonder. Kinetic receptions and hypotextual activations hark to but also interpret and transform the original text. Herodotus's canonicity is expanded with each act of reception. I would stop short, however, of saying that this can-onicity becomes a predetermining monolith or that reception always means referring to a stable "meaning" fixed unalterably in the *Histories*. As we have seen in different instances, reception often returns us to a point of indetermi-nacy and ambiguity in Herodotus. Reception is an antiphonal process that valorizes a source even as it also fragments and parcels that source out into the "halo of the multiple."

"Who decides that a work is finished and where does that certainty reside—in signatures, submissions, and declarations by artists? In the judgments of critics, viewers, and readers?" So asks Susan Stewart, ruminating on the no-tion of finality.[3] She goes on ultimately to contend that, even for supposedly finished works, the "task of art itself is ongoing and unending."[4] At the close of this book, I suggest that such a framing applies to the creative acts of re-ception encountered herein. Their effect is rather more to continue and to rework Herodotus than to stabilize him. For all the monumental qualities of the *Histories*, its repurposing and adaptation repeatedly figure Herodotus as ongoing. In some sense, reception adds an ellipsis to the sprawling text that resulted from Herodotus's own original questing. To return to Aristotle, whose formulations helped to launch this book, it seems only fitting that in his remarks on the continuous style in prose (λέξις εἰρομένη), he tags Herodotus as representative of a syntactical mode that "has no end in itself, and stops only when the narrated matter is complete" (οὐδὲν ἔχει τέλος καθ' αὑτήν, ἂν μὴ τὸ πρᾶγμα λεγόμενον τελειωθῇ, *Rh.*1409a30–31). Aristotle, like

---

[3] Stewart 2020: 230.
[4] Stewart 2020: 256.

Solon, orients us toward the end—indeed, he says that having the end in view is what we all want (τὸ γὰρ τέλος πάντες βούλονται καθορᾶν, 1409a31–32). But maybe the end is not what we all want. The Imperial Greek authors we have encountered challenge the idea of an end, and they challenge the ends of our own reading. Their dazzling receptions show us that no final boundary contains Herodotus's *Histories* and the unending wish to inquire.

Bibliography

Aboulafia, M. 1986. *The Mediating Self: Mead, Sartre, and Self-Determination*. New Haven.

Adams, C., and J. Roy (eds.). 2007. *Travel, Geography, and Culture in Ancient Greece, Egypt, and the Near East*. Oxford.

Aicher, P. 2013. "Herodotus and the Vulnerability Ethic in Ancient Greece." *Arion* 21.2: 55–99.

Akujärvi, J. 2005. *Researcher, Traveler, Narrator: Studies in Pausanias' Periegesis*. Lund.

Akujärvi, J. 2012a. "Pausanias," in de Jong 2012: 235–55.

Akujärvi, J. 2012b. "Pausanias' *Periegesis*, Dionysius Periegetes, Eustathius' Commentary, and the Construction of the Periegetic Genre," in D. Searby, E. B. Witakowska, and J. Heldt (eds.), *ΔΩΡΟΝ ΡΟΔΙΠΟΙΚΙΛΟΝ: Studies in Honor of Jan Olof Rosenqvist*. Uppsala: 41–52.

Alcock, S. E. 1993. *Graecia Capta: The Landscapes of Roman Greece*. Cambridge.

Alcock, S. E. 1996. "Landscapes of Memory and the Authority of Pausanias," in Bingen 1996: 241–67.

Alcock, S. E. 2001. "The Peculiar Book IV and the Problem of the Messenian Past," in Alcock, Cherry, and Elsner 2001: 142–66.

Alcock, S., J. F. Cherry, and J. Elsner (eds.). 2001. *Pausanias: Travel and Memory in Roman Greece*. Oxford.

Allen, K. H. 2003. "Becoming the 'Other': Attitudes and Practices at Attic Cemeteries," in C. Dougherty and L. Kurke (eds.), *The Cultures within Greek Culture*. Cambridge: 207–36.

Alonso-Núñez, J. 1988. "Herodotus' Ideas about World Empires." *AncSoc* 19: 125–33.

Ambaglio, D. 1991. "La Periegesi di Pausania e la storiografia greca tradita per citazioni." *QUCC* 39: 129–38.

Anderson, G. 1976a. *Lucian: Theme and Variation in the Second Sophistic*. Leiden.

Anderson, G. 1976b. "Lucian's Classics: Some Short Cuts to Culture." *BICS* 23: 59–68.

Anderson, G. 1976c. *Studies in Lucian's Comic Fiction*. Leiden.

Anderson, G. 1977. "Patterns in Lucian's Prolaliae." *Philologus* 121: 313–15.

Anderson, G. 1982. "Lucian: A Sophist's Sophist." *YCS* 27: 61–92.

Anderson, G. 1993. *The Second Sophistic: A Cultural Phenomenon in the Roman Empire*. London.

Anderson, G. 2000. "Some Uses of Storytelling in Dio," in Swain 2000a: 143–60.

Ando, C. 1999. "Was Rome a *polis*?" *ClAnt* 18.1: 5–34.

Andrade, N. J. 2013. *Syrian Identity in the Greco-Roman World*. Cambridge.

Anhalt, E. K. 2008. "Seeing is Believing: Four Women on Display in Herodotus' *Histories*." *NECJ* 35.4: 269–80.

Ankersmit, F. 1994. *History and Tropology: The Rise and Fall of Metaphor*. Berkeley.

Anzaldúa, G. 2007 [1987]. *Borderlands: The New Mestizo = La frontera*. 3rd ed. San Francisco.

Appiah, K. A. 2005. *The Ethics of Identity*. Princeton.

Arafat, K. W. 1996. *Pausanias' Greece: Ancient Artists and Roman Rulers*. Cambridge.

338 BIBLIOGRAPHY

Arbib, M. 2012. *How the Brain Got Language: The Mirror System Hypothesis*. Oxford.

Armayor, O. K. 1978. "Did Herodotus Ever Go to Egypt?" *Journal of the American Research Center in Egypt* 15: 59–73.

Armayor, O. K. 1985. *Herodotus' Autopsy of the Fayoum: Lake Moeris and the Labyrinth of Egypt*. Amsterdam.

Arrighetti, G. 1993. "Riflessione sulla letteratura e biografia presso i Greci," in F. Montanari (ed.), *La philologie grecque à l'époque hellénistique et romaine*. Vandoeuvres: 211–62.

Asheri, D., A. B. Lloyd, and A. Corcella (eds.). 2007. *A Commentary on Herodotus I–IV*. Oxford.

Auberger, J. 2011. "Pausanias le Périégète et la Seconde Sophistique," in Schmidt and Fleury 2011: 133–45.

Aujac, G. (ed.). 1978. *Denys d'Halicarnasse: Opuscules rhétoriques*. Tome I. Paris.

Aujac, G. (ed.). 1981. *Denys d'Halicarnasse: Opuscules rhétoriques*. Tome III. Paris.

Aujac, G. (ed.). 1988. *Denys d'Halicarnasse: Opuscules rhétoriques*. Tome II. Paris.

Aujac, G. (ed.). 1991. *Denys d'Halicarnasse: Opuscules rhétoriques*. Tome IV. Paris.

Aujac, G. (ed.). 1992. *Denys d'Halicarnasse: Opuscules rhétoriques*. Tome V. Paris.

Avery, J. R. 1997. "Herodotean Presences in Lucian." Dissertation, New Haven.

Bäbler, B. 2002. "'Long-Haired Greeks in Trousers': Olbia and Dio Chrysostom (Or. 36, 'Borystheniticus')." *Ancient Civilizations* 8.3–4: 311–27.

Bäbler, B. 2003. "Behoste Griechen im Skythenland: Erscheinungsformen und Wahrnehmung antiker Kultur in ihren Grenzbereichen," in Nesselrath 2003: 113–27.

Bäbler, B. 2007. "Dio Chrysostom's Construction of Olbia," in Braund and Kryzhitskiy 2007: 145–60.

Bakker, E. J. 2002. "The Making of History: Herodotus' *Histories' apodeixis*," in Bakker, de Jong, and van Wees 2002: 3–32.

Bakker, E. J., I. J. F. de Jong, and H. van Wees (eds.). 2002. *Brill's Companion to Herodotus*. Leiden.

Baragwanath, E. 2008. *Motivation and Narrative in Herodotus*. Oxford.

Baragwanath, E. 2017. "Intertextuality and Plural Truths in Xenophon's Historical Narrative," in Hau and Ruffell 2017: 155–71.

Baragwanath, E., and M. de Bakker (eds.). 2012. *Myth, Truth, and Narrative in Herodotus*. Oxford.

Barrow, R. H. 1967. *Plutarch and His Times*. London.

Barth, H. 1968. "Zur Bewertung und Auswahl des Stoffes durch Herodotus (Die Begriffe θῶμα, θωμάζω, θωμάσιος und θωμαστός)." *Klio* 50: 93–110.

Barthes, R. 1977 [1967]. "The Death of the Author," in *Image-Music-Text*. Trans. S. Heath. London: 142–48.

Bartky, E. 2002. "Aristotle and the Politics of Herodotus' *History*." *Review of Politics* 64.3: 445–68.

Bartley, A. (ed.). 2009. *A Lucian for Our Times*. Newcastle.

Bassi, K. 2014. "Croesus' Offerings and the Value of the Past in Herodotus' *Histories*," in Ker and Pieper 2014: 173–96.

Bassi, K. 2016. *Traces of the Past: Classics between History and Archaeology*. Ann Arbor.

Baumbach, M., and P. von Möllendorff. 2017. *Ein literarischer Prometheus: Lukian aus Samosata und die Zweite Sophistik*. Heidelberg.

Beck, M. (ed.). 2014. *A Companion to Plutarch*. Malden, MA.

Beecroft, A. 2008. "World Literature without a Hyphen: Towards a Typology of Literary Systems." *NLR* 54: 87–100.

BIBLIOGRAPHY   339

Beloe, W. 1812. *Herodotus*. London.

Benjamin, W. 1936. "The Storyteller: Reflections on the Works of Nikolai Leskov," in H. Arendt (ed.), 1968, *Illuminations*. Trans. H. Zohn. New York: 83–110.

Benjamin, W. 1950. "Theses on the Philosophy of History," in H. Arendt (ed.), 1968, *Illuminations*. Trans. H. Zohn. New York: 253–64.

Bichler, R. 2000. *Herodots Welt: Der Aufbau der Historie am Bild der fremden Länder und Völker, ihrer Zivilisation und ihrer Geschichte*. Berlin.

Bichler, R. 2006. "Über Grenzen und ihre Relativität im Licht von Herodots *Historien*," in B. Burtscher-Bechter, P. Haider, B. Mertz-Baumgartner, and R. Rollinger (eds.), *Grenzen und Entgrenzungen: Historische und kulturwissenschaftliche Überlegungen am Beispiel des Mittelmeerraums*. Saarbrücken: 155–70.

Bichler, R., and R. Rollinger. 2000. *Herodot*. Hildesheim.

Bidez, J., and F. Cumont. 1938. *Les mages hellénisés*. 2 vols. Paris.

Billault, A. 2005. "Dion Chrysostome, Protagoras et Platon dans le discours XXXVI, 'Borysthénitique.'" *REA* 107.2: 727–43.

Bingen, J. (ed.). 1996. *Pausanias Historien*. Vandoeuvres.

Biriotti, M., and N. Miller (eds.). 1993. *What Is an Author?* Manchester.

Blank, D. 2011. "Reading between the Lies: Plutarch and Chrysippus on the Uses of Poetry," in J. Allen, E. K. Emilsson, W.-R. Mann, and B. Morison (eds.), *Oxford Studies in Ancient Philosophy* 40: 237–64.

Blösel, W. 2013. "Quellen—Kritik: Herodots Darstellung der Athener," in B. Dunsch and K. Ruffing (eds.), *Herodots Quellen—Die Quellen Herodots*. Wiesbaden: 255–72.

Boake, J. W. 1975. "Plutarch's Historical Judgement with Special Reference to the *De Herodoti Malignitate*." Dissertation, Toronto.

Bompaire, J. 1958. *Lucien Écrivain: Imitation et Création*. Paris.

Bonner, S. F. 1939. *The Literary Treatises of Dionysius of Halicarnassus: A Study in the Development of Critical Method*. Cambridge.

Booth, K. J. 2013. "Embodied Mind and the Mimetic Basis for Taking the Role of the Other," in Burke and Skowroński 2013: 137–48.

Borg, B. E. (ed.). 2004. *Paideia: The World of the Second Sophistic*. Berlin.

Borgeaud, P. 2004 [1996]. *Mother of the Gods: From Cybele to the Virgin Mary*. Trans. L. Hochroth. Baltimore.

Bost-Pouderon, C. (ed.). 2011. *Dion de Pruse dit Dion Chrysostome—Oeuvres: Premier discours à Tarse (Or. XXXIII), Second discours à Tarse (Or. XXXIV), Discours à Célènes de Phrygie (Or. XXXV), Discours borysthénitique (Or. XXXVI)*. Paris.

Bowen, A. 1992. *Plutarch: The Malice of Herodotus*. Warminster.

Bowersock, G. W. 1965. *Augustus and the Greek World*. Oxford.

Bowersock, G. W. 1979. "Historical Problems in Late Republican and Augustan Classicism," in Flashar 1979: 57–75.

Bowersock, G. W. 1989. "Herodotus, Alexander, and Rome." *American Scholar* 58.3: 407–14.

Bowie, E. L. 1970. "Greeks and Their Past in the Second Sophistic." *P&P* 46.1: 3–41.

Bowie, E. L. 1989. "Poetry and Poets in Asia and Achaea," in S. Walker and A. Cameron (eds.), *The Greek Renaissance in the Roman Empire: Papers from the Tenth British Museum Classical Colloquium, BICS* supp. 55. London: 198–205.

Bowie, E. L. 1991. "Hellenes and Hellenism in the Writers of the Early Second Sophistic," in S. Saïd (ed.), *ΕΛΛΗΝΙΣΜΟΣ: Quelques jalons pour une histoire de l'identité grecque, Actes du colloque de Strasbourg, 25–27 octobre 1989*. Leiden: 183–204.

340 BIBLIOGRAPHY

Bowie, E. L. 1996. "Past and Present in Pausanias," in Bingen 1996: 207–30.

Bowie, E. L. 2001. "Inspiration and Aspiration: Date, Genre, and Readership," in Alcock, Cherry, and Elsner 2001: 21–32.

Bowie, E. L. 2004. "Poetry and Music in the Life of Plutarch's Statesmen," in L. de Blois, J. Bons, T. Kessels, and D. M. Schenkeveld (eds.), *The Statesman in Plutarch's Works*, Vol. 1. Leiden: 115–23.

Bowie, E. L. 2008a. "Literary Milieux," in T. Whitmarsh (ed.), *The Cambridge Companion to the Greek and Roman Novel*. Cambridge: 17–38.

Bowie, E. L. 2008b. "Plutarch's Habits of Citation: Aspects of Difference," in Nikolaidis 2008: 143–58.

Bowie, E. L. 2013. "Marathon in the Greek Culture of the Second Century AD," in C. Carey and M. Edwards (eds.), *Marathon—2,500 Years*. London: 241–53.

Bowie, E. L. 2014. "Poetry and Education," in Beck 2014: 177–90.

Bowie, E. L. 2018. "The Lesson of Book 2," in Harrison and Irwin 2018: 53–74.

Bowra, C. M. 1966. *Landmarks in Greek Literature*. Cleveland.

Branham, R. B. 1985. "Introducing a Sophist: Lucian's Prologues." *TAPhA* 115: 237–43.

Branham, R. B. 1989. *Unruly Eloquence: Lucian and the Comedy of Traditions*. Cambridge, MA.

Branscome, D. 2013. *Textual Rivals: Self-Presentation in Herodotus' Histories*. Ann Arbor.

Braund, D. 2007. "Greater Olbia: Ethnic, Religious, Economic, and Political Interactions in the Region of Olbia, c. 600–100 BCE," in Braund and Kryzhitskiy 2007: 33–77.

Braund, D., and S. Kryzhitskiy (eds.). 2007. *Classical Olbia and the Scythian World, from the Sixth Century BC to the Second Century AD*. Proceedings of the British Academy. Oxford.

Bridges, E., E. Hall, and P. J. Rhodes (eds.). 2007. *Cultural Responses to the Persian Wars 472 BCE–2003 CE*. Oxford.

Brown, T. 1988. "Herodotus in Egypt." *AncW* 17: 77–87.

Brubaker, R., and F. Cooper. 2000. "Beyond 'Identity.'" *Theory and Society* 29.1: 1–47.

Burke, F. T., and K. Skowroński (eds.). 2013. *George Herbert Mead in the Twenty-First Century*. Lanham.

Burke, S. 1992. *The Death and Return of the Author: Criticism and Subjectivity in Barthes, Foucault, and Derrida*. Edinburgh.

Burke, S. 1995. *Authorship: From Plato to the Postmodern—A Reader*. Edinburgh.

Burrow, C. 2019. *Imitating Authors: Plato to Futurity*. Oxford.

Callero, P. L. 2003. "The Sociology of the Self." *Annual Review of Sociology* 29: 115–33.

Chamberlain, D. 2001. "'We the Others': Interpretive Community and Plural Voice in Herodotus." *ClAnt* 20.1: 5–34.

Chambers, M., W. E. H. Cockle, J. C. Shelton, and E. G. Turner (eds.). 1981. *The Oxyrhynchus Papyri*, Vol. XLVIII. London.

Chaniotis, A. 2015. "Das kaiserzeitliche Gymnasion in Aphrodisias," in P. Scholz and D. Wiegandt (eds.), *Das kaiserzeitliche Gymnasion*. Berlin: 111–32.

Chiasson, C. 1986. "The Herodotean Solon." *GRBS* 27: 249–62.

Chrysanthou, C. 2015. "P. Oxy. LXXI 4808: *Bios*, Character, and Literary Criticism." *ZPE* 193: 25–38.

Chrysanthou, C. 2018. *Plutarch's Parallel Lives: Narrative Technique and Moral Judgement*. Berlin.

Chrysanthou, C. 2020. "Plutarch and the 'Malicious' Historian." *ICS* 45.1: 49–79.

BIBLIOGRAPHY 341

Clarke, K. 1999a. *Between Geography and History: Hellenistic Constructions of the Roman World*. Oxford.

Clarke, K. 1999b. "Universal Perspectives in Historiography," in Kraus 1999: 249–79.

Clarke, K. 2018. *Shaping the Geography of Empire: Man and Nature in Herodotus' Histories*. Oxford.

Cobet, C. G. 1877. "Ad Dionis Chrysostomi orationes." *Mnemosyne* 5.1: 56–102.

Cobet, J. 1971. *Herodots Exkurse und die Frage der Einheit seines Werkes*. Wiesbaden.

Cohoon, J. W. 1939. *Dio Chrysostom: Discourses 12–30*. Cambridge, MA.

Connolly, J. 2001. "Problems of the Past in Imperial Greek Education," in Too 2001: 339–72.

Connolly, J. 2007a. "Being Greek/Being Roman: Hellenism and Assimilation in the Roman Empire," in W. Brandes et al. (eds.), *Millennium Jahrbuch zu Kultur und Geschichte der ersten Jahrtausends n. Chr.* Berlin: 21–42.

Connolly, J. 2007b. "The New World Order: Greek Rhetoric in Rome," in Worthington 2007: 139–65.

Connor, W. R. 1993. "The Ionian Era of Athenian Civic Identity." *PAPHS* 37.2: 194–206.

Cooley, A. 2009. *Res Gestae Divi Augusti: Text, Translation, and Commentary*. Cambridge.

Corcella, A. 2013 [1984]. "Herodotus and Analogy," in Munson 2013b: 51–97.

Coverley, M. 2006. *Psychogeography*. London.

Cribiore, R. 2001. *Gymnastics of the Mind: Greek Education in Hellenistic and Roman Egypt*. Princeton.

Cueva, E. P., and S. N. Byrne (eds.). 2014. *A Companion to the Ancient Novel*. Malden, MA.

Damon, C. 1991. "Aesthetic Responses and Technical Analysis in the Rhetorical Writings of Dionysius of Halicarnassus." *MH* 48: 33–58.

Darbo-Peschanski, C. 1987. *Le discours du particulier: Essai sur l'enquête Hérodotéenne*. Paris.

Davis, L. 2009. "Certain Knowledge from Herodotus," in *The Collected Stories of Lydia Davis*. New York: 325.

De Jong, A. F. 2003. "Dions Magierhymnen: Zoroastrischer Mythos oder griechische Phantasie?" in Nesselrath 2003: 157–78.

De Jong, I. J. F. 2002. "Narrative Unity and Units," in Bakker, de Jong, and van Wees 2002: 245–66.

De Jong, I. J. F. (ed.) 2012. *Space in Ancient Greek Literature*. Leiden.

De Jonge, C. C. 2005. "Dionysius of Halicarnassus and the Method of Metathesis." *CQ* 55.2: 463–80.

De Jonge, C. C. 2008. *Between Grammar and Rhetoric: Dionysius of Halicarnassus on Language, Linguistics, and Literature*. Leiden.

De Jonge, C. C. 2011. "Dionysius of Halicarnassus and the *Scholia* on Thucydides' Syntax," in S. Matthaios, F. Montanari, and A. Rengakos (eds.), *Ancient Scholarship and Grammar: Archetypes, Concepts and Contexts*. Berlin: 451–78.

De Jonge, C. C. 2012. "Dionysius and Longinus on the Sublime: Rhetoric and Religious Language." *AJPh* 133.2: 271–300.

De Jonge, C. C. 2014. "The Attic Muse and the Asian Harlot: Classicizing Allegories in Dionysius and Longinus," in Ker and Pieper 2014: 388–409.

De Jonge, C. C. 2017. "Dionysius of Halicarnassus on Thucydides," in R. Balot, S. Forsdyke, and E. Foster (eds.), *The Oxford Handbook of Thucydides*. Oxford: 641–58.

De Jonge, C. C. 2019. "Dionysius and Horace: Composition in Augustan Rome," in Hunter and de Jonge 2019a: 242–66.

342 BIBLIOGRAPHY

Delcourt, A. 2005. *Lecture des Antiquités romaines de Denys d'Halicarnasse*. Brussels.

De Man, P. 1986. "Reading and History," in *The Resistance to Theory*. Minneapolis: 54–72.

Dench, E. 2007. "Ethnography and History," in Marincola 2007a: 493–503.

Dench, E. 2017. "Ethnicity, Culture, and Identity," in Richter and Johnson 2017: 99–114.

Desideri, P. 1978. *Dione di Prusa: Un intellettuale greco nell'impero romano*. Florence.

Desideri, P. 1989. "Teoria e prassi storiografica di Plutarco: Una proposta di lettura della coppia Emilio Paolo-Timoleonte." *Maia* 41: 199–215.

Desideri, P. 2000. "City and Country in Dio," in Swain 2000a: 93–107.

Destrée, P., and P. Murray (eds.). 2015. *A Companion to Ancient Aesthetics*. Malden, MA.

Dewald, C. 1987. "Narrative Surface and Authorial Voice in Herodotus' *Histories*." *Arethusa* 20.1–2: 147–70.

Dewald, C. 1997. "Wanton Kings, Pickled Heroes, and Gnomic Founding Fathers: Strategies of Meaning at the End of Herodotus' *Histories*," in D. H. Roberts, F. M. Dunn, and D. Fowler (eds.), *Classical Closure: Reading the End in Greek and Latin Literature*. Princeton: 62–82.

Dewald, C. 1998. "Introduction" and "Notes" for *Herodotus: The Histories*. Trans. R. Waterfield. Oxford World's Classics. Oxford.

Dewald, C. 2002. "I Didn't Give My Own Genealogy," in Bakker, de Jong, and van Wees 2002: 267–89.

Dewald, C. 2009. "The Figured Stage: Focalizing the Initial Narratives of Herodotus and Thucydides," in Rusten 2009: 114–47.

Dewald, C. 2012. "Myth and Legend in Herodotus' First Book," in Baragwanath and de Bakker 2012: 59–86.

Dewald, C. and J. Marincola (eds.). 2006. *The Cambridge Companion to Herodotus*. Cambridge.

Dickey, E. 2007. *Ancient Greek Scholarship*. New York.

Dihle, A. 1956. *Studien zur griechischen Biographie*. Göttingen.

Dihle, A. 1977. "Der Beginn des Attizismus." *A&A* 23: 162–77.

Dihle, A. 2007. "Zur Datierung der Schrift des Demetrios *Über den Stil*." *RhM* 148: 298–313.

Diller, H. 1962. "Die Hellenen-Barbaren-Antithese im Zeitalter der Perserkriege," in H. Schwabl (ed.), *Grecs et Barbares: Six exposés et discussions*. Vandoeuvres: 39–82.

Doran, R. 2015. *The Theory of the Sublime from Longinus to Kant*. Cambridge.

Dorati, M. 2005. "Pausania e il modello erodoteo: La tradizioni di Fliunte," in M. Giangiulio (ed.), *Erodoto e il "modello erodoteo": Formazione e transmissione della tradizioni storiche in Grecia*. Trento: 315–48.

Dorati, M. 2011. "Travel Writing, Ethnographical Writing, and the Representation of the Edges of the World in Herodotus," in Rollinger, Truschnegg, and Bichler 2011: 273–312.

Dowden, K. 2015. "Dio Chrysostom (707)," in I. Worthington et al. (eds.), *Brill's New Jacoby*. http://dx.doi.org/10.1163/1873-5363_bnj_a707.

Drews, R. 1973. *Greek Accounts of Eastern History*. Washington, D.C.

Drexler, H. 1972. *Herodot-Studien*. Hildesheim.

Duff, T. 1999. *Plutarch's Lives: Exploring Virtue and Vice*. Oxford.

Duff, T. 2007-8. "Plutarch's Readers and the Moralism of the *Lives*." *Ploutarchos* n.s. 5: 3–18.

Duff, T. 2011. "Plutarch's *Lives* and the Critical Reader," in G. Roskam and L. Van der Stockt (eds.), *Virtues for the People: Aspects of Plutarchan Ethics*. Leuven: 59–82.

Duff, T. 2014. "The Prologues," in Beck 2014: 333–49.

BIBLIOGRAPHY 343

Dührsen, N. C. 2005. "Wer war der Verfasser des rhetorischen Lehrbuchs *Über den Stil* (Περὶ ἑρμηνείας)?" *RhM* 150: 242–71.

Dunsch, B., and K. Ruffing (eds.). 2013. *Herodots Quellen–Die Quellen Herodots.* Wiesbaden.

Ebert, J. 1986. "Das Literaten-Epigramm aus Halikarnass." *Philologus* 130: 37–43.

Ehrhardt, C. 1988. "Herodot," in *Reallexikon für Antike und Christentum* XIV: 849–61.

Ek, S. 1942. *Herodotismen in der Archäologie des Dionys von Halikarnass: Ein Beitrag zur Beleuchtung des Beginnenden Klassizismus.* Lund.

Ellis, B. A. (ed.). 2015a. *God in History: Reading and Rewriting Herodotean Theology from Plutarch to the Renaissance. Histos* supplements 4. Newcastle.

Ellis, B. A. 2015b. "Introduction: Mortal Misfortunes, θεὸς ἀναίτιος, and τὸ θεῖον φθονερόν: The Socratic Seeds of Later Debate on Herodotus' Theology," in Ellis 2015a: 17–40.

Ellis, B. A. 2017. "Fictional Truth and Factual Truth in Herodotus," in Hau and Ruffell 2017: 104–29.

Elsner, J. 1992. "Pausanias: A Greek Pilgrim in the Roman World." *P&P* 135.1: 3–29.

Elsner, J. 1994. "From the Pyramids to Pausanias and Piglet: Monument, Travel, and Writing," in S. Goldhill and R. Osborne (eds.), *Art and Text in Ancient Greek Culture.* Cambridge: 224–54.

Elsner, J. 1995. *Art and the Roman Viewer: The Transformation of Art from the Pagan World to Christianity.* Cambridge.

Elsner, J. 1997. "The Origins of the Icon: Pilgrimage, Religion and Visual Culture in the Roman East as 'Resistance' to the Centre," in S. E. Alcock (ed.), *The Early Roman Empire in the East.* Oxford: 178–99.

Elsner, J. 2001a. "Describing Self in the Language of the Other: Pseudo (?) Lucian at the Temple of Hierapolis," in Goldhill 2001: 123–53.

Elsner, J. 2001b. "Structuring 'Greece': Pausanias' *Periegesis* as a Literary Contract," in Alcock, Cherry, and Elsner 2001: 3–20.

Eshleman, K. 2012. *The Social World of Intellectuals in the Roman Empire: Sophists, Philosophers, and Christians.* Cambridge.

Evans, S. 2008. "The Recitation of Herodotus," in Pigoń 2008: 1–16.

Ewald, B. 2004. "Men, Muscle, and Myth: Attic Sarcophagi in the Cultural Context of the Second Sophistic," in Borg 2004: 229–75.

Fehling, D. 1989 [1971]. *Herodotus and His "Sources": Citation, Invention, and Narrative Art.* Trans. J. G. Howie. Leeds.

Fields, D. 2013. "The Reflections of Satire: Lucian and Peregrinus." *TAPhA* 143: 213–45.

Flashar, H. (ed.). 1979. *Le classicisme à Rome aux 1ers siècles avant et après J.-C.* Vandoeuvres.

Fornara, C. 1971. *Herodotus: An Interpretive Essay.* Oxford.

Fornara, C. 1977. *Archaic Times to the End of the Peloponnesian War (Translated Documents of Greece and Rome).* Cambridge.

Fornara, C. 1983. *The Nature of History in Ancient Greece and Rome.* Berkeley.

Fornara, C. 1990. "Human History and the Constraint of Fate in Herodotus," in J. Allison (ed.), *Conflict, Antithesis, and the Ancient Historian.* Columbus: 25–45.

Forsdyke, S. 2006. "Herodotus, Political History, and Political Thought," in Dewald and Marincola 2006: 224–41.

Foucault, M. 1977. "What Is an Author?," in D. F. Bouchard (ed.), *Language, Counter-Memory, Practice.* Oxford: 113–38.

344 BIBLIOGRAPHY

Fowler, R. L. 1996. "Herodotos and His Contemporaries." *JHS* 116: 62–87.

Fowler, R. L. 2001. "Early *Historiê* and Literacy," in Luraghi 2001a: 95–115.

Fowler, R. L. 2010. "Gods in Early Greek Historiography," in J. Bremmer and A. Erskine (eds.), *The Gods of Ancient Greece: Identities and Transformations*. Edinburgh: 318–34.

Fox, M. 1993. "History and Rhetoric in Dionysius of Halicarnassus." *JRS* 83: 31–47.

Fox, M. 2001. "Dionysius, Lucian, and the Prejudice against Rhetoric in History." *JRS* 91: 76–93.

Fox, M. 2011. "The Style of the Past: Dionysius of Halicarnassus in Context," in Schmitz and Wiater 2011: 93–114.

Fox, M. 2019. "The Prehistory of the Roman *polis* in Dionysius," in Hunter and de Jonge 2019a: 180–200.

Fox, M., and N. Livingstone. 2007. "Rhetoric and Historiography," in Worthington 2007: 542–61.

Frateantonio, C. 2009. *Religion und Städtekonkurrenz: Zum politischen und kulturellen Kontext von Pausanias' Periegese*. Berlin.

Frazer, J. G. 1898. *Pausanias's Description of Ancient Greece*. 6 vols. London.

Free, A. 2015. *Geschichtsschreibung als Paideia: Lukians Schrift "Wie man Geschichte schreiben soll" in der Bildungskultur des 2. Jhs. n. Chr.* Munich.

Gabba, E. 1981. "True History and False History in Classical Antiquity." *JRS* 71: 50–62.

Gabba, E. 1982. "Political and Cultural Aspects of the Classicistic Revival of the Augustan Age." *ClAnt* 1: 43–65.

Gabba, E. 1991. *Dionysius and the History of Archaic Rome*. Berkeley.

Gadamer, H.-G. 1965. "Hermeneutics and Historicism." Supplement I to Gadamer 1975 [1960]: 528–67.

Gadamer, H.-G. 1975 [1960]. *Truth and Method*. Trans. J. Weinsheimer and D. G. Marshall. London.

Gagné, R. 2006. "What Is the Pride of Halicarnassus?" *ClAnt* 25.1: 1–33.

Gagné, R. 2019. "Hyperboreans, Arimaspians and Issedones: Mirages of Ethnicity and the Distant North in Book 4 of the Histories," in T. Figueira and C. Soares (eds.), *Ethnicity and Identity in Herodotus*. London: 85–102.

Gangloff, A. 2007. "Peuples et préjugés chez Dion de Pruse et Lucien de Samosate." *REG* 120.1: 64–86.

Gelzer, T. 1979. "Klassizismus, Attizismus, und Asianismus," in Flashar 1979: 1–41.

Genette, G. 1997 [1982]. *Palimpsests: Literature in the Second Degree*. Trans. C. Newman and C. Doubinsky. Lincoln.

Georgiadou, A., and D. Larmour. 1994. "Lucian and Historiography." *ANRW* 34.2: 1449–1509.

Georgiadou, A., and D. Larmour. 1998. *Lucian's Science Fiction Novel True Histories: Interpretation and Commentary*. Leiden.

Georgiadou, A. and K. Oikonomopoulou (eds.). 2017. *Space, Time and Language in Plutarch*. Berlin.

Gibson, C. 2004. "Learning Greek History in the Ancient Classroom: The Evidence of the Treatises on *Progymnasmata*." *CPh* 99.2: 103–29.

Gibson, C. 2008. *Libanius's* Progymnasmata: *Model Exercises in Greek Prose Composition and Rhetoric*. Translated with an introduction and notes. Atlanta.

Gilhuly, K., and N. Worman (eds.). 2014. *Space, Place, and Landscape in Ancient Greek Literature and Culture*. Cambridge.

BIBLIOGRAPHY 345

Gill, C. 1983. "The Question of Character-Development: Plutarch and Tacitus." *CQ* 33: 469–87.

Gill, C. 1990. "The Character-Personality Distinction," in Pelling 1990a: 1–31.

Gill, C., and T. P. Wiseman (eds.). 1993. *Lies and Fiction in the Ancient World*. Exeter.

Godley, A. D. 1921–1924. *Herodotus: The Persian Wars*. 4 vols. Cambridge, MA.

Goldhill, S. 1993. "The Sirens' Song: Authorship, Authority and Citation," in Biriotti and Miller 1993: 137–54.

Goldhill, S. (ed.). 2001. *Being Greek under Rome*. Cambridge.

Goldhill, S. 2002. *The Invention of Prose*. Oxford.

Goldhill, S. 2010. "What Is Local Identity? The Politics of Cultural Mapping," in Whitmarsh 2010a: 46–68.

Goold, G. P. 1961. "A Greek Professorial Circle at Rome." *TAPhA* 92: 168–92.

Gould, J. 1989. *Herodotus*. London.

Gould, J. 1991. *Give and Take in Herodotus: The Fifteenth Annual J. L. Myres Memorial Lecture*. Oxford.

Gould, J. 1994. "Herodotus and Religion," in Hornblower 1994: 91–106.

Gozzoli, S. 1976. "Polibio e Dionigi d'Alicarnasso." *SCO* 25: 149–76.

Gray, V. J. 1987. "*Mimesis* in Greek Historical Theory." *AJPh* 108.3: 467–86.

Greenwood, E. J. M. 2018. "Surveying Greatness and Magnitude in Herodotus," in Harrison and Irwin 2018: 163–86.

Grene, D. 1987. *Herodotus: The History*. Chicago.

Grethlein, J. 2006. "The Manifold Uses of the Epic Past: The Embassy Scene in Herodotus 7.153–63." *AJPh* 127.4: 485–509.

Grethlein, J. 2010. *The Greeks and Their Past: Poetry, Oratory, and History in the Fifth Century BCE*. Cambridge.

Griffin, J. 2014. "The Emergence of Herodotus." *Histos* 8: 1–24 (= Griffin, J. 1990. "Die Ursprünge der Historien Herodots," in W. Ax (ed.), *Memoria Rerum Veterum: Neue Beiträge zur antiken Historiographie und alten Geschichte*. Stuttgart: 51–82).

Griffiths, A. 1999. "Euenius the Negligent Nightwatchman," in R. Buxton (ed.), *From Myth to Reason: Studies in the Development of Greek Thought*. Oxford: 169–82.

Gruen, E. 2011. *Rethinking the Other in Antiquity*. Princeton.

Gurd, S. 2012. *Work in Progress: Literary Revision as Social Performance in Ancient Rome*. Oxford.

Gurlitt, W. 1890. *Über Pausanias*. Graz.

Habicht, C. 1985. *Pausanias' Guide to Ancient Greece*. Berkeley.

Hadas, M. 1954. *Ancilla to Classical Reading*. New York.

Hall, E. 1989. *Inventing the Barbarian: Greek Self-Definition through Tragedy*. Oxford.

Hall, J. 1997. *Ethnic Identity in Greek Antiquity*. Cambridge.

Halliwell, S. 1986. *Aristotle's Poetics*. London.

Halliwell, S. 1988. *Plato: Republic 10, with Translation and Commentary*. Warminster.

Halliwell, S. 2002. *The Aesthetics of Mimesis: Ancient Texts and Modern Problems*. Princeton.

Hanson, V. D. 2002. *Carnage and Culture: Landmark Battles in the Rise to Western Power*. New York.

Harloe, K. 2010. "Pausanias as Historian in Winckelmann's *History*." *CRJ* 2.2: 174–96.

Harrison, T. 2000. *Divinity and History: The Religion of Herodotus*. Oxford.

346 BIBLIOGRAPHY

Harrison, T. 2003. "Upside Down and Back to Front: Herodotus and the Greek Encounter with Egypt," in R. Matthews and C. Roemer (eds.), *Ancient Perspectives on Egypt*. London: 145–55.

Harrison, T. 2009. "Herodotus and the Certainty of Divine Retribution," in A. B. Lloyd (ed.), *What Is a God? Studies in the Nature of Greek Divinity*. Swansea: 101–22.

Harrison, T. 2020. "Reinventing the Barbarian." *CPh* 115.2: 139–63.

Harrison, T., and E. Irwin (eds.). 2018. *Interpreting Herodotus*. Oxford.

Harrison, T., and J. Skinner (eds.). 2020. *Herodotus in the Long Nineteenth Century*. Cambridge.

Hartog, F. 1988 [1980]. *The Mirror of Herodotus: The Representation of the Other in the Writing of History*. Trans. J. Lloyd. Berkeley.

Hartog, F. 2001. *Memories of Odysseus: Frontier Tales from Ancient Greece*. Trans. J. Lloyd. Chicago.

Hartog, F. 2013 [1979]. "Imaginary Scythians: Space and Nomadism" in Munson 2013b: 245–66.

Hau, L. I. 2016. *Moral History from Herodotus to Diodorus Siculus*. Edinburgh.

Hau, L., and I. Ruffell (eds.). 2017. *Truth and History in the Ancient World: Pluralising the Past*. London.

Hawes, G. 2016. "Pausanias and the Footsteps of Herodotus," in Priestley and Zali 2016: 322–45.

Heath, M. 1989a. "Dionysius of Halicarnassus 'On Imitation.'" *Hermes* 170: 370–73.

Heath, M. 1989b. *Unity in Greek Poetics*. Oxford.

Heer, J. 1979. *La personnalité de Pausanias*. Paris.

Helmbold, W. C., and E. N. O'Neil. 1959. *Plutarch's Quotations*. Baltimore.

Hershbell, J. P. 1993. "Plutarch and Herodotus: The Beetle in the Rose." *RhMP* 135.2: 143–63.

Hershbell, J. P. 1997. "Plutarch's Concept of History: Philosophy from Examples." *AncSoc* 28: 225–43.

Hidber, T. 1996. *Das Klassizistische Manifest des Dionys von Halikarnass: Die Praefatio zu De Oratoribus Veteribus*. Stuttgart.

Hinds, S. 1998. *Allusion and Intertext: Dynamics of Appropriation in Roman Poetry*. Cambridge.

Hirzel, R. 1895. *Der Dialog: Ein literarhistorischer Versuch*. Vols. 1–2. Leipzig.

Hogan, P. P. 2014. *A Student Commentary on Pausanias Book 1*. Ann Arbor.

Hogan, P. P. 2017. "*Pausanias Politicus*: Reflections on Theseus, Themistocles, and Athenian Democracy in Book 1 of the *Periegesis*." *CW* 110.2: 187–210.

Hohti, P. 1975. "Über die Notwendigkeit bei Herodot." *Arctos* 9: 31–37.

Hollmann, A. 2011. *The Master of Signs: Signs and the Interpretation of Signs in Herodotus' Histories*. Cambridge, MA.

Hölscher, T. 2003. "Images of War in Greece and Rome: Between Military Practice, Public Memory, and Cultural Symbolism." *JRS* 93: 1–17.

Holub, R. C. 1984. *Reception Theory: A Critical Introduction*. London.

Homeyer, H. 1965. *Lukian: Wie man Geschichte schreiben soll*. Munich.

Homeyer, H. 1967. "Zu Plutarchs *De Malignitate Herodoti*." *Klio* 49: 181–87.

Hornblower, S. 1991. *A Commentary on Thucydides, Volume I: Books I–III*. Oxford.

Hornblower, S. (ed.). 1994. *Greek Historiography*. Oxford.

Hornblower, S. 2006. "Herodotus' Influence in Antiquity," in Dewald and Marincola 2006: 306–18.

BIBLIOGRAPHY   347

Hornblower, S. 2010. *A Commentary on Thucydides, Volume III: 5.25–8.109*. Oxford.

Hornblower, S. 2011. "The Religious Dimension to the Peloponnesian War, or, What Thucydides Does Not Tell Us," in *Thucydidean Themes*. Oxford: 25–53.

Hornblower, S. 2015. *Lykophron: Alexandra*. Oxford.

Householder, F. W. 1941. *Literary Quotation and Allusion in Lucian*. New York.

Houser, J. S. 2002. "*Eros* and *Aphrodisia* in the Works of Dio Chrysostom," in M. C. Nussbaum and J. Sihvola (eds.), *The Sleep of Reason: Erotic Experience and Sexual Ethics in Ancient Greece and Rome*. Chicago: 327–53.

Hunter, R. L. 2009. *Critical Moments in Classical Literature*. Cambridge.

Hunter, R. L. 2014. *Hesiodic Voices: Studies in the Ancient Reception of Hesiod's* Works and Days. Cambridge.

Hunter, R. L. 2018. *The Measure of Homer: The Ancient Reception of the* Iliad *and the* Odyssey. Cambridge.

Hunter, R. L. 2019. "Dionysius of Halicarnassus and the Idea of the Critic," in Hunter and de Jonge 2019a: 37–55.

Hunter, R., and C. de Jonge (eds.). 2019a. *Dionysius of Halicarnassus and Augustan Rome*. Cambridge.

Hunter, R., and C. de Jonge. 2019b. "Introduction," in Hunter and de Jonge 2019a: 1–33.

Hunter, R., and D. A. Russell (eds.). 2011. *Plutarch:* How to Study Poetry (De audiendis poetis). Cambridge.

Hunter, V. J. 1982. *Past and Process in Herodotus and Thucydides*. Princeton.

Hunzinger, C. 1995. "La notion de θῶμα chez Hérodote." *Ktema* 20: 47–70.

Hunzinger, C. 2015. "Wonder," in Destrée and Murray 2015: 422–37.

Hutton, W. 2005a. "The Construction of Religious Space in Pausanias," in J. Elsner and I. Rutherford (eds.), *Pilgrimage in Greco-Roman and Early Christian Antiquity*. Oxford: 291–318.

Hutton, W. 2005b. *Describing Greece: Landscape and Literature in the* Periegesis *of* Pausanias. Cambridge.

Hutton, W. 2008. "The Disaster of Roman Rule: Pausanias 8.27.1." *CQ* 58: 622–37.

Hutton, W. 2009. "Pausanias the Novelist," in G. A. Karla (ed.), *Fiction on the Fringe: Novelistic Writing in the Post-Classical Age*. Leiden: 151–70.

Hutton, W. 2010. "Pausanias and the Mysteries of Hellas." *TAPhA* 140.2: 423–59.

Hutton, W. 2017. "Pausanias," in Richter and Johnson 2017: 357–70.

Immerwahr, H. R. 1960. "*Ergon*: History as Monument in Herodotus and Thucydides." *AJPh* 81.3: 261–90.

Immerwahr, H. R. 1966. *Form and Thought in Herodotus*. Cleveland.

Ingenkamp, H. G. 2016. "De Plutarchi Malignitate," in Opsomer, Roskam, and Titchener 2016: 229–42.

Inglese, L. 2003. "Aspetti della fortuna di Erodoto in Plutarco." *RCCM* 45: 221–44.

Innes, D., H. Hine, and C. Pelling (eds.). 1995. *Ethics and Rhetoric: Classical Essays for Donald Russell on His Seventy-Fifth Birthday*. Oxford.

Irwin, E. 2009. "Herodotus and Samos: Personal or Political?" *CW* 102.4: 395–416.

Irwin, E. 2013. "The Significance of Talthybius' Wrath (Hdt. 7.133–37)," in K. Geus, E. Irwin, and Th. Poiss (eds.), *Herodots Wege des Erzählens: Logos und Topos in den Historien*. Frankfurt: 223–60.

Irwin, E. 2014. "Ethnography and Empire: Homer and the Hippocratics in Herodotus' Ethiopian *Logos*, 3.17–26." *Histos* 8: 25–75.

348 BIBLIOGRAPHY

Irwin, E. 2015. "Dionysius of Halicarnassus' *On Thucydides* and Thucydides' Rhetoric of the Episodic," in C. Werner, A. Dourado-Lopes, and E. Werner (eds.), *Tecendo narrativas: Unidade e episódio na literatura grega antiga*. São Paulo: 121–99.

Irwin, E., and E. Greenwood (eds.). 2005. *Reading Herodotus: A Study of the Logoi of Book 5 of Herodotus' Histories*. Cambridge.

Isager, S. 1998. "The Pride of Halicarnassus: *Editio Princeps* of an Inscription from Salmakis." *ZPE* 124: 1–14.

Itkonen, E. 2005. *Analogy as Structure and Process: Approaches in Linguistics, Cognitive Psychology, and Philosophy of Science*. Philadelphia.

Ivantchik, A. I. 1999. "Une légende sur l'origine des Scythes (Hdt. IV, 5–7) et le problème des sources du *Scythicos logos* d'Hérodote." *REG* 112: 141–92.

Ivantchik, A. I. 2011. "The Funeral of the Scythian Kings: The Historical Reality and the Description of Herodotus (4.71–72)," in L. Bonfante (ed.), *The Barbarians of Ancient Europe: Realities and Interactions*. Cambridge: 71–106.

Jacob, C. 1980–81. "Paysages hantés et jardins marveilleux: La Grèce imaginaire de Pausanias." *L'ethnographie* 76.1: 35–67.

Jacoby, F. 1913. "Herodotos." *Realencyclopädie der classischen Altertumswissenschaft*. supp. II: 205–520.

Jacoby, K. (ed.). 1885–1905. *Dionysii Halicarnasei antiquitatum Romanarum quae supersunt*. 4 vols. Leipzig.

Jauss, H. R. 1982 [1970]. "Literary History as a Challenge to Literary Theory," in *Toward an Aesthetic of Reception*. Trans. T. Bahti. Minneapolis: 3–45.

Jerram, C. S. 1991 [1879]. *Luciani Vera Historia*. Mundelein, IL.

Jones, C. P. 1966. "Towards a Chronology of Plutarch's Works." *JRS* 56.1–2: 61–74.

Jones, C. P. 1971. *Plutarch and Rome*. Oxford.

Jones, C. P. 1978. *The Roman World of Dio Chrysostom*. Cambridge, MA.

Jones, C. P. 1982. "Plutarch ca. AD 40–ca. 120," in T. J. Luce (ed.), *Ancient Writers: Greece and Rome*, II: *Lucretius to Ammianus Marcellinus*. New York: 961–83.

Jones, C. P. 1986. *Culture and Society in Lucian*. Cambridge, MA.

Jones, C. P. 2001. "Pausanias and His Guides," in Alcock, Cherry, and Elsner 2001: 33–39.

Jones, C. P. 2004. "Multiple Identities in the Age of the Second Sophistic," in Borg 2004: 13–21.

Jost, M. 2007. "Pausanias in Arkadia: an Example of Cultural Tourism," in Adams and Roy 2007: 104–22.

Kadir, D. 2004. "To World, to Globalize: Comparative Literature's Crossroads." *CLS* 41.1: 1–9.

Karttunen, K. 2002. "The Ethnography of the Fringes," in Bakker, de Jong, and van Wees 2002: 457–74.

Kennedy, G. A. 1994. *A New History of Classical Rhetoric*. Princeton.

Kennedy, G. A. 2003. *Progymnasmata: Greek Textbooks for Prose Composition and Rhetoric*. Leiden.

Ker, J. 2000. "Solon's *Theôria* and the End of the City." *ClAnt* 19.2: 304–29.

Ker, J., and C. Pieper (eds.). 2014. *Valuing the Past in the Greco-Roman World: Proceedings from the Penn-Leiden Colloquia on Ancient Values VII*. Leiden.

Khellaf, K. 2018. "Incomplete and Disconnected: Polybius, Digression, and Its Historiographical Afterlife," in N. Miltsios and M. Tamiolaki (eds.), *Polybius and His Legacy*. Berlin: 167–201.

BIBLIOGRAPHY 349

Kim, L. 2010a. *Homer between History and Fiction in Imperial Greek Literature.* Cambridge.

Kim, L. 2010b. "The Literary Heritage as Language: Atticism and the Second Sophistic," in E. Bakker (ed.), *A Companion to the Ancient Greek Language.* Malden, MA: 468–82.

Kim, L. 2014. "Archaizing and Classicism in the Literary Historical Thinking of Dionysius of Halicarnassus," in Ker and Pieper 2014: 357–87.

Kim, L. 2017a. "Literary History in Imperial Greece: Dionysius' *On Ancient Orators*, Plutarch's *On the Oracles of the Pythia*, Philostratus' *Lives of the Sophists*," in J. Grethlein and A. Rengakos (eds.), *Griechische Literaturgeschichtsschreibung: Traditionen, Probleme und Konzepte.* Berlin: 212–47.

Kim, L. 2017b. "Poetry, Extravagance, and the Invention of the 'Archaic' in Plutarch's *On the Oracles of the Pythia*," in Georgiadou and Oikonomopoulou 2017: 87–98.

Kindstrand, J. F. 1981. *Anacharsis: The Legend and the Apophthegmata.* Uppsala.

Kindt, J. 2006. "Delphic Oracle Stories and the Beginning of Historiography: Herodotus' Croesus *Logos*." *CPh* 101: 34–51.

Kingsley, K. S. Forthcoming. *Herodotus and the Presocratics: Inquiry and Intellectual Culture in the Fifth Century.*

Kirk, A. 2014. "The Semantics of Showcase in Herodotus' *Histories*." *TAPhA* 144.1: 19–40.

Kirkland, N. B. 2018. "Herodotus and Pseudo-Herodotus in the *Vita Herodotea*." *TAPA* 148.2: 299–329.

Kirkland, N. B. 2019. "The Character of Tradition in Plutarch's *On the Malice of Herodotus*." *AJPh* 140.3: 477–511.

König, A., R. Langlands, and J. Uden (eds.). 2020. *Literature and Culture in the Roman Empire, 96–235: Cross-Cultural Interactions.* Cambridge.

König, J. 2005. *Athletics and Literature in the Roman Empire.* Cambridge.

König, J. 2011. "Self-Promotion and Self-Effacement in Plutarch's *Table Talk*," in F. Klotz and K. Oikonomopoulou (eds.), *The Philosopher's Banquet: Plutarch's Table Talk in the Intellectual Culture of the Roman Empire.* Oxford: 179–203.

König, J. 2012. *Saints and Symposiasts: The Literature of Food and the Symposium in Greco-Roman and Early Christian Culture.* Cambridge.

Konstan, D. 1987. "Persians, Greeks, and Empire." *Arethusa* 20.1–2: 59–74.

Konstan, D. 2004. "'The Birth of the Reader': Plutarch as a Literary Critic." *Scholia* 13: 3–27.

Konstan, D. 2010. "Anacharsis the Roman, or Reality *vs.* Play," in Mestre and Gómez 2010: 183–90.

Kraus, C. S. (ed.). 1999. *The Limits of Historiography: Genre and Narrative in Ancient Historical Texts.* Leiden.

Kurke, L. 2011. *Aesopic Conversations: Popular Tradition, Cultural Dialogue, and the Invention of Greek Prose.* Princeton.

Lacey, J. 2011. *The First Clash: The Miraculous Greek Victory at Marathon and Its Impact on Western Civilization.* New York.

Lachenaud, G. 1978. *Mythologies, religion et philosophie de l'Histoire dans Hérodote.* Paris.

Lachenaud, G. 1981. "Notice," in *Plutarque: Oeuvres Morales*, Vol. 12. Paris: 107–28.

Laird, A. 2001. "Ringing the Changes on Gyges: Philosophy and the Formation of Fiction in Plato's *Republic*." *JHS* 121: 12–29.

Laird, A. 2003. "Fiction as a Discourse of Philosophy in Lucian's *Verae Historiae*," in S. Panayotakis, M. Zimmerman, and W. Keulen (eds.), *The Ancient Novel and Beyond.* Leiden: 115–27.

350 BIBLIOGRAPHY

Lamberton, R. 2001. *Plutarch*. New Haven.

Langlands, R. 2020. "Plutarch and Roman Exemplary Ethics: Cultural Interactions," in König, Langlands, and Uden 2020: 75–94.

Lateiner, D. 1989. *The Historical Method of Herodotus*. Toronto.

Lather, A. 2017. "Taking Pleasure Seriously: Plutarch on the Benefits of Poetry and Philosophy." *CW* 110.3: 323–49.

Lattimore, R. 1939. "The Wise Adviser in Herodotus." *CPh* 34.1: 24–35.

Legrand, P. 1932. "*De la malignité d'Hérodote*." *Mélanges Gustave Glotz* II: 535–47.

LeJeune, P. 1982. "The Autobiographical Contract," in Tz. Todorov (ed.), *French Literary Theory Today: A Reader*. Cambridge: 192–222.

Leo, F. 1901. *Die Griechisch-Römische Biographie nach ihrer Literarischen Form*. Leipzig.

Levi, P. 1971. *Pausanias: Guide to Greece*. Vols. 1–2. New York.

Levi, P. 1977. "The Style of Pausanias," review of Strid 1976. *CR* 27: 178–80.

Lightfoot, J. L. 2003. *Lucian: "On the Syrian Goddess."* Oxford.

Lightfoot, J. L. 2014. *Dionysius Periegetes: Description of the Known World (with Introduction, Text, Translation, and Commentary)*. Oxford.

Ligota, C. 2007. "Lucian on the Writing of History—Obsolescence Survived," in C. Ligota and L. Panizza (eds.), *Lucian of Samosata Vivus et Redivivus*. London: 45–70.

Lincoln, B. 2018. *Apples and Oranges: Explorations in, on and with Comparison*. Chicago.

Lloyd, A. B. 1975. *Herodotus: Book II, Introduction*, Vol. 1. Leiden.

Lloyd, A. B. 1990. "Herodotus on Egyptians and Libyans," in G. Nenci and O. Reverdin (eds.), *Hérodote et les peuples non grecs*. Vandoeuvres: 215–53.

Lloyd, A. B. 1995. "Herodotus on Egyptian Buildings: A Test Case," in A. Powell (ed.), *The Greek World*. London: 273–301.

Lloyd-Jones, H. 1999. "The Pride of Halicarnassus." *ZPE* 124: 1–14.

Luce, T. J. (ed.). 1982. *Ancient Writers: Greece and Rome*, II: *Lucretius to Ammianus Marcellinus*. New York.

Luce, T. J. 1989. "Ancient Views on the Causes of Bias in Historical Writing." *CPh* 84.1: 16–31.

Luraghi, N. (ed.). 2001a. *The Historian's Craft in the Age of Herodotus*. Oxford.

Luraghi, N. 2001b. "Local Knowledge in Herodotus' *Histories*," in Luraghi 2001a: 138–60.

Luraghi, N. 2003. "Dionysios von Halikarnassos zwischen Griechen und Römern," in U. Eigler, U. Gotter, N. Luraghi, and U. Walter (eds.), *Formen römischer Geschichtsschreibung von den Anfängen bis Livius: Gattungen–Autoren–Kontexte*. Darmstadt: 268–86.

Luraghi, N. 2009. "The Importance of Being λόγιος." *CW* 102.4: 439–56.

Macaulay, G. C. 1890. *The History of Herodotus*. London.

Maciver, C. 2016. "Truth, Narration, and Interpretation in Lucian's *Verae Historiae*." *AJPh* 137.2: 219–50.

Macleod, M. D. 1972–1987. *Luciani Opera*. 4 vols. Oxford.

Macleod, M. D. 1991. *Lucian: A Selection*. Warminster.

MacQueen, B. D. 2008. "The Stepchildren of Herodotus: the Transformation of History into Fiction in Late Antiquity," in Pigoń (ed.): 329–48.

Malkin, I. (ed.). 2001. *Ancient Perceptions of Greek Ethnicity*. Washington, DC.

Marcus, S. 2019. *The Drama of Celebrity*. Princeton.

Marincola, J. 1987. "Herodotean Narrative and the Narrator's Presence." *Arethusa* 20.1–2: 121–37.

Marincola, J. 1989. "Thucydides 1.22.2." *CPh* 84.3: 216–23.

BIBLIOGRAPHY 351

Marincola, J. 1994. "Plutarch's Refutation of Herodotus." *AncW* 25.2: 191–203.

Marincola, J. 1997. *Authority and Tradition in Ancient Historiography*. Cambridge.

Marincola, J. 1999. "Genre, Convention, and Innovation in Greco-Roman Historiography," in Kraus 1999: 281–324.

Marincola, J. 2001. *Greek Historians*. Oxford.

Marincola, J. (ed.). 2007a. *A Companion to Greek and Roman Historiography*. Malden, MA.

Marincola, J. 2007b. "Odysseus and the Historians." *SyllClass* 18: 1–79.

Marincola, J. 2010. "Plutarch, 'Parallelism,' and the Persian-War Lives," in N. Humble (ed.), *Plutarch's Lives: Parallelism and Purpose*. Swansea: 121–43.

Marincola, J. 2012a. "The Fairest Victor: Plutarch, Aristides, and the Persian Wars." *Histos* 6: 91–113.

Marincola, J. 2012b. "Introduction: A Past without Historians," in J. Marincola, Ll. Llewellyn-Jones, and C. Maciver (eds.), *Greek Notions of the Past in the Archaic and Classical Eras: History without Historians*. Edinburgh: 1–13.

Marincola, J. 2015a. "Defending the Divine: Plutarch on the Gods of Herodotus," in Ellis 2015a: 41–84.

Marincola, J. 2015b. "Plutarch, Herodotus, and the Historian's Character," in R. Ash, J. Mossman, and F. Titchener (eds.), *Fame and Infamy: Essays on Characterization in Greek and Roman Biography and Historiography*. Oxford: 83–96.

Marincola, J. 2016. "History without Malice: Plutarch Rewrites the Battle of Plataea," in Priestley and Zali 2016: 101–19.

Martin, H. M. 1995. "Moral Failure without Vice in Plutarch's Athenian *Lives*." *Ploutarchos* 12: 13–18.

Martin, P.-M. 1993. "De l'universel à l'éternel: La liste des hégémonies dans la preface des *Antiquités romaines*." *Pallas* 39: 193–214.

Martin, R. P. 1996. "The Scythian Accent: Anacharsis and the Cynics," in R. B. Branham and M.-O. Goulet-Cazé (eds.), *The Cynics: The Cynic Movement in Antiquity and Its Legacy*. Berkeley: 136–55.

Martindale, C. 1993. *Redeeming the Text: Latin Poetry and the Hermeneutics of Reception*. Cambridge.

Martindale, C. 2007. "Reception," in C. Kallendorf (ed.), *A Companion to the Classical Tradition*. Malden, MA: 297–311.

Martindale, C. 2010. "Leaving Athens: Classics for a New Century?" *Arion* 18.1: 135–48.

Martindale, C. 2013. "Reception—A New Humanism? Receptivity, Pedagogy, the Transhistorical." *CRJ* 5.2: 169–83.

Martindale, C., and R. F. Thomas (eds.). 2006. *Classics and the Uses of Reception*. Malden, MA.

Marušič, J. 2011. "Poets and *Mimēsis* in the *Republic*," in P. Destrée and F.-G. Herrmann (eds.), *Plato and the Poets*. Leiden: 217–40.

Matijašić, I. 2018. *Shaping the Canons of Ancient Greek Historiography*. Berlin.

McCann, G. 1993. "Distant Voices, Real Lives: Authorship, Criticism, Responsibility," in Biriotti and Miller 1993: 72–82.

McInerney, J. 2014. "Pelasgians and Leleges: Using the Past to Understand the Present," in Ker and Pieper 2014: 25–55.

McWilliams, S. 2013. "Hybridity in Herodotus." *Political Research Quarterly* 66.4: 745–55.

Mead, G. H. 1982. *The Individual and the Social Self: Unpublished Work of George Herbert Mead*. Ed. D. Miller. Chicago.

Mead, G. H. 2015 [1934]. *Mind, Self & Society*. Chicago.

352 BIBLIOGRAPHY

Meadows, A. 1995. "Pausanias and the Historiography of Classical Sparta." *CQ* 89: 92–113.

Mensch, P. 2014. *Herodotus: Histories*. With Introduction and Notes by J. Romm. Indianapolis.

Merrifield, A. 1993. "Place and Space: A Lefebvrian Reconciliation." *Transactions of the Institute of British Geographers* 18.4: 516–531.

Mestre, F. 2003. "Anacharsis, the Wise Man from Abroad." *Lexis* 21: 303–17.

Mestre, F., and P. Gómez (eds.). 2010. *Lucian of Samosata, Greek Writer and Roman Citizen*. Barcelona.

Mikalson, J. 2003. *Herodotus and Religion in the Persian Wars*. Chapel Hill.

Moggi, M. 1996. "L'*Excursus* di Pausania sulla Ionia," in Bingen 1996: 79–116.

Moles, J. 1978. "The Career and Conversion of Dio Chrysostom." *JHS* 98: 79–100.

Moles, J. 1995. "Dio Chrysostom, Greece, and Rome," in Innes, Hine, and Pelling 1995: 177–92.

Moles, J. 1996. "Herodotus Warns the Athenians." *Leeds International Latin Seminar* 9: 259–84.

Moles, J. 2002. "Herodotus and Athens," in Bakker, de Jong, and van Wees 2002: 33–52.

Moles, J. 2005. "The Thirteenth Oration of Dio Chrysostom: Complexity and Simplicity, Rhetoric and Moralism, Literature and Life." *JHS* 125: 112–38.

Möller, M. 2004. *Talis oratio–qualis vita: Zu theorie und praxis mimetischer verfahren in der griechisch-römischen literaturkritik*. Heidelberg.

Momigliano, A. 1958. "The Place of Herodotus in the History of Historiography." *History* 43: 1–13 (= Momigliano 1966: 127–42).

Momigliano, A. 1961–62. "Historiography on Written Tradition and Historiography on Oral Tradition." *Atti della Academia delle Scienze di Torino* 96: 1–12 (= Momigliano 1966: 211–20).

Momigliano, A. 1966. *Studies in Historiography*. New York.

Momigliano, A. 1975. *Alien Wisdom: The Limits of Hellenization*. Cambridge.

Momigliano, A. 1978. "Greek Historiography." *H&T* 17.1: 1–28.

Momigliano, A. 1990. *The Classical Foundations of Modern Historiography*. Berkeley.

Montiglio, S. 2005. *Wandering in Ancient Greek Culture*. Chicago.

Morgan, J. 1993. "Make-Believe and Make Believe: The Fictionality of the Greek Novels," in Gill and Wiseman 1993: 175–229.

Morgan, T. 1998. *Literate Education in the Hellenistic and Roman Worlds*. Cambridge.

Morrison, A. D. 2020. *Apollonius Rhodius, Herodotus and Historiography*. Cambridge.

Most, G. W. 2011. "Principate and System," in Schmitz and Wiater 2011: 163–79.

Moyer, I. S. 2002. "Herodotus and an Egyptian Mirage: The Genealogies of the Theban Priests." *JHS* 122: 70–90.

Moyer, I. S. 2011. *Egypt and the Limits of Hellenism*. Cambridge.

Munson, R. V. 2001. *Telling Wonders: Ethnographic and Political Discourse in the Work of Herodotus*. Ann Arbor.

Munson, R. V. (ed.). 2013a. *Herodotus, Vol. 1: Herodotus and the Narrative of the Past*. Oxford Readings in Classical Studies. Oxford.

Munson, R. V. (ed.). 2013b. *Herodotus, Vol. 2: Herodotus and the World*. Oxford Readings in Classical Studies. Oxford.

Murray, O. 1972. "Herodotus and Hellenistic Culture." *CQ* 22.2: 200–213.

Musti, D. 1984. "L'itinerario di Pausania: Dal viaggio alla storia." *QUCC* 46: 7–18.

Musti, D. 1996. "La struttura del discorso storico in Pausania," in Bingen 1996: 9–34.

Musti, D., and L. Beschi (eds.). 1982. *Pausania: Guida della Grecia*, Vol. 1: *L'Attica*. Milan.

BIBLIOGRAPHY   353

Myres, J. L. 1907. "A History of the Pelasgian Theory." *JHS* 27: 170–225.

Nachtergael, G. 1977. *Les Galates en Grèce et les Sôtéria de Delphes.* Brussels.

Nenci, G. 1951. "Ecateo di Mileto e la questione del suo razionalismo." *RAL* 6: 51–58.

Nesselrath, H.-G. 1990. "Lucian's Introductions," in Russell 1990a: 111–40.

Nesselrath, H.-G. 1993. "Utopie-Parodie in Lukians *Wahren Geschichten*," in W. Ax and R. F. Glei (eds.), *Literaturparodie in Antike und Mittelalter.* Trier: 41–56.

Nesselrath, H.-G. 1995. "Herodot und die Enden der Erde." *MH* 52: 20–44.

Nesselrath, H.-G. 2002. "Homerphilologie auf der Insel der Seligen: Lukian *VH* II 20," in M. Reichel and A. Rengakos (eds.), *Epea Pteroenta: Beiträge zur Homerforschung. Festschrift für Wolfgang Kullmann zum 75. Geburtstag.* Stuttgart: 151–62.

Nesselrath, H.-G. (ed.). 2003. *Dion von Prusa: Menschliche Gemeinschaft und göttliche Ordnung: Die Borysthenes-Rede.* Darmstadt.

Nightingale, A. W. 2004. *Spectacles of Truth in Classical Greek Philosophy: Theôria in Its Cultural Context.* Cambridge.

Nikolaidis, A. G. (ed.). 2008. *The Unity of Plutarch's Work: Moralia Themes in the* Lives, *Features of the* Lives *in the* Moralia. Berlin.

Nikolaidis, A. G. 2014. "Morality, Characterization, and Individuality," in Beck 2014: 350–72.

Ní Mheallaigh, K. 2005. "'Plato Alone Was Not There': Platonic Presences in Lucian." *Hermathena* 179: 89–103.

Ní Mheallaigh, K. 2008. "Pseudo-Documentarism and the Limits of Ancient Fiction." *AJPh* 129.3: 403–31.

Ní Mheallaigh, K. 2009. "Monumental Fallacy: The Teleology of Origins in Lucian's *Verae Historiae*," in Bartley 2009: 11–28.

Ní Mheallaigh, K. 2010. "The Game of the Name: Onymity and the Contract of Reading in Lucian," in Mestre and Gómez 2010: 121–32.

Ní Mheallaigh, K. 2014. *Reading Fiction with Lucian: Fakes, Freaks and Hyperreality.* Cambridge.

Ní Mheallaigh, K. 2020. *The Moon in the Greek and Roman Imagination.* Cambridge.

Nörenberg, H.-W. 1973. "Untersuchungen zum Schluss der Περιήγησις τῆς Ἑλλάδος des Pausanias." *Hermes* 101.2: 235–52.

Oakley, S. 2019. "The Expansive Scale of the *Roman Antiquities*," in Hunter and de Jonge 2019a: 127–60.

Opsomer, J., G. Roskam, and F. B. Titchener (eds.). 2016. *A Versatile Gentleman: Consistency in Plutarch's Writing. Studies Offered to Luc Van der Stockt on the Occasion of His Retirement.* Leuven.

Payen, P. 1997. *Les îles nomades: Conquérir et resister dans l'Enquête d'Hérodote.* Paris.

Pearson, L. (ed.). 1965. *Plutarch's Moralia XI.* Cambridge, MA.

Peirano, I. 2010. "Hellenized Romans and Barbarized Greeks: Reading the End of Dionysius of Halicarnassus' *Antiquitates Romanae*." *JRS* 100: 32–53.

Pelling, C. B. R. 1988a. "Aspects of Plutarch's Characterization." *ICS* 13.2: 257–74 (= Pelling 2002a: 283–300).

Pelling, C. B. R. 1988b. *Plutarch: Life of Antony.* Cambridge.

Pelling, C. B. R. 1989. "Plutarch: Roman Heroes and Greek Culture," in M. Griffin and J. Barnes (eds.) *Philosophia Togata.* Oxford: 199–232.

Pelling, C. B. R. (ed.). 1990a. *Characterization and Individuality in Greek Literature.* Oxford.

354 BIBLIOGRAPHY

Pelling, C. B. R. 1990b. "Childhood and Personality in Greek Biography," in Pelling 1990a: 213–33 (= Pelling 2002a: 301–38).

Pelling, C. B. R. 1990c. "Truth and Fiction in Plutarch's *Lives*," in Russell 1990a: 19–52 (= Pelling 2002a: 143–70).

Pelling, C. B. R. 1995. "The Moralism of Plutarch's *Lives*," in Innes, Hine, and Pelling 1995: 205–20 (= Pelling 2002a: 237–52).

Pelling, C. B. R. 1996. "The Urine and the Vine: Astyages' Dreams at Herodotus 1.107–8." *CQ* 46.1: 68–77.

Pelling, C. B. R. 1997. "East Is East and West Is West—Or Are They? National Stereotypes in Herodotus." *Histos* 1: 51–66.

Pelling, C. B. R. 2000. "Rhetoric, *Paideia*, and Psychology in Plutarch's *Lives*," in L. Van der Stockt (ed.), *Rhetorical Theory and Praxis in Plutarch*. Leuven: 331–39 (= Pelling 2002a: 339–48).

Pelling, C. B. R. 2002a. *Plutarch and History: Eighteen Studies*. Swansea.

Pelling, C. B. R. 2002b. "'You for Me and Me for You': Narrator and Narratee in Plutarch's *Lives*," in Pelling 2002a: 267–82.

Pelling, C. B. R. 2004. "Plutarch," in I. J. F. de Jong, R. Nünlist, and A. Bowie (eds.), *Narrators, Narratees, and Narratives in Ancient Greek Literature*. Leiden: 403–22 (= Pelling 2002b).

Pelling, C. B. R. 2006. "Homer and Herodotus," in M. J. Clarke, B. G. F. Currie, and R. O. A. M. Lyne (eds.), *Epic Interactions: Perspectives on Homer, Virgil, and the Epic Tradition Presented to Jasper Griffin by Former Pupils*. Oxford: 75–104.

Pelling, C. B. R. 2007. "*De Malignitate Plutarchi*: Plutarch, Herodotus, and the Persian Wars," in Bridges, Hall, and Rhodes 2007: 145–64.

Pelling, C. B. R. 2009. "Bringing Autochthony Up-to-Date: Herodotus and Thucydides." *CW* 102: 471–83.

Pelling, C. B. R. 2011."Herodotus and Samos." *BICS* 54.1: 1–18.

Pelling, C. B. R. 2016. "Plutarch the Multiculturalist: Is West Always Best?" *Ploutarchos* n.s. 13: 33–51.

Pelling, C. B. R. 2019. *Herodotus and the Question Why*. Austin.

Penick, D. A. 1902. "Herodotus in the Greek Renascence." Dissertation, Baltimore.

Pernot, L. 1995. "Le plus panégyrique des historiens." *Ktema* 20: 125–36.

Pfundtner, J. 1866. *Pausanias periegeta imitator Herodoti*. Königsberg.

Pigoń, J. (ed.). 2008. *The Children of Herodotus: Greek and Roman Historiography and Related Genres*. Newcastle.

Pirenne-Delforge, V. 2008. *Retour à la source: Pausanias et la religion grecque. Kernos* supp. 20. Liège.

Popescu, V. 2014. "Lucian's *True Stories*: Paradoxography and False Discourse," in M. Futre Pinheiro, G. Schmeling, and E. Cuevas (eds.), *The Ancient Novel and the Frontiers of Genre: Fluid Contexts*. Ancient Narrative Supplementum 18. Groningen: 39–58.

Porod, R. 2009. "Lucian and the Limits of Fiction in Ancient Historiography," in Bartley 2009: 29–46.

Porter, J. I. 2001. "Ideals and Ruins: Pausanias, Longinus, and the Second Sophistic," in Alcock, Cherry, and Elsner 2001: 63–93.

Porter, J. I. (ed.). 2006a. *Classical Pasts: The Classical Traditions of Greece and Rome*. Princeton.

Porter, J. I. 2006b. "Feeling Classical: Classicism and Ancient Literary Criticism," in Porter 2006a: 301–51.

BIBLIOGRAPHY 355

Porter, J. I. 2006c. "What Is 'Classical' about Classical Antiquity?" in Porter 2006a: 1–65.

Porter, J. I. 2010. *The Origins of Aesthetic Thought in Ancient Greece: Matter, Sensation, and Experience*. Cambridge.

Porter, J. I. 2016. *The Sublime in Antiquity*. Cambridge.

Poster, M. 2002. "The Digital Subject and Cultural Theory," in D. Finkelstein and A. McCleery (eds.), *The Book History Reader*. London: 486–93.

Pretzler, M. 2004. "Turning Travel into Text: Pausanias at Work." *G&R* 51.2: 199–216.

Pretzler, M. 2007a. "Greek Intellectuals on the Move: Travel and *Paideia* in the Roman Empire," in Adams and Roy 2007: 123–38.

Pretzler, M. 2007b. *Pausanias: Travel Writing in Ancient Greece*. London.

Prier, R. A. 1989. *Thauma Idesthai: The Phenomenology of Sight and Appearance in Archaic Greek*. Tallahassee.

Priestley, J. 2014. *Herodotus and Hellenistic Culture: Literary Studies in the Reception of the Histories*. Oxford.

Priestley, J., and V. Zali (eds.). 2016. *Brill's Companion to the Reception of Herodotus in Antiquity and Beyond*. Leiden.

Pritchett, W. K. 1975. *Dionysius of Halicarnassus: On Thucydides*. Berkeley.

Pritchett, W. K. 1993. *The Liar School of Herodotus*. Amsterdam.

Pritchett, W. K. 1999. *Pausanias Periegetes II*. Amsterdam

Purves, A. 2010. *Space and Time in Ancient Greek Narrative*. Cambridge.

Purves, A. 2013. "Haptic Herodotus: History and the Senses," in S. Butler and A. Purves (eds.), *Synaesthesia and the Ancient Senses*. London: 27–41.

Raaflaub, K. A. 1987. "Herodotus, Political Thought, and the Meaning of History." *Arethusa* 20.1–2: 221–48.

Raaflaub, K. A. 2002. "Herodot und Thukydides: Persischer Imperialismus im Lichte der athenischen Sizilienpolitik," in N. Ehrhardt and L.-M. Günther (eds.), *Widerstand–Anpassung–Integration: Die griechische Staatenwelt und Rom, Festschrift für Jürgen Deininger*. Stuttgart: 11–40.

Rawson, E. 1985. *Intellectual Life in the Late Roman Republic*. Baltimore.

Reardon, B. P. 1971. *Courants littéraires grecs des IIe et IIIe siècles après J.-C*. Paris.

Redfield, J. 1985. "Herodotus the Tourist." *CPh* 80.2: 97–118.

Regenbogen, O. 1956. "Pausanias." *RCA* supp. 8: 1057–97.

Rhodes, P. J. 1994. "In Defense of Greek Historians." *G&R* 41: 156–71.

Richter, D. S. 2005. "Lives and Afterlives of Lucian of Samosata." *Arion* 13: 75–100.

Richter, D. S. 2011. *Cosmopolis: Imagining Community in Late Classical Athens and the Early Roman Empire*. Oxford.

Richter, D. S. 2017. "Lucian of Samosata," in Richter and Johnson 2017: 327–44.

Richter, D. S., and W. A. Johnson (eds.). 2017. *The Oxford Handbook to the Second Sophistic*. Oxford.

Richter, G. M. A. 1965. *The Portraits of the Greeks*. 3 vols. London.

Riegl, A. 1982 [1903]. "The Modern Cult of Monuments: Its Character and Its Origins." Trans. K. W. Forster and D. Ghirardo. *Oppositions* 25: 20–51.

Riemann, K. 1967. "Das Herodoteische Geschichtswerk in der Antike." Dissertation, Munich.

Riffaterre, M. 1983. *Text Production*. Trans. T. Lyons. New York.

Robert, C. 1909. *Pausanias als Schriftsteller: Studien und Beobachtungen*. Berlin.

Rollinger, R., B. Truschnegg, and R. Bichler (eds.). 2011. *Herodot und das Persische Weltreich = Herodotus and the Persian Empire*. Wiesbaden.

356 BIBLIOGRAPHY

Romm, J. S. 1989. "Herodotus and Mythic Geography: The Case of the Hyperboreans." *TAPhA* 119: 97–113.

Romm, J. S. 1992. *The Edges of the Earth in Ancient Thought: Geography, Exploration, and Fiction*. Princeton.

Rood, T. 2009. "Thucydides' Persian Wars," in Rusten 2009: 148–75 (= Kraus 1999: 141–68).

Rood, T. 2012. "Herodotus," in de Jong 2012: 121–40.

Rood, T. 2020. "From Ethnography to History: Herodotean and Thucydidean Traditions in the Development of Greek Historiography," in Harrison and Skinner 2020: 20–45.

Ros, J. G. A. 1938. *Die Metabolē (Variatio) als Stilprinzip des Thukydides*. Paderborn.

Roskam, G. 2017. "Discussing the Past: Moral Virtue, Truth, and Benevolence in Plutarch's *On the Malice of Herodotus*," in Georgiadou and Oikonomopoulou 2017: 161–74.

Roueché, C. 1993. *Performers and Partisans at Aphrodisias in the Roman and Late Roman Periods*. JRS Monograph 6. London.

Russell, D. A. 1963. "Plutarch's *Life* of Coriolanus." *JRS* 53: 21–29.

Russell, D. A. 1966. "The Loeb *Moralia* Again." *CR* 16.2: 180–82.

Russell, D. A. 1972. *Plutarch*. London.

Russell, D. A. 1979. "Classicizing Rhetoric and Criticism: The Pseudo-Dionysian *Exetasis* and *Mistakes in Declamation*," in Flashar 1979: 113–30.

Russell, D. A. 1980. "*De Imitatione*," in D. West and T. Woodman (eds.), *Creative Imitation and Latin Literature*. Cambridge: 1–16.

Russell, D. A. 1981. *Criticism in Antiquity*. London.

Russell, D. A. 1983. *Greek Declamation*. Cambridge.

Russell, D. A. (ed.). 1990a. *Antonine Literature*. Oxford.

Russell, D. A. 1990b. "*Ēthos* in Oratory and Rhetoric," in Pelling 1990a: 197–212.

Russell, D. A. 1990c. "Greek Criticism of the Empire," in G. A. Kennedy (ed.), *The Cambridge History of Literary Criticism*, Vol. 1: *Classical Criticism*. Cambridge: 297–329.

Russell, D. A. 1992. *Dio Chrysostom: Orations VII, XII, XXXVI*. Cambridge.

Russell, D. A. 1993. "Self-Disclosure in Plutarch and Horace," in G. W. Most, H. Petersmann, and A. M. Ritter (eds.), *Philanthropia kai eusebeia: Festschrift für Albrecht Dihle zum 70. Geburtstag*. Göttingen: 426–37.

Russell, D. A. 1995. "On Reading Plutarch's *Lives*," in Scardigli 1995: 75–94 (= Russell, D.A. 1966. "On Reading Plutarch's *Lives*." *G&R* 13: 139–54).

Russell, D. A., and M. Winterbottom (eds.). 1972. *Ancient Literary Criticism*. Oxford.

Rusten, J. (ed.). 2009. *Thucydides*. Oxford Readings in Classical Studies. Oxford.

Rusten, J. 2013. "ΔΗΛΟΣ ΕΚΙΝΗΘΗ: An 'Imaginary Earthquake' on Delos in Herodotus and Thucydides." *JHS* 133: 135–45.

Rutherford, I. 2001. "Tourism and the Sacred: Pausanias and the Traditions of Greek Pilgrimage," in Alcock, Cherry, and Elsner 2001: 40–52.

Rutherford, R. 2018. "Herodotean Ironies." *Histos* 12: 1–48.

Rütten, U. 1997. *Phantasie und Lachkultur: Lukians Wahre Geschichten*. Tübingen.

Sacks, K. S. 1983. "Historiography in the Rhetorical Works of Dionysius of Halicarnassus." *Athenaeum* 60.1–2: 65–87.

Said, E. 1983. "On Originality," in *The World, the Text, and the Critic*. Cambridge, MA: 126–39.

Saïd, S. 1993. "Le 'je' de Lucien," in M.-F. Baslez, P. Hoffmann, and L. Pernot (eds.), *L'invention de l'autobiographie d'Hésiode à saint Augustin*. Paris: 253–70.

Saïd, S. 1994. "Lucien Ethnographe," in A. Billault (ed.), *Lucien de Samosate*. Paris: 149–70.

BIBLIOGRAPHY 357

Saïd, S. 2001. "The Discourse of Identity in Greek Rhetoric from Isocrates to Aristides," in Malkin 2001: 275–99.

Salmeri, G. 1982. *La politica e il potere: Saggio su Dione di Prusa*. Catania.

Salmeri, G. 2000. "Dio, Rome, and the Civic Life of Asia Minor," in Swain 2000a: 53–92.

Sartre, J.-P. 1956. *Being and Nothingness*. Trans. H. E. Barnes. New York.

Scardigli, B. (ed.) 1995. *Essays on Plutarch's Lives*. Oxford.

Schenkeveld, D. M. 1975. "Theories of Evaluation in the Rhetorical Treatises of Dionysius of Halicarnassus." *MPhL* 1: 93–107.

Schenkeveld, D. M. 1982. "The Structure of Plutarch's *De Audiendis Poetis*." *Mnemosyne* 34: 60–71.

Schepens, G. 1975. "Some Aspects of Source Theory in Greek Historiography." *AncSoc* 6: 257–74.

Schepens, G. 1980. *L' "autopsie" dans la méthode des historiens grecs du v' siècle avant J.-C.* Brussels.

Schepens, G. 2007. "History and *Historia:* Inquiry in the Greek Historians," in Marincola 2007a: 39–55.

Schepens, G., and K. Delcroix. 1996. "Ancient Paradoxography: Origin, Evolution, Production and Reception,' in O. Pecere and A. Stramaglia (eds.), *La letteratura di consumo nel mondo greco-latino*. Casini: 373–460.

Schmidt, T. 2010. "Sophistes, barbares et identité grecque: Le cas de Dion Chrysostome," in Schmidt and Fleury 2011: 105–19.

Schmidt, T. and P. Fleury (eds.). 2011. *Perceptions of the Second Sophistic and Its Times (Regards sur la Seconde Sophistique et son époque)*. Toronto.

Schmitz, T. A., and N. Wiater (eds.). 2011. *The Struggle for Identity: Greeks and Their Past in the First Century BCE*. Stuttgart.

Schofield, M. 1991. *The Stoic Idea of the City*. Cambridge.

Schreyer, J. 2017. "The Past in Pausanias: Its Narration, Structure and Relationship with the Present," in S. Rocchi and C. Mussini (eds.), *Imagines Antiquitatis: Representations, Concepts, Receptions of the Past in Roman Antiquity and the Early Italian Renaissance*. Berlin: 49–64.

Schubert, C. 2010. *Anacharsis der Weise: Nomade, Scythe, Grieche*. Tübingen.

Schultze, C. 2019. "Ways of Killing Women: Dionysius on the Deaths of Horatia and Lucretia," in Hunter and de Jonge 2019a: 161–79.

Sciolla, L. 1988. *Gli artifici della finzione poetica nella "Storia Vera" di Luciano*. Foggia.

Seavey, W. 1991. "Forensic Epistolography and Plutarch's *de Herodoti malignitate*." *Hellas* 2.1: 33–45.

Segre, M. 2004 [1927]. *Pausania come fonte storica: Con un'appendice sulle Fonti storiche di Pausania per l'età ellenistica*. Rome.

Shannon-Henderson, K. 2020. "Constructing a New Imperial Paradoxography: Phlegon of Tralles and His Sources," in König, Langlands, and Uden 2020: 159–78.

Shapiro, S. O. 1996. "Herodotus and Solon." *ClAnt* 15.2: 348–64.

Shrimpton, G. S. 1997. *History and Memory in Ancient Greece*. Montreal.

Sidebottom, H. 2002. "Pausanias: Past, Present, and Closure." *CQ* 52.2: 494–99.

Sidwell, K. 2004. *Lucian: Chattering Courtesans and Other Sardonic Sketches*. Trans. with introduction and notes. New York.

Simmel, G. 1971 [1908]. "The Stranger," in *On Individuality and Social Forms* (ed. D. N. Levine). Chicago: 143–49.

Skinner, J. E. 2012. *The Invention of Greek Ethnography: From Homer to Herodotus*. Oxford.

358   BIBLIOGRAPHY

Skinner, J. E. 2020. "Imagining Empire through Herodotus," in Harrison and Skinner 2020: 117–53.

Skinner, Q. 1969. "Meaning and Understanding in the History of Ideas." *H&T* 8.1: 3–53.

Smith, B. H. 1983. "Contingencies of Value." *Critical Inquiry* 10.1: 1–35.

Smith, S. D. 2009. "Lucian's *True Story* and the Ethics of Empire," in Bartley 2009: 79–92.

Smolin, N. I. 2018. "Divine Vengeance in Herodotus' *Histories*." *JAH* 6.1: 2–43.

Sourvinou-Inwood, C. 2003. "Herodotus (and Others) on Pelasgians: Some Perceptions of Ethnicity," in P. Derow and R. Parker (eds.), *Herodotus and His World*. Oxford: 103–44.

Spawforth, A. 1994. "Symbol of Unity? The Persian-Wars Tradition in the Roman Empire," in Hornblower 1994: 233–47.

Spawforth, A. 2012. *Greece and the Augustan Cultural Revolution*. Cambridge.

Spiro, F. 1959 [1903]. *Pausanias: Graeciae Descriptio*. 3 vols. Leipzig.

Stadter, P. A. 1988. "The Proems of Plutarch's *Lives*" *ICS* 13.2: 275–95.

Stadter, P. A. 1992. "Herodotus and the Athenian Archê." *ASNP*. 22.3: 781–809.

Stadter, P. A. 1997. "Plutarch's *Lives*: The Statesman as Moral Actor," in C. Schrader, V. Ramón, and J. Vela (eds.), *Plutarco y la historia: Actas del V Simposio Español sobre Plutarco, Zaragoza, 20–22 de Junio de 1996*. Zaragoza: 65–81.

Stadter, P. A. 2000. "The Rhetoric of Virtue in Plutarch's *Lives*," in L. Van der Stockt (ed.), *Rhetorical Theory and Praxis in Plutarch: Acta of the IVth International Congress of the International Plutarch Society, Leuven, July 3–6, 1996*. Leuven: 493–510.

Stadter, P. A. 2003–4. "Mirroring Virtue in Plutarch's *Lives*." *Ploutarchos* n.s. 1: 89–95.

Stadter, P. A. 2012. "Speaking to the Deaf: Herodotus, His Audience, and the Spartans at the Beginning of the Peloponnesian War." *Histos* 6: 1–14.

Stewart, D. R. 2013. "'Most Worth Remembering': Pausanias, Analogy, and Classical Archaeology." *Hesperia* 82.2: 231–61.

Stewart, S. 2020. *The Ruins Lesson: Meaning and Material in Western Culture*. Chicago.

Strasburger, H. 2013 [1955]. "Herodotus and Periclean Athens," in Munson 2013a: 295–320.

Strauss, B. 2005. *The Battle of Salamis: The Naval Encounter That Saved Greece—and Western Civilization*. New York.

Strid, O. 1976. *Über Sprache und Stil des 'Periegeten' Pausanias*. Uppsala.

Swain, S. 1996. *Hellenism and Empire: Language, Classicism, and Power in the Greek World, AD 50–250*. Oxford.

Swain, S. (ed.) 2000a. *Dio Chrysostom: Politics, Letters, and Philosophy*. Oxford.

Swain, S. 2000b. "Reception and Interpretation," in Swain 2000a: 13–50.

Szelest, H. 1953. *De Pausaniae clausulis* (Auctarium Maeandreum, Vol. III). Warsaw.

Tagore, R. 2001 [1907]. "World Literature," in S. Chaudhuri (ed.), *Rabindranath Tagore: Selected Writings on Literature and Language*. Oxford: 138–50.

Tamiolaki, M. 2013. "Lucien précurseur de la *Liar School of Herodotus*: Aspects de la réception d'Hérodote dans l'*Histoire Vraie*," in J. Alaux (ed.), *Hérodote: Formes de pensée, figures du récit*. Rennes: 145–58.

Tamiolaki, M. 2015. "Satire and Historiography: The Reception of Classical Models and the Construction of the Author's Persona in Lucian's *De historia conscribenda*." *Mnemosyne* 68: 917–36.

Tamiolaki, M. 2016. "Writing for Posterity in Ancient Historiography: Lucian's Perspective," in A. Lianeri (ed.), *Future Time in and through Ancient Historiography*. Berlin: 267–82.

Tamiolaki, M. 2017. "Lucian on Truth and Lies in Ancient Historiography: The Theory and Its Limits," in Hau and Ruffell 2017: 267–83.

BIBLIOGRAPHY 359

Tatum, J. 1997. "Herodotus the Fabulist," in M. Picone and B. Zimmermann (eds.), *Der antike Roman und seine mittelalterlicher Rezeption*. Basel: 29–48.

Teodorsson, S.-T. 1997. "Ethical Historiography: Plutarch's Attitude to Historical Criticism," in C. Schrader, V. Ramón, and J. Vela (eds.), *Plutarco y la historia: Actas del V Simposio Español sobre Plutarco*. Zaragoza: 439–47.

Thomas, R. 1989. *Oral Tradition and Written Record in Classical Athens*. Cambridge.

Thomas, R. 2000. *Herodotus in Context: Ethnography, Science, and the Art of Persuasion*. Cambridge.

Thomas, R. 2001a. "Ethnicity, Genealogy, and Hellenism in Herodotus," in Malkin 2001: 213–33.

Thomas, R. 2001b. "Herodotus' *Histories* and the Floating Gap," in Luraghi 2001a: 198–210.

Thomas, R. 2011. "Herodotus's Persian Ethnography," in Rollinger, Truschnegg, and Bichler 2011: 237–54.

Thomas, R. 2013. "Ethnicity, Genealogy, and Hellenism in Herodotus," in Munson 2013b: 339–59.

Todorov, Tz. 1973 [1970]. *The Fantastic: A Structural Approach to a Literary Genre*. Trans. R. Howard. Ithaca.

Too, Y. L. (ed.). 2001. *Education in Greek and Roman Antiquity*. Leiden.

Trapp, M. 1990. "Plato's *Phaedrus* in Second-Century Greek Literature," in Russell 1990a: 141–73.

Trapp, M. 1995. "Sense of Place in the Orations of Dio Chrysostom," in Innes, Hine, and Pelling 1995: 163–75.

Trapp, M. 2000. "Plato in Dio," in Swain 2000a: 213–39.

Trapp, M. 2005. "Dio's *Borystheniticus*," review of Nesselrath 2003. *CR* 55.1: 77–78.

Trapp, M. 2012. "Dio Chrysostom and the Value of Prestige," in G. Roskam, M. de Pourcq, and L. Van Der Stockt (eds.), *The Lash of Ambition: Plutarch, Imperial Greek Literature and the Dynamics of Philotimia*. Leuven: 119–41.

Trapp, M. 2020. "With All Due Respect to Plato: The *Platonic Orations* of Aelius Aristides." *TAPA* 150.1: 85–113.

Treu, K. 1961. "Zur Borysthenitica des Dion Chrysostomos," in J. Irmscher and D. B. Šelov (eds.), *Griechische Städte und einheimische Völker des Schwarzmeergebietes: Eine Aufsatzsammlung*. Berlin: 137–54.

Tribulato, O. 2016. "Herodotus' Reception in Ancient Greek Lexicography and Grammar: From the Hellenistic to the Imperial Age," in Priestley and Zali 2016: 169–92.

Ungefehr-Kortus, C. 1996. *Anacharsis, der Typus des edlen, weisen Barbaren*. Frankfurt am Main.

Ursin, F. 2019. *Freiheit, Herrschaft, Wiederstand: Griechische Erinnerungskultur in der hohen Kaiserzeit (1.-3. Jahrhundert n. Chr.)*. Wiesbaden.

Usher, S. (ed.). 1974. *Dionysius of Halicarnassus: Critical Essays*, Vol. I. Cambridge, MA.

Usher, S. (ed.) 1985. *Dionysius of Halicarnassus: Critical Essays*, Vol. II. Cambridge, MA.

Van der Stockt, L. 1992. *Twinkling and Twilight: Plutarch's Reflections on Literature*. Brussels.

Vannicelli, P. 2001. "Herodotus' Egypt and the Foundations of Universal History," in Luraghi 2001a: 211–40.

Vasunia, P. 2001. *The Gift of the Nile: Hellenizing Egypt from Aeschylus to Alexander*. Berkeley.

Veyne, P. 1988. *Did the Greeks Believe in Their Myths? An Exercise in Constitutive Imagination*. Trans. P. Wissing. Chicago.

360 BIBLIOGRAPHY

Veyne, P. 1999. "L'identité grecque devant Rome et l'empereur." *REG* 112: 510–67.

Viidebaum, L. 2019. "Dionysius and Lysias' Charm," in Hunter and de Jonge 2019a: 106–24.

Vlassopoulos, K. 2013. *Greeks and Barbarians*. Cambridge.

Von Arnim, H. 1898. *Leben und Werke des Dio von Prusa*. Berlin.

Von Arnim, H. 1962 [1893–1896]. *Dionis Prusaensis quem vocant Chrysostomum quae extant omnia*. 2 vols. Berlin.

Von Möllendorff, P. 2000. *Auf der Suche nach der Verlogenen Wahrheit: Lukians Wahre Geschichten*. Munich.

Von Möllendorff, P. 2014. "Mimet(h)ic *Paideia* in Lucian's *True History*," in Cueva and Byrne 2014: 522–34.

Walbank, F. 2007. "Fortune (*Tychē*) in Polybius," in Marincola 2007: 349–55.

Walker, J. 2012. *The Genuine Teachers of This Art: Rhetorical Education in Antiquity*. Columbia.

Ward, A. 2008. *Herodotus and the Philosophy of Empire*. Waco.

Wardman, A. 1974. *Plutarch's Lives*. London.

Waterfield, R. 1998. *Herodotus: The Histories*. With Introduction and Notes by C. Dewald. Oxford World's Classics. Oxford.

Weaire, G. 2002. "The Relationship between Dionysius of Halicarnassus' *De Imitatione* and *Epistula ad Pompeium*." *CPh* 97.4: 351–59.

Weaire, G. 2005. "Dionysius of Halicarnassus' Professional Situation and the *De Thucydide*." *Phoenix* 59: 246–66.

Webb, R. 2001. "The *Progymnasmata* as Practice," in Too 2001: 289–316.

Webb, R. 2006. "Fiction, *Mimesis*, and the Performance of the Past in the Second Sophistic," in D. Konstan and S. Saïd (eds.), *Greeks on Greekness: Viewing the Past under the Roman Empire*. Cambridge: 27–46.

Węcowski, M. 2004. "The Hedgehog and the Fox: Form and Meaning in the Prologue of Herodotus." *JHS* 124: 143–64.

Wells, J. 1923. *Studies in Herodotus*. Oxford.

West, S. 1985. "Herodotus's Epigraphical Interests." *CQ* 35.2: 278–305.

West, S. 1991. "Herodotus' Portrait of Hecataeus." *JHS* 111: 144–60.

West, S. 2007. "Herodotus and Olbia," in Braund and Kryzhitskiy 2007: 79–92.

West, S. 2009. "Herodotus in Lycophron," in C. Cusset and E. Prioux (eds.), *Lycophron: Éclats d'obscurité*. Saint-Étienne: 81–93.

West, S. 2011. "The Papyri of Herodotus," in D. Obbink and R. Rutherford (eds.), *Culture in Pieces: Essays on Ancient Texts in Honour of Peter Parsons*. Oxford: 69–83.

Wheeldon, M. J. 1989. "'True Stories': The Reception of Historiography in Antiquity," in A. Cameron (ed.), *History as Text: The Writing of Ancient History*. London: 36–63.

White, H. 1973. *Metahistory: The Historical Imagination in Nineteenth-Century Europe*. Baltimore.

Whitmarsh, T. 1998. "Reading Power in Roman Greece: The *Paideia* of Dio Chrysostom," in Y. L. Too and N. Livingstone (eds.), *Pedagogy and Power: Rhetorics of Classical Learning*. Cambridge: 192–213.

Whitmarsh, T. 2001a. "'Greece Is the World': Exile and Identity in the Second Sophistic," in Goldhill 2001: 269–305.

Whitmarsh, T. 2001b. *Greek Literature and the Roman Empire: The Politics of Imitation*. Oxford.

Whitmarsh, T. 2005. *The Second Sophistic*. Cambridge.

Whitmarsh, T. 2006a. "Quickening the Classics: The Politics of Prose in Roman Greece," in Porter 2006a: 353–74.

Whitmarsh, T. 2006b. "True Histories: Lucian, Bakhtin, and the Pragmatics of Reception," in Martindale and Thomas 2006: 104–15.

Whitmarsh, T. (ed.). 2010a. *Local Knowledge and Microidentities in the Imperial Greek World*. Cambridge.

Whitmarsh, T. 2010b. "Thinking Local," in Whitmarsh 2010a: 1–16.

Whitmarsh, T. 2013. *Beyond the Second Sophistic: Adventures in Greek Postclassicism*. Berkeley.

Whitmarsh, T. 2015. "The Mnemology of Empire and Resistance: Memory, Oblivion, and Periegesis in Imperial Greek Culture," in K. Galinsky and K. Lapatin (eds.), *Cultural Memories in the Roman Empire*. Los Angeles: 49–65.

Wiater, N. 2011a. *The Ideology of Classicism: Language, History, and Identity in Dionysius of Halicarnassus*. Berlin.

Wiater, N. 2011b. "Writing Roman History—Shaping Greek Identity: The Ideology of Historiography in Dionysius of Halicarnassus," in Schmitz and Wiater 2011: 61–92.

Wiater, N. 2019. "Experiencing the Past: Language, Time and Historical Consciousness in Dionysian Criticism," in Hunter and de Jonge 2019a: 56–82.

Wilamowitz-Moellendorf, U. von. 1995. "Plutarch as Biographer," in Scardigli 1995: 47–74 (= *Reden und Vorträge*, ii (5) 1967 [1922]: 247–79).

Wilson, A. 2004. "Foucault on the 'Question of the Author': A Critical Exegesis." *Modern Language Review* 99.2: 339–63.

Wilson, N. G. 2015. *Herodotea: Studies on the Text of Herodotus*. Oxford.

Wiseman, T. P. 1993. "Lying Historians: Seven Types of Mendacity," in Gill and Wiseman 1993: 122–46.

Wisse, J. 1995. "Greeks, Romans and the Rise of Atticism," in J. G. J. Abbenes, S. R. Slings, and I. Sluiter (eds.), *Greek Literary Theory after Aristotle: A Collection of Papers in Honor of D. M. Schenkeveld*. Amsterdam: 65–79.

Wood, C. 2016. "'I Am Going to Say': A Sign on the Road of Herodotus' *Logos*." *CQ* 66.1: 13–31.

Woodman, A. J. 1988. *Rhetoric in Classical Historiography: Four Studies*. London.

Woolf, G. 1994. "Becoming Roman, Staying Greek: Culture, Identity, and the Civilizing Process in the Roman East." *CCJ* 40: 116–43.

Worman, N. 2002. *The Cast of Character: Style in Greek Literature*. Austin.

Worman, N. 2015a. "The Aesthetics of Ancient Landscapes," in Destrée and Murray 2015: 291–306.

Worman, N. 2015b. *Landscape and the Spaces of Metaphor in Ancient Literary Theory and Criticism*. Cambridge.

Worthington, I. (ed.). 2007. *A Companion to Greek Rhetoric*. Malden, MA.

Xenophontos, S. 2016. *Ethical Education in Plutarch: Moralising Agents and Contexts*. Berlin.

Yates, D. C. 2019. *States of Memory: The Polis, Panhellenism, and the Persian War*. Oxford.

Zadorojnyi, A. V. 2006. "King of His Castle: Plutarch, *Demosthenes* 1–2." *CCJ* 52: 102–27.

Zeitlin, F. I. 2001. "Visions and Revisions of Homer," in Goldhill 2001: 195–266.

Ziegler, K. 1951. "Plutarchos," in *Realencyclopädie der classischen Altertumswissenschaft* 21.1. Stuttgart: 636–962.

Ziegler, K. 1957–1971. *Plutarchi Vitae Parallelae*. 3 Vols. 2nd Edition. Leipzig.

Index of Passages

Due to the use of para id indexing, indexed terms that span two pages (e.g., 52– 53) may, on occasion, appear on only one of those pages.

Aelius Theon
  66–67: 15n.50
  71: 58n.50
  91–92: 15n.50
  115–116: 15n.50
  118: 15n.50
Aeschylus
  *Ag.*659: 285n.77
Aphthonius
  Prog.
    8.8: 13n.42
    12.1: 15n.51
Aristotle
  Cat.
    8b26–28: 46
    8b35–36: 46
    9a10–13: 46–47
  Gen. an.
    3.5.755b6: 1–2, 199n.45
  Hist. an.
    491b22–26: 114n.29
  Poet.
    1448 b16–18: 154–55
    1450b8–9: 134–35
    1451a38: 3n.5, 3n.6
    1451b6–7: 2–3
    1451b7–11: 2–3
  Rh.
    1378a6–13: 45–46n.29
    1389b15–21: 114n.29, 117n.34,
      120n.47
    1409a24–b1: 3n.8
    1409a30–31: 334–35
    1409a31–32: 334–35
Cicero
  Leg.
    1.1.5: 16–17

Orat.
  25: 88n.43
  30–32: 55n.42
  37–39: 108–9n.15
Demetrius
  Eloc.
    112–13: 56n.44
    181: 49n.36, 108n.13, 229n.114
Dio Chrysostom
  FGrHist 707: 160n.31
  Or.
    12.16–20: 160n.31
    13.4: 154–55
    13.9: 154–55
    18.9: 152n.1
    18.10: 31–32, 152
    32: 155–56
    32.44: 247n.38
    33.52: 155–56
    35.18–24: 155–56
    36.1–2: 159
    36.2–3: 164–65
    36.3: 162n.36
    36.4–5: 165–66
    36.7: 166–67
    36.8–9: 168–69
    36.9–12: 170
    36.13: 170–71
    36.15–17: 173
    36.18: 171–72
    36.21–27: 174–76
    36.28: 176
    36.31: 171–72
    36.38–39: 176
    36.39: 181n.80
    36.41: 178
    36.42–55: 179–81

364 INDEX OF PASSAGES

Dio Chrysostom (*cont.*)
36.42: 179–80, 181
36.43: 179, 181n.80
36.51: 177
36.55–56: 179–80
36.60: 181–82
36.61: 182
40.12: 154–55
47.7: 154–55
47.9–11: 154–55
53.9–10: 149–50
77/78.32: 154n.6

Diodorus Siculus
1.66.10: 16n.58
1.69.7: 16n.58
9.6.1: 249n.44

Diogenes Laertius
1.101–5: 247n.37
1.103–4: 247n.38
1.104: 243n.23
1.105: 248n.40

Dionysius of Halicarnassus
Amm. I
1–2: 70n.82
Amm. II
1: 48n.35
2.2: 48n.35
17.2: 48n.35
Ant. Rom.
1.1.2: 75–76
1.1.3: 37n.7
1.2.1–3.3: 76–77
1.2.1: 96–97
1.3.3–4: 91–92, 93
1.3.4: 84n.33
1.3.5: 96–97
1.3.6: 78n.18
1.4.2: 83–84
1.5.1: 80–81
1.5.3: 96–97
1.6.2: 96–97
1.6.3: 83–84
1.6.5: 76–77, 101n.65
1.7.2: 74n.1
1.8.2: 77–78
1.8.3: 96–97
1.89.1: 81

1.89.3: 82
1.89.4: 82
1.90.1: 80–81, 83–84
2.6.2: 102n.68
2.17.1–4: 79–80n.24
2.17.3: 83–84
2.18.1: 79–80n.24
3.11.4: 81n.29
4.24.2: 102n.68
7.47.1: 102n.68
7.70.2: 74n.1
11.1.4–5: 86–87
14.6: 81n.29
14.6.4–5: 101–2
14.6.5: 85
20.13.2: 79–80n.24
Comp.
3.12: 67–69
3.13–14: 60–61
3.14: 44, 48–49
3.16–17: 60–61
3.18: 67–69
4: 79–80
4.7: 67–69
4.8: 95
4.9: 95
4.10: 95–96
4.11: 95
4.19–20: 68n.75
5.12: 69n.78
9: 47–48n.32
10.5: 49, 108n.13, 229n.114
11.5: 69n.78
11.6: 49–50
11.8: 49–50
11.9: 50
11.10: 49–50
12.8–12: 60–61
16.5: 67–69
19: 47–48n.32, 66n.72
19.1: 66
19.10: 66
19.11–12: 50
19.12: 66
19.13: 66
22: 51n.38

INDEX OF PASSAGES 365

24: 47–48n.32
32: 47–48n.32
De imit.
  Epitome fr. 1.1–5: 62–63
  fr. 2: 60n.56
  fr. 3.3: 60–61
Dem.
  22.2–5: 53n.40
  24: 51n.38
  41.1: 97–98
  41.3: 60–61, 68n.76
  41.5: 98–99
  46–47: 66n.72
Din.
  7.5–6: 59
Lys.
  11: 51n.38
Orat. Vett.
  1.1: 38n.10
  1.4: 88n.42
  1.7: 87–88, 102–3
  2–3: 87–88
  3.1–2: 99
  4.1–2: 37, 76–77
  4.2: 38n.13
  4.4: 35n.2
Pomp.
  1–2: 53n.39
  1: 48n.35
  1.2: 38n.11
  1.3: 89n.46
  3–6: 38–39
  3: 66n.72
  3.1–6: 38–42
  3.1: 38–39
  3.2–6: 39–40
  3.2: 38n.13, 49, 89
  3.6–7: 42–43
  3.6: 41–42
  3.9: 43n.26, 71
  3.11: 56n.44, 66–67
  3.12: 50n.37, 67, 68n.77, 95–96
  3.14: 60–61, 89–91
  3.15: 45, 55, 71
  3.16: 51
  3.17: 51
  3.18: 46–47

3.21: 56n.44
4.1: 75–76
4–5: 43n.24
4.22–23: 69
4.3: 53–54
6.1–11: 78n.17
Thuc.
  1.3: 70
  1.4: 70
  2.3: 71, 147n.108
  4.1: 51–52
  4.3: 51–52
  5–6: 91n.49
  5.3: 75–76
  5.5: 90
  8.1: 55, 89n.46
  16.4: 75–76
  23.7: 60–61
  24.1: 48n.35
  24.12: 75–76
  27: 51n.38
  27.1–4: 52–53
  27.1: 49
  29: 53n.39
  33: 53n.39
  49–51: 54
  49.2: 54
  49.3: 38n.13, 54–55
  51.1: 56
Eustathius
  Il. 1.6.6–7 = 4.20: 15–16
Heraclitus
  DK 22 B 93: 268–69
Hermogenes
  Id.
    2.4 (330–36 Rabe): 229n.114
    2.12 (408 Rabe): 16n.58
  Prog.
    22: 58n.50
Herodotus
  proem: 2n.3, 41–42, 64, 182–83, 267
  1.1–2: 289–90
  1.4.2: 126
  1.5: 63n.64
  1.5.3: 69–70, 91–92, 239–40, 268–69,
    280–81, 290–91, 311n.55
  1.5.4: 180–81

366   INDEX OF PASSAGES

Herodotus (*cont.*)
1.5.3–4: 172, 289, 297–98
1.6: 49
1.8.2: 44–45, 218n.93
1.8.3: 281n.65
1.20: 241n.16
1.23–24: 241n.16
1.27: 241n.16
1.29–32: 277–78, 295n.103
1.30.1: 251, 252–53
1.30.2: 86–87, 240–42, 251
1.32: 284–85
1.32.1: 127, 278–79
1.32.2: 180–81
1.32.3–4: 255–56
1.32.4: 278–79
1.32.8: 278
1.32.9: 278–79
1.33: 248–49
1.56: 187n.5
1.57: 220
1.59: 241n.16
1.74–75: 241n.16
1.91: 281, 281n.65
1.93.1: 318–19
1.95.1: 68n.75, 298n.8
1.107–8: 178–79
1.117.2: 298n.8
1.120: 178–79
1.128: 178–79
1.133.2: 37n.9
1.135: 169–70
1.137: 278n.55
1.139: 68n.76, 137n.85
1.140.3: 178–79
1.145: 273n.44
1.148: 273n.44
1.157: 83–84
1.157.2: 186–87
1.160: 220
1.170: 241n.16
1.172: 220
1.172.1: 187
1.185.1: 317–18
1.185.3: 317–18, 318–19n.76
1.194.1: 319n.78
1.207.2: 180–81, 186, 248–49
2.2.5: 199–200

2.3.1: 208
2.3.2: 181n.79
2.4.1: 199–200
2.5: 220n.97
2.7.1: 207n.66
2.10: 303n.26
2.10.1: 206
2.11.1: 208n.70
2.12.1: 206
2.18.1: 206
2.19.3: 224n.105
2.20.1: 224–25, 298n.8
2.21: 318–19n.76
2.22.2: 207
2.23: 198
2.24: 205n.60
2.27: 205n.60
2.28.1–2: 224–25
2.29.1: 201–2n.53
2.32–33: 204–5
2.33: 303n.26
2.35: 199–200
2.35.1: 204–5
2.45.1–3: 327–28
2.49–53: 214
2.51: 187n.5
2.53.1–3: 314
2.53.1: 290–91
2.56: 205n.60
2.57.3: 214
2.59.3: 221
2.62: 221
2.65.2: 68n.75
2.66: 204–5
2.69: 204–5
2.81: 214
2.91.1: 238n.7
2.93: 205n.60
2.93.6: 206–7n.65
2.99.1: 207–8
2.104: 205n.60
2.109.3: 214
2.113.3: 181n.79
2.115.3: 181n.79
2.119: 199–200
2.120.5: 289–90
2.123: 68n.76
2.123.1: 201–2n.53, 262n.6

INDEX OF PASSAGES 367

2.125: 205n.60
2.138.2: 37n.9
2.143: 233–34
2.146: 68n.76
2.148–149.1: 202–4
2.148.1: 322–23
2.148.6: 318–19n.76, 322–23
2.149.1: 317–18
2.161: 281
2.161.3: 281n.65
2.171: 214
2.173: 197–98
2.175.1–2: 317–18
2.175.1: 319n.78
2.175.3: 317–18, 318–19n.76
2.177.2: 214
3.12.1: 319n.78
3.17–26: 196n.36
3.33: 285n.75
3.37: 285n.75
3.38: 217–18
3.38.1–2: 250n.53
3.40–43: 281
3.40.3: 248–49
3.47.3: 319n.78
3.48–53: 241n.16
3.56: 137n.86
3.61–79: 178–79
3.64: 281n.65
3.72.1: 181n.79
3.106.1: 169n.53, 244–45
3.111.1: 318–19n.76
3.112: 318–19
3.113: 229–30
3.113.1: 318–19
3.116: 313
3.120–26: 281
4.11: 258n.70
4.13.1: 313
4.14–16: 312
4.17: 160n.31
4.17.1: 166n.48
4.18: 160n.31
4.18.3: 162
4.20: 168n.50
4.20.2: 162, 167–68
4.24: 160n.31
4.28.2: 37n.9

4.30: 69–70
4.30.1: 318–19n.76
4.32–35: 146n.106
4.36: 146
4.42.1: 318–19n.76
4.46–47.1: 163n.41
4.46.1–3: 163
4.46.1: 239
4.46.2: 239–40
4.46.3: 171–72
4.47.2–58: 163n.41
4.47.1: 163
4.53: 160
4.53.1–4: 161–62
4.53.3: 318–19
4.53.5–6: 161
4.76–80: 163n.41
4.76.1: 166
4.76.1–2: 238
4.76.3–5: 238–39
4.76.5: 245–46
4.77.1–2: 240
4.78–79: 160n.31
4.78.4–5: 167–68
4.79: 281
4.80.5: 167–68
4.82: 161, 319n.78
4.85.2: 161, 319n.78
4.93–96: 160
4.99–101: 163n.41
4.99: 301–2
4.99.1: 301
4.99.3: 301n.22
4.100–102: 168n.50
4.103–17: 163n.41
4.107: 168n.50
4.118: 160
4.119: 168n.50
4.123: 258n.70
4.125: 168n.50
4.127: 258n.70
4.129.1: 319n.78
4.199.1: 319n.78
4.205: 284n.73
5.9: 69–70n.79
5.9.3: 180–81
5.18.4: 126n.57
5.33: 281n.65

368 INDEX OF PASSAGES

Herodotus (*cont.*)
5.42–48: 66n.71
5.45: 68n.76
5.52: 68n.76
5.54: 68n.76
5.55: 18–19, 66n.71
5.63: 137n.86
5.65: 66n.71
5.67: 68n.76
5.78: 100–1, 295n.103
5.83–87: 312
5.90: 137n.86
5.92: 241n.16
5.92.δ.1: 281n.65
5.95: 241n.16
5.97: 295n.103
5.97.2: 100–1
5.97.3: 225–26
6.27.1: 268–69
6.55: 313n.57
6.64: 281n.65
6.98: 295n.103
6.98.1–3: 265
6.98.2: 100–1
6.121.1: 317
6.123.1: 317
6.129.4: 145
6.131: 295n.103
6.131.2: 100–1
6.135.3: 281n.65
6.136–40: 187n.5
7.6.4: 281n.65
7.8–11: 86n.36
7.10: 290n.89
7.10.ε: 172, 248–49
7.17.2: 281
7.19.2: 178–79
7.37.2–3: 178–79
7.46.2: 248–49
7.60: 220
7.61–100: 286–87
7.96.1: 68n.75
7.99.1: 318n.74, 318–19n.76
7.113: 178–79
7.129.4: 267
7.132–37: 271n.41
7.132–33: 271–72
7.134: 271–72
7.137.1–2: 272

7.139.1: 68n.75, 100–1, 314
7.140–43: 259n.71
7.144: 301n.21
7.152.3: 262n.6, 278n.55, 314n.60
7.164.1: 278n.55
7.171: 68n.75
7.187.1: 319n.78
7.191: 178–79
7.235: 241n.16
8.8.2: 319n.77
8.26.2–3: 252n.55
8.35.2: 37n.9
8.37.2: 319n.78
8.91: 37n.9
8.144.2: 83
9.27.4: 187n.4
9.65.2: 318–19n.76, 319n.78
9.73: 295n.103
9.73.3: 100–1
9.84: 220
9.100.2: 273n.45
9.109.2: 281
9.120–21: 295n.103
9.122: 86n.36
9.122.3: 172
Homer
*Il.*5.63: 225–26
*Od.*1.1–4: 241n.18
Inscriptions
IAph 2007 12.27 = *MAMA*
viii 418: 14
Literaten-Epigramm (*IG* XII 1, 145;
SEG 36, 975): 13–14
Res Gestae Divi Augusti
3: 92–93
9.2: 92–93
10.2: 92–93
13: 92–93
25.2: 92n.53
26–29: 92n.53
Salmakis Inscription (*SEG* 48. 1330;
SGO 01/12/02): 14
Josephus
*Ap.*1.16: 13
[Longinus]
Subl.
1.4: 328n.96
4.7: 16–17, 126n.57
7.1: 328n.96

INDEX OF PASSAGES   369

7.4: 328n.96
8.1: 331–32
9.2: 328n.96
9.3: 328n.96
10: 331–32
10.3: 328n.96
13.3: 14
14.1: 17n.59
22.1: 16–17, 328n.96
22.3: 17n.59
25.1: 17n.59
26.2: 16–17, 58, 297–98
30.1: 328n.96
35.4–5: 328n.96
36.3: 328n.96
38.3: 17n.59
38.4: 16–17
39.3: 328n.96
39.4: 328n.96
43.1: 16–17
44.1: 328n.96
44.8: 328n.96

Lucian

Anach.
5: 250
10–12: 252–53
14: 251, 257n.66
15: 252
17: 253–54
18–19: 257
20: 258–59
21: 257
32: 255
34: 253
37: 256–57
38: 257–58

Demon.
23: 178n.74
25: 178n.74

Dom.
20: 218n.93

Her.
1: 189–91, 229–30
2–8: 192–93
7: 247

Hist. conscr.
3: 195
4: 195n.29
9–10: 229n.114

29: 218n.93
39–42: 195
50: 41n.20, 195, 218n.94
61: 195

Philops.
14: 178n.74
15: 178n.74

Scyth.
1: 243–44
2: 242–43n.20, 243–44
3: 243–44, 246
4: 243–44
5: 244–45
5–7: 243
8: 244n.26, 246nn.32–33
9: 247

Salt.
78: 218n.93

Ver. Hist.
1.1–5: 197–98
1.4: 233–34
1.5: 217, 229
1.7–8: 211–12
1.7: 232–33
1.10–11: 216
1.11–17: 213
1.17: 217–18
1.22: 215
1.23–27: 213–14
1.25: 217
1.26: 218–19
1.29: 197–98, 222–23
1.30–33: 225–27
1.32: 232–33
2.3: 232–33
2.5: 229, 234
2.6: 229–30
2.10: 228–29
2.12: 230–31, 233n.122
2.14–15: 233n.122
2.20: 230
2.28: 198n.43, 231–32, 233–34
2.31: 228, 234

Marcellinus

Vit. Thuc.
35: 53n.39
48–49: 67n.74

Menander Rhetor
2.3.5: 229n.114

370 INDEX OF PASSAGES

Nicolaus of Damascus
  FGrHist 90 F 125: 78n.17
Pausanias
  1.1.1: 299–300
  1.3.2: 295n.103
  1.5.1: 311
  1.12.2: 320n.82, 321–22
  1.13.9: 320n.82
  1.17.1: 304–5
  1.18: 305n.29
  1.18.3: 305–6
  1.18.5: 305–6
  1.19.1: 305–6
  1.19.6: 320n.82, 321–22
  1.20.1–2: 305–6
  1.20.3: 305–6
  1.20.4: 282, 305–6
  1.20.5: 284–85
  1.20.7: 282–83, 295n.103
  1.21.3: 303n.27, 306
  1.23.2: 311
  1.23.10: 311n.56
  1.24.6: 312–13
  1.24.7: 320n.82
  1.24.8: 275n.47, 303n.27
  1.26.4: 290–91, 298n.8, 311, 319–20
  1.27.9: 275n.47
  1.35.7: 320n.82
  1.39.3: 299n.15
  2.11.1: 286
  2.15.4: 311n.56
  2.16.4: 328n.98
  2.17.4: 262n.6
  2.22.3: 303n.27
  2.30.4: 311–12, 311n.56
  2.30.9: 311n.54
  3.17.7: 311n.56
  3.22.4: 303n.27
  3.26.3: 320–21
  4.29.7: 286–87
  4.29.8–9: 289n.84, 293
  4.29.13: 279
  4.30.3: 279–80
  4.30.5–6: 279–80
  4.35.9–11: 319–20
  5.5.2: 320n.82
  5.10.1: 322–23
  5.10.2–11.10: 322–23
  5.13.7: 303n.27
  5.14.1: 320n.82

  5.14.3: 320n.82
  5.25.11: 278n.55
  5.27.5–6: 303n.27
  6.2.10: 320n.82
  6.3.8: 262n.6, 278n.55, 314n.60
  6.22.1: 303n.27
  7.5.4: 320–21
  7.17.1–3: 295n.103
  7.17.1: 292–93
  7.23.5–9: 270–71
  7.24.1: 271
  7.24.3–4: 270–71
  7.24.5: 273
  7.24.6: 273, 274–75
  7.24.7–11: 274–75
  7.24.9: 273, 274–75
  7.24.11–12: 273–74
  7.24.13: 303n.27
  7.25.1: 273–74
  7.27.12: 303n.27
  8.2.7: 303n.27
  8.7.3: 320n.82
  8.8.3: 327
  8.17.3: 303n.27, 320n.82
  8.17.4: 319–20
  8.17.6: 323
  8.18.2: 323
  8.18.3: 323
  8.18.4: 323, 324n.89
  8.18.5: 324–25
  8.18.6: 324
  8.24.1–12: 276–77
  8.24.9: 277
  8.24.13–14: 277
  8.27: 286–87
  8.27.1: 295n.103
  8.30.2–32.5: 286–87
  8.33.1–4: 287–88
  8.38.6: 325
  8.38.10: 303n.27
  8.42.7: 320–21
  9.7.5–6: 295n.103
  9.13.11: 266–67n.27
  9.17.6: 284n.73
  9.19.5: 316n.65
  9.21.1: 319–20
  9.22.4: 303n.27
  9.30.1: 285n.75
  9.30.3: 313–14
  9.32.10: 278n.55

Subject Index

Due to the use of para id indexing, indexed terms that span two pages (e.g., 52– 53) may, on occasion, appear on only one of those pages.

Anacharsis, 236–60
  in the *Anacharsis*, 247–60
  in the *Histories*, 237–42
  in the *Scythian*, 242–47
Aristeas of Proconnesus, 312–13
Aristotle
  on *ethos* (character), 132–33, 134–35
  on habit and disposition, 46–47
  on Herodotus, 1–2, 199n.45, 334–35
  on history-writing, 2–4
  on malice (*kakoêtheia*), 111n.22,
    114n.29, 117n.34, 120n.47
  on recognition, 154–55
  on wonder, 317n.71
Artemisia, 142–43, 318n.74
Asianism, 87–88, 87–88nn.39–43, 102–3,
  309–10
Athens, 100–2, 143n.99, 237n.3, 243–46,
  247, 271n.41, 281–83, 285–86, 304–8
Atticism, 21n.76, 87n.39, 262, 309–10,
  309n.43
authorship, ideas of, 25–27, 31, 31n.106,
  193–94n.23, 232n.119
autochthony, 244–45, 245nn.29–30
autopsy, 155–56, 159–60, 202–10, 213–14,
  217–20, 231–34, 306–8. *See also*
  Herodotus and the *Histories*

Barthes, Roland, 127
Benjamin, Walter, 20–21, 31–32
Borysthenes. *See* Dio Chrysostom
Burrow, Colin, 24–25, 37n.7, 47n.31

Cicero, 16–17, 38n.10, 51n.38, 55n.42,
  56n.43, 108–9n.15, 152n.1
cities, as thematic locus in Herodotean
  reception, 160n.29, 166, 171–72,
  173–77, 286–95

classicality and classicizing, 10–11, 11n.35,
  20–21, 36, 43n.25, 76–77, 101–2
Croesus, 94–96, 180–81, 240–42, 247–50,
  251–53, 255–56, 277–79, 281, 290–
  91, 295n.103

Davis, Lydia, 1–2
De Man, Paul, 9n.28, 11–12nn.36–38,
  30n.103
Demosthenes, 50, 53n.40, 59–60n.55, 66,
  100n.61, 309–10
Dio Chrysostom, 21–22, 149–50, 152–85,
  333–34
  Borysthenes, geography of, 159–64
  Borysthenites, ethnography of, 164–73
  Borystheniticus (*Or.* 36), 157–83
  Hellenism and Greekness, representations
    of, 157–58, 166–68, 169, 173, 174,
    181–83
  literary techniques, 153–56
  Magi and Magian hymn, 157–58,
    173–83
  Olbia, 157–58, 159–61, 159n.26 (*see also*
    Borysthenes, geography of)
  Prusa and Prusans, 157–58, 160n.29,
    163–64, 168–70, 172n.61, 173,
    181–83
  Zoroastrianism, 157n.20, 175–76,
    177n.73, 178, 181–82
Dionysius of Halicarnassus, 7–8, 35–72,
  73–104, 332–33
  alogos aesthesis (intuitive perception),
    47–48, 47–48n.32, 51–52, 51n.38
  coherence of corpus, 75–77
  diathesis (disposition), 45–47
  ethos (character), 36–57, 71
  explicit assessment of historiographers
    by, 38–43, 89–92, 94–96

374 SUBJECT INDEX

Dionysius of Halicarnassus (*cont.*)
  globalism and unity, Herodotus's role in
    ideas of, 87–103
  imitation of Herodotus by, 57–58,
    61–71
  laypersons, 47–57
  mimesis and imitation, 51, 58–61, 86–87
  narrative style of, 65–72
  prohairesis (deliberate choice), 36–38,
    69–70, 75–77, 86, 91–92
  rhetorical works, 35–72
  Roman Antiquities, 73–104
  Rome and Roman history, 77–87, 88–89,
    92–94, 96–97, 99, 101–2
divinity, ideas of, 106n.3, 127, 263–95

earthquakes, 264–69, 273–76
Egypt, Herodotus's representation of, 127–28,
  196n.36, 197–98, 199–210, 199n.45,
  214, 221–22, 224–25, 265n.21,
  318n.73, 319n.78, 322–23, 327–28
empire, 92–101, 177. *See also* Rome
Ethiopians, 145, 155–56, 196n.36, 209n.73
ethnography, 28n.100, 80n.25, 81–86, 93–
  94n.54, 144–45, 155–56, 156n.17,
  160n.31, 162–64, 167–70, 186–87,
  187n.5, 196–97, 196n.36, 199–200,
  207–9, 211–34, 213n.83, 317n.69,
  319–20
ethos (character). *See* Dionysius of
  Halicarnassus: *ethos*; Plutarch: *ethos*

Fehling, Detlev, 8, 11, 201n.52
Foucault, Michel, 25–27

Gadamer, Hans-Georg, 9–12, 61–62,
  154–55, 183–84
Genette, Gérard, 19, 29, 197–98n.41
Getae, the, 157–58, 160, 160n.31
global literature, 27–29, 74–75, 102–3
Greekness, 79–88, 143, 165–70, 173, 181–82,
  211–12, 225–28, 247, 296n.1, *See*
  also identity

Halicarnassus, 13, 14, 28, 55n.42, 142–43
Hecataeus of Miletus, 149–50, 201–2n.53,
  233–34
Hegesias of Magnesia, 88n.42, 95, 309–10

Herodotus and the *Histories*
  ambiguity of, 117–18, 152–53, 200–10, 295
  aspects of ancient reputation, 13–17
  aspects of twentieth-century reception, 4–6
  autopsy in, 201–2n.53, 205–7, 205–6n.61,
    208–10
  bribery by and of, 136–37
  connections between ancient and
    modern receptions?, 7–9
  globalism of, 27–29, 87–97, 291
  ideas of instability in, 143, 186–87,
    248–49, 278–79, 290–91
  narratorial style or narratology of,
    31–32, 65–72, 162–64, 200–10 (*see*
    also Herodotus: voice of)
  papyri, 14–15, 199n.45
  philobarbaros, 127–28, 130, 142–43
  political warnings of, 100–1, 283n.70,
    295n.103
  religious ideas in, 264–69 (*see also*
    divinity, ideas of)
  representation of space in, 297–99, 301–3
  role in rhetorical education, 5n.15, 14–15
  sensibility of, 29–34
  voice of, 26–27, 31, 58, 201n.50, 209,
    209n.71, 221–22, 269n.33 (*see also*
    Herodotus: narratorial style or
    narratology of)
  wonder, 192n.20, 317–20
Hinds, Stephen, 19–20, 24n.85
Hippocleides, 145
Hobbes, Thomas, 8
hodology, as metaphor for narrative, 69n.78,
  91–92, 239–40, 297–98, 298n.8
Homer, 14, 15–16, 56n.44, 67, 149–50,
  168–70, 198–99, 225–26, 230,
  231–34, 271, 279–81, 313–15
Hyperboreans and Hypernotians, 146

identity. *See also* Greekness
  complexities of, 27–29, 164–73, 177,
    181–82, 186–89, 196–97, 212,
    214–15, 309–10
  in Imperial Greek literature, 32,
    32n.110
  individual, 132–33, 143 (*see also*
    Plutarch: *ethos*)
  Romans as Greek, 79–81, 82, 84–85

SUBJECT INDEX 375

imitation, concepts of, 20–25, 27, 61–65. *See also* Dionysius of Halicarnassus; Plutarch
intertextuality, 24–25, 154–55, 193–94, 233, 275–76, 292–93
hypotextual activation, 19, 27, 30, 65, 102–3, 181, 242–43, 275–76
Ionic and Ionicism, 17, 30, 61–62, 189–90, 192–93, 309–10

Jacoby, Felix, 5–6, 14n.48, 199n.45
Jauss, Hans Robert, 9n.26, 9n.28, 11–12
Josephus, 13

Kadir, Djelal, 27–29, 74–75

Literaten-Epigramm, 13–14
Longinus, *On the Sublime*, 14, 16–17, 42n.21, 58, 126n.57, 297–98, 328n.96, 331–32
Lucian, 21n.77, 186–235, 236–60, 333–34
  Anacharsis, 247–60
  mediation in, 251–53
  "nomadic" argumentation in, 254–55, 257
  parallels with Solon-Croesus exchange, 250–60
  perspectival inversions of, 247–50, 254
  reversed identities in, 258, 259
  explicit references to Herodotus by, 189–94, 229–30
  Herodotus and Aëtion, 189–94
  How to Write History, 61n.62, 188n.9, 195, 195n.29
  performance, representation of Herodotus's by, 191–94
  Scythian, the, 242–47
  as self-conscious reception artist, 187–90, 191–200
  True Histories, 19, 197–200, 210–35
  ideas of truth in, 195–96, 220, 223–25, 233–34
  Isle of the Blessed episode, 228–35
  metaliterary aspects of, 197–200, 210–11, 229–30
  moon episode, 213–20

relation to historiography, 195–97, 199–200, 205, 210–11, 217–18, 224–25, 228, 232–33
representations of ethnography in, 211–34
representations of subjectivity in, 196–97, 210–11, 212, 214–15, 217–18, 220–28, 231
self-othering in, 214–15, 218–20, 227–28, 233–34

Magi. *See* Dio Chrysostom
Magnesia ad Sipylum, 296, 306–7, 310n.49
malice (*kakoêtheia*). *See* Plutarch
Marathon, Battle of, 136–37, 236
Marcus, Sharon, 19–20
Martindale, Charles, 9n.26, 12n.41
Mead, George Herbert, 214–15, 225–26
Megalopolis, 286–95
mimesis. *See* imitation
Momigliano, Arnaldo, 5–6

Nicolaus of Damascus, 78, 79–80, 154n.8
nomadism, 163–64, 239–40, 249–50, 256, 258, 259n.71

Ocean, 197–99, 229
Olbia. *See* Dio Chrysostom
Olympia, 191–92, 193–94, 322–23

Pausanias, 261–95, 296–329, 333–34
ideas of divinity and fate in, 266n.25, 269–95
imitation of Herodotus, nature of, 261–63, 275–76, 299–304, 308
judgment of literary talents of, 262, 294
language of, 263n.10, 301nn.22–23, 309–10
narrative style of, 270, 277
origin of, 296, 303n.27, 306–7
political tone of, 271n.41, 282n.66, 295, 295n.103
religious aspects of, 326–28, 326n.93
role of fortune in, 279–81, 286–95
self-differentiation from Herodotus, 308–15
space in, 276, 298–301, 303–8
wonder, 315–29

376 SUBJECT INDEX

Pergamene Library, 13
Persia and Persians, 85–86, 100–1, 127–28,
    129–30, 169–70, 173–74
Persian Wars, reception of, 10, 15–16, 41–
    42, 80–81, 118–19, 118n.38, 121,
    143n.98, 192–93
Philostratus, 6n.19, 21–22, 106n.4, 153n.3,
    188n.11
Phocylides, 170–74
Photius, 16–17
Plato, 64n.67, 116n.31, 117–19, 154n.7,
    158, 169n.53, 174–76, 177n.73,
    179n.75, 188n.7, 225n.106,
    241n.16, 248n.41, 317n.72
Plutarch, 8, 105–51, 332–33
    ambiguity, ideas of, 117, 142–43
    ethos (character), ideas of, 107–10, 113–
        17, 122–25, 132–33, 139–43
    complexity of, 141–43
    legibility of, 114, 116, 122–25, 134–35
    history, ideas of, 118–19, 123–25,
        147–48
    ichnê (signs), 110–13, 127, 140–41
    implicit comparison with Herodotus,
        143–47
    malice (*kakoêtheia*), 113–17
    mimesis (imitation), ideas of, 117–21
    negative exemplarity in, 137–39
    On the Malice of Herodotus, 106–13,
        117–18, 120–21, 125–28, 136–39,
        141–43, 144–51
    Parallel Lives, 122–43
    possibilities of Herodotean reception
        in, 105–6
    prohairesis (deliberate choice), 118–19,
        134, 135–36
    psychologizing in, 125–28, 130–36
    role as critic, 111–13, 146–51
Polybius, 4n.12, 41n.20, 78–80, 88n.45,
    91–92
progymnasmata, 14–15, 14n.48, 44n.27,
    58n.50
prohairesis (deliberate choice). *See*
    Dionysius of Halicarnassus;
    Plutarch
Prusa and Prusans. *See* Dio Chrysostom
psychogeography, 297–99

reception, concepts of, 7–20, 332–33
    distinguished from reputation, 12–17
    kinetic reception, 18–20, 30, 193–94,
        228, 234, 261, 309–10, 313
Rome
    Atticism at, 21n.76
    centrality to Dionysius of
        Halicarnassus's rhetorical
        program, 73–74, 75–77
    complex role in Imperial Greek
        literature, 22n.78, 143nn.99–100,
        236n.1, 253n.58, 282n.66, 283n.71
    as empire, 77–79, 87–89, 91–94, 96–97,
        99–100, 177
    relation to Greekness, 75, 79–82, 83–87,
        101–3, 188n.11, 255n.64

Said, Edward, 22–24, 25, 118n.40
Salmakis Inscription, 14, 15–16
Sartre, Jean-Paul, 214–15, 219–20
Scythia and Scythians, 157–73, 237–59,
    301–3
Second Sophistic, the, 21–22
self. *See* identity; Lucian: *True Histories*
Simmel, Georg, 156
Smith, Barbara Herrnstein, 10
Solon, 127, 179n.75, 180–81, 214, 240–59,
    277–79, 281, 284–85, 290–91
sophists, 21–22, 191–92, 259n.72, 268–69
Stewart, Susan, 297–98, 334–35
Strabo, 78, 272, 290n.90
Sulla, 281–86
Sunium, 299–303

Talthybius, 270, 271–72, 275–76
Themistocles, 146, 300–1
Theopompus, 11n.34, 38–39, 43n.24, 78n.17
Thucydides
    ancient rhetorical treatises, presence in,
        11n.34
    assessment by Cicero, 35n.1,
        108–9n.15
    assessment by Dionysius of
        Halicarnassus, 38–43, 45, 48n.35,
        49–50, 51–57, 70–71, 91–92
    assessment by Longinus, 17n.59
    autopsy, 205–6n.61

SUBJECT INDEX   377

Delian earthquake, presentation
  of, 266
fundamental figure in Herodotean
  reception, 1–6
kinetic reception of Herodotus,
  18–19
minimal religious dimension of, 269
papyri of, 14–15
as stylistic model or counter-model,
  67–69, 95–96, 309–10
Thurii, 142–43, 303
Todorov, Tzvetan, 196–97, 197n.40,
  216n.92, 224n.103, 225n.106,
  227–28
Toxaris, 242–47

travel, 159–60, 188n.11, 200n.48, 208–10,
  240–42, 244–45, 275n.48, 297–98

voice. *See* Herodotus: voice of

White, Hayden, 67
wonder (*thauma, thôma*), 32, 176, 192, 199–
  200, 202–6, 218–20, 291, 315–29. *See
  also* Herodotus; Pausanias

Xenophon, 11n.34, 38–39, 43n.24, 331–32
Xerxes, 97–104, 172, 178–79, 271–72, 282,
  284n.72, 290n.89

Zoroastrianism. *See* Dio Chrysostom

Printed in the USA
CPSIA information can be obtained
at www.ICGtesting.com
BVHW051906010823
668110BV00009B/95/J